1995 Children's Writer's & Illustrator's Market

Distributed in Canada by McGraw-Hill Ryerson,
300 Water St., Whitby, Ontario L1N 9B6.
Also distributed in Australia by
Kirby Books, Private Bag No. 19, P.O. Alex-
andria NSW/2015.

Managing Editor, Market Books Department:
Constance J. Achabal;
Supervising Editor: Michael Willins.

Children's Writer's & Illustrator's Market.

International Standard Serial Number
0897-9790
International Standard Book Number
0-89879-679-2

Cover illustration by John Steven Gurney
Portraits by Leslie Sowers Slaughter

Attention Booksellers: This is an annual directory of F&W Publications.
Returns accepted between January 1, 1996 and March 31, 1996.

1995

Children's Writer's & Illustrator's Market

Edited by
Alice P. Buening
and
Christine Martin

WRITER'S DIGEST BOOKS
Cincinnati, Ohio

Contents

The Markets

Page 95

Page 212

Resources

Page 293

Page 117

From the Editors

"It's important for me to always be aware who my audience is," says illustrator Will Hillenbrand. "And for me, children are the truest, most honest, and most satisfying audience . . . "

And he's right. That's why the calling to create material for children is such a special one. Whether you're a children's writer, illustrator, animator, photographer or songwriter, the work you do entertains, instructs and delights young minds, making impressions that can last a lifetime.

Children's Writer's & Illustrator's Market is an important tool in helping you reach your young audience. In creating this, our seventh edition, we've worked hard to gather new markets and up-to-date listing information, as well as conducting enlightening interviews to give you added insights into the children's field.

As part of our effort to better address the concerns of illustrators, you can hear more from Will Hillenbrand in an in-depth interview on page 5, where he explains how he became a children's illustrator, and shares examples of work from his picture books. Hillenbrand's insights are not just beneficial for illustrators, however. We urge anyone chasing a dream to read his story.

Equally inspiring is our First Books feature on page 15. This year we talked to Staton Rabin, whose first children's picture book was a work of historical fiction about World War I; Yumi Heo, a new author and illustrator with a unique style that mixes oil paint, pencil and collage; and Juddi Morris, author of a nonfiction book for ages 10 and up. These three women recall the very different paths they took to getting their first children's books on the shelves.

Sally E. Stuart, nationally recognized expert on Christian writing, marketing and publishing, shares her tips for selling work in the vast religious market in Don't Miss Out! Explore the Children's Religious Market, on page 22. We have also included a special sidebar on Jewish publishing at the end of that article.

One big change we made this year was combining audio and video markets for children in a single section now called Audiovisual & Audiotape. In the last few years, the children's entertainment industry has been booming, and the lines have begun to blur between audio and video. You can read more about these exciting developments in the section introduction on page 225. We've also included Insider Reports with Jeffrey Aikman of JEF Films (our first ever audiovisual interview) and Joseph Porrello of Peter Pan Industries.

In addition to those two interviews, you'll find seven other Insider Reports throughout this book. In Book Publishers, Sasha Alyson of Alyson Publications talks about the consequences of producing material that can be controversial. Arthur A. Levine, author and editor-in-chief of Knopf Books for Young Readers discusses multiculturalism and the children's field in general. And illustrators can gain perspective from both sides of the drawing board from award-winning illustrator Carole Byard and Rosanne Main, freelance designer/art director for Orchard Books.

You'll find two interviews in Magazines. First Steve Charles, editor of *Turtle Magazine* and *U.S. Kids*, publications of the Children's Better Health Institute, shares his views on writing for kids. Next you'll hear from Al Matano, editor and art director of *Scienceland*, a picture book magazine designed to teach science and reading.

Finally, young writers and illustrators—and parents and teachers—should be sure to read our interview with Marty Kusmierski in Young Writer's & Illustrator's Markets. Kusmierski is the founder of the Tyketoon Young Author Publishing Company which produces books created completely by kids.

Note that we've included artwork with all of our Insider Reports this year, in addition to sprinkling it throughout the book. We've picked some great pieces in a variety of styles and media. If you're an illustrator or photographer, be sure to read Show Us What You've Sold! on page 40, and perhaps *your* work can appear in the pages of our next edition.

We continue to add editorial comments within listings (including the more than 100 new ones) to give you added information that we believe is important and useful. For example, we have included comments to help you sort through the Simon & Schuster/Macmillan merger, and to let you know which publishers want material submitted through agents.

We feel sure that by using the 1995 *Children's Writer's & Illustrator's Market* your work will reach its special audience. But remember *you* are *our* audience. Please write or call to let us know what we're doing right and what we can do better. Tell us who you'd like to hear from or where you sold your work. After all, our goal is to continue to give you opportunities to entertain, instruct and delight young minds.

Alice P. Buening   Christine Martin

How to Use Children's Writer's & Illustrator's Market

As a children's writer, illustrator or photographer first picking up *Children's Writer's & Illustrator's Market*, you may not know quite how to start. Your impulse may be to flip through the book, quickly make a list of contacts who purchase freelance material, and submit to them in hopes that someone will buy your work.

But there's more to it. Before you begin to submit manuscripts, illustrations or photos to the markets listed here, you've got to do some research. Editors, art directors and producers don't have time to sort through stacks of inappropriate submissions, so the more you know about a company that interests you—whether it be a book publisher, a greeting card company, or a film production house—the better chance you have of getting work accepted.

Besides providing listings, this directory includes a number of tools to help you determine which markets are the best ones for your work. By using these tools, as well as researching on your own (for instance, checking into specific publishers' styles by finding their books in libraries or bookstores, or sending for sample copies of magazines that interest you), you are turning the odds in your favor.

Start with the indexes

This directory has over 600 potential buyers of freelance material and more than 100 listings (all marked with an asterisk [*]) are new in this edition. The easiest way to narrow down the listings, to learn which ones publish the type of material you're interested in submitting, is to start with the indexes.

In most listings of book publishers and magazines, you will find four age categories: "Picture books" (or "picture-oriented material") are written/illustrated for preschoolers to 8-year-olds; "young readers" are for 5- to 8-year-olds; "middle readers" are for 9- to 11-year-olds; and "young adults" are for those ages 12 and up. These age breakdowns may vary slightly from publisher to publisher, but they can help you identify buyers who may be interested in your work.

If you have a manuscript about teenage sports heroes, identify and contact those book publishers who publish titles for young adults. If you have an exciting short story about dragons, princes and princesses that would interest 6-year-olds, search for magazine markets catering to young readers. The Age-Level Index in the back of this book can help you quickly accomplish this task.

Using the Age-Level Index in combination with the Subject Index will further hone your list of potential markets. The Subject Index lists book and magazine publishers by the fiction and nonfiction subjects they are seeking.

If you're a writer trying to place a health article written for middle readers, make a list of those markets under Health in the Magazines: Nonfiction section of the Subject Index. Then go to the Age-Level Index and compare your list with the list of magazines under Middle Readers. Circle those that are the same, and read the circled listings to discover submission procedures.

If you're an illustrator or photographer, use the Subject Index to determine which publishers are seeking your preferred subject matter. If you enjoy painting or photographing animals, for instance, consider sending samples to book and magazine publishers listed under Animals and, perhaps, Nature/Environment. Of course, read the listings for the potential markets to discover the type of work the art directors prefer and what type of samples they will keep on file.

Study the listings

Many listings use the "Tips" section to describe the freelancing credentials they seek or to impart special advice for selling to their companies. Look for additional information about specific markets in the form of comments from the editors of this book set off by bullets (●) within the listings.

Besides providing subject information, markets also state the average word lengths for the fiction and nonfiction material they seek. To guarantee you are sending an editor or art director exactly what he wants, see if specific submission guidelines are available and send for them.

Throughout this book, the abbreviations "ms" or "mss" refer to "manuscript" or "manuscripts," respectively. The letters "SASE" stand for self-addressed, stamped envelope, while SAE (self-addressed envelope) is often used in conjunction with IRC (International Reply Coupon). Many markets require SASEs and you must include one if you want your work returned. IRCs are required when sending mail to countries other than your own.

In the Book Publishers section a solid block [■] appears before markets that subsidy publish manuscripts. In Contests & Awards a double dagger [‡] indicates contests open to students.

If you're a parent or teacher you may be interested in Young Writer's & Illustrator's Markets. The markets in this section encourage submissions from children—and your students or kids may have material that could get published. Some markets, however, require a written statement from a teacher or parent, noting the work is original. Also watch for age limits.

Along with information for writers, markets provide information for photographers and illustrators. If you're a photographer, check under the Photography subhead to see what format a buyer prefers. For example, some want 35mm color transparencies, others want b&w prints. Most important, note the type of photos a buyer wants to purchase and the procedures for submitting. It's not uncommon for a market to want a résumé and promotional literature, as well as tearsheets from previous work. Listings also note whether model releases and/or captions are required.

Illustrators will find numerous markets in which samples are kept on file for possible future assignments. If you are both a writer and illustrator, look for markets that accept manuscript/illustration packages.

In researching listings you will also find payment information. Some markets pay on acceptance, others on publication. Some pay a flat rate for manuscripts and artwork, others pay advances and royalties. Know how a market operates. This will keep you from being shocked when you discover your paycheck won't arrive until your manuscript is published—18 months after it was accepted. For details about contracts and other business tips, see The Business of Children's Writing & Illustrating.

Inspiration is the Only 'In' You Need: A Will Hillenbrand Story

by Alice P. Buening

Will Hillenbrand is a master storyteller, telling tales through his pencils, pens and paintbrushes. To learn his stories he's ventured (in his imagination) to different periods in time and exotic places like China, Africa and South America. He's hung out with dogs and cats and visited zoos. Most of all, he's paid attention to the world around him, believing that, for a storyteller, every experience is important.

Leaving behind his job at an advertising agency, Hillenbrand began his career in picture book illustration in 1990 with *Traveling to Tondo*, by Verna Aardema. To date he has 12 picture books to his credit (and that number is growing). He's worked with publishers the likes of Holiday House, Harcourt Brace, Houghton Mifflin, Knopf and Macmillan. He's illustrated books by established authors like Eric A. Kimmel (who retells a Jewish folktale in *Asher and the Capmakers*), as well as talented newcomers such as Roxanne Dyer Powell (whose enchanting 1994 debut was *Cat, Mouse and Moon*).

Will Hillenbrand

Among his latest projects are a Chinese folktale, complete with three magical genie-like monks, entitled *The Treasure Chest*, by Rosalind C. Wang (Holiday House), to be released in March 1995; and *The House That Drak Built*, by Judy Sierra (Harcourt Brace), a spooky story featuring a haunted house and a group of little trick-or-treaters, due out in the fall—just in time for Halloween.

Here, the Cincinnati-based artist tells his own tale. He talks about how he developed his love of the story, and how he created a structure in his life that would allow him to pursue his dream. He also shares insights on approaching a new manuscript, and advice for budding illustrators wishing to break into the competitive market of children's book publishing.

Tell me about your background. What drew your interest to children's books?

The reason I do children's books now is that I was read to as a child and shown pictures. I was told stories by my grandmother and my father—sometimes they

Alice P. Buening is co-editor of this edition of Children's Writer's & Illustrator's Market. She has also assisted on the 1995 edition of Artist's & Graphic Designer's Market and has previously worked on Writer's Digest magazine, The Artist's Magazine and Decorative Artist's Workbook.

were just family tales, especially from my grandmother. She had it down to a pattern where we'd ask for a specific story. That kind of background was a foundation.

I began my first real lessons with an art teacher in junior high. It was then I thought this would be something I would consider as a career.

After that, you attended the Art Academy of Cincinnati. What kind of courses did you take?

At the Art Academy, the experience was really good because there was a broad base. We had foundation courses in design, and other things. But eventually we progressed to courses which always had drawing in every class—different kinds of drawing, but every time you looked at your schedule, drawing was going to be a part of it.

I also had classes in printmaking and photography. All of the experiences were very useful for someone who does picture books. You end up dealing with things like typography—it's not something you can wish away. You can't let these things daunt you and say, "I can't do this because . . . "

I had also worked in television during college, and I had an opportunity to continue to work at a TV station, but I knew I was more interested in print because it's a more private kind of thing—you don't need to be plugged in, you don't need a certain piece of equipment. It's simple, economical, and as far as books go, a great invention. [When you read] you can do it at your own pace. You can begin where you want. You can take it to bed with you.

So I knew I wanted to be in print, but it wasn't that defined yet.

I know you worked in advertising after college. When did you finally decide to go into children's book illustration?

When I began dating Jane, who became my wife, she had just graduated from Capital University in Columbus, Ohio, where she was an elementary school teacher. I began getting involved in doing [classroom] bulletin boards for her about illustrators like Tomie DePaola, and it started rekindling the embers of that early storytelling. I started wanting to learn more about these people. Jane would go to literature conferences and tell me she saw Tomie DePaola. I'd say, "Next time you have to go to one of those conferences, let me know—I'll take off work and join you." So [my interest] began to build.

At that point I started thinking that there was a possible change ahead, but I knew my portfolio wasn't prepared. My daily task was doing design work, not illustration. But it was also being a communicator—being able to take a huge amount of information and focus it down to a small, digestible amount for an audience. And that training benefited me.

How then did you get your portfolio prepared?

It's a little like the old Yankee thing, "You can't get there from here." Before you can be clever about the pictures you make, you have to be clever enough to come up with a structure that's going to allow you to do it. If you can solve that mystery, you've made it.

What structure did you come up with?

When Jane and I were dating, she still lived in Columbus and I lived in Cincinnati, and we saw each other once a week usually. After that date, I'd do a watercolor painting of what we did that weekend. I came up with that structure for two

Hillenbrand used a light touch to capture the sprightly title character in The King
Who Tried to Fry an Egg on His Head *as the king triumphantly proclaims he'll let the
Sun, the Moon, and the Raven marry his three daughters to bring prosperity to his
impoverished household. The Russian roots of the folktale, adapted by Mirra Gins-
burg, are reflected in the costuming and architecture featured throughout this story
of a foolish, yet good-hearted, king.*

In this illustration from Asher and the Capmakers, by Eric A. Kimmel, Hillenbrand depicts the title character surrounded by his family on Hanukkah Eve as he prepares to depart on what becomes (much to Asher's surprise) a fantastic journey. The tale is rooted in the lore of Ireland, England and Eastern Europe, and Hillenbrand researched the cultures, clothing and architecture of the period. Hillenbrand is currently working on illustrations for a version of Ali Baba & the Forty Thieves *by Kimmel, who has written, adapted and retold dozens of tales.*

reasons. I wanted to do it for Jane as something special to keep our communication going—and visually I can communicate things often that words can't.

But I also knew it was a weekly exercise. If we saw *The Nutcracker*, I'd draw my own Nutcracker—it wouldn't be as it was on stage, but I might draw a puppet theater with the Nutcracker coming out. It was the structure that allowed me to exercise, almost like an athlete who knows to get to the pros you have to practice. It was extremely useful in two ways. I ended up marrying Jane, and I was able to exercise the kind of muscles I needed. I exercised my imagination.

Eventually, Jane went to a lit conference and found out about a three-week [book illustration] class she thought I might want to take. I had two weeks of vacation from work, so it didn't quite fit, but I took it anyway because I was interested in having a real experience [in which] I would have made a book. I knew at the end of it that I would find out whether I liked [illustrating books] or whether I hated it. The book was not great, but it was a book, and it allowed me to begin to send work to publishers in New York and Boston.

Then how did you finally make the jump from your advertising career to your illustration career?

Eventually, I knew I had to take another step. As you probably know, when you work on salary, you agree to an approximate 40-hour week, but that's not always the case. And they use the best hours you have. When you come home, unless you're a night owl, it's hard to get that energy level back up. I knew I needed to talk to my employer about working on a part-time schedule.

I was lucky. The fellow that was my boss wanted to be a novelist when he was younger, so he understood what I wanted to do and the transition required. He essentially said, "If you can do what you do now in three days a week, then you can do it." I got paid less, and I did about the same amount of work, but I knew I wanted to be able to do books.

What was your first assignment?

My first book was a chapter book called *Awfully Short for the First Grade* (by Elvira Woodruff). [Doing a chapter book] was a useful way to get into picture books. When I got my contract, I was overwhelmed. I think Margery Cuyler (of Holiday House) was wise to give me a chapter book first to let me get my feet wet.

I've had experience with some very fine editors. One of the really useful things I did when I began thinking about getting my portfolio together is spend hours and hours in children's bookstores reading and looking. I wanted to understand [the industry] better. Going to the library and reading stories was extremely useful not only in getting to know what is appropriate and essential for good storytelling, but to begin to know what publishers my work might be right for.

On my first visit to New York, I just went to four publishers. I spent one day there. I ended up coming back with the contract for *Awfully Short*. But within a year, I had three different contracts from three different publishers—three of the four.

What kind of working relationships do you have with your editors and authors?

I asked one of my editors, Liz Van Doren of Harcourt Brace, to define herself to me [as an editor]. She said, "I'm ready for that question—I'm a midwife. I'll help you in your labor, but when that book is finished it's yours, and I'll hand it right back to you. In your labor I'll be by your bedside but you'll feel every bit of the pain and all the joy." And that's as good a description as I can think of.

Most often I work directly with editors. Very seldom will I ever work with an author. The editor will be the useful go-between. For example, Margery Cuyler sent the book dummy for *Asher and the Capmakers* to Eric Kimmel, and he took out about a third of the text because he thought the pictures were working well enough that they didn't need to be supported. It's the editor's discretion. They know [the author] better than I. So I don't work with [authors] directly.

And you think this is best?

I just recently read an article from *The New York Times* about how to do picture books, and it began talking about Sir John Tenniel. He illustrated both *Alice's Adventures in Wonderland* and the following book (*Through the Looking Glass & What Alice Found There*). I think there were 90-some illustrations—Lewis Carroll was happy with only one of them. A battle royal went on between them.

It's important to be able to say the visual part is distinct from the writing part. The author is the author of the text; the illustrator is the author of the pictures. Now, if something's technically wrong—an element, a dress color, a sock—that needs to be changed, period. But to me it's the illustrator's sole right to interpret how it's done.

So you have control over all of the elements of a book—the background, how the characters are going to look, etc.?

When you do a story about a cat, you need to lose yourself in what the cat is. You build the relationships. You costume the characters. You need to consider every level—subplots, background, setting—for the continuity of the story.

When a manuscript is given to me, that's it. Sometimes the publisher will tell me that because of publishing limitations we're doing 8 × 10 this time, or it has to be horizontal. But aside from that, the drama begins. Then I have to immerse myself in the story.

All my books look very different unless you know how I approach things, then you can see the continuity from the approach. But essentially, they all have a slightly different character—that's because I look for the story to be my jumping-off point. And the personality of the story should come out before the personality of the illustration. They should be married, but the story should be more important.

You've done Russian, Jewish and South American tales, and you've just finished working on a Chinese folktale. How much research do you do into specific cultures for the stories you illustrate?

I have an eclectic range of books that I'm interested in. It stems partly from publishers being more open to publishing multicultural literature. It also fits very well with my interest—being a visual interpreter, and an interpreter for children.

If I get a book that's a Chinese folktale, yes, there's a lot of research I'll do. And if I look at the bottom line, I'm not compensated for every hour in that sense. But I'm interested, because it's a good story. And when I get that assignment, it's like someone giving me a ticket to China, and saying, "Here are the people you'll meet."

What's even more fascinating is that they're not people who are living now. It can be 500 or 600 years ago or more. It can be a certain dynasty. It's a fascinating journey. [When I got the manuscript for the Chinese folktale] I began collecting a pile of books and magazines about China. If I was at a used book sale, I'd look for the Chinese books they had. I put it all in my "China pile."

How did you research your first picture book, Traveling to Tondo?

When I got *Traveling to Tondo*, the editor told me [the main character] was a civet cat. I said, "Fine. What's a civet cat?" She said, "I don't know, but you'll find out." And surely I did. I went to common resources, encyclopedias and things. Not much there—just illustrations of the cat.

Eventually, that led me to take a trip to the Philadelphia Zoo, so I could see a civet cat [in person] and draw it. Ultimately, a story will tell you what you need to do if you're really listening to it.

I had pretty much made a model [of the civet cat] from the pictures I'd seen in magazines, but it was just a two-dimensional picture. I had no idea how it moved.

It's like if you imagine someone saying, "I want to tell you about an animal that's in another country. It's called a rabbit. I've got a picture of it." And you see it's a little fur-ball with a round body, an oval head and long ears. But you still don't know much about it. If you had someone to tell you about it, you'd know more.

Hillenbrand explored Chinese folklore—full of magical elements and supernatural characters—as well as the ancient lyric artwork of China, to illustrate The Treasure Chest, *by Rosalind C. Wang. The main characters, Laifu and Pearl, are rewarded for an act of kindness by visits from three magical monks housed in bamboo poles. Here the pair meet the third monk in the story. The folktale was passed down to Wang through generations of oral tradition.*

But if you see that animal's character, if you're able to sit and watch it and see how it moves, and how its body shifts like a Slinky. And when it's hopping it's like a rubberband, going and coming, going and coming. The movement of the animal [goes hand in hand] with the movement of the story.

And when you draw it, you're like an editorial cartoonist doing a caricature of a president. It's not the way the president looks, but the way the cartoonist interprets him. The cartoonist exaggerates so you know him in a different way, but you say, "That's exactly him." It's an internalization, a personalization, of that character.

You have to do everything you need to do to satisfy yourself, and create that pile. There are things you need to know. For example, in an African tale, what the huts looked like, what the vegetation looked like, what the animals look like.

If you do find something [in your research] that you personally like, you can include it, but it shouldn't be the linchpin of the story.

Do you have an example from one of your books?

In the case of *Traveling to Tondo*, I found that in the part of Africa [where the story took place], there was a tradition that on the day you were to marry, if a pied wagtail (which is a bird) was sitting on the doorstep of the groom's house, you would have a successful marriage. The shaman could come by and put a few pieces of birdseed on your doorstep to attract the bird. But that did not guarantee a successful marriage, although the bird may arrive and make you feel better.

So I found out what a pied wagtail looked like [and included one in the book]. I put a few pieces of black seed on the ground, because the marriage [to take place in the book] never happens.

Now since I know this, I know a legend. I know something more about the culture and the way the people behave. It wasn't important for understanding the story, but the story became more interesting. And when I include [things like that], I talk to children about them, then they become storytellers of the specific, and it becomes more personal for them.

You frequently visit schools and give presentations for kids at bookstores. Do you think this kind of communication with children is important for your career?

I like to see children around each other. They're fascinating to watch. It's important for me to always be aware who my audience is. And for me, children are the truest, most honest, and the most satisfying audience — they are uncluttered; they're not going to analyze; they're going to look at the heart of the story.

When I make a presentation I know I have to change my personality from how I am at my desk. Primarily what I talk to children about is process. One of the essential ideas I use is that your first idea is a great idea, but the best idea may be the twentieth idea.

I don't say, "I did this [book] the first time I sat down." I show them how it builds, idea on idea, just like a drawing does, the first stroke to the next and the next — and pretty soon those abstract marks become something.

Part of Hillenbrand's preparation for Cat, Mouse and Moon, by Roxanne Dyer Powell, involved borrowing a neighbor's cat to observe feline mannerisms and personality, apparent in this detail from one of his illustrations. The artist used a variety of colors — purples, blues, greens, browns and greys — applied with spray bottles to create a background that wouldn't swallow up the stealthy, curious black kitty as readers spy on his nighttime prowl.

What advice can you offer aspiring illustrators about the market?

It comes down to how much you want it. Because if you really want to do it, you'll find your way. This book you produce (*Children's Writer's & Illustrator's Market*), is an extremely beneficial, helpful guide.

When I get phone calls [from illustrators or writers], and I get lots of them, I refer them to your book or Uri Shulevitz's book (*Writing With Pictures: How to Write and Illustrate Children's Books*). Many ask me if I'll illustrate their manuscripts and I say no. They ask if I'll read their manuscripts and I say no.

Why won't you read manuscripts?

Because, I'm thinking about writing one of my own, and if my idea was similar [to one of theirs], and I went with my idea, and they never got theirs published, they'd think I was taking their work, so I won't do it. The best advice I can give them, and usually what they don't want to hear, is if you've got a manuscript, send it to an editor. Go to a resource. Look up a publisher. Then submit it. You have your most likely chance by following that path.

And what do you think about writers having their manuscripts illustrated before submitting them?

Finding someone to draw pictures for your story is useless, absolutely useless. There are all kinds of pitfalls in doing it. If it's a good story, it has some merit, period. And editors are trained to see that. They might read it and think it reminds them of Ed Young, and they might call him and tell him to do it—so why mess around with someone down the block when you can have Ed Young?

A lot of people think that, as in Hollywood, you have to have an "in." The only "in" you need is inspiration.

But what is the market like now?

It may be harder now to break into the market than it was five or ten years ago. That was more of a golden age, more things were being published. Not necessarily better things, just more. You need to prepare as broadly as you can and have a lot of tenacity—and it comes back to how much you want to do it. If you go into the office at 8:30 a.m., maybe you should get up at four in the morning, so you can put in a few hours of your best time.

Sometimes you sit down and nothing comes of it, but it's an act of faith. You know what you want to do, you have a goal, and you're persistent. And it does happen. It comes from the activity—all the times that you sat there and it didn't, but you kept working.

At this point, you've done a dozen picture books. Are you able to pick your own projects—tell a publisher, "I want this one, I don't want that one."?

Yeah, that happens now. But usually the publishers I work with know what I'm interested in because of our relationship. The things I get that aren't right are from publishers who have seen my work but don't know me that well.

Now I think I have a pretty good idea of the publishers I like to work with and which ones print quality books and market them well.

I've learned that when you say yes to a book, you commit. You know you're not going to be the same person when you've gone through the experience. You know you're going to grow. You're going to know the story so intimately that after you see that cover with your name on it, you'll say, "Well, it should say my name, I earned it."

But now I'm able to be more selective, although early on I was very fortunate to get some really good manuscripts. *Traveling to Tondo* couldn't have been a better first picture book to do.

I think it's real important to look to the very finest publishers. I recommend to anyone to not think you have to start with a smaller publisher and work your way up. If you like and admire and respect a certain publisher, go directly to them, even if you have to keep working to get better. It's better than going to a third-rate publisher, and being able to say, "I got published," but your book is on paper that's going to fall apart.

Is Traveling to Tondo *your favorite of the books you've illustrated?*

A professor I had always said the cliché answer: "My favorite is the book I'm working on right now." The one I'm working on needs to be my favorite, so I'll pay attention to it and nurture it and give it everything it needs. It has to be my favorite because I need to love it.

I feel very fortunate and grateful I can do what I do. There are no words for it—it's my real dream-come-true, not knowing what the dream was in the beginning, but loving stories. What I remember most from my childhood is the voice of my father telling a story. When he read *The Night Before Christmas*, it was right from the encyclopedia. But the pictures came up here [in my mind]. Now I think, "What would I be doing now if I didn't have an adult that read to me?" Nothing in the visual world could inspire me like that . . . across the board, it's magic.

© 1991 Will Hillenbrand.

Traveling to Tondo, *an African tale retold by Verna Aardema, was Hillenbrand's first picture book. In this illustration he depicts the civet cat with his friends the pigeon, the tortoise and the snake (who has just devoured an antelope). The story takes place deep in the rainforest, captured in rich, muted earthtones.*

First Books

by Christine Martin

As an aspiring writer or illustrator, it's natural to wonder about your chances of breaking into the children's book market. With increased competition and restrictions on unsolicited manuscripts, the question of whether newcomers can get their books published is a legitimate one. The answer, however, is "Yes, they can!"

For the past two years, we have brought you stories of both writers and illustrators who have made their way inside the doors of children's book publishing and have seen their "first books" on store shelves. This year is no exception. Here you will discover three individuals who had their first children's books published just last year.

How did we locate these folks? Staton Rabin called us to say that after 15 rejections she sold her first fiction picture book. Illustrator Yumi Heo was one of the "talents new to the children's book scene" included in "Flying Starts," a semiannual feature in *Publishers Weekly*. And writer Juddi Morris came to our attention in a conversation with Cheryl Peremes, publicity and promotion manager at Walker and Company.

Staton Rabin
Casey Over There (Harcourt Brace & Company)

From the moment Staton Rabin finished the manuscript for *Casey Over There*, she says her first thought was, "Well, I've finally done it. I've written a picture book that works." And her second thought was, "My God. Nobody's going to notice!"

Rabin's concern stemmed from the fact that she intentionally limited her text. "Over the years, as I've read picture books, I've noticed those written by illustrators have text that is well-integrated with the pictures. Those made by two separate people (writer and illustrator) tend to have text that doesn't really need pictures," she says. "My goal was to write a picture book text almost as an illustrator would—one that *needed* pictures to work and that, hopefully, would

Christine Martin *is co-editor of this edition of* Children's Writer's & Illustrator's Market. *She is also editor of the 1995* Poet's Market, *has edited* The Art and Craft of Poetry *by Michael J. Bugeja, and has worked on previous editions of* Novel & Short Story Writer's Market.

result in a synergistic relationship between words and art."

As a graduate of New York University's film school and a freelance story analyst for Warner Bros. Pictures and Laurel Entertainment, Rabin wrote a picture book that juxtaposed two locations. Her story is about a family whose oldest son, Casey, joins the army and sails to France to fight in World War I. While Casey is sitting in muddy trenches and awaiting mail from overseas, his younger brother, Aubrey, at home in Brooklyn, New York, is playing kick the can, riding the Coney Island Ferris wheel, and writing Casey letters. When months go by without any response from Casey, a concerned Aubrey writes a letter to Uncle Sam—and receives a reply from President Woodrow Wilson.

Though Rabin, who lives in Tarrytown, New York, knew the book was good when she wrote it, she feared editors wouldn't understand what she was trying to do. At the time, she had a children's book agent who agreed to represent her for a previous manuscript which never sold, so Rabin promptly sent the agent the manuscript for *Casey*. After four unsuccessful tries at submitting it to publishers for her, the agent gave up and dropped Rabin as a client.

Still believing in her manuscript, Rabin sent it to a number of other publishers on her own. At first, her efforts were also unsuccessful. In fact, the book was rejected a total of 15 times—and Rabin had already become discouraged—by the time Jeannette Larson pulled the manuscript out of the slush pile at Harcourt Brace. Within six weeks Rabin received word that Harcourt was very interested, and two weeks later, she was offered a contract.

"I know Harcourt likes historical fiction, but the truth is it was the luck of the manuscript happening to land on Jeannette's desk that resulted in the sale. She understood the book and isn't locked into convention as much as some editors are," Rabin says. "I think she liked *Casey* because it has a warm family feeling. I think she also believed there would be a market for a book about World War I."

A history buff, who, like young Aubrey, wrote letters to famous people as she was growing up, Rabin chose World War I because it occurred around the time her father was born in Brooklyn. Part of her research for the book was asking him about life in his old neighborhood, such as what kinds of games he played as a boy. She also fact-checked details about World War I and drew on her father's own experiences in World War II.

"I believe historical fiction for kids should be accurate," Rabin says. "But I also believe good historical fiction not only can but must vary from historical fact to some degree in order to make a worthwhile story. Any event that *could* have happened, but may or may not have, is certainly appropriate for historical fiction. How much you alter depends to some degree on the fame of the events and the people involved. The better known they are, the less you should tamper with them. In *Casey*, Woodrow Wilson gets a letter from a little boy and answers it. Did it happen? No. But based on what I know of Wilson's character, such an event was in keeping with it."

While the book was published in April of 1994, Rabin actually wrote *Casey Over There* during the Persian Gulf War. "I was upset about our participation in that war, yet have deep respect for veterans since my father's a veteran. It was the tug of war between my feelings of support for our soldiers and dismay and distress at our fighting the war that prompted me to write *Casey*," she says. "I felt that if I set the story during World War I instead of the present it would give kids—and me—a safe emotional distance from the subject, to better be able to deal with it."

In a starred review, *Publishers Weekly* called *Casey Over There* "an excellent picture-book introduction to the topic of war and its effect on families." Yet, besides being especially relevant to the lives of children whose relatives are veterans or active duty servicemen and women, *Casey* has universal appeal. It is a book about separation from loved ones, Rabin says, something all kids have experienced, whether through travel, divorce, illness, or other events beyond their control.

Although Rabin has had other material for children published, this was her first fiction picture book *and* it was the first picture book for self-taught, San Diego, California, artist Greg Shed, whose sepia-shaded gouache paintings capture the era of the text. "Harcourt gave me the best support possible by hiring Greg," Rabin says. "He put his heart and soul into the art. He used his family and friends as models for the book's characters and did lots of research about what Brooklyn looked like in 1917 and what soldiers looked like in battle.

"In *Casey Over There*, I wrote a book that *requires* pictures to contrast the lives of its two main characters," Rabin says. "The emotional impact of the book depends on the way the artist can depict this contrast and visibly establish warm family relationships that bridge the geographical gap between the soldier and his family. Without Greg's terrific art, *Casey Over There* would be only half a story."

Yumi Heo
The Rabbit's Judgment (Henry Holt and Company, Inc.)

Unlike most illustrators, Yumi Heo began her art experience when she was four or five years old. It was around that time her mother gave her a box of crayons—and she has been drawing and painting ever since.

Born and raised in South Korea, Heo was encouraged to draw throughout her childhood and began more formal training at age 14, when her mother sent her to an art studio to study every day after school. She earned a Bachelor of Fine Arts in graphic design from Sangji University and worked as a graphic designer in Korea until coming to the United States in 1989.

Wanting to study more, Heo had followed up on an ad in a Korean art magazine for the School of Visual Arts in New York City. It was an exciting step, and one that would eventually lead her, quite by accident, to discover the field of children's books.

While at school, Heo created a project about a grocery boycott carried out by African-Americans against Korean-owned stores in Brooklyn, New York. Then she created puppets about the same subject. Eventually one of her thesis teachers suggested she put the ideas together.

"That is how I started," says Heo, who now lives in White Plains, New York, and occasionally does editorial illustrations for such publications as *The New Yorker*, *Ms. Magazine* and *McCall's*. "In school I did a book with puppets and began to take it around to publishers. My teacher recommended Henry Holt and

Company and I made an appointment with editor Laura Godwin. She loved the style of my book, but the subject was not appropriate for their list."

After graduation, Heo kept trying to make the rounds but got few appointments. "When you get lucky, publishers will say, 'Why don't you come in and show your book?' And often they will refer you to someone else," she says. When you don't get lucky, you just have to continue sending out samples.

About six months after her first contact with Holt, Heo received a call from Godwin who had a manuscript for a Korean folktale. "She sent me the book and asked me to do samples," Heo explains. "I did three and she loved them. And the next day I got the contract."

The manuscript Heo was given was actually one of 64 folktales recorded by Suzanne Crowder Han in *Korean Folk and Fairy Tales*, published in 1991 by Hollym Corporation in Seoul, Korea. Godwin had seen Han's book and, believing some of the stories would make good picture books, asked Han to rework the narrative.

A native of South Carolina, Han had gone to Korea as a Peace Corps volunteer in 1977 and continues to make her home in Seoul. In an initial effort to learn the language, however, she had encouraged Korean friends to tell her stories. After becoming proficient in the language, she then studied various interpretations of their folktales and recorded the stories in her own words.

As for the folktale manuscript she received, Heo says Han's interpretation is very close to the story she remembers from when she was little. Though different characters are used in the tale, the version Han tells is about a rabbit who solves a dispute between a man and the hungry tiger he just rescued from a deep pit.

To help create the illustrations, Heo located a book about animals and drew a realistic tiger and rabbit. She kept drawing the tiger and rabbit, and altering them, until she was happy with the characters. After making about ten sketches of each animal in her notebook, Heo went to work on the final art, combining pencil, oil paint and collage.

The resulting book, *The Rabbit's Judgment*, published in March of 1994, is the first picture book for both Han and Heo and includes a Korean translation alongside the English text. "I am very proud they also put the text in Korean," Heo says. "I felt it was part of my duty, being a Korean, to show a bit of Korean culture to America. I think this book is also important for Koreans because the style of illustration is more modern. I never saw a book in Korea like this."

But *The Rabbit's Judgment* is not Heo's only book — it's only the first book she's illustrated. Six months later, in September of 1994, *One Afternoon*, the first picture book Heo both wrote and illustrated was published by Orchard Books. The story is about a boy named Minho who spends an afternoon doing errands with his mother.

In many ways, *One Afternoon* is the result of Heo's earlier meetings with editors. While still at the School of Visual Arts, Heo had also met Harold Underdown, now an editor at Orchard, who was looking for illustrators with new styles. Though Underdown was not interested in Heo's book about a boycott in Brooklyn, he liked her style and encouraged her to write a story about something she knew, the Korean immigrant experience. Another person Heo met said, "You're so good at doing store scenes, why don't you do something about stores?"

Heo decided to combine the two suggestions, but wondered what story could use all the different stores. Then she recalled all the new sights and sounds she experienced when she first arrived in New York—the sounds were different in the streets and at all the stores. She would write a book highlighting all the different sounds at all the different places!

Though writing the actual story of going from store to store did not take long, Heo wanted to incorporate the sounds into her illustrations. "But when I hear a sound, I think in Korean," she says. "So I had to do research at the library to look for the sounds." Heo found onomatopoeic words, such as "kaching" and "clickety clack," and, by putting them in various typefaces, made them graphic design elements.

The result is a delightful picture book filled with lively, detailed illustrations and sounds youngsters can imitate. Yet, when *One Afternoon* received a starred review in *Publishers Weekly*, Heo was a bit overwhelmed. "I never thought I would be a writer," she says. "When I tried to write, it was very difficult. This is not my first language. It surprises me that I could do it. Sometimes I don't believe I'm doing it, even now."

Yet Heo *is* doing it. In addition to recently illustrating another picture book for Holt based on a tale in Han's original collection (*The Rabbit's Escape*, due out in the spring of this year), she has also just finished writing and illustrating her second picture book for Orchard (*Father's Rubber Shoes*, due out this fall).

Overall, Heo says, the best advice she received was to write from her own experience. "It's the only way you are different from others. You don't have to look for ideas. They're in you. I think that's very important. I also like to tell beginners that when you see editors and art directors and they tell you something, it is better for you to try their suggestions instead of saying 'What do they know?' If I hadn't taken their advice, I wouldn't be here."

Juddi Morris
The Harvey Girls (Walker and Company)

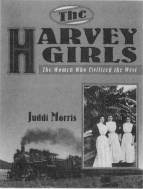

''Just call me a late bloomer,'' says Juddi Morris of Paso Robles, California. "I didn't become a writer until after my husband's death and my son Christopher was an adult."

Actually, Morris had already spent several years working at a string of odd jobs when she noticed an article in the *Los Angeles Times* about the Harvey Girls, women who ventured west in the late 19th century to work as waitresses in restaurants owned by Fred Harvey along the Santa Fe railroad line—women who were often credited for "civilizing" the West as they carried out their duties.

"After reading the piece," Morris says, "I knew three things: One, this was one of the most sparkling chapters in American history. Two, these were gutsy women—spunky and adventurous when those qualities weren't admired in the female sex. And three, I would write a book about them someday."

And just like that, Morris broke the cardinal rule most actors and writers live by—she quit her job. Then she bought a secondhand typewriter and, though she had never written anything longer than letters to friends and family, disciplined herself to work four hours at a time. "Naive as I was, I knew I didn't know how to write a book," she says. "So I decided to start writing magazine articles and work up."

Morris admits she knew nothing about publishing, "like how *hard* it is to get your byline in print," but she was lucky. The first piece she wrote, about a suitcase coming open on a baggage carousel at New York's John F. Kennedy Airport, sold to *Westways*, a California travel magazine.

"From then on I lived closer with the *Writer's Market* than I ever did with a human being," she says. "It was always by my side and when it wasn't, I was thinking of a religious market on, say, page 535 that sounded right for the piece I'd just done on church cookbooks, or would that humorous essay about a couple being served an awful child-cooked breakfast in bed work for *Woman's World*?

"Coming to writing late, I had years of ideas stacked like cordwood and they were, and are, all grist for the mill. I wrote travel articles, essays, fillers, you name it. The *Writer's Market* was my security blanket, rapidly becoming underlined, pasted-in, tattered and torn—my guide to the world of freelance roulette."

After four years of freelancing, coping with hundreds of rejections, and acceptances, and obtaining a firmer grasp on her craft, Morris recalled the story of those Harvey Girls and decided to see if anyone would be interested. She spent a couple of months doing research and then wrote an article entitled "The Dish That Won the West." The response was overwhelming! In fact, Morris ended up selling one-time rights for the article to nearly 20 magazines around the United States. "I knew then," she says, "that these were my nonfiction heroines."

Convinced that children, especially girls, need strong role models, Morris believed the Harvey Girls would be the perfect subject for a book for ages ten and up. So she began to research further, traveling to "towns and wide spots in the road where there used to be Harvey Houses [as Harvey's restaurants and hotels were called]. I spent hours at universities, museums, and historical societies in Arizona, New Mexico, Kansas and Colorado—any place that had Santa Fe Railroad or Harvey Corporation papers," she says.

Since many Harvey Houses remained in operation until after World War II, when railroad passenger service began to decline, Morris was also able to locate and interview former Harvey Girls. "In my travels I'd hear of a Harvey Girl who would then tell me about another, and that Harvey Girl knew another, and on it went," she explains. "It was wonderful! The women were gracious, eager to talk, and a joy to interview. Being a Harvey Girl still loomed large in their lives."

By the time Morris finished the manuscript, she had *Children's Writer's & Illustrator's Market* close at hand and queried several publishing houses about the project, but with no luck. Then a friend, children's writer Elizabeth Van Steenwyk, suggested she query Mary Rich, who had just moved to Walker & Company. Morris did and was delighted to learn Rich was interested.

"Mary thought the manuscript needed more focus and asked for changes up front before offering a contract," Morris says. "From day one, I trusted Mary and realized her suggestions would make a better book. So I made the changes—more than one time. I'll admit I wondered why I was doing all that work without a contract, but Mary never lost confidence in the project and I kept reminding myself that, although I had a track record with magazines, I was new to the children's book world that she knew very well."

In the end, Morris's revisions resulted in the publication of *The Harvey Girls: The Women Who Civilized the West* in July of 1994. Throughout its 112 pages, divided into eight chapters and featuring black and white photographs culled from museums, historical societies and Harvey Girls, Morris shares the story of Fred Harvey and the women who traveled west in response to his need for reliable help to work in his chain of quality eating establishments.

Believing "truth shouldn't be boring," Morris included a number of anecdotes, often quoting former Harvey Girls and other sources. By all accounts, she succeeded in writing a text that entertains as well as informs. A review in *School Library Journal* said, "The narrative is lively, conversational, and spiced with wry humor that will interest even reluctant readers." Another review referred to *The Harvey Girls* as "a book for history buffs of all ages."

Throughout the process of writing and revising the book, Morris was boosted by the support of other writers. "On the day I signed the contract, my writer's group threw a champagne party for me," she says. "Believe me, this was going beyond the call of duty, for these people had heard all the manuscript changes and had given me helpful critiques. Not only that, they listened to my whining and doubts with patience and good grace.

"The support of other writers is tremendously important. I knew no other writers when I got into the business. The day a mutual friend told me about another writer in my town, I nearly flipped. I called her within 15 minutes. She felt isolated, too. As soon as I actively started looking for other people in the business, they seemed to come out of the woodwork. After we got together for the first time we were a functioning group that is still going strong. Writing is lonely work, and it's easy to start feeling you're the last person left in Dodge."

Besides finding a support network, Morris's advice to writers is to trust editors. "My work has only improved from listening, making the suggested changes, and pushing my own ego out of the way," she says. "I have enough rejections I could probably paper my whole house. Never, ever give up. Don't take rejections personally. And, finally, it's never too late to try something new. I'm living proof. Now is the time to start making your dreams come true."

Don't Miss Out! Explore the Children's Religious Market

by Sally E. Stuart

If you have not explored your options in the religious area, you are missing sales to more than a third of your potential markets. Thirty-five percent of the periodicals in this market guide, for example, are religious. Once you discover religious magazines *and* book publishers, you'll be surprised at the range of options and at the apparent "coming of age" in this long-established, but expanding market.

"The best way to break into the religious market is to write for magazines before trying to sell a book," says Diane Stortz, children's book editor at Standard Publishing. "You can establish credibility that way; editors see that you can deliver. Plus you get great practice at your craft." Another benefit of starting with religious periodicals is that because so many are denominational publications with non-overlapping readerships, you can sell your material over and over — if you only sell one-time rights.

Sunday school take-home papers

A number of the "magazines" Stortz refers to are actually Sunday school take-home papers — eight-page leaflets (some 4 or 16 pages), published quarterly in weekly editions — that are distributed to children and teens in Sunday school classes. Because many denominations produce 52 of these every year (for each age-group), there is a tremendous demand for good material.

A typical take-home paper features a fiction piece but often adds a short article, a poem, and games, crafts or activities appropriate for the age-group. Some publications require an explicit religious message, but many accept an implicit message or a strong character-building tone. Avoid religious jargon or unexplained use of Christian symbols or symbolism that many children will not understand. Although a number of periodicals are denominational, it is not necessary to be intimately familiar with the doctrines of each group. Write from a Christian and/or religious world view and avoid doctrinal issues.

The articles and poetry used in take-home papers are often related to nature/creation or the Bible. Poems might include a Bible story told in rhyme, a look at nature or creation that reveals an implicit reverence for God, or a fun poem to delight a child. Some editors prefer true stories as opposed to fiction. Most are open to true stories about children who have done something significant or are living out their faith in specific ways.

Almost all social issues can be dealt with, generally from a conservative view-

Sally E. Stuart *is a nationally recognized expert on Christian writing, marketing and publishing. She is the author of the* Christian Writers' Market Guide, *a contributing editor for* The Christian Communicator, *and has sold more than 850 articles to nearly 100 different publications. Stuart lives in Aloha, Oregon, and speaks at Christian writers' conferences nationwide.*

point. "Social issues can certainly be addressed through the pages of Christian young people's magazines," says Randy Fishell, associate editor at *Guide Magazine*. "We have discovered, however, that such qualities as mystery, action and discovery are the vehicles that seem to work best in holding young readers' interest. If social issues are tackled, they must be addressed in an engaging way."

These papers also include how-to pieces on games, parties, crafts, recipes or family activities; a variety of word-puzzles; and jokes and short humor pieces. Because the papers are dated, they use a lot of holiday-related material.

For someone wanting to break into the religious market, take-home papers offer the best opportunity to learn what works and what doesn't. The sheer volume of material used improves your chances of being accepted. However, it's wise to send for guidelines and sample copies of publications that interest you and study them carefully. The publications put out by your own denomination are logical places to start, since you may already be familiar with them.

Magazines

The religious magazine market for children seems to be growing, although there have been casualties. (Perhaps parents who are used to getting take-home papers free at church are reluctant to subscribe.) These magazines are generally sponsored by religious ministries, rather than denominations, and are slick, full-color magazines that rival any in the general market. They include such publications as *Focus on the Family Clubhouse* (and *Clubhouse, Jr.*) and *Guideposts for Kids*. Mostly monthly, these magazines have highly visual, competitive appeal for children or teens.

"We strive to give kids a biblical perspective on today's problems to teach them *how* to think rather than *what* to think," explains Mary Lou Carney, editor at *Guideposts for Kids*. "Basic values like kindness, patience, self-discipline and honesty run through the magazine like arteries. They are shown, not told."

Periodicals in general

For the most part, topics deemed acceptable by religious children's magazines parallel those acceptable in all children's magazines. Publications for both children and teens are also showing an increasing interest in multicultural material.

Many publishers seek material on announced themes. If you send for a theme list from publishers who offer them, and submit pieces to fit those themes, you will greatly increase your chances of selling in this market.

The taboos in the religious market vary. Most editors do not like talking animals, fantasy or science fiction (although there are exceptions). Most do not publish material dealing with Santa Claus or the secular aspects of Christmas; some object to references to Halloween, ghosts, witches, etc.

No matter what you write, avoid being "preachy." Says Elaina Meyers, editor at *R-A-D-A-R*, "Our writers make references to prayer, Bible reading, and church attendance throughout their stories, rather than trying to tack [a moral] on at the end." Sister Anne Joan Flanagan, managing editor of *My Friend*, a Catholic magazine, adds, "Write as you would for adults; respect the reader. You wouldn't be moralistic or explicitly drag out every point for an adult reader—so why do it for kids?" And Janet Knight, editor at *Pockets*, simply says, "Avoid the words 'ought' and 'should.' "

Teen publications

Religious publications for teens vary from black and white and one- or two-color take-home papers to full-color, visually animated magazines. More than half of the teen publications are monthly or bimonthly magazines, and a third are weekly take-home papers. The take-home papers follow the same basic format as children's publications, but the magazines contain a wide variety of features of interest to teens, comparable to those in the general market. Several teen publications have recently ceased publication or are revamping as they attempt to keep up with the market's changing needs.

Teen publications use a lot of fiction, but they are also looking for a variety of nonfiction topics as revealed in this list of possible topics for *Straight*, a teen publication that regularly appears on *Writer's Digest* magazine's annual list of the top 100 magazine markets: controversial issues, Christian living, divorce, environment, ethnic, health, holidays, self-help, humor, profiles, money, music, siblings, experiences, dating and friends.

Book markets

If you watch the best-seller lists of Christian children's books, you'll notice the majority are children's versions of the Bible or Bible-story books, plus a few children's novels for 8- to 12-year-olds. Although most periodicals shy away from fantasy or science fiction, the best-seller book list often includes such titles as *The Lion, the Witch and the Wardrobe*, by C.S. Lewis, or a series of fantasy books by best-selling author Frank Peretti.

Even books that are not explicitly Christian can make it onto this best-seller list (which is based on sales in Christian bookstores). For more than a year, Robert Munsch's *Love You Forever*—a book with no religious content—has been as high as number two.

Although Christian bookstores stock such titles, few religious book publishers are willing to publish books that are not specifically religious. Spending some time in the children's section of a religious bookstore will give you a good feel for what is meant by "specifically religious." Most picture books tend to be illustrated Bible stories, or books on prayer or other virtues. Biographies of religious heroes or saints are also popular, along with books that deal with children's problems or making good choices.

"If stories are taken from the Bible, they should follow the biblical account closely," explains Ruth Geisler, family and children's resources editor at Concordia Publishing House. "We encourage humor and delightful touches of all kinds in our Bible story series, but because we espouse a conservative doctrine, our Bible stories are biblically accurate. Fictional characters may be used to add reader interest or provide detail, but nothing should contradict the Scriptural text."

"Instead of preaching, offer the truth as part of the thought process or experience of a character in the story," says Len Goss, editorial director at Crossway Books. "When the actions, words or thoughts of your character forcefully communicate your message, then readers will have been given a positive example that they will want to imitate."

Christmas is considered the only strong book-giving holiday by most Christian children's publishers, so you'll find Christmas books in the stores by June. Some houses also publish books on Easter or other religious holidays.

Most religious children's books are sold in religious bookstores. For the most part, only best sellers, such as the most popular children's Bibles or Bible-story books, make it into mainstream stores. The Christian Booksellers Association estimates there are 8,000 to 10,000 Christian bookstores nationwide, so religious children's books do get exposure.

Middle-grade fiction

As in the general children's market, publishers are looking for picture books, young readers, middle readers and teen/young adult books (although the market for teens is more limited). While working on the 1994-95 *Christian Writers' Market Guide*, I found a slight decrease in the number of publishers interested in young adult/teen fiction, while the number interested in picture books had increased since the previous edition. Today, it appears most publishers are looking for series books for middle readers and up.

Novels for 8- to 12-year-olds are actually the most open market for juveniles. Publishers are especially interested in contemporary realism, historical, humorous, adventure and mystery books. They are also interested in a wide range of ideas. Don't feel the need to create a family with two parents, two kids and a dog—consider the variety of today's families. "I want racial and ethnic authors who write [fiction about] what life is like in their communities," says Alice Pepplar, children's book editor at Augsburg Fortress Publishers. "No animals or talking trees, etc. [Or] stories about the nuclear, idealized family of the 1950s."

The top-selling juvenile genre in secular publishing is horror, even for very young kids, says Geisler (Concordia). "[With] the largest bulk of kids in the United States moving into middle school, ready for series fiction, and parents seeking material with wholesome, Christian values, juvenile Christian fiction will boom."

Liz Duckworth, managing editor, Children and Youth, at Victor Books adds, "The teen population should reach all-time peaks in the year 2006, so publishers should be ready with young adult fiction next."

Other opportunities

Besides religious periodicals and books, other outlets exist for religious writers—even young ones. Here are a few more possibilities for getting your work sold or recognized:

• *Markets for kids.* Most take-home papers and magazines are open to submissions from young readers. Standard Publishing's *Straight*, for example, publishes fiction and poetry from readers. Teen publications, especially, use teen poetry almost exclusively.

• *Curriculum markets.* There are also markets open to those interested in writing curriculum for children or teens. These are lesson plans put out by both denominational and non-denominational publishers and used by Sunday school teachers in local churches. Lessons are written to very strict guidelines and always on assignment, usually in units of 13. Curriculum writing requires an intimate knowledge of the religious field as a whole and the specific denomination in particular. Qualified writers may write to curriculum publishers, giving their background and experience, and request an assignment.

• *Special contests.* Watch for publisher-sponsored contests especially for religious material. For example, *Pockets* magazine sponsors an annual fiction writing contest for unpublished work, with winning entries appearing in the magazine. Published book writers, on the other hand, are eligible for the Gold Medallion Book Awards, from the Evangelical Christian Publishing Association. (For additional information on these and other contests, turn to the Contests & Awards section.)

Support for Christian writers

One of the best places to learn about writing for the Christian market is at a Christian writers' conference. The number of conferences across the country has increased dramatically over the last five years. Although some major ones have ceased, they have been replaced with local, one- to three-day seminars.

Attending seminars will provide you with expert instruction on how to write, a feel for what is expected in this market, along with an opportunity to meet and discuss projects with editors. You'll find Christian writers' conferences in the Conferences & Workshops section, and a complete list appears in the *Christian Writers' Market Guide* (for order information, write to 17768 SW Pointe Forest, Aloha OR 97006).

Although there are no publications that specifically deal with writing for the religious children's market, *The Christian Communicator* (P.O. Box 5168, Phoenix AZ 85010) is the leading publication for writers in the field and regularly carries articles on the children's market.

Some writers' organizations even offer correspondence courses on religious children's writing. The Christian Writer's Guild (260 Fern Lane, Hume CA 93628); The Writing Academy (6512 Colby Ave., Des Moines IA 50311-1713); and Christian Writers Institute (177 E. Crystal Lake Ave., Lake Mary FL 32746) all have courses available.

Jewish publishing

One of the oldest publishing houses in the country, the Jewish Publication Society (JPS), produces only Jewish titles. While this may seem like a highly specialized area, it's not a market that can be ignored. Although they make up less than two percent of the American population, the "People of the Book" buy more books per capita than any other group, according to a report in Children's Writer.

While publishers such as JPS, Jewish Lights Publishing, Behrman House and Kar-Ben Copies publish exclusively children's titles with Jewish themes, many mainstream houses publish Jewish titles as well. For example, Eric Kimmel's Jewish folktale Asher and the Capmakers *was published by Holiday House and Tambourine published Arthur A. Levine's* All the Lights in the Night. *Most mainstream Jewish titles, however, must have a universal appeal.*

If this market interests you, keep in mind that, just as in Christian material for children, Jewish books can have a broad range of formats and themes. A Jewish title could be anything from a board book about Hanukkah to a young adult novel about a boy in a Jewish family to a nonfiction reference about the Holocaust. But unlike Christianity, Judaism is not just a religion—it's a culture. Jews have their own language, customs, even food. And there are about a dozen Jewish holidays each year, including Hanukkah and Passover, that can be addressed in books.

Refer to the Subject Index at the back of this book under the Religious heading for publishers that produce both Jewish and Christian titles. Magazines such as Shofar, *which publishes Jewish material by adults* and *children, are market possibilities as well. Also note that several listings in the Contests & Awards section are specifically for Jewish material.*

The Business of Children's Writing & Illustrating

When a writer, illustrator or photographer decides to market her talents she will encounter many unexpected problems, and develop numerous questions about the field. "What is the proper way to submit my work?" "Do I need an agent?" "How much should I be paid for my material?" This article answers your questions—and exposes you to the business techniques needed to properly market your work.

Researching markets

There are two basic elements to submitting your work successfully: good research and persistence. Read through the listings in this book and familiarize yourself with the companies that interest you—study the specific needs and the required submission procedures of each. Editors and art directors hate to receive inappropriate submissions because handling them wastes precious time. By randomly sending out material without knowing the markets' needs, you're sure to meet with rejection.

If you're interested in submitting to a particular magazine, write to request a sample copy. For a book publisher, obtain a book catalog and check a library or bookstore for titles produced by that publisher. By studying such materials carefully, you can better acquaint yourself with that market's writing and illustration styles and formats.

Most of the book publishers and magazines listed (as well as many special markets such as greeting card and paper product companies) offer some sort of writer's/artist's/photographer's guidelines. Read these guidelines *before* submitting work.

Formats for submission

Throughout the listings you will read requests for particular elements to include when initially contacting markets. Every submission should be directed to a specific person. It is a good idea to call the company to confirm a contact name before sending anything. You do not need to speak to the contact person directly; merely ask the receptionist or secretary if the person still works there and if he still handles the submissions.

Query letters. A query letter should be no more than a one-page, well-written piece to arouse an editor's, art director's or producer's interest in your work. Queries are usually required from writers submitting nonfiction material to a publisher. In the query letter for a nonfiction piece you want to convince the editor your idea is perfect for his readership and you're the writer qualified to do the job. Note any previous writing experience in your letter and include published samples to prove your credentials, especially samples related to the subject matter about which you're querying.

Many query letters from writers start with leads similar to those of actual manuscripts. Next, briefly outline the work and include facts, anecdotes, interviews or other pertinent information that give the editor a feel for the manuscript's premise. Your goal is to entice him to want to know more. End your letter with a straightforward request to write (or submit) the work, and include information on its approximate length, date it could be completed, and the availability of accompanying photos or artwork.

More and more, queries are being requested for fiction manuscripts because slush piles at many publishing houses have become virtually uncontrollable. As the number of submissions continues to skyrocket, a number of publishers have stopped accepting unsolicited submissions. While some will now only accept agented material, many are still open to queries. For a fiction query, explain the story's plot, main characters, conflict and resolution. Just as in nonfiction queries, make the editor eager to see more. For more information on writing good queries, consult *How to Write Irresistible Query Letters*, by Lisa Collier Cool (Writer's Digest Books).

Cover letters. Some editors prefer to review complete manuscripts, especially for fiction. In such cases, the cover letter serves as your introduction, establishes your credentials as a writer, and gives the editor an overview of the manuscript.

If an editor asked for a manuscript because of a query, note this in your cover letter. Also, if an earlier rejection letter included an invitation to submit other work, mention that as well. Editors should know the work was solicited.

For an illustrator or photographer, the cover letter serves as an introduction to the art director or producer and establishes credentials as a professional. Explain what services you can provide as well as what type of follow-up contact you plan to make, if any. When sending samples of your work, indicate whether they should be returned or filed. Never send original work! If you wish to have the samples returned, include a self-addressed, stamped envelope (SASE). Cover letters, like queries, should be no longer than one page.

Résumés. Often writers, illustrators and photographers are asked to submit résumés with their cover letters and samples. Résumés can be created in a variety of formats ranging from a single page listing information to color brochures featuring your work. Keep the résumé brief, and focus on your achievements, including your clients and the work you've done for them, as well as your educational background and any awards you've received. Do not use the same résumé you use for a typical job application.

Book proposals. Throughout the listings in the Book Publishers section you will find references to the submission of a synopsis, outline and sample chapters. Depending on an editor's preference, some or all of these components, as well as inclusion of a cover letter, make up a book proposal.

A synopsis summarizes the book. Such a summary covers the basic plot of the book (including the ending), is easy to read and flows well.

An outline can also be used to set up fiction but is more effective as a tool for nonfiction. The outline covers your book chapter by chapter and provides highlights of each. If you are developing an outline for fiction include major characters, plots and subplots, and length of the book. An outline can run to 30 pages depending on the complexity of your manuscript.

Sample chapters give a more comprehensive idea of your writing skill. Some editors may request the first two or three chapters to see how your material is set up; others may request beginning, middle and ending chapters to get a better feel for the entire plot. Be sure to determine what the editor needs to see before investing time in writing and/or revising sample chapters.

Manuscript formats. If an editor wants you to submit a complete manuscript, you should follow some basic guidelines. In the upper left corner of your title page, type your legal name (not pseudonym), address, phone number and Social Security number (publishers must have this to file payment records with the government). In the upper right corner, type the approximate word length. All material in the upper corners should be typed single-spaced. Then type the title (centered) almost halfway down the page with the word "by" two spaces under that and your name or pseudonym two spaces under "by."

The first page should also include the title (centered) one-third of the way down. Two spaces under that type "by" and your name or pseudonym. To begin the body of your manuscript, drop down two double spaces and indent five spaces for each new paragraph. There should be 1¼ inch margins around all sides of a full typewritten page. (Manuscripts with wide margins are more readable and easier to edit.) Set your computer or typewriter on double-space for the manuscript body. From page two to the end of your manuscript include your last name followed by a comma and the title (or key words of the title) in the upper left corner. The page number should go in the top right corner. Drop down two double spaces to begin the body of each page. If you're submitting a novel, type each chapter title one-third of the way down the page. For more information on manuscript formats read *Manuscript Submission*, by Scott Edelstein (Writer's Digest Books).

Picture books. The majority of editors prefer to see complete manuscripts for picture books. When typing the text of a picture book, it is not necessary to include page breaks or supply art. As echoed in the interviews throughout this book, editors prefer to find the illustrators for picture books. Most of the time, a writer and an illustrator who work on the same book never meet. In this kind of arrangement, the editor acts as a go-between in case either the writer or illustrator has any problems with text or artwork. *How to Write and Sell Children's Picture Books*, by Jean E. Karl (Writer's Digest Books), offers advice on preparing text and marketing your work.

If you are an illustrator who has written your own book, create a dummy or storyboard containing both art and text. Then submit it along with your complete manuscript and sample pieces of final art (color photocopies or slides—no originals). Publishers interested in picture books specify in their listings what should be submitted. For a step-by-step guide on creating a good dummy, refer to Frieda Gates's book, *How to Write, Illustrate, and Design Children's Books* (Lloyd-Simone Publishing Company).

Mailing and recording submissions

Your primary concern in packaging material is to ensure it arrives undamaged. If your manuscript is fewer than six pages it is safe to simply fold it in thirds and send it out in a #10 (business-size) envelope. For a self-addressed, stamped envelope (SASE) you can then fold another #10 envelope in thirds or insert a #9 (reply) envelope which fits in a #10 neatly without any folding. Some editors like receiving a manuscript folded in half in a 6×9 envelope. For larger manuscripts use a 9×12 envelope both for mailing the submission out and as a SASE for its return. The SASE can be folded in half. Book manuscripts require a sturdy box (such as a typing paper or envelope box) for mailing. Include a self-addressed mailing label and return postage.

If asked to send artwork and photographs, remember they require a bit more care in packaging to guarantee they arrive in good condition. Sandwich illustrations and photos between heavy cardboard that is slightly larger than the work, and securely tape the cardboard together. Write your name and address on each piece in case the inside material becomes separated. For the packaging use either a manila envelope, foam-padded envelope, brown paper or a mailer with plastic air bubbles as a liner. Bind non-joined edges with reinforced mailing tape and affix a typed mailing label or clearly write your address.

Mail material first class to ensure quick delivery. Also, first-class mail is forwarded for one year if the addressee has moved, and can be returned if undeliverable. If you are concerned about your material safely reaching its destination, consider other mailing options, such as UPS or certified mail. If material needs to reach your editor, art director or producer quickly, you can elect to use overnight delivery services.

Throughout this book you will occasionally see the term International Reply Coupon (IRC). Keep in mind markets outside your own country cannot use your country's postage when returning a manuscript to you. When mailing a submission to another country, include a self-addressed envelope and IRCs. Your post office can help you determine, based on the package's weight, the correct number of IRCs to include to ensure its return.

If it is not necessary for an editor to return your work, such as with photocopies, don't include return postage. Instead, track the status of your submission by enclosing a postage-paid reply postcard with options for the editor to check, such as "Yes, I am interested," "I'll keep the material on file," or "No, the material is not appropriate for my needs at this time."

Some writers, illustrators and photographers simply include a deadline date. If nothing is heard from the editor, art director or producer by the specified date, the manuscript, artwork or photos are automatically withdrawn from consideration. Because many publishing houses and companies are overstocked with material, a minimum deadline should be at least three months.

One thing you should never do is use a company's fax number to send queries, manuscripts or samples. Only use a fax number after acquiring proper authorization so you don't disrupt the company's internal business.

It's important to keep track of the material you submit. When recording each submission be sure to include the date it was sent, the business and contact name, and any enclosures such as samples of writing, artwork or photography. Keep copies of the article or manuscript you send together with related correspondence for easier follow up. When you sell rights to a manuscript, artwork or photos you can "close" your file by noting the date the material was accepted, what rights were purchased, the publication date and payment.

Many times writers, illustrators and photographers devote their attention to submitting material, then fail to follow up on overdue responses because they feel the situation is out of their hands. If you don't hear from a market within its stated response time, wait a month and then follow up with a note inquiring about the status of your submission. Include the title or description, date sent, and SASE for response. Ask the contact person when he anticipates making a decision. By doing this you may refresh the memory of a buyer who temporarily forgot about your submission, or revise a troublesome point to make your work more enticing to him. At the very least you will receive a definite "no," thereby freeing you to send your material to another market.

Simultaneous submissions

If you opt for simultaneous submissions—sending the same material to several editors at the same time—be sure to inform each editor your work is being considered elsewhere. Doing so is a professional courtesy encouraged throughout the field. Most editors are reluctant to receive simultaneous submissions but understand the frustration experienced by hopeful freelancers who must wait many months for a response. In some cases, an editor may actually be more inclined to read your manuscript sooner because he knows it's being considered elsewhere.

The Society of Children's Book Writers and Illustrators, however, warns against simultaneous submissions, for fear they will eventually cause publishers to quit accepting unsolicited material altogether. Also, since simultaneously submitted manuscripts are not specifically tailored to any one publisher, SCBWI feels the act will result in less than serious consideration of work received. The official recommendation of the SCBWI is to submit to one publisher at a time, but wait only three months (note you will do so in your cover letter). If no response is received, then send a note withdrawing your manuscript from consideration. SCBWI considers simultaneous submissions acceptable only if you have a manuscript dealing with a timely issue.

It is especially important to keep track of submissions when you are submitting simultaneously. This way if you get an offer on that manuscript, you can instruct the other publishers to withdraw your work from consideration.

Agents and representatives

Many children's writers, illustrators or photographers, especially those who are just beginning, are confused about whether to enlist the services of an agent or representative. The decision is strictly one that each writer, illustrator or photographer must decide for herself. Some are confident with their own negotiation skills and feel acquiring an agent or rep is not in their best interest. Others feel uncomfortable in the business arena or are not willing to sacrifice valuable creative time for marketing.

Enough demand for children's material exists that breaking into children's publishing without an agent is easier than breaking into the adult market without one. Also, some agents avoid working with children's books because traditionally low advances and trickling royalty payments over long periods of time make children's books less lucrative. Writers targeting magazine markets do not need the services of an agent. In fact, it's practically impossible to find one interested in marketing articles and short stories, as there simply isn't enough financial incentive.

One benefit of having an agent, though, is it may expedite the process of getting your work reviewed, especially with publishers who don't accept unagented submissions (a policy becoming more and more common in children's publishing). If an agent has a good reputation and submits your manuscript to an editor, that manuscript may actually bypass the first-read stage (which is done by editorial assistants and junior editors) and end up on the editor's desk sooner. And illustrators and photographers who live elsewhere often seek representatives based in New York City when they want their work shown to New York City publishers.

When agreeing to have a reputable agent represent you, remember that she should be familiar with the needs of the current market and evaluate your manuscript/artwork/photos accordingly. She should also determine the quality of your piece and whether it is saleable. Upon selling your manuscript, your agent should negotiate a favorable contract and clear up any questions you have about monetary payments. One advantage to having an agent be the "go-between" is that she acts as the "bad guy" during negotiations. This allows you, as an individual, to preserve your good faith with the publisher.

Keep in mind that however reputable the agent or rep is, she has limitations. Representation does not guarantee sale of your work. It just means an agent or rep sees potential in your writing, art or photos. Though an agent or rep may offer criticism or advice on how to improve your work, she cannot make you a better writer, artist or photographer or give you fame.

Literary agents typically charge a 15 percent commission from the sale of writing; art and photo representatives usually charge a 25 to 30 percent commission. Such fees are taken from advances and royalty earnings. If your agent sells foreign rights to your work, she will deduct a higher percentage because she will most likely be dealing with an overseas agent with whom she must split the fee.

Some agents offer reading services. If you are a new writer, you will probably be charged a fee of less than $75. Many times, if an agent agrees to represent you, the fee will be reimbursed (though not always). If you wish to use an agency's critique service, expect to pay $25-200 depending on the length of the manuscript. The purpose of a critique service is not to polish the manuscript, but to offer advice based on the agent's knowledge of what sells in juvenile publishing.

Prior to using a reading or critique service, find out up front what results to expect. Beware of agencies that derive most of their income from reading and critique services. Unfortunately, some in this business are more interested in earning their money from services than from selling books.

Other standard fees incurred from an agent include miscellaneous expenses such as photocopying, phone bills, postage or messenger services. Before signing a contract with an agent, find out the exact terms, such as the rate of commission charged and the expenses you will be expected to pay.

Be advised that not every agent is open to representing a writer, artist or photographer who lacks an established track record. Your manuscript, artwork or photos, and query or cover letter, must be attractive and professional looking. Your first impression must be that of an organized, articulate person.

Feel free to investigate an agent or rep before contacting her. Determine, for instance, how familiar and successful she is with selling to children's publishers. For a detailed directory of literary agents, refer to *Guide to Literary Agents*; for listings of art reps, consult the 1995 *Artist's & Graphic Designer's Market*; and for photo reps, see the 1995 *Photographer's Market* (all Writer's Digest Books).

Negotiating contracts and royalties

Negotiation is a two-way street on which, hopefully, both parties will feel mutual satisfaction prior to signing a contract.

Book publishers pay authors and artists in royalties, a percentage of either the wholesale or retail price of each book sold. From large publishing houses, the author usually receives an advance issued against future royalties before the book is published. Half of the advance amount is issued upon signing the book contract; the other half is issued when the book is finished. For illustrations, one-third of the advance should be collected upon signing the contract; one-third upon delivery of sketches; and one-third upon delivery of finished art.

After your book has sold enough copies to earn back your advance, you will start to get royalty checks. Some publishers hold a reserve against returns, meaning a percentage of royalties is held back in case books are returned. If you have such a reserve clause in your contract, make sure to find out the exact percentage of total sales that will be withheld and the time period the publisher will hold this money. You should be reimbursed this amount after a reasonable time period, such as a year. Royalty percentages vary with each publisher, but there are standard ranges.

According to the latest figures from SCBWI, picture book writers can expect advances of $3,500-5,000; picture book illustrators' advances range from $7,000-10,000; text and illustration packages can score $8,000-10,000. Royalties for picture books are generally about 5 percent (split between the author and illustrator), but can go as high as 10 percent. Those who both write and illustrate a book, of course, receive the full royalty.

Advances for chapter books and middle grade novels vary slightly from picture books. Hardcover titles can fetch authors advances of $4,000-6,000 and 10% royalties; paperbacks bring in slightly lower advances of $3,000-5,000 and royalties of 6-8 percent. Fees for young adult novels are generally the same, but additional length may bring fees and royalties up a bit.

As you might expect, advance and royalty figures vary from house to house and are affected by such factors as the time of year and the state of the economy. Some smaller houses may not even pay royalties, just flat fees. First-time writers and illustrators generally start on the low end of the scale, while established and high-profile writers are paid more.

Writers will find price structures for magazines based on a per-word rate or range for a specific length of article. Artists and photographers have a few more variables to contend with before contracting their services.

Payment for illustrations and photos can be set by such factors as whether the piece(s) will be black and white or four-color, how many are to be purchased, and the artist's or photographer's prior experience. Determine an hourly rate by using the annual salary of a staff artist doing similar work in an economically similar geographic area (try to find an artist or photographer willing to share this information), then dividing that salary by 52 (the number of weeks in a year) and again by 40 (the number of hours in a work week). To figure in overhead expenses such as rent, utilities, supplies, etc., multiply the hourly rate you came up with by 2.5. Research again to be sure your rate is competitive.

Once you make a sale you will probably sign a contract. A contract is an agreement between two or more parties that specifies the fees to be paid, services rendered, deadlines, rights purchased and, for artists and photographers, whether original work is returned. Most companies have standard contracts for writers, illustrators and photographers. The specifics (such as royalty rates, advances, delivery dates, etc.) are typed in after negotiations.

Though it is okay to conduct negotiations over the telephone, be sure to obtain a written contract once both parties have agreed on terms. Do not depend on oral stipulations; written contracts protect both parties from misunderstandings. Watch for clauses that may not be in your best interest, such as "work-for-hire." When you do work for hire, you give up all rights to your creations. Several reputable children's magazines, such as *Highlights for Children*, buy all rights, and many writers and illustrators believe it is worth the concession in order to break into the field. However, once you've entered the field, it's in your best interest to keep the rights to your work.

Be sure you know whether your contract contains an option clause. This clause requires the author to give the publisher a first look at her next work before marketing it to other publishers. Though it is editorial etiquette to give the publisher the first chance at publishing your next work, be wary of statements in the contract which could trap you. Don't allow the publisher to consider the next project for more than 30 days and be specific about what type of work should actually be considered "next work" (for example, if the book under contract is a young adult novel, specify that the publisher will only receive an exclusive look at your next young adult novel).

If there are clauses that appear vague or confusing, get legal advice. The time and money invested in counseling up front could protect you from more serious problems later. If you have an agent or rep, she will review any contract.

One final note. When a book goes out of print, a publisher will sell any existing copies to a wholesaler who, in turn, sells the copies to stores at a discount. When the books are "remaindered" to a wholesaler, they are usually sold at a price just above the cost of printing. When negotiating a contract with a publisher you may want to discuss the possibility of purchasing the remaindered copies before they are sold to a wholesaler. Then you can market the copies you purchased and still make a profit.

Copyright protection

A copyright is a form of protection provided to creators of original works, published or unpublished. The Copyright Act of 1976 (which went into effect January 1, 1978) states that work is protected as soon as it's created. International recognition of copyright protection is provided in the Berne Convention, ratified in March 1989, which prevents foreign piracy of works copyrighted in the U.S. and allows prosecution of foreign copyright infringers in foreign courts.

While works are protected once they are created, to proceed with an infringement lawsuit, the work must be registered. A person who infringes upon a registered copyright is subject to greater liabilities, even when no damages or profits are made as a result of the infringement. Some feel a copyright notice should be included on all work, registered or not. Others feel it is not necessary and a copyright notice will only confuse publishers about whether the material is registered (acquiring rights to previously registered material is a more complicated process).

Although it is not necessary to include a copyright notice on unregistered work, if you don't feel your work is safe without a copyright notice, it is your right to include one. Including a copyright notice – © (*year of work, your name*) – should help ensure your work against plagiarism.

Registration is a legal formality intended to make copyright public record. As stated, registration of work is necessary to file any infringement suits. Also, registration can help you win more money in a court case. By registering work within three months of publication or before an infringement occurs, you are eligible to collect statutory damages and attorney's fees. If you register later than three months after publication, you will qualify only for actual damages and profits.

Keep in mind that ideas and concepts are not copyrightable, but expressions of those ideas and concepts are. A character type or basic plot outline is not subject to a copyright infringement lawsuit. Also, titles, names, short phrases or slogans, and lists of contents are not subject to copyright protection, though titles and names may be protected through the Trademark Office.

In general, copyright protection ensures the writer, illustrator or photographer the power to decide how her work is used and allows her to receive payment for each use. Essentially a copyright also encourages the creation of new works by guaranteeing the power to sell rights to them in the marketplace. The copyright holder can print, reprint or copy her work; sell or distribute copies of her work; or prepare derivative works such as plays, collages or recordings. The Copyright

Law is designed to protect a writer's, illustrator's or photographer's work (copyrighted on or after January 1, 1978) for her lifetime plus 50 years.

If you collaborate with someone else on a written or artistic project, the copyright will last for the lifetime of the last survivor plus 50 years. The creators' heirs may hold a copyright for an additional 50 years. After that, the work becomes public domain. In addition, works created anonymously or under a pseudonym are protected for 100 years, or 75 years after publication. Incidentally, this latter rule is also true of work-for-hire agreements. Under work-for-hire you relinquish your copyright to your "employer." Try to avoid agreeing to such terms.

For *members* of the Society of Children's Book Writers and Illustrators, in-depth information about copyrights and the law is available. Send a self-addressed, stamped envelope to the Society of Children's Book Writers and Illustrators, 22736 Vanowen St., Suite 106, West Hills CA 91307 and request their brochure, "Copyright Facts for Writers."

For more information about the proper procedure to register works, contact the Copyright Office, Library of Congress, Washington DC 20559. The forms available are **TX** for writing (books, articles, etc.); **VA** for pictures (photographs, illustrations); and **PA** for plays and music. (To order copyright forms by phone, call (202)707-9100.) For information about how to use the copyright forms, request a copy of Circular I on Copyright Basics. All of these forms are free. Send the completed registration form along with the stated fee and a copy of the work to the Copyright Office. You can register a group of articles, illustrations or photos if it meets these criteria:

- the group is assembled in order, such as in a notebook;
- the works bear a single title, such as "Works by (*your name*)";
- it is the work of one writer, artist or photographer;
- the material is the subject of a single claim to copyright.

It is a publisher's responsibility to register your book for copyright. If you have previously registered the same material, you must inform your editor and supply the previous copyright information. Otherwise, the publisher cannot register the book in its published form.

For specific answers to questions about copyright (but not legal advice), call the Copyright Public Information Office at (202)707-3000 weekdays between 8:30 a.m. and 5 p.m. EST.

Rights for writers, illustrators & photographers

The copyright law specifies that a writer, illustrator or photographer generally sells one-time rights to her work unless she and the buyer agree otherwise in writing. Be forewarned that some editors may not be aware of this. Many publications will want more exclusive rights from you than just one-time usage of your work; some will even require you to sell all rights. Be sure you are monetarily compensated for the additional rights you relinquish. It is always to your benefit to retain as much control as possible over your work.

Writers who only give up limited rights to their work can then sell reprint rights to other publications, foreign rights to international publications, or even movie rights, should the opportunity arise. Likewise, artists and photographers can sell their work to other markets such as to paper-product companies who may use an image on a calendar or greeting card. Illustrators and photographers may even sell original work after it has been published. And there are now galleries throughout the U.S. that display the work of children's illustrators.

Exercising more control over ownership of your work gives you a greater marketing edge for resale. If you must give up all rights to a work, carefully consider the price you are being offered to determine whether you'll be compensated for the loss of other sales.

Rights acquired through the sale of a book manuscript are explained in each publisher's contract. Take time to read through relevant clauses to be sure you understand what rights each contract is specifying before signing. Make sure your contract contains a clause allowing all rights to revert back to you in the event the publisher goes out of business. These are the rights you will most often be selling to publishers, periodicals and producers in the marketplace:

• *One-time rights*—The buyer has no guarantee that he is the first to use a piece. One-time permission to run written work, illustrations or photos is acquired, then the rights revert back to the creator.

• *First rights*—The creator sells the rights to use the work for the first time in any medium. All other rights remain with the creator. When material is excerpted from a soon-to-be-published book for use in a newspaper or periodical, first serial rights are also purchased.

• *First North American serial rights*—This is similar to first rights, except that companies who distribute both in the U.S. and Canada will stipulate these rights to ensure that a company in the other country won't come out with simultaneous usage of the same work.

• *Second serial (reprint) rights*—In this case newspapers and magazines are granted the right to reproduce a work that already has appeared in another publication. These rights are also purchased by a newspaper or magazine editor who wants to publish part of a book after the book has been published. The proceeds from reprint rights are often split 50/50 between the author and his publishing company.

• *Simultaneous rights*—Use of such rights occurs among magazines with circulations that don't overlap, such as many religious publications. Many spiritual stories, illustrations or photos are appropriate for a variety of denominational periodicals. (For information on other aspects of the religious market, see Don't Miss Out! Explore the Children's Religious Market on page 22.) Be sure you submit to a publication that allows simultaneous submissions, and be sure to state in your cover letter that the submission is being considered elsewhere (to a non-competing market).

• *All rights*—Rights such as these are purchased by publishers who pay premium usage fees, have an exclusive format, or have other book or magazine interests from which the purchased work can generate more mileage. (Some magazines that purchase all rights to artwork use the same work again several years later.) When the writer, illustrator or photographer sells all rights to a market she no longer has any say in who acquires rights to use her piece.

Synonymous with purchase of all rights is the term "work-for-hire." Under such an agreement the creator of a work gives away all rights—and her copyright—to the company buying her work. It's best to avoid such agreements; they're not in your best interest. If a market insists on acquiring all rights to your work, see if you can negotiate for the rights to revert back to you after a reasonable period of time. If they agree to such a proposal, get it in writing.

• *Foreign serial rights*—Be sure before you market to foreign publications that you have only sold North American—not worldwide—serial rights to previous markets. If so, you are free to market to publications you think may be interested in material that has appeared in a North American-based periodical.

• *Syndication rights*—This is a division of serial rights. For example, if a syndicate prints portions of a book in installments in its newspapers, it would be syndicating second serial rights. The syndicate would receive a commission and leave the remainder to be split between the author and publisher.

● *Subsidiary rights* — These include serial rights, dramatic rights, book club rights or translation rights. The contract should specify what percentage of profits from sales of these rights go to the author and publisher.

● *Dramatic, television and motion picture rights* — During a specified time the interested party tries to sell a story to a producer or director. Many times options are renewed because the selling process can be lengthy.

● *Display rights* — Watch out for these. They're also known as "Electronic Publishing Rights" or "Data, Storage and Retrieval." Usually listed under subsidiary rights, they're not clear. They refer to many means of publication not yet fully developed. If a display rights clause is listed in your contract, try to negotiate its elimination. Otherwise, demand the clause be restricted to things designed to be read only. By doing this, you maintain your rights to use your work for things such as games and interactive software.

Business records

It is imperative to keep accurate business records to determine if you are making a profit as a writer, illustrator or photographer. Keep a bank account and ledger apart from your personal finances. Also, if writing, illustrating or photography is secondary to another freelance career, maintain separate business records from that as well.

If you're just starting, you will likely accumulate some business expenses prior to showing any profit. To substantiate your income and expenses to the IRS, keep all invoices, cash receipts, sales slips, bank statements, cancelled checks and receipts related to travel expenses and entertaining clients. For entertainment expenditures record the date, place and purpose of the business meeting as well as gas mileage.

Be sure to file all receipts in chronological order; if you maintain a separate file for each month, it will provide for easier retrieval of records at year's end. Keeping receipts is important for all purchases, big and small. Don't take the small purchases for granted. Enough of them can result in a rather substantial sum.

When setting up a single-entry bookkeeping system, record income and expenses separately. It may prove easier to use some of the subheads that appear on Schedule C (the form used for recording income from a business) of the 1040 tax form. This way you can easily transfer information onto the tax form when filing your return. In your ledger include a description of each transaction — date, source of income (or debts from business purchases), description of what was purchased or sold, the amount of the transaction, and whether payment was by cash, check or credit card.

You don't have to wait until January 1 to start keeping records, either. The moment you first make a business-related purchase or sell an article, book manuscript, illustration or photo begin tracking your profits and losses. If you keep records from January 1 to December 31 you are using a calendar-year accounting period. Any other accounting period is known as a fiscal year.

You also can choose between two types of accounting methods — the cash method and the accrual method. The cash method is used more often: You record income when it is received and expenses when they are disbursed. Under the accrual method you report income at the time you earn it rather than when it is actually received. Similarly, expenses are recorded at the time they are incurred rather than when you actually pay them. If you choose this method keep separate records for "accounts receivable" and "accounts payable."

Taxes

To successfully (and legally) compete in the business of writing or illustrating, you must know what income you should report and deductions you can claim. Yet before you can do this, you must prove to the IRS that you are in business to make a profit, that your writing, illustrating or photography is not merely a hobby. Under the Tax Reform Act of 1986 it was determined you should show a profit for three years out of a five-year period to attain professional status. What does the IRS look for as proof of your professionalism? Keeping accurate financial records (see previous section on business records), maintaining a business bank account separate from your personal account, the time you devote to your profession and whether it is your main or secondary source of income, and your history of profits and losses. The amount of training you have invested in your field—as well as your expertise—is also a contributing factor.

If your business is unincorporated, you will fill out tax information on Schedule C of Form 1040. If you're unsure of what deductions you can take, request the appropriate IRS publication containing this information. Under the Tax Reform Act, only 50 percent of business meals, entertainment and related tips, and parking charges are deductible. Other deductible expenses allowed on Schedule C include: car expenses for business-related trips, professional courses and seminars, depreciation of office equipment (such as a computer), dues and publications, and miscellaneous expenses, such as postage used for business needs, etc.

If you're working out of a home office, a portion of your mortgage interest (or rent), related utilities, property taxes, repair costs and depreciation may be deducted as business expenses—under special circumstances. To learn more about the possibility of home office deductions, consult IRS Publication 587, Business Use of Your Home.

The method of paying taxes on income not subject to withholding is called "estimated tax" for individuals. If you expect to owe more than $500 at year's end and if the total amount of income tax that will be withheld during the year will be less than 90% of the tax shown on the current year's return, you will generally make estimated tax payments. Estimated tax payments are made in four equal installments due on April 15, June 15, September 15 and January 15 (assuming you're a calendar-year taxpayer). For more information, request Publication 505, Self-Employment Tax.

Depending on your net income you may be liable for a Social Security tax. This is a tax designed for those who don't have Social Security withheld from their paychecks. You're liable if your net income is $400 or more per year. Net income is the difference between your income and allowable business deductions. Request Schedule SE, Computation of Social Security Self-Employment Tax, if you qualify.

If completing your income tax return proves to be too complex, consider hiring an accountant or contact the IRS for assistance. In addition to numerous publications to instruct you in various facets of preparing a tax return, the IRS also has walk-in centers in some cities.

Insurance

As a self-employed professional be aware of what health and business insurance coverage is available to you. Unless you're a Canadian who is covered by national health insurance or a fulltime freelancer covered by your spouse's policy, health insurance will no doubt be one of your biggest expenses. Under the terms of the Consolidated Omnibus Budget Reconciliation Act (COBRA) of 1985, if you leave a job with health benefits, you are entitled to continue that coverage for at least 18 months at the insurer's cost plus a small administration charge. Eventually, though, you must search for your own health plan. Keep in mind you may also need disability and life insurance.

Disability insurance is offered through many private insurance companies and state governments, and pays a monthly fee that covers living and business expenses during periods of long-term recuperation from a health problem. The amount of money paid is based on the recipient's annual earnings.

Before contacting any insurance representative, talk to other writers, illustrators or photographers to find which insurance companies they recommend. If you belong to a writers' or artists' organization, be sure to contact them to determine if any insurance coverage for professionals is offered to members. Such group coverage may prove less expensive and yield more comprehensive coverage than an individual policy.

Key to Symbols

* *Symbol indicating a listing is new in this edition*
■ *Symbol indicating a market subsidy publishes manuscripts*
‡ *Symbol indicating a contest is open to students*
● *Symbol indicating a comment from the editors of* Children's Writer's & Illustrator's Market

---

Important Market Listing Information

● *Listings are based on questionnaires, phone calls and updated copy. They are not advertisements nor are markets reported here necessarily endorsed by the editors of this book.*
● *Information in the listings comes directly from the companies and is as accurate as possible, but situations may change and needs may fluctuate between the publication of this directory and the time you use it.*
● Children's Writer's & Illustrator's Market *reserves the right to exclude any listing that does not meet its requirements.*

Show Us What You've Sold!

Les Gray created this dad diligently shampooing his daughter's hair, as well as five other illustrations, for "Daddy Stays Home with Me," by Lois G. Grambling. The short story, which appeared in the October/November issue of Humpty Dumpty's Maga- *zine, is a sweet tale told from the perspective of a little girl.* Humpty Dumpty's *is for an audience ages 4-6 and uses uncomplicated, colorful artwork on almost every page.*

Throughout *Children's Writer's & Illustrator's Market you'll find similar examples of artwork purchased by book publishers and magazines. How would you like to see your work in our next edition? Send us a tearsheet, photo, or good quality photocopy of work—done on a freelance basis—which was purchased by a market listed in this book. Include information about who purchased it and how it was used, as well as your name, address and telephone number. (Send to CWIM Artwork, 1507 Dana Ave., Cincinnati OH 45207.) If we pick your illustration or photo, we'll pay $50 to the owner of the rights, and both you and the publisher will receive a copy of the 1996* Children's Writer's & Illustrator's Market *absolutely free!*

The Markets

Book Publishers

The children's book industry, which just a few years ago seemed to be growing by leaps and bounds, has begun to mature. Sales have leveled off, and marketing consultants Veronis, Suhler & Associates predict slow growth in consumer spending on children's titles in the next five years. Stores and publishers report an increase in returns, buyers are becoming more cautious in purchasing new titles, and publishers are still relying heavily on their backlists for sure sales.

Even Macmillan, a stable force in children's publishing for nearly 75 years, was not immune to corporate takeover and downsizing, merging with Simon & Schuster in late 1993. The two houses, which entered the merger with 16 imprints between them, have been condensed to six imprints—Atheneum Books for Young Readers, Macmillan Books for Young Readers, Simon & Schuster Books for Young Readers, Margaret K. McElderry Books, Aladdin Paperbacks and Little Simon. The company is using the name Simon & Schuster. (For a good breakdown and explanation, see the new information in this year's listings and the August 1994 issue of *Children's Book Insider*.)

All told, it only makes sense that publishing houses deluged with submissions must be more selective in determining which manuscripts to purchase. More and more houses have adopted a "does not accept unsolicited manuscripts" policy. A number of them will now only accept material through agents. (Watch for information on agented material, as well as editorial comments on policy changes, within the listings. Also, refer to the Business of Children's Writing & Illustrating for more information on agents.)

While such news may initially be disheartening for newcomers to the children's field, the end result is sure to be a curb in "over publishing" and the production of stronger titles—ones that will attract the attention of both bookstore owners and prospective book buyers. Many publishers believe the key is to focus their lists, to specialize, to find and fill the niches unaddressed by the book boom of the '80s. For example, among our new listings in this year's book you'll find publishers such as McClanahan Book Company which produces board-, work- and storybooks for the very young reader and Oliver Press which specializes in collective biographies. This means children's writers and illustrators must study the market even more carefully than in the past, submit highly polished work and persevere.

Be wary of trends

In her September-October editorial in *The Horn Book Magazine*, Editor-in-Chief Anita Silvey, citing as examples the work of Maurice Sendak, Dr. Seuss, Patricia MacLachlan and Lois Lowry, says that in the last 50 years in children's publishing, "the books that changed the industry were published *contrary* to all trends. By going against the current wisdom creators and publishers set new standards and directions and gave children and young adults some of their finest books."

Arthur Levine, editor-in-chief of Knopf Books for Young Readers (see the Insider Report on page 100) points out that because of lengthy production time, what appears in bookstores is not always a reflection of what publishers are currently working on. Writers trying to keep up with trends may actually be a few *years* behind. So, ultimately, it's the substance of your submission, not the topic, that's important to a prospective publisher.

As always, the key to marketing both children's writing and illustration is to match your interests with that of the publisher. To help you locate markets seeking the work you're creating, we've included a Subject Index at the back of this book. This index lists book and magazine publishers according to their fiction and nonfiction needs and/or interests. Use the Age-Level Index in conjunction with the Subject Index and you'll narrow the list of possible markets even further.

For instance, if you write historical fiction for middle readers and you're trying to place a book manuscript, go first to the Subject Index. Locate the fiction categories under Book Publishers and find History. Make a list of the book publishers listed there. Now go to the Age-Level Index and see if any of the publishers on your list are included under the heading Middle Readers. Circle them. Read the listings for those publishers and see if your work matches their needs.

Expanding categories

Talk of topical trends aside, some types of children's books appear to be more popular than others. Picture books, for instance, was the booming category for many years. Now, however, their status is changing. In fact, a report in *Publishers Weekly* noted that picture books was the major area in which retailers were noticing a slowdown in growth—and increased price resistance.

Yet, while picture books may be a concern in the retail sector, nonfiction picture books are expanding their audience and, perhaps, their slice of the educational market. No longer are picture books with nonfiction subjects just for preschoolers and elementary school children. In fact, artwork and photographs are being integrated into nonfiction books aimed at even older readers.

While picture books is an area to watch, other categories are also expanding. One area that's undoubtedly booming is the easy-to-read market, comprising the first books children read on their own. Another area in which interest is increasing, though much more slowly, is that of historical fiction for middle readers. The growth in this area, as well as the growth in nonfiction picture books, is due in large part to teachers who are incorporating more trade books into their classrooms.

Though Veronis, Suhler & Associates forecast a decrease in the growth rate of consumer spending on books, they also predict an increase in the growth rate of educational and professional spending, particularly on the elementary through high school level. This not only means the above categories could expand even further, but it also translates into increased opportunities for writers and illustrators.

Finally, while the interest in science fiction and fantasy books appears to be growing in the young adult market, horror has taken a firm hold on the best seller lists in the form of the series. Editors expect teen horror to be the most popular genre of the decade.

Why are today's teens reading the latest novel by R.L. Stine or Christopher Pike (the "superstars" of the genre) instead of the romances so popular in the

'80s? Part of the reason is that young adult horror novels appeal to both boys and girls, though the protagonists are primarily female. Similar to romances, the suspense-filled plots are written in a predictable formula. In addition, the books are very teen-centered; adults are merely peripheral characters. And these stories of graphic violence and multiple murders have room for a bit of romance. Watch for this category to continue to expand with books for 8- to 12-year-olds in which editors are looking for "creepy suspense rather than serial killers," reports *Children's Writer*.

Subsidy publishing

Some writers who are really determined to get their work into print, but who receive rejections from royalty publishers, may look to subsidy publishers as an option. Subsidy publishers ask writers to pay all or part of the costs of producing a book. Some of the listings in this section give percentages of subsidy-published material and are marked with a solid block (■).

Aspiring writers should strongly consider working solely with publishers who pay. Such publishers will be active in marketing work because they profit only through these efforts. Subsidy publishers, on the other hand, make their money from writers who pay to have their books published. In fact, some operations are more interested in the contents of your wallet than the contents of your book. And you must do your own marketing and promotion. Though there are reputable subsidy publishers, those considering such services should take a "buyer beware" attitude. Any contracts offered by these houses should be carefully inspected by a lawyer or someone qualified to analyze these types of documents.

If you're interested in publishing your book just to share it with friends and relatives, self publishing is a viable option. In self publishing, you oversee all of the book production details. A local printer may be able to help you, or you may want to arrange some type of desktop computer publishing.

Whatever course you choose, don't treat writing for children as a starter course into the world of "real writing." Creating a children's book is *not* a quick and easy project. Actually, aspects of the craft make writing for this audience more difficult. Writing for children *is* real writing, and what follows in this section are listings of *real* markets—one of which might make your dreams of being published a reality.

*ABC, ALL BOOKS FOR CHILDREN, The All Children's Co., Ltd., 33 Museum St., London WC1A 1LD United Kingdom. (171)436-6300. Fax: (171)240-6923. Imprints: softbABCks (paperback); factbABCks (nonfiction). Book publisher. Unsolicited Manuscripts: Carol Mackenzie. Publisher: Sue Tarsky. Publishes 40 picture books/year. 50% of books by first-time authors.
Fiction: Picture books: adventure, animal, concept, contemporary, multicultural, nature/environment. Average word length: picture books—under 1,000. Recently published *Angelina Ice Skates*, by Katharine Holabird, illustrated by Helen Craig; *Three Bags Full*, by Ragnhild Scamell, illustrated by Sally Hobson; *Somebody and the Three Blairs*, by Marilyn Tolhurst, illustrated by Simone Abel.
Nonfiction: Picture books, young readers, middle readers: concept, history nature/environment.
How to Contact/Writers: Picture books: Submit complete manuscript. Nonfiction: Query. Reports on queries in 1 month; ms in 2-3 months. Publishes a book 12-18 months after acceptance. Will consider simultaneous submissions.
Illustration: Works with 15 illustrators/year. Will review ms/illustration packages. Will review artwork for future assignments. Uses color artwork only.
How to Contact/Illustrators: Ms/illustration packages: Submit ms with 2 color photocopies. Reports in 1 month. Samples returned with SASE (IRC); samples filed. Original artwork returned at job's completion.

Terms: "Payment decided on individual basis." Sends galleys to authors; color proofs to illustrators. Book catalog available for SAE.

ADVOCACY PRESS, P.O. Box 236, Santa Barbara CA 93102. (805)962-2728. Fax: (805)963-3580. Division of The Girls Incorporated of Greater Santa Barbara. Book publisher. Editorial Contact: Bill Sheehan. Publishes 2-4 children's books/year.
Fiction: Picture books, young readers, middle readers: animal, concepts in self-esteem, fantasy, gender equity, nature/environment. "Illustrated children's stories incorporate self-esteem, gender equity, self-awareness concepts." Recently published *Nature's Wonderful World in Rhyme* (birth-age 12, collection of poems); *Shadow and the Ready Time* (32-page picture book). "Most publications are 32-48 page picture stories for readers 4-11 years. Most feature adventures of animals in interesting/educational locales."
How to Contact/Writers: "Because of the required focus of our publications, most have been written inhouse." Reports on mss in 1-2 months. Include SASE.
Illustration: "Require intimate integration of art with story. Therefore, almost always use local illustrators." Average about 30 illustrations per story. Will review ms/illustration packages.
How to Contact/Illustrators: Ms/illustration packages: Query first.
Terms: Authors and illustrators paid by royalty.
Tips: "We are not presently looking for new titles."

■**AEGINA PRESS/UNIVERSITY EDITIONS, INC.,** 59 Oak Lane, Spring Valley, Huntington WV 25704. (304)429-7204. Book publisher. Estab. 1983. Managing Editor: Ira Herman. Art Coordinator: Angela Hall. Publishes 3 picture books/year; 4 young readers/year; 4 middle readers/year; 6 young adults/year. 40% of books by first-time authors; 5% of books from agented writers; "most new titles are subsidy published."
Fiction: All levels: adventure, animal, fantasy, humor, poetry, religion, romance, science fiction, sports, suspense/mystery. "Will consider most categories." Average word length: picture books—1,000; young readers—2,000; middle readers—10,000; young adults—20,000. Recently published *Terry the Tractor*, by Mike Rucker, illustrated by Bob Burchett (ages 4-7, picture book); *Johnny Long Tail*, by Peter Leggett and Linda Bricker, illustrated by Anna Finkel (ages 5-8, animal story); *The Ghost of Deadman's Hollow*, by Ronald Talney (young adult mystery).
Nonfiction: All levels: animal, history, nature/environment, sports, textbooks. "Will consider all types of manuscripts, especially those usable in classrooms." Recently published *The Boy with a Paintbox, The Story of Paul Cezanne*, by Rosalind Hoover, with art reproductions of Paul Cezanne (ages 6-10, biographical fiction); and *Adelma Goes Herbing*, by Margaret S. Messing, illustrated by Nicole Bastiaanse (ages 4-8, nonfiction herb book).
How to Contact/Writers: Fiction/nonfiction: Submit complete ms. Reports on queries in 1 week; mss in 1 month. Publishes a book 5-6 months after acceptance. Will consider simultaneous submissions.
Illustration: Works with 20 illustrators/year. Will review ms/illustration packages. Will review artwork for future assignments. Contact: Angela Hall, art coordinator. Primarily uses b&w artwork.
How to Contact/Illustrators: Ms/illustration packages: Query first. Illustrations only: Query with nonreturnable samples. "We generally use our own artists. We will consider outside art. Artists should send photocopies or nonreturnable samples." Reports on art samples in 1 month.
Terms: Pays authors in royalties of 10-15% based on retail price. Pays freelance artists per project ($60 minimum). Payment "negotiated individually for each book." Sends galleys to authors. Book catalog available for $2 and SAE and 4 first-class stamps; ms guidelines for #10 envelope and 1 first-class stamp.
Tips: "Focus your subject and plotline. For younger readers, stress visual imagery and fantasy characterizations. A cover letter should accompany the manuscript, which states the approximate length (not necessary for poetry). A brief synopsis of the manuscript and

a listing of the author's publishing credits (if any) should also be included. Queries, sample chapters, synopses and completed manuscripts are welcome."

AFRICA WORLD PRESS, P.O. Box 1892, Trenton NJ 08607. (609)771-1666. Book publisher. Editor: Kassahun Checole. Publishes 20-30 picture books/year; 10 young reader and young adult titles/year; 15 middle readers/year. Books concentrate on African-American life.
Fiction: Picture books, young readers: adventure, concept, contemporary, folktales, history, multicultural. Middle readers, young adults: adventure, contemporary, folktales, history, multicultural. Publishes very little fiction.
Nonfiction: Picture books, young readers, middle readers, young adults: concept, history, multicultural. Does not want to see self-help, gender or health books.
How to Contact/Writers: Query; submit outline/synopsis and 2 sample chapters. Reports on queries in 30-45 days; mss in 3 months. Will consider previously published work.
Illustration: Works with 10-20 illustrators/year. Will review ms/illustration packages. Contact: Kassahun Checole, editor. Will review artwork for future assignments.
How to Contact/Illustrators: Ms/illustration packages: Query. Illustrations only: Query with samples. Reports in 3 months.
Terms: Pays authors royalty based on retail price. Pays illustrators by the project or royalty based on retail price. Book catalog available for SAE; ms and art guidelines available for SASE.

AFRICAN AMERICAN IMAGES, 1909 W. 95th St., Chicago IL 60643. (312)445-0322. Fax: (312)445-9844. Book publisher. Editor: Jawanza Kunjufu. Publishes 2 picture books/year; 1 young reader title/year; 1 middle reader title/year; 1 young adult title/year. 90% of books by first-time authors.
Fiction/Nonfiction: All levels: black culture. "We publish books from an Africentric frame of reference that promote self-esteem, collective values, liberation and skill development." Does not want to see poetry, essays, novels, autobiographies, biographies, religious materials or mss exclusively addressing the continent of Africa.
How to Contact/Writers: Fiction/nonfiction: Submit complete ms. Reports in 2 months. Publishes a book 9 months after acceptance. Will consider simultaneous submissions. Include SASE for return of ms.
Illustration: Editorial will review ms/illustration packages.
How to Contact/Illustrators: Ms/illustration packages: Submit 3 chapters of ms with 1 piece of final art. Illustrations only: Submit tearsheets. Reports on art samples in 2 weeks. Original artwork returned at job's completion.
Terms: Buys ms outright. Illustrator paid by the project. Book catalog, ms/artist's guidelines free on request.

ALADDIN PAPERBACKS, 24th Floor, 866 Third Avenue, New York NY 10022. (212)702-9043. Paperback imprint of Simon & Schuster Children's Publishing Division.
 • Aladdin publishes primarily reprints of successful hardcovers from other Simon & Schuster imprints. They publish very little original material. Send SASE for writer's and artist's guidelines.

ALYSON PUBLICATIONS, INC., 40 Plympton St., Boston MA 02118. (617)542-5679. Book publisher. Editorial Contact: Sasha Alyson. Publishes 4 (projected) picture books/year; 1 (projected) young adult title/year. "Alyson Wonderland is the line of children's books. We are looking for diverse depictions of family life for children of gay and lesbian parents."
Fiction: All levels: adventure, anthology, contemporary and multicultural. "We like books that incorporate all racial, religious and body types, as well as dealing with children with gay and lesbian parents—which all our books must deal with. Our YA books should deal with issues faced by kids growing up gay or lesbian." Recently published *Anna Day and*

The solid block before a listing indicates the market subsidy publishes manuscripts.

Small Press Welcomes Controversial Subjects

In recent years major book publishers have been a little more willing to look at adult fiction dealing with subjects previously thought too controversial. Among these have been books dealing with gay and lesbian issues, characters and themes. Right now it's a fairly good (albeit competitive) market for gay and lesbian adult fiction in that, in addition to several successful small presses, more commercial publishing opportunities exist. Yet, children's fiction dealing with gay and lesbian subjects is still a hard sell to most major publishers.

A reason for this difference, says Sasha Alyson, whose company, Alyson Publications, includes a line of books for the children of gay and lesbian parents, is that large houses are willing to take some risks with adult fiction, because fiction ac-

Sasha Alyson

counts for only a small part of their income. On the other hand, children's fiction has always included a strong backlist and for most publishers their children's book lines represent a major source of income—a "cash cow," so to speak, that few are willing to put at risk. So, writers of children's books dealing with controversial subjects and sensitive issues may have a harder time selling such manuscripts to large houses.

Small press publishers have known this for a long time and many have built their businesses by publishing good books that were in some way considered too controversial, too sensitive, or just too different for the commercial publishers. Alyson Publications is no exception. "When I started, I was doing whatever was of interest to me. After a year or two I realized that I had to specialize, so I specialized in gay books and that was very definitely the right way to go. We quickly become the largest and best known of several small gay presses."

Alyson took the same approach with the development in 1990 of Alyson Wonderland, a line of books for children ages 2 to 12 who have gay or lesbian parents or family members. "With the children's books it was the same as for our adult line. By really identifying one area and getting to know it, trying to get to know who the readers are, the reviewers, the booksellers, we've clearly been able to fill that niche. I've made a point during my publishing career to look for chances to talk to booksellers about what books they think we should be doing, and I've gotten a lot of good suggestions that way. At one of the American Booksellers Association conventions I talked to a couple of booksellers from Denver and they said they were getting more and more gay and lesbian

Lynette Schmidt created these jolly jesters and their jar of jellybeans for Alyson Wonderland's The Duke Who Outlawed Jellybeans, *written by Johnny Valentine. The collection of fairy tales features nontraditional families coupled with traditional ogres, dragons, frogs and royalty depicted in Schmidt's colorful paintings and soft black and white illustrations.*

parents coming in looking for books for their kids and they had nothing to give them."

Alyson Publications was one of the first presses to publish a line of books aimed at gay and lesbian teens and young adults, but the Alyson Wonderland line for younger children was a very new direction for the publisher. "We've done about 15 children's books at this point and it's definitely been an experiment for us. We're trying to figure out what the best ways are to integrate gay and lesbian issues into children's books, and we've done books that take quite a range of approaches. What we've found so far is books that focus just on having gay parents don't hold a child's interest. On the other hand, if the gay parents are just there in the background but the book doesn't deal with that at all, it's too slight a theme and gay parents don't feel the book meets their needs. So it's the books that find a balance—that actively deal with the issues but don't focus on them exclusively—we find most successful."

Alyson is looking for a story that not only portrays a child with gay or lesbian parents, but one that also has an interesting story line or predicament to hold readers' interest. "It must deal with some of the differences that come up because the child has gay or lesbian parents without dwelling on them."

Despite his experience publishing in the gay and lesbian field, Alyson was surprised at the variety of issues these children face. For example, Alyson says he met a divorced gay father whose daughter had trouble understanding the difference between a lifestyle choice and ethnicity. Thinking in these terms, she thought since her father was gay, she, too, must be "half gay." Another issue these children confront is whether to tell their friends about gay family members, and what to do if siblings disagree about telling others.

"What we don't see enough of right now and what we're really looking for is some good illustrators—either illustrators just interested in drawing or those who have a text. It's much easier to work with a manuscript than it is to find good illustrations. We'd like to see a proposal for a book with at least one sample illustration and a story. We might have some advice on how to change the story but if the illustrations are good we'd be willing to work with it." Interested illustrators should note that Alyson also publishes a few coloring books.

Alyson's advice to writers is similar to what he does with his press. "Talk to the kids and talk to some parents—that's the first step. Then try to do an interesting, fun story that's not preachy, that's not trying to get a message across but that does give kids a chance to see others in their situation dealing with some of the real-life issues they face. The setting may be real or fantasy, but the story must at least grapple with some of these. And please don't avoid writing a book because you think it might be controversial."

—*Robin Gee*

the O-Ring, by Elaine Wickens; and *One Dad, Two Dads, Brown Dad, Blue Dads*, by Johnny Valentine.

How to Contact/Writers: Submit outline/synopsis and sample chapters (young adults); submit complete manuscript (picture books/young readers). Reports on queries in 1 month; on mss in 6 weeks. Include SASE.

Illustration: Works with 4 illustrators/year. Will review mss/illustration packages. Will review artwork for future assignments.

How to Contact/Illustrators: Submit "representative art that can be *kept on file*. Good quality photocopies are OK."

Terms: Pays authors and illustrators royalties. Prefers to discuss terms with the authors and artists. "We *do* offer advances." Book catalog and/or ms guidelines free on request.

Tips: "We only publish kids' books aimed at the children of gay or lesbian parents."

AMERICAN BIBLE SOCIETY, 1865 Broadway, New York NY 10023. (212)408-1235. Fax: (212)408-1435. Book publisher. Estab. 1816. Product Development Manager: Charles Houser. Publishes 2 picture books/year; 4 young readers/year; 4 young adults/year. Publishes books with spiritual/religious themes based on the Bible.

Nonfiction: All levels: activity books, multicultural, religion, self-help, nature/environment, reference, social issues and special needs. Multicultural needs include intercity lifestyle; African-American, Hispanic/Latino, Native American, Asian; mixed groups (such as choirs, classrooms, church events). "Unsolicited mss will be returned unread! We prefer published writing samples with résumés so that we can contact copywriters when an appropriate project comes up." Recently published *God Loves You: Proverbs from the Bible* (ages 4-6, full color cover and 42 full color interior illustrations).

How to Contact/Writers: All manuscripts developed inhouse. Query with résumé and writing samples. Contact: Barbara Bernstengel. Unsolicited mss rejected. No credit lines given.

Illustration: Works with 2-5 illustrators/year. Editorial will review artwork for possible future assignments. Contact: Charles Houser. "Would be more interested in artwork for children and teens which is influenced by the visual 'vocabulary' of videos."

How to Contact/Illustrators: Ms/illustration packages: "Query first." Illustrations only: Query with samples; arrange a personal interview to show portfolio; send "résumés, tearsheets and promotional literature to keep; slides will be returned promptly." Reports on queries in 6 weeks. Factors used to determine payment for ms/illustration package include "nature and scope of project; complexity of illustration and continuity of work; number of illustrations." Pays illustrators $200-30,000; based on fair market value. Sends 2 complimentary copies of published work to illustrators. Original artwork returned at job's completion. Book catalog free on request.

Photography: Contact: Charles Houser. Buys stock and assigns work. Looking for "nature, scenic, multicultural, intergenerational people shots." Model/property releases required. Uses any size b&w prints; 35mm, $2\frac{1}{4} \times 2\frac{1}{4}$ and 4×5 transparencies. Photographers should query with samples; arrange a personal interview to show portfolio; provide résumé, promotional literature or tearsheets.

Terms: Photographers paid by the project (range: $800-5,000); per photo (range $150-1,500). Credit line given on most projects. Most photos purchased on one-time use basis. ABS owns all publication rights to illustrations and mss.

AMERICAN EDUCATION PUBLISHING, Suite 145, 150 E. Wilson Bridge Rd., Columbus OH 43085-2328. (614)848-8866. Book publisher. Director, Retail Product Development: Diane Mangan. Publishes 6-8 picture books/year. 20% of books by first-time authors; 80% of books developed inhouse.

Fiction: Picture books: adventure, animal, concept, contemporary. Young readers: adventure, animal, concept, contemporary, fantasy, folktales, humor. Does not want to see dinosaurs, talking animals and environment. Published *The Wind, The Alphabet* and *The Colors*, all by Monique Felix (8×8 softcover for toddlers).

Nonfiction: Picture books: activity books, animal, concept and science. Young readers: activity books, animal, concept, hobbies and science. Does not want to see dinosaurs, environment. Published *Gnat* and *Fire* both by Kitty Benedict (8×8 softcover for beginners).

How to Contact/Writers: Fiction/Nonfiction: Submit outline/synopsis and 3 sample chapters. Reports on queries in 2 months; mss in 3-4 months. Publishes a book 6-8 months after acceptance. Will consider simultaneous submissions and previously published work.

Illustration: Works with 5 illustrators/year. Will review ms/illustration packages. Will review artwork for future assignments. Contact: Julia Breedlove, creative manager.

How to Contact/Illustrator: Ms/illustration packages: Submit ms with 2 pieces of final art. Illustrations only: Query with samples, résumé, tearsheets. Reports in 2 months. Samples returned with SASE; samples kept on file. Original artwork returned at job's completion.

Terms: Pays authors royalty of 5-10% based on wholesale price or work purchased outright. Pays illustrators by the project or royalty of 5-10% based on wholesale price. Sends galleys to authors.

*ANDERSEN PRESS LIMITED, 20 Vauxhall Bridge Rd., London SWIV 2SA England. (71)973-9720. Fax: (71)233-6263. Book publishers. Contact: Editor. Publishes 24 picture books/year; 12 young readers/year; 6 middle readers/year; and 2 young adult titles/year. 10% of books by first-time authors.

Fiction: Picture books: adventure, animal, contemporary, fantasy, folktales, humor, multicultural, nature/environment. Young readers: adventure, contemporary, fantasy, multicultural, suspense/mystery. Middle readers: contemporary, humor, multicultural, science fiction, suspense/mystery. Young adults: contemporary, science fiction, suspense/mystery.

AQUILA COMMUNICATIONS LTD., 2642 Diab St., St. Laurent, Quebec H4S 1E8 Canada. (514)338-1065. Fax: (514)338-1948. Book publisher. Manager: Mike Kelada. 100% of books by first-time authors. "We specialize in teaching French as a second language."

How to Contact/Writers: Fiction: Submit outline/synopsis and 5 sample chapters. Nonfiction: Submit outline/synopsis and 10 sample chapters. Reports on queries/mss in 1 week to 2 months. Will consider previously published work.

Illustration: Will review ms/illustration packages. Will review artwork for future assignments. Uses b&w and color artwork.

How to Contact/Illustrators: Ms/illustration packages: Submit ms with copies of artwork. Illustrations only: Submit photocopies of sample artwork. Reports in 3 weeks. Cannot return samples; samples filed.

Photography: Purchases photos from freelancers. Buys stock and assigns work.

*ARCADE PUBLISHING, 141 Fifth Ave., New York NY 10010. (212)475-2633. Subsidiary of Little Brown & Co. Book publisher. President and Publisher: Richard Seaver. Publishes 8-12 picture books/year; 3-5 young reader titles/year; 5-8 middle reader titles/year. 50% of books from agented writers. 25% of books by first-time authors.

• Arcade Publishing is currently not accepting unsolicited manuscripts.

Fiction: Young readers, middle readers. Published *I Am the Ocean*, by Suzanna Marshak (ages 4-8, picture book).

Nonfiction: Will consider general nonfiction—"all ages." Published *Water's Way*, by Lisa Westberg Peters, illustrated by Ted Rand (ages 4-7, picture book).

How to Contact/Writers: Fiction/Nonfiction: Query. Reports on queries in 2 months. Publishes ms 18 months after acceptance. Will consider simultaneous submissions.

Illustration: Will review ms/illustration packages.

How to Contact/Illustrators: "*No* original art—send slides or color photocopies." Illustrations only: Submit tearsheets and slides. Reports on ms/art samples in 3 weeks. Original artwork returned at job's completion.

Terms: Pays authors in variable royalties or buys ms outright for $400-3,000; "also flat fees per b&w books and jackets." Offers average advance of $2,500. Sends galleys to authors; book catalog for 8×10 SASE; ms guidelines for SASE.

ARCHWAY/MINSTREL BOOKS, 1230 Avenue of the Americas, New York NY 10020. (212)698-7000. Fax: (212)698-7337. Imprint of Pocket Books. Book publisher—Minstrel

Books (ages 7-11) and Archway Paperbacks (ages 12-16). Editorial Director: Patricia Mac-Donald. Publishes originals and reprints.

Fiction: Middle readers: animal stories, adventures, fantasy, funny school stories, thrillers. Young adults: adventure, contemporary stories, horror, suspense. Recently published (Archway) *Bury Me Deep*, by Christopher Pike and *Fear Street* cheerleaders trilogy, by R.L. Stine; *Help Wanted*, by Richie Tenkersley Cusick. Recently published (Minstrel) *Aliens Ate My Homework*, by Bruce Coville; *My Babysitter is a Vampire*, by Ann Hodman; and *My Crazy Cousin Courtney*, by Judi Miller.

Nonfiction: Middle readers: environment, sports. Young adults: sports, popular media figures.

How to Contact/Writers: Fiction/nonfiction: Query; submit outline/synopsis and sample chapters. SASE mandatory.

Terms: Pays authors in royalties.

*ARTISTS & WRITERS GUILD BOOKS, 850 Third Ave., New York NY 10022. (212)753-8500. Imprint of Western Publishing Co. Editorial Director: Alice Bregman. Book publisher. Quality trade books for preschool through middle readers, including fiction and nonfiction picture books and storybooks.

• Also see listing for Golden Books.

How to Contact/Writers: "Material accepted only through agent."

Illustration: Will sometimes review ms/illustration packages. Will review an illustrator's work for possible future assignments. Contact: Remo Consentino or Georg Brewer, art directors.

How to Contact/Illustrators: Ms/illustration packages: Query first.

Terms: Pays authors in royalties based on retail price.

ATHENEUM BOOKS FOR YOUNG READERS, 866 Third Ave., New York NY 10022. (212)702-2000. Simon & Schuster Children's Publishing Division. Book publisher. Vice President/Editorial Director: Jonathan Lanman. Editorial Contacts: Marcia Marshall, senior editor; Ana Cerro, associate editor. Publishes 15-20 picture books/year; 4-5 young readers/year; 20-25 middle readers/year; 10-15 young adults/year. 20% of books by first-time authors; 50% of books from agented writers.

Fiction: Picture books and middle readers: animal, contemporary, fantasy. Young readers and young adults: contemporary, fantasy.

Nonfiction: All levels: animal, biography, education, history.

How to Contact/Writers: Fiction/Nonfiction: Query; will consider complete picture book ms; submit outline/synopsis and sample chapters for longer works. Reports on queries in 6-8 weeks; mss in 3 months. Publishes a book 18-24 months after acceptance. Will consider simultaneous submissions from previously unpublished authors; "we request that the author let us know it is a simultaneous submission."

Illustration: Editorial will review ms/illustration packages.

How to Contact/Illustrators: Ms/illustration packages: Query first, 3 chapters of ms with 1 piece of final art. Illustrations only: Submit résumé, tearsheets. Reports on art samples only if interested. Original artwork returned at job's completion.

Terms: Pays authors in royalties of 8-12½% based on retail price. Illustrators paid royalty or flat fee depending on the project. Sends galleys to authors; proofs to illustrators. Book catalog available for 9 × 12 SAE and 5 first-class stamps; ms guidelines for #10 SAE and 1 first-class stamp.

*AUGSBURG FORTRESS, PUBLISHERS, 426 S. Fifth St., Box 1209, Minneapolis MN 55440. (612)330-3300. Fax: (612)330-3455. Acquisition Editor: Alice Peppler. Managing Editor: Ann Rehfeldt. Publishes 5-7 picture books/year; 6-8 middle readers/year; 3-4 devotionals/year. 5% of books by first-time authors. Publishes fiction with Christian characters and themes only.

Fiction: Picture books: multicultural. Middle readers, young adults: history, multicultural. Looking for stories of Christian children from American multicultural homes—also from single parent homes. Also very interested in historical fiction for ages 10-14. Does not want to see picture books or young readers (send inquiries only). Average length: middle readers—100 pages; young adults—200 pages.

How to Contact/Writers: Query. Reports in 3 months. Publishes a book 1-1½ years after acceptance. Will consider simultaneous and previously published submissions.

Illustration: Works with 10 illustrators/year. Will review ms/illustration packages. Will review artwork for future assignments.

How to Contact/Illustrators: Illustrations only: Query with samples, resume, promo sheet and client list. Reports back only if interested. Samples returned with SASE; samples filed. Originals not returned.

Terms: Pays authors royalty. Pays illustrators by the project (range: varies).

Tips: Looking for authors "who are familiar with Lutheran and other mainline church denominations and more books about today's families—not the families of the 1970s or even 1950s."

AVON BOOKS/BOOKS FOR YOUNG READERS (AVON FLARE, AVON CAMELOT AND YOUNG CAMELOT), 1350 Avenue of the Americas, New York NY 10019. (212)261-6817. Division of The Hearst Corporation. Book publisher. Editorial Director: Gwen Montgomery. Senior Editor: Anne E. Dunn. Editorial Assistant: Stephanie Siegel. Publishes 25-30 middle readers/year; 20-25 young adults/year. 10% of books by first-time authors; 20% of books from agented writers.

Fiction: Middle readers: comedy, contemporary, problem novels, sports, spy/mystery/adventure. Young adults: contemporary, problem novels, romance. Average length: middle readers—100-150 pages; young adults—150-250 pages. Avon does not publish preschool picture books.

Nonfiction: Middle readers: hobbies, music/dance, sports. Young adults: music/dance, "growing up." Average length: middle readers—100-150 pages; young adults—150-250 pages.

How to Contact/Writers: Fiction: Submit complete ms. Nonfiction: Submit outline/synopsis and sample chapters. Reports on queries in 1 month; mss in 3-4 months. Publishes a book 18-24 months after acceptance. Will consider simultaneous submissions.

Illustration: Very rarely will review ms/illustration packages.

How to Contact/Illustrators: "Send samples we can keep. Need line art and cover art."

Terms: Pays authors in royalties of 6% based on retail price. Average advance payment is "very open." Sends galleys to authors; sometimes sends dummies to illustrators. Book catalog available for 9×12 SAE and 4 first-class stamps; ms guidelines for #10 SASE.

Tips: "We have three young readers imprints: Young Camelot, books for beginner readers; Avon Camelot, books for the middle grades; and Avon Flare, young adults. Our list includes both individual titles and series, with the emphasis in our paperback originals on high quality recreational reading—a fresh and original writing style; identifiable, three dimensional characters; a strong, well-paced story that pulls readers in and keeps them interested." Writers: "Make sure that you really know what a company's list looks like before you submit work. Is your work in line with what they usually do? Is your work appropriate for the age group that this company publishes for? Keep aware of what's in your bookstore (but not what's in there for too long!)" Illustrators: "Submit work to art directors and people who are in charge of illustration at publishers. This is usually not handled entirely by the editorial department."

BANDANNA BOOKS, 319-B Anacapa St., Santa Barbara CA 93101. (805)962-9915. Fax: (805)564-3278. Book Publisher. Editor: Sasha Newborn. Fiction Editor: Joan Blake. Publishes 1 young adult title/year. "Most books have been translations in the humanist tradition. Looking for themes of intellectual awakening."

The asterisk before a listing indicates the listing is new in this edition.

Fiction: Young adults (16 and older): history and autobiographical. No religious, fantasy. Average word length: 60,000. Published *The First Detective*, by Edgar Allan Poe and *Benigna Machiavelli*, by Charlotte Perkins Gilman.

How to Contact/Writers: Fiction: Submit outline/synopsis and 1 sample chapter. Reports on queries in 1 month; mss in 3 months. Publishes a book up to a year after acceptance. Will consider simultaneous submissions.

Illustration: Works with 2 illustrators/year. Will review ms/illustration packages. Contact: Sasha Newborn, publisher. Will review artwork for future assignments. Uses b&w artwork only. Prefers woodblock, scratchboard artwork.

How to Contact/Illustrators: Ms/illustration packages: Submit ms with dummy. Illustrations only: Query with samples, portfolio and tearsheets. Reports back only if interested. Cannot return samples.

Terms: Pays authors royalty of 5-10% based on retail price; also advances (average amount: $200). Pays illustrators by the project (range: $25-200). Sends galleys to authors. Ms and art guidelines not available.

*B&B PUBLISHING, INC., Interactive Education Technologies, 820 Wisconsin St., P.O. Box 96, Wallworth WI 53184. (414)275-9474. Fax: (414)275-9530. Book publisher, independent book producer/packager. Managing Director: Katy O'Shea. Publishes 8 young adult titles/year. All titles are nonfiction, educational, usually curriculum related. "We do not do fiction unless it is based on fact (i.e., historical), has an educational theme, and could fit a curriculum area."

Nonfiction: Middle readers, young adults: biography, careers, concept, geography, history, multicultural, nature/environment, reference, science, social issues. Multicultural needs include smaller ethnic groups, sociological perspective, true stories; no folktales. "Please no personal war experiences, most such material is unsuitable for younger readers." Average word length: middle readers—15,000; young adults—20,000. Recently published *Awesome Almanac® California*, by Skip Press (ages 12 and up, reference); and *Awesome Almanac® Florida*, by Sima Star and Jean F. Blashfield (ages 12 and up, reference).

How to Contact/Writers: Fiction/nonfiction: Query. Submit outline/synopsis and 1 sample chapter. Reports in 2 months. Usually publishes a book 1 year after acceptance. Will consider simultaneous and previously published submissions. "Send SASE."

Illustration: Works with 3-4 illustrators/year. Will review ms/illustration packages. Contact: Katy O'Shea, managing director. Will review artwork for future assignments.

How to Contact/Illustrators: Ms/illustration packages: Query. Submit sample chapter with illustration. Illustrations only: Query with samples, resume, promo sheet and tearsheets. Reports back in 2 months; only if interested on non-manuscript sample submissions. Samples returned with SASE; samples filed. Original artwork returned at job's completion.

Photography: Buys photos from freelancers. Contact: Margie Benson, photo editor. Buys stock and assigns work. Photos used vary by project—wonders of the world, nature/environment, etc. Uses color or b&w prints and 35mm, $2\frac{1}{4} \times 2\frac{1}{4}$, 4×4 or 8×10 transparencies. Submit cover letter, resume, published samples, stock photo list and promo piece.

Terms: Pays authors royalty of 1-10% on net receipts. Work purchased outright from authors ($500-4,000). Offers advances (up to $2,000). Pays illustrators by the project. Pays photographers by the project or per photo. Sends galleys to authors; dummies to illustrators. Ms guidelines available for SASE.

BANTAM DOUBLEDAY DELL, 1540 Broadway, New York NY 10036. (212)354-6500. Book publisher Vice President/Publisher: Craig Virden. Vice President/Editor-in-Chief: Beverly Horowitz. Publishes 12 picture books/year; 12 young reader titles/year; 60 middle reader books/year; 60 young adult titles/year. 10% of books by first-time authors; 70% of books from agented writers.

● Bantam Doubleday Dell ranks the sixth, based on net sales, of the top 12 children's publishers.

Fiction: Picture books: adventure, animal, contemporary, easy-to-read, fantasy, humor. Young readers: animal, contemporary, humor, easy-to-read, fantasy, sports, suspense/mystery. Middle readers: adventure, animal, contemporary, humor, easy-to-read, fantasy, sports, suspense/mystery. Young adults: adventure, contemporary issues, humor, coming-of-age, suspense/mystery. Recently published *Spite Fences*, by Trudy Krisher; *Driver's Ed*, by Caroline Cooney; *Bill*, by Chap Reaver.

Nonfiction: "Bantam Doubleday Dell Books for Young Readers publishes a very limited number of nonfiction titles."

How to Contact/Writers: Submit through the agent only. "All unsolicited manuscripts returned unopened with the following exceptions: Unsolicited manuscripts are accepted for the Delacorte Press Prize for a First Young Adult Novel contest (see Contests and Awards section) and the Marguerite de Angeli Prize for a First Middle Grade Novel contest (see Contests and Awards section)." Reports on queries in 6-8 weeks; mss in 3 months.

Illustration: Number of illustrations used per fiction title varies considerably.

How to Contact/Illustrators: Query first. Do not send originals. Cannot return samples; samples filed. "If you submit a dummy, please submit the text separately." Illustrations only: Submit tearsheets, rèsumè, samples that do not need to be returned. Reports on ms/art samples only if interested. Original artwork returned at job's completion.

Terms: Pays authors advance and royalty. Pays illustrators advance and royalty or flat fee.

BARRONS EDUCATIONAL SERIES, 250 Wireless Blvd., Hauppauge NY 11788. (516)434-3311. Fax: (516)434-3723. Book publisher. Estab. 1945. Managing/Acquisitions Editor: Grace Freedson. Publishes 20 picture books/year; 20 young readers/year; 20 middle reader titles/year; 10 young adult titles/year. 25% of books by first-time authors; 25% of books from agented writers.

Fiction: Picture books: animal, concept, multicultural, nature/environment. Young readers: adventure, multicultural, nature/environment, suspense/mystery. Middle readers: adventure, horror, multicultural, nature/environment, problem novels, suspense/mystery. Young adults: horror, problem novels. Recently published *Bartholomew's Dream*, by Patti Farmer, illustrated by Amy Wummer; *Bon Jours Mes Amis*, by Irene Bowers, illustrated by Unda Weller (preschool language book/cassette package); and *I Am a Pilot*, by Cynthia Benjamin, illustrated by Miriam Sagasti (pre-school picture book).

Nonfiction: Picture books: concept, reference. Young readers: how-to, reference, self help, social issues. Middle readers: hi-lo, how-to, reference, self help, social issues. Young adults: how-to, self help, social issues.

How to Contact/Writers: Fiction: Query. Nonfiction: Submit outline/synopsis and sample chapters. "Submissions must be accompanied by SASE for response." Reports on queries in 1 month; mss in 6-8 months. Publishes a book 1 year after acceptance. Will consider simultaneous submissions.

Illustration: Works with 10 illustrators/year. Will review ms/illustration packages. Will review artwork for future assignments. Contact: Grace Freedson.

How to Contact/Illustrators: Ms/illustration packages: Query first; 3 chapters of ms with 1 piece of final art, remainder roughs. Illustrations only: Submit tearsheets or slides plus résumé. Reports in 3-8 weeks.

Terms: Pays authors in royalties of 10-16% based on wholesale price or buys ms outright for $2,000 minimum. Pays illustrators by the project based on retail price. Only interested in agented material. Sends galleys to authors; dummies to illustrators. Book catalog, ms/artist's guidelines for 9×12 SAE.

Tips: Writers: "We are predominately on the lookout for preschool storybooks and concept books. No YA fiction/romance or novels." Illustrators: "We are happy to receive a sample illustration to keep on file for future consideration. Periodic notes reminding us of your work is acceptable." Children's book themes "are becoming much more contemporary and relevant to a child's day-to-day activities."

***■BEAUTIFUL AMERICA PUBLISHING COMPANY**, 9725 S.W. Commerce Circle, Wilsonville OR 97070. (503)682-0173. Fax: (503)682-0175. Imprint of Little America (children's).

A bullet has been placed within some listings to introduce special comments by the editors of Children's Writer's & Illustrator's Market.

Book publisher. Editor: Jaime Thoreson. Art Director: Heather Kier. Publishes 2 middle readers titles/year. 50% of books by first-time authors; 50% subsidy published.
Fiction: Middle readers: animal, environmentally and/or morally conscious. Average word length: middle readers—60-90 pages. Recently published *The Christmas Collie*.
Nonfiction: Middle readers: animal, environmentally and/or morally conscious. Average word length: 60-90 pages. Recently published *Melody's Mystery*.
How to Contact/Writers: Fiction/Nonfiction: Query. Submit outline/synopsis. Reports on mss in 6 months. Publishes a book 1-2 years after acceptance.
Illustration: Works with 3 illustrators/year. Will review artwork for future assignments. Contact: Heather Kier, art director.
How to Contact/Illustrators Ms/illustration packages: Submit ms with dummy. Illustrations only: Query with samples. Reports only if interested. Samples returned with SASE; samples filed if artist doesn't want samples back. Original artwork returned at job's completion.
Photography: Buys photos from freelancers. Contact: Jaime Thoreson, photo-librarian. Buys stock and assigns work. Model/property releases required; captions required. "Absolutely no prints accepted." Uses 35mm, 2¼×2¼, 4×5 or 8×10 transparencies. Submit resume, published samples and promo piece.
Terms: Pays authors royalty on retail price. Offers advances. Pays illustrators by the project. Pays photographers by the project, per photo, royalty. Book catalog available for 9×12 SAE and 2 first-class stamps.

BEHRMAN HOUSE INC., 235 Watchung Ave., West Orange NJ 07052. (201)669-0447. Fax: (201)669-9769. Book publisher. Project Editor: Adam Siegel. Publishes 3 young reader titles/year; 3 middle reader titles/year; 3 young adult titles/year. 12% of books by first-time authors; 2% of books from agented writers. Publishes books on all aspects of Judaism: history, cultural, textbooks, holidays.
Nonfiction: All levels: history, religion, Jewish educational textbooks. Average word length: young reader—1,200; middle reader—2,000; young adult—4,000. Recently published *My Jewish Year*, by Adam Fisher (ages 8-9); and *Let's Discover the Bible*, by Shirley Rose, illustrated by Lane Yerkes (grades K-2).
How to Contact/Writers: Fiction/nonfiction: Submit outline/synopsis and sample chapters. Reports on mss/queries in 2 months. Publishes a book 2½ years after acceptance. Will consider simultaneous submissions.
Illustration: Will review ms/illustration packages. Will review artwork for future assignments.
How to Contact/Illustrators: Ms/illustration packages: "Query first." Illustrations only: Query with samples; send unsolicited art samples by mail. Reports on queries in 1 month; mss in 2 months.
Photography: Purchases photos from freelancers. Contact: Adam Siegel. Buys stock and assigns work. Uses photos of families involved in Jewish activities. Uses color and b&w prints. Photographers should query with samples. Send unsolicited photos by mail. Submit portfolio for review.
Terms: Pays authors in royalties of 3-8% based on retail price or buys ms outright for $1,000-5,000. Offers advance (average amount: $500). Pays illustrators by the project (range: $500-5,000). Sends galleys to authors; dummies to illustrators. Book catalog free on request.
Tips: Looking for "religious school texts" with Judaic themes.

BERKLEY PUBLISHING GROUP, 200 Madison Ave., New York NY 10016. Imprints: Berkley, Joye, Diamond, Ace, Pacer. Book publisher. Senior Editor: Gary Goldstein. "We are mainly publishing young adult horror, thrillers and romance."
Fiction: Young adults: problem novels, romance, suspense/horror. Average word length: young adults—55,000.
How to Contact/Writers: Fiction: Submit outline/synopsis and 3 sample chapters. Reports on queries in 2 weeks; mss in 2-3 months. Publishes a book in 12-18 months after acceptance.
Terms: Pays authors royalty based on retail price. Offers advance. Sends galleys to authors.

BESS PRESS, P.O. Box 22388, Honolulu HI 96823. (808)734-7159. Editor: Revé Shapard. Publishes 1-2 picture books/year; 1-2 young readers/year; 0-1 middle readers/year. 60% of books by first-time authors. "Books must be about Hawaii, Asia or the Pacific."
Fiction: Picture books, young readers: adventure, animal, anthology, concept, contemporary, folktales, hi-lo, history, humor, multicultural, nature/environment, sports, suspense/mystery. Middle readers: adventure, animal, anthology, contemporary, folktales, hi-lo, history, humor, multicultural, nature/environment, problem novels, sports, suspense/mystery. Young adults: adventure, anthology, contemporary, hi-lo, history, humor, multicultural, problem novels, sports, suspense/mystery. Recently published *The Little Makana*, by Helen M. Dano, illustrated by Wren (ages 3-8); *Too Many Curls*, by Marilyn Kahalewai (ages 3-8, picture book); *Let's Call Him Lau-wili-wili-humuhumu-nukunuku-nukunuku-apuaa-oioi*, by Tim Myers, illustrated by Daryl Arakaki (ages 3-8, picture book).
Nonfiction: Picture books: activity books, biography, concept, geography, hi-lo, history, multicultural, reference, sports, textbooks. Young readers: activity books, biography, geography, hi-lo, history, multicultural, reference, sports, textbooks. Middle readers, young adults: biography, geography, hi-lo, history, multicultural, reference, sports, textbooks. Published *Filipino Word Book*, by Teresita V. Ramos and Josie Clausen, illustrated by Jerri Asuncion and Boboy Betco (ages 5-11, introductory language book); *Flowers of Hawaii Coloring Book*, by Wren (ages 3-8, coloring book); Keiki's First Books, by Maile and Wren (toddlers, concept books).
How to Contact/Writers: Fiction/nonfiction: Submit complete ms. Reports on queries in 2 weeks; on mss in 3-4 weeks. Publishes a book 6-12 months after acceptance. Will consider simultaneous submissions and previously published work.
Illustration: Works with 3 illustrators/year. Will review ms/illustration packages. Contact: Revé Shapard, editor. Will review artwork for future assignments.
How to Contact/Illustrators: Ms/illustration packages: Submit ms with dummy. Illustrations only: Query with samples. Reports in 3 weeks. Samples returned with SASE; samples filed. Original artwork returned at job's completion.
Terms: Pays authors royalty of 2½-10% based on wholesale price or work purchased outright. Pays illustrators by the project, royalty of 2½-5% based on wholesale price. Sends galleys to authors; dummies to illustrators. Book catalog available for SASE; ms and art guidelines available for SASE.
Tips: Looks for "books with commercial or educational appeal in our primary markets—Hawaii, Asia, the Western United States and libraries."

BETHANY HOUSE PUBLISHERS, 11300 Hampshire Ave. S., Minneapolis MN 55438. (612)829-2500. Book publisher. Children's Book Editor: Barbara Lilland. Managing Editor: Lance Wubbels. Publishes 16 young readers/year; 16 young adults/year. Publishes books with spiritual and religious themes.
Fiction: Middle readers, young adults: adventure, contemporary, problem novels, romance, suspense/mystery. Does not want to see poetry or science fiction. Average word length: young readers—20,000; young adults—35,000. Published *Too Many Secrets*, by Patricia H. Rushford (young adult/teens, mystery-adventure series); *Becky's Brainstorm*, by Elaine L. Schulte (young readers, adventure series with strong Christian values theme); *Mandie and the Fiery Rescue*, by Lois Leppard (young readers, adventure series).
Nonfiction: Middle readers, young adults: religion, self-help, social issues. Published *Can I Be a Christian Without Being Weird?*, by Kevin Johnson (early teens, devotional book); *Dear Judy, Did You Ever Like a Boy (who didn't like you?)*, by Judy Baer (young adult/teen, advice book on social issues).
How to Contact/Writers: Fiction/Nonfiction: Query. Reports on queries in 1 month; mss in 2 months. Publishes a book 9-12 months after acceptance. Will consider simultaneous submissions and previously published work.
Illustration: Works with 4 illustrators/year. Will review/ms/illustration packages. Will review artwork for future assignments.
How to Contact/Illustrators: Ms/illustration packages: Query. Illustrations only: Query with samples. Reports in 6 weeks. Samples returned with SASE.
Terms: Pays authors royalty based on retail price. Pays illustrators by the project. Sends galleys to authors. Book catalog available for 11 × 14 SAE and 5 first-class stamps.

Tips: "Research the market, know what is already out there. Study our catalog before submitting material. We look for an evangelical message woven delicately into a strong plot and topics that seek to broaden the reader's experience and perspective."

BETHEL PUBLISHING, 1819 S. Main, Elkhart IN 46516. (219)293-8585. Book publisher. Contact: Senior Editor. Publishes 1-2 young readers/year; 1-2 middle readers/year.
Fiction: Young readers: animal, religion. Middle readers and young adults: adventure, religion. Does not want to see "New-Age—Dungeon & Dragons type." Published *The Great Forest*, by Jean Springer (ages 9-14, religion); *Pordy's Prickly Problem*, by Janette Oke (ages 7-12, religion); *Peace Porridge*, by Marjie Douglas (ages 8-13, religion). Does not want to see workbooks, cookbooks, coloring books, books on theological studies, poetry or preschool/elementary age stories. Average word length: 30,000-50,000.
Nonfiction: Young readers, middle readers and young adults: religion.
How to Contact/Writers: Fiction/nonfiction: Query. Submit complete ms. Reports on queries in 3 weeks; mss in 3 months. Publishes a book 1 year after acceptance. Will consider simultaneous submissions and previously published work.
Illustration: Works with 2 illustrators/year. Will review ms/illustration packages. Will review artwork for future assignments.
How to Contact/Illustrators: Ms/illustration packages: Query. Reports in 1 month. Samples returned with SASE. Originals not returned.
Photography: Purchases photos from freelancers. Contact: Senior Editor. Buys stock. Model/property releases required. Uses color and b&w glossy prints; 35mm and 2¼×2¼ transparencies. Photographers should send cover letter.
Terms: Pays authors royalty of 5-10% on wholesale price. Pays illustrators by the project. Photographers paid by the project. Sends galleys to authors. Book catalog available for 9×12 SAE and 3 first-class stamps. Ms guidelines available for SASE. Artist's guidelines not available.

BLUE HERON PUBLISHING, INC., 24450 N.W. Hansen Rd., Hillsboro OR 97124. (503)621-3911. Book publisher. Publisher: Dennis Stovall. Publishes 1-2 young adult titles/year. Wants "reprints of YA classics. Only interested in the previously described from Northwest authors."
Fiction: Young adults: adventure, anthology, animal, contemporary, history, nature/environment. Average word length: young adult—60,000. Published reprints by Lensey Namioka (YA, adventure); *Death Walk*, by Walt Morey (YA, adventure novel); *Morning Glory Afternoon*, by Irene Bennett Brown (YA, historical adventure/romance).
Nonfiction: Middle readers, young adults: history, nature/environment, writing/publishing.
How to Contact/Writers: Nonfiction: Query. Reports on queries in 4-6 weeks; mss in 6 weeks. Publishes a book 18 months after acceptance. Will consider simultaneous submissions, electronic submissions via disk or modem and previously published work.
Illustration: Will review artwork for future assignments (only Northwest artists). Contact: Linny Stovall, publisher.
How to Contact/Illustrators: Illustrations only: Query with samples.
Terms: Pays authors royalty of 5-8% on retail price. Pays illustrators by the project (range: $100-600). Sends galleys to authors; dummies to illustrators. Book catalog available for 6×9 SAE and 52¢ postage. Ms guidelines available.

BOYDS MILLS PRESS, 815 Church St., Honesdale PA 18431. (800)949-7777. Fax: (717)253-0179. Imprint: Wordsong (poetry). Book publisher. Manuscript Coordinator: Beth Troop. Art Director: Tim Gillner. 5% of books from agented writers.

"Picture books" are geared toward preschoolers to 8-year-olds; "Young readers" are for 5- to 8-year-olds; "Middle readers" are for 9- to 11-year-olds; and "Young adults" are for those ages 12 and up.

Fiction: All levels: adventure, animal, contemporary, folktales, history, humor, multicultural, poetry, special needs, sports. Middle readers, young adults: suspense/mystery. Multicultural themes vary. "Please query us on the appropriateness of suggested topics for middle grade and young adult. For all other submissions send entire manuscript." Does not want to see talking animals, coming of age novels, and fantasy/science fiction. Recently published *Wanda's Roses*, by Pat Brisson (ages 4-8, contemporary picture book); *Bitter Bananas*, by Isaac Olaeye (ages 4-8, picture book—multicultural); *First Apple*, by Ching Yeung Russell (ages 7-10, middle grade—multicultural); and *Music of Their Hooves*, by Nancy Springer (ages 8-12, poetry—animals).

Nonfiction: Picture books, young readers, middle readers: activity books, animal, arts/crafts, history, multicultural, nature/environment. Picture books, young readers: concept. Young readers, middle readers, young adult: geography. Does not want to see reference/curricular text. Recently published *Wildlife Rescue*, by Jennifer Owings Dewey (ages 8 and up, middle readers, nature/environment).

How to Contact/Writers: Fiction/nonfiction: Submit complete manuscript or submit through agent. Query on middle reader, young adult and nonfiction. Reports on queries/mss in 1 month.

Illustration: Works with 70-100 illustrators/year. Will review ms/illustration packages. Will review artwork for future assignments. Contact: Tim Gillner, art director.

How to Contact/Illustrators: Ms/illustration packages: Submit complete ms. Illustrations only: Query with samples; send résumé and slides.

Photography: Buys photos from freelancers. Contact: Tim Gillner, art director. Assigns work.

Terms: Authors paid royalty or work purchased outright. Offers advances. Illustrators paid by the project, royalty. Catalog available for 9×12 SASE. Ms and art guidelines available for free.

Tips: "Picture books—with fresh approaches, not worn themes—are our strongest need at this time. Check to see what's already on the market before submitting your story."

BRADBURY PRESS, was incorporated into Macmillan Books for Young Readers, an imprint of Simon & Schuster Children's Publishing Division.

BRIGHT RING PUBLISHING, 1900 N. Shore Dr., Box 5768, Bellingham WA 98227-5768. (206)734-1601 or (800)480-4ART. Fax: (206)676-1271. Estab. 1985. Editor: MaryAnn Kohl. Publishes 1 young reader title/year. 50% of books by first-time authors. Uses only recipe format—"but no cookbooks unless woven into another subject like art, music, science."

• Bright Rings Science Arts received the 1993 Benjamin Franklin Award for best education book and the 1993 National Press Association Communicator Award for best instructional book.

Nonfiction: Young readers and middle readers: activity books involving art ideas, hobbies, cooking, how-to, multicultural, music/dance, nature/environment, science. "No picture books, no poetry, no stories of any kind and no crafts." Average length: "about 125 ideas/book." Multicultural needs include: arts of world cultures or related to kids' literature. "We are moving into only recipe-style resource books in any variety of subject areas—useful with children 2-12. 'Whole language' is the buzz word in early education—so books to meet the new demands of that subject will be needed." Recently published: SCRIBBLE ART: *Independent Creative Art Experiences for Children*; MUDWORKS: *Creative Clay, Dough, and Modeling Experiences*; and SCIENCE ARTS: *Discovering Science Through Art Experiences* (all by Mary Ann Kohl).

How to Contact/Writers: Nonfiction: submit complete ms. Reports on queries in 2 weeks; mss in 6 weeks. Publishes a book 1 year after acceptance. Will consider simultaneous submissions.

Illustration: Works with 2 illustrators/year. Will review ms/illustration packages. Prefers to review "black line (drawings) for text." Will review artwork for future assignments.

How to Contact/Illustrators: Ms/illustration packages: "Query first." Illustrations only: Query with samples; send tearsheets and "sample of ideas I request after query." Reports in 6-8 weeks.

Terms: Pays authors in royalties of 3-10% based on net sales. Work purchased outright (range: $500-2,000). Pays illustrators $500-2,000. Also offers "free books and discounts for future books." Book catalog, ms/artist's guidelines for business-size SAE and 29¢ postage.
Tips: "Bright Ring Publishing is not looking for picture books, juvenile fiction, or poetry at this time. We are, however, highly interested in creative activity and resource books for children to use independently or for teachers and parents to use with children. Must work for pre-school through age 12. We cannot accept book ideas which require unusual packaging such as attached toys or unique binding or paper."

*CAMBRIDGE EDUCATIONAL, P.O. Box 2153, Charleston WV 25328-2153. (800)468-4227. Fax: (800)FAX-ONUS (329-6687). Editor: Denny Keiffer. Publishes 10-20 middle readers/year; 20-40 young adult titles/year. 15-20% of books by first-time authors.
Nonfiction: Middle readers and young adults: activity books, arts/crafts, careers, concept, geography, history, how-to, nature/environment, science, self-help, social issues, sports. Recently published *Underdeveloped and Overexposed: Putting Your Self-Esteem in Focus*, by K. Lordan (ages 9-adult, self-help); and *Basic Office Skills*, by DeFaila (ages 9-adult, self-help).
How to Contact/Writers: Submit outline/synopsis. Reports on queries in 1-2 weeks; mss in 1-2 months. Publishes a book 6 months after acceptance. Will consider simultaneous submissions, electronic submissions via disk or modem, and previously published work.
Illustration: Uses both b&w and color artwork.
How to Contact/Illustrators: Ms/illustration packages: Query. Illustrations only: Query with samples and tearsheets. Samples returned with SASE; samples not filed. Originals not returned.
Photography: Buys photos from freelancers. Contact: Charlotte Angel, production director. Buys stock and assigns work. Model/property releases required. Uses 5×7 glossy b&w prints, 35mm, $2\frac{1}{4} \times 2\frac{1}{4}$, or 4×5 transparencies. Submit letter.
Terms: Pays authors royalty of 15-20% based on retail price. Work purchased outright from authors ($1,500-5,000). Offers advances (average amount: $1,000). Pays illustrators by the project (range: $250-1,000). Pays photographers by the project (range: $250-1,000); per photo (range: $50-500). Book catalog available for 9×12 SAE and 7 first-class stamps; ms and art guidelines available for SASE.
Tips: Looking for "more titles to break down cultural diversity barriers; self-help or career oriented titles; more titles dealing with controversial issues facing children."

*CANDLEWICK PRESS, 2067 Massachusetts Ave., Cambridge MA 02140. (617)661-3330. Fax: (617)661-0565. Book publisher. Editorial Assistant: M.T. Anderson. Design Coordinator: Aimee Smith. Publishes 120 picture books/year; 6 young readers/year; 10 middle readers/year; and 6 young adult titles/year. 5% of books by first-time authors.
• Candlewick cannot accept unsolicited manuscripts.
Fiction: Picture books, young readers: animal, contemporary, fantasy, folktales, history. Middle readers, young adults: adventure, animal, anthology, contemporary, fantasy, folktales, history, poetry.
Nonfiction: Picture book, young readers, middle readers: animal, biography, history, music/dance, nature/environment. Young adults: animal, biography, history, music/dance.
How to Contact/Writers: Reports on queries in 3 weeks; mss in 3 months. Publishes a book 12-18 months after acceptance. Will consider simultaneous submissions. Only interested in agented material.
Illustration: Works with 50 illustrators/year. Will review artwork for future assignments.
How to Contact/Illustrators: Ms/illustration packages: "General samples only please." Illustrations only: Submit résumé and portfolio. "We prefer to see a variety of the artist's style." Samples returned with SASE; samples filed. Original artwork returned at job's completion.
Terms: Pays authors royalty of 5-10% based on retail price. Offers advances. Pays illustrators 5-10% royalty based on retail price. Sends galleys to authors; dummies to illustrators. Book catalog available for 9×12 SAE and $1.67 postage.

CAROLINA WREN PRESS/LOLLIPOP POWER BOOKS, 120 Morris St., Durham NC 27701. (919)560-2738. Book publisher. Carolina Wren, Estab. 1976; Lollipop Power, Estab. 1971.

Both are nonprofit, small presses. Children's Editor: Ruth A. Smullin. Designer: Martha Scotford. Publishes an average of 1 picture book/year.

• Carolina Wren will not be reviewing manuscripts until April, 1995. Contact them at that time for current status.

Fiction: Picture books:. bilingual (English/Spanish), multicultural, multiracial, nonsexist. Average length: 30 pages. Recently published *I Like You to Make Jokes With Me, But Don't Touch Me*, by Ellen Base, illustrated by Margo LeMieux (bilingual).

How to Contact/Writers: "Query and request guidelines; enclose SASE with request. All manuscripts must be typed, double-spaced and accompanied by SASE of appropriate size with sufficient postage. If you do not wish your manuscript returned, you may simply enclose SASE for our response. Do not send illustrations." Reports on queries/ms in 3 months. Publishes a book 2-3 years after acceptance.

Illustration: Will review ms/illustration packages. Contact: Martha Scotford, designer. Will review artwork for future assignments.

How to Contact/Illustrators: Query with tearsheets. Reports on art samples only if SASE enclosed. Original artwork returned at job's completion.

Terms: Pays authors in royalties of 5% of print-run based on retail price, or cash, if available. Pays illustrators in royalties of 5% of print-run based on retail price, or cash, if available.

Tips: "Lollipop Power Books offer alternative points of view to prevailing stereotypes. Our books show children: girls and women who are self-sufficient, with responsibilities beyond those of home and family; boys and men who are emotional and nurturing and involved in domestic responsibilities; families that use day care or alternative child care; families that consist of one parent only, working parents, or extended families; realistic portrayals of children of all races and ethnic groups, who have in common certain universal feelings and experiences. We believe that children must be taken seriously. Our books present their problems honestly and without condescension. Lollipop Power Books must be well-written stories that will appeal to children. We are not interested in preachy tales where message overpowers plot and character. We are looking for good stories told from a child's point of view. Our current publishing priorities are: a) African-American, Hispanic or Native American characters; b) bilingual books (English/Spanish); c) books that show gay men or lesbian women as ordinary people who can raise children. To request a catalog, send a 9 × 12 envelope with postage sufficient for 2 ounces."

CAROLRHODA BOOKS, INC., 241 First Ave. N., Minneapolis MN 55401. (612)332-3344. Book publisher. Estab. 1969. Submissions Editor: Rebecca Poole. Publishes 5 picture books/year; 25 young reader titles/year; 30 middle reader titles/year. 20% of books by first-time authors; 10% of books from agented writers.

Fiction: Picture books: folktales, multicultural, nature/environment, special needs. Young readers, middle readers: historical. Average word length: picture books—1,000-1,500; young readers—2,000. Recently published *Pub, Slug, and Doug the Thug*, by Carol Saller; and *A Place to Belong*, by Emily Crofford.

Nonfiction: Picture books: animal, hobbies, nature/environment. Young readers, middle readers: animal, biography, history, hobbies, multicultural, nature/environment, science, social issues, special needs. Multicultural needs include biographies. Average word length: young readers— 2,000; middle readers—6,000. Recently published *What I Had Was Singing: The Story of Marian Anderson*, by Jeri Ferris; and *Grand Canyon*, by Patrick Cone.

How to Contact/Writers: Fiction/nonfiction: Submit complete ms. Reports on queries in 3-4 weeks; mss in 3 months. Publishes a book 18 months after acceptance. Will consider simultaneous submissions. Must enclose SASE.

Illustration: Will review ms/illustration packages. Will review artwork for future assignments. "Do not send originals."

How to Contact/Illustrators: Ms/illustration packages: Submit at least one sample illustration (in form of photocopy, slide, duplicate photo) with full ms. Illustrations only: Query with samples; send résumé/slides. "We like illustrators to send samples we can keep on file." Reports on art samples only if interested.

Photography: Purchases photos from freelancers. Buys stock and assigns work.
Terms: Buys ms outright for variable amount. Factors used to determine final payment: color vs. b&w, number of illustrations, quality of work. Sends galleys to authors; dummies to illustrators. Book catalog available for 9×12 SAE and 3 first-class stamps; ms guidelines for #10 SAE and 1 first-class stamp.
Tips: Writers: "Research the publishing company to be sure it is in the market for the type of book you're interested in writing. Familiarize yourself with the company's list. We specialize in beginning readers, photo essays and books published in series. We do very few single-title picture books and no novels. For more detailed information about our publishing program, consult our catalog. We do not publish any of the following: textbooks, workbooks, songbooks, puzzles, plays and religious material. In general, we suggest that you steer clear of alphabet books; preachy stories with a moral to convey; stories featuring anthropomorphic protagonists ('Amanda the Amoeba,' 'Frankie the Fire Engine,' 'Tonie the Tornado'); and stories that revolve around trite, unoriginal plots. Be sure to avoid racial and sexual stereotypes in your writing, as well as sexist language." (See also Lerner Publications.)

CHARIOT BOOKS, 20 Lincoln Ave., Elgin IL 60120. (708)741-9558. An imprint of Chariot Family Products and a division of David C. Cook Publishing Co. Book publisher. Design Coordinator: Helen Lannis. Managing Editor: Julie Smith. Publishes 20-30 picture books/year; 6-8 young readers/year; 10-15 middle readers/year; 4-6 young adult titles/year. Less than 5% of books by first-time authors; 15% of books from agented authors. "All books have overt Christian values, but there is no primary theme."
● This publisher does not read unsolicited manuscripts.
Illustration: Works with 20 illustrators/year. Will review artwork for future assignments. Contact: Helen Lannis, design coordinator.
How to Contact/Illustrators: Illustrations only: Query with samples; send résumé, promo sheet, portoflio, tearsheets. "Send color material I can keep." Reports only if interested. Samples returned with SASE; samples filed. Original artwork returned at job's completion.
Terms: Pays illustrators by the project, royalty or work purchased outright. Sends dummies to illustrators. Ms guidelines available for SASE.

CHARLESBRIDGE, 85 Main St., Watertown MA 02172. (617)926-0329. Subsidiary of Mastery Education. Book publisher. Publishes 10 nonfiction picture books/year. Managing Editor: Elena Dworkin Wright. Publishes nature or science picture books.
Fiction: Multicultural fiction for ages 6-10 (picture books) about childhood events in country of origin or immigration or visit to US.
Nonfiction: Picture books: geography, nature/environment, science. "We look for accurate biological and behavioral information about animals in their appropriate environment." Average word length: picture books—1,500. Recently published: *This Is Our Earth*, by Laura Benson (picture book); *Can We Be Friends? Partners in Nature*, by Alexandra Wright (picture book); and *Itse Selu-Cherokee Harvest Festival*, by Dan Pennington (picture book).
How to Contact/Writers: Nonfiction: Submit complete ms. Reports on mss in 1 month. Publishes a book 1-2 years after acceptance.
Illustration: Works with 5 illustrators/year. Will review ms/illustration packages. Will review artwork for future assignments. Uses color artwork only.
How to Contact/Illustrators: Illustrations only: Query with samples; provide résumé, tearsheets to be kept on file. Reports back only if interested. Does not return original artwork at job's completion.

Always include a self-addressed, stamped envelope (SASE) with submissions within your own country. When sending material to other countries, include a self-addressed envelope (SAE) and International Reply Coupons (IRCs).

Support Essential to Illustrator's Success

In art school, Carole Byard had been required to major in "something which would allow you to make a living," in addition to her first love, fine art. Sensing the similarity between illustration and her figure-oriented painting, and drawn to the prospect of joining other African-American illustrators in the field, Byard chose illustration. But a year after graduating from the New York-Phoenix School of Design, she was still trying to get her first job. Then her aunt helped her acquire an agent, and in a month, she had two children's book projects from Doubleday.

Carole Byard

"Even though school had prepared me, it had only been exercises, and I was really afraid I didn't know what to do," Byard remembers. When she got the contracts, she became even more unsure, and her agent suggested she call Tom Feelings, the African-American illustrator whose work she most admired. When Byard couldn't bring herself to do it, her agent contacted him and soon thereafter, Byard got a call from Feelings himself. "He said he heard I was working on my first book and would come over and take a look. I was shocked," she says.

This visit, in which Feelings shared his work and technique, and told Byard she was doing "just fine," boosted her confidence and gave her needed support. Feelings also said it was a privilege to illustrate books about African-Americans because the need was so great. "And he told me something I'll always remember: 'Whatever you do, do it with love.' That's always been in my mind."

In order to "do it with love," Byard must believe in a project from the start, and she is very selective about the book illustration she takes on. "What feels good to me is a story with feelings, that has some intimacy in it, that has something presented in a new or different way that may be helpful or meaningful to the reader."

Working Cotton, a moving account of a day in the life of an African-American family working the cotton fields of California in the 1950s, is an example of a story Byard immediately loved. "I read the text and it was about real people, something I felt was missing in the world of children's books; it was about work and about children who worked. It showed how hard Black people work in this country." Other appeals were the sparse text, which presented Byard with great artistic freedom, and that the story dealt with the land. "I like to draw people who work with the land, and in my fine art, I use earth and nature a lot."

Like many illustrators, Byard often uses her family members as models for her work. For example, her brother works with his hands and spends a great deal of time in his garden. His hands were the model for the father's hands in *Working Cotton*. To depict the setting accurately, she referred to photographs she was sent by the author, Sherley Anne Williams, and did an immense amount of research at the library. "I wanted to know everything I could about cotton fields," Byard says. *Working Cotton* went on to become a Caldecott Honor Book in 1993, and it was then that she finally met the author.

In the past 20 years, Byard, who now resides in New York City, has illustrated 15 books, done magazine and album cover illustration, and dedicated most of her time to fine art—painting, sculpture and murals. While the majority of her income comes from book illustration royalties, she has gallery representation, has taught, and has received grants and fellowships for her fine art. One grant allowed her to spend three months in Africa, and African influence can be seen in her books *African Dream* and *Cornrows*, both of which won her the Coretta Scott King Award for illustration.

While Byard started out working in black and white, mostly charcoal, her recent children's books tend to be in the rich colors of acrylic and pastel, which is one of the major changes she has seen in the world of children's books. The most significant change, though, is "that now there are books about all the children," she says.

Byard advises aspiring children's book illustrators to write to the Center for Multicultural Children's Literature, a place where established children's book illustrators and writers come together to help those who are entering the field. They advise, steer to publishers and mentors, and hold an annual fall conference. (Send SASE to CMCL, 10 E. 53rd St., 30th Floor, New York NY 10022.)

Presently Byard is writing and illustrating two books for Scholastic based on one of the major inspirations in her life, her father. She is also creating two ceramic murals paying tribute to writer Langston Hughes for the lobby of the Langston Hughes Elementary School in Brooklyn. For Byard, it's a project that is both a challenge and an honor.

—Lauri Miller

Carole Byard captures African-American children hard at work in this acrylic illustration from Working Cotton, by Sherley Anne Williams, published by Harcourt Brace. The book received a Caldecott Honor Award in 1993.

© 1993 Carole Byard.

Terms: Pays authors in royalties or work purchased outright. Pays illustrators by the project. Sends galleys to authors.
Tips: Wants "picture books that have humor and are factually correct."

*CHELSEA HOUSE PUBLISHERS, 300 Park Ave. S., New York NY 10010. (212)677-4010. Fax: (212)677-9414. Art Director: Bob Mitchell. Publishes 40 middle readers/year; 80 young adult titles/year. 50% of books by first-time authors.
Nonfiction: Middle readers, young adults: biography, history, multicultural, science, sports. Average word length: middle readers—10,000; young adults—20,000.
How to Contact/Writers: Nonfiction: Submit outline/synopsis and 1 sample chapter. Reports on queries/mss in 1 month. Publishes a book 9 months after acceptance. Will consider electronic submissions via disk or modem.
Illustration: Works with 40 illustrators/year. Will review artwork for future assignments. Uses color artwork only.
How to Contact/Illustrators: Illustrations only: Arrange personal portfolio review. Reports in 1 month. Samples returned with SASE; samples filed. Original artwork returned at job's completion.
Terms: Work purchased outright from authors. Pays illustrators by the project. Sends galleys to authors. Book catalog and ms guidelines available for SAE.

CHICAGO REVIEW PRESS, 814 N. Franklin St., Chicago IL 60610. (312)337-0747. Book publisher. Editorial Director: Amy Teschner. Art Director: Fran Lee. Publishes 1 middle reader/year; "about 4" young adult titles/year. 50% of books by first-time authors; 30% of books from agented authors. "We publish art activity books for young children and project books in the arts and sciences for ages 10 and up (our Ziggurat Series). We do not publish fiction."
Nonfiction: Young readers, middle readers and young adults: activity books, arts/crafts, geography, hobbies, how-to, science. "We're interested in hands-on, educational books; anything else probably will be rejected." Average word length: young readers and young adults—175 pages. Recently published *Huzzah Means Hooray: Activities from the Days of Damsels, Jesters, and Blackbirds in a Pie,* by Laurie Carlson (ages 3-9); *Happy Birthday, Grandma Moses: Activities for Special Days Throughout the Year,* by Clare Bonfanti Braham and Maria Bonfanti Esche (ages 3-9); and *Video Cinema: Techniques and Projects for Beginning Filmmakers,* by John Parris Frantz (ages 11 and up). Reports on queries/mss in 2 months. Publishes a book 1-2 years after acceptance. Will consider simultaneous submissions and previously published work.
Illustration: Works with 2 illustrators/year. Will review ms/illustration packages. Will review artwork for future assignments. Contact: Fran Lee, art director.
How to Contact/Illustrators: Ms/illustration packages: Submit 1-2 chapters of ms with corresponding pieces of final art. Illustrations only: Query with samples, résumé. Reports back only if interested. Original artwork "usually" returned at job's completion.
Photography: Buys photos from freelancers ("but not often"). Contact: Fran Lee, art director. Buys stock and assigns work. Wants "instructive photos. We consult our files when we know what we're looking for on a book-by-book basis." Uses b&w prints.
Terms: Pays authors royalty of 7½-12½% based on retail price. Offers advances ("but not always") of $500-1,500. Pays illustrators by the project (range varies considerably). Pays photographers by the project (range varies considerably). Sends galleys to authors. Book catalog available for SASE; ms guidelines available for SASE.
Tips: "We're looking for original activity books for small children and the adults caring for them—new themes and enticing projects to occupy kids' imaginations and promote their sense of personal creativity. We like activity books that are as much fun as they are constructive. For older kids, age 10 and up, we publish Ziggurat Books—activity books geared to teach a discipline in the arts or sciences. As for the future, we expect parents to become increasingly engaged in their children's educations. Our Ziggurat books are intended to encourage children to pursue interests and talents inspired but not thoroughly covered by their schoolwork or other influences. We think parents are buying our books so their kids can pick up where a particularly exciting lesson or museum visit left off. When a kid becomes curious about say, videography or graphic design, we want to provide the

challenging hands-on book that will cultivate enthusiasm while teaching him or her all about that intriguing subject."

CHILDREN'S BOOK PRESS, Suite 4, 6400 Hollis St., Emeryville CA 94608. (510)655-3395. Contact: Emily Romero. Publishes 3 picture books/year. 50% of books by first-time authors. "Children's Book Press is a nonprofit publisher of bilingual and multicultural children's literature. We publish folktales and contemporary stories reflecting the traditions and culture of the emerging majority in the United States and from countries around the world. Our goal is to help broaden the base of children's literature in this country to include more stories from the African-American, Asian-American, Hispanic and Native American communities as well as the diverse Spanish-speaking communities throughout the Americas."
Fiction: Picture books: contemporary, multicultural. Average word length: picture books— 800-1,600.
How to Contact/Writers: Fiction: Submit complete ms to Submissions Editor. Reports on mss in 1-12 months. Publishes a book 1 year after acceptance. Will consider simultaneous submissions.
Illustration: Works with 3 illustrators/year. Will review ms/illustration packages. Will review artwork for future assignments. Uses color artwork only.
How to Contact/Illustrators: Ms/illustration packages: Send ms with 3 or 4 color photocopies. Illustrations only: Send slides. Reports in 1-12 months. Samples returned with SASE. Original artwork returned at job's completion.
Terms: Pays authors royalty. Pays illustrators by the project. Book catalog available for SAE; ms guidelines available for SASE.
Tips: "Vocabulary level should be approximately third grade (eight years old) or below. Keep in mind, however, that many of the young people who read our books may be nine, ten, or eleven years old or older. Their life experiences are often more advanced than their reading level, so try to write a story that will appeal to a fairly wide age range. We are especially interested in humorous stories."

*CHILDREN'S LIBRARY PRESS, P.O. Box 1919, Joshua Tree CA 92252. Book Publisher. Editor-in-Chief: Teresa Bjornson. Publishes 4-5 picture books/year. 80% of books by first-time authors.
● This publisher is still working on its first titles.
Fiction: Picture books: adventure, animal, anthology, concept, contemporary, fantasy, folktales, history, humor, multicultural, nature/environment, science fiction, suspense/mystery.
Nonfiction: Picture books: animal, cooking, geography, history, hobbies, nature/environment, science.
How to Contact/Writers: Fiction/Nonfiction: Submit complete ms. Reports on queries/mss in 6 months. Publishes a book 2 years after acceptance. Will consider simultaneous submissions.
How to Contact/Illustrators: Only interested in agented material.
Terms: Pays authors royalty based on wholesale price (amount determined on a per-book basis). Offers advances (amount varies). Sends galleys to authors.
Tips: Looking for "simple, well-written texts."

CHILDRENS PRESS, 5440 N. Cumberland, Chicago IL 60656. (312)693-0800. Book publisher. Vice President of Editorial: M.F. Dyra. Creative Director: M. Fiddle. Publishes 20 picture books and 30 middle readers/year. 5% of books by first-time authors. Publishes informational (nonfiction) for K-6; picture books for young readers K-3.
Fiction: Picture books, young readers: adventure, animal, concept, contemporary, folktales, multicultural. Middle readers: contemporary, hi-lo, humor, multicultural. Young adults: hi-lo. Does not want to see young adult fiction, romance or science fiction. Average word length: picture book—300; middle readers—4,000.
Nonfiction: Picture books: arts/crafts, biography, concept, geography, hi-lo, history, hobbies, how-to, multicultural, nature/environment, science, special needs. Young readers: animal, arts/crafts, biography, careers, concept, geography, health, hi-lo, history, hobbies, multicultural, nature/environment, science, social issues, sports. Middle readers: hi-lo, his-

tory, multicultural, reference, science. Average word length: picture books—400; young readers—2,000; middle readers—8,000; young adult—12,000.

How to Contact/Writers: Fiction: Query; submit outline/synopsis or submit outline/synopsis and 1 sample chapter. Nonfiction: Query; submit outline/synopsis. Reports in 2-3 months. Publishes book 18 months after acceptance. Will consider simultaneous submissions.

Illustration: Works with 14 illustrators/year. Will review ms/illustration packages. Contact: M. Fiddle, creative director. Will review artwork for future assignments. Uses color artwork only.

How to Contact/Illustrators: Illustrations only: Query with samples or arrange personal portfolio review. Reports back only if interested. Samples returned with SASE. Samples filed. Originals not returned.

Photography: Purchases photos from freelancers. Contact: Jan Izzo, photo editor. Buys stock and assigns work. Model/property releases and captions required. Uses color and b&w prints; 2¼×2¼, 35mm transparencies. Photographers should send cover letter and stock photo list.

Terms: Pays authors royalty of 5% based on net or work purchased outright (range: $500-1,000). Offers average advances of $1,000. Pays illustrators by the project (range: $1,800-3,500). Photographers paid per photo (range: $50-100). Sends galleys to authors; dummies to illustrators. Book catalog available for SAE; ms guidelines for SASE.

Tips: "Never write down to reader; keep language lively."

CHILDREN'S WRITER'S & ILLUSTRATOR'S MARKET, 1507 Dana Ave., Cincinnati OH 45207. Publication of Writer's Digest Books. Contact: Alice P. Buening. Publishes this annual directory of freelance markets for children's writers and illustrators. Send b&w or color samples—photographs, photostats or good quality photocopies of artwork. "Since *Children's Writer's & Illustrator's Market* is published only once a year, submissions are kept on file for the next upcoming edition until selections are made. Material is then returned by SASE." Buys one-time rights. Buys 10-20 illustrations/year. "I need examples of art that have been sold to one of the listings in *CWIM*. Thumb through the book to see the type of art I'm seeking. The art must have been freelanced; it cannot have been done as staff work. Include the name of the listing that purchased the work, what the art was used for and the payment you received." Pays $50 to holder of reproduction rights and free copy of *CWIM* when published.

■CHINA BOOKS, 2929 24th St., San Francisco CA 94110. (415)282-2994. Fax: (415)282-0994. Book publisher. Independent book producer/packager. Estab. 1960. Art Director: Wendy Lee. 10% of books by first-time authors; 10% of books from agented writers. 10% subsidy published.

Fiction: Picture books: animal, anthology, folktales, health, history, multicultural, nature/environment, poetry. Young readers: animal, contemporary, folktales, health, history, multicultural, nature/environment, religion. Middle readers: animal, contemporary, fantasy, folktales, nature/environment, poetry. Subjects must relate to China or Chinese-Americans. Published *The Moon Maiden & Other Asian Folktales*, adapted and illustrated by Hua Long (ages 10-12).

Nonfiction: Picture books, young readers, middle readers: activity books, arts/crafts, biography, cooking, geography, history, hobbies, multicultural, music/dance, nature/environment, religion, sports. Average word length: young readers—2,000; middle readers—4,000. Subjects must relate to China or Chinese-Americans.

How to Contact/Writers: Fiction/nonfiction: Query; submit outline/synopsis and sample chapters. Reports on queries in 1 month; mss in 2 months. Publishes a book 9 months after acceptance. Will consider simultaneous and electronic submissions via disk or modem.

Illustration: Works with 10 illustrators/year. Will review ms/illustration packages. Will review artwork for future assignments.

How to Contact/Illustrators: Illustrations only: Query with samples, tearsheets.

Photography: Buys stock and assigns work. Looking for Chinese or Chinese-American subjects. Uses color and b&w prints; 35mm and 2¼×2¼ transparencies. Query with samples.

Terms: Pays authors in royalties of 8-10% based on retail price; buys ms outright for $100-500. Offers average advance payment of "1/3 of total royalty." Pays illustrators by the project (range: $100-500); royalties of 8% based on retail price. Pays photographers by the project (range: $50-500); per photo (range: $25-100); royalty of 4-8% based on retail price. Sends galleys to authors; dummies to illustrators. Book catalog free on request; ms/artist's guidelines for SASE.

Tips: Looks for "something related to China or to Chinese-Americans."

CHRONICLE BOOKS, 275 Fifth St., San Francisco CA 94103. (415)777-7240. Fax: (415)495-2478. Book publisher. Assistant Editor: Molly Ker. Director of Children's Books: Victoria Rock. Publishes 18-20 (both fiction and nonfiction) picture books/year; 2-4 middle readers nonfiction titles/year; 2-4 beginning readers or middle readers fiction/year. 10-50% of books by first-time authors; 10-50% of books from agented writers.

Fiction: Picture books: animal, folktales, history, multicultural, nature/environment. Young readers: animal, folktales, history, multicultural, nature/environment, poetry. Middle readers: animal, history, multicultural, nature/environment, poetry, problem novels. Young adults: multicultural needs include "projects that feature diverse children in everyday situations." Recently published *The Night I Followed the Dog*, by Nina Laden (ages 5-9); and *Alejandro's Gift*, by Richard E. Albert and Sylvia Long (ages 3-8).

Nonfiction: Picture books: animal, history, multicultural, nature/environment, science. Young readers: animal, arts/crafts, cooking, geography, history, multicultural and science. Middle readers: animal, arts/crafts, biography, cooking, geography, history, multicultural and nature/environment. Young adults: biography and multicultural. Recently published *The Car Book* and *The Bake-a-Cake Book*, by Marie Meijer (ages 3-8); *The Eyes of Gray Wolf*, by Jonathan London and Jon Van Zyle (ages 3-8); and *Among the Orangutans: The Biruté Galdikas Story*, by Evelyn Gallardo (ages 8-12).

How to Contact/Writers: Fiction and nonfiction: Submit complete manuscript (picture books); submit outline/synopsis and 3 sample chapters (for older readers). Reports on queries/mss in 2-12 weeks. Publishes a book 1-3 years after acceptance. Will consider simultaneous submissions, as long as they are marked "multiple submission." Will not consider submissions by fax.

Illustration: Works with 15-20 illustrators/year. Will review ms/illustration packages. "Indicate if project *must* be considered jointly, or if editor may consider text and art separately." Will review artwork for future assignments. Wants "unusual art, something that will stand out on the shelves. Either bright and modern or very traditional. Fine art, not mass market."

How to Contact/Illustrators: Submit samples of artist's work (not necessarily from book, but in the envisioned style). Slides, tearsheets and color photocopies OK. (No original art.) Dummies helpful. Résumé helpful. "If samples sent for files, generally no response — unless samples are not suited to list, in which case samples are returned. Queries and project proposals responded to in same time frame as author query/proposals."

Photography: Purchases photos from freelancers. Works on assignment only. Wants nature/natural history photos.

Terms: Generally pays authors in royalties based on retail price "though we do occasionally work on a flat fee basis." Advance varies. Illustrators paid royalty based on retail price or flat fee. Sends proofs to authors and illustrators. Book catalog for 9 × 12 SAE and 8 first-class stamps; manuscript guidelines for #10 SASE.

Tips: "Chronicle Books publishes an eclectic mixture of traditional and innovative children's books. We are interested in taking on projects that have a unique bent to them — be it in subject matter, writing style, or illustrative technique. As a small list, we are looking for books that will lend our list a distinctive flavor. Primarily we are interested in fiction and nonfiction picture books for children ages infant-8 years, and nonfiction books for children ages 8-12 years. We are also interested in developing a middle grade/YA fiction program, and are looking for literary fiction that deals with relevant issues. Our sales reps are witnessing a resistance to alphabet books. And the market has become increasingly competitive. The '80s boom in children's publishing has passed, and the market is demanding high-quality books that work on many different levels."

CLARION BOOKS, 215 Park Ave. S., New York NY 10003. (212)420-5889. Houghton Mifflin Company. Book publisher. Editor and Publisher: Dorothy Briley. Art Director: Anne Diebel. Publishes 20 picture books/year; 7 young reader titles/year; 14 middle reader titles/year; 4 young adult titles/year. 10% of books by first-time authors; 15% of books from agented writers.

● To learn more about Clarion's illustration needs, read the interview with Anne Diebel in the 1994 edition of *Children's Writer's & Illustrator's Market*.

Fiction: All levels: adventure, animal, contemporary, fantasy, folktales, history, humor, multicultural, nature/environment, science fiction, sports, family stories. Average word length: picture books—50-1,000; young readers—1,000-2,500; middle readers—10,000-30,000; young adults—20,000-30,000.

Nonfiction: All levels: animal, biography, concept, geography, history, multicultural, nature/environment, science, social issues. Average word length: picture books—750-1,000; young readers—1,000-2,500; middle readers—10,000-30,000.

How to Contact/Writers: Fiction: Send complete ms. Nonfiction: Query. Reports on queries in 1 month; mss in 2-3 months. Publishes a book 18-24 months after acceptance. Will consider simultaneous submissions. "Address all submissions to Dorothy Briley."

Illustration: Works with 30 illustrators/year. Will review ms/illustration packages. Will review artwork for future assignments.

How to Contact/Illustrators: Ms/illustration packages: "Query first." Illustrations only: Query with samples. Reports on art samples only if interested. Original artwork returned at job's completion.

Terms: Pays in royalties of 10% based on retail price, shared 50/50 by author and illustrator. Offers advance (average amount: $2,500-5,000). Sends galleys to authors; dummies to illustrators. Ms/artist's guidelines free on request with #10 SASE; book catalog free on request with 9 × 12 SASE ($1.05 postage).

*CLEAR LIGHT PUBLISHERS, 823 Don Diego, Santa Fe NM 87501. (505)989-9590. Fax: (505)989-9519. Book publisher. Publisher: Harmon Houghton. Publishes 3 middle readers/year; 3 young adult titles/year.

Nonfiction: Middle readers and young adults: multicultural, American Indian only.

How to Contact/Writers: Fiction/Nonfiction: Submit complete ms. Will consider simultaneous submissions. Reports in 3 months.

Illustration: Will review ms/illustration packages.

How to Contact/Illustrators: Ms/illustration packages: Submit ms with dummy. Contact: Harmon Houghton, publisher.

Terms: Pays authors royalty of 10% based on wholesale price. Offers advances (average amount: up to 50% of expected net sales). Sends galleys to authors.

Tips: Looking for "authentic American Indian art and folklore."

COBBLEHILL BOOKS, 375 Hudson St., New York NY 10014. (212)366-2628. Affiliate of Dutton Children's Books, a division of Penguin Books USA Inc. Book publisher. Editorial Director: Joe Ann Daly. Executive Editor: Rosanne Lauer.

Fiction: Picture books, young readers: adventure, animal, contemporary, easy-to-read, sports, suspense/mystery. Middle readers: adventure, contemporary, problem novels, sports, suspense/mystery. Young adults: adventure, suspense/mystery.

Nonfiction: Picture books, young readers: animal, nature/environment, sports. Middle readers: nature/environment.

How to Contact/Writers: Fiction/nonfiction: Query. Will consider simultaneous submissions "if we are informed about them."

How to Contact/Illustrators: Illustrations only: Submit samples to keep on file, no original artwork. Original artwork returned at job's completion.

Terms: Pays authors in royalties. Pays illustrators royalties or a flat fee. Book catalog available for 8½ × 11 SAE and 2 first-class stamps; ms guidelines available for #10 SASE.

Refer to the Business of Children's Writing & Illustrating for up-to-date marketing, tax and legal information.

CONCORDIA PUBLISHING HOUSE, 3558 S. Jefferson Ave., St. Louis MO 63118. (314)268-1000. Book publisher. Family and Children's Resources Editor: Ruth Geisler. Art Director: Ed Luhmann. "Concordia Publishing House publishes a number of quality children's books each year. Most are fiction, with some nonfiction, based on a religious subject."

Fiction/Nonfiction: "Reader interest ranges from picture books to young adults. All books must contain explicit Christian content." Published *Little Visits on the Go*, by Mary Manz Simon (family devotional book and audio tape); *The Biggest Bully in Brookdale*, by Carol Gormon (The Tree House Kids series, grades 2-3, first chapter books); *God Loves Me — So What*, by Guy Doud (preteen and teen, Christian living).

How to Contact/Writers: Fiction: Query. Submit complete ms (picture books); submit outline/synopsis and sample chapters (novel-length). Reports on queries in 1 month; mss in 2 months. Publishes a book 1 year after acceptance. Will consider simultaneous submissions.

Illustration: Will review artwork for future assignments. Contact: Ed Luhmann, art director.

How to Contact/Illustrators: Illustrations only: Query with samples.

Terms: Pays authors in royalties based on retail price or outright purchase (minimum $500). Sends galleys to author. Ms guidelines for 1 first-class stamp and a #10 envelope.

Tips: "Do not send finished artwork with the manuscript. If sketches will help in the presentation of the manuscript, they may be sent. If stories are taken from the Bible, they should follow the Biblical account closely. Liberties should not be taken in fantasizing Biblical stories."

*COOL KIDS PRESS, 1098 N.W. Boca Raton Blvd., Boca Raton FL 33432. (407)750-9826. Fax: (407)750-9869. Imprint of Cool Hand Communication. Book publisher. Editorial Director: Lisa McCourt. Publishes 8 picture books/year; 3 young readers/year; 3 middle readers/year; 3 young adult titles/year. 25% of books by first-time authors.

Fiction: Picture books, young readers: adventure, animal, concept, contemporary, humor, multicultural, nature/environment, sports. Middle readers: adventure, animal, contemporary, humor, multicultural, nature/environment, problem novels, romance, sports, suspense/mystery. Young adults: adventure, contemporary, humor, multicultural, problem novels, romance, suspense/mystery. Multicultural needs include titles that portray ethnic diversity, not titles *about* various cultures. Does not want to see religious material. Average word length: picture books — 100-1,500. Recently published *Sam and Spot*, by John O'Brien (ages 4-8, picture book); *Daisy the Firecow*, by Viki Woodworth (ages 4-8, picture book); and *"I've Done This Before, Miss!"*, by Michael Ratnett and June Goulding (ages 4-8, picture book).

Nonfiction: Picture books: careers, concept, self help, social issues. Young readers: careers, self help, social issues. Middle readers, young adults: self help, social issues. "We're a very new juvenile imprint, and while we plan to incorporate nonfiction titles into future lists, we have not published any to date."

How to Contact/Writers: Fiction: Submit complete manuscript. Submit outline/synopsis and 3 sample chapters (for longer works). Nonfiction: Query. Reports on queries in 3 weeks; mss in 2 months. Publishes a book 1 year after acceptance. Will consider simultaneous submissions.

Illustration: Works with 12-15 illustrators/year. Will review ms/illustration packages. Contact: Lisa McCourt, editorial director. Will review artwork for future assignments. Uses color artwork only. "We use a wide variety."

How to Contact/Illustrators: Ms/illustration packages: Query, submit ms with dummy or submit ms with some final art. "We look at submissions no matter how they come in." Illustrations only: Query with samples; provide résumé, promo sheet, client list. Samples are returned with SASE only; samples filed "unless the illustrator has requested it be returned."

Photography: Buys photos from freelancers. Contact: Lisa McCourt, editorial director. Works on assignment only. Uses "object photos for Dorling Kindersley type concept book." Submit cover letter, résumé, published sample, client list, promo piece (color).

Terms: Pays authors and illustrators royalty. Offers advances. Sends galleys to authors; dummies to illustrators. Book catalog available for SAE.

Tips: Wants "original stories that are either outrageously funny or very touching, or deliver a social message (in any format)."

COTEAU BOOKS LTD., 401-2206 Dewdney Ave., Regina, Sasketchewan S4R 1H3 Canada. (306)777-0170. Thunder Creek Publishing Co-op Ltd. Book publisher. Managing Editor: Shelley Sopher. Publishes 1-2 juvenile and/or young adult books/year, 9-12 books/year. 10% of books by first-time authors.
Fiction: Middle readers, young adults: adventure, contemporary, fantasy, history, humor, multicultural, nature/environment, suspense/mystery. "No didactic, message pieces, nothing religious."
How to Contact/Writers: Fiction: Submit complete ms. Reports on queries in 1 month; mss in 4 months. Publishes a book 1-2 years after acceptance. Coteau Books publishes Canadian writers only; mss from the US are returned unopened.
Illustration: Will review artwork for possible future assignments. Contact: Val Jakubowski, production coordinator.
How to Contact/Illustrators: Illustrations only: Submit nonreturnable samples. Reports only if interested. Original artwork returned at job's completion. Only Canadian illustrators are used.
Photography: "Very occasionally buys photos from freelancers." Buys stock and assigns work.
Terms: Pays authors in royalties of 5-12½% based on retail price. Other method of payment: "signing bonus." Pays illustrators by the project (range: $500-2,000) or royalty of 5% maximum based on retail price. Sends galleys to authors; dummies to illustrators. Book catalog free on request with 9 × 12 SASE (IRC).

CRESTWOOD HOUSE, 250 James St., Morristown NJ 07960. Imprint of Silver Burdett Press, Simon & Schuster Education Group. Book publisher. Editor: Debby Biber. See Silver Burdett Press listing.

CROCODILE BOOKS, USA, 99 Seventh Ave., Brooklyn NY 11215. (718)797-4292. Imprint of Interlink Publishing Group, Inc. Book publisher. Vice President: Ruth Moushabeck. Publishes 16 picture books/year. 25% of books by first-time authors.
• No unsolicited manuscripts are accepted by this publisher.
Fiction: Picture books: animal, contemporary, history, spy/mystery/adventure.
Nonfiction: Picture book: history, nature/environment.
Terms: Pays authors in royalties. Sends galleys to author; dummies to illustrator.

*CROCODILE CREEK PRESS/EUROPEAN TOY COLLECTION, 6643 Melton Rd., Portage IN 46368. (219)763-3234. Fax: (219)762-1740. Book Publisher. Children's Book Development Director: Beth Mullaney. Publishes 4-8 picture books/year; and 4-8 young readers/year. 50% of books by first-time authors.
• Crocodile Creek is opening up a new division to publish children's books, some with product tie-ins. See also Crocodile Creek's listing in the Special Markets section of this book.
Fiction: Picture books: adventure, animal, anthology, concept, contemporary, fantasy, folktales, history, humor, nature/environment. Young readers: animal, concept, folktales, humor. Average word length: picture books—150-300; young readers—500-2,000.
Nonfiction: Picture books: activity books, animal, arts/crafts, concept, cooking, geography, health, history, how-to, multicultural, music/dance, nature/environment, science. Young readers: activity books, animal, arts/crafts, concept, geography, history, how-to, multicultural, music/dance, nature/environment, science. Average word length: picture books—150-300; young readers—500-2,000.
How to Contact/Writers: Fiction/Nonfiction: Query. Reports on queries in 4-6 weeks; mss in 4-6 months. Publishes a book 1-2 years after acceptance. Will consider simultaneous submissions and previously published work.
Illustration: Will review ms/illustration packages. Will review artwork for future assignments. Contact: Beth Mullaney.

How to Contact/Illustrators: Ms/illustration packages: Submit ms with 4 pieces of final art. Illustrations only: Query with samples; provide promo sheet, client list and tearsheets. Reports in 4-6 weeks. Samples not returned. Original artwork returned at job's completion.
Terms: Pays authors royalty of 4-8% based on wholesale price. Offers advances (amount varies). Pays illustrators variably, "according to several factors."
Tips: "Rather than focusing on a large number of titles, we will be focusing on a limited number of titles that reflect high standards in both design and writing. Imagination, insight, wonder, awe, delight, humor, compassion and poetry will be the hallmarks of the books we choose to publish."

CROSSWAY BOOKS, Good News Publishers, 1300 Crescent, Wheaton IL 60187. (708)682-4300. Fax: (708)682-4785. Book Publisher. Editorial Director: Leonard Goss. Publishes 1-2 picture books/year; 6-10 young readers/year; 6 middle readers/year; 5-10 young adult titles/year. "Crossway Books is committed to publishing books that bring Biblical reality to readers and that examine crucial issues through a Christian world view."
Fiction: Picture books: religion. Young readers: adventure, contemporary, fantasy, history, humor, religion. Middle readers: adventure, contemporary, fantasy, history, humor, religion, science fiction, suspense/mystery, supernatural, Christian realism. Young adults: contemporary, fantasy, history, humor, religion, science fiction, suspense/mystery, supernatural, Christian realism. Does not want to see horror novels, romance or prophecy novels. Published *Tell Me the Secrets*, by Max Lucado, illustrated by Ron DiCianni.
Nonfiction: Middle readers, young adults: history, reference, religion, social issues. Does not want to see celebrity books, popular trend books, popular experience books or books attempting cultural synthesis.
How to Contact/Writers: Fiction/nonfiction: Submit outline/synopsis. Reports on queries/mss in 4-6 weeks. Publishes a book 6-10 months after acceptance. Will consider simultaneous submissions.
Illustration: Works with 5 illustrators/year. Will review ms/illustration packages. Will review artwork for future assignments.
How to Contact/Illustrators: Ms/illustration packages: Query. Illustrations only: Query with samples; provide resume, promo sheet and client list.
Terms: Pays authors royalty of 14% based on net sales. Pays illustrators by the project. Sends galleys to authors; dummies to illustrators. Book catalog available; ms guidelines available for SASE.

CROWN PUBLISHERS (CROWN BOOKS FOR CHILDREN), 201 E. 50th St., New York NY 10022. (212)940-7742. Imprint of Random House, Inc. See Random House listing.

CSS PUBLISHING, 628 S. Main St., Lima OH 45804. (419)227-1818. Book publisher. Editor: Terry Rhoads. Publishes books with religious themes.
Fiction: Picture books, young readers, middle readers, young adults: religion. Needs children's sermons (object lesson) for Sunday morning worship services; dramas for Advent, Christmas or Epiphany involving children for church services; activity and craft ideas for Sunday school or mid-week services for children (particularly pre-school and first and second grade). Does not want to see secular picture books. Published *That Seeing, They May Believe*, by Kenneth Mortonson (lessons for adults to present during worship services to pre-schoolers-third graders); *What Shall We Do With This Baby?*, by Jan Spence (Christmas Eve worship service involving youngsters from newborn babies to high school youth); *Miracle in the Bethlehem Inn*, by Mary Lou Warstler (Advent or Christmas drama involving pre-schoolers to high school youth and adults).
Nonfiction: Picture books, young readers, middle readers, young adults: religion. Needs children's sermons (object lesson) for Sunday morning workship services; dramas for Advent, Christmas or Epiphany involving children for church services; activity and craft ideas for Sunday school or mid-week services for children (particularly pre-school and first and second grade). Does not want to see secular picture books. Published *Mustard Seeds*, by Ellen Humbert (activity/bulletins for pre-schoolers-first graders to use during church); *This Is The King*, by Cynthia Cowen.

How to Contact/Writers: Reports on queries in 1 week; mss in 1-6 months. Publishes a book 9 months after acceptance. Will consider simultaneous submissions.

Tips: "We are seeking material for use by clergy, Christian education directors and Sunday school teachers for mainline Protestant churches. Our market is mainline Protestant clergy."

MAY DAVENPORT, PUBLISHERS, 26313 Purissima Rd., Los Altos Hills CA 94022. (415)948-6499. Book publisher. Independent book producer/packager. Estab. 1976. Editor: May Davenport. Publishes 1-2 picture books/year; 2-3 young adult titles/year. 99% of books by first-time authors. Seeks books with literary merit. "We are overstocked with picture book/elementary reading material."

Fiction: Young adults: contemporary, history, humor, suspense/mystery. Average word length: 40,000-60,000. Recently published *Something in the Air*, by Anne Derson (a Migg McClue Mystery, grades 4-5, paper); *Blow Away Seaweeds*, by May Davenport (grades 8-12, hardback); *Tug of War*, by Barbara A. Scott (grades 8-12, paper); *A Fine Line*, by Constance D. Casserly (grades 8-12, paper).

Nonfiction: Activity books to read alone or aloud, or to color. Recently published *History of Papa Frog*, by William F. Meisburger (Spanish/English, grades 1-2, paper); *Sumo, The Wrestling Elephant*, by Esther Lee (Spanish/English, grades 1-2, paper).

How to Contact/Writers: Fiction: Query. Reports on queries in 1-2 weeks; mss in 2-4 weeks. "We do not answer queries or manuscripts which do not have SASE attached." Publishes a book 6-12 months after acceptance.

Illustration: Works with 2-3 illustrators/year.

How to Contact/Illustrators: Illustrations only: "Send samples for our files for future reference."

Terms: Pays authors in royalties of 15% based on retail price. Pays "by mutual agreement, no advances." Pays illustrators by the project. Book listing, ms guidelines free on request with SASE.

Tips: Writers: "Make readers laugh with your imaginative words. However, if you do not have a humorous literary talent, forget it."

DAVIS PUBLICATIONS, INC., 50 Portland St., Worcester MA 01608. (508)754-7201. Fax: (508)753-3834. Book publisher. Acquisitions Editors: Claire M. Golding (grades K-8) and Helen Ronan (grades 9-12). Publishes 10 titles total/year. 30% of books by first-time authors. "We publish books for the art education market (elementary through high school), both technique-oriented and art appreciation resource books and textbooks."

Nonfiction: Middle readers, young adults: activity books about art and art-related textbooks; multicultural books detailing the arts of other cultures (Hispanic, Native American, African-American, Asian); textbooks. Recently published *Discovering Drawing*, by Ted Rose; *African Arts and Cultures*, by Jacqueline Chanda; *The Visual Experience*, by Jack Hobbs and Richard Salome; and *William Sidney Mount*, by Nancy Howard.

How to Contact/Writers: Submit outline/synopsis and 1 sample chapter. Reports on queries in 3 months; mss in 6 months. Publishes a book 1 year after acceptance. Will consider simultaneous submissions and electronic submissions via disk.

Illustration: Works with 2 illustrators/year. "We use a combination of photos and line drawings" (200-300/nonfiction title). Will review ms/illustration packages. Will review artwork for future assignments. "We are not major purchasers of illustrations; we generally need clear, informative line art that can be used to explain, demonstrate and elucidate art procedures and materials."

How to Contact/Illustrators: Query with samples. Reports in 1 month.

Photography: "Rarely" purchases photos from freelancers. Contact: Holly Hanson. "Usually need photos of particular artists, artworks or art forms." Model/property releases required; captions required. Publishes photo concept books. Uses 5×7 and 8×10 glossy, b&w prints and 4×5 and 8×10 transparencies.

Terms: Pays authors royalties of 10-12½% based on wholesale price. Pays illustrators by the project (range $50-300). Sends galleys to authors. Book catalog available for $8½ \times 11$ SASE; ms guidelines available for 6×9 SASE.

Tips: Seeking "nonfiction titles on art techniques, media and history/appreciation. We do not publish children's story/picture books; rather, we publish educational books for use by art teachers, art students and amateur artists."

DAWN PUBLICATIONS, 14618 Tyler Foote, Nevada City CA 95959. (916)292-3482. Fax: (916)292-4258. Book publisher. Publisher: Bob Rinzler. Publishes works with holistic themes dealing with nature, parenting and health issues.

Fiction: All levels: adventure, animal, folktales, multicultural and nature/environment.

Nonfiction: All levels: multicultural, nature/environment, social issues, parenting, values and morals. Recently published *A Walk in the Rainforest*, by Kristin Pratt; *I Celebrate Nature*, by Diane Iversen.

How to Contact/Writers: Fiction/nonfiction: Query; submit complete ms; submit outline/synopsis and sample chapters. Reports on queries/mss in 2 weeks. Publishes a book 1 year after acceptance. Will consider simultaneous submissions and previously published work.

Illustration: Works with 3 illustrators/year. Will review ms/illustration packages. Will review artwork for future assignments.

How to Contact/Illustrators: Ms/illustration packages: Query; submit complete package; submit chapters of ms. Illustrations only: Query with samples, résumé.

Terms: Pays authors royalty based on wholesale price. Offers advance. Pays illustrators by the project or royalties based on wholesale price. Sends galleys to authors; dummies to illustrators. Book catalog available for 6×9 SASE.

T.S. DENISON CO. INC., 9601 Newton Ave. S., Minneapolis MN 55431. Fax: (612)888-9641. Editor: Baxter Brings. 25% of books by first-time authors. "We publish only teacher resource/activity books."

Nonfiction: Young readers, middle readers: activity books, animal, arts/crafts, careers, history, multicultural, music/dance, nature/environment, reference, science, social issues, textbooks. Average length: middle readers—150 pages. Published *Let's Meet Famous Composers*, by Harriet Kinghorn, illustrated by Margo De Paulis (grades 3-6, teacher resource); *Toddler Calendar*, by Elaine Commius, illustrated by Anita Nelson (Pre-K, teacher resource); *Fairy Tale Mask*, by Gwen Rives Jones, illustrated by Darcy Myers (grades 1-3, teacher resource).

How to Contact/Writers: Query; submit complete ms; submit outline/synopsis and 2 sample chapters. Reports on queries/mss in 2 months. Publishes a book 12-18 months after acceptance. Will consider simultaneous submissions and electronic submissions via disk or modem.

Illustration: Works with 15 illustrators/year. Will review artwork for future assignments.

How to Contact/Illustrators: Illustrations only: Query with samples; arrange a personal interview to show portfolio. Reports in 1 month. Original artwork not returned at job's completion.

Terms: Pays authors royalty of 4-8% based on retail price (direct mail). Work purchased outright (range: $300-1,000). Pays illustrators by the project (range: $300-500 for covers; $25 for b&w; $15-30/hour for inside illustration). Book catalog available for 9×12 SAE and 3 first-class stamps; ms guidelines available for SASE.

DIAL BOOKS FOR YOUNG READERS, Penguin Books USA Inc., 375 Hudson St., New York NY 10014. (212)366-2800. Editor-in-Chief: Phyllis J. Fogelman. Publishes 70 picture books/year; 10 young reader titles/year; 5 middle reader titles/year; 10 young adult titles/year.

• Dial no longer accepts unsolicited manuscripts; only agented material will be read.

Fiction: Picture books: adventure, animal, contemporary, fantasy, folktales, history, nature/environment, poetry, religion, science fiction, sports, suspense/mystery. Young readers: animal, contemporary, easy-to-read, fantasy, folktales, history, nature/environment, poetry, science fiction, sports, mystery/adventure. Middle readers, young adults: animal, contemporary, fantasy, folktales, history, health-related, nature/environment, poetry, problem novels, religion, science fiction, sports, spy/mystery/adventure. Published *Brother Eagle, Sister Sky*, illustrated by Susan Jeffers (all ages, picture book); *Amazing Grace*, by Mary Hoffman (ages 4-8, picture book); and *Soul Looks Back in Wonder*, by Tom Feelings, Maya Angelou, et al (ages 7 and up, poetry picture book.)

Nonfiction: Uses very little nonfiction but will consider submissions of outstanding artistic and literary merit. Picture books: animal, biography, history, nature/environment, sports. Young readers: activity books, animal, biography, history, nature/environment, religion, sports. Middle readers: animal, biography, careers, health, history, nature/environment, religion, sports. Young adults: animal, biography, careers, health, history, hobbies, music/dance, nature/environment, religion, sports. Recently published *Big-Top Circus*, by Neal Porter (ages 4-8, picture book); *Hand, Heart, and Mind*, by Lou Ann Walker (middle readers).

How to Contact/Writers: Only interested in agented material.

Illustration: Will review ms/illustration packages. Prefers to use own artists for mss submitted by authors. Will review work for possible future assignments.

How to Contact/Illustrators: Ms/illustration packages: Query first or submit 1 piece of final color art and sketches. Illustrations only: Query with samples; submit portfolio for review; arrange a personal interview to show portfolio; provide tearsheets to be kept on file.

Photography: Contact: Toby Sherry. Model/property releases required with submissions. Publishes photo essays. Uses b&w, glossy prints and 35mm, 2¼ × 2¼, 4 × 5 transparencies. Send samples to be kept on file.

Terms: Pays authors and illustrators in royalties based on retail price. Average advance payment "varies." Ms guidelines for SASE.

DILLON PRESS, INC., 250 James St., Morristown NJ 07960. Imprint of Silver Burdett Press, Simon & Schuster Education Group. Book Publisher. Editor: Debbie Biber. See Silver Burdett listing.

■DIMI PRESS, 3820 Oak Hollow Lane, SE, Salem OR 97302-4774. (503)364-7698. Fax: (503)364-9727. Book publisher. "For children's books, we do subsidy publishing. We have not published any children's books, but will."

Fiction: Young adults: adventure.

Nonfiction: Middle readers, young adults: biography, how-to, nature/environment, self help.

How to Contact/Writers: Fiction/nonfiction: Query. Submit outline/synopsis and 1 sample chapter. Reports on queries in 1 month; mss in 2 months. Publishes a book 3-9 months after acceptance.

Terms: Pays authors royalty of 5-10% based on wholesale price. Book catalog available for #10 SAE and 1 first-class stamp.

■DISCOVERY ENTERPRISES, LTD., 134 Middle St., Lowell MA 01852. (508)459-1720. Fax: (508)937-5779. Book publisher and independent book producer/packager. Executive Director: JoAnne Weisman. Publishes 6 middle readers books/year. 40% of books by first-time authors; subsidy publishes 10%. Publishes all nonfiction—serious histories and biographies, 15,000-20,000 words for ages 12-adult. Needs pen & ink drawings for history series.

Nonfiction: Young readers, middle readers, young adults: biography, history, plays. "No sports figures, religious leaders, pop stars or current entertainers for biographies." Average word length: middle readers 15,000-20,000; young adults 15,000-20,000. Published *J. Robert Oppenheimer and the Birth of the Atomic Age*, by Kenneth M. Deitch and Joseph Yeamans (ages 12-adult, biography); *Marjory Stoneman Douglas: Guardian of the Everglades*, by Kem Knapp Sawyer, illustrated by Leslie Carow (ages 10-adult, biography); *Pride and Promise: The Harlem Renaissance*, by Kathryn Cryan-Hicks (ages 12-adult, historical); *Humor in the*

Leslie Carow rendered this lush portrait for the cover of Marjory Stoneman Douglas: Guardian of the Everglades, by Kem Knapp Sawyer. The book is part of Discovery Enterprises' biography series. JoAnne Weisman of Discovery was impressed with Carow's "excellent and accurate research, attention to detail, and beautiful composition in portraying the remarkable 104-year-old woman who has been instrumental in preserving the ecology of the Everglades."

Classroom: A New Approach to Critical Thinking, by Prof. Fred Stopsky (guide to teaching methods for teachers of grades 2-12); *Edna Hibel: Her Life and Her Art*, by Olga Cossi (ages 10-adult, biography).

How to Contact/Writers: Nonfiction: Query. Submit outline/synopsis and 3 sample chapters. Looking for historical plays for grades 4-8. Reports on queries in 1-2 weeks "only if SASE provided"; mss in 3-6 months. Publishes a book 6-12 months after acceptance. Will consider simultaneous submissions.

Illustration: Works with 6-8 illustrators/year. Will review ms/illustration packages after query only. Will review artwork for future assignments. Contact: JoAnne Weisman, executive director. "No preference in medium or style, but artist must be able to do portraits, as these are biographies."

How to Contact/Illustrators: Ms/illustration packages: Submit 2-3 chapters of ms with copies of 4-6 pieces of final art. Send samples of artwork—color copies OK with text. Illustrations only: Query with samples; provide resume, promotional literature and tearsheets to be kept on file. Reports in 4-6 weeks. Original artwork returned at job's completion "but not for 2 years."

Photography: Photographers should contact JoAnne Weisman, executive director. Uses all types of photos. Model/property releases required; captions required. Interested in stock photos, historical subjects. Uses 35mm, 2¼ × 2¼ and 4 × 5 transparencies. Photographers should query with samples; provide resume, business card, promotional literature and tearsheets to be kept on file.

Terms: Pays authors royalty of 5-10% based on wholesale price or outright purchase ($300-1,500). Offers $1,000 advance on book assignments only. Pays playwrights 10% on net sales only. No advance. Pays illustrators by the project (range: $100-1,500) or royalty of 5-10% based on wholesale price. Photographers paid per photo (range: $25-400). Sends galleys to authors; dummies to illustrators. Book catalog available for #10 SASE.

Tips: Wants "neat, clean artwork, presented professionally." For writers, good cover letter, outline and sample chapters necessary. "Watch for grammatical errors. I prefer separate submissions from artists and authors. Carefully research and accurately illustrate art for histories and biographies in any medium. We are looking for biographies of women in sciences/computers; curriculum guides regarding Turn of the Century for grades 5-8; historical plays." Sees trend toward more nonfiction for use in classrooms to supplement or replace textbooks, as well as more emphasis on multi-racial books, women's history, peace, etc.

DISNEY PUBLISHING, Subsidiary of Walt Disney Co., 500 S. Buena Vista, Burbank CA 91521. Prefers not to share information.
- Disney Publishing ranks the 12th, based on net sales, of the top 12 children's publishers.

DISTINCTIVE PUBLISHING CORP., P.O. Box 17868, Plantation FL 33318-7868. (305)975-2413. Fax: (305)972-3949. Book publisher. Independent book producer/packager. Editor: F. Knauf. Publishes 1-2 books/year. 95% of books by first-time authors.

Fiction: Picture books, young readers: adventure, animal, fantasy, multicultural, nature/environment and sports. Middle readers: animal, multicultural, nature/environment, religion, sports and suspense/mystery. Young adults/teens: nature/environment, religion, sports, suspense/mystery. "We will consider all submissions." Recently published *Ships of Children*, by Richard Taylor (middle-young adult, adventure); and *Daniel and the Ivory Princess*, written and illustrated by Kevin Martin.

Nonfiction: Picture books, young readers: animal, biography, careers, geography, history, social issues. "As with fiction we will consider all submissions."

How to Contact/Writers: Nonfiction: Submit complete ms. Reports on queries in 1-2 weeks; mss in 1-3 months. Publishes book 6-12 months after acceptance. Will consider simultaneous submissions and previously published work.

Illustration: Works with 3-5 illustrators/year. Will review ms/illustration packages. Contact: Alan Erdlee, publisher. Will review artwork for future assignments.

How to Contact/Illustrators: Ms/illustration packages: Submit complete package. Illustrations only: Query with samples, résumé and promo sheet. Reports in 1 month. Original artwork is returned at job's completion.

Photography: Buys photos from freelancers. Buys stock and assigns work. Contact: Alan Erdlee, publisher. Type of photos used depends on project. Model/property release required; captions required. Interested in stock photos. Publishes photo concept books. Uses 4 × 6 glossy color prints, 2¼ × 2¼ transparencies. Photographer should query with samples; query with résumé of credits; provide résumé, business card, tearsheets to be kept on file.
Terms: Pays authors royalty of 6-15% based on wholesale. "Each project is different." Offers advances. Pays illustrators by the project (range: $100-1,000) or royalty of 3-10%. Photographers are paid by the project or per photo. Sends galleys to author; dummies to illustrators. Book catalog available for 9 × 12 SASE.
Tips: Best chance of selling to this market is with adventure and educational mss.

DORLING KINDERSLEY, INC., 95 Madison Ave., New York NY 10016. (212)213-4800. Book publisher. Assistant Editor, Children's Books: C. Decaire. Publishes 10 picture books/ year. 50% of books by first-time authors; 50% of books from agented authors (fiction list only).
Fiction: Picture books: adventure, contemporary, folktales, history, multicultural, nature/ environment. Multicultural needs include relationship stories/family stories. Does not want to see fiction with licensed characters. Average word length: picture books—48 pages.
Nonfiction: Young readers: activity books, animal, arts/crafts, geography, history, nature/ environment, science and sports. "We produce almost all nonfiction inhouse." Does not want to see "manuscripts imitating books we've already published, suggestions for fiction series, long fiction and alphabet books." Average length: young readers—32 pages. Recently published Look Closer series, Eyewitness Books and Eyewitness Explorers Guides.
How to Contact/Writers: Fiction/nonfiction: Submit agented ms. Reports on queries/mss in 4 months. Publishes a book about 18 months after acceptance. Will consider simultaneous submissions.
Illustration: Works with about 10 illustrators/year. Will review ms/illustration packages. Contact: C. Decaire, assistant editor. Will review artwork for future assignments.
How to Contact/Illustrators: Ms/illustration packages: Submit ms with dummy. Illustrations only: Query with samples; provide promo sheet and tearsheets. Reports only if immediately interested. Otherwise samples go in file. Samples returned with SASE (if requested).
Photography: Purchases photos from freelancers. Contact: Dirk Kaufman, designer. Works on assignment only. Photographers should submit cover letter and résumé.
Terms: Pays author royalty based on retail price. Pays illustrators by the project or royalty. Pays photographers by the project. Sends galleys to authors; dummies to illustrators. Book catalog available for 9 × 12 SAE and 3 first-class stamps; ms guidelines available for SASE; artist's guidelines not available.
Tips: A writer has the best chance of selling well-written picture book stories that work internationally. Also, innovative manuscripts that combine fiction and nonfiction. "See our recently published book, *Mr. Frog Went A-Courting*, by Gary Chalk."

*DOWN EAST BOOKS, P.O. Box 679, Camden ME 04843. (207)594-9544. Fax: (207)594-7215. Book publisher. Editor: Karin Womer. Publishes 1-2 young or middle readers/year. 90% of books by first-time authors. All books pertain to Maine/New England region.
Fiction: All levels: adventure, animal, history, nature/environment. Recently published *Silas the Bookstore Cat*, by Karen Mather (young-middle readers, animal); and *Junior—A Little Loon Tale*, by John Hassett (middle readers, animal/conservation).
Nonfiction: All levels: animal, geography, nature/environment. Recently published *Wild Fox*, by Cherie Mason (middle readers, animal/nature).
How to Contact/Writers: Fiction/Nonfiction: Query. Reports on queries/mss in 2 weeks to 2 months. Publishes a book 6-18 months after acceptance. Will consider simultaneous and previously published submissions.
Illustration: Works with 2-3 illustrators/year. Will review ms/illustration packages. Contact: Karin Womer, editor. Will review artwork for future assignments.
How to Contact/Illustrators: Ms/illustration packages: Query. Illustrations only: Query with samples. Reports in 2 weeks to 2 months. Samples returned with SASE; samples filed sometimes. Original artwork returned at job's completion.

Terms: Pays authors royalty (varies widely). Pays illustrators by the project or by royalty (varies widely). Sends galleys to authors; dummies to illustrators. Book catalog available. Manuscript guidelines available for SASE.

DUTTON CHILDREN'S BOOKS, 375 Hudson St., New York NY 10014. (212)366-2600. Penguin USA. Prefers not to share information.

*E.M. PRESS, INC., P.O. Box 4057, Manassas VA 22110. (703)439-0304. Book publisher. Publisher/Editor: Beth Miller. Publishes 2 middle readers/year; 2 young adult titles/year. 50% of books by first-time authors.
Fiction: Middle readers, young adults: adventure. Recently published *The Search For Archerland*, by H.R. Coursen (adventure, 12 and up); *Some Brief Cases of Inspector Alec Stuart of Scotland Yard*, by Archibald Wagner MD (mystery, 12 and up).
Nonfiction: Middle readers, young adults: animal, history, how-to, self help, social issues, sports.
How to Contact/Writers: Fiction: Query. Submit outline/synopsis. Nonfiction: Query. Reports on queries in 6 weeks. Publishes a book 18 months after acceptance. Will consider simultaneous submissions.
Terms: Pays authors royalty on wholesale price. Offers varied advances. Sends galleys to authors. Manuscript guidelines for SASE.

EAKIN PRESS, P.O. Box 90159, Austin TX 78709-0159. (512)288-1771. Imprint of Sunbelt Media, Inc. Book publisher. President: Edwin M. Eakin. Publishes 4 picture books/year; 2 young readers/year; 6 middle readers/year; 2 young adult titles/year. "We publish children's books about Texas or the Southwest; picture books for preschool, grades 1, 2 and 3; middle reader books 25-35,000 words, nonfiction for grades 4-7; young adult books for grades 7-12." 50% of books by first-time authors.
Fiction: Publishes picture books and chapter books for preschool-grade 3. Also young adult fiction (40,000-50,000 words).
Nonfiction: Publishes middle readers (grades 4-7; 25,000-35,000 words) and young adult (40,000-50,000 words).
How to Contact/Writers: Fiction/Nonfiction: Query. Reports on queries in 1 week; mss in 1 month. Publishes ms 12-18 months after acceptance. Will consider simultaneous submissions.
Illustration: Works with 5 illustrators/year. Will review ms/illustration packages. Will review artwork for future assignments.
How to Contact/Illustrators: Ms/illustration packages: Submit ms with dummy. Samples returned with SASE. Reports in 2 weeks. Samples returned with SASE. Original artwork returned at job's completion.
Terms: Pays authors royalty of 10-15% net to publisher. Pays illustrators by the project (range: $350-600). Sends galleys to authors; dummies to illustrators. Book catalog available for SAE and $1.05 postage; ms and art guidelines available for SASE.

WM. B. EERDMANS PUBLISHING COMPANY, 255 Jefferson Ave. SE, Grand Rapids MI 49503. (616)459-4591. Book publisher. Children's Book Editor: Amy Eerdmans. Publishes 6 picture books/year; 4 young readers/year; 4 middle readers/year.
Fiction: All levels: fantasy, parables, problem novels, religion, retold Bible stories from a Christian perspective.
Nonfiction: All levels: biography, history, nature/environment, religion.
How to Contact/Writers: Fiction/Nonfiction: Query; submit complete ms. Reports on queries in 1-2 weeks; mss in 4-6 weeks.

The Subject Index, located before the General Index, lists book and magazine publishers by their fiction and nonfiction needs.

Illustration: Reviews ms/illustration packages. Will review illustrator's work for possible future assignments. Contact: Willem Mineur, art director.

How to Contact/Illustrators: Illustrations only: Submit résumé, slides or color photocopies. Reports on ms/art samples in 1 month. Original artwork returned at job's completion.

Terms: Pays authors in royalties of 5-10%. Pays illustrators royalty or permission fee. Sends galleys to authors; dummies to illustrators. Book catalog free on request; ms and/or artist's guidelines free on request.

Tips: "We're looking for fiction and nonfiction that project a positive spiritual message and imply Christian values. We are also looking for material that will help children explore their faith. Accept all genres."

ENSLOW PUBLISHERS INC., 44 Fadem Rd., Box 699, Springfield NJ 07081. Vice President: Brian D. Enslow. Estab. 1978. Publishes 30 middle reader titles/year; 30 young adult titles/year. 30% of books by first-time authors.

Nonfiction: Young readers, middle readers, young adults: activity books, animal, biography, careers, health, history, hobbies, nature/environment, sports. Average word length: middle readers-5,000; young adult-15,000. Published *Louis Armstrong*, by Patricia and Fredrick McKissack (grades 2-3, biography); *Lotteries: Who Wins, Who Loses?*, by Ann E. Weiss (grades 6-12, issues book).

How to Contact/Writers: Nonfiction: Query. Reports on queries/mss in 2 weeks. Publishes a book 18 months after acceptance. Will not consider simultaneous submissions.

Illustration: Number of illustrations used for nonfiction: middle readers—20; young adults—20.

How to Contact/Illustrators: Provide résumé, business card or tearsheets to be kept on file.

Terms: Pays authors royalties or work purchased outright. Sends galleys to authors. Book catalog/ms guidelines available for $2.

FACTS ON FILE, 460 Park Ave. S., New York NY 10016. (212)683-2244. Book publisher. Executive Editor, Young Adult Publications: James Warren. Editor: Nicole Bowen. Publishes 35-40 young adult titles/year. 5% of books by first-time authors; 25% of books from agented writers; additional titles through book packagers, co-publishers and unagented writers.

Nonfiction: Middle readers, young adults: animal, biography, careers, geography, health, history, multicultural, nature/environment, reference, religion, science, social issues and sports. Recently published *Martin Luther King, Jr. and the Freedom Movement*, by Lillie Patterson; *Charles Darwin: The Evolution of a Naturalist*, by Richard Milner; and *Contemporary Women Scientists*, by Lisa Yount.

How to Contact/Writers: Nonfiction: Submit outline/synopsis and sample chapters. Reports on queries in 6-8 weeks. Publishes a book 10 months after acceptance. Will consider simultaneous submissions. Sends galleys to authors. Book catalog free on request.

Tips: "Most projects have high reference value and fit into a series format."

FALCON PRESS PUBLISHING CO., SkyHouse, P.O. Box 1718, Helena MT 59624. (406)442-6597. Book publisher, independent book producer/packager (SkyHouse). Publishes 6 middle readers/year; 2 young adults/year. Focuses on nature/environment and outdoor recreation.

Nonfiction: Picture books: animal, geography, nature/environment. Young readers, young adults: animal, nature/environment. Middle readers: animal, biography, history, nature/environment. Does not want to see anthropomorphized animal stories. Average word length: picture books—650; middle readers—6,500; young adults—20,000-40,000. Published *The Battle of the Little Bighorn*, by Mark Henckel (ages 8-12, history); *Montana Wildlife*, by Gayle C. Shirley (ages 8 and up, animal field guide); *Where Dinosaurs Still Rule*, by Debbie Tewell (ages 8 and up, nature); *Four-Legged Legends of Montana*, by Gayle C. Shirley (young adult, animal).

How to Contact/Writers: Query, submit outline/synopsis. Reports on queries/mss in 2-3 months. Publishes a book 18 months after acceptance. Will consider simultaneous submissions, electronic submissions via disk or modem.

Illustration: Works with 4 illustrators/year.

How to Contact/Illustrators: Illustrations only: Query with samples, résumé, slides, tear-sheets. "Do not send original artwork; we cannot return it." Reports in 2-3 months; "will not respond to unsolicited artwork."

Terms: Pays authors 5-15% royalty based on wholesale price, or work purchased outright ($750 minimum). Pays illustrators by the project, royalty based on wholesale price. Sends galleys to authors. Book catalog available for 9 × 12 SAE and 2 first-class stamps; ms guidelines available for SASE; artist guidelines not available.

Tips: "Research each publishing house before you submit to make sure your manuscript is appropriate for it." Looking for "books that fit into our existing history and natural history series."

FARRAR, STRAUS & GIROUX, 19 Union Square W., New York NY 10003. (212)741-6934. Book publisher. Children's Books Editor-in-Chief: Margaret Ferguson. Estab. 1946. Publishes 21 picture books/year; 6 middle reader titles/year; 5 young adult titles/year. 5% of books by first-time authors; 5% of books from agented writers.

Fiction: "Original and well-written material for all ages." Published *Tell Me Everything*, by Carolyn Coman (ages 12 up).

How to Contact/Writers: Fiction/nonfiction: Query; submit outline/synopsis and sample chapters. Reports on queries in 6 weeks; mss in 12 weeks. Publishes a book 18 months after acceptance. Will consider simultaneous submissions.

Illustration: Will review ms/illustration packages.

How to Contact/Illustrators: Ms/illustration packages: Submit ms with 1 example of final art, remainder roughs. Illustrations only: Query with tearsheets. Reports on art samples only if interested. Original artwork returned at job's completion.

Terms: "We offer an advance against royalties for both authors and illustrators." Sends galleys to authors; dummies to illustrators. Book catalog available for 6½ × 9½ SAE and 56¢ postage; ms guidelines for 1 first-class stamp.

Tips: "Study our catalog before submitting. We will see illustrator's portfolios by appointment."

FAWCETT JUNIPER, 201 E. 50 St., New York NY 10022. (212)751-2600. Imprint of Ballantine/DelRey/Fawcett Books. Book publisher. Editor-in-Chief/Vice President: Leona Nevler. Publishes 36 young adult titles/year.

Fiction: Middle readers: contemporary, romance, science fiction. Young adults: contemporary, fantasy, romance.

How to Contact/Writers: Fiction: Query.

Terms: Pays authors in royalties.

THE FEMINIST PRESS AT THE CITY UNIVERSITY OF NEW YORK, 311 E. 94th St., New York NY 10128. (212)360-5790. Book publisher. Senior Editor: Susannah Driver. Publishes 1-2 middle reader, young reader and young adult books/year.

How to Contact/Writers: Fiction/Nonfiction: Query. Reports on queries/mss in 2-3 weeks. Publishes a book 1-2 years after acceptance.

Illustration: Works with 1 illustrator/year. Will review ms/illustration packages. Uses primarily b&w artwork.

Terms: Pays authors royalty. Offers advances (average amount: $100). Pays illustrators by the project or royalty; "depends on project." Sends galleys to authors. Book catalog available; ms guidelines available.

FIESTA CITY PUBLISHERS, Box 5861, Santa Barbara CA 93150-5861. (805)733-1984. Book publisher. Editorial contact: Ann Cooke. Publishes 1 middle reader/year; 1 young adult/year. 25% of books by first-time authors. Publishes books about cooking and music or a combination of the two.

Nonfiction: Young adult: cooking, music/dance, self-help. Average word length: 30,000. Does not want to see "cookbooks about healthy diets or books on rap music." Published *Kids Can Write Songs, Too!* (revised second printing), by Eddie Franck; *Bent-Twig*, by Frank

E. Cooke, with some musical arrangements by Johnny Harris (a 3-act musical for young adolescents).

How to Contact/Writers: Query. Reports on queries in 2 weeks; on mss in 1 month. Publishes a book 1 year after acceptance. Will consider simultaneous submissions.

Illustration: Works with 1 illustrator/year. Will review ms/illustrations packages (query first). Contact: Frank E. Cooke, president.

How to Contact/Illustrators: Send résumé.

Terms: Pays authors royalty based on wholesale price.

Tips: "Write clearly and simply. Do not write 'down' to young adults (or children). Looking for self-help books on current subjects, original and unusual cookbooks, and books about music, or a combination of cooking and music."

*FITZHENRY & WHITESIDE LTD., 195 Allstate Pkwy., Markham, Ontario L3R 4T8 Canada. (905)477-9700. Fax: (905)477-9179. Book publisher. Vice President: Robert W. Read. Publishes 2 picture books/year; 5 young readers/year; 5 middle readers/year; 5 young adult titles/year. 15% of books by first-time authors. Publishes mostly nonfiction — social studies, biography, environment. Prefers Canadian subject or perspective.

Fiction: Picture books: folktales, history, multicultural, nature/environment and sports. Young readers: contemporary, folktales, health, history, multicultural, nature/environment and sports. Young readers: contemporary, folktales, health, history, multicultural, nature/environment and sports. Middle readers: adventure, contemporary, folktales, history, humor, multicultural, nature/environment and sports. Young adults: adventure, contemporary, folktales, history, multicultural, nature/environment, sports and suspense/mystery. Average word length: young readers — 5,000-10,000; middle readers — 2,000-5,000; young adults — 10,000-20,000.

Nonfiction: Picture books: arts/crafts, biography, history, multicultural, nature/environment, reference and sports. Young readers: arts/crafts, biography, geography, history, hobbies, multicultural, nature/environment, reference, religion and sports. Middle readers: arts/crafts, biography, careers, geography, history, hobbies, multicultural, nature/environment, reference, social issues and sports. Young adults: arts/crafts, biography, careers, geography, health, hi-lo, history, multicultural, music/dance, nature/environment, reference, social issues and sports. Average word length: young readers — 500-1,000; middle readers — 2,000-5,000; young adults — 10,000-20,000. Recently published *Indians of the Northwest*, by Stan Garrod (ages 8-12, nonfiction native studies); *Wolf Island*, by Celia Godkin (ages 5-10, environment/nature); and *Wayne Gretzky*, by Fred McFadden (ages 8-12, sports biography).

How to Contact/Writers: Fiction: Submit outline/synopsis and 1 sample chapter. Nonfiction: Submit outline/synopsis. Reports in 3 months. Publishes a book 1 year after acceptance. Will consider simultaneous submissions.

Illustration: Works with 5-10 illustrators/year. Will review ms/illustration packages. Will review artwork for future assignments.

How to Contact/Illustrators: Ms/illustration packages: Submit outline and sample illustration (copy). Illustrations only: Query with samples and promo sheet. Reports in 3 months. Samples returned with SASE; samples filed if no SASE.

Photography: Buys photos from freelancers. Buys stock and assigns work. Captions required. Uses b&w 8×10 prints; 35mm and 4×5 transparencies. Submit stock photo list and promo piece.

Terms: Pays authors royalty of 10%. Offers "modest" advances. Pays illustrators by the project and royalty. Pays photographers per photo. Sends galleys to authors; dummies to illustrators.

Tips: "We respond to quality."

FOUR WINDS PRESS, was incorporated into Simon & Schuster Books for Young Readers, an imprint of Simon & Schuster Children's Publishing Division.

FRANKLIN WATTS, 11th Floor, 95 Madison Ave., New York NY 10016. (212)951-2650. Subsidiary of Grolier Inc. Book publisher. Editorial contact: John Selfridge. 10% of books by first-time authors; 5% of books from agented writers.

Nonfiction: Young readers: activity books. Middle readers: activity books, animal, arts/ crafts, biography, cooking, geography, health, history, multicultural, music/dance, nature/ environment, reference, religion, science, social issues, special needs, sports. Young adults: arts/crafts, biography, geography, health, history, multicultural, music/dance, nature/environment, reference, religion, science, social issues, special needs, sports. Does not want to see fiction or poetry. Average word length: middle readers—5,000; young adult/teens—16,000-35,000.

How to Contact/Writers: Query. No mss. SASE.

Illustration: Works with 10-20 illustrators/year. Will review ms/illustration packages. Will review artwork for future assignments. Contact: Vicki Fischman, art director.

How to Contact/Illustrators: Query with samples, résumé; promo sheet; client list. Original artwork returned at job's completion.

Photography: Purchases photos from freelancers. Contact photo editor. Buys stock and assigns work.

Terms: Pays authors royalties and buys photos outright. Illustrators paid by the project. Book catalog for 10×13 SASE.

Tips: Looks for children's nonfiction grades 5-8 or 9-12.

FREE SPIRIT PUBLISHING, Suite 616, 400 First Ave. N., Minneapolis MN 55401-1730. (612)338-2068. Fax: (612)337-5050. Book publisher. Publisher/President: Judy Galbraith. Publishes 1-2 young readers/year; 3-4 middle reader titles/year; 3-4 young adult titles/year. 80% of books by first-time authors. "Our books pertain to the education and psychological well being of young people."

● This publisher received several awards in 1994 for children's publishing. *Sofia and the Heartmender* received *Skipping Stones* magazine's Multicultural Honor Award; won Best Children's Book from the Midwest Independent Publisher's Association (MIPA); and was a finalist for Best Picture Book from the Publishers Marketing Association. *Bringing Up Parents* won Best Self-Help Book from MIPA; *A Gebra Named Al* was selected for the American Booksellers Association's "Children's Books Mean Business" exhibit and received an award of merit for Best Children's Book from MIPA.

Fiction: All levels: contemporary, mental health, multicultural, problem novels and special needs. Recently published *Sofia and the Heartmender*, by Marie Olofsdotter (ages 5 and up, self-esteem/assertiveness); *A Gebra Named Al*, by Wendy Isdell (ages 11 and up, fantasy/ adventure that explores math and chemistry basics); and *The Worst Speller in Jr. High*, by Caroline Janover (ages 11 and up, novel that explores new school/dyslexia/dating/friendship/family relationships). Multicultural needs include books that help kids accept/respect people who are different in a variety of ways; not books that explore specific cultures. Does not want to see poetry; anything related to religion or spirituality (fiction and nonfiction); books with animal or other nonhuman characters (fiction or nonfiction).

Nonfiction: All levels: health, hobbies, multicultural, nature/environment, self-esteem, social issues, special needs, psychology, education. Recently published *Respecting Our Differences: Getting Along in a Changing World*, by Lynn Duvall (ages 12 and up, diversity/ tolerance of others); *The Power to Prevent Suicide: A Guide for Teens Helping Teens*, by Richard E. Nelson, Ph.D., and Judith C. Galas (ages 11 and up, suicide awareness/prevention/intervention); *Becoming Myself: True Stories about Learning from Life*, by Cassandra Walker Simmons (ages 11 and up, self-esteem/character development/values).

How to Contact/Writers: Nonfiction: Submit résumé, outline/synopsis and sample chapters. Reports on queries/mss in 3 months. Publishes a book 12-18 months after acceptance. Write or call for catalog and submission guidelines.

Illustration: Works with 5 illustrators/year. Will review ms/illustration packages. Will review work for future assignments. "We don't keep files of artist's samples inhouse." Contact: Nancy Tuminelly, graphic designer, Maclean & Tuminelly, Suite 626, 400 First Ave. N., Minneapolis MN 55401. "MacLean & Tuminelly is a firm that designs and produces our books."

How to Contact/Illustrators: Ms/illustrations packages: Query with samples.

Terms: Pays authors in royalties of 7-12% based on wholesale price. Offers advance payment of $500-$1,000. Pays illustrators by the project. Sends galleys to authors. Book catalog free on request.

Tips: Does not accept unsolicited artists' or photographers' samples. Wants to see "a book that helps kids help themselves, or that helps adults help kids help themselves; one that complements our list without duplicating current titles; one that is written in a direct, straightforward manner (no jargon, please); one that teaches without preaching or being condescending."

*FRIENDSHIP PRESS, Room 860, 475 Riverside Dr., New York NY 10115. (212)870-2497. National Council of Churches of Christ in the USA. Book publisher. Editorial Contact: Margaret Larom. Art Director: Paul Lansdale. Publishes 1-2 picture books/year; 1 young reader title/year; 1 middle reader title/year; 1 young adult title/year. 75% of books commissioned for set themes.

Fiction: All levels: multicultural, mission and religion. Average word length: young adults—20,000-40,000. Book catalog free on request. Published *Pearlmakers*, by Vilma May Fuentes (grades 1-6, stories about the Philippines); *Aki and the Banner of Names*, by Atsuko Gōda Lolling (grades 1-6, stories about Japan).

Nonfiction: All levels: activity books, geography, multicultural, social issues, mission and religion. Average word length: middle readers—10,000; young adults—10,000.

How to Contact/Writers: Fiction and nonfiction: Query. Reports on queries in 1 month; mss in 6 months. Publishes a book 18 months after acceptance. Will consider simultaneous submissions. Ms guidelines free on request.

Illustration: Works with 1 illustrator/year. Will review ms/illustration packages. Will review artwork for future assignments. Contact: Paul Lansdale, art director.

How to Contact/Illustrators: Ms/illustration packages: Submit 3 chapters of ms with 1 piece of final art. Illustrations only: Submit résumé and tearsheets. Reports only if interested. Original artwork returned at job's completion.

Terms: Buys ms outright for $25-1,200. Pays illustrators by the project (range: $25-1,200). Sends galleys to authors; dummies to illustrators. Book catalog and ms guidelines free on request.

Tips: Seeking "a book that illustrates what life is like for children in other countries, especially Christian children, though not exclusively."

LAURA GERINGER BOOKS, 10 E. 53rd St., New York NY 10022. (212)207-7554. Fax: (212)207-7192. Imprint of HarperCollins Publishers. Editorial Director: Laura Geringer. Publishes 10-12 picture books/year; 2 middle readers/year; 2-4 young adult titles/year. 20% of books by first-time authors; 50% of books from agented authors.

Fiction: Picture books: adventure, animal, contemporary, fantasy, folktales, history, nature/environment, poetry. Young readers: adventure, anthology, animal, contemporary, fantasy, folktales, health-related, history, nature/environment, poetry, sports, suspense/mystery. Middle readers, young adults: adventure, anthology, animal, contemporary, fantasy, folktales, health-related, history, nature/environment, poetry, problem novels, sports, suspense/mystery. Average word length: picture books—250-1,200. Published *Santa Calls*, by William Joyce (all ages, picture book); *The Borning Room*, by Paul Fleischman (ages 10 and up, middle grade); *The Tub People*, by Pam Conrad (preschool-3 years, picture book); and *What Hearts*, by Bruce Brooks (age 10-young adult).

How to Contact/Writers: Fiction: Submit complete ms. Reports on queries in 2-4 weeks; mss in 3-4 months. Publishes a book 1½-3 years after acceptance. Will consider simultaneous submissions.

Illustration: Works with 20-25 illustrators/year. Average number of illustrations used for fiction: picture books—12-18; middle readers—10-15. Will review ms/illustration packages. Will review artwork for future assignments. Contact: Laura Geringer or Harriett Barton, art director.

How to Contact/Illustrators: Ms/illustration packages: Submit complete package. Illustrations only: Query with samples; submit portfolio for review; provide résumé, business card, promotional literature or tearsheets to be kept on file. Reports in 2-4 weeks. Original artwork returned at job's completion.

Terms: Pays authors royalties of 5-6¼% (picture book) or 10-12% (novel) based on retail price. Offers advances. Pays illustrators royalties of 5-6%. Sends galleys to authors; proofs to illustrators. Book catalog available for 9×11 SASE; ms guidelines available for SASE.

Tips: "Write about what you *know*. Don't try to guess our needs. And don't forget that children are more clever than we give them credit for!" Wants "artwork that isn't overly 'cutesy' with a strong sense of style and expression."

*GIBBS SMITH, PUBLISHER, P.O. Box 667, Layton UT 84041. (801)544-9800. Imprint: Peregrine Smith Books. Book publisher. Editorial Director: Madge Baird. Publishes 6 picture books/year. 10% of books by first-time authors. 50% of books from agented authors.

Fiction: Picture books: multicultural, nature/environment. Young readers: adventure, animal, fantasy, folktales, history, humor, multicultural, nature/environment. Middle readers: adventure, animal, fantasy, folktales, history, humor, multicultural, nature/environment. Average word length: picture books—2,000-3,000.

Nonfiction: Picture books: activity, biography, how-to, multicultural, nature/environment, western/cowboy. Young readers: activity, multicultural, nature/environment. Middle readers: activity, arts/crafts, biography, cooking, history, how-to, multicultural, nature/environment. Average word length: picture books—up to 4,000.

How to Contact/Writers: Fiction/nonfiction: Query. Submit several chapters or complete ms. Reports on queries in 3 weeks; reports on mss in 6-8 weeks. Publishes a book 1-2 years after acceptance. Will consider simultaneous submissions. Ms returned with SASE.

Illustration: Works with 6-8 illustrators/year. Contact: Linda Nimori, associate editor. Will review ms/illustration packages. Will review artwork for future assignments.

How to Contact/Illustrators: Ms/illustration packages: Query. Submit ms with 3-5 pieces of final art. Illustrations only: Query with samples; provide résumé, promo sheet, slides (duplicate slides, not originals). Reports back only if interested. Samples returned with SASE; samples kept on file. Original artwork returned at job's completion.

Terms: Pays authors royalty of 4-7½% based on wholesale price or work purchased outright ($500 minimum). Offers advances (average amount: $1,000). Pays illustrators by the project or royalty of 4-5% based on wholesale price. Sends galleys to authors; color proofs to illustrators. Book catalog available for 9×12 SAE and $2.13 postage. Ms/artist's guidelines not available.

Tips: "We target ages 5-11." Wants "multi-dimensional products (book, tape, toy, etc.)."

GLOBE FEARON EDUCATIONAL PUBLISHER, 1 Lake St., Upper Saddle River NJ 07458. Imprint of Paramount Publishing. Book publisher. Production Director: Penny Gibson. Publishes 100 special education, low level, remedial titles/year.

Fiction: Young adults: hi-lo, multicultural, special needs. Average word length: 10,000-15,000.

Nonfiction: Young adults: biography, careers, health, hi-lo, history, multicultural, nature/environment, science, special needs, textbooks.

How to Contact/Writers: Fiction/nonfiction: Query "but, we don't respond to all queries." Reports on queries in 6 months; mss in 12-18 months.

Illustration: Works with 20 illustrators/year. Will review samples/portfolio. Contact: Penny Gibson, production director. Will review artwork for future assignments.

How to Contact/Illustrators: Illustrations only: Query with samples, résumé, promo sheet, portfolio, slides, client list, tearsheets; arrange personal portfolio review. Reports in 2 months. Samples returned with SASE. "We prefer to keep on file."

Photography: Buys photos from freelancers. Buys stock and assigns work. "We don't accept general submissions. We commission as needed." Model/property releases required.

The asterisk before a listing indicates the listing is new in this edition.

Uses wide range of color and b&w prints. Submit cover letter, résumé, published samples, slides, client list, stock photo list, portfolio, promo piece.

Terms: Work purchased outright ($2,500 minimum). Pays illustrators by the project. Pays photographers by the project. Sometimes sends galleys to authors.

Tips: "Be very sure the house you approach publishes the type of work you do. Make sure your work has solid, carefully crafted development with no dangling details."

DAVID R. GODINE, PUBLISHER, 300 Massachusetts, Boston MA 02115. (617)536-0761. Book publisher. Estab. 1970. Contact: Editorial Department. Publishes 3-4 picture books/year; 2 young reader titles/year; 3-4 middle reader titles/year. 10% of books by first-time authors; 20% of books from agented writers.

• This publisher is no longer considering unsolicited manuscripts of any type.

Fiction: Picture books: animal. Young readers: adventure, animal, easy-to-read, fantasy, folk or fairy tales. Middle readers: animal, fantasy, folk or fairy tales. Recently published *The Last Giants*, by François Place (award-winning illustrated fable); *No Effect*, by Daniel Hayes (YA fiction); and *Rotten Island*, by William Steig.

How to Contact/Writers: Fiction: Query. Publishes a book 2 years after acceptance.

Illustration: Query.

How to Contact/Illustrators: Ms/illustration packages: "Roughs and one piece of finished art plus either sample chapters for very long works or whole ms for short works." Illustrations only: "Slides, with one full-size blow-up of art." Reports on art samples in 3 weeks. Original artwork returned at job's completion.

Terms: Pays authors in royalties based on retail price. Number of illustrations used determines final payment. Pay for separate authors and illustrators "differs with each collaboration." Illustrators paid by the project. Sends galleys to authors; dummies to illustrators. Book catalog/ms guidelines free on request.

GOLDEN BOOKS, 850 Third Ave., New York NY 10022. (212)753-8500. Imprint of Western Publishing Co. Co-Editorial Director: Marilyn Salomon. Book publisher. 100% of books from agented authors.

• Also see listing for Artists & Writers Guild Books.

Fiction: Board books, novelty books, picture books: "accepts a variety of age-appropriate subject matter." Middle readers: series lines.

Nonfiction: Picture books: history, nature/environment, sports. Young and middle readers: animal, education, history, nature/environment, sports.

How to Contact/Writers: "Material accepted only through agent."

Illustration: Will sometimes review ms/illustration packages. Will review an illustrator's work for possible future assignments. Contact Remo Cosentino and Georg Brewer, art directors.

How to Contact/Illustrators: Ms/illustration packages: Query first.

Terms: Pays authors in royalties based on retail price.

*GRAPEVINE PUBLICATIONS, INC., P.O. Box 2449, Corvallis OR 97339-2449. (503)754-0583. Fax: (503)754-6508. Book publisher. Managing Editor: Chris Coffin. Publishes 1 picture book/year; 1 young readers/year. 100% of books by first-time authors.

Fiction: Picture books, young readers, middle readers: all categories considered. Average length: picture books—16-32 pages; young readers—32 pages; middle readers—64 pages.

How to Contact/Writers: Submit complete ms. Reports in 6 weeks. "Due to volume received, we report *only* on material of interest." Publishes a book 1 year after acceptance. Will consider simultaneous and previously published submissions.

Illustration: Works with 1 illustrator/year. Contact: Chris Coffin. Will review illustration packages. Will review artwork for future assignments.

How to Contact/Illustrators: Ms/illustration packages: Submit ms with dummy. Illustrations only: Query with samples; provide tearsheets. Reports only if interested. Samples returned with SASE; samples filed.

Terms: Pays authors royalty of 9% on wholesale price. Pays illustrators by the project. Sends galleys to authors; dummies to illustrators.

Tips: "Test books on kids other than those who know you. Match the 'look and feel' of text and illustrations to the subject and age level." Wants "early/middle reader fiction with polished writing and 'timeless' feel."

GREEN TIGER PRESS, INC., Green Tiger Press was incorporated into Simon & Schuster Books for Young Readers, an imprint of Simon & Schuster Children's Publishing Division.

GREENHAVEN PRESS, 10911 Technology Place, San Diego CA 92127. (619)485-7424. Book publisher. Estab. 1970. Senior Editor: Bonnie Szumski. Publishes 40-50 young adult titles/year. 35% of books by first-time authors.
Nonfiction: Middle readers: biography, controversial topics, history, issues. Young adults: biography, history, nature/environment. Other titles "to fit our specific series." Average word length: young adults—15,000-25,000.
How to Contact/Writers: Query only. "We accept no unsolicited manuscripts. All writing is done on a work-for-hire basis."
Terms: Buys ms outright for $1,500-3,000. Offers advances. Sends galleys to authors. Book catalog available for 9 × 12 SAE and 65¢ postage.
Tips: "Get our guidelines first before submitting anything."

GREENWILLOW BOOKS, 1350 Avenue of the Americas, New York NY 10019. (212)261-6500. Imprint of William Morrow & Co. Book publisher. Editor-in-Chief: Susan Hirschman. Art Director: Ava Weiss. Publishes 50 picture books/year; 10 middle readers books/year; 10 young adult books/year.
Fiction: Will consider all levels of fiction; various categories.
How to Contact/Writers: Submit complete ms to editorial department "not specific editor." Do not call. Reports on mss in 10-12 weeks. Publishes a book 18-24 months after acceptance. Will consider simultaneous submissions.
Illustration: Will review ms/illustration packages.
How to Contact/Illustators: Illustrations only: Query with samples, résumé.
Terms: Pays authors royalty. Offers advances. Pays illustrators royalty or by the project. Sends galleys to authors. Book catalog available for 9 × 12 SAE with $2 postage; ms guidelines available for SASE.

GROSSET & DUNLAP, INC., 200 Madison Ave., New York NY 10016. (212)951-8700. Imprint of The Putnam & Grosset Group. Book publisher. Editor-in-chief: Judy Donnelly. Art Director: Ronnie Ann Herman. Publishes 5 picture books/year; 8 young readers/year; 12 middle readers/year; 5 young adult titles/year; 25 board books/year; 25 novelty books/year. 5% of books by first-time authors; 50% of books from agented authors. Publishes fiction and nonfiction for mass market; novelty and board books.
Fiction: Picture books: animal, concept. Young readers: adventure, animal, concept, history, nature/environment, sports. Most categories will be considered. "We publish series fiction, but not original novels in the young adult category." Sees too many trade picture books. Published *Yo! It's Captain Yo-Yo*, by Jon Buller and Susan Schade (grades 2-3, All Aboard Reading); *Snakes*, by Pat Demuth, illustrations by Judity Moffatt (grades 1-3, All Aboard Reading); *Nina, Nina Ballerina*, by Jane O'Connor, illustrations by DyAnne DiSalvo-Ryan (preschool-grade 1, All Aboard Reading).
Nonfiction: Picture books: animal, concept, nature/environment. Young readers: activity books, animal, arts/crafts, biography, concept, history, sports. Published *Your Insides*, by Joanna Cole (ages 4-6, human body); *Dinosaur Bones!*, by C.E. Thompson, illustrations by Paige Billin-Frye (ages 4-8, book and mobile); *Zoom!*, written and illustrated by Margaret A. Hartelius (ages 4-8, paper airplane kit).
How to Contact/Writers: Fiction/Nonfiction: Query. Reports in 2-4 weeks on queries; 1-2 months on mss. Publishes book 1-2 years after acceptance. Will consider simultaneous submissions.
Illustrations: Works with 50 illustrators/year. Will review ms/illustration packages. Will review artwork for future assignments. Contact: Ronnie Ann Herman, art director.
How to Contact/Illustrators: Ms/illustration packages: Query. Illustrations only: Query with samples; provide résumé, promo sheet, portfolio, slides, tearsheets. "Portfolio drop-

off on Wednesdays." Reports only if interested. Original artwork returned at job's completion.

Photography: Buys photos from freelancers. Contact: Ronnie Ann Herman, art director. Buys stock. Uses photos of babies and toddlers, interactive children, animals—full color. Publishes photo concept books. Uses color prints; 35mm, 2¼×2¼, 4×5 and 8×10 transparencies. To contact, photographers should query with samples, send unsolicited photos by mail, submit portfolio, provide promotional literature or tearsheets to be kept on file.

Terms: Pays authors royalty or by outright purchase. Offers advances. Pays illustrators by the project or by royalty. Photographers paid by the project or per photo. Book catalog available for 9×12 SASE. Ms guidelines available for SASE.

*GRYPHON HOUSE, P.O. Box 207, Beltsville MD 20704-0207. (301)595-9500. Fax: (301)595-0051. Book publisher. Editor-in-Chief: Kathy Charner.

Nonfiction: Parent and teacher resource books. Recently published *Games to Play with Two Year Olds*, by Jackie Silberg; *Preschool Art*, by Maryann Kohl; *Theme Storming*, by Becker Et Al; *450 More Story Stretchers*, by Shirley Raines.

How to Contact/Writers: Query. Submit outline/synopsis and 2 sample chapters. Reports on queries in 3 weeks; mss in 3 months. Publishes a book 18 months after acceptance. Will consider simultaneous submissions, electronic submissions via disk or modem.

Illustration: Uses b&w artwork only.

How to Contact/Illustrators: Illustrations only: Query with samples, promo sheet. Reports back only if interested. Samples are filed. Original artwork returned at job's completion.

Photography: Buys photos from freelancers. Contact: Kathy Charner, editor-in-chief. Buys stock and assigns work. Submit cover letter, published samples, stock photo list.

Terms: Pays authors royalty based on retail price. Offers advances. Pays illustrators by the project. Pays photographers by the project or per photo. Sends galleys to authors. Ms guidelines available for SASE.

Tips: "We are looking for books of creative, participatory learning experiences that have a common conceptual theme to tie them together. The books should be on subjects that teachers want to do on a daily basis in the classroom. If a book caters to a particular market in addition to teachers, that would be a plus."

HARCOURT BRACE & CO., 1250 Sixth Ave., San Diego CA 92101. (619)699-6810. Children's Books Division which includes: Harcourt Brace Children's Books, Gulliver Books, Voyager Paperbacks, Odyssey Paperbacks, Jane Yolen Books. Book publisher. Attention: Manuscript Submissions, Children's Books Division. Publishes 40-45 picture books/year; 15-20 middle reader titles/year; 8-12 young adult titles/year. 20% of books by first-time authors; 50% of books from agented writers.

 • The staff of Harcourt Brace's children's book department is no longer accepting unsolicited manuscripts. Only query letters and manuscripts submitted by agents will be considered.

Fiction: Picture books, young readers: animal, contemporary, fantasy, history. Middle readers, young adults: animal, contemporary, fantasy, history, problem novels, romance, science fiction, sports, spy/mystery/adventure. Average word length: picture books—"varies greatly"; middle readers—20,000-50,000; young adults—35,000-65,000.

Nonfiction: Picture books, young readers: animal, biography, history, hobbies, music/ dance, nature/environment, religion, sports. Middle readers, young adults: animal, biography, education, history, hobbies, music/dance, nature/environment, religion, sports. Average word length: picture books—"varies greatly"; middle readers—20,000-50,000; young adults—35,000-65,000.

How to Contact/Writers: Fiction/nonfiction: Query. Reports on queries in 6-8 weeks.

Illustration: Will review ms/illustration packages. Art Director of Children's Books, Michael Farmer, will review an illustrator's work for possible future assignments.

How to Contact/Illustrators: Ms/illustration packages: "picture books ms—complete ms acceptable. Longer books—outline and 2-4 sample chapters." Send several samples of art; no original art. Illustrations only: Submit résumé, tearsheets, color photocopies, color stats all accepted. "Please DO NOT send original artwork or transparencies. Include SASE for

David Wilgus brought fantasy to life in graphite for Here There Be Unicorns, *by Jane Yolen, his third project for Harcourt Brace & Company. "David's realistic style of art brings a sense of reality to Jane Yolen's imaginative prose," says Art Director Michael Farmer. "His artwork is proof that books can be expressively and powerfully illustrated in black and white, and that drawing, in addition to other forms of illustration, is a skill that deserves exposure."*

return, please." Reports on art samples in 6-10 weeks. Original artwork returned at job's completion.

Terms: Pays authors in royalties based on retail price. Pays illustrators by the project. Sends galleys to authors; dummies to illustrators. Book catalog available for 9 × 12 SASE; ms/artist's guidelines for business-size SASE.

Tips: "Become acquainted with Harcourt Brace's books in particular if you are interested in submitting proposals to us."

HARPERCOLLINS CHILDREN'S BOOKS, 10 E. 53rd St., New York NY 10022. (212)207-7044. Fax: (212)207-7192. Contact: Submissions Editor. Book publisher.

Fiction: All levels: adventure, animal, concept, contemporary, fantasy, folktales, humor, history, multicultural, nature/environment, poetry, problem novels, sports, suspense/mystery. Published *The Magic Wood*, by Henry Treece (ages 6 and up, picture book); and *The Noisy Giants' Tea Party*, by Kate and Jim McMullan (ages 3-8, picture book).

• HarperCollins ranks the fourth, based on net sales, of the top 12 children's publishers.

Nonfiction: All levels: activity books, animal, arts/crafts, biography, concept, geography, hi-lo, history, hobbies, multicultural, music/dance, nature/environment, reference, science, social issues, sports. Published *Marie Curie & Radium*, by Steve Parker (ages 8-12); *The Pigman & Me*, by Paul Zindel (ages 12 up, young adult); and *The Moon of the Deer*, by Jean Craighead George (ages 8-12, middle reader).

How to Contact/Writers: Fiction/nonfiction: Query, submit outline/synopsis and sample chapters. Reports on queries in 1 month; mss in 4 months.

Illustration: Works with 20 illustrators/year. Will review ms/illustration packages (preferable to see picture books without art). Contact: Laura Geringer, editorial director or Caitlyn Dlouhy, development editor. Will review work for possible future assignments. (No original art, please).

How to Contact/Illustrators: Ms/illustrations packages: Query first. Illustrations only: Query with samples, portfolio, slides, arrange personal portfolio review.

Terms: Pays authors in royalties based on retail price; 10-12% for novels, 5-6½% for picture books. Pays illustrators royalty of 5-6½% based on retail price.

HARVEST HOUSE PUBLISHERS, 1075 Arrowsmith, Eugene OR 97402. (503)343-0123. Book publisher. Manuscript Coordinator: LaRae Weikert. Publishes 1-2 picture books/year; 2 young reader titles/year; 2 young adult titles/year. 25% of books by first-time authors. Books follow a Christian theme.
Fiction: Picture books: easy-to-read. Young readers: contemporary, easy-to-read. Middle readers: contemporary, mystery. Young adults: mystery, problem novels, romance.
Nonfiction: All levels: religion.
How to Contact/Writers: Fiction/nonfiction: Query; submit outline/synopsis and sample chapters; submit complete ms. Reports on queries in 2-4 weeks; mss in 6-8 weeks. Publishes a book 1 year after acceptance. Will consider simultaneous submissions. Send SASE with original packet for return of submissions.
Illustration: Will review ms/illustration package. Will review artwork for future assignments.
How to Contact/Illustrators: Ms/illustration packages: Submit 3 chapters of ms with copies (do not send originals) of art and any approximate rough sketches. Illustrations only: Send résumé, tearsheets. Submit to production manager. Reports on art samples in 2 months.
Terms: Pays authors in royalties of 10-15%. Average advance payment: "negotiable." Pays illustrator: "Sometimes by project." Sends galleys to authors; sometimes sends dummies to illustrators. Book catalog, ms guidelines free on request.

THE HEARST BOOK GROUP, 1350 Avenue of the Americas, New York NY 10019. See listings for Avon Books and Morrow Junior Books.
• The Hearst Book Group ranks ninth, based on net sales, of the top 12 children's publishers.

HENDRICK-LONG PUBLISHING COMPANY, P.O. Box 25123, Dallas TX 75225. Book publisher. Vice President: Joann Long. Publishes 1 picture book/year; 4 young reader titles/year; 4 middle reader titles/year. 20% of books by first-time authors.
Fiction: Middle readers: history books on Texas and the Southwest. No fantasy or poetry. Recently published *I Love You, Daisy Phew*, by Ruby C. Tolliver, illustrated by Joyce Haynes (ages 9 and above); *Twelve Days in Texas*, by Donna D. Cooner, illustrated by Bob Leland (all ages).
Nonfiction: Middle readers, young adults: history books on Texas and the Southwest, biography, multicultural. Especially interested in Spanish, African American, Asian multicultural themes. Recently published *Hats Are for Watering Horses*, by Mary Blount Christian, illustrated by Lyle Miller (all ages); *New Medicine*, by Jeanne Williams, illustrated by Michael Taylor (ages 12 and above).
How to Contact/Writers: Fiction/Nonfiction: Query with outline/synopsis and sample chapter. Reports on queries in 2 weeks; mss in 2 months. Publishes a book 18 months after acceptance. No simultaneous submissions. Include SASE.
Illustration: Works with 2-3 illustrators/year. Number of illustrations used for fiction and nonfiction: picture books—22; middle readers—11; young readers-11. Uses primarily b&w artwork. Will review artwork for future assignments. Contact: Joann Long.
How to Contact/Illustrators: Query first. Submit résumé or promotional literature or photocopies or tearsheets—no original work sent unsolicited. Material kept on file. No reply sent.
Terms: Pays authors in royalty based on selling price. Advances vary. Pays illustrators by the project. Sends galleys to authors; dummies to illustrators. Book catalog for $1, 52¢ postage and large SAE; ms guidelines for 1 first-class stamp and #10 SAE.

HERALD PRESS, 616 Walnut Ave., Scottdale PA 15683. (412)887-8500. Fax: (412)887-3111. Division of Mennonite Publishing House. Estab. 1908. Publishes 1 picture storybook/year; 1 young reader title/year; 2-3 middle reader titles/year; 1-2 young adult titles/year. Editorial Contact: S. David Garber. Art Director: Jim Butti. 20% of books by first-time authors; 3% of books from agented writers.
• Herald Press's *Why Are Your Fingers Cold?*, by Larry McKaughan, illustrated by Joy Dunn Keenan, received a Silver Angel Award of Merit.

Fiction: Young readers, middle readers, young adults: contemporary, history, problem novels, religious, self-help, social concerns. Recently published *Katie and the Lemon Tree*, by Esther Bender; *Where the Eagles Fly*, by Ruth Nulton Moore; and *Polly*, by Mary C. Borntrager and S. David Garber. Does not want stories on fantasy, science fiction, war, drugs, cops and robbers.

Nonfiction: Young readers, middle readers, young adults: how-to, religious, self-help, social concerns. Recently published *Storytime Jamboree*, by Peter Dyck; and *We Knew Jesus*, by Marian Hostetler (both fiction and nonfiction collections).

How to Contact/Writers: Fiction/nonfiction: "Send to Book Editor, the following: (1) a one-page summary of your book, (2) a one- or two-sentence summary of each chapter, (3) the first chapter and one other, (4) your statement of the significance of the book, (5) a description of your target audience, (6) a brief biographical sketch of yourself, and (7) SASE for return of the material. You may expect a reply in about a month. If your proposal appears to have potential for Herald Press, a finished manuscript will be requested. Herald Press depends on capable and dedicated authors to continue publishing high-quality Christian literature." Reports on queries in 1 month; mss in 2 months. Publishes a book 12 months after acceptance. Will consider simultaneous submissions but prefers not to.

Illustration: Works with 3 illustrators/year. Will review ms/illustration packages. Will review artwork for future assignments. Contact: Jim Butti, art director.

How to Contact/Illustrators: Illustrations only: Query with samples. Send résumé, tearsheets and slides.

Photography: Purchases photos from freelancers. Contact: Debbie Cameron. Buys stock and assigns work.

Terms: Pays authors in royalties of 10-12% based on retail price. Pays for illustrators by the project (range: $220-600). Sends galleys to authors. Book catalog for 3 first-class stamps; ms guidelines free on request.

Tips: "We invite book proposals from Christian authors in the area of juvenile fiction. Our purpose is to publish books which are consistent with Scripture as interpreted in the Anabaptist/Mennonite tradition. Books that are honest in presentation, clear in thought, stimulating in content, appropriate in appearance, superior in printing and binding, and conducive to the spiritual growth and welfare of the reader."

*HI-TIME PUBLISHING CORPORATION, P.O. Box 13337, Milwaukee WI 53213. (414)466-2420. Editor: Lorraine M. Kukulski.

Nonfiction: Young adults: religion.

How to Contact/Writers: Reports on queries in 2-4 weeks; mss in 4-6 weeks.

Photography: Buys photos from freelancers. Buys stock and assigns work.

Terms: Ms guidelines available for SASE.

HOLIDAY HOUSE INC., 425 Madison Ave., New York NY 10017. (212)688-0085. Fax: (212)421-6134. Book publisher. Vice President/Editor-in-Chief: Margery Cuyler. Associate Editor: Ashley Mason. Publishes 30 picture books/year; 3 young reader titles/year; 10 middle reader titles/year; 3 young adult titles/year. 20% of books by first-time authors; 10% from agented writers.

● For more information on Holiday House, read the interview with Margery Cuyler in the 1994 *Children's Writer's & Illustrator's Market.*

Fiction: Picture book: animal, folktales, sports. Young reader: contemporary, history, sports, spy/mystery/adventure. Middle reader: contemporary, fantasy, history, sports, spy/mystery/adventure. Recently published *Dumbstruck*, by Sara Pennypacker (humorous middle-grade fantasy); *Peeping Beauty*, by Mary Jane Auch (humorous picture book).

Nonfiction: Picture books: biography, history, nature. Young reader: biography, history, nature/environment, sports. Middle reader: biography, history, nature/environment, sports. Recently published *Looking at Penguins*, by Dorothy Hinshaw Patent (young reader, nature/environment); *The Wright Brothers*, by Russell Freedman (middle reader, historical); *The Sioux*, by Virginia Driving Hawk Sneve, illustrated by Ronald Hamler (picture book).

How to Contact/Writers: Fiction/nonfiction: Submit complete ms. Reports on queries in 2 weeks; on mss in 6 weeks. Publishes a book 10 months after acceptance. Will consider simultaneous submissions.

Illustration: Works with 25 illustrators/year. Will review ms/illustration packages. Will review artwork for future assignments. Ashley Mason will also view artists' portfolios in-house.

How to Contact/Illustrators: Ms/illustration packages: Query first. Illustrations only: Submit résumé and tearsheets. Reports within 6 weeks with SASE or if interested (if no SASE). Original art work returned at job's completion.

Terms: Pays authors royalties. Pays illustrators royalties. Ms/artist's guidelines #10 SASE.

HENRY HOLT & CO., INC., 115 W. 18th St., New York NY 10011. (212)886-9200. Book publisher. Editor-in-Chief/Vice President/Associate Publisher: Brenda Bowen. Publishes 20-30 picture books/year; 60-80 young reader titles/year; 10 middle reader titles/year; 10 young adult titles/year. 5% of books by first-time authors; 40% of books from agented writers.

How to Contact/Writers: Fiction/nonfiction: Submit complete ms. Reports on queries/mss in 2 months. Publishes a book 12-18 months after acceptance. Will consider simultaneous submissions.

Illustration: Will review ms/illustration packages.

How to Contact/Illustrators: Ms/illustration packages: Random samples OK. Illustrations only: Submit tearsheets, slides. Do *not* send originals. Reports on art samples only if interested. If accepted, original artwork returned at job's completion.

Terms: Pays authors/illustrators royalty based on retail price. Sends galleys to authors; dummies to illustrators.

HOMESTEAD PUBLISHING, Box 193, Moose WY 83012. Book publisher. Editor: Carl Schreier. Publishes 15 picture books/year; 2 young reader titles/year; 2 middle reader titles/year; 2 young adult titles/year. 30% of books by first-time authors; 1% of books from agented writers.

Fiction: Average word length: young readers—1,000; middle readers—5,000; young adults—5,000-150,000.

Nonfiction: Picture books, middle readers: animal (wildlife), biography, history, nature/environment. Young readers: nature/environment (wildlife). Young adults: history, nature/environment (wildlife). Average word length: young readers—1,000; middle readers—5,000; young adults—5,000-250,000.

How to Contact/Writers: Fiction/nonfiction: Query; submit outline/synopsis and sample chapters. Reports on queries/mss in 1 month. Publishes a book 1 year after acceptance. Will consider simultaneous submissions.

Illustration: Will review ms/illustration packages. Prefers to see "watercolor, opaque, oil" illustrations.

How to Contact/Illustrators: Ms/illustration packages: "Query first with sample writing and art style." Illustrations only: Submit résumés, style samples. Reports on art samples in 1-2 months. Original artwork returned at job's completion with SASE.

Terms: Pays authors in royalties of 5-10% based on wholesale price. Work purchased outright "depending on project." Pay illustrators by the project (range: $50-10,000) or royalty of 3-10% based on wholesale price. Sends galleys to authors; dummies to illustrators.

HOUGHTON MIFFLIN CO., Children's Trade Books, 222 Berkeley St., Boston MA 02116. (617)351-5000. Book publisher. Vice President/Director: Walter Lorraine. Senior Editor: Matilda Welter. Editors: Audrey Bryant, Margaret Raymo. Coordinating Editor: Laura Hornik. Art Director: Amy Bernstein. Averages 50-55 titles/year. Publishes hardcover originals and trade paperback reprints.

- Two of Houghton Mifflin's titles were honored with medals in 1994—Lois Lowry's *The Giver* (Newbery Medal recipient) and Allen Say's *Grandfather's Journey* (Caldecott Medal recipient). Houghton Mifflin ranks tenth, based on net sales, of the top 12 children's publishers.

Fiction: All levels: all categories except religion. "We do not rule out any theme, though we do not publish specifically religious material." Recently published *The Giver*, by Lois

Lowry (novel); *Owl in Love*, by Patrice Kindl (ages 10 and up, novel); and *The Sweetest Fig*, by Chris Van Allsburg (all ages, picture book).

Nonfiction: Recently published *Grandfather's Journey*, by Allen Say (all ages, picture book); and *Amish Home*, by Raymond Bial (ages 7-14, photo essay).

How to Contact/Writers: Fiction: Submit complete ms. Nonfiction: Submit outline/synopsis and sample chapters. Reports on queries in 2 weeks; on mss in 1-8 weeks.

Illustration: Works with 60 illustrators/year. Will review ms/illustration packages. Will review artwork for future assignments.

How to Contact/Illustrators: Query with samples (colored photocopies are fine); provide tearsheets.

Terms: Pays standard royalty; offers advance. Illustrators paid by the project and royalty. Book catalog free with SASE.

HUNTER HOUSE PUBLISHERS, P.O.Box 2914, Alameda CA 94501-0914. Fax: (510)865-4295. Book publisher. Independent book producer/packager. Editor: Lisa Lee. Publishes 1-2 young adult titles/year. 80% of books by first-time authors; 5% of books from agented writers.

Nonfiction: Young adults: health, multicultural, self-help, social issues. "We emphasize that all our books try to take multicultural experiences and concerns into account. We would be interested in a social issues or self-help book on multicultural issues." Books are therapy/personal growth-oriented. Does not want to see books for young children; "fiction; illustrated picture books; autobiography." Published *Turning Yourself Around: Self-Help Strategies for Troubled Teens*, by Kendall Johnson, Ph.D.; *Safe Dieting for Teens*, by Linda Ojeda, Ph.D.

How to Contact/Writers: Nonfiction: Query; submit overview and chapter-by-chapter synopsis, sample chapters and statistics on your subject area, support organizations or networks and marketing ideas. "Testimonials from professionals or well-known authors are important." Reports on queries in 1 month; mss in 4 months. Publishes a book 18 months after acceptance. Will consider simultaneous submissions.

Illustration: Works with 1 illustrator/year. Will review ms/illustration packages. Will review artwork for future assignments. Contact: Paul Frindt or Lisa Lee. Uses primarily b&w artwork.

How to Contact/Illustrators: Query with samples. Provide résumé and client list. Contact: Lisa Lee.

Photography: Purchases photos from freelancers. Contact: Paul Frindt. Buys stock images.

Terms: Pays authors royalty of 12-15% based on wholesale price or work purchased outright. Pays illustrators by the project. Sends galleys to authors. Book catalog available for 9 × 12 SAE and 79¢ postage; ms guidelines for standard SAE and 1 first-class stamp.

Tips: Wants therapy/personal growth workbooks; teen books with solid, informative material. "No fiction! Please, no fiction."

HUNTINGTON HOUSE PUBLISHERS, P.O. Box 53788, Lafayette LA 70505. (318)237-7049. Book publisher. Editor-in-Chief: Mark Anthony. Publishes 2 young readers/year. 100% of books by first-time authors. "All books have spiritual/religious themes."

Fiction: Picture books: folktales, religion. Young readers: folktales, history, religion. Middle readers, young adults: contemporary, folktales, history, religion. Does not want to see romance, nature/environment, multicultural. Average word length: picture books—12-50; young readers—100-300; middle readers—4,000-15,000; young adults/teens—10,000-40,000. Published *Greatest Star of All*, by Greg Gulley and David Watts (ages 9-11, adventure/religion).

Nonfiction: Picture books: animal, religion. Young readers, middle readers, young adults/teens: biography, history, religion. No nature/environment, multicultural. Average word length: picture books—12-50; young readers—100-300; middle readers—4,000-15,000; young adult/teens—10,000-40,000. Published *To Grow By Storybook Readers*, by Marie Le Doux and Janet Friend (preschool to age 8, textbook).

How to Contact/Writers: Fiction/Nonfiction: Query. Submit outline/synopsis, table of contents and proposal letter. One or two sample chapters are optional. Send SASE. Reports on queries in 1 month; mss in 2 months. Publishes a book 8 months after acceptance. Will consider simultaneous submissions.

Illustration: Works with 2 illustrators/year. Will review ms/illustration packages. Will review artwork for future assignments.

How to Contact/Illustrators: Ms/illustration packages: Query; submit ms with dummy. Illustrations only: Query with samples; send résumé and client list. Ms/illustration packages: Reports in 1 month. Illustrations only: Reports only if interested. Samples returned with SASE; samples filed. Original artwork returned at job's completion.

Photography: Buys photos from freelancers. Contact: Managing Editor. Buys stock images. Model/property releases required. Submit cover letter and résumé to be kept on file.

Terms: Pays authors royalty of 10% based on wholesale price. Pays illustrators by the project (range: $50-250) or royalty of 10% based on wholesale price. Sends galleys to authors; dummies to illustrators. Book catalog available for #10 SAE and 2 first-class stamps; ms guidelines for SASE.

HYPERION BOOKS FOR CHILDREN, 114 Fifth Ave., New York NY 10011. (212)633-4400. Fax: (212)633-4833. An operating unit of Walt Disney Publishing Group, Inc. Book publisher. Editorial Director: Andrea Cascardi. 30% of books by first-time authors; 40% of books from agented authors. Publishes various categories.

Fiction: Picture books, young readers, middle readers, young adults: adventure, animal, anthology (short stories), contemporary, fantasy, folktales, history, humor, multicultural, poetry, science fiction, sports, suspense/mystery. Middle readers, young adults: problem novels, romance. Published *Rescue Josh McGuire*, by Ben Mikaelsen (ages 10-14, adventure).

Nonfiction: All trade subjects for all levels.

How to Contact/Writers: Fiction: Submit complete ms. Nonfiction: Submit outline/synopsis and 2 sample chapters. Reports on mss in 4 months.

Illustration: Works with 100 illustrators/year. "Picture books are fully illustrated throughout. All others depend on individual project." Will review ms/illustration packages. Will review artwork for future assignments. Contact: Ellen Friedman, art director.

How to Contact/Illustrators: Ms/illustration packages: Submit complete package. Illustrations only: Submit résumé, business card, promotional literature or tearsheets to be kept on file. Reports back only if interested. Original artwork returned at job's completion.

Photography: Contact: Ellen Friedman, art director. Works on assignment only. Publishes photo essays and photo concept books. Provide résumé, business card, promotional literature or tearsheets to be kept on file.

Terms: Pays authors royalty based on retail price. Offers advances. Pays illustrators and photographers royalty based on retail price or a flat fee. Sends galleys to authors; dummies to illustrators. Book catalog available for 9 × 12 SAE and 3 first-class stamps; ms guidelines available for SASE.

*HYPERION PRESS LIMITED, 300 Wales Ave., Winnipeg, Manitoba R2M 2S9 Canada. (204)256-9204. Fax: (204)255-7845. Book Publisher. Editor: Dr. M. Tutiah. Publishes authentic-based, retold folktales/legends for ages 4-12.

Fiction: Young readers, middle readers: folktales/legends. Recently published *A Sled Dog for Moshi*, by Jeanne Bushey, illustrated by Germaine Arnaktauyok; *The Hummingbirds' Gift*, by Stefan Czernecki and Timothy Rhodes, illustrated by Stefan Czernecki; and *Som See and the Magic Elephant*, by Jamie Oliviero, illustrated by Jo'Anne Kelly (all ages 5-9, picture books).

How to Contact/Writers: Fiction: Query. Reports on mss in 3 months.

Illustration: Will review artwork for future assignments.

How to Contact/Illustrators: Ms/illustration packages: Query. Samples returned with SASE.

Terms: Pays authors royalty. Pays illustrators by the project. Sends galleys to authors; dummies to illustrators. Book catalog available for 8½ × × 11 SAE and $1.40 postage (Canadian).

IDEALS CHILDREN'S BOOKS, 1501 County Hospital Rd., Nashville TN 37218. Imprint of Hambleton-Hill Publishing Inc. Book publisher. Manuscript Contact: Tama Montgomery.

Art Contact: Leslie Anderson. Publishes 40-50 picture books/year; 5-8 young reader titles/year. 5-10% of books by first-time authors; 5-10% of books from agented writers.
Fiction: Picture books: adventure, animal, concept, contemporary, easy-to-read, folktales, history, multicultural, nature/environment. sports. Average word length: picture books—200-1,200; young readers—1,200-2,400. Published *Nobiah's Well*, by Donna Guthrie (ages 4-8); and *Alpha Zoo Christmas*, by Susan Harrison (ages 4-8).
Nonfiction: Picture books, young readers: activity books, animal, biography, history, hobbies, music/dance, nature/environment, sports. Does not want "ABC" and counting books of a general nature. "Only interested in them if they relate to specific themes." Average word length: picture books—200-1,200; young readers—1,000-2,400. Published: *The Blue Whale*, by Melissa Kim (ages 6-10); and *How's the Weather?*, by Melvin and Gilda Berger (ages 5-9, early reader).
How to Contact/Writers: Fiction/nonfiction: Submit complete ms. Reports on queries/mss in 3-6 months. Publishes a book 18-24 months after acceptance. Must include SASE for response.
Illustration: Works with 20 illustrators/year. Number of illustrations used for fiction and nonfiction: picture books—12-18; young readers—12-18. Will review ms/illustration packages. Will review artwork for future assignments. No cartoons—tight or loose, but realistic watercolors, acrylics.
How to Contact/Illustrators: Ms/illustration packages: Submit ms with 1 color photocopy of final art and remainder roughs. Illustrations only: Submit résumé and tearsheets showing variety of styles. Reports on art samples only if interested. "No original artwork, please."
Terms: "All terms vary according to individual projects and authors/artists."
Tips: "Trend is placing more value on nonfiction and packaging. We are not interested in young adult romances." Illustrators: "Be flexible in contract terms—and be able to show as much final artwork as possible." Work must have strong storyline with realistic characters. Shows little interest in anthropomorphism.

INCENTIVE PUBLICATIONS, INC., 3835 Cleghorn Ave., Nashville TN 37215. (615)385-2934. Editor: Leslie Britt. Approximately 20% of books by first-time authors.
Nonfiction: Young reader, middle reader, young adult: education. Recently published *The Definitive Middle School Guide*, by Imogene Forte and Sandra Schurr (grades 5-8, resource book for middle school teachers and administrators); and *Everything You Need To Know To Be a Successful Whole Language Teacher*, by Judith Cochran (grades K-6, tips and strategies for whole language instruction).
How to Contact/Writers: Nonfiction: Submit outline/synopsis, sample chapters and SASE. Usually reports on queries/mss in approximately 1 month. Typically publishes a book 18 months after acceptance. Will consider simultaneous submissions.
Terms: Pays in royalties or work purchased outright. Book catalog for SAE and 90¢ postage.
Tips: "We buy only teacher resource material. Please do not submit fiction!"

JALMAR PRESS, #204, 2675 Skypark Dr., Torrance CA 90505. (310)784-0016. Fax: (310)784-1379. Subsidiary of B.L. Winch and Associates. Book publisher. Estab. 1971. President: B.L. Winch. Publishing Assistant: Jeanne Iler. Publishes 3 picture books and young reader titles/year. 10% of books by first-time authors. Publishes self-esteem (curriculum content related), drug and alcohol abuse prevention, peaceful conflict resolution, stress management, whole brain learning and gender equity materials.
Fiction: All levels: concept, self-esteem. Does not want to see "children's fiction books that have to do with cognitive learning (as opposed to affective learning) and autobiographical work." Recently published *Hilde Knows: Someone Cries for the Children*, by Lisa Kent, illustrated by Mikki Machlen (child abuse); *Scooter's Tail of Terror: A Fable of Addiction and Hope*, by Larry Shles (ages 5-105). "All submissions must teach (by metaphor) in the areas listed above."
Nonfiction: All levels: activity books, concept, how-to, social issues, textbooks within areas specified above. Does not want to see autobiographical work. Recently published *Esteem Builders Program*, by Michele Berpa, illustrated by Bob Brochett (for school use—6 books, tapes, posters).

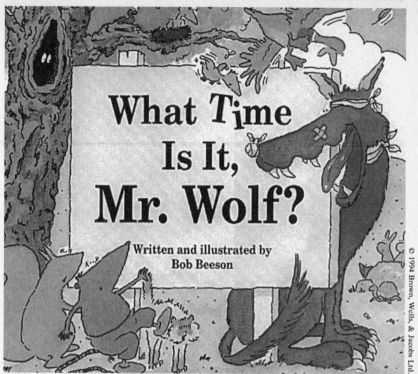

© 1994 Brown, Wells, & Jacobs Ltd.

Ideals Children's Books' title What Time Is It Mr. Wolf?, *written and illustrated by Bob Beeson, features a clock in the corner of each spread to teach kids about time as they follow the day's activities of a mouse, a squirrel and a bumbling wolf. The publisher was attracted to Beeson's "funny, lively, colorful style with lots of movement from page to page."*

How to Contact/Writers: Fiction/nonfiction: Submit complete ms. Reports on queries/mss in 1-6 months. Publishes a book 6-12 months after acceptance. Will consider simultaneous submissions.

Terms: Pays authors 7-12% royalty based on net receipts. Average advance "varies." Book catalog free on request.

Tips: Wants "thoroughly researched, tested, practical, activity-oriented, curriculum content and grade/level correlated books on self-esteem, peaceful conflict resolution, stress management, drug and alcohol abuse prevention and whole brain learning and books bridging self-esteem to various 'trouble' areas, such as 'at risk,' 'dropout prevention,' etc."

JEWISH LIGHTS PUBLISHING, P.O. Box 237, Woodstock VT 05091. (802)457-4000. A division of LongHill Partners, Inc. Book publisher. President: Stuart M. Matlins. Publishes 1 picture book/year; 1 young readers/year. 50% of books by first-time authors; 50% of books from agented authors. All books have spiritual/religious themes.

Fiction: Picture books: multicultural. Young readers: spirituality. "We are not interested in anything other than spirituality."

Nonfiction: All levels: spirituality. Published *God's Paintbrush*, by Rabbi Sandy Eisenberg Sasso and Annette Carroll Compton (K-4, spiritual).

How to Contact/Writers: Fiction/Nonfiction: Query. Submit outline/synopsis. Reports on queries in 1 month; mss in 3 months. Publishes a book 6 months after acceptance. Will consider simultaneous submissions and previously published work.

Illustration: Works with 3 illustrators/year. Will review ms/illustration packages. Will review artwork for future assignments.

How to Contact/Illustrators: Ms/illustration packages: Query. Illustrations only: Query with samples; provide résumé. Reports in 1 month. Samples returned with SASE; samples filed. Original artwork not returned at job's completion.

Terms: Pays authors royalty of 10% of revenue received. Offers advances. Pays illustrators by the project or royalty. Pays photographers by the project, per photo or royalty. Sends galleys to authors; dummies to illustrators. Book catalog available for 9×12 SAE and 59¢ postage.

JEWISH PUBLICATION SOCIETY, 1930 Chestnut St., Philadelphia PA 19103. (215)564-5925. Editor-in-Chief: Dr. Ellen Frankel. Children's Editor: Bruce Black. Book publisher. All work must have Jewish content.

Fiction: Picture books, young readers, middle readers and young adults: adventure, contemporary, folktales, history, mystery, problem novels, religion, romance, sports. Recently published *The Wise Shoemaker of Studena*, by Syd Lieberman, illustrated by Martin Lemelman (ages 3-8, picture book); *The Star and the Sword*, by Pamela Melnikoff (ages 10 and up, historical fiction).

Nonfiction: Picture books: biography, history, religion. Young readers, middle readers, young adults: biography, history, religion, sports. Recently published *I.B. Singer: The Life of a Storyteller*, by Lila Perl, illustrated by Donna Nuff (ages 10 and up, biography); *Leonard Bernstein: A Passion for Music*, by Johanna Hurwitz, illustrated by Sonia O. Lisker (ages 10 and up, biography).

How to Contact/Writers: Fiction/nonfiction: Query, submit outline/synopsis and sample chapters. Will consider simultaneous submissions (please advise).

Illustration: Will review ms/illustration packages.

How to Contact/Illustrators: Ms/illustration packages: Query first or send 3 chapters of ms with 1 piece of final art, remainder roughs. Illustrations only: Query with photocopies; arrange a personal interview to show portfolio.

Terms: Pays authors in royalties based on retail price.

Tips: Writer/illustrator currently has best chance of selling picture books to this market.

BOB JONES UNIVERSITY PRESS/LIGHT LINE BOOKS, 1500 Wade Hampton Blvd. Greenville SC 29614. (803)242-5100, ext. 4315. Book publisher. Editor: Mrs. Gloria Repp. Publishes 4 young reader titles/year; 4 middle reader titles/year; 4 young adult titles/year. 50% of books by first-time authors.

Fiction: Young readers: adventure, animal, contemporary, easy-to-read, history, sports, spy/mystery. Middle readers: adventure, animal, contemporary, history, problem novels, sports, spy/mystery. Young adults/teens: adventure, contemporary, history, problem novels, sports, spy/mystery. Average word length: young readers—20,000; middle readers—30,000; young adult/teens—50,000. Published *The Treasure of Pelican Cove*, by Milly Howard (grades 2-4, adventure story); *Right Hand Man*, by Connie Williams (grades 5-8, contemporary).

Nonfiction: Young readers: animal, biography, nature/environment. Middle readers: animal, biography, history, nature/environment. Young adults/teens: biography, history, nature/environment. Average word length: young readers—20,000; middle readers—30,000; young adult/teens—50,000. Published *With Daring Faith*, by Becky Davis (grades 5-8, biography); *Morning Star of the Reformation*, by Andy Thomson (grades 9-12, biography).

How to Contact/Writers: Fiction: "Send the complete manuscript or five sample chapters for these genres: Christian biography, modern realism, historical realism, regional realism and mystery/adventure. Query with a synopsis and five sample chapters for these genres: fantasy and science fiction (no extra-terrestrials). We do not publish these genres: romance, poetry and drama." Nonfiction: Query, submit complete manuscript or submit outline/synopsis and sample chapters. Reports on queries in 3 weeks; mss in 2 months. Publishes book "approximately one year" after acceptance. Will consider simultaneous and electronic submissions via IBM-compatible disk or modem.

Terms: Buys ms outright for $1,000-1,500. Book catalog and ms guidelines free on request.

Tips: "Write something fresh and unique to carry a theme of lasting value. We publish only books with high moral tone, preferably with evangelical Christian content. Stories should reflect the highest Christian standards of thought, feeling and action. The text should make no reference to drinking, smoking, profanity or minced oaths. Other unacceptable story elements include unrelieved suspense, sensationalism and themes advocating secular attitudes of cynicism, rebellion or materialism."

JUST US BOOKS, INC., 301 Main St., Orange NJ 07050. (201)676-4345. Fax: (201)677-0234. Imprint of Afro-Bets Series. Book publisher; "for selected titles" book packager. Estab. 1988. Vice President/Publisher: Cheryl Willis Hudson. Publishes 4-6 picture books/year; "projected 6" young reader/middle reader titles/year. 33% books by first-time authors. Looking for "books that reflect a genuinely authentic African or African-American experience. We try to work with authors and illustrators who are from the culture itself." Also publishes *Harambee*, a newspaper for young readers, 6 times during the school year. (Target age for *Harambee* is 10-13.)

Fiction: Picture books, young readers, middle readers: adventure, contemporary, easy-to-read, history, multicultural (African-American themes), sports. Average word length: "varies" per picture book; young reader — 500-2,000; middle reader — 5,000. Wants African-American themes. Gets too many traditional African folktales. Published *Land of the Four Winds*, by Veronica Freeman Ellis, illustrated by Sylvia Walker (ages 6-9, picture book).

Nonfiction: Picture books, young readers, middle readers: activity books, biography, concept, history, multicultural (African-American themes). Published *Book of Black Heroes Vol. 2: Great Women in the Struggle*, by Toyomi Igus.

How to Contact/Writers: Fiction/Nonfiction: Query or submit outline/synopsis for proposed title. Reports on queries in 6-8 weeks; ms in 8 weeks "or as soon as possible." Publishes a book 12-18 months after acceptance. Will consider simultaneous submissions (with prior notice).

Illustration: Works with 4-6 illustrators/year. Will review ms/illustration packages ("but prefer to review them separately"). Will review artwork for future assignments.

How to Contact/Illustrators: Ms/illustration packages: "Query first." Illustrations only: Query with samples; send résumé, promo sheet, slides, client list, tearsheets; arrange personal portfolio review. Reports in 2-3 weeks. Original artwork returned at job's completion "depending on project."

Photography: Purchases photos from freelancers. Buys stock and assigns work. Wants "African-American themes — kids age 10-13 in school, home and social situations for *Harambee* (newspaper)."

Terms: Pays authors royalty based on retail price or work purchased outright. Royalties based on retail price. Pays illustrators by the project or royalty based on retail price. Sends galleys to authors; dummies to illustrators. Book catalog for business-size SAE and 65¢ postage; ms/artist's guidelines for business-size SAE and 65¢ postage.

Tips: "Multicultural books are tops as far as trends go. There is a great need for diversity and authenticity here. They will continue to be in the forefront of children's book publishing until there is more balanced treatment on these themes industry wide." Writers: "Keep the subject matter fresh and lively. Avoid 'preachy' stories with stereotyped characters. Rely more on authentic stories with sensitive three-dimensional characters." Illustrators: "Submit 5-10 good, neat samples. Be willing to work with an art director for the type of illustration desired by a specific house and grow into larger projects."

KABEL PUBLISHERS, 11225 Huntover Dr., Rockville MD 20852. (301)468-6463. Fax: (301)468-6463. Manager: John Aker. Publishes 1-3 picture books/year; 1-3 young readers/year; 1-3 middle readers/year; 1-3 young adult titles/year. 20% of books by first-time authors.

"Picture books" are geared toward preschoolers to 8-year-olds; "Young readers" are for 5- to 8-year-olds; "Middle readers" are for 9- to 11-year-olds; and "Young adults" are for those ages 12 and up.

Fiction: Will consider any children's fiction category.

Nonfiction: Will consider any children's nonfiction category.

How to Contact/Writers: Fiction/Nonfiction: Submit complete ms (typewritten), outline/synopsis. Reports on queries in 2-4 weeks. Publishes a book 3-6 months after acceptance. Will consider disk submissions in Word Perfect format.

Illustration: Will review ms/illustration packages. Uses primarily b&w artwork only.

How to Contact/Illustrators: Ms/illustration packages: Submit ms with final art. Reports in 2-4 weeks. Cannot return samples; samples filed. Originals not returned.

Terms: Pays authors 4 author's copies free as royalty; 10% gross after sale of 250 copies. Pays illustrators by the project. Sends galleys to authors (1 proof). Ms/artist's guidelines are not available.

Tips: "Colored illustrations are possible with author's subsidy."

KAR-BEN COPIES, INC., 6800 Tildenwood Lane, Rockville MD 20852. (301)984-8733. Fax: (301)881-9195. Book publisher. Estab. 1975. Vice President: Madeline Wikler. Publishes 10 picture books/year; 10 young reader titles/year. 20% of books by first-time authors.

Fiction: Picture books: folktales, multicultural, religion, special needs — only if connected to a Jewish theme. Average word length: picture books — 2,000. Recently published *Kingdom of Singing Birds*, by Miriam Aroner; *Hillel Builds a House*, by Shoshana Lepon; *Sammy Spider's First Hanukkah*, by Sylvia Rouss; and *Matzah Ball, A Passover Story*, by Mindy Avra Portnoy.

Nonfiction: Picture books, young readers, middle readers: religion — Jewish interest. Average word length: picture books — 2,000. Published *Jewish Holiday Crafts for Little Hands*, by Ruth Brinn; *Tell Me a Mitzvah*, by Danny Siegel; *My First Jewish Word Book*, by Roz Schanzer.

How to Contact/Writers: Fiction/nonfiction: Submit complete ms. Reports on queries/ms in 6 weeks. Publishes a book 1 year after acceptance. Will consider simultaneous submissions. "We don't like them, but we'll look at them — as long as we *know* it's a simultaneous submission."

Illustration: Works with 6-10 illustrators/year. Will review ms/illustration packages. Will review artwork for future assignments. Prefers "4-color art to any medium that is scannable."

How to Contact/Illustrators: Ms/illustration packages: Submit whole ms and sample of art (no originals). Illustrations only: Submit tearsheets, photocopies, promo sheet or anything representative that does *not* need to be returned. Enclose SASE for response. Reports on art samples in 4 weeks.

Terms: Pays authors in royalties of 6-8% based on net sales or work purchased outright (range: $500-2,000). Offers advance (average amount: $1,000). Pays illustrators royalty of 6-8% based on net sales or by the project (range: $500-3,000). Sends galleys to authors. Book catalog free on request. Ms guidelines for #10 SAE and 1 first-class stamp.

Tips: Looks for "books for young children with Jewish interest and content, modern, nonsexist, not didactic. Fiction or nonfiction with a *Jewish* theme — can be serious or humorous, life cycle, Bible story, or holiday-related."

*KEY PORTER BOOKS, 70 The Esplanade, Toronto, Ontario M5E 1R2 Canada. (416)862-7777. Fax: (416)862-2304. Book publisher. Vice President/Editor-in-Chief: Susan Renouf. Publishes 4 picture books/year; 4 young readers/year. 30% of books by first-time authors.

Fiction: Picture books, young readers: adventure, contemporary, folktales, humor and nature/environment. Does not want to see religious material. Average word length: picture books — 1,500; young readers — 5,000.

Nonfiction: Picture books: animal, history, nature/environment, reference, science. Middle readers: animal, careers, history, nature/environment, reference, science and sports. Average word length: picture books — 1,500; middle readers — 15,000. Recently published *How on Earth: A Question and Answer Book About How Animals & Plants Live*, by Ron Orenstein (ages 8-10, nature/environment); *Super Skaters: World Figure Skating Stars*, by Steve Milton (ages 8 and up, sports); and *Underwater Explorers*, by Arlene Moscovitch (ages 9-11, career).

How to Contact/Writers: Fiction/Nonfiction: Submit outline/synopsis and 2 sample chapters. Reports in 2 months. Publishes a book 12-18 months after acceptance, depending on quality, length and format. Will consider simultaneous submissions.
Illustration: Will review ms/illustration packages. Contact: Susan Renouf, editor-in-chief. Will review artwork for future assignments.
How to Contact/Illustrators: Ms/illustration packages: Submit ms with 2-3 pieces of final art. Illustrations only: Query with samples; provide résumé, promotional literature and tearsheets. Reports in 2 months. Samples returned with SASE; samples filed. Original artwork returned at job's completion.
Photography: Buys photos from freelancers. Contact: Renée Dykeman, trade editor. Buys stock and assigns work. Captions required. Uses 35mm transparencies. Submit cover letter, résumé, duplicate slides, stock photo list.
Terms: Pays authors royalty of 4-10% based on retail price. Offers advances (average amount: $4,000-20,000, Canadian). Pays illustrators by the project (range: $4,000-20,000, Canadian). Pays photographers by the project (range: $4,000-10,000, Canadian); per photo (range: $50-250, Canadian); royalty (range: 4-10% of retail price). Sends galleys to authors; dummies to illustrators. Book catalog available for 8½ × 11 SAE and 2 first-class stamps; ms guidelines available for SASE.

KNOPF BOOKS FOR YOUNG READERS, 29th Floor, 201 E. 20th St., New York NY 10022. (212)254-1600. Random House, Inc. Book publisher. Estab. 1915. Publishing Director: Simon Boughton. Editor-in-Chief: Arthur Levine. Publisher, Apple Soup Books: Anne Schwartz. 90% of books published through agents.
Fiction: Upmarket picture books: adventure, animal, contemporary, fantasy, retellings of folktales, original stories. Young readers: adventure, animal, contemporary, nature/environment, science fiction, sports, suspense/mystery. Middle readers: adventure, animal, fantasy, nature/environment, science fiction, sports, suspense/mystery. Young adult: adventure, contemporary, fantasy, science fiction—very selective; few being published currently.
Nonfiction: Picture books, young readers—middle readers: animal, biography, nature/environment, sports.
How to Contact/Writers: Fiction/nonfiction: Submit through agent only. Publishes a book 12-18 months after acceptance. Will consider simultaneous submissions.
Illustration: Will review ms/illustration packages (through agent only). Will review an illustrator's work for possible future assignments. Contact: Art Director.
Terms: Pays authors in royalties. Book catalog free on request.

*KRUZA KALEIDOSCOPIX, INC., Box 389, Franklin MA 02038. (508)528-6211. Book publisher. Picture Books Editor: Jay Kruza. Young/middle Editor: Russ Burbank. Art Director: Brian Sawyer. Publishes 4 picture books/year; 2 young reader titles/year; 1 middle reader title/year. 50% of books by first-time authors.
Fiction: Picture books, young readers: animal, fantasy, history. Average word length: picture books—200-500; young readers—500-2,000; middle readers—1,000-10,000.
Nonfiction: Picture books: animal, history, nature/environment. Young readers: animal, history, nature/environment, religion. Middle readers: biography, sports.
How to Contact/Writers: Fiction/nonfiction: Query; submit outline/synopsis and sample chapters; submit complete ms. Reports on queries/mss in 2-8 weeks.
Illustration: Will review artwork for future assignments. Prefers to see "realistic" illustrations.
How to Contact/Illustrators: Illustrations only: "Submit actual work sample photocopies in color, and photos." Reports on art samples only if interested.
Terms: Buys ms outright for $250-500. Pays illustrators $25-100/illustration. Ms/artist's guidelines available for #10 SASE.
Tips: Writers: "Rework your story several times before submitting it without grammatical or spelling mistakes. *Our company charges a $3 reading fee per manuscript* to reduce unprepared manuscripts." Illustrators: "Submit professional looking samples for file. The correct manuscript may come along." Wants ms/illustrations "that teach a moral. Smooth prose that flows like poetry is preferred. The story will be read aloud. Vocabulary and language should fit actions. Short staccato words connote fast action; avoid stories that solve prob-

Editor's Advice: Get Back to the Basics of Good Writing

"Multiculturalism" has been a misunderstood catchword in children's book publishing during the past few years. Many writers wrongly assume that simply featuring a non-white character or culture can ensure a manuscript's publication. Editors do strive for diversity in voice and subject matter, but the bottom line when it comes to success in this field remains the same—good writing, according to Arthur A. Levine, editor-in-chief of Knopf Books for Young Readers.

With more than a decade of experience in children's literature, Levine knows of what he speaks. Before coming to Knopf in 1994, he was editor-in-chief of G.P. Putnam's Sons and worked on their Whitebird line of folktales. He's also the author of five children's books, including *All the Lights in the*

Arthur A. Levine

Night (Tambourine Books, 1991), which was nominated for the National Jewish Book Award; and, most recently, *The Boy Who Drew Cats* (Dial Books, 1994), a retelling of a Japanese folktale.

As both author and editor, the Brown University graduate has become an acute observer of the industry's increasing sophistication. "We subject the folktales we review to the same scrutiny that any other form of writing would get," says Levine. "In folktales, we're looking for a great story first, not just a cultural curiosity."

Multicultural publishing is not just limited to folklore either. Levine looks for material that "speaks to a psychological and cultural reality—both through traditional tales and contemporary literature." In either case, Knopf keeps an eye out for the basics of good craftsmanship: a solid plot, vivid imagery, distinctive characters, and such qualities as emotional appeal, or sense of humor.

Knopf publishes books geared toward many age-groups, from preschoolers to young adults. Right now Levine is particularly in need of quality literary fiction for the middle grades. "There is plenty of mediocre stuff available," he adds. "I want truly distinguished writing."

So how much stock should you place in the latest trend if you're seeking a publisher for your book? Not much, cautions Levine. If you've done your research, you'll be aware of what is being published; but don't rely on what appears to be the latest trend or simply allow a writer's guide listing to dictate your submission target. Because the production time required for book publication can range from months to years, what you see in the bookstores is not always a true reflection of today's hottest topic. Thus, writers tend to be two years behind any trend, continuing to submit material that doesn't address an editor's needs, says Levine. So forget about getting an edge on the competition based solely on your subject matter—substance is more important.

Once you've refined a particular manuscript until it's the best it can be, find the right market for your work. Levine advises writers to spend several months reading publications in their field. Comb the shelves of a good bookstore and note the publishers you most admire. (You can also browse the shelves of a library. Check publication dates on the copyright pages to find the most recent books.) Only after you've followed these steps should you consult a marketing resource (such as *Children's Writer's & Illustrator's Market*) to pinpoint your market and obtain submission information. If you bypass the research phase, you're more than likely to find rejection. The process is similar to shopping for a gift, says Levine. "If you're giving a book to a friend, you take certain steps to ensure the book is in the recipient's taste. You should do the same with an editor."

Another error novice writers often make is coupling their submissions with illustrations. Editors work with illustrators as well as writers and consider it their job to match text and art. They may wish to pair an unknown writer with a prominent artist, or vice versa.

Success in this field doesn't take any magic, but it does take knowledge, creativity and common sense. Write well, research, and get to know an editor's taste before you approach him or her with your work. "I hope what I've published reflects a consistent set of standards," says Levine of his career. And if you do your homework, you'll know that.

—*Jennifer Hogan-Redmond*

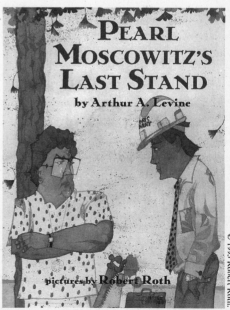

One of the several books by author and editor Arthur A. Levine, Pearl Moscowitz's Last Stand (Tambourine Books), is illustrated in the distinctive watercolor style of Robert Roth. Roth's cover illustration depicts the stand off between Pearl, the main character, and a city worker who is trying to cut down the last tree in her neighborhood. The story was sparked by a similar incident involving Levine's own mother.

© 1993 Robert Roth.

lems by the 'wave of a wand' or that condone improper behavior. Jack of Beanstalk fame was a dullard, a thief and even a murderer. We seek to purchase all rights to the story and artwork. Payment may be a lump sum in cash."

LAREDO PUBLISHING CO. INC., 22930 Lockness Ave., Torrance CA 90501. (310)517-1890. Fax: (310)517-1892. Book publisher. Vice President: Clara Kohen. Publishes 5 picture books/year; 15 young readers/year. 10% of books by first-time authors. Spanish language books only.

Fiction: Picture books: multicultural (Spanish). Young readers: adventure, animal, fantasy, folktales, health, multicultural (Spanish), poetry. Middle readers: adventure, animal, contemporary, fantasy, folktales, health, multicultural (Spanish), nature/environment, poetry. Published *Pregones*, by Alma Flor Ada (middle readers, personal experience in Spanish); *Pajaritos*, by Clarita Kohen (young readers, counting book in Spanish); *El Conejoyel Coyote*, by Clarita Kohen (young readers, folktale in Spanish).

Nonfiction: Published *Los Aztecas*, by Robert Nicholson (middle readers, history, culture and traditions of the Aztecs in Spanish); *Los Sioux*, by Robert Nicholson (middle readers; history, culture and traditions of the Sioux in Spanish); *La Antigua China*, by Robert Nicholson (middle readers; history, culture and traditions of the Chinese in Spanish).

How to Contact/Writers: Fiction: Submit complete ms. Reports on mss in 3 months. Publishes a book 1 year after acceptance. Will consider simultaneous submissions.

Illustration: Works with 20 illustrators/year. Will review ms/illustration packages. Uses color artwork only.

How to Contact/Illustrators: Illustrations only: Query with samples, promo sheet. Reports in 2 months. Samples returned with SASE. Originals not returned.

Terms: Pays authors royalty of 5-7% based on wholesale price. Offers advances (varies). Pays illustrators by the project (range: $250-500). Sends galleys to authors; dummies to illustrators.

Tips: "We will only accept manuscripts in Spanish."

LEE & LOW BOOKS, INC., 228 E. 45th St., New York NY 10017. (212)867-6155. Fax: (212)338-9059. Book publisher. Editor-in-Chief: Elizabeth Szabla. Publishes 8-10 picture books/year. 50% of books by first-time authors. "We publish only multicultural themes.

Fiction: Fiction or poetry that reflects the experiences of children of color, as well as children from countries/cultures outside the US. "We are not considering folktales or animal stories." Average word length: picture books—1,000-1,500 words. Recently published *Baseball Saved Us*, by Ken Mochizuki, illustrated by Dom Lee (ages 4-10, picture book); and *Bein' with You This Way*, by W. Nikola-Lisa, illustrated by Michael Bryant (ages 2-6, picture book).

Nonfiction: Picture books: biography and multicultural. Average word length: picture books—1,500. Recently published *Zora Hurston and the Chinaberry Tree*, by William Miller, illustrated by Cornelius Van Wright and Ying-Hwa Hu (ages 4-10, picture book).

How to Contact/Writers: Fiction/Nonfiction: Submit complete ms. Reports in 1-2 months. Publishes a book 12-18 months after acceptance. Will consider simultaneous submissions.

Illustration: Works with 8-10 illustrators/year. Will review ms/illustration packages. Contact: Elizabeth Szabla, editor-in-chief. Will review artwork for future assignments. Uses color artwork only.

How to Contact/Illustrators: Ms/illustration packages: Submit ms with dummy. Illustrations only: Query with samples, résumé, promo sheet and tearsheets. Reports in 1-2 months. Samples returned with SASE; samples filed. Original artwork returned at job's completion.

Photography: Buys photos from freelancers. Works on assignment only. Model/property releases required. Submit cover letter, résumé, promo piece and book dummy.

Terms: Pays authors royalty based on retail price. Offers advances. Pays illustrators royalty based on retail price plus advance against royalty. Photographers paid royalty based on retail price plus advance against royalty. Sends galleys to authors; dummies to illustrators. Book catalog available for 9 × 12 SAE and 75¢ postage; ms and art guidelines available for SASE.

This charming illustration by Michael Bryant captures children's joy of "just bein' together" in Lee & Low's Bein' with You This Way, *by W. Nikola-Lisa. The picture book relays — in rap — the story of an African-American girl who visits the park on a sunny afternoon and rounds up a diverse group of playmates who discover that "despite their physical differences, they're all really the same."*

LERNER PUBLICATIONS CO., 241 First Ave. N., Minneapolis MN 55401. (612)332-3344. Fax: (612)332-7615. Book publisher. Editor: Jennifer Martin. Publishes 9 young readers/year; 62 middle readers/year; 5 young adults/year. 20% of books by first-time authors; 5% of books from agented writers. "Most books are nonfiction for children, grades 3-9."
Fiction: Middle readers: adventure, contemporary, hi-lo, multicultural, nature/environment, sports, suspense/mystery. Young adults: contemporary, hi-lo, history, multicultural, nature/environment, problem novels, sports, suspense/mystery. "Especially interested in books with ethnic characters." Recently published the Kerry Hill Casecrackers series, by Joan Warner and Peggy Nicholson (grades 4-7, mystery).
Nonfiction: Middle readers, young adults: animal, arts/crafts, biography, careers, concept, cooking, geography, health, hi-lo, history, hobbies, how-to, multicultural, music/dance, nature/environment, sports, science/math, social issues, self-help, special needs. Multicultural material must contain authentic details. Does not want to see textbooks, workbooks, song books, audiotapes, puzzles, plays, religious material, books for teachers or parents, picture or alphabet books. Average word length: young readers — 3,000; middle readers — 7,000; young adults — 12,000. Recently published *J.M. Barrie: The Magic Behind Peter Pan*, by Susan Aller (grades 5 and up, Lerner Biographies series); *Shaquille O'Neal: Center of Attention*, by Brad Townsend (grades 4-9, Sports Achievers series).
How to Contact/Writers: Fiction: Submit outline/synopsis and sample chapters. Nonfiction: Query; submit outline/synopsis and sample chapters. Reports on queries in 3-4 weeks; mss in 3 months. Publishes a book 12-18 months after acceptance. Will consider simultaneous submissions.
Illustration: Works with 1-2 illustrators/year. Will review ms/illustration packages. Will review artwork for future assignments. "We tend to work only with local talent." Contact: Art Director.
How to Contact/Illustrators: Query with samples and résumé.
Photography: Contact: Photo Research Department. Buys stock and assigns work. Model/property releases required. Publishes photo essays. Photographers should query with samples.
Terms: Pays authors royalty or work purchased outright. Pays illustrators by the project. Sends galleys to authors. Book catalog available for 9 × 12 SAE and $1.90 postage; ms guidelines for 4 × 9 SAE and 1 first-class stamp.

Tips: Wants "straightforward, well-written nonfiction for children in grades 3-9 backed by solid current research or scholarship. Before you send your manuscript to us, you might first take a look at the kinds of books that our company publishes. We specialize in publishing high-quality educational books for children from second grade through high school. Avoid sex stereotypes (e.g., strong, aggressive, unemotional males/weak, submissive, emotional females) in your writing, as well as sexist language." (See also Carolrhoda Books, Inc.)

LION BOOKS, PUBLISHER, Suite B, 210 Nelson, Scarsdale NY 10583. (914)725-2280. Imprint of Sayre Ross Co. Book publisher. Editorial contact: Harriet Ross. Publishes 5 middle readers/year; 10 young adults/year. 50-70% of books by first-time authors. Publishes books "with ethnic and minority accents for young adults, including a variety of craft titles dealing with African and Asian concepts."

Nonfiction: Activity, art/crafts, biography, history, hobbies, how-to, multicultural. Average word length: young adult—30,000-50,000.

How to Contact/Writers: Query, submit complete ms. Reports on queries in 3 weeks; ms in 2 months.

How to Contact/Illustrators: Reports in 2 weeks.

Terms: Work purchased outright (range: $500-5,000). Average advance: $1,000-2,500. Illustrators paid $500-1,500. Sends galleys to author. Book catalog free on request.

LITTLE, BROWN AND COMPANY, 34 Beacon St., Boston MA 02108. (617)227-0730. Book publisher. Editor-in-Chief: Maria Modugno. Art Director: Susan Lu. Estab. 1837. Publishes 30% picture books/year; 10% young reader titles/year; 30% middle reader titles/year; 10% young adult titles/year.

• Little, Brown ranks 11th, based on net sales, of the top 12 children's publishers.

Fiction: Picture books: adventure, animal, contemporary, fantasy, folktales, history, humor, multicultural, nature/environment. Young readers: adventure, animal, contemporary, fantasy, history, humor, multicultural, nature/environment, science fiction, suspense/mystery. Middle readers: adventure, contemporary, fantasy, history, humor, multicultural, nature/environment, science fiction, suspense/mystery. Young adults: contemporary, health, humor, multicultural, nature/environment, suspense/mystery. Multicultural needs include "any material by, for and about minorities." No "rhyming texts, anthropomorphic animals that learn a lesson, alphabet and counting books, and stories based on an event rather than a character." Average word length: picture books—1,000; young readers—6,000; middle readers—15,000-25,000; young adults—20,000-40,000. Published *Honkers*, by Jane Yolen (ages 4-8, picture book); *Babysitting for Benjamin*, by Valiska Gregory (ages 4-8, picture book); *Howling for Home*, by Joan Carris (ages 7-9, first chapter book); *Dear Mom, Get Me Out of Here!*, by Ellen Conford (ages 8-12, middle reader).

Nonfiction: Picture books: animal, biography, concept, history, multicultural, nature/environment. Young readers: activity books, biography, multicultural. Middle readers: activity books, arts/crafts, biography, cooking, geography, history, multicultural. Young adults: multicultural, self-help, social issues. Average word length: picture books—2,000; young readers—4,000-6,000; middle readers—15,000-25,000; young adults—20,000-40,000. Published *In the Shogun's Shadow*, by John Langone (ages 10 and up, young adult); *Faith Ringgold*, by Robyn Turner (ages 6-10, picture book).

How to Contact/Writers: Submit through agent or, if previously published, submit with list of writing credits.

Illustration: Works with 40 illustrators/year. Will review artwork for future assignments.

How to Contact/Illustrators: Illustrations only: Query art director with samples/slides; provide résumé, promo sheet or tearsheets to be kept on file. Reports on art samples in 6-8 weeks. Original artwork returned at job's completion.

Photography: Works on assignment only. Model/property releases required; captions required. Publishes photo essays and photo concept books. Uses 35mm transparencies. Photographers should provide résumé, promo sheets or tearsheets to be kept on file.

Terms: Pays authors royalties of 3-10% based on retail price. Offers advance (average amount: $2,000-10,000). Pays illustrators by the project (range: $1,500-5,000) or royalty of 3-10% based on retail price. Photographers paid by the project, by royalty based on retail price. Sends galleys to authors; dummies to illustrators. Book catalog, manuscript/artist's guidelines free on request.

Tips: "Publishers are cutting back their lists in response to a shrinking market and relying more on big names and known commodities. In order to break into the field these days, authors and illustrators research their competition and try to come up with something outstandingly different."

LODESTAR BOOKS, 375 Hudson St., New York NY 10014. (212)366-2627. Fax: (212)366-2011. Affiliate of Dutton Children's Books, a division of Penguin Books, USA, Inc. Estab. 1980. Editorial Director: Virginia Buckley. Senior Editor: Rosemary Brosnan. Publishes 10 picture books/year; 8-10 middle readers/year; 5 young adults/year (25 books/year). 5-10% of books by first-time authors; 50% through agents.

● This publisher has received numerous awards in recent years including the Coretta Scott King Honor Book Award and other awards from the American Library Association and the *Boston Globe-Horn Book*.

Fiction: Picture books: adventure, animal, contemporary, folktales, humor, multicultural, nature/environment. Young readers: adventure, animal, contemporary, humor, multicultural, nature/environment. Middle reader: adventure, animal, contemporary, folktales, humor, multicultural, nature/environment, suspense/mystery. Young adult: adventure, contemporary, history, humor, multicultural, nature/environment. Multicultural needs include "well-written books with good characterization. Prefer books by authors of same ethnic background as subject, but not absolutely necessary." No commercial picture books, science fiction or genre novels. Published *Little Eight John*, by Jan Wahl with illustrations by Wil Clay (ages 5-8, picture book); *Jericho's Journey*, by G. Clifton Wisler (ages 10-14, historical novel); *Celebrating the Hero*, by Lyll Becerra de Jenkins (ages 12 and up, a novel set in Columbia).

Nonfiction: Picture books: activity books, animal, concept, geography, history, multicultural, nature/environment, science, social issues. Young reader: animal, concept, geography, history, multicultural, nature/environment, science, social issues, sports. Middle reader: animal, biography, careers, geography, history, multicultural, music/dance, nature/environment, science, social issues, sports. Young adult: history, multicultural, music/dance, nature/environment, social issues, sports. Multicultural needs include authentic, well-written books about African-American, Native American, Hispanic and Asian-American experiences. Also, books on Jewish themes. Published *The Giant Book of Animal Worlds*, by Anita Ganeri, illustrations by John Butler (ages 7-10, giant board book on animal habitats); *Twins on Toes: A Ballet Debut*, by Joan Anderson, photographs by George Ancona (ages 8-12); *Witnesses to Freedom: Young People Who Fought for Civil Rights*, by Belinda Rochelle (ages 8-12).

How to Contact/Writers: Fiction: Submit synopsis and sample chapters or submit complete ms. Nonfiction: Query or submit synopsis and sample chapters. Reports on queries in 1 month; mss in 3 months. Publishes a book 12-18 months after acceptance. Will consider simultaneous submissions.

Illustration: Works with approximately 12 illustrators/year. Will review ms/illustration packages. Will review artwork for possible future assignments.

How to Contact/Illustrators: Ms/illustration packages: Submit "manuscript and copies of art (no original art please)." Illustrations only: Query with samples; send portfolio or slides. Drop off portfolio for review. Reports back only if interested. Original art work returned at job's completion.

Photography: Buys photos from freelancers (infrequently).

Terms: Pays authors and illustrators royalties of 5% each for picture books; 8% to author, 2% to illustrator for illustrated novel; and 10% for novel based on retail price. Sends galleys to author. Book catalog for SASE; manuscript guidelines for #10 SAE and 1 first-class stamp.

 A bullet has been placed within some listings to introduce special comments by the editors of **Children's Writer's & Illustrator's Market.**

Tips: Wants "well-written books that show awareness of children's and young people's lives, feelings and problems; arouse imagination and are sensitive to children's needs. More books by African-American, Hispanic, Asian-American and Native American writers. More novelty and interactional books."

LOOK AND SEE PUBLICATIONS, P.O. Box 64216, Tucson AZ 85728-4216. (602)529-2857. Book publisher. "We self-publish the children's activity books we write." Publishes 2 young readers/year. Publishes "history and cultures of the Southwest national parks."
Nonfiction: Middle readers, young adults: activity books.
How to Contact/Writers: Query. "We are not interested in having manuscripts submitted." Reports on queries in 1 month.
Illustration: Works with 1-2 illustrators/year. Will review artwork for future assignments. Uses primarily b&w artwork but "also interested in color transparencies. Most of the art we use is done in charcoal or pen & ink."
How to Contact/Illustrators: Ms/illustration packages: Query. Illustrations only: Query with samples. Reports back only if interested. Cannot return samples; samples filed. Originals returned with SASE.
Terms: Pays illustrators by the project. Sends dummies to illustrators. Book catalog available for 4¼ × 9½ SAE and 1 first-class stamp.

*JAMES LORIMER & CO., 35 Britain St., Toronto, Ontario M5A 1R7 Canada. (416)362-4762. Book publisher. Publishing Assistant: M. Tate. Publishes 3 middle readers/year; 2 young adult titles/year. 20% of books by first-time authors. Uses Canadian authors only; wants realistic, contemporary material with Canadian settings.
Fiction: Middle readers: adventure, contemporary, hi-lo, multicultural, problem novels, sports and suspense/mystery. Young adults: contemporary, multicultural, problem novels and sports. Canadian settings featuring characters from ethnic/racial/cultural minorities — prefers author from same background. Does not want to see fantasy, science fiction, verse, drama and short stories. Average word length: middle readers — 12,000; young adults — 25,000. Recently published *The Great Pebble Creek Bike Race*, by Kathy Stinson (ages 7-10, sport/adventure); *Gallop for Gold*, by Sharon Siamon (ages 7-10, dventure novel); *Curve Ball*, by John Danakas (ages 9-12, sport novel).
How to Contact/Writers: Submit outline/synopsis and 2 sample chapters. Reports on queries in 2 months; mss in 6 months. Publishes a book 8 months after acceptance.
Illustration: Works with 3 illustrators/year. Prefers realistic style.
How to Contact/Illustrators: Illustrations only: Submit promo sheet, photocopies OK. Reports only if interested. Samples returned with SASE; samples filed. Original artwork returned at job's completion.
Photography: Buys photos from freelancers. Contact: M. Tate, publishing assistant. Buys stock and assigns work. Uses color prints and 35mm transparencies. Submit letter.
Terms: Pays authors royalty of 6-10% based on retail price. Offers advances (average amount: $500). Pays illustrators by the project (range: $300-450). Pays photographers by the project (range: $250-350). Sends galleys to authors. Ms and art guidelines available for SASE.
Tips: "Follow submission guidelines and research the market — read current kids' books, talk to kids." Wants realistic novels, set in Canada, dealing with social issues. Recent trends include hi-lo and multicultural.

LUCAS/EVANS BOOKS INC., 407 Main St., Chatham NJ 07928. Executive Director: Barbara Lucas. Editor and Production Manager: Cassandra Conyers. Estab. 1984. Book packager specializing in children's books, preschool through high school age. Books prepared from inception to camera-ready mechanicals for all major publishers.
Fiction/Nonfiction: Particularly interested in series ideas, especially for middle grades and beginning readers. All subject categories except problem novels and textbooks considered. Published fiction titles: *Ghost Dog*, by Ellen Leroe (Hyperion); *Song for the Ancient Forest*, by Nancy Luenn (Atheneum); *Second-Grade Friends*, by Miriam Cohen (Scholastic). Published nonfiction titles: *They Had a Dream*/ Epoch Biography by Jules Archer (Viking),

and *The Kids' Cookbook*, by West Village Nursery School (Outlet); *Science Source Books* (Facts on File series).

How to Contact/Writers: Query. Reports on queries in 2 months.

Illustration: Works with 15-20 illustrators/year.

How to Contact/Illustrators: Query with samples; provide résumé, promo sheet, slides, client list, tearsheets, arrange personal portfolio review. "Color photocopies of art welcome for our file."

Terms: Offers authors and illustrators royalty-based contracts with advances based on retail price. Work purchased outright.

Tips: Prefers experienced authors and artists but will consider unpublished work. "There seems to be an enormous demand for early chapter books, although we will continue our efforts to sell to publishers in all age groups and formats. We are interested in series since publishers look to packagers for producing time-consuming projects."

LUCENT BOOKS, P.O. Box 289011, San Diego CA 92128-9009. (619)485-7424. Sister Company to Greenhaven Press. Book publisher. Editor: Bonnie Szumski. 50% of books by first-time authors; 10% of books from agented writers.

• This publisher does not accept unsolicited manuscripts.

Nonfiction: Middle readers, young adults: education, health, topical history, nature/environment, sports, "any overviews of specific topics — i.e., political, social, cultural, economic, criminal, moral issues." No fiction. Average word length: 15,000-25,000. Published *The Persian Gulf War*, by Don Nardo (grades 6-12, history); *Photography*, by Brad Steffens (grades 5-8, history); and *Rainforests*, by Lois Warburton (grades 5-8, overview).

How to Contact/Writers: "Writers should query first; we do writing by assignment only. If you want to write for us, send SASE for guidelines."

Illustration: "We use photos, mostly." Uses primarily b&w artwork. Will review ms/illustration packages. Will review artwork for future assignments. "Prefers 7×9 format — 4-color cover."

How to Contact/Illustrators: Ms/illustration packages: Query first. Illustrations only: Query with samples; provide résumé, business card, promotional literature or tearsheets to be kept on file.

Terms: "Fee negotiated upon review of manuscript." Sends galleys to authors. Ms guidelines free on request.

Tips: "Books must be written at a 7th-8th-grade reading level. There's a growing market for quality nonfiction. Tentative topics: free speech, tobacco, alcohol, discrimination, immigration, poverty, the homeless in America, space weapons, drug abuse, terrorism, animal experimentation, endangered species, AIDS, pollution, gun control, etc. The above list is presented to give writers an example of the kinds of titles we are seeking. If you are interested in writing about a specific topic, please query us by mail before you begin writing to be sure we have not assigned a particular topic to another author. The author should strive for objectivity. There obviously will be many issues on which a position should be taken — e.g. discrimination, tobacco, alcoholism, etc. However, moralizing, self-righteous condemnations, maligning, lamenting, mocking, etc. should be avoided. Moreover, where a pro/con position is taken, contrasting viewpoints should be presented. Certain moral issues such as abortion and euthanasia, if dealt with at all, should be presented with strict objectivity."

LUCKY BOOKS, P.O. Box 1415, Winchester VA 22604. (703)662-3424. Book publisher. Co-Publishers: Mac S. Rutherford and Donna Rutherford. Publishes 1-2 picture books/year; 1-2 young readers/year. 90% of books by first-time authors.

Fiction: Picture books, young readers: adventure, animal, fantasy, nature/environment, poetry. Middle readers: animal, mystery, science fiction. No religion. Average word length: picture books — 500-1,500; young readers — 3,000-6,000. Published *Prince*, by Margery Van Susteren (8 and up, pet story); *Zonkey The Donkey*, by Virginia Athey, illustrated by Donna Rutherford (pre-school, poetic); *When the Zebras Came for Lunch*, by Barbara Van Curen (pre-school, fantasy). "We do not want to be limited by category. Quality of work is important to Lucky Books."

Nonfiction: Picture books: animal. Young readers: animal, arts/crafts, nature/environment. Middle readers: animal, arts/crafts, history, hobbies, sports. Not interested in how-to. Average word length: picture books—500-1,500.

How to Contact/Writers: Fiction: Submit complete ms. Nonfiction: Query. Reports on queries in 1-2 months; mss in 3-4 months. Publishes a book 1-1½ years after acceptance (varies greatly).

Illustration: Works with 1-2 illustrators/year. Will review ms/illustration packages. Contact: Donna Rutherford, co-publisher. Will review artwork for future assignments.

How to Contact/Illustrators: Ms/illustration packages: Submit ms with 2-3 pieces of final art. Illustrations only: Query with samples, résumé, slides. Reports back only if interested. Samples returned with SASE; samples filed.

Terms: Pays authors royalty of 3-6% based on wholesale or retail price. Pays illustrators by the project (range: $500-1,000) or royalty of 1-3% based on wholesale or retail price.

Tips: Looking for "more artistic/fine art layouts with simple message (pre-school)."

*McCLANAHAN BOOK COMPANY, 23 W. 26th St., New York NY 10010. (212)725-1515. Fax: (212)725-5911. Book publisher. Executive Editor: Lauren Ariev. Creative Director: Dave Werner. Publishes 90 picture books/year. Publishes boardbooks, workbooks and storybooks for the very young reader.

Fiction: Board storybooks.

How to Contact/Writers: Submit complete ms. Reports on queries in 1 month; mss in 3 months. Will consider simultaneous submissions.

How to Contact/Illustrators: Illustrations only: Query with samples. Reports back in 1 month. Samples returned with SASE; samples filed. Original artwork returned at job's completion.

Photography: Buys photos from freelancers. Contact: Dave Werner, creative director. Works on assignment only. Uses photos of children or photos for catalog/sell sheet. Uses color prints. Submit cover letter, samples.

Terms: Pays authors on work-for-hire basis (flat fee). Pays illustrators/photographers by the project.

MARGARET K. McELDERRY BOOKS, 866 Third Ave., New York NY 10022. (212)702-7855. Fax: (212)605-3045. Imprint of Simon & Schuster Children's Publishing Division. Publisher: Margaret K. McElderry. Art Director: Nancy Williams. Publishes 10-12 picture books/year; 2-4 young reader titles/year; 8-10 middle reader titles/year; 5-7 young adult titles/year. 25% of books by first-time authors; 33% of books from agented writers.

Fiction: Picture books: folktales, multicultural. Young readers: adventure, contemporary, fantasy, history, multicultural. Middle readers: adventure, contemporary, fantasy, history, multicultural. Young adult: contemporary, fantasy. "Always interested in publishing picture books and beginning reader stories by people of color about cultures and people other than Caucasian American. We see too many rhymed picture book manuscripts which are not terribly original or special." Average word length: picture books—500; young readers—2,000; middle readers—10,000-20,000; young adults—45,000-50,000. Recently published *My Dad*, by Niki Daly; *Out of the Blue*, by Sarah Ellis; and *Stories from Shakespeare*, by Geraldine McCaughrean.

Nonfiction: Young readers, middle readers: biography, history. Average word length: picture books—500-1,000; young readers—1,500-3,000; middle readers—10,000-20,000; young adults—30,000-45,000. Recently published *Hiawatha: Messenger of Peace*, by Dennis Fradin (ages 7-11); *To Hold This Ground: A Desperate Battle At Gettysburg*, by Susan Provost Beller (ages 10 and up); and *The Mystery of the Ancient Maya*, by Carolyn Meyer and Charles Gallenkamp (ages 12 and up).

How to Contact/Writers: Fiction/nonfiction: Submit complete ms. Reports on queries in 2 weeks; mss in 3 months. Publishes a book 12-18 months after acceptance. Will consider simultaneous submissions (only if indicated as such).

Illustration: Works with 20-30 illustrators/year. Contact: Nancy Williams, art director.

How to Contact/Illustrators: Ms/illustration packages: Submit ms (complete) and 2 or 3 copies of finished art. Illustrations only: Query with samples; provide, promo sheet or tearsheets; arrange personal portfolio review. Reports on art samples in 6-8 weeks. Original artwork returned at job's completion.

Terms: Pays authors royalty based on retail price. Pay illustrators by the project or royalty based on retail price. Photographers paid by the project. Sends galleys to authors; dummies to illustrators. Book catalog, ms/artist's guidelines free on request with 9 × 12 SASE.

Tips: Sees "more sales of beginning chapter books; more sales of poetry books; constant interest in books for the youngest baby market; more need for multicultural biographies and folktales."

MACMILLAN BOOKS FOR YOUNG READERS, 866 Third Ave., New York NY 10022. Imprint of Simon & Schuster Children's Publishing Division.
- Macmillan Books for Young Readers is not accepting unsolicited manuscripts at this time. They will be reviewing this policy in 1996.

MAGE PUBLISHERS INC., 1032 29th St. NW, Washington DC 20007. (202)342-1642. Book publisher. Editorial contact: A. Sepehri. Publishes 2-3 picture books/year.

Fiction: Contemporary/myth, Persian heritage. Average word length: 5,000.

Nonfiction: Persian heritage. Average word length: 5,000.

How to Contact/Writers: Fiction/Nonfiction: Query. Reports on queries/ms in 3 months. Will consider simultaneous submissions.

Illustration: Will review ms/illustration packages submitted by authors/artists. Will review artwork for possible future assignments.

How to Contact/Illustrators: Illustrations only: Submit résumé and slides. Reports in 3 months. Original artwork returned at job's completion.

Terms: Pays authors in royalties. Sends galleys to authors. Book catalog free on request.

MAGINATION PRESS, 19 Union Square West, New York NY 10003. (212)924-3344. Brunner/Mazel, Inc. Book publisher. Editor-in-Chief: Susan Kent Cakars. Publishes 4-8 picture books and young reader titles/year. Publishes "books dealing with the psycho/therapeutic treatment or resolution of children's serious problems—written by mental health professionals."

Fiction: Picture books, young readers: concept, mental health, multicultural, problem novels, special needs. Published *Gentle Willow: A Story for Children About Dying*, by Joyce C. Mills, Ph.D. (ages 4-8); *Sammy's Mommy Has Cancer*, by Sherry Kohlenberg (ages 4-8); *What About Me? When Brothers & Sisters Get Sick*, by Allan Peterkin, M.D. (ages 4-8).

Nonfiction: Picture books, young readers: concept, mental health, how-to, multicultural, psychotherapy, special needs. Published *Putting on the Brakes: Young People's Guide to Understanding Attention Deficit Hyperactivity Disorder (ADHD)*, by Patricia O. Quinn, M.D. and Judith M. Stern, M.A. (ages 8-13).

How to Contact/Writers: Fiction/nonfiction: Submit complete ms. Reports on queries/ mss: "up to 3 months (may be only days)." Publishes a book 1 year after acceptance.

Illustration: Works with 4-8 illustrators/year. Reviews ms/illustration packages. Will review artwork for future assignments.

How to Contact/Illustrators: Illustrations only: Query with samples. Original artwork returned at job's completion.

Terms: Pays authors in royalties. Offers vary but low advance. Pays illustrators by the project, $2,000 maximum, or royalty of 2% maximum. Sends galleys to authors. Book catalog and ms guidelines on request with SASE.

*MARLOR PRESS, INC., 4304 Brigadoon Dr., St. Paul MN 55126. (612)484-4608. Fax: (612)490-1188. Book publisher. Editorial Director: Marlin Bree. Publishes 2 young readers/year. 100% of books by first-time authors.

Always include a self-addressed, stamped envelope (SASE) with submissions within your own country. When sending material to other countries, include a self-addressed envelope (SAE) and International Reply Coupons (IRCs).

Nonfiction: Young readers: activity books, hobbies. Middle readers: activity books. ecently published *Kids' Squish Book*, by Doris and Marlin Bree (ages 4-12, kids' activity book); *Kids' Vacation* (ages 6-12, diary and activity book for kids while traveling).
How to Contact/Writers: Query. Reports on queries in 6 weeks; mss in 2 months. Publishes a book 8-12 months after acceptance. Will consider simultaneous and previously published submissions.
Illustration: Will review ms/illustration packages. Contact: Marlin Bree, editorial director.
How to Contact/Illustrators: Ms/illustration packages: Query. Reports in 6 weeks.
Terms: Pays authors 10% royalty based on wholesale price. Pays illustrators by the project. Sends galleys to authors; dummies to illustrators. Book catalog available for #10 SAE and 2 first-class stamps. Ms guidelines available for SASE.

MEADOWBROOK PRESS, 18318 Minnetonka Blvd., Deephaven MN 55391. (612)473-5400. Fax: (612)475-0736. Book publisher. Senior Editor: Dale Howard. Submissions Editor: David Tobey. Art Director: Amy Unger. Publishes 2-4 middle readers/year; 2-4 young readers/year. 20% of books by first-time authors; 10% of books from agented writers. Publishes children's activity books, gift books, humorous poetry anthologies and story anthologies.
Fiction: Picture books, young readers and middle readers: humorous poetry anthologies (no single-author poetry books). "Poems representing people of color encouraged." Recently published *The New Adventures of Mother Goose*; *Kids Pick the Funniest Poems*; and *A Bad Case of the Giggles* (all children's poetry anthologies).
Nonfiction: Young readers, middle readers: activity books. "Books which include multicultural activities are encouraged." Recently published: *Kids' Party Games and Activities*, by Penny Warner; *Free Stuff for Kids* (activity book); and *Kids' Holiday Fun* (activity book).
How to Contact/Writers: Fiction/Nonfiction: Query, submit outline/synopsis and sample chapters or submit complete ms with SASE. Reports on queries/mss in 1-3 months. Publishes a book 9-12 months after acceptance. Send a business-sized SAE and 2 first-class stamps for free writer's guidelines and book catalog before submitting ideas. Will consider simultaneous submissions.
Illustration: Works with 2-3 illustrators/year. Will review artwork for future assignments. Contact: Amy Unger, art director.
How to Contact/Illustrators: Ms/illustration packages: Query. Illustrations only: Submit résumé, promo sheet and tearsheets. Reports back only if interested. Samples not returned; samples filed.
Photography: Buys photos from freelancers. Buys stock and assigns work. Model/property releases required. Submit cover letter.
Terms: Pays authors in royalties of 5-7½% based on retail price. Offers average advance payment of $2,000-4,000. Pays illustrators: $100-10,000; ¼-¾% of total royalties. Pays photographers per photo ($250). Book catalog available for 5×11 SASE and 2 first-class stamps; ms guidelines available for SASE.
Tips: Illustrators: "Develop a commercial style—compare your style to that of published illustrators, and submit your work when it is judged 'in the ball park.' " Writers: "Don't send in just anything. Our catalog and guidelines are free for a SASE. Send for them. See what works for us, what we publish. 98% of rejected material comes from writers who never bothered to do their homework on us and find out what we do publish, first. As a result, their ideas are a total miss for our market from the word 'go.' " Poets: "Send in only your best work. If you're writing a structured poem, stick rigidly to meter and beat. Our philosophy favors clear ideas clearly communicated. Poems that leave their message a mystery don't work well in our market."

JULIAN MESSNER, 250 James St., Morristown NJ 07960. Imprint of Silver Burdett Press, Simon & Schuster Education Group. Book Publisher. Editor: Adrianne Ruggiero. See Silver Burdett Press listing.

■**METAMORPHOUS PRESS,** P.O. Box 10616, Portland OR 97210. (503) 228-4972. Book publisher. Acquisitions Editor: Lori Stephens. Estab. 1982. 10% of books from agented writers. Subsidy publishes 10%.

Nonfiction: Picture books: education. Young readers: education, music/dance. Middle readers: education, music/dance, self-help/esteem. Young adults: education, music/dance, self-help/esteem.

How to Contact/Writers: Fiction: Query. Nonfiction: Query; submit outline/synopsis and sample chapters. Reports on queries in 6-12 months. Publishes a book 1-2 years after acceptance. Will consider simultaneous and electronic submissions via disk or modem.

Illustration: Will review ms/illustration packages.

How to Contact/Illustrators: Ms/illustration packages: Query. Illustrations only: "vitae with samples of range and style." Reports on art samples only if interested.

Terms: Pays authors royalty of 10% based on wholesale price. Illustrators paid by author. Sends galleys to authors; dummies to illustrators. Book catalog available for large SAE and 52¢ postage.

Tips: Looks for "books that relate and illustrate the notion that we create our own realities, self-reliance and positive outlooks work best for us—creative metaphors and personal development guides given preference."

MILKWEED EDITIONS, Suite 400, 430 First Ave. North, Minneapolis MN 55401-1743. (612)332-3192. Book Publisher. Writers Contact: Children's reader. Illustrators Contact: Art Director. Publishes 4 middle readers/year; 0-1 young adult titles/year. 25% of books by first-time authors. "Works must embody humane values and contribute to cultural understanding. There is no primary theme."

Fiction: Middle readers, young adults: adventure, animal, contemporary, fantasy, history, humor, multicultural, nature/environment, problem novels, science fiction, suspense/mystery. Does not want to see anthologies, folktales, health, hi-lo, poetry, religion, romance, sports. Average length: middle readers—110-350 pages; young adults—110-350 pages. Published *Gildaen*, by Emilie Buchwald (middle reader, fantasy); *I Am Lavina Cumming*, by Susan Lowell (middle reader, contemporary).

Nonfiction: Middle readers, young adults: biographies. Average length: middle readers—110-350 pages; young adults—110-350 pages. "We have not published any nonfiction as of yet."

How to Contact/Writers: Fiction/nonfiction: Query; submit complete manuscript. Reports on queries in 2-3 weeks; mss in 1-6 months. Publishes a book 10-12 months after acceptance. Will consider simultaneous submissions.

Illustration: Works with 3 illustrators/year. Will review ms/illustration packages. Will review artwork for future assignments.

How to Contact/Illustrators: Ms/illustration packages: Query; submit manuscript with dummy. Illustrations only: Query with samples; provide resume, promo sheet, slides, tearsheets and client list. Reports in 4-6 weeks. Samples returned with SASE; samples filed. Originals returned at job's completion.

Terms: Pays authors royalty of 7½% based on retail price. Offers advance against royalties. Sends galleys to authors. Book catalog available for $1 to cover postage; ms guidelines available for SASE.

THE MILLBROOK PRESS, 2 Old New Milford Rd., Brookfield CT 06804. (203)740-2220. Book publisher. Manuscript Coordinator: Sarah DeCapua. Art Director: Judie Mills. Publishes 4 picture books/year; 40 young readers/year; 50 middle readers/year; 10 young adult titles/year. 10% of books by first-time authors; 10% of books from agented authors. Publishes nonfiction, concept-oriented/educational books.

Nonfiction: All levels: activity books, animal, arts/crafts, biography, careers, concept, geography, health, history, hobbies, multicultural, music/dance, nature/environment, reference, social issues, sports, science. No fiction or poetry. Average word length: picture books—minimal; young readers—5,000; middle readers—10,000; young adult/teens—20,000. Recently published *Frog Counts to Ten*, by John Liebler (grades K-3, picture book); *The Scopes Trial: Defending the Right to Teach*, by Arthur Blake (grades 4-6, history); *The U.S. Health Care Crisis*, by Victoria Sherrow (grades 7-up, contemporary issues).

How to Contact/Writers: Query. Submit outline/synopsis and 1 sample chapter. Reports on queries/mss in 1 month.

Illustration: Work with 12 illustrators/year. Will review ms/illustration packages. Will review artwork for future assignments. Contact: Judie Mills, art director.
How to Contact/Illustrators: Ms/illustration packages: Query; submit 1 chapter of ms with 1 piece of final art. Illustrations only: Query with samples; provide résumé, business card, promotional literature or tearsheets to be kept on file. Reports back only if interested.
Photography: Buys photos from freelancers. Buys stock and assigns work.
Terms: Pays author royalty of 5-7½% based on wholesale price or work purchased outright. Offers advances. Pays illustrators by the project, royalty of 3-7% based on wholesale price. Sends galleys to authors. Book catalog for SAE; ms guidelines for SASE.

MISTY HILL PRESS, 5024 Turner Rd., Sebastopol CA 95472. (707)823-7437. Book publisher. Editor-in-Chief: Sally Karste. 100% of books by first-time authors.
Fiction: Middle readers, young adults: history. Published *Trails to Poosey*, by Olive Cooke (young adults, historical fiction).
Nonfiction: Middle readers, young adults: history.
How to Contact/Writers: Fiction/nonfiction: Submit outline/synopsis and sample chapters. Reports on queries/ms in 2 weeks. Publishes a book 8 months after acceptance. Will consider simultaneous submissions.
Terms: Pays illustrators by the project. Sends galleys to authors.
Tips: Looking for "historical fiction: substantial research, good adventure or action against the historical setting."

MOREHOUSE PUBLISHING CO., 871 Ethan Allen Hwy., Ridgefield CT 06877. (203)431-3927. Fax: (203)431-3964. Book publisher. Estab. 1884. Editor: Deborah Grahame-Smith. Publishes 4 picture books/year. 75% of books by first-time authors.
Fiction: Picture books: animal, fantasy, folktales, multicultural, religion. Young readers: animal, fantasy, folktales, multicultural. Middle readers: fantasy, folktales, multicultural, poetry, religion. Young adults: fantasy, multicultural, poetry. Multicultural themes include "working together for the betterment of God's world." Does not want to see "anything other than traditional Christian values."
Nonfiction: Picture books: nature/environment, religion. Young readers: biography, nature/environment, religion. Middle readers: biography, religion, social issues. Young adults: biography, social issues.
How to Contact/Writers: Fiction/nonfiction: Submit outline/synopsis and sample chapters to Deborah Grahame-Smith. Reports on queries in 4-6 weeks; mss in 3 months. Publishes a book 1 year after acceptance.
Illustration: Works with 3 illustrators/year. Will review ms/illustration packages. Will review artwork for future assignments.
How to Contact/Illustrators: Ms/illustration packages: Submit 3 chapters of ms with 1 piece of final art. Illustrations only: Submit résumé, tearsheets. Reports on art samples in 4-6 weeks. Original artwork returned at job's completion. Contact: Gail Eltringham, art director.
Photography: Buys photos from freelancers. Buys stock images. Uses photos of children/youth in everyday life experiences.
Terms: Pays authors royalty of 6-15% based on retail price and purchases more outright. Offers average advance payment of $500. Pay illustrators by the project. Sends galleys to authors. Book catalog free on request.
Tips: Writers: "Prefer authors who can do their own illustrations. Be fresh, be fun, not pedantic, but let your work have a message." Illustrators: "Work hard to develop an original style." Looks for ms/illustration packages "with a religious or moral value while remaining fun and entertaining."

JOSHUA MORRIS PUBLISHING, 221 Danbury Rd., Wilton CT 06897. (203)761-9999. Fax: (203)761-5655. Subsidiary of Reader's Digest, Inc. Contact: Acquisition Editor. Art Direc-

Refer to the Business of Children's Writing & Illustrating for up-to-date marketing, tax and legal information.

tor: Julia Sabbagh. "We publish mostly early concept books and books for beginning readers. Most are in series of four titles and contain some kind of novelty element (i.e., lift the flap, die cut holes, book and soft toy, etc.). We publish 300-400 books per year." 5% of books by first-time authors; 5% of books from agented authors; 90% of books published on commission (book packaging).

Fiction: Picture books and young readers: activity books, adventure, animal, concept, nature/environment, reference, religion. Middle readers: animal, nature/environment, religion. Does not want to see poetry, short stories, science fiction. Average word length: picture books—300-400. Published *Whooo's There?*, by Lily Jones (ages 3-7, sound and light); *Ghostly Games*, by John Speirs, with additional text by Gill Speirs (ages 8-12, puzzle).

Nonfiction: Picture books, young readers and middle readers: activity books, animal, nature/environment, religion. Average word length: varies. Published *Alan Snow Complete Books (Dictionary, Atlas* and *Encyclopedia)*, by Alan Snow (ages 3-7, first reference); *Rain Forest Nature Search*, by Paul Sterry (ages 7-12, puzzle/activity).

How to Contact/Writers: Fiction/Nonfiction: Query. Nonfiction: Query. Reports on queries/mss in 3-4 months. Publishes a book 12-18 months after acceptance. Will consider simultaneous submissions and previously published work.

Illustration: Will review ms/illustration packages. Will review artwork for future assignments. Contact: Julie Sabbagh, art director.

How to Contact/Illustrators: Ms/illustration packages: Query. Illustrations only: Query with samples (nonreturnable). Provide résumé, promo sheet or tearsheets to be kept on file. Reports back only if interested. Original artwork returned (only if requested).

Photography: Buys stock and assigns work. Contact: Patricia Jennings, art director. Uses photos of animals and children. Model/property releases required. Publishes photo concept books. Uses 4×6 glossy, color prints and 4×5 transparencies. Submit résumé, promo sheet or tearsheets to be kept on file.

Terms: Pays authors royalty or work purchased outright. Offers advances. Pays illustrators by the project or royalty. Photographers paid per photo.

Tips: Best bets with this market are "innovative concept and beginning readers, and books that have a novelty element."

MORROW JUNIOR BOOKS, 1350 Avenue of the Americas, New York NY 10019. Division of the Hearst Corporation. Does not accept unsolicited manuscripts.

JOHN MUIR PUBLICATIONS, INC., P.O. Box 613, Santa Fe NM 87504-0613. (505)982-4078. Book publisher. Editorial Contact: Ken Luboff. Publishes 25 middle reader nonfiction picture books/year.

Nonfiction: Middle readers: animal, arts/crafts, biography, concept, hobbies, multicultural, nature/environment, science, social issues. Average word length: middle readers—12,000-15,000. Published *Kids Explore Series* (4 titles), by different authors (middle readers); *Kids Explore America's Hispanic Heritage, Kids Explore America's African-American Heritage*, etc.

How to Contact/Writers: Query. Reports on queries/mss in 4-6 weeks. Publishes a book 8-12 months after acceptance. Will consider simultaneous submissions.

Illustration: Reviews ms/illustration packages. Production Director, Kathryn Lloyd, will review artwork for future assignments.

How to Contact/Illustrators: Ms/illustration packages: Query, outline and 1 chapter for illustration; 4 original finished pieces and roughs of ideas. Illustrations only: Submit résumé and samples of art that have been reproduced or samples of original art for style.

Photography: Purchases photos from freelancers. Buys stock images. Buys "travel, animal" photos.

Terms: Pays authors on work-for-hire basis, occasionally royalties. Some books are paid by flat fee for illustration or by the project. Book catalog free on request.

Tips: "We want nonfiction books for 8- to 12-year-old readers that can sell in bookstores as well as gift stores, libraries and classrooms."

NAR PUBLICATIONS, P.O. Box 233, Barryville NY 12719. (914)557-8713. Book publisher. 50% of books by first-time authors; 100% of books from agented writers.

• This publisher is no longer soliciting manuscripts.
Fiction: "No young adult novels or books. Short picture books with limited text preferred."
How to Contact/Writers: Fiction/nonfiction: Query. Reports in 3 weeks. Publishes a book 9 months after acceptance. Will consider simultaneous and electronic submissions via disk.
Terms: Buys ms outright. Book catalog for 1 first-class stamp and #10 SAE.
Tips: "We have only published two books for children. Preschool to age 8 has best chance of acceptance. We no longer accept unagented manuscripts."

NATUREGRAPH PUBLISHER, INC., P.O. Box 1075, Happy Camp CA 96039. (916)493-5353. Fax: (916)493-5240. Contact: Barbara Brown. Publishes 2 adult titles/year, usable by young adults. ("We are not geared to young adult as such.") 100% of books by first-time authors.
Nonfiction: Young adult/teens: animal, nature/environment, Native American. Average word length: young adults—70,000.
How to Contact/Writers: Nonfiction: Query. Reports on queries in 2 weeks; mss in 2 months. Publishes a book 18 months after acceptance.
Photography: Buys photos from freelancers. Buys stock images.
Terms: Pays authors in royalties of 8-10% based on wholesale price. Pays illustrators by the project. "Authors are responsible for artwork of text. Publisher takes care of cover art or photography." Sends galleys to authors. Book catalog is free on request.

NEW DISCOVERY BOOKS, 250 James St., Morristown NJ 07960. Imprint of Silver Burdett Press, Simon & Schuster Education Group. Book publisher. Editor: Debbie Biber. See Silver Burdett Press listing.

NORTHLAND PUBLISHING, P.O. Box 1389, Flagstaff AZ 86002. (602)774-5251. Book publisher. Editor: Betti Albrecht. Art Director: Trina Stahl. Publishes 6 picture books/year; 2 young readers/year. 75% of books by first-time authors. Primary theme is West and Southwest regionals, Native American folktales.
Fiction: Picture books and young readers: animal, contemporary, folktales, history, multicultural/bilingual, nature/environment. "Our Native American folktales are enjoyed by readers of all ages, child through adult." No religion, science fiction, anthology. Average word length: picture books—800; young readers—1,500. Published *Master Birds*, retold by Vee Brown, illustrated by Baje Whitethorne (ages 7 and up); *Carlos the Squash Plant*, by Jan Romero Stevens, illustrated by Jeanne Arnold (ages 5 and up, bilingual Spanish/English book); *Building a Bridge*, by Lisa Shook Begaya, illustrated by Libba Tracy (ages 5 and up).
Nonfiction: Picture books and young readers: animal, multicultural, nature/environment. Average word length: picture books—1,500; young readers—1,500.
How to Contact/Writers: Fiction/Nonfiction: Query; submit complete ms with cover letter. Reports on queries in 1 month; mss in 2 months. "Acknowledgment sent immediately upon receipt." If ms and art are complete at time of acceptance, publication usually takes 1 year. Will consider simultaneous submissions.
Illustration: Works with 6-8 illustrators/year. Will review ms/illustration packages. Will review artwork for future assignments. Uses color artwork only.
How to Contact/Illustrators: Ms/illustration packages: Submit ms with samples; slides or color photocopies. Illustrations only: Query with samples, promo sheet, slides, tearsheets. Reports in 1 month. Samples returned with SASE. Original artwork returned at job's completion.
Terms: Pays authors/illustrators royalty of 4-7% based on wholesale price. Offers advances. "This depends so much on quality of work and quantity needed." Sends galleys to authors; dummies to illustrators. Ms guidelines available for SASE.
Tips: Receptive to "Native American folktales (must be retold by a Native American author)."

NORTHWORD PRESS, INC., P.O. Box 1360, Minocqua WI 54548. (715)356-7644. Managing Editor: Barbara Harold. Production Coordinator: Russ Kuepper. Publishes 10 picture books/year. 50% of books by first-time authors; 10% of books from agented authors. Publishes books pertaining to nature, wildlife and the environment. Also Native American topics.

Fiction: Picture books, young readers: animal, nature/environment. Does not want to see "anything without a strong nature/animal focus; no moralizing animal/nature stories (didactic)."

Nonfiction: Picture books, young readers: activity books, animal, nature/environment. Average word length: picture books—500-3,000; young readers—2,500-3,000. Published *Moose for Kids*, by Jeff Fair (ages 4-10, photo picture book); *Who Lives Here?*, by Dawn Baumann Brunke (ages 4-10, animal and habitat coloring guide series).

How to Contact/Writers: Fiction: Query. Nonfiction: Query; submit outline/synopsis and 1 sample chapter. Reports on queries in 2 months; mss in 3 months. Publishes a book 9-12 months after acceptance. Will consider simultaneous submissions.

Illustration: Works with 1-3 illustrators/year. Will review ms/illustration packages. Will review artwork for future assignments. Contact: Russ Kuepper, production coordinator.

How to Contact/Illustrators: Ms/illustration packages: Query. Submit 1 chapter of ms with 3 pieces of final art. Illustrations only: Query with samples. Reports back only if interested. Original artwork returned at job's completion.

Photography: Buys photos from freelancers. Contact: Larry Mishkar, photo editor. Uses nature and wildlife photos, full-color. Buys stock and assigns work. Model releases required. Publishes photo concept books. Uses color prints and 35mm transparencies. Query with samples. "Not responsible for damage to, or loss of, unsolicited materials."

Terms: Pays authors royalty based on wholesale price or work purchased outright. Offers negotiable advances. Pays illustrators by the project. Pays photographer by the project, per photo or royalty. Sends galleys to authors. Book catalog available for 9 × 12 SAE and 2 first-class stamps; ms guidelines available for SASE.

Tips: "The three key words are 'educational,' 'nature' and 'wildlife.' Beyond that, we're looking for fun, unusual and well-written manuscripts. We are expanding our children's line."

*THE OLIVER PRESS, INC., 2709 Lyndale Ave. S., Minneapolis MN 55408. Phone/fax: (612)871-9554. Book publisher. Editor: James Satter. Publishes 8 young adult titles/year. 10% of books by first-time authors. "We publish collective biographies of people who made an impact in one area of history, including science, government, archaeology, business and crime."

Nonfiction: Young adults: biography, history and science. "Authors should only suggest ideas that fit into one of our existing series." Average word length: young adult—20,000 words. Recently published *Great Justices of the Supreme Court*, by Nathan Aaseng (ages 10 and up, collective biography); *Women Inventors and Their Discoveries*, by Ethlie Ann Vare and Greg Ptacek (ages 10 and up, collective biography); and *The World's Greatest Explorers*, by William Scheller (ages 10 and up, collective biography).

How to Contact/Writers: Query. Submit outline/synopsis. Reports in 1 month. Publishes a book approximately 1 year after acceptance.

Photography: Buys photos from freelancers. Contact: James Satter, editor. Buys stock images. Looks primarily for photos of people in the news. Captions required. Uses 8 × 10 b&w prints. Submit cover letter, résumé and stock photo list.

Terms: Work purchased outright from authors for $750-1,250. Pays photographers per photo (range: $20-50). Sends galleys to authors upon request. Book catalog available for SASE; ms and art guidelines available for SASE.

Tips: "Authors should read some of the books we have already published before sending a query to The Oliver Press. Authors should propose collective biographies for one of our existing series."

*OPEN HAND PUBLISHING INC., P.O. Box 22048, Seattle WA 98122. (206)447-0597. Book publisher. Manuscript Editor: Pat Andrus. Publishes 1-3 children's books/year. 50% of books by first-time authors. Multicultural books: African-American theme or bilingual.
 • Open Hand is not currently accepting manuscripts.

Fiction: Picture books: folktales, history and African-American. Young readers and middle readers: history and African-American. Young adult/teens: African-American. Average

Illustrating Books Takes More Than Talent

Rosanne Main

"I've always loved children's books, and I knew creating them would be rewarding," says Rosanne Main, freelance designer/art director for Orchard Books. So she hatched a plan to trade a successful career as an art director in advertising for a more meaningful one in children's book publishing.

Before launching her dream career, Main researched the market. "I was amazed at the vast number of children's publishers!" she says. As she paged through picture books, Main was impressed by the quality within the field of "trade books" (titles carried by bookstores and libraries).

Enrolling in several evening courses on illustration and book design, Main learned important technical skills, like keeping gutters (the creases in the middle of the book between pages) clear of pertinent images. If you can't attend classes, advises Main, consult *How to Write and Illustrate Children's Books* by Treld Pelkey Bicknell and Felicity Trotman (North Light Books) or *How to Write, Illustrate, and Design Children's Books* by Frieda Gates (Lloyd-Simone). You'll find instructions for creating a storyboard and book dummy, valuable additions to an illustrator's portfolio.

An updated, book-oriented portfolio led Main to fulltime freelance design and art directing projects for various publishing houses. After chalking up five years in her new field, she approached Orchard Books because she shared their commitment to making quality children's books that stand the test of time. She's enjoyed designing and art directing for Orchard on a freelance basis for the past two years.

An important part of Main's work is reviewing countless submissions and selecting just the right illustrators for the books she is assigned. With so many submissions, you'd think it would be easy. Yet, Main says finding skilled illustrators who are also punctual with deadlines and flexible to work with is a challenge. To find such illustrators, art directors and designers search through files, pour over resource books such as *Creative Black Book*, attend student portfolio reviews, and seek referrals from colleagues.

How can *you* impress art directors? Take the time to visit libraries and bookstores to examine a publisher's books, and request guidelines and catalogs *before* you submit, says Main. That way, you won't mail drawings intended for toddlers to a publisher of historical biographies geared toward older children.

Review Orchard Books' catalog and you'll notice lively, imaginative portrayals of children (from toddlers to preteens), and their families and pets, illustrated in a variety of styles. You'll see many multicultural books among Orchard's releases, and a long list of awards and honors, including the Newbery Medal and Newbery and Caldecott Honor Book awards—all clues to the subject matter and quality of work Orchard seeks.

When submitting material to Orchard or elsewhere, your goals determine whom to contact and what to send. If you illustrate your own stories, send art and text to the editor, preferably in dummy form, as well as a typed manuscript. If you seek work as an illustrator, not a writer, mail 8 × 10 tearsheets or postcards of your work to the art department. Main prefers 8 × 10 samples because they are easier to file.

If your samples impress her, Main may request a portfolio review. Art directors gauge skill by checking key elements in your portfolio. Be sure to include sequential drawings. "You'd be surprised how difficult that is!" says Main. Show characters from different angles, with a variety of expressions and poses.

"Some artists draw wonderful animals, objects and landscapes, but have a hard time drawing faces, so they show people from the back." Wait to include people (if you intend to include them at all) once you've mastered them.

Finally, don't think you have to find a writer before submitting. "This is a common misconception," says Main. Likewise, if a writer asks you to illustrate a story, it's best to decline. "Paired submissions" are discouraged because matching a writer's words to an artist's style is a delicate balance and an art in itself. "Publishers prefer making the match themselves," says Main. Author-illustrated stories are acceptable because art and words from the same person tend to naturally complement each other.

These days, as Main examines a new book, she often does so with baby Jessie Lynn perched on her lap, to make sure each page pleases its intended audience as well as the grown-ups. Knowing her daughter's eyes brighten as she points to a colorful illustration makes the hard work of shepherding a manuscript to press worthwhile, and makes her career in children's books even more rewarding than she imagined.

—*Mary Cox*

Chris Raschka brings to life "two lonely characters, one black, one white" with simple, bright watercolor and charcoal illustrations and big, bold lettering in Yo! Yes?, his second picture book for Orchard. "Yow!," the final illustration in the 34-word book, which Raschka also wrote and designed, shows the joy of the two boys who have become friends after a chance meeting on the street. Yo! Yes? was well-received and chosen as a Caldecott Honor Book in 1994.

length: picture books—32-64 pages; young readers—64 pages; middle readers—64 pages; young adult/teens—120 pages.

Nonfiction: All levels: history and African-American. Average length: picture books—32-64 pages; young readers—64 pages; middle readers—64 pages; young adult/teens: 64-120 pages.

How to Contact/Writers: Fiction/nonfiction: Query. Reports on queries in 3 weeks; reports on mss in 5 weeks. Publishes a book 12-18 months after acceptance. Will consider simultaneous submissions.

Illustration: Will review ms/illustration packages. Contact: P. Anna Johnson, publisher. Will review artwork for future assignments.

How to Contact/Illustrators: Ms/illustration packages: Query. Illustrations only: Query with samples. Reports in 3 weeks. Original artwork returned "depending on the book."

Terms: Pays authors royalty of 5-10% based on wholesale price. Offers advances ("only under special circumstances"). Pays illustrators by the project; commission for the work. Sends galleys to authors. Book catalog available for SAE and 2 first-class stamps; ms guidelines available for SAE and 1 first-class stamp.

ORCA BOOK PUBLISHERS, P.O. Box 5626 Station B, Victoria, British Columbia V8R 6S4 Canada. (604)380-1229. Fax: (604)380-1892. Book publisher. Children's Books Editor: Ann Featherstone. Publishes 6 picture books/year; 1 or 2 middle readers/year; 1 or 2 young adult titles/year. 25% of books by first time authors. "We only consider authors and illustrators who are Canadian or who live in Canada."

Fiction: Picture books: contemporary, fairy tales, folktales, humor, nature/environment. Middle readers: adventure, contemporary, history, multicultural, nature/environment, problem novels, special needs, suspense/mystery. Young adults: contemporary, history, multicultural, nature/environment, problem novels, special needs. "Please, no cute little woodland creatures looking for their mother, name or home. Spare us also from *Alice in Wonderland* clones, where children meet talking animals that take them on 'exciting' adventures." Average word length: picture books—500-2,000; middle readers—25,000-35,000; young adult—35,000-60,000. Published *Thistle Broth*, by Richard Thompson, illustrated by Henry Fernandes; *Waiting for the Whales*, by Sheryl McFarlane, illustrated by Ron Lightburn.

Nonfiction: Picture books, young readers, middle readers: animal, nature/environment. "We have enough whale stories to hold us for a while." Average word length: picture books—300-500; middle readers—2,000-3,000. Published *Siwiti—A Whale's Story*, by Alexandra Morton, photographs by Robin and Alexandra Morton (ages 6-12, animal).

How to Contact/Writers: Fiction: Submit complete ms if picture book; submit outline/synopsis and 3 sample chapters. Nonfiction: Query with SASE. "All queries or unsolicited submissions should be accompanied by a SASE." Reports on queries in 3-6 weeks; mss in 1-3 months. Publishes book 12-18 months after acceptance.

Illustration: Works with 6 illustrators/year. Will review ms/illustration packages. Will review artwork for future assignments.

How to Contact/Illustrators: Ms/illustration packages: Submit ms with 3-4 pieces of final art. "Reproductions only, no original art please." Illustrations only: Query with samples; provide resume, slides. Reports in 6-8 weeks. Samples returned with SASE; samples filed. Original artwork returned at job's completion if picture books.

Terms: Pays authors royalty of 5-10% if picture book based on retail price. Offers advances (average amount: $500). Pays illustrators royalty of 5% minimum based on retail price or advance on royalty of $500. Sends galleys to authors. Book catalog available for legal or

---

Market conditions are constantly changing! If you're still using this book and it is 1996 or later, buy the newest edition of Children's Writer's & Illustrator's Market *at your favorite bookstore or order directly from Writer's Digest Books.*

8½ × 11 manila SAE and 2 first-class stamps. Ms guidelines available for SASE. Art guidelines not available.

Tips: "American authors and illustrators should remember that the U.S. stamps on their reply envelopes cannot be posted in any country outside of the U.S."

ORCHARD BOOKS, 95 Madison Ave., New York NY 10016. (212)686-7070. Division and imprint of Grolier, Inc. Book publisher. President and Publisher: Neal Porter. "We publish between 60 and 70 books yearly including fiction, poetry, picture books, and photo essays." 10-25% of books by first-time authors.
- This publisher has received numerous awards in the last few years for children's literature. The book *Missing May*, by Cynthia Rylant, received the 1993 Newbery Medal. Chris Raschka's *Yo! Yes* was a 1994 Caldecott Honor Book. Angela Johnson's *Toning the Sweep* won the Coretta Scott King Award.

Fiction: All levels: animal, anthology, contemporary, fantasy, folktales, history, humor, multicultural, nature/environment, poetry, science fiction, sports, suspense/mystery. Does not want to see anthropomorphized animals. Recently published *The Barn*, by Avi; *The Ear, the Eye, and the Arm*, by Nancy Farmer (both novels).

Nonfiction: Picture books, young readers: animal, history, multicultural, nature/environment, science, social issues. "We publish nonfiction on a very selective basis."

How to Contact/Writers: Send mss to attention of Submissions Committee. Fiction: Submit entire ms. Nonfiction: Submit outline/synopsis and sample chapters. Reports on queries in 2 weeks; mss in 1 month (longer for novels). Average length of time between acceptance of a book-length ms and publication of work "depends on the editorial work necessary. If none, about 8 months or longer if schedule of books dictates."

Illustration: Works with 40 illustrators/year. Editorial will review ms/illustration packages. "It is better to submit ms and illustration separately unless they are by the same person, or a pairing that is part of the project such as husband and wife." Will review artwork for future assignments. Contact: Art Department.

How to Contact/Illustrators: Ms/illustration packages: 3 chapters of ms with 1 piece of final art, remainder roughs. Illustrations only: Submit "tearsheets or photocopies or photostats of the work." Reports on art samples in 1 month. Samples returned with SASE. Original artwork returned at job's completion.

Terms: Pays authors in royalties "industry standard" based on retail price. Sends galleys to authors; dummies to illustrators. Book catalog free on request with 8½ × 11 SASE with 4 oz. postage.

OUR CHILD PRESS, 800 Maple Glen Lane, Wayne PA 19087-4797. (610)964-0606. Fax: (610)293-9038. Book publisher. President: Carol Hallenbeck. 90% of books by first-time authors.

Fiction/Nonfiction: All levels: adoption, multicultural, special needs. Word length: Open. Published *Don't Call Me Marda*, by Sheila Kelly Welch; *Is That Your Sister?* by Catherine and Sherry Burin; and *Oliver: A Story About Adoption*, by Lois Wichstrom.

How to Contact/Writers: Fiction/Nonfiction: Query or submit complete ms. Reports on queries/mss in 3 months. Publishes a book 6-12 months after acceptance.

Illustration: Works with 2 illustrators/year. Reviews ms/illustration packages. Will review artwork for future assignments.

How to Contact/Illustrators: Query first. Submit résumé, tearsheets and photocopies. Reports on art samples in 2 months. Original artwork returned at job's completion.

Terms: Pays authors in royalties of 5-10% based on wholesale price. Pays illustrators royalties of 5-10% based on wholesale price. Book catalog for business-size SAE and 52¢ postage.

Tips: Won't consider anything not related to adoption.

RICHARD C. OWEN PUBLISHERS, INC., Dept. CWIM-95, P.O. Box 585, Katonah NY 10536. (914)232-3903. Book publisher. Editor/Art Director: Janice Boland. Publishes 3-13 young readers/year. 90% of books by first-time authors. Publishes "child focused, meaningful books about characters and situations with which five, six, and seven-year-old children can identify. We include multicultural stories that present minorities in a positive and natural way. Our stories show the diversity in America."

Fiction: Picture books, young readers: contemporary, folktales, humor, multicultural, nature/environment. Does not want to see holiday, religious themes, moral teaching stories. No talking animals with personified human characteristics, jingles and rhymes, holiday stories, alphabet books, lists without plots, stories with nostalgic views of childhood, soft or sugar-coated tales. No stereotyping. Average word length: 40-100 words.

Nonfiction: Picture books, young readers: animals, careers, multicultural, nature/environment. Wants lively stories. No "encyclopedic" type of information stories. Average word length: 40-100 words.

How to Contact/Writers: Fiction/nonfiction: Submit complete ms. "*Must* request guidelines first with #10 SASE." Reports on mss in 2-6 weeks. Publishes a book 2-3 years after acceptance. Will consider simultaneous submissions.

Illustration: Works with 3-10 illustrators/year. Will review artwork for future assignments. Uses color artwork only.

How to Contact/Illustrators: Send color copies/reproductions or photos of art or provide tearsheets. Must request guidelines first. Reports only if interested. Samples filed.

Photography: Buys photos from freelancers. Contact: Janice Boland, art director. Wants photos that are child oriented; not interested in portraits. "Natural, bright, crisp and colorful—of children and of subjects and compositions attractive to children." Sometimes interested in stock photos for special projects. Uses 35mm, 2¼ × 2¼, color transparencies.

Terms: Pays authors royalties of 5% based on "monies we receive." Offers no advances. Pays illustrators and photographers by the project (variable). Sends galleys to authors. Ms/artist guidelines available for SASE.

Tips: Seeking "stories (both fiction and nonfiction) that have charm, magic, impact and appeal; that children living in today's society will want to read and reread; books with strong storylines, child-appealing language, action and interesting, vivid characters." Multicultural needs include "Ethnic true-to-life tales, folktales, Indian legends and stories about specific culture environments. We want our books to reflect the rich cultural heritage and diversity of this country without stereotyping." Trend is toward "quality books that portray various cultures in rich and interesting ways; well-constructed and developed books that make these cultures accessible to all."

PACIFIC PRESS, P.O. Box 7000, Boise ID 83707. (208)465-2500. Fax: (208)465-2531. Book publisher. Acquisitions Editor: Jerry D. Thomas. Publishes 2-4 picture books, 2-4 young readers, 2-4 middle readers, 4-6 young adult titles/year. 5% of books by first-time authors. Seventh-day Adventist Christian publishing house which publishes books pertaining to religion, spiritual values (strong spiritual slant).

Fiction: Picture books, young readers: religion. Middle readers: adventure, animal, contemporary, religion, suspense/mystery. Young adults: adventure, animal, religion, suspense/mystery. "All books have spiritual/religious themes." Does not want to see fantasy or totally non-factual stories. "We prefer true stories that are written in fiction style." Average word length: picture books—500-1,000; young readers—6,000-7,000; middle readers—25,000-33,000; young adult/teens—33,000-75,000. Recently published *500 Degrees in the Shade*, by Andy Demsky (teens); the Detective Zack series, by Jerry D. Thomas (8-12); and A Child's Steps to Jesus series by Linda Porter Carlyle (ages 3-7).

Nonfiction: All levels: religion. "We publish very little nonfiction for children. All manuscripts must have a religious/spiritual/health theme." Average word length: picture books—500-1,000; young readers—6,000-7,000; middle readers—25,000-33,000; young adult/teens—33,000-80,000. Recently published *Just Like You and Me*, by Ginger Ketting (ages 3-6).

How to Contact/Writers: Fiction: Submit complete ms; submit outline/synopsis and 2 sample chapters. Nonfiction: Query; submit complete ms; submit outline/synopsis and 2 sample chapters. Reports on queries in 1 month; mss in 2 months. Publishes a book 6-12 months after acceptance. Will consider simultaneous submissions and electronic submissions via disk or modem.

Illustration: Works with 4-6 illustrators/year. Will review artwork for future assignments. Contact: Randy Maxwell, advertising director.

How to Contact/Illustrators: Ms/illustration packages: Submit complete package. Illustrations only: Query with samples; submit portfolio for review. Reports in 2 weeks. Original artwork returned at job's completion.
Terms: Pays authors royalty of 6-16% based on wholesale price. Offers advances ($300-500). Pays illustrators by the project (range: $500-750); 6% royalty based on wholesale price. Sends galleys to authors. Book catalog available for 9×12 SASE. Ms guidelines available for SASE.
Tips: "Character building stories with a strong spiritual emphasis have the best chance of being published by our press. Also, adventure, and mystery stories that incorporate spirituality and character building are especially welcome."

PANDO PUBLICATIONS, 5396 Laurie Lane, Memphis, TN 38120. (901)682-8779. Book publisher. Estab. 1988. Owner: Andrew Bernstein. Publishes 2-6 middle readers/year; 2-6 young adults/year. 20% of books by first-time authors.
Fiction: Animal, concept, folktales, history, nature/environment. No poetry, science fiction, religion.
Nonfiction: Middle readers, young adults: activity books, animal, arts/crafts, biography, concept, cooking, geography, history, hobbies, how-to, multicultural, nature/environment, reference, science, social issues, special needs, sports. Average length: middle readers—175 pages; young adults—200 pages.
How to Contact/Writers: Fiction/Nonfiction: Query only. "All unsolicited manuscripts are destroyed. Please, no phone calls." Reports on queries in 6 months; on mss in 7 months. Publishes a book 1 year after acceptance. Will consider simultaneous submissions. "Prefers" electronic submissions via disk or modem.
Illustration: Works with 2 illustrators/year. Editorial will review all illustration packages.
How to Contact/Illustrators: Ms/illustrations: Query first. Illustrations only: Query with samples. Reports on art samples in 3 months. Original artwork returned at job's completion.
Terms: Pays authors royalty of 7-10% based on retail price. Offers average advance payment of "⅓ royalty due on first run." Sends galleys to authors; dummies to illustrators. "Book descriptions available on request."
Tips: Writers: "Find an untapped market then write to fill the need." Illustrators: "Find an author with a good idea and writing ability. Develop the book with the author. Join a professional group to meet people—ABA, publishers' groups, as well as writers' groups and publishing auxiliary groups. Talk to printers." Looks for "how-to books, but will consider anything."

PARENTING PRESS, INC., P.O. Box 75267, Seattle WA 98125. (206)364-2900. Fax: (206)364-0702. Book publisher. Estab. 1979. Associate Publisher: Carolyn Threadgill. Publishes 4-5 books/year for parents or/and children and those who work with them. 40% of books by first-time authors.
Fiction: Publishes social skills books, problem-solving books, safety books, dealing-with-feelings books that use a "fictional" vehicle for the information. "We rarely publish straight fiction." Recently published *Bully on the Bus*, by Carl W. Bosch, illustrations by Rebekah J. Strecker (ages 7-11); *On The Wings of a Butterfly*, by Marilyn Maple, Ph.D., illustrations by Sandy Haight (ages 6-11); *I'm Mad*, by Elizabeth Crary, illustrations by Jean Whitney (ages 3-9); and *I Want It*, by Elizabeth Crary, illustrated by Marina Megal.
Nonfiction: Picture books: health, social skills building. Young readers: health, social skills building books. Middle readers: health, social skills building. No books on "new baby; coping with a new sibling; cookbooks; manners; books about disabilities (which we don't publish at present); animal characters in anything; books that tell children what they should do, instead of giving options." Average word length: picture books—500-800; young readers—1,000-2,000; middle readers—up to 10,000. Published *Kids to the Rescue*, by Maribeth and Darwin Boelts (ages 4-12).
How to Contact/Writers: Fiction: "We publish educational books for children in story format. *No straight fiction*." Nonfiction: Query. Reports on queries in 2 weeks; mss in 1 month, "after requested." Publishes a book 10-11 months after acceptance. Will consider simultaneous submissions.

Illustrations: Works with 3 illustrators/year. Will review ms/illustration packages. "We do reserve the right to find our own illustrator, however." Will review artwork for future assignments. Contact: John Shoemaker.

How to Contact/Illustrators: Ms/illustration packages: Query. Illustrations only: Submit "résumé, samples of art/drawings (no original art); photocopies or color photocopies okay."

Terms: Pays authors in royalties of 4% based on net. Outright purchase of ms, "negotiated on a case-by-case basis. Not common for us." Offers average advance of $150. Pays illustrators (for text) by the project; 3-4% royalty based on wholesale price. Pays illustrators (for covers) by the project ($300-800). Sends galleys to authors; dummies to illustrators. Book catalog/ms guidelines for #10 SAE and 1 first-class stamp.

Tips: Writers: "Query publishers who already market to the same audience. We often get manuscripts (good ones) totally unsuitable to our market." Illustrators: "We pay attention to artists who are willing to submit an illustration on speculation." Looking for "social skills building books for children, books that empower children, books that encourage decision making, books that are balanced ethnically and in gender."

PAULIST PRESS, 997 Macarthur Blvd., Mahwah NJ 07430. (201)825-7300. Fax: (201)825-8345. Book publisher. Estab. 1865. Editor: Karen Scialabba. Publishes 9-11 picture books/year; 6-7 young reader titles/year; 3-4 middle reader titles/year. 70% of books by first-time authors; 30% of books from agented writers.

Fiction: Picture books: animal, concept, folktales, health, history, multicultural, nature/environment, religion, special needs. Young readers, middle readers: concept, contemporary, folktales, health, history, multicultural, nature/environment, religion, special needs. Young adults: anthology, concept, contemporary, history, multicultural, nature/environment, religion, special needs. Average length: picture books—24 pages; young readers—24-32 pages; middle readers—64 pages. Recently published *Sometimes You Just Have to Tell Somebody*, by Ruth V. Cullen, illustrated by Emil Antonucci (ages 9-11, moral/value concept book); *The Hurt*, by Teddi Doleski, illustrated by William Hart McNichols (ages 6-8, moral/value concept book); and *Love Is Always There*, by Lisa Kent, illustrated by Mikki Machlin (ages 4-10, moral/value concept book).

Nonfiction: Picture books: activity books, animal, biography, concept, health, history multicultural, nature/environment, religion, social issues, special needs. Young readers: activity books, animal, arts/crafts, biography, concept, health, history, multicultural, nature/environment, religion, social issues, special needs, textbooks. Middle readers: activity books, animal, biography, concept, health, history, multicultural, nature/environment, religion, self help, social issues, special needs, textbooks. Young adults: biography, careers, concept, cooking, health, history, multicultural, nature/environment, religion, self help, social issues, special needs, textbooks. Recently published *A Child's Bible, Old and New Testaments*, (The Old Testament rewritten for children, by Ann Edwards; The New Testament rewritten for children, by Shirley Steen ages 9-11); and *First Bible Stories*, by Lawrence Waddy, illustrated by Mark Mitchell (ages 5-9 years).

How to Contact/Writers: Fiction/nonfiction: Submit complete ms. Reports on queries in 1-2 months; mss in 2-3 months. Publishes a book 12-16 months after acceptance.

Illustration: Works with 10-12 illustrators/year. Editorial will review all varieties of ms/illustration packages. Contact: Karen Scialabba, children's book editor.

How to Contact/Illustrators: Ms/illustration packages: Complete ms with 1 piece of final art, remainder roughs. Illustrations only: Submit résumé, tearsheets. Reports on art samples in 6 weeks. Original artwork returned at job's completion, "if requested by illustrator."

Photography: Buys photos from freelancers. Contact: Karen Scialabba. Works on assignment only. Uses inspirational photos.

Terms: Pays authors royalty of 8% based on retail price. Offers average advance payment of $450-$650. Pays illustrators by the project (range: $50-100) or royalty of 2-6% based on retail price. Factors used to determine final payment: color art, b&w, number of illustrations, complexity of work. Pay for separate authors and illustrators: Author paid by royalty rate; illustrator paid by flat fee, sometimes by royalty. Sends galleys to authors; dummies to illustrators.

Tips: Not interested in reviewing novels. Looking for "concept books for young readers that explore self-esteem, community involvement and care, social issues, families and spiritual development."

*PAVILION BOOKS LTD., 26 Upper Ground, London SE1 9PD. (071)620-1666. Fax: (071)620-1314. Imprint: Pavilion Children's Books. Book publisher. Children's Editor: Jo Fletcher-Watson. Publishes 4-6 picture books/year; 10-15 middle readers/year. 5-10 young adult titles/year. 10% of books are by first-time authors. Publishes mostly 'classic' children's stories and collections of myths/legends etc.
Fiction: Picture books: contemporary, folktales, humor. Young readers: anthology, folktales. Middle readers, young adults: anthology, contemporary, folktales. Does not want to see poetry, science fiction. Average word length: picture books—250-300; middle readers—10,000-20,000; young adults—40,000-50,000.
How to Contact/Writers: Submit complete manuscript (if short). Submit outline/synopsis and 2 sample chapters. Reports on mss in 6 weeks. Will consider previously published submissions.
Illustration: Works with 10 illustrators/year. Contact: Jo Fletcher-Watson. Will review ms/illustration packages. Will review artwork for future assignments.
How to Contact/Illustrators: Ms/illustration packages: Query. Illustrations only: Query with samples. Reports in 6 weeks. Samples returned with SASE; samples filed. Original artwork returned at job's completion.
Terms: Pay varies depending on individual titles. Sends galleys to authors.

*PEACHTREE PUBLISHERS, LTD., 494 Armour Circle NE, Atlanta GA 30324. (404)876-8761. Fax: (404)875-2578. Book publisher. Editorial: Helen Harriss.
Fiction: Picture books: adventure, animal, concept, fantasy, history, nature/environment. Young readers: adventure, animal, concept, fantasy, history, nature/environment, poetry. Middle readers: adventure, animal, history, nature/environment. Young adults: history, humor, nature/environment. Does not want to see science fiction, romance.
Nonfiction: Picture books: animal, history, nature/environment. Young readers, middle readers, young adults: animal, biography, history, nature/environment. Does not want to see sports, religion.
How to Contact/Writers: Fiction/Nonfiction: Submit complete manuscript. Reports on queries in 2-3 months; mss in 4 months. Publishes a book 1-1½ years after acceptance. Will consider simultaneous and previously published submissions.
Illustration: Works with 4 illustrators/year. Editorial will review manuscript/illustration packages. Will review artwork for future assignments.
How to Contact/Illustrators: Ms/illustration packages: Submit ms. Illustrations only: Query with samples, résumé, slides, color copies to keep on file. Reports back only if interested. Samples returned with SASE; samples filed.
Terms: Book catalog available for SAE. Manuscript guidelines for SASE.

■PEARTREE, P.O. Box 14533, Clearwater FL 34629-4533. (813)531-4973. Book publisher. Owner: Barbara Birenbaum. Publishes 1-5 young readers/year; 1-5 middle readers/year. 50% of books by first-time authors; 50% subsidy publishes. "Publishes events (i.e. Liberty Centennial, Groundhog Day) and general stories with 'lessons,' no Christian themes."
Fiction: Books for readers/grades 2-6: adventure, animal, environment/nature, safety, contemporary, hi-lo, holidays, multicultural. Does not want to see material on religion, science fiction, suspense, sports (per se), anthology or folktales.
How to Contact/Writers: Query with SASE. Reports on queries in 2 weeks; mss in 3-6 months. Publishes book 9 months after acceptance. Will consider simultaneous submissions and previously published work.

The asterisk before a listing indicates the listing is new in this edition.

Illustration: Works with 3 illustrators/year. Will review ms/illustration packages. Uses primarily b&w artwork with text.

How to Contact/Illustrators: Ms/illustration packages: Query; then submit ms with dummy. Illustrations only: Query with samples and SASE. Samples returned with SASE; samples filed ("if we anticipate an interest").

Terms: Work purchased outright. Other methods of payment include profits from sales of books. Pays illustrators by the project (range—$10 per illustration to $200 per book). Sends galleys to authors.

Tips: "We will consider publishing and marketing books as subsidy when major houses reject titles. Be willing to get illustrations in books at minimum cost. Understand that small presses offer budding artists/writers chance to get in print and 'launch' careers on shoe-string budgets."

PELICAN PUBLISHING CO. INC., 1101 Monroe St., Gretna LA 70053. (504)368-1175. Book publisher. Estab. 1926. Editor: Nina Kooij. Production Manager: Dana Bilbray. Publishes 6 picture books/year; 2 middle reader titles/year. 20% of books from agented writers.

Fiction: Picture books, young readers: folktales, history, multicultural, nature/environment, religion. Middle readers: folktales, history, multicultural, nature/environment, religion, suspense/mystery. Multicultural needs include stories about Native Americans and African-Americans. Does not want animal stories, general Christmas stories, "day at school" or "accept yourself" stories. Average word length: picture books—32 pages; middle readers—112 pages. Recently published *Toby Belfer's Seder: A Passover Story Retold*, by Gloria Teles Pushker (ages 5-8), describes the Jewish holiday; *Little Freddie's Legacy*, by Kathryn Cocquyt, illustrated by Sylvia Corbett (novel about a horse running a famous race in Ireland) (ages 8-12).

Nonfiction: Young readers: biography, health, history, multicultural, music/dance, nature/environment, religion. Middle readers: biography, cooking, health, history, multicultural, music/dance, nature/environment, religion, sports. Published *Floridians All*, by George S. Fichter, illustrated by George Cardin (ages 8-12, collection of biographies on famous Florida figures).

How to Contact/Writers: Fiction/Nonfiction: Query. Reports on queries in 1 month; mss in 3 months. Publishes a book 12-18 months after acceptance.

Illustration: Works with 5 illustrators/year. Will review ms/illustration packages. Will file artwork for future assignments.

How to Contact/Illustrators: Ms/illustration packages: Query first. Illustrations only: Query with samples (no originals). Reports on ms/art samples only if interested.

Terms: Pays authors in royalties; buys ms outright "rarely." Sends galleys to authors.

Tips: No anthropomorphic stories, pet stories (fiction or nonfiction), fantasy, poetry, science fiction or romance. Writers: "Be as original as possible. Develop characters that lend themselves to series and always be thinking of new and interesting situations for those series. Give your story a strong hook—something that will appeal to a well-defined audience. There is a lot of competition out there for general themes." Looks for: "writers whose stories have specific 'hooks' and audiences, and who actively promote their work." Foresees more books on divorced families in the future.

PENGUIN USA, 375 Hudson St., New York NY 10014. See listings for Dial Books for Young Readers, Dutton Children's Books, and Puffin Books.

● Penguin USA ranks fifth, based on net sales of the top 12 children's publishers.

PERSPECTIVES PRESS, P.O. Box 90318, Indianapolis IN 46290-0318. (317)872-3055. Book publisher. Estab. 1982. Publisher: Pat Johnston. Publishes 1-3 picture books/year; 1-3 young reader titles/year. 95% of books by first-time authors.

Fiction/Nonfiction: Picture books, young readers: adoption, foster care, donor insemination or surrogacy. Does not want young adult material. Published *Lucy's Feet*, by Stephanie Stein, illustrated by Kathryn A. Imler.

How to Contact/Writers: Fiction/nonfiction: Query or submit outline/synopsis and sample chapters. "No query necessary on picture books." Reports on queries in 2 weeks; mss in 6 weeks. Publishes a book 6-10 months after acceptance. Will consider simultaneous submissions.

Illustration: Works with 1-2 illustrators/year.

How to Contact/Illustrators: Illustrators only: Submit promo sheet and client list. Reports on art samples only if interested.

Terms: Pays authors royalties of 5-15% based on net sales or by work purchased outright. Pays illustrators royalty or by the project. Sends galleys to authors; dummies to illustrators. Book catalog, ms guidelines available for #10 SAE and 2 first-class stamps.

Tips: "Do your homework! I'm amazed at the number of authors who don't bother to check that we have a very limited interest area and subsequently submit unsolicited material that is completely inappropriate for us. For children, we focus *exclusively* on issues of adoption and interim (foster) care plus families built by donor insemination or surrogacy; for adults we also include infertility issues."

PHILOMEL BOOKS, 200 Madison Ave., New York NY 10016. (212)951-8700. Imprint of The Putnam & Grosset Group. Book publisher. Editorial Director: Patricia Gauch. Associate Editor: Michael Green. Editorial Contact: David Bridge. Art Director: Cecilia Yung. Publishes 30 picture books/year; 5-10 young reader titles/year. 20% of books by first-time authors; 80% of books from agented writers.

Fiction: All levels: adventure, animal, fantasy, folktales, history, nature/environment, special needs, poetry, multicultural. Middle readers, young adults: problem novels. No concept picture books, mass-market "character" books, or series.

Nonfiction: All levels: arts/crafts, biography, history, multicultural, music/dance. "Creative nonfiction on any subject." Average length: "not to exceed 150 pages."

How to Contact/Writers: Fiction/Nonfiction: Query; submit outline/synopsis and sample chapters. Reports on queries in 4-6 weeks. Publishes a book 2 years after acceptance.

Illustration: Works with 20-25 illustrators/year. Will review ms/illustration packages. Will review artwork for future assignments.

How to Contact/Illustrators: Ms/illustration packages: Query first. Illustrations only: Query with samples. Send resume, promo sheet, portfolio, slides, client list, tearsheets or arrange personal portfolio review. Reports on art samples in 2 months. Original artwork returned at job's completion.

Terms: Pays authors in royalties. Average advance payment "varies." Illustrators paid by advance and in royalties. Sends galleys to authors; dummies to illustrators. Book catalog, ms/artist's guidelines free on request with SASE (9×12 envelope for catalog).

Tips: Wants "unique fiction or nonfiction with a strong voice and lasting quality. Discover your own voice and own story—and persevere." Looks for "something unusual, original, well-written. Fine art. The genre (fantasy, contemporary, or historical fiction) is not so important as the story itself, and the spirited life the story allows its main character. We are also interested in receiving adolescent novels, particularly novels that contain regional spirit, such as a story about a young boy or girl written from a Southern, Southwestern or Northwestern perspective."

PIPPIN PRESS, 229 E. 85th St., Gracie Station, Box 1347, New York NY 10028. (212)288-4920. Fax: (212)563-5703. Children's book publisher. Estab. 1987. Publisher/President: Barbara Francis. Publishes 6-8 books/year. "Not interested in young adult books." *Query letter must precede all submissions.*

Fiction: Picture books, young readers, middle readers: adventure, animal, fantasy, folktales, humor, history, multicultural, nature/environment, suspense/mystery. Multicultural needs include "original material rather than retellings or adaptations; written by a person of the particular ethnic group." Average word length: picture books—750-1,500; young readers—2,000-3,000; middle readers—6,000-10,000. Recently published *The Spinner's Daughter*, by Amy Littlesugar, illustrated by Robert Quackenbush; *The Sounds of Summer*, by David Updike, illustrated by Robert Andrew Parker (ages 7-10); and *Windmill Hill*, by Hope Slaughter, illustrated by Edward Frascino (ages 7-10).

Nonfiction: Picture books, young readers, middle readers: animal, arts/crafts, biography, geography, history, multicultural, music/dance, nature/environment, science, social issues. Published *James Madison and Dolley Madison and Their Times*, written and illustrated by

Robert Quackenbush (ages 7-11); *Take Me to Your Liter,* by Charles Keller, illustrated by Gregory Filling (ages 7-11, science and math jokes). No young adult books.

How to Contact/Writers: Fiction/nonfiction: Query with SASE. No unsolicited mss. Reports on queries in 2-3 weeks; solicited mss in 2-3 months. Publishes a book 1-2 years after acceptance. Will consider simultaneous submissions.

Illustration: Works with 6-8 illustrators/year. Send query with SASE before sending any artwork. Contact: Barbara Francis.

How to Contact/Illustrators: Illustrations only: Query; provide samples, résumé, client list and tearsheets. "I see illustrators by appointment." Reports on art samples only if interested. Original artwork returned at job's completion.

Photography: Buys photos from freelancers. Contact: Barbara Francis.

Terms: Pays authors in royalties. Pays illustrators royalties or by the project. Sends galleys to authors; dummies to illustrators. "The illustrator prepares the dummy on picture books; dummies for longer books prepared by the designer are submitted to the illustrator." Book catalog available for 6×9 SASE; ms/artist's guidelines for #10 SASE.

Tips: "We receive too many unsolicited mss even though our guidelines specify *query only.* We will be publishing more transitional books, i.e. picture storybooks for ages 7-10 and more imaginative nonfiction for ages 6-10. We are looking for chapter books, especially humorous ones, and will continue to publish writers and illustrators with track records."

*PLANET DEXTER, One Jacob Way, Reading MA 01867. (617)944-3700. Imprint of Addison-Wesley Publishing Co. Book Publisher. Contact: Liz Doyle. Publishes 10-15 young readers, middle readers/year. 25% of books by first-time authors. Publishes nonfiction interactive books—mainly math and science. No fiction, poetry, whole language or early readers at all. "All of our products are 'book and thing' packages; all proposals should address the 'thing' that would accompany the book (e.g.: calculator, dice, cards). The 'thing' is an integral part of the product and not just a 'value-added item.' "

Nonfiction: Young readers, middle readers: hobbies, how-to, nature/environment, science, math. No curriculum-oriented or textbook-style manuscripts; no characters or narratives. Average word length: middle readers—10,000; young readers—5,000. Recently published *Planet Dexter's Calculator Mania* (comes with calculator); *Planet Dexter's Money Madness* (comes with real U.S. coins); and *Planet Dexter's Roddy!* (comes with Cuisenaire rods)—all math titles developed inhouse.

How to Contact/Writers: Query. Submit outline/synopsis and 2 sample chapters with SASE. Reports in 6-8 weeks. Publishes a book 18 months after acceptance.

Illustration: Works with 1-2 illustrators/year. Uses color artwork only.

Terms: Pay authors royalty. Work purchased outright from authors. Offers advances. Pays illustrators/photographers by the project. Sends final ms to authors for review; dummies to illustrators. Ms guidelines available for SASE.

Tips: "The more thorough a proposal, the better. Include outline, competition analysis, marketing 'hooks,' etc. Children's publishing is as competitive as adult's, so preparation on the author's part is key. We want fun, hip, irreverent, educational titles—books that kids learn from without realizing it (we call it 'stealth learning')."

PLAYERS PRESS, INC., P.O. Box 1132, Studio City CA 91614. (818)789-4980. Book publisher. Estab. 1965. Vice President/Editorial: R. W. Gordon. Publishes 2-10 young readers dramatic plays and musicals/year; 2-10 middle readers dramatic plays and musicals/year; 4-20 young adults dramatic plays and musicals/year. 35% of books by first-time authors; 1% of books from agented writers.

Fiction: "We use all categories (young readers, middle readers, young adults) but only for dramatic plays and/or musicals. No novels or storybooks."

Nonfiction: "Any children's nonfiction pertaining to the entertainment industry, performing arts and how-to for the theatrical arts only."

How to Contact/Writers: Fiction/nonfiction: Submit plays or outline/synopsis and sample chapters of entertainment books. Reports on queries in 2-4 weeks; mss in 3-4 months. Publishes a book 10 months after acceptance. No simultaneous submissions.

Illustration: Associate Editor will review artwork for future assignments.

How to Contact/Illustrators: Ms/illustration packages: Query first. Illustrations only: Submit résumé, tearsheets. Reports on art samples only if interested.

Terms: Pays authors in royalties of 2-20% based on retail price. Pay illustrators by the project; royalties range from 2-5%. Sends galleys to authors; dummies to illustrators. Book catalog available for $1.

Tips: Looks for "plays/musicals and books pertaining to the performing arts only."

■**POCAHONTAS PRESS, INC.**, 832 Hutcheson Dr., Blacksburg VA 24060-3259. (703)951-0467. Book Publisher. Editorial contact: Mary C. Holliman. Publishes 1-2 middle readers/year. Subsidy publishes 50%.

Nonfiction: Middle readers, young adults/teens: biography, careers, history, hobbies, multicultural, nature/environment, science, sports and textbooks. No pre-school or fiction. Recently published *Quarter-Acre of Heartache*, by C.C. Smith (young adult, Indian battle to save reservation); *Mountain Summer*, by Bill Mashburn; *Talking Together—A Parent's Guide to the Development, Enrichment, and Problems of Speech and Language*, by Katherine F. Schetz and Stuart Cassell, illustrated by Pamela Taylor (for adults and young adults).

How to Contact/Writers: Query; submit outline/synopsis and sample chapters. Reports on queries in 3-4 weeks; mss in 1-2 months. Publishes a book "probably as much as a year" after acceptance.

Illustrations: Will review all varieties of ms illustration packages. Prefers "black ink, though will sometimes accept pencil drawings. No color." Contact: David B. Wallace, editorial associate.

Terms: Pays authors in royalties of 5-10% based on actual receipts. Pays illustrators either by the project $20/hour or in royalties of 5-10% based on actual receipts. Sends galleys to authors; dummies to illustrators. Book catalog free on request. Ms guidelines not available.

Tips: "Have respect for your child reader, and remember that the actual reader is often an adult. Don't talk down and make jokes or references that are beyond the child's experience. Please, avoid the caricature and the scary." Looks for "a story, well told, about a real person, not necessarily well known, who has done something interesting or unusual or achieved something from a poor start." Pocahontas Press is "currently overloaded with manuscripts ready to publish, and won't be able to consider any for some time."

*POLYCHROME PUBLISHING CORPORATION, 4509 N. Francisco, Chicago IL 60625. (312)478-4455. Fax: (312)478-0786. Book publisher. Contact: Editorial Board. Publishes 2-4 picture books/year; 1-2 middle readers/year; and 1-2 young adult titles/year. 50% of books are by first-time authors. Books aimed at children of Asian ancestry in the United States.

Fiction: All levels: adventure, contemporary, history, multicultural. Multicultural needs include Asian American children's experiences. Not interested in animal stories, fables, fairy tales, folk tales. Recently published *Nene and the Horrible Math Monster*, by Marie Villanueva; *Stella: On the Edge of Popularity*, by Lauren Lee.

Nonfiction: All levels: history, multicultural. Multicultural needs include Asian-American themes.

How to Contact/Writers: Fiction/Nonfiction: Submit complete manuscript. Reports on queries in 3-4 months; mss in 4-6 months. Publishes a book 1-2 years after acceptance. Will consider simultaneous submissions.

Illustration: Works with 4 illustrators/year. Will review ms/illustration packages. Contact: Editorial Board. Will review artwork for future assignments.

How to Contact/Illustrators: Ms/illustration packages: Submit ms with bio of author re story background. Illustrations only: Query with résumé and samples (can be photocopies) of drawings of multicultural children. Reports back only if interested. Samples returned with SASE; samples filed "only if under consideration for future work."

Terms: Pays authors royalty of 2-10% based on wholesale price. Work purchased outright ($25 minimum). Pays illustrators 2-10% royalty based on wholesale price. Sends galleys to authors; dummies to illustrators. Book catalog available for #10 SAE and 52¢. Manuscript guidelines available for SASE.

Tips: Wants "stories about experiences that will ring true with Asian Americans."

■**THE PRESERVATION PRESS**, 1785 Massachusetts Ave. NW, Washington DC 20036. (202)673-4057. Fax: (202)673-4172. Subsidiary of the National Trust for Historic Preservation. Book publisher. Director: Scott Gerloff. Publishes 3 picture books/year; 2 young readers/year; 1 middle reader/year. 20% of books by first-time authors; 25% of books from agented authors; 40% subsidy published. Publishes books about architecture; "preservation of cultural sites and objects."
Nonfiction: Picture books, young readers, middle readers and young adults: activity books, history, architecture, American culture. Recently published *Under Every Roof*, by Patricia Brown Glenn (young reader, architecture); *Bridges Go From Here To There*, by Forrest Wilson (young reader, architecture); *Daily Life in a Victorian House*, by Laura Wilson (middle reader).
How to Contact/Writers: Submit outline/synopsis and 1 sample chapter. Reports on queries in 3 weeks; mss in 2 months. Publishes a book 12-18 months after acceptance. Will consider simultaneous submissions and previously published work.
Illustration: Will review ms/illustration packages.
How to Contact/Illustrators: Ms/illustration packages: Submit 1-2 chapters of ms with 3-4 pieces of final art. Reports in 3-4 weeks. Original artwork returned at job's completion.
Photography: Photographers should provide résumé, business card, promotional literature and tearsheets to be kept on file.
Terms: Pays authors royalty of 5-15% based on retail price. Offers advances of $800-1,600. Pays illustrators and photographers flat fee. Sends galleys to authors; dummies to illustrators. Book catalog available for 9 × 12 SAE and 2 first-class stamps.
Tips: Looks for "an energetic, hands-on approach for kids to gain an appreciation for the variety and depth of their American cultural heritage."

THE PRESS OF MACDONALD & REINECKE, Imprint of Padre Productions, Box 840, Arroyo Grande CA 93421-0840. (805)473-1947. Book publisher. Estab. 1974. Editor: Lachlan P. MacDonald. 80% of books by first-time authors; 5% of books from agented authors.
Fiction: Middle readers, young adults: folktales, history, nature. No fantasy, mystery, detective, westerns, romances. Average length: middle reader—120-140 pages.
Nonfiction: Middle readers, young adults: history, nature/environment. Average length: middle readers—120 pages.
How to Contact/Writers: Fiction: Submit outline/synopsis and sample chapters. Nonfiction: Submit complete ms. Reports on queries in 2 weeks; mss in 4 months. Publishes a book 1 year after acceptance. Will consider simultaneous submissions.
Illustration: Works with 8-12 illustrators/year. Will review ms/illustration packages.
How to Contact/Illustrators: Illustrations only: Submit tearsheets. Reports on art samples only if interested.
Terms: Pays authors in royalties based on retail price. Illustrators paid by the project. Sends galleys to authors; dummies to illustrators. Book catalogs for 9 × 12 SAE and 52¢ in first-class postage. Ms guidelines/artist's guidelines for #10 SASE.
Tips: Writers: "Concentrate on nonfiction that recognizes changes in today's audience and includes minority and gender considerations without tokenism. The Press of MacDonald & Reinecke is devoted to highly selected works of drama, fiction, poetry and literary nonfiction. Juveniles must be suitable for 140-page books appealing to both boys and girls in the 8-14 year range of readers." Illustrators: "There is a desperate lack of realism by illustrators who can depict proportionate bodies and anatomy. The flood of torn-paper and poster junk is appalling." Looks for: "A book of historical nonfiction of U.S. regional interest with illustrations that have 19th century elegance and realistic character representations, about topics that still matter today."

The Subject Index, located before the General Index, lists book and magazine publishers by their fiction and nonfiction needs.

PRICE STERN SLOAN, Inc., 11150 Olympic Blvd., Los Angeles CA 90064. (310)477-6100. A Member of the Putnam & Grosset Group. Subsidiaries: Troubador Press. Book publisher. Contact: Editorial Assistant. Publishes 0-4 picture books/year; 20-40 young reader titles/year; 10-20 middle reader titles/year; 0-6 young adult titles/year. 35% of books by first-time authors; 65% of books from agented writers; 10% from packagers.

Fiction: Young readers, middle readers: novelty, mass-market projects. Recently published *Fly Away Home*, by K.D. Plum (ages 2 and up, die-cut story book); *Little Box Books*, by Chuck Reasoner (ages 3 and up, 4 die-cut board books in a box with a plastic handle); *The Night Before Halloween House*, by C.J. Ochetree (ages 6 and up, die-cut house for readers to assemble and decorate with stickers).

Nonfiction: Young readers, middle readers, young adults: novelty, mass-market projects. Recently published *Slam-o-Rama*, by Ann Braybrooks (ages 5 and up, book of games with play materials included); *Tell Me About When I Was a Baby*, by Lisa Rojany (ages 3 and up, pop-up book); *Mad Mysteries*, by David LaRochelle (ages 6 and up, puzzle game book).

How to Contact/Writers: Fiction/nonfiction: Query; submit outline/synopsis and entire ms or 1-3 sample chapters. Reports on queries/mss in 2-3 months. Publishes a book 1 year after acceptance. Will consider simultaneous submissions and previously published work, if stated.

Illustration: Will review ms/illustration packages. Will review artwork for future assignments. "Please do not send original artwork."

How to Contact/Illustrators: Ms/illustration packages: Query; submit 1-3 chapters of ms with 1-2 pieces of final art (color copies—no original work). Illustrations only: Query with samples; provide résumé, promo sheet, portfolio, tearsheets to be kept on file. Reports in 2-3 months.

Photography: Contact: Art Director. Buys stock and assigns work. Model/property releases required.

Terms: Pays authors royalty or work purchased outright. Offers advances. Pays photographers by the project or per photo. Book catalog available for 9 × 12 SAE and 5 first-class stamps. Ms/artist's guidelines available.

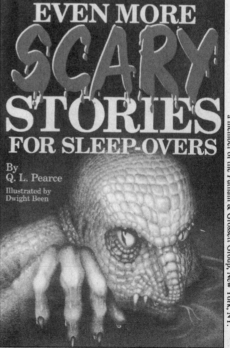

Dwight Been worked in gouache and colored pencil to concoct this creepy, slimy, scaly, ready-to-grab-you creature for the cover of Even More Scary Stories for Sleep-Overs, *by Q.L. Pierce. The artist also rendered 11 spooky black and white pencil drawings for the book's interior. The collection is the fourth in the series of hair-raising tales of suspicious deaths, swamps, and prehistoric superslime published by Price Stern Sloan.*

PROMETHEUS BOOKS, 59 John Glenn Dr., Amherst NY 14228-2197. Book publisher. Acquisitions Editor: Steven L. Mitchell. Publishes 1-2 titles/year. 40% of books by first-time authors; 50% of books from agented writers. Publishes books on moral education, critical thinking, skepticism.
Nonfiction: All levels: sex education, moral education, critical thinking, science, skepticism. Average word length: picture books—2,000; young readers—10,000; middle readers—20,000; young adult/teens—60,000. Published *Wonder-workers! How They Perform the Impossible*, by Joe Nickell (ages 9-14, skepticism); *How Do You Know It's True?*, by Hy Ruchlis (ages 12-15, critical thinking); *Maybe Right, Maybe Wrong*, by Dan Barker (ages 7-12, moral education); *The Tree of Life: The Wonders of Evolution*, by Ellen Jackson (ages 4-9, science).
How to Contact/Writers: Submit complete ms with sample illustrations (b&w). Reports on queries in 1-2 months; mss in 2-3 months. Publishes a book 12-18 months after acceptance. SASE required for return of ms/proposal.
Illustration: Works with 1-2 illustrators/year. Will review ms/illustration packages. "We will keep samples in a freelance file, but freelancers are rarely used."
How to Contact/Illustrators: "Prefer to have full work (manuscript and illustrations); will consider any proposal." Include résumé, photocopies.
Terms: "Contract terms vary with projects." Pays authors royalties. "Author hires illustrator; we do not contract with illustrators." Sends galleys to author. Book catalog is free on request.
Tips: "Book should reflect secular humanist values, stressing nonreligious moral education, critical thinking, logic, and skepticism. Authors should examine our book catalog to learn what sort of manuscripts we're looking for."

PUFFIN BOOKS, 375 Hudson St., New York NY 10014-3567. (212)366-2000. An imprint of Viking Children's Books. The majority of Puffin's list is now reprints, therefore it no longer accepts unsolicited submissions.

PUMPKIN PRESS PUBLISHING HOUSE/A WAY TO GROW, P.O. Box 139, Shasta CA 96087. (916)244-3456. Book publisher. President: Dick Bozzi. Vice President/Production: David Fleming. Editor: Susan Olson Higgins. Publishes 2-3 picture books/year; 2-3 young readers/year; 1-2 middle readers/year.
• This press is not accepting manuscripts until mid-1995.
Fiction: All levels: adventure, animal, concept, contemporary, folktales, health, history, humor, multicultural, nature/environment, poetry, religious (Christian), sports.
Nonfiction: All levels: activity books, animal, biography, concept, geography, history, music/dance, nature/environment, religion, science, social issues.
How to Contact/Writers: Submit complete ms. Reports on queries in 3 weeks; on mss in 6 months.
Illustration: Works with 3 illustrators/year. Will review ms/illustration packages. Will review artwork for future assignments. Contact: Design Dept.
How to Contact/Illustrators: Ms/illustration packages: Submit ms with dummy.
Terms: Work purchased outright from authors. Pays illustrators by the project. Book catalog available for SASE. Ms/artist's guidelines not available.
Tips: "Fresh, fun, original manuscripts focused on pre-school to third-grade children."

G.P. PUTNAM'S SONS, 200 Madison Ave., New York NY 10016. (212)951-8700. Imprint of Putnam and Grosset Group. Book publisher. Executive Editor: Refna Wilkin. Art Director: Cecilia Yung. Publishes 25 picture books/year; 4 middle readers/year; 7 young adult titles/year. 5% of books by first-time authors; 50% of books from agented authors.
• Putnam ranks seventh, based on net sales, of the top 12 children's publishers.
Fiction: Picture books: adventure, concept, contemporary, folktales, humor. Young readers: adventure, contemporary, folktales, history, humor, special needs, suspense/mystery. Middle readers: adventure, contemporary, history, humor, special needs, suspense/mystery. Young adults: contemporary, humor, problem novels, special needs. "Multicultural books should reflect different cultures accurately but unobtrusively." Regarding special needs, "stories about physically or mentally challenged children should portray them accurately

and without condescension." Does not want to see series, romances, sports fiction. Very little fantasy. Average word length: picture books—200-1,500; middle readers—10,000-30,000; young adults—40,000-50,000. Recently published *Mirette on the High Wire*, by Emily Arnold McCully; *Mayfield Crossing*, by Vaunda Nelson; *Mary Marony Hides Out*, by Suzy Kline.

Nonfiction: Picture books: multicultural. Young readers: biography, history, multicultural. Middle readers and young adults: biography, history, multicultural, social issues. No hard science, series. Average word length: picture books—200-1,500; middle readers: 10,000-30,000; young adults: 30,000-50,000. Recently published *Freedom's Children*, by Ellen Levine; *Speaking Out*, by Susan Kuklin; *Harriet Beecher Stowe and the Beecher Preachers*, by Jean Fritz.

How to Contact/Writers: Fiction/nonfiction: Query; submit outline/synopsis and 3 sample chapters. No unsolicited mss. Reports on queries in 1 month; mss in 8-10 weeks. Publishes a book two years after acceptance. Will consider simultaneous submissions on queries only.

Illustration: Works with 40 illustrators/year. Will review ms/illustration packages. Will review artwork for future assignments.

How to Contact/Illustrators: Query. Reports in 6-8 weeks. Samples returned with SASE; samples filed. Original artwork returned at job's completion.

Terms: Pays authors royalty based on retail price. Pays illustrators by the project or royalty. Sends galleys to authors. Books catalog and ms guidelines available for SASE.

*QUESTAR PUBLISHERS, INC., 305 W. Adams, P.O. Box 1720, Sisters OR 97759. (503)549-1144. Imprint: Gold 'n' Honey. Book publisher. Editorial Coordinator: Brenda Saltzer. Art Director: David Uttley. Publishes 3-5 picture books/year; 5-8 young readers/year; 1-2 middle readers/year; and 1-2 adult titles/year. 10% of books by first-time authors. Publishes spiritual/religious titles.

Fiction: All levels: religion. Average word length: picture books—150-250; young readers—4,000-16,000; middle readers—10,000-30,000; young adults—20,000-50,000. Recently published *Adventures in South America*, by Jeannette Windle (middle readers); *The First Step Bible*, by Mack Thomas (picture book); and *When Stars Come Out*, by L.J. Saltgast (picture book).

Nonfiction: All levels: religion. Average word length: picture books—150-250; young readers—4,000-16,000; middle readers—10,000-30,000; young adults—20,000-50,000. Recently published *Somewhere Angels* and *Someday Heaven*, both by Larry Libby (middle readers).

How to Contact/Writers: Fiction/Nonfiction: Query. Reports on queries in 3 months; mss in 6 months. Publishes a book 2 years after acceptance.

Illustration: Works with 8-12 illustrators/year. Will review artwork for future assignments. Uses color artwork only.

How to Contact/Illustrators: Ms/illustration packages: Query. Illustrations only: Query with samples, résumé, promo sheet. Reports back only if interested. Samples filed.

Photography: Buys photos from freelancers. Contact: David Uttley, art director. Buys stock and assigns work. Uses children, animals and nature photos. Model/property releases required; captions required. Uses 35mm, 2¼ × 2¼, 4 × 5 transparencies. Submit cover letter, résumé, published samples, color promo piece.

Terms: Pays royalty based on wholesale price. Pays illustrators by the project or royalty. Pays photographers by the project or per photo. Sends galleys to authors.

RANDOM HOUSE BOOKS FOR YOUNG READERS, 201 E. 50th St., New York NY 10022. (212)940-7742. Random House, Inc. Book publisher. Vice President/Editor-in-Chief: Kate Klimo. Vice President/Executive Art Director: Cathy Goldsmith. 100% of books published through agents; 2% of books by first-time authors.

● They now accept agented material only. Random House ranks second, based on net sales, of the top 12 children's publishers.

Fiction: Picture books: animal, easy-to-read, history, sports. Young readers: adventure, animal, easy-to-read, history, sports, suspense/mystery. Middle readers: adventure, history, science, sports, suspense/mystery.

Nonfiction: Picture books: animal. Young readers: animal, biography, hobbies. Middle readers: biography, history, hobbies, sports.

How to Contact/Writers: Fiction/Nonfiction: Submit through agent only. Publishes a book 12-18 months after acceptance. Will consider simultaneous submissions.

Illustration: Will review ms/illustration packages (through agent only). Will review an illustrator's work for possible future assignments.

Terms: Pays authors in royalties; sometimes buys mss outright. Sends galleys to authors. Book catalog free on request.

■**READ'N RUN BOOKS,** P.O. Box 294, Rhododendron OR 97049. (503)622-4798. Subsidiary of Crumb Elbow Publishing. Book publisher. Publisher: Michael P. Jones. Publishes 3 picture books/year; 5 young reader titles/year; 2 middle reader titles/year; 5 young adult titles/year. 50% of books by first-time authors; 8% of books from agented writers; 12% subsidy published.

Fiction: Picture books, young readers, middle readers: religion, suspense/mystery, animal, folktales, multicultural, anthology, nature/environment, science fiction, concept, hi-lo, poetry, contemporary, history, problem novels, sports. Young adults: all categories considered.

Nonfiction: Picture books: activity books, history, nature/environment, social issues, animal, hobbies, reference, art/crafts, biography, multicultural, science, textbooks, career, hi-lo." Young readers: animal, arts/crafts, biography, career, concept, geography, health, hi-lo, history, hobbies, how-to, multicultural, music/dance, nature/environment, reference, religion, science, self help, social issues, sports, textbooks. Middle readers: animal, arts/crafts, biography, careers, hi-lo, history, hobbies, multicultural, nature/environment, reference, science, social issues, textbooks. Young adults: animal, arts/crafts, biography, careers, cooking, hi-lo, history, hobbies, multicultural, nature/environment, reference, science, social issues, textbooks.

How to Contact/Writers: Fiction/Nonfiction: Query. Reports on queries/mss in 2 months "or sooner depending upon work load." Publishes a book about 8 months to a year after acceptance depending on workload and previously committed projects. Will consider simultaneous submissions. "If samples and manuscripts are not accompanied by a SASE, we will not return, nor will we maintain them. We are overwhelmed by responses."

Illustration: Works with 25 illustrators/year. Reviews ms/illustration packages. Publisher, Michael P. Jones, will review illustrator's work for possible future assignments. "Black & white, 8×10 or 5×7 illustrations. No color work for finished artwork, but color work is great to demonstrate the artist's talents."

How to Contact/Illustrators: Ms/illustration packages: Query with entire ms and several pieces of the artwork. Illustrations only: Query with samples; provide portfolio, slides and tearsheets. Reports on ms/art samples in 1-2 months. Original artwork returned at job's completion.

Photography: Purchases photos from freelancers. Contact: Michael P. Jones. Buys stock and assigns work. Looking for wildlife, history, nature. Model/property releases required; photo captions optional. Publishes photo essays and photo concept books. Uses 5×7 or 8×10 b&w prints; 4×5 or 35mm transparencies. To contact, photographers should query with samples.

Terms: Pays in published copies only. Sends galleys to authors; dummies to illustrators. Book catalog available for $2. Ms/artists' guidelines available for 1 first-class stamp and #10 SAE.

Tips: "Don't give up. The field can seem cruel and harsh when trying to break into the market. Roll with the punches." Wants natural history and historical books. Sees trend toward "more computer generated artwork."

 The solid block before a listing indicates the market subsidy publishes manuscripts.

*RIZZOLI BOOKS FOR CHILDREN, 300 Park Ave. S., New York NY 10010. (212)387-3653. Fax: (212)387-3535. Book publisher. Senior Editor: M. Soares. Publishes 6-10 picture books/year; 2-3 middle readers/year; 2-3 young adult titles/year. 80% of books by first-time authors. Rizzoli Books seeks to introduce children to the world of fine art, architecture, literature and music through artbooks, picture books and biographies. The work of historic and contemporary figures is of interest, in addition to contemporary stories and folk tales. **Fiction:** Young readers: adventure, anthology, contemporary, folktales, multicultural. Middle readers, young adults: adventure, anthology, contemporary, folktales, history, multicultural, poetry. Average word length: picture books—500-750; middle readers—2,500; and young readers—4,000. Recently published *Dave's and Jane's Adventures with Lewis & Clark*, by Bob Knox (ages 7-12); *The Prince & the Salmon People*, by Claire Murphy, illustrated by Duane Pasco (ages 7-up); and *Nightingale and the Wind*, by Paul Mandelstein, illustrated by Pamela Palmer (8-up). **Nonfiction:** Young readers: biography, history, multicultural. Middle readers: arts/crafts, biography, cooking, history, multicultural, music/dance, nature/environment. Young adults: biography, cooking, history, multicultural. Multicultural needs include music, poetry, dance, biography. Average word length picture books 500-750; middle readers—2,500; young adults—4,000. Special needs include music, poetry, dance, biography. Average word length: picture books—500-750; middle readers—2,500; young adults—4,000. Recently published *The Will & The Way*, by Karen Hudson (ages 8-12, biography of African-American architect); *Walking The Log*, by Bessie Nickens (ages 7-up, stories and painting about growing up in rural South); and *Who Has Seen The Wind?*, Museum of Fine Arts, Boston (all ages, an illustrated collection of poetry for young people). **How to Contact/Writers:** Fiction/Nonfiction: Query; submit complete ms. Reports in 2 weeks on queries; mss in 4-6 weeks. Publishes a book 1 year after acceptance. Will consider simultaneous submissions. **Illustration:** Will review ms/illustration packages. Contact: M. Soares. **How to Contact/Illustrators:** Ms/illustration package: Query; submit ms with dummy. Illustrations only: Submit résumé and promo sheet. Original artwork returned at job's completion. **Terms:** Pays authors royalty of 3-10% based on wholesale price. Offers advances (average $2,000-3,000). Pays illustrators by the project (range: $2,000-4,000) or royalty of 3-10% based on wholesale price. Sends galleys to authors; dummies to illustrators. Ms and art guidelines available for SASE.

*ROSEBRIER PUBLISHING CO., 1510 Perkinsville Dr., Box 106, Boone NC 28607. Independent book producer/packager. Editorial Contact: Beverly Donadio. Publishes 1 picture book/year. 50% of books by first-time authors. **Fiction:** Picture books; fantasy, nature/environment. Middle readers: adventure, fantasy, nature/environment, religion. No violence. **How to Contact/Writers:** Submit complete ms. Reports on queries/ms in 6 months. Publishes a book 6 months after acceptance. **Illustration:** Uses 20 illustrations in a picture book. Editorial will review ms/illustration packages. Uses color artwork only. **How to Contact/Illustrators:** Ms/illustration packages: Submit 3 chapters of ms with 1 piece of art. Illustrations only: provide tearsheets to be kept on file. **Terms:** Pays authors in royalties.

THE ROSEN PUBLISHING GROUP, 29 E. 21st St., New York NY 10010. (212)777-3017. Book publisher. Estab. 1950. Editorial Contact: Gina Strazzabosco. Publisher: Roger Rosen. Publishes 25 middle readers/year; 50 young adults/year. 35% of books by first-time authors; 3% of books from agented writers. **Nonfiction:** Young adults: careers, hi-lo, multicultural, special needs, psychological self-help. No fiction. Average word length: middle readers—10,000; young adults—40,000. Published *Everything You Need to Know When a Parent is in Jail*, (hi-lo, young adult, The Need to Know Library); *The Value of Trust*, by Rita Milios (young adult, The Encyclopedia of Ethical Behavior); *Careers as an Animal Rights Activist*, by Shelly Field (young adult, The Career Series).

How to Contact/Writers: Submit outline/synopsis and sample chapters. Reports on queries/mss in 1-2 months. Publishes a book 9 months after acceptance.

Photography: Buys photos from freelancers. Contact: Roger Rosen. Works on assignment only.

Terms: Pays authors in royalties or work purchased outright. Sends galleys to authors. Book catalog free on request.

Tips: "Target your manuscript to a specific age group and reading level and write for established series published by the house you are approaching."

WILLIAM H. SADLIER, INC., 9 Pine St., New York NY 10005. (212)227-2120. Textbook publisher. President: William S. Dinger. "We publish texts for Roman Catholic religious studies. We are looking for writers whose stories might be used in our religious education programs."

Fiction: All levels: religion. "Multicultural themes are important."

Nonfiction: All levels: religious education textbooks. Average word length: 25-30 words per lesson in each text for all age levels.

Terms: Pays authors "fee for stories" (authors are work for hire).

Tips: "We are looking for engaging stories that will involve the child especially primary grades, ages 3-8."

ST. ANTHONY MESSENGER PRESS, 1615 Republic St., Cincinnati OH 45210. (513)241-5615. Fax: (513)241-0399. Book publisher. Managing Editor: Lisa Biedenbach. 25% of books by first-time authors. "All books nurture and enrich Catholic Christian life. We also look for books for parents and religious educators."

Nonfiction: Middle readers, young adults: religion. Does not want to see fiction, story books, picture books for preschoolers.

How to Contact/Writers: Query; submit outline/synopsis and sample chapters. Reports on queries in 2-4 weeks; mss in 4-6 weeks. Publishes a book 12-18 months after acceptance.

Illustration: Works with 2 illustrators/year. Will review ms/illustration packages. Will review artwork for future assignments. "We design all covers and do most illustrations in-house." Uses primarily b&w artwork. Contact: Mary Alfieri, art director.

How to Contact/Illustrators: Ms/illustration packages: Query with samples; résumé. Reports on queries in 2-4 weeks.

Photography: Purchases photos from freelancers. Contact: Mary Alfieri, art director. Buys stock and assigns work.

Terms: Pays authors royalties of 10-12% based on net receipts. Offers average advance payment of $600. Pays illustrators by the project. Pays illustrators by the project. Sends galleys to authors. Book catalog and ms guidelines free on request.

Tips: "We're looking for programs to be used in schools and parishes — stories with Catholic themes for sacramental preparation; proven programs for religious education of children and teens to be used by parents and parishes."

ST. PAUL BOOKS AND MEDIA, 50 St. Paul's Ave., Jamaica Plain MA 02130. (617)522-8911. Daughters of St. Paul. Book publisher. Estab. 1934. Editor: Sister Mary Mark, fsp. Art Director: Sister Mary Joseph. Publishes 1-2 picture books/year; 1-2 young reader titles/year. 20% of books by first-time authors.

Fiction: All levels: contemporary, religion. Average word length: picture books — 150-300; young readers — 1,500-5,000.

Nonfiction: All levels: biography (saints), devotionals, religion. Average word length: picture books — 200; young readers — 1,500-5,000; middle readers — 10,000; young adults — 20,000-50,000.

How to Contact/Writers: Fiction/Nonfiction: Submit outline/synopsis and sample chapters. Reports on queries in 3-8 weeks; on mss in 3 months. Publishes a book 2-3 years after acceptance. No simultaneous submissions.

Illustration: Works with 20 illustrators/year. Will review ms/illustration packages. Will review artwork for future assignments. Style/size of illustration "varies according to the title."

How to Contact/Illustrators: Ms/illustration packages: "Outline first with art samples." Illustrations only: Query with samples; send promo sheets or tearsheets. Reports on art samples in 3-8 weeks.

Photography: Buys photos from freelancers. Contact: Sister Helen Rita. Buys stock. Looking for children, animals—active interaction. Uses 4×5 or 8×10 b&w prints; 35mm or 4×5 transparencies.

Terms: Pays authors in royalties of 4-12% based on gross sales. Illustrations paid by the project. Photographers paid by the project, $15-200. Book catalog for 9×12 SAE and 5 first-class stamps. Manuscript guidelines for legal-size SAE and 1 first-class stamp.

Tips: "We are a Roman Catholic publishing house looking for devotional material for all ages (traditional and contemporary prayer-forms); obviously, material should be consonant with Catholic doctrine and spirituality!"

*SASQUATCH BOOKS, 1008 Western Ave., #300, Seattle WA 98110. (206)467-4300. Fax: (206)467-4338. Book Publisher. Acquisitions Editor: Stephanie Irving. Art Director: Nancy Deahl. Publishes 2-3 picture books/year; and 2-3 young readers/year. 40% of books by first-time authors. "Most of our books have something to do with the greater Northwest (Northern California to Alaska) or the Pacific Rim. Most are nonfiction."

Fiction: Picture books, young readers: adventure, animal, folktales, multicultural, nature/environment, special needs. Multicultural needs include Native American, Pacific Rim, Black. "We've also published one book about a little hearing dog and would consider others for the physically or mentally challenged." Does not want to see science fiction, poetry or religion. Average word length: picture books—less than 200; young readers—300-500.

Nonfiction: Picture books, young readers: activity books, animal, arts/crafts, cooking, geography, how-to, multicultural, music/dance, nature/environment, special needs. Multicultural needs include Native American, Pacific Rim, Black. Average word length: picture books—less than 200; young readers—200-600. Recently published *Red Hot Peppers*, by Bob and Diane Boardman (ages 8 and up, jump rope book with tape and rope included); *Seya's Song*, by Ron Hirschi (ages 3 and up, Native American story that shows relationship of salmon to people and seasons); and *Wild, Wild West*, by Constance Perenyi (ages 4 and up, wildlife habitats of western North America).

How to Contact/Writers: Fiction: Query; submit complete ms. Nonfiction: Query; submit outline/synopsis and 2 sample chapters. Reports on queries in 1 month; mss in 3 months. Publishes a book 1 year after acceptance. Will consider simultaneous submissions.

Illustration: Works with 4-5 illustrators/year. Will review ms/illustration packages. Contact: Stephanie Irving, acquisitions editor. Will review artwork for future assignments. Contact: Nancy Deahl, art director.

How to Contact/Illustrators: Illustrations only: Query with samples; provide resume, promo sheets and slides. Reports in 3 months. Samples returned with SASE; "good ones" filed. Original artwork returned at job's completion.

Photography: Buys photos from freelancers. Contact: Nancy Deahl, art director. Works on assignment only.

Terms: Pays authors royalty of 6-10% based on retail price (split with illustrator). Offers advances (average amount: $2,000.) Pays illustrators royalty of 6-10% based on retail price (split with author). Pays photographers royalty of 6-10%. Sends galleys to authors; dummies to illustrators. Book catalog available upon request; ms guidelines available for SASE.

SCHOLASTIC HARDCOVER, 555 Broadway, New York NY 10012.
- Does not currently accept unsolicited work. Scholastic ranks eighth, based on net sales, of the top 12 children's publishers.

SCIENTIFIC AMERICAN BOOKS FOR YOUNG READERS, W.H. Freeman and Company, 41 Madison Ave., New York NY 10010. (212)576-9450. Fax: (212)689-2383. Book publisher. Executive Editor: Marc Gave. Approximately 30 titles/year. 25% of books from agented authors. Publishes science, social science, math subjects.

Fiction: "We publish fiction with science or math content if there is real learning *and* entertainment value. In the picture book category are the *Mouse & Mole* books, by Doug

Cushman and *The Rajah's Rice*, by David Barry. Successful midgrade series include *Dinosaur Detective*, by B.B. Calhoun and *Mathnet Casebooks*, by David D. Connell and Jim Thurman."

Nonfiction: All levels: science, math, nature/ecology, health, anthropology, related biography. All material should have substance but must not resemble a textbook. All books are heavily illustrated. Recently published *One Small Square* series, by Donald M. Silver, illustrated by Patricia J. Wynne (ages 7-12, ecosystems); *Science Superstars* series (ages 8-12, biographies); *In the Air and Everywhere*, by Jody Marshall, illustrated by Elizabeth McClelland (ages 8 and up, pop-up book of birds); *Incredible Edible Science*, by Tina Seelig (ages 9-14, cooking chemistry).

How to Contact/Writers: Fiction/Nonfiction: Query. Reports on queries in 1 month; reports on mss in 2 months. Will consider simultaneous submissions.

Illustration: Will review ms/illustration packages. Will review artwork for future assignments. Contact: Maria Epes, art director, children's books.

How to Contact/Illustrators: Ms/illustration packages: Query. Illustrations only: Query with samples (reply only upon request); submit portfolio for review; provide tearsheets. Reports in 1 month.

Photography: Buys photos from freelancers. Contact: Maria Epes, art director, children's books. Uses scientific subjects. Model/property release required. May publish photo essays. Uses 35mm transparencies. Photographers should query with samples; submit portfolio for review; provide tearsheets.

Terms: Pays authors royalty based on net sales receipts. Offers advances. Pays illustrators by the project or royalty. Photographers paid by the project or per photo. Sends galleys to authors. Book catalog available. Ms and art guidelines available for SASE.

Tips: "Study the publishers' lists to find out who is publishing what. Don't send anything out to a publisher without finding out if the publisher is interested in receiving such material." Looking for "well-researched, well-written, thoughtful but lively books on a focused aspect of science, social science (anthropology, psychology—not politics, history), with lots of kid interest, for ages 4-14. Also now considering toddler material."

CHARLES SCRIBNER'S SONS, was incorporated into Atheneum Books for Young Readers, an imprint of Simon & Schuster Children's Publishing Division.

SEACOAST PUBLICATIONS OF NEW ENGLAND, Suite 165, 2800A Lafayette Rd., Portsmouth NH 03801. Book publisher. Founder: Paul Peter Jesep. Publishes 1-3 young readers/year. 100% of books by first-time authors. Mss "*must* have New England theme."

Fiction: Young readers, middle readers: adventure, animal, contemporary, fantasy, folktales, history, nature/environment. Fiction must be related to New England. Average word length: young readers—1,400. Published *Lady-Ghost of the Isles of Shoals*, illustrated by John Bowdren (ages 5-8); *A December Gift from the Shoals*, illustrated by John Bowdren; *I Saw A Whale!*, by Virginia Kroll.

Nonfiction: Young readers, middle readers: animal, biography, geography, history, nature/environment. Average word length: 1,400. "SPNE wants short manuscripts that 'celebrate' New England's heritage, culture, folklore and mind-set."

How to Contact/Writers: Fiction/Nonfiction: Query. Reports on queries in 2 months; on mss in 4 months. Publishes a book 16-20 months after acceptance. Will consider simultaneous submissions. "Do not send manuscripts without being asked."

Illustrations: Works with 1-2 illustrators/year. Will review ms/illustration packages. Will review artwork for future assignments. Uses primarily b&w artwork.

How to Contact/Illustrators: Ms/illustration packages: Submit ms with 2 pieces of final art. Illustrations only: Query with samples; provide résumé and client list. Reports in 6 weeks. Samples returned with SASE. Originals not returned.

Photography: Buys photos from freelancers. Contact: Paul Peter Jesep. Buys stock and assigns work. Wants photos of scenic New England. Model/property releases required; captions required. Uses b&w prints. Submit cover letter and résumé.

Terms: Work purchased outright (range: $100-400). Pays illustrators by the project (range: $100-300). Photographers paid per photo ($25 minimum). Ms and art guidelines available for SASE.

Tips: Wants "a very unique New England theme—will consider most short children's manuscripts on any of the six New England states, particularly stories about pirates, ghosts, marine life and 18th and 19th century historical figures. The first book issued by Seacoast Publications of New England was about a group of islands off the Maine-New Hampshire coast called the Isles of Shoals. Although the Shoals are rich in pirate lore, ghost stories and New England history, there are few children's books on the topic." No phone calls.

*SEEDLING PUBLICATIONS, INC., 4079 Overlook Dr. E., Columbus OH 43214-2931. Phone/fax: (614)451-2412. Vice President: Josie Stewart. Publishes 5-10 young readers/year. 20% of books by first-time authors. Publishes books for the beginning reader.
Fiction: Young readers: adventure, animal, concept, contemporary, fantasy, folktales, hi-lo, multicultural, nature/environment, poetry, special needs and sports. Does not want to see texts longer than 16 pages or over 150-200 words. Averge word length: young readers—100. Recently published *Staying with Grandma Norma*, by L. Salem and J. Stewart (ages 3-7, paperback early reader); *Our House Had a Mouse*, by Denise Worthington (ages 3-7, paperback early reader).
Nonfiction: Young readers: animal, biography, careers, concept, cooking, hi-lo, hobbies, how-to, multicultural, music/dance, nature/environment, science, special needs and sports. Does not want to see texts longer than 16 pages or over 150-200 words. Average word length: young readers—100. Recently published *Taking Care of Rosie*, by L. Salem and J. Stewart (ages 3-7, early reader).
How to Contact/Writers: Fiction/Nonfiction: Submit complete ms. Reports in 3 months. Publishes a book 1 year after acceptance. Will consider simultaneous submissions.
Illustration: Works with 5-10 illustrators/year. Will review ms/illustration packages. Contact: Josie Stewart, vice president. Uses color artwork only.
How to Contact/Illustrators: Ms/illustration package: Submit ms with dummy. Illustrations only: Arrange personal portfolio review. Reports in 3 months. Samples returned with SASE; samples filed.
Photography: Buys photos from freelancers. Contact: Josie Stewart, vice president. Works on assignment only. Model/property releases required. Uses color prints and 35mm transparencies. Submit cover letter and color promo piece.
Terms: Pays authors royalty of 5% based on retail price. Work purchased outright from authors. Pays illustrators and photographers by the project. Book catalog available for 1 first-class stamp.

HAROLD SHAW PUBLISHERS, P.O. Box 567, 388 Gundersen Dr., Wheaton IL 60189. (708)665-6700. Book publisher. Estab. 1967. Director of Editorial Services: Joan Guest. Publishes young adult fiction infrequently "as exceptional manuscripts become available." 10% of books by first-time authors; 5% of books from agented writers.
Fiction: Young adults: adventure, problem novels, including religious themes. Average length: young adults—112-250 pages. Published *The Sioux Society*, by Jeffrey Asher Nesbit (ages 13 and up, novel); *Light at Summer's End*, by Kimberly M. Ballard (ages 13 and up, novel).
How to Contact/Writers: Reports on queries in 4-6 weeks; mss in 8-10 weeks. Publishes a book 1 year after acceptance. Will consider simultaneous queries.
Terms: Pays authors in royalties of 5-10% based on retail price. Sends pages to authors. Book catalog available for SAE and $1.25; ms guidelines for SASE.
Tips: "We no longer accept illustrator or photographer packages."

*SHOESTRING PRESS, Box 1223, Edmonton, Alberta T5J 2M4 Canada. Book publisher. Contact: Editor. Publishes 2 picture books/year; 1 young readers/year; 1 middle readers/

"Picture books" are geared toward preschoolers to 8-year-olds; *"Young readers"* are for 5- to 8-year-olds; *"Middle readers"* are for 9- to 11-year-olds; and *"Young adults"* are for those ages 12 and up.

year; 10 young adult titles/year. 40% of books by first-time authors; subsidy publishes 20%. No primary theme, publishes various categories.

Fiction: Picture books, young readers, middle readers, young adults: adventure, folktales, Indian legends. Average word length: picture books—3,000; young readers—7,500; middle readers—4,000; young adult—20,000.

Nonfiction: Picture books: geography, Indian legends. Young readers, middle readers, young adults: Indian legends.

How to Contact/Writers: Fiction/Nonfiction: Query; submit outline/synopsis. Reports on queries in 4 months; mss in 6 months. Publishes book 15 months after acceptance.

Illustration: Works with 2 illustrators/year. Will review ms/illustration packages. Will review artwork for future assignments. Uses primarily b&w artwork.

How to Contact/Illustrators: Ms/illustration packages: Query. Illustrations only: Query with samples; provide résumé portfolio. Reports in 4 months. Samples returned with SASE; samples filed for 6 months. Originals not returned.

Terms: Pays authors royalty of 5-10% based on wholesale price. Pays illustrators royalty. Ms and art guidelines available for SASE.

*SILVER BURDETT PRESS, 250 James St., Morristown NJ 07960. (201)285-8031. Fax: (201)326-6683. Simon & Schuster Education Group. Imprints: Crestwood House, Dillon Press, Julian Messner, New Discovery. Book publisher. Senior Editor: Dorothy Goeller. Publishes 40 young readers/year and 40 young adults/year. 1% of books by first-time authors.

Fiction/Nonfiction: "Our list ranges from pre-school to young adult books, both fiction and nonfiction. This also includes Crestwood House which is a hi-lo nonfiction imprint." Considers all fiction and nonfiction categories. Recently published *Riddle by the River, The United States Holocaust Memorial Museum, The White Stallions* and *Insects*.

How to Contact/Writers: Fiction/Nonfiction: Submit outline/synopsis and 1 sample chapter. Reports on queries in 6 months; mss in 12 months. Publishes a book 1 year after acceptance. Will consider simultaneous and electronic submissions via disk or modem. Only interested in agented material.

Illustration: Works with 40 illustrators/year. Will review ms/illustration packages. Contact: Dorothy Goeller, senior editor. Will review artwork for future assignments.

How to Contact/Illustrators: Ms/illustration packages: Submit ms with dummy. Illustrations only: Submit résumé and portfolio. Only interested in agented material. Reports only if interested. Samples returned with SASE.

Photography: Buys photos from freelancers. Contact: Debbie Biber, senior product editor. Buys stock and assigns work. Captions required. Uses color or b&w prints, ½-full page. Submit published samples and client list.

Terms: Pays authors royalty of 3-7½% based on wholesale or retail price or work purchased outright from authors, $5,000 minimum. Offers advances (average amount: $7,500). Pays illustrators by the project (range: $500-10,000) or royalty of 3-7½% based on wholesale or retail price. Sends galleys to authors; dummies to illustrators. Book catalog available for 9×11 SAE and $2.60 postage.

SILVER MOON PRESS, 126 Fifth Ave., New York NY 10011. (212)242-6499. Book publisher. Managing Editor: Eliza Booth. Publishes 2 picture books/year; 2 books for grades 1-3; 10 books for grades 4-6. 25% of books by first-time authors; 10% books from agented authors.

Fiction: All levels: historical and mystery. Average word length: varies. Recently published *Children of Flight Pedro Pan*, by Maria Acierno (ages 8-12, historical novel); *Mr. Peale's Bones*, by Tracey West (ages 8-12, historical novel); *A Spy in the King's Colony* (ages 8-12, historical mystery novel).

Nonfiction: All levels. Recently published *Sports Lab*, by Robert Sheely (ages 8-12, sports science); *Get Inside: Baseball*, by Paul Almonte; *Get Inside: A Ranch*, by Barbara Morgenroth (ages 8-12, insiders' guides); *Melting Pots: Family Stories and Recipes*, by Judith Weber (ages 6-8, family).

How to Contact/Writers: Fiction/Nonfiction: Query. Reports on queries in 2-4 weeks; mss in 1-2 months. Publishes a book 1-2 years after acceptance. Will consider simultaneous submissions, electronic submissions via disk or modem, previously published work.

How to Contact/Illustrators: Ms/illustration packages: Query. Illustrations only: Query with samples, résumé, client list; arrange personal portfolio review. Reports only if interested. Samples returned with SASE. Original artwork returned at job's completion.

Photography: Buys photos from freelancers. Buys stock and assigns work. Uses archival, historical, sports photos. Captions required. Uses color, b&w prints; 35mm, 2¼ × 2¼, 4 × 5, 8 × 10 transparencies. Submit cover letter, résumé, published samples, client list, promo piece.

Terms: Pays authors royalty or work purchased outright. Pays illustrators by the project, royalty. Pays photographers by the project, per photo, royalty. Sends galleys to authors; dummies to illustrators. Book catalog available for SAE.

SIMON & SCHUSTER BOOKS FOR YOUNG READERS, 866 Third Ave., New York NY 10022. (212)702-2000. Imprint of Simon & Schuster Children's Publishing Division. Vice President/Editorial Director: Stephanie Owens Lurie. Art Director: Lucille Chomowicz. Publishes 75 books/year.

• Simon & Schuster ranks third, based on net sales, of the top 12 children's publishers.

Fiction: Picture books: animal, contemporary, folktales, history, multicultural, poetry. Young readers: animal, adventure, contemporary, fantasy, folktales, history, humor, multicultural, poetry, mystery. Middle readers: adventure, animal, contemporary, fantasy, history, humor, multicultural, mystery. Young adults: contemporary, multicultural, poetry, suspense/mystery. Does not want to see picture books with anthropomorphic animals; didactic stories; problem novels. Recently published *Uncle Jed's Barbershop*, by Margaree Mitchell, illustrated by James Ransome, (ages 4-7, picture book); *My Rotten Redheaded Older Brother*, by Patricia Polacco, (ages 4-7, picture book); *The Crying for a Vision*, by Walter Wangerin, (ages 12 and up, young adult novel); and *Duppy Talk: West Indian Tales of Mystery and Magic*, by Gerald Hausman, (ages 9 and up, middle readers).

Nonfiction: Picture books: animal, biography, history, multicultural, nature/environment, religion, science. Young readers: animal, arts/crafts, biography, cooking, history, multicultural, nature/environment, religion, science. Middle readers: animal, art/crafts, biography, cooking, history, multicultural, nature/environment, religion, science. Young adults: social issues. "We're looking for multicultural manuscripts that portray a variety of cultures honestly and sensitively."

How to Contact/Writers: Fiction: Submit complete ms to Editorial Director. Reports on queries/mss in 3 months. Publishes book 1-2 years after acceptance. Will consider simultaneous submissions.

Illustration: Works with 75 illustrators/year. Editorial will review all varieties of ms/illustration packages. Will review artwork for future assignments. Contact: Lucille Chomowicz, art director.

How to Contact/Illustrators: Ms/illustration packages: Submit entire ms, prints, slides or color photocopies of illustrations and dummy to Editorial Director. Illustrations only: Query with samples; provide promo sheet, tearsheets. Do not submit original artwork. Reports only if interested. Original artwork returned at job's completion.

Terms: Pays authors royalty (varies) based on retail price. Pays illustrators by the project or royalty (varies) based on retail price. Photographers paid royalty. Book catalog, ms/ artist's guidelines free on request.

Tips: "We're looking for picture books centered on a strong, fully-developed protagonist who grows or changes during the course of the story; YA novels that are challenging and psychologically complex; also imaginative and humorous middle fiction. And we want nonfiction that is as engaging as fiction."

SOUNDPRINTS, 165 Water St., P.O. Box 679, Norwalk CT 06856. (203)838-6009. Book publisher. Assistant Editor: Dana Rau. Publishes 12 picture books/year. 10% of books by first-time authors; 10% of books from agented authors. Subjects published include North American wildlife and habitats.

Fiction: Picture books: animal, nature/environment. No fantasy or anthropomorphic animals. Average word length: picture books—700. Recently published *Dolphin's First Day*, by Kathleen Weidner Zoehfeld, illustrated by Steven James Petruccio (grades PS-2, picture book); *Woodchuck at Blackberry Road*, by C. Drew Lamm, illustrated by Allen Davis (grades PS-2 picture book); and *Swan Flyway*, by Dana Limpert, illustrated by Jo-Ellen Bosson (grades K-3, picture book).

How to Contact/Writers: Query. Reports on queries/mss in 6-8 weeks. Publishing time "can vary from one to two years, depending on where it can fit in our publishing schedule." Will consider simultaneous submissions. "Do NOT send manuscripts without reading our guidelines first."

Illustration: Works with 6-10 illustrators/year. Will review ms/illustration packages "if subject matter is appropriate." Will review artwork for future assignments. Uses color artwork only. Illustrations are usually full bleed 2-page spreads.

How to Contact/Illustrators: Ms/illustration packages: Query. Illustrations only: Query with samples; provide résumé, portfolio, promo sheet, slides. "If interest is generated, additional material will be requested." Reports in 1 month. Samples returned with SASE. Original artwork returned at job's completion.

Terms: Pays authors royalty or outright purchase. Offers advances. Pays illustrators by the project or royalty. Book catalog for 8¼ × 11 SAE and 98¢ postage; ms guidelines for SASE. "It's best to request both guidelines and catalog. Both can be sent in self-addressed envelope at least 8½ × 11 with 98¢ postage."

Tips: Wants a book that "features North American wildlife and habitats with great accuracy while capturing the interest of the reader/listener through an entertaining storyline."

THE SPEECH BIN, INC., 1965 25th Ave., Vero Beach FL 32960. (407)770-0007. Fax: (407)770-0006. Book publisher. Senior Editor: Jan J. Binney. Publishes 10-12 books/year. 50% of books by first-time authors; less than 15% of books from agented writers. "Nearly all our books deal with treatment of children (as well as adults) who have communication disorders of speech or hearing or children who deal with family members who have such disorders (e.g., a grandparent with Alzheimer's disease or stroke)."

Fiction: Picture books: animal, easy-to-read, fantasy, health, special needs. Young readers, middle readers, young adult: health, special needs.

Nonfiction: Picture books, young readers, middle readers, young adults: activity books, health, textbooks, special needs. Published *Chatty Hats and Other Props*, by Denise Mantione; *Holiday Hoopla: Holiday Games for Language & Speech*, by Michele Rost; and *Speech Sports*, by Janet M. Shaw.

How to Contact/Writers: Fiction/Nonfiction: Query. Reports on queries in 4-6 weeks; mss in 2-3 months. Publishes a book 10-12 months after acceptance. "Will consider simultaneous submissions *only* if notified; too many authors fail to let us know if manuscript is simultaneously submitted to other publishers! We *strongly* prefer sole submissions."

Illustration: Works with 4-5 illustrators/year ("usually inhouse"). Will review ms/illustration packages. Will review artwork for future assignments.

How to Contact/Illustrators: "Query first!" Submit tearsheets (no original art). SASE required for reply or return of material. Original artwork returned at job's completion.

Photography: Photographers should contact Jan J. Binney, senior editor. Buys stock and assigns work. Looking for scenic shots. Model/property releases required. Uses glossy b&w prints, 35mm or 2¼ × 2¼ transparencies. Submit résumé, business card, promotional literature or tearsheets to be kept on file.

Terms: Pays authors in royalties based on retail price. Pay illustrators by the project. Photographers paid by the project or per photo. Sends galleys to authors. Book catalog for 3 first-class stamps and 9 × 12 SAE; ms guidelines for #10 SASE.

*SRI RAMA PUBLISHING, Box 2550, Santa Cruz CA 95063. (408)426-5098. Book publisher. Estab. 1975. Secretary/Manager: Karuna K. Ault. Publishes 1 or fewer young reader titles/year.

Illustration: Illustrations used for fiction. Will review artwork for possible future assignments. Contact: Josh Gitomer, graphic design director. Not reviewing at this time, however.

Terms: "We are a nonprofit organization. Proceeds from our sales support an orphanage in India, so we encourage donated labor, but each case is worked out individually." Pays illustrators $200-1,000. Sends galleys to authors; dummies to illustrators. Book catalog free on request.

STANDARD PUBLISHING, 8121 Hamilton Ave., Cincinnati OH 45231. (513)931-4050. Book publisher. Director: Mark Taylor. Children's Editor: Diane Stortz. Creative Director: Coleen Davis. Publishes 4-8 board books/year; 25 picture books/year; 8-10 easy readers/year; 8-10 coloring and activity books/year. 25-40% of books by first-time authors; 1% of books from agented writers. Publishes well-written, upbeat books with a Christian perspective.
Fiction: Board/picture books: animal, contemporary, religion (Bible stories). Young readers: adventure, animal, contemporary, religion. Middle readers: adventure, contemporary, religion. Young adults: contemporary, mystery, religion, sports. Average word length: board/picture books—400-1,000; young readers—1,000.
Nonfiction: Board/picture books, young readers: concept, Bible background, nature/environment, sports. Average word length: picture books—400-1,000; young readers—1,000.
How to Contact/Writers: Fiction/Nonfiction: Send complete ms. Reports on queries/mss in 2 months. Publishes a book 18 months after acceptance. Will consider simultaneous and electronic submissions via disk or modem.
Illustration: Works with 6-10 illustrators/year. Will review artwork for future assignments. Contact: Coleen Davis, creative director.
How to Contact/Illustrators: Illustrations only: Submit cover letter and photocopies. Reports on art samples only if interested.
Terms: Pays authors royalties of 5-10% based on wholesale price or work purchased outright (range $250-1,000). Sends galleys to authors. Book catalog available for 8½ × 11 SAE; ms guidelines for letter-size SASE.
Tips: "We look for manuscripts that help draw children into a relationship with Jesus Christ; help children develop insights about what the Bible teaches; make reading an appealing and pleasurable activity."

*STARBURST PUBLISHERS, P.O. Box 4123, Lancaster PA 17604. (717)293-0939. Editorial Director: Ellen Hake. Publishes 1-3 picture books/year. 60% of books by first-time authors; 10% of books from agented authors. "Only looking for Bible-related books."
Nonfiction: All levels: religion. Only interested in Bible related themes. Recently published *A Child's Guide to the Lord's Prayer*; and *Dinosaurs*, by Phil Phillips.
How to Contact/Writers: Submit outline, 3 sample chapters, bio, photo and SASE. Reports on queries in 2-3 weeks; mss in 6-8 weeks. Publishes a book less than 1 year after acceptance. Will consider simultaneous submissions.
Illustration: Works with 2 illustrators/year. Will review ms/illustration packages. Contact: Ellen Hake, editorial director. Will review artwork for future assignments.
How to Contact/Illustrators: Ms/illustration packages: Query; submit ms with 3 pieces of final art. Illustrations only: Query with samples; provide résumé. Reports on queries in 1 month. Cannot return samples. Original artwork returned at job's completion.
Terms: Pays authors royalty of 6-16% based on net price to retailer. Pays illustrators by the project ($100 minimum). Sends galleys to authors; dummies to illustrators. Book catalog available for 9 × 12 SAE and 5 first-class stamps; ms guidelines available for SASE.

STEMMER HOUSE PUBLISHERS, INC., 2627 Caves Rd., Owings Mills MD 21117. (410)363-3690. Fax: (410)363-8459. Book publisher. Estab. 1975. President: Barbara Holdridge. Publishes 1-3 picture books/year. "Sporadic" numbers of young reader, middle reader, young adult titles/year. 60% of books by first-time authors.
Fiction: Picture books: animal, ecology, folktales, multicultural, nature/environment. Young reader, middle reader: history. Does not want to see anthropomorphic characters. Published *Grandma's Band*, by Brad Bowles, illustrations by Anthony Clon (ages 4-6); *The Pied Piper*, by Sharon Chmeloy, illustrations by Pat and Robin DeWitt (ages 4-8); *Why Buffalo Roam*, by L. Michael Kershen, illustrations by Monica Hansen.
Nonfiction: Picture books: young readers: animal, arts/crafts, biography, multicultural, music/dance, nature/environment. Published *The Hawaiian Coral Reef Coloring Book*, by Katherine Orr; *The First Teddy Bear*, by Helen Kay, illustrations by Susan Kranz.

How to Contact/Writers: Fiction/Nonfiction: Query; submit outline/synopsis and sample chapters. Reports on queries in 2 weeks; mss in 6 weeks. Publishes a book 18 months after acceptance. Will consider simultaneous submissions.

Illustration: Works with 3 illustrators/year. Will review ms/illustration packages. Will review artwork for future assignments.

How to Contact/Illustrators: Ms/illustration packages: Query first with several photocopied illustrations. Illustrations only: Submit tearsheets and/or slides (with SASE for return). Reports in 2 weeks.

Terms: Pays authors royalties of 4-10% based on wholesale price. Offers average advance payment of $300. Pays illustrators royalty of 4-5% based on wholesale price. Sends galleys to authors. Book catalog for 9 × 12 SASE.

Tips: Writers: "Simplicity, literary quality and originality are the keys." Wants to see ms/illustration packages.

STERLING PUBLISHING CO., INC., 387 Park Ave. S., New York NY 10016. (212)532-7160. Fax: (212)213-2495. Book publisher. Acquisitions Director: Sheila Anne Barry. Publishes 30 middle readers/year. 10% of books by first-time authors.

Nonfiction: Middle readers: activity books, animal, arts/crafts, geography, ghosts, hi-lo, hobbies, how-to, humor, true mystery, nature/environment, reference, science, sports, supernatural incidents. "Since our books are highly illustrated, word length is seldom the point. Most are 96-128 pages." Does not want to see fiction, poetry, story books or personal narratives. Published *Traveler's Guide to the Solar System*, by Patricia Barnes-Svarney (ages 10 and up, an imaginative trip to nine planets and a look at what it would be like to live on them); *World's Best Outdoor Games*, written and illustrated by Glen Vecchione (ages 9 and up); *Paper Action Toys*, by E. Richard Churchill, illustrated by James Michaels (ages 9 and up, easy to follow instructions for making dozens of moving projects with everyday materials).

How to Contact/Writers: Reports on queries/mss in 1-12 weeks. "If we are interested it may take longer." Publishes a book 6-18 months after acceptance. Will consider simultaneous submissions.

Illustration: Works with 7-10 illustrators/year. Will review ms/illustration packages. Will review artwork for future assignments.

How to Contact/Illustrators: Ms/illustration packages: "Query first." Illustrations only: "Send sample photocopies of line drawings; also examples of some color work." Original artwork returned at job's completion "if possible, but usually held for future needs."

Terms: Pays authors in royalties of up to 10%; "standard terms, no sliding scale, varies according to edition." Pays illustrators royalty, by the project. Sends galleys to authors. Ms guidelines for SASE.

Tips: Looks for "humor, hobbies, science books for middle-school children." Also, "mysterious occurrences, activities and fun and games books."

*THE SUMMIT PUBLISHING GROUP, Suite 500, 1227 W. Magnolia, Fort Worth TX 76104. Book publisher. Managing Editor: Mike Towle. Art Director: David Sims.

Nonfiction: All levels: activity books, arts/crafts, careers, health, hobbies, how-to, self help. Average word length: picture books—5,000; young readers—5,000. Recently published *You Can Do It!*; series includes cheerleading, ballet, balloon animals, card tricks, painting T-shirts, sock puppets.

How to Contact/Writers: Submit complete ms. Reports in 1-3 months. Publishes a book 4-6 months after acceptance. Will consider simultaneous and previously published submissions. Prefers no agents.

Always include a self-addressed, stamped envelope (SASE) with submissions within your own country. When sending material to other countries, include a self-addressed envelope (SAE) and International Reply Coupons (IRCs).

Illustration: Works with 4-6 illustrators/year. Will review ms/illustration packages. Contact: Mike Towle, managing editor. Will review artwork for future assignments. Uses primarily b&w artwork (some color).

How to Contact/Illustrators: Ms/illustration packages: Submit with 4-5 pieces of final art. Illustrations only: Query with samples, résumé, portfolio, slides, client list and tearsheets. Reports back only if interested in 3 months. Samples filed.

Photography: Buys photos from freelancers. Contact: Dave Sims, art director. Model/property release required; captions required. Uses 5×7, 8×10 b&w prints; 35mm, 4×5 transparencies. Submit cover letter, résumé, published samples, slides, client list.

Terms: Pays authors royalty of 5-12% based on wholesale price. Work purchased outright from authors. Rarely offers advances. Sends galleys to authors; dummies to illustrators. Ms guidelines available for SASE.

SUNBELT MEDIA, INC./EAKIN PRESS, P.O. Box 90159, Austin TX 78709. (512)288-1771. Fax: (512)288-1813. Book publisher. Estab. 1978. President: Ed Eakin. Publishes 2 picture books/year; 3 young readers/year; 10 middle readers/year; 2 young adult titles/year. 50% of books by first-time authors; 5% of books from agented writers.

Fiction: Picture books: animal. Middle readers, young adults: history, sports. Average word length: picture books—3,000; young readers—10,000; middle readers—15,000-20,000; young adults—20,000-30,000. "90% of our books relate to Texas and the Southwest."

Nonfiction: Picture books: animal. Middle readers and young adults: history, sports. Recently published *Sam and the Speaker's Chair*.

How to Contact/Writers: Fiction/Nonfiction: Query. Reports on queries in 2 weeks; mss in 6 weeks. Publishes a book 18 months after acceptance. Will consider simultaneous and electronic submissions via disk.

Illustration: Will review all varieties of ms/illustration packages.

How to Contact/Illustrators: Ms/illustration packages: Query. Illustrations only: Submit tearsheets. Reports on art samples in 2 weeks.

Terms: Pays authors royalties of 10-15% based on net to publisher. Pays for separate authors and illustrators: "Usually share royalty." Pays illustrators royalty of 10-15% based on wholesale price. Sends galleys to authors. Book catalog, ms/artist's guidelines for SASE.

Tips: Writers: "Be sure all elements of manuscript are included—include bio of author or illustrator." Submit books relating to Texas only.

SUNDANCE PUBLISHERS & DISTRIBUTORS, P.O. Box 1326 Newtown Rd., Littleton MA 01460. (508)486-9201. Book publisher. Publisher: Gare Thompson. Art Director: Patricia Rotonda. Publishes 12 picture books/year. 25% of books by first-time authors; 25% of books from agented authors. Multicultural, usually rhyming books, 300-500 words.

Nonfiction: Picture books: biography, geography, multicultural, photo essays. Young readers, young adults: geography, multicultural (all groups, strong contemporary narratives). Middle readers: careers, geography, multicultural. Multicultural needs include "all groups; strong, contemporary narratives." Average word length: picture books—300-500; young readers—1,500-4,000; middle readers—10,000-20,000; young adults—15,000-30,000. Published *Regalia: Native American Dress & Dance*, by Russell Peters, photos by Richard Haynes (ages preschool-8, "Big Books").

How to Contact/Writers: Fiction: Query (for young readers and up); submit complete ms (for picture books). Nonfiction: Query. Reports on queries in 6-10; mss in 2-3 months. Publishes a book "less than one year" after acceptance.

Illustration: Works with 15-20 illustrators/year. Will review ms/illustration packages. Contact: Forrest Stone, editor-in-chief. Will review artwork for future assignments.

How to Contact/Illustrators: Ms/illustration packages: Query; submit ms with dummy. Illustration only: Query with samples. Reports only if interested. Samples returned with SASE; samples "sometimes" filed. Original artwork "usually" returned.

Photography: Buys photos from freelancers. Contact: Patricia Rotondo, art director. Buys stock and assigns work. Uses series of multicultural subjects. Model/property releases required; captions required. Uses 4×5 transparencies. Photographers should submit cover letter, résumé, published samples, client list.

Terms: "Fees vary, depending on project."

Tips: "We're a school publisher. Only submit school material to us."

TAB BOOKS, Blue Ridge Summit PA 17294-0850. (717)794-2191. A Division of McGraw-Hill, Inc. Book publisher. Editor-in-Chief: Kim Tabor. Publishes 6 young readers/year; 6 young adults/year. 50% of books by first-time authors. 10% of books by agented authors.

Nonfiction: All levels: activity books, geography, multicultural, nature/environment, science. Young adults: geography, nature/environment, science. "We intend to broaden our children's science publishing area by adding books for nonscience teachers who are faced with teaching science and enviornmental awareness to children in the primary and elementary grades." Published *Weather in the Lab: Simulate Nature's Phenomena*, by Thomas Richard Baker (grade 10+, weather experiments); *From Field to Lab: 200 Life Science Experiments for the Amateur Biologist*, by James Witherspoon (grade 10+, life science experiments); *Insect Biology: 49 Science Fair Projects*, by H. Steven Dashefsky (grades 6+, science fair projects).

How To Contact/Writers: Query; submit outline/synopsis and sample chapters. Reports on queries in 2 months; mss in 3 months. Publishes a book 9-12 months after acceptance. Does not want to see fiction.

Illustration: Works with approximately 8-12 illustrators/year. Will review ms/illustration packages and artwork for future assignments.

How To Contact/Illustrators: Query first; submit resume, tearsheets, photocopies. Reports back only if interested. Originals returned at job's completion.

Terms: Authors paid royalty of 8-15% based on wholesale price. Illustrators paid by the project. "Terms vary from project to project." Book catalog and ms guidelines are free on request.

Tips: Looks for "science topics which are fun and educational and include activities adults and children can work on together. Projects should be designed around inexpensive, household materials and should require under two hours for completion."

TAMBOURINE BOOKS, 1350 Sixth Ave., New York NY 10019. Imprint of William Morrow & Co. Inc. Book publisher. Editor-in-Chief: Paulette Kaufmann. Art Director: Golda Laurens. Publishes 50 picture books/year; 4 middle readers/year; 2 young adults/year.

Fiction/Nonfiction: No primary theme for fiction or nonfiction — publishes various categories.

How to Contact/Writers: Fiction/Nonfiction: Submit complete ms. Reports on mss in 1-3 months.

Illustration: Will review ms/illustration packages. Will review artwork for future assignments.

How to Contact/Illustrators: Ms/illustration packages: Submit complete package. Illustrations only: Submit portfolio for review; provide résumé, business card, promotional literature or tearsheets to be kept on file. Original artwork returned at job's completion.

Terms: Pays authors royalty based on retail price. Offers advances. Pays illustrators royalty. Sends galleys to authors. Book catalog available for 9×12 SASE; ms guidelines available for SASE.

TEXAS CHRISTIAN UNIVERSITY PRESS, Box 30783, Fort Worth TX 76129. (817)921-7822. Fax: (817)921-7822. Book Publisher. Editorial Contact: Judy Alter. Art Director: Tracy Row. Publishes 1 young adult title/year. 75% of books by first-time authors. Only publishes historical works set in Texas.

Fiction: Young adults/teens: Texas history. Average word length: 35,000-50,000. Recently published *Josefina and the Hanging Tree*, by Isabelle Ridout Marvin (grades 6-9); *Whistle Punk*, by Alice Chapin and Kent Ross; and *A House Divided*, by Marj Gurasich. Does not want to see picture books, inspirational fiction.

Nonfiction: Young adults/teens: Texas biography, Texas history. Average word length: 35,000-50,000.

How To Contact/Writers: Fiction/Nonfiction: Query. Reports on queries in 1 week; mss in 1 month. Publishes a book 1-2 years after acceptance.

Kathy Osborn created this great, wise ruler for Ferida Wolff's The Emperor's Garden, *published by Tambourine Books. Osborn's simple shapes, interesting texture, vivid color, and unusual perspective work in perfect harmony with Wolff's tale of a "poor, but agreeable" Chinese village, whose residents set out to honor their emperor by building a splendid garden for him. The villagers end up in jealous arguments over the garden's name—arguments put to rest by the emperor himself.*

Illustration: Works with 1 illustrator/year. Will review mss/illustration packages. Will review artwork for future assignments. Contact: Tracy Row, art director.

How To Contact/Illustrators: Ms/illustration packages: Query with samples. Reports back to artists within 1 week. Originals returned to artist at job's completion.

Terms: Pays in royalty of 10% based on net price. Pays illustrators by the project. Book catalog free on request. Ms guidelines free on request.

Tips: Wants "well written, thoroughly researched historical fiction set in Texas. We are interested in fiction portraying various ethnicities."

THISTLEDOWN PRESS LTD., 633 Main St., Saskatoon, Saskatchewan S7H 0J8 Canada. (306)244-1722. Book publisher. Contact: Patrick O'Rourke. Publishes numerous middle reader and young adult titles/year. "Thistledown originates books by Canadian authors only, although we have co-published titles by authors outside Canada. We do not publish children's picture books."

Fiction: Middle readers: animal, folktales. Young adults: adventure, contemporary, folktales, humor, multicultural, suspense/mystery, sports. Average word length: middle readers—35,000; young adults—40,000. Published *The Blue Jean Collection*, by various authors (young adult, short story anthology); *Fish House Secrets*, by Kathy Stinson (young adult); *The Mystery of the Missing Will*, by Jeni Mayer (middle reader, mystery series).

How to Contact/Writers: Submit outline/synopsis and sample chapters. Reports on queries in 3 weeks, mss in 3-6 months. Publishes a book about one year after acceptance. No simultaneous submissions.

Illustration: Works with 2-3 illustrators/year. Contact: A.M. Forrie, art director.
How to Contact Illustrators: Illustrations only: Query with samples, promo sheet, slides, tearsheets.
Terms: Pays authors in royalty of 10-14% based on retail price. Pays illustrators by the project (range: $250-750). Sends galleys to authors. Book catalog free on request. Ms guidelines for #10 envelope and IRC.

TICKNOR & FIELDS, Books for Young Readers, 215 Park Ave. S., New York NY 10003. (212)420-5800. Imprint of Houghton Mifflin Company. Book publisher. Art Director: David Saylor. Publishes 25 picture books/year; 15 young readers/year; 10 middle readers/year; 10 young adults/year. 30% of books by first-time authors; 70% of books from agented authors.
Illustration: Works with 60 illustrators/year. Will review ms/illustration packages. Will review artwork for future assignments.
How to Contact/Illustrators: Ms/illustration packages: Submit ms with dummy. Illustrations only: Submit promo sheet, slides or tearsheets. Reports in 1 month. Samples returned with SASE. Samples filed "if we like them." Original artwork returned at job's completion.
Photography: Buys photos from freelancers. Works on assignment only. Model/property releases required. Uses b&w or color prints; 35mm, 2¼ × 2¼, 4 × 5 or 8 × 10 transparencies. Submit cover letter, published samples, slides or promo piece.
Terms: Pays illustrators and photographers by the project or royalty.

*TITAN BOOKS, 42-44 Dolben St., London SE1 0UP England. (071)620-0200. Fax: (071)620-0032. Book publisher. Managing Director: Katy Wild. Studio Manager: Chris Teather. Publishes 4 young adult titles/year. Publishes fantasy or film and TV tie-in titles (Batman, *Jurassic Park*, Star Trek, *Aliens*, etc.).
  • Titan has just moved into the area of children's books.
Fiction: Young adults: contemporary, fantasy, horror, humor, science fiction, suspense/mystery. Recently published *Batman: Knightfall and Beyond*.
Nonfiction: Young adults: biography, film & TV, how-to, music/dance.
How to Contact/Writers: Fiction/Nonfiction: Submit outline/synopsis. Reports in 2 months. Publishes a book 6-9 months after acceptance. Will consider simultaneous and electronic submissions and previously published work.
Illustration: Will review ms/illustration packages. Contact: Katy Wild, managing director. Will review artwork for future assignments.
How to Contact: Ms/illustration packages: Submit ms with dummy. Illustrations only: Query with samples. Reports in 2 months. Samples are returned; samples filed. Original artwork returned at job's completion.
Photography: Buys photos from freelancers. Contact: Chris Teather, studio manager. Buys stock images. Captions required. Uses 8 × 10 color or b&w prints and 35mm, 4 × 5 transparencies. Submit cover letter, published samples, stock photo list.
Terms: Pays authors royalty. Offers advances. Sends galleys to author. Book catalog available for SASE (IRC). Ms guidelines available for SASE (IRC).

TOR BOOKS, Forge, Orb, 175 Fifth Ave., New York NY 10010. Director Educational Sales: Kathleen Doherty. Educational Sales Coordinator: Amy Riddley. Publishes 50 picture books/year; 5-10 young readers/year; 20 middle readers/year; 5-10 young adults/year.
Fiction: Young readers, middle readers, young adults: Will consider anything except religious themes and poetry. "We are interested and open to books which tell stories from a wider range of perspectives. We are interested in materials that deal with a wide range of issues." Average word length: picture books—5,000; young readers—20,000; middle readers—10,000; young adults—20,000-40,000. Published *The Furious Flycycle*, by Jan Wahl/Ted Erik (ages 6-12/children's, fully illustrated); *The Eyes of Kid Midas*, by Neal Shusterman (ages 10-16, young adult novel).
Nonfiction: Does not want to see religion, cooking. Average word length: picture books—5,000; young readers—20,000; middle readers—10,000; young adults—40,000. Published *Strange Science: Planet Earth*, by Q.L. Pearce; *Stargazer's Guide*, by Q.L. Pearce (ages 6-12, guide to constellations, illustrated).

How to Contact/Writers: Fiction/Nonfiction: Submit outline/synopsis and 3 sample chapters. Reports on queries in 1 month; mss in 2 months.

Illustration: Works with 40 illustrators/year. Will review ms/illustration packages. Will review artwork for future assignments. Contact: Stefan M. Gerard, Educational Sales Coordinator.

How to Contact/Illustrators: Ms/illustration packages: Submit ms with dummy. Illustrations only: Query with samples. Reports only if interested. Samples returned with SASE; samples kept on file.

Terms: Pays authors royalty. Offers advances. Pays illustrators by the project. Book catalog available for 9 × 12 SAE and 3 first-class stamps.

Tips: "Get an agent. Allow him/her to direct you to publishers who are most appropriate. It saves time and effort."

*TRANSWORLD PUBLISHERS LIMITED, 61-63 Uxbridge Rd., London W5 5SA England. (081)579-2652. Fax: (081)579-5479. Imprints are Doubleday, Corgi, Yearling, Bantam. Book publisher. Editorial Director Children's and Young Adult Publishing: Philippa Dickinson. Publishes 6 picture books/year; 12 young readers/year; 12 middle readers/year; and 6 young adult titles/year.

Fiction: Picture books: adventure, animal, anthology, contemporary, fantasy, folktales, humor, multicultural, nature/environment, poetry, suspense/mystery. Young readers: adventure, animal, anthology, contemporary, fantasy, folktales, humor, multicultural, nature/environment, poetry, sports, suspense/mystery. Middle readers: adventure, animal, anthology, contemporary, fantasy, folktales, humor, multicultural, nature/environment, problem novels, romance, sports, suspense/mystery. Young adults: adventure, contemporary, fantasy, humor, multicultural, nature/environment, problem novels, romance, science fiction, suspense/mystery. Average word length: picture books — 800; young readers — 1,500-6,000; middle readers — 10,000-15,000; young adults — 20,000-45,000. Recently published *Hacker*, by Malorie Blackman (8, computer assisted adventure); *The Suitcase Kid*, by Jacqueline Wilson (8-11, contemporary); and *Horse Pie*, by Dick King-Smith (6-8, animal novel).

How to Contact/Writers: Submit outline/synopsis and 3 sample chapters. Reports on queries in 1-2 months; mss in 2-3 months. Will consider simultaneous and previously published submissions.

Illustration: Works with 50 illustrators/year. Will review ms/illustration packages. Contact: Senior Children's Editor. Will review artwork for future assignments.

How to Contact/Illustrators: Ms/illustration packages: Submit ms with dummy. Illustrations only: Query with samples. Reports in 1 month. Samples are returned with SASE (IRC).

Photography: Buys photos from freelancers. Contact: Liz Masters, art department. Buys stock images. Photo captions required. Uses color or b&w prints. Submit cover letter, published samples.

Terms: Pays authors royalty. Offers advances. Pays illustrators by the project or royalty. Pays photographers by the project or per photo. Sends galleys to authors; dummies to illustrators.

*TRICYCLE PRESS, P.O. Box 7123, Berkeley CA 94707. Acquisitions Editor: Nicole Geiger. Publishes 5 picture books/year; 1 young adult/year. 30% of books by first-time authors.

Fiction: Picture books: concept, folktales, health, multicultural, nature/environment. Middle readers: health, multicultural, nature/environment. Average word length: picture books-1,200. Recently published *Fairies from A to Z*, by Adrienne Keith and Wendy Wallin Malinow (ages 3 and up); and *Amelia's Notebook*, by Marissa Moss (ages 7-9, picture book).

Nonfiction: Picture books: activity books, arts/crafts, concept, geography, health, how-to, nature/environment, science, self help, social issues. Young readers: activity books, arts/crafts, health, how-to, nature/environment, science, self help, social issues. Middle readers: Activity books, health, nature/environment, science, self help. Young adults: careers, concept, health, how-to, reference, self help, social issues. Recently published *Ask Me If I Care: Voices from an American High School*, by Nancy Rubin (ages 14 and up); *More Mudpies: 101 Alternatives to Television*, by Nancy Blakey (ages 2-12, activity book); and *Pretend Soup* *and Other Real Recipes: A Cookbook for Preschoolers and Up,* by Mollie Katzen and Ann Henderson (ages 3-6, children's cookbook).

How to Contact/Writers: Fiction: Submit complete ms for picture books; submit outline/synopsis and 3 sample chapters for anything else. Nonfiction: Submit complete ms. Reports on queries/mss in 8-10 weeks. Publishes a book 1 year after acceptance. Will consider simultaneous submissions.

Illustration: Works with 6 illustrators/year. Will review ms/illustration package. Contact: Nicole Geiger, acquisitions editor. Will review artwork for future assignments.

How to Contact/Illustrators: Ms/illustration packages: Submit ms with dummy. Illustrations only: Query with samples, promo sheet, tearsheets. Reports back only if interested. Samples returned with SASE; samples filed. Original artwork returned at job's completion unless work for hire.

Terms: Pays authors 15% royalty (but lower if illustrated ms) based on wholesale price. Offers advances. Pays illustrators by the project or royalty. Sends galleys to authors. Book catalog for 9 × 12 SAE and 98¢. Ms guidelines for SASE.

Tips: "We are looking for something a bit outside the mainstream and with lasting appeal (no one-shot-wonders). Lately we've noticed a sacrifice of quality writing for the sake of illustration."

TROLL ASSOCIATES, 100 Corporate Dr., Mahwah NJ 07430. Book publisher. Editor: Marian Frances.

Fiction: Picture books: animal, contemporary, folktales, history, nature/environment, poetry, sports, suspense/mystery. Young readers: adventure, animal, contemporary, folktales, history, nature/environment, poetry, science fiction, sports, suspense/mystery. Middle readers: adventure, anthology, animal, contemporary, fantasy, folktales, health-related, history, nature/environment, poetry, problem novels, romance, science fiction, sports, suspense/mystery. Young adults: problem novels, romance and suspense/mystery.

Nonfiction: Picture books: activity books, animal, biography, careers, history, hobbies, nature/environment, sports. Young readers: activity books, animal, biography, careers, health, history, hobbies, music/dance, nature/environment, sports. Middle readers: activity books, animal, biography, careers, health, history, hobbies, music/dance, nature/environment, religion, sports. Young adults: health, music/dance.

How to Contact/Writers: Fiction: Query or submit outline/synopsis and 3 sample chapters. Nonfiction: Query. Reports in 2-4 weeks.

Illustration: Will review ms/illustration packages. Contact: Marian Frances, editor. Will review artwork for future assignments.

How to Contact/Illustrators: Illustrations only: Query with samples; arrange a personal interview to show portfolio; provide résumé, promotional literature or tearsheets to be kept on file. Reports in 2-4 weeks.

Photography: Interested in stock photos. Model/property releases required.

Terms: Pays authors royalty or work purchased outright. Pays illustrators by the project or royalty. Photographers paid by the project.

TROPHY BOOKS, 10 E. 53rd St., New York NY 10022. Subsidiary of HarperCollins Children's Books Group. "Trophy is primarily a paperback reprint imprint. We do not publish original illustrated manuscripts."

TUDOR PUBLISHERS, INC., P.O. Box 38366, Greensboro NC 27438. Contact: Pam Cocks. Publishes 1 middle readers/year; 2 young adults/year. 30% of books by first-time authors. Primarily publishes young adult novels and fiction.

Fiction: Young adults: contemporary, folktales, multicultural (African-American, Native American), problem novels, suspense/mystery. Does not want to see romance. Word length

A bullet has been placed within some listings to introduce special comments by the editors of **Children's Writer's & Illustrator's Market.**

varies. Published *The Mean Lean Weightlifting Queen*, by Mark Emerson (young adult novel).

Nonfiction: Middle readers, young adults: biography, multicultural (folklore, history), reference, science, social issues, sports, textbooks. Average word length: middle readers—10,000-12,000; young adults—15,000-25,000. Published *Bill Clinton: President from Arkansas*, by Gene L. Martin and Aaron Boyd (young adult, biography).

How to Contact/Writers: Fiction: Submit outline/synopsis and 3 sample chapters. Nonfiction: Submit outline/synopsis and 1-3 sample chapters. Reports on queries in 2 weeks; mss in 1 month. Publishes a book 9-12 months after acceptance.

Terms: Pays authors royalty of 8-10% based on wholesale price. Offers "occasional modest advance." Sends galleys to authors. Book catalog available for #10 SAE and 1 first-class stamp.

TYNDALE HOUSE PUBLISHERS, INC., 351 Executive Dr., P.O. Box 80, Wheaton IL 60189. (708)668-8300. Book publisher. Children's editorial contact: Marilyn Dellorto. Children's illustration contact: Marlene Muddell. Publishes approximately 20 children's titles/year.

• Tyndale House no longer reviews unsolicited manuscripts.

Fiction: Middle readers: adventure, religion, suspense/mystery.

Nonfiction: Picture books: activity books, religion. Young readers: religion.

How to Contact/Writers: Fiction/Nonfiction: Query. Reports on queries in 6 weeks; mss in 3 months.

Illustration: Uses full-color for book covers, b&w or color spot illustrations for some nonfiction. Contact: Marlene Muddell.

How to Contact/Illustrators: Illustrations only: Query with photocopies (color or b&w) of samples, résumé.

Photography: Buys photos from freelancers. Contact: Marlene Muddell. Works on assignment only.

Terms: Pay rates for authors and illustrators vary. Only interested in agented material.

Tips: "All accepted manuscripts will appeal to Evangelical Christian children and parents."

UNIVERSITY CLASSICS, LTD. PUBLISHERS, One Bryan Rd., P.O. Box 2301, Athens OH 45701. (614)592-4543. Book publisher. President: Albert H. Shuster. Publishes 1 young readers/year; 1 middle readers/year; 1 young adult title/year. 50% of books by first-time authors.

• This publisher is "booked for the next two years" in children's fiction and nonfiction. Do not submit work (manuscripts or illustrations) to them.

Fiction: Picture books: animal, concept, health, nature/environment. Young readers: concept, health, nature/environment, special needs. Middle readers: health, nature/environment, problem novels, special needs. Young adults: health, nature/environment, special needs. Average word length: young readers—1,200; middle readers—5,000. Published *Toodle D. Poodle*, by Katherine Oaha/Dorathyre Shuster (grades 4-6, ages 10-12); *The Day My Dad and I Got Mugged*, by Howard Goldsmith (grades 5-8, ages 12-15).

Nonfiction: Picture books: activity books, animal, arts/crafts, concept, health, nature/environment, self help, special needs. Young readers: activity books, animal, arts/crafts, concept, health, nature/environment, self help, special needs, textbooks. Middle readers, young adults: arts/crafts, concept, health, nature/environment, self help, special needs, textbooks. Average word length: young readers—1,200; middle readers—5,000. Published *Fitness and Nutrition: The Winning Combination*, by Jane Buch (ages 13-17, textbook); *The Way We Live: Practical Economics*, by John Shaw (ages 13-adult, textbook); *Ride Across America: An Environmental Commitment*, by Lucian Spataro (ages 13-17, trade).

Illustration: Works with 2 illustrators/year.

Terms: Pays authors royalty of 5-12% based on retail price. Pays illustrators by the project. Book catalog available for #10 SAE and 2 first-class stamps.

Tips: "Consumers are looking more for educational than fictional books, and this will continue."

■**UNIVERSITY EDITIONS, INC.**, Subsidiary of Aegina Press, Inc., 59 Oak Lane, Spring Valley, Huntington WV 25704. (304)429-7204. Book publisher. Managing Editor: Ira Herman. Art Coordinator: Angela Hall. Publishes 3 picture books/year; 4 young readers/year; 4 middle readers/year; 4 young adult titles/year. 40% of books by first-time authors; 5% of books from agented authors. "Most new titles are subsidy published."

Fiction: Picture books, young readers: adventure, animal, fantasy, history, poetry, science fiction, suspense/mystery. Middle readers: adventure, animal, fantasy, history, nature/environment, poetry, romance, science fiction, suspense/mystery. Young adults: adventure, animal, fantasy, nature/environment, romance, science fiction, suspense/mystery. Average word length: picture books—1,000; young readers—2,000; middle readers—10,000; young adults—20,000. Recently published *The Clumsy Tooth Fairy*, by Lucille D'Amore Zegers, illustrated by Michalino Pusatera (ages 4-7); *From the Dragon's Tale*, by Diane and Joe Notaro, illustrated by Gary Lehman (ages 6-8, fantasy); and *There's a Blue Bear in the Bathtub and My Mother Is Mad*, by Sandra Potts, illustrated by Gary Laronde (ages 4-6, picture book).

Nonfiction: Picture books: animal, history, nature/environment, religion. Young readers: animal, biography, history, religion, science, sports. Middle readers: animal, biography, history, nature/environment, religion, science, sports. Young adults: animal, careers, history, nature/environment, religion, science, sports. Average word length: picture books—1,000; young readers—2,000; middle readers—10,000; young adults—20,000. Recently published *Art Japanese Style*, by Charlene Stewart McCree, illustrated by Susan Kemnitz, (ages 5-10).

How to Contact/Writers: Fiction/Nonfiction: Submit complete ms. Reports on queries in 1 week; mss in 1 month. Publishes a book 6 months after acceptance.

Illustration: Works with 15 illustrators/year. Will review ms/illustration packages. Contact: Angela Hall, art coordinator. Will review artwork for future assignments.

How to Contact/Illustrators: Ms/illustration packages: Submit ms with dummy or submit ms with 5 pieces of final art. Illustrations only: Query with samples; photocopies OK; samples will not be returned. Reports in 1 month. Samples not filed.

Terms: Pays authors royalty of 10-15% based on retail price, "negotiated individually for each book." Pays illustrators by the project ($60 minimum), "negotiated individually for each book." Sends galleys to authors. Book catalog available for $2, 10×13 SAE and 4 first-class stamps; ms guidelines available for SASE.

*USBORNE PUBLISHING LTD., 83-85 Saffron Hill, London ECIN 8RT England. (071)430-2800. Fax: (071)430-1562. Managing Designer: Amanda Barlow. 10-15% of books by first-time authors. Publishes about 100 titles/year.

• Usborne is not interested in unsolicited manuscripts, only illustrations.

Fiction: Young readers: adventure, animal, health, history, nature/environment, poetry, sports. Middle readers: adventure, animal, fantasy, health, history, nature/environment, poetry, science fiction, sports, suspense/mystery. Young adults: adventure, animal, fantasy, history, nature/environment, poetry, science fiction, sports.

Nonfiction: Picture books: activity books, animal, arts/crafts, cooking, geography, history, hobbies, how-to, music/dance, nature/environment, reference, religion, science, sports, math, languages, puzzles. Recently published *Usborne Book of Face Painting*, by Chris Caudron and Caro Childs (8-12, illustration and color photography); *Usborne Book of Europe*, by Rebecca Treays (10 up, history/politics); *First Book of Music*, by Emma Danes (introduction to musical instruments).

Illustration: Works with 150 illustrators/year. Will review artwork for future assignments.

How to Contact/Illustrators: Illustrations only: Query with samples, portfolio, slides; arrange personal portfolio review. Reports back only if interested. Samples are returned with SASE; samples filed.

Terms: Pays illustrators by the project "Depends entirely on type of book, style etc." Book catalog for 11×4 and U.K. postage.

VICTOR BOOKS, Scripture Press, 1825 College Ave., Wheaton IL 60187. (708)668-6000. Fax: (708)668-3806. Book publisher. Children's Editor: Liz Duckworth. Publishes 9 picture books/year; 6 middle readers/year. "No young readers at this point, but open to them." 20% of books by first-time authors; 10% of books from agented authors. All books are related to Christianity.

Fiction: Picture books: adventure, animal, contemporary, religion. Young readers: adventure, animal, contemporary, religion, science fiction, sports, suspense/mystery. Middle readers: adventure, contemporary, history, religion, sports, suspense/mystery. Does not want to see stories with "Christian" animals; no holiday legends. Recently published *What Twos Can Do*, by Jane Morton (ages 1-3, board book); *The Morning of the World*, by Bob Hartman (ages 4-7, picture book); *Wings of an Angel*, by Sigmund Browner (ages 8-12, middle reader); *The Long Way Home*, by Jerry Jerman (ages 8-12, middle reader).

Nonfiction: Picture books: biography, religion. Young readers: biography, history, religion. Middle readers: biography, history, religion, sports. No ABC books or biographies of obscure/not well-known people.

How to Contact/Writers: Fiction/Nonfiction: Submit complete ms for picture books. Submit outline/synopsis and 2 sample chapters for middle readers. Reports on queries in 2 months; mss in 3 months. Publishes a book 18 months after acceptance. Will consider simultaneous submissions.

Illustration: Will review ms/illustration packages. Will review artwork for future assignments. Contact: Paul Higdon, art director.

How to Contact/Illustrators: Ms/illustration packages: Submit complete package. Illustrations only: Submit portfolio for review; provide résumé, promotional literature or tearsheets to be kept on file. Reports back only if interested. Originals not returned.

Photography: Contact: Paul Higdon, art director. Uses photos of children. Model/property releases required. Buys stock images. Photographers should submit portfolio for review; provide résumé, promotional literature or tearsheets to be kept on file.

Terms: Pays authors royalty of 5-10% based on wholesale price, outright purchase $125-2,500. Offers advance "based on project." Pays illustrators by the project, royalty of 5% based on wholesale price. Photographers paid by the project, per photo. Sends galleys to authors. Book catalog available for 9×12 SAE and 2 first-class stamps. Ms guidelines available for SASE.

Tips: "In general children's books I see trends toward increasingly high quality. It's a crowded field, so each idea must be fresh and unique. Ask yourself, 'Does this book belong primarily on the shelf of a *Christian* bookstore?' That's how we distribute so your answer should reflect that."

VICTORY PUBLISHING, 3504 Oak Dr., Menlo Park CA 94025. (415)323-1650. Book publisher. Publisher: Yolanda Garcia. 95% of books by first-time authors. "All books pertain to instruction of elementary age children—specifically bilingual, Spanish/English."

Fiction: Young readers: concept, poetry. Middle readers: poetry. Does not want to see mystery, religion, fantasy, sports.

Nonfiction: Young readers, middle readers: activity books, arts/crafts, concept, cooking, how-to, self-helf. No animals.

How to Contact/Writers: Fiction/Nonfiction: Query. Submit outline/synopsis and 2 sample chapters. "Must send SASE." Reports on queries in 3 weeks; mss in 1-2 months. "Must send SASE." Publishes a book 1 year after acceptance.

Illustration: Works with 1-2 illustrators/year. Will review ms/illustration packages. Will review artwork for future assignments. Contact: Veronica Garcia, illustrator.

How to Contact/Illustrators: Ms/illustration packages: Query. Illustration only: Query with samples; provide résumé, promo sheet to be kept on file. Reports on queries in 3 weeks. Samples returned with SASE (if requested); samples filed. "Originals are purchased."

Terms: Work purchased outright from authors (average amount: $100-500). Pays illustrators by the project or set amount per illustration depending on complexity. Sends dummies to illustrators.

Tips: Wants "teacher resources for elementary school—bilingual Spanish/English activity books."

■**W.W. PUBLICATIONS**, P.O. Box 373, Highland MI 48357-0373. (813)585-0985. Subsidiary of American Tolkien Society. Independent book producer. Editorial Contact: Phil Helms. 75% of books by first-time authors. Subsidy publishes 75%.

Fiction/Nonfiction: All ages: fantasy, Tolkien-related.
How to Contact/Writers: Fiction: Query. Submit outline/synopsis of complete ms. Reports on queries in 4-6 weeks; 2-3 months on mss. Publishes a book 3-6 months after acceptance. Will consider simultaneous submissions.
Illustrations: Reviews all illustration packages. Prefers 8½ × 11 b&w and ink.
How to Contact/Illustrators: Query with samples. Reports on ms/art samples in 3 months. Original artwork returned at job's completion if requested.
Terms: Pays author free copies. Sends galleys to author if requested; dummies to illustrators. Book catalog for 1 first-class stamp and #10 SAE.
Tips: "Tolkien-oriented only."

WALKER AND CO., 435 Hudson St., New York NY 10014. (212)727-8300. Division of Walker Publishing Co. Inc. Book publisher. Estab. 1959. Editor: Mary Rich. Publishes 3-5 picture books/year; 10-15 middle readers/year; 15 young adult titles/year. 10-15% of books by first-time authors; 65% of books from agented writers.
Fiction: Picture books: fantasy, history. Young readers: animal, history, fantasy. Middle readers: fantasy, science fiction, history. Young adults: fantasy, history, science fiction. Recently published *King Kendrick's Splinter*, by Sally Derby, illustrated by Leonid Gore (picture book); *The Dirty War*, by Charles Slaughter (young adult); *Red Dirt Jessie*, by Anna Myers (middle grade).
Nonfiction: Picture books, young readers, middle readers, young adults: animal, biography, education, history, hobbies, music/dance, nature/environment, religion, science, sports. Recently published *To the Top of the World: Adventures with Arctic Wolves*, by Jim Brandenburg (photo essay); *The Fire Curse and Other True Medical Mysteries*, by David Drotar.
How to Contact/Writers: Fiction/nonfiction: Submit outline/synopsis and sample chapters. Reports on queries/mss in 2-3 months. Will consider simultaneous submissions.
Illustration: Editorial will review ms/illustration packages.
How to Contact/Illustrators: Ms/illustration packages: 5 chapters of ms with 1 piece of final art, remainder roughs. Illustrations only: Tearsheets. Reports on art samples only if interested. Original artwork returned at job's completion.
Terms: Pays authors in royalties of 5-10% based on wholesale price "depends on contract." Offers average advance payment of $2,000-4,000. Pays illustrators by the project (range: $500-5,000); royalties from 50%. Sends galleys to authors. Book catalog available for 9 × 12 SASE; ms guidelines for SASE.
Tips: Writers: "Don't take rejections personally and try to consider them objectively. We receive more than 20 submissions a day. Can it be improved?" Illustrators: "Have a well-rounded portfolio with different styles." Looks for "original picture books and quality nonfiction for young and middle readers."

WARD HILL PRESS, P.O. Box 04-0424, Staten Island NY 10304. (718)816-9449. Editorial Assistant: Elizabeth Davis. Publishes 3-6 middle readers/year; 3-6 young adults/year. 90% of books by first-time authors.
Fiction: Middle readers, young adults: folktales, multicultural novels. Average word length: middle readers—20,000; young adults—20,000.
Nonfiction: Middle readers, young adults: biography, history, multicultural, social issues. Multicultural needs include biographies of figures from diverse cultures. Does not want to see biographies of mainstream personalities or pop entertainers. Average word length: middle readers—20,000; young adults—20,000. Published *Zora Neale Hurston: A Storyteller's Life*, by Janelle Yates, illustrated by David Adams (ages 10 and up, biography).
How to Contact/Writers: Fiction/Nonfiction: Query. Reports on queries in 6-8 weeks; mss in 6-8 weeks. Publishes a book 1 year after acceptance. Will consider previously published work.
Illustration: Works with 3-6 illustrators/year.
How to Contact/Illustrators: Ms/illustration packages: Query. Illustrations only: Query with samples; provide résumé. Reports in 1-2 months. Samples returned with SASE; samples filed. Originals not returned.

Terms: Pays authors royalty of 5-8% based on retail price. Offers advances (average amount: $800). Pays illustrators royalty of 3-5% based on retail price. Sends galleys to authors; dummies to illustrators. Book catalog available for 4×9½ SAE and 1 first-class stamp. "We send manuscript guidelines only after seeing query."

WATERFRONT BOOKS, 85 Crescent Rd., Burlington VT 05401. (802)658-7477. Book publisher. Publisher: Sherrill N. Musty. Some books by first-time authors.
Fiction: "Special issues for children only." Picture books, young readers, middle readers, young adults: mental health, family/parenting, health, special issues involving barriers to learning in children.
Nonfiction: "Special issues for children only." Picture books, young readers, middle readers, young adults: education, guidance, health, mental health, social issues. "We publish books for both children and adults on any subject that helps to lower barriers to learning in children: mental health, family/parenting, education and social issues. We are now considering books for children on bettering the environment."
How to Contact/Writers: Fiction/Nonfiction: Query. Reports on queries in 2 weeks; mss in 6 weeks. Publishes a book 6 months after acceptance.
Illustration: Will review ms/illustration packages.
How to Contact/Illustrators: Ms/illustration packages: Query first. Illustrations only: Résumé, tearsheets. Reports on art samples only if interested.
Terms: Pays authors in royalties of 10-15% based on wholesale price. Pays illustrators by the job. Sends galleys to authors; dummies to illustrators. Book catalog available for #10 SAE and 1 first-class stamp.
Tips: "Have your manuscript thoroughly reviewed and even copyedited, if necessary. If you are writing about a special subject, have a well-qualified professional in the field review it for accuracy and appropriateness. It always helps to get some testimonials before submitting it to a publisher. The publisher then knows she/he is dealing with something worthwhile."

WEIGL EDUCATIONAL PUBLISHERS, 1900A 11th St. SE., Calgary, Alberta T2G 3G2. (403)233-7747. Book publisher. Publisher: Linda Weigl.
Fiction: Middle readers: folktales, multicultural, nature/environment.
Nonfiction: Young reader, middle reader, young adult: resources involving activity books, careers, education, health, history, nature/environment, social studies. Average length: young reader, middle reader, young adult—64 pages. Recently published *Career Connections Series II*, (middle readers); *Digging for Dinosaurs*, (young readers, middle readers); and *Introducing Japan*, (young readers, middle readers).
How to Contact/Writers: Nonfiction: Submit query and résumé. Reports on queries in 3 weeks; mss in 6 months. Publishes a book 2 years after acceptance. Will consider simultaneous submissions.
Illustration: Works with 1 illustrator/year. Will review ms/illustration packages. Will review artwork for future assignments. Contact: A. Woodrow, project coordinator.
How to Contact/Illustrators: Ms/illustration packages: Query first. Illustrations only: Query with samples. Reports back only if interested or when appropriate project comes in.
Photography: Buys photos from freelancers. Buys stock and assigns work. Wants political, juvenile, multicultural photos. Contact: A. Woodrow.
Terms: Pays authors royalty or work purchased outright. Pays illustrators by the project. Sends galleys to author; dummies to illustrator. Book catalog free on request.
Tips: Looks for "a manuscript that answers a specific curriculum need, or can be applied to a curriculum topic with multiple applications (e.g. career education)."

The Subject Index, located before the General Index, lists book and magazine publishers by their fiction and nonfiction needs.

*DANIEL WEISS ASSOCIATES, INC., 11th Floor, 33 W. 17th St., New York NY 10011. (212)645-3865. Fax: (212)633-1236. Independent book producer/packager. Editorial Assistant: Sigrid Berg. Publishes 30 young readers/year; 40 middle readers/year; and 70 young adults/year. 25% of books by first-time authors. "We do mostly series!"

Fiction: Young readers: adventure, animal, contemporary, fantasy, suspense/mystery. Middle readers, young adults: adventure, anthology, contemporary, problem novels, romance, sports, suspense/mystery.

How to Contact/Writers: Submit outline/synopsis and 2 sample chapters. Reports on queries in 1 month; mss in 2 months. Publishes a book 1 year after acceptance. Will consider simultaneous submissions.

Illustration: Works with 20 illustrators/year. Will review ms/illustration packages. Contact: Paul Matarazzo, art director. Will review artwork for future assignments.

How to Contact/Illustrators: Ms/illustration packages: Submit ms with dummy. Illustrations only: Provide promo sheet. Reports in 2 months. Samples returned with SASE. Original artwork returned at job's completion.

Terms: Pays authors royalty of 4%. Work purchased outright from authors, $1,000 minimum. Offers advances (average amount: $3,000). Pays illustrators by the project. Ms guidelines available if SASE sent.

WESTERN PUBLISHING, 1220 Mound Ave., Racine WI 53404. See the listings for Artists & Writers Guild Books and Golden Books.
- Western Publishing ranks first, based on net sales, of the top 12 children's publishers.

*WHISPERING COYOTE PRESS, INC., Suite 1150, 300 Crescent Court, Dallas TX 75201. Editor/Publisher: Lou Alpert. Publishes 6 picture books/year. 20% of books from first-time authors.

Fiction: Picture books: adventure, animal, fantasy, folktales, humor, nature/environment. Does not want to see number, alphabet, death, handicap and holiday books. Average word length: picture books—under 2,000. Recently published *Itsy Bitsy Spider*, written and illustrated by Iza Trapani (4-8, picture book); *It's Raining, It's Pouring*, by Kin Eagle, illustrated by Rob Gilbert (picture book).

How to Contact/Writers: Submit complete ms. Reports on queries in 3 months. Publishes a book 1½-3 years after acceptance. Will consider simultaneous submissions.

Illustration: Works with 6 illustrators/year. Will review ms/illustration packages. Contact: Lou Alpert, editor/publisher. Uses color artwork only.

How to Contact/Illustrators: Ms/illustration packages: Submit ms with dummy or 3-4 pieces of final art. Illustrations only: Submit color copies or a half dozen pieces for file. Reports back only if interested. Samples returned with SASE; samples filed. Originals not returned.

Terms: Pays authors royalty of 4% based on retail price. Offers advances. Pays illustrators royalty of 4%. Book catalog available for #10 SAE and 1 first-class stamp. Manuscript and art guidelines available for SASE.

WHITEBIRD BOOKS, 200 Madison Ave., New York NY 10016. An imprint of Putnam and Grosset Group. See the listing for G.P. Putnam's Sons.

ALBERT WHITMAN & COMPANY, 6340 Oakton St., Morton Grove IL 60053-2723. (708)581-0033. Book publisher. Editor-in-Chief: Kathleen Tucker. Publishes 30 books/year. 15% of books by first-time authors; 15% of books from agented authors. "We publish various categories, but we're mostly known for our concept books—books that deal with children's problems or concerns."

Fiction: Picture books: adventure, animal, contemporary, fantasy, folktales, health, nature/environment. Young readers and middle readers: adventure, animal, contemporary, fantasy, folktales, health, history, multicultural, nature/environment, problem novels, special needs, sports, suspense/mystery. Does not want to see "religion-oriented, ABCs, pop-up, romance, counting or any book that is supposed to be written in." Published *Two of Everything*, by Lily Toy Hong (picture book); *Kathy's Hats*, by Trudy Krisher (ages 7-10, concept).

Nonfiction: Picture books, young readers and middle readers: animal, careers, health, history, hobbies, multicultural, music/dance, nature/environment, special needs, sports. Does not want to see "religion, any books that have to be written in, biographies of living people." Published *Hampsters*, by Jerome Wexler (grades 2-8, young readers/middle readers); *Theodore Roosevelt Takes Charge*, by Nancy Whitelaw (ages 8 and up, middle readers).

How to Contact/Writers: Fiction/Nonfiction: Submit complete ms. Reports on queries in 4-6 weeks; mss in 2 months. Publishes a book 18 months after acceptance. Will consider simultaneous submissions "but let us know if it is one" and previously published work "if out of print."

Illustration: Will review ms/illustration packages. Contact: Editorial. Will review artwork for future assignments. Uses more color art than b&w.

How to Contact/Illustrators: Ms/illustration packages: Submit all chapters of ms with any pieces of final art. Illustrations only: Query with samples. Send slides or tearsheets. Reports back only if interested. Original artwork returned at job's completion.

Photography: Photographers should contact Editorial. Publishes books illustrated with photos but not stock photos—desires photos all taken for project. "Our books are for children and cover many topics; photos must be taken to match text. Books often show a child in a particular situation (e.g., a First Communion, a sister whose brother is born prematurely)." Photographers should query with samples; send unsolicited photos by mail.

Terms: Pays authors royalty. Offers advances. Pays illustrators royalty. Sends galleys to authors; dummies to illustrators. Book catalog available for 9×12 SAE and 5 first-class stamps. Ms guidelines available for SASE.

Tips: "In both picture books and nonfiction, we are seeking stories showing life in other cultures and the variety of multicultural life in the U.S. We also want fiction and nonfiction about mentally or physically challenged children—some recent topics have been AIDS, asthma, cerebral palsy."

*JOHN WILEY & SONS, INC., 605 Third Ave., New York NY 10158. (212)850-6206. Fax: (212)850-6095. Book publisher. Editor: Kate Bradford. Publishes 15 middle readers/year; 2 adult titles/year. 20% of books by first-time authors. Publishes educational nonfiction, primarily science, nature and activities.

Nonfiction: Middle readers: activity books, animal, arts/crafts, cooking, geography, health, hobbies, how-to, nature/environment, reference, science, self help. Young adults: activity books, arts/crafts, health, hobbies, how-to, nature/environment, reference, science, self help. Average word length middle readers—20,000-40,000. Recently published *Dinosaurs for Every Kid*, by Janice Van Cleave, (8-12, science activities); *Roller Coaster Science*, by Jim Wiese, (8-12, science activities); and *Earth-Friendly Toys*, by George Pfiffner, (8-12, crafts).

How to Contact/Writers: Query. Submit outline/synopsis and 2 sample chapters. Reports on queries in 1 month; mss in 3 months. Publishes a book 1 year after acceptance. Will consider simultaneous and previously published submissions.

Illustration: Works with 10 illustrators/year. Will review ms/illustration packages. Will review artwork for future assignments. Uses primarily black & white artwork.

How to Contact/Illustrators: Ms/illustration packages: Query. Illustrations only: Query with samples, résumé, client list. Reports back only if interested. Samples filed. Original artwork returned at job's completion.

Terms: Pays authors royalty of 7% based on wholesale price. Offers advances. Pays illustrators by the project. Sends galleys to authors. Book catalog available for SAE.

Tips: "There's a glut of children's publishing in many areas. Horror fiction and merchandise seem to be the hottest areas. Electronic publishing for kids is coming on strong."

WILLIAMSON PUBLISHING CO., Box 185, Charlotte VT 05445. (802)425-2102. Fax: (802)425-2199. Book publisher. Editorial Director: Susan Williamson. Publishes 10-12 young readers titles/year. 70% of books by first-time authors; 20% of books from agented authors. Publishes "very successful nonfiction series (Kids Can! Series) on subjects such as nature, creative play, arts/crafts, geography."

• Williamson's titles have received several awards in the last few years. In 1994, *Kids Make Music* won a Benjamin Franklin Award for best juvenile/YA nonfiction.

ECOART! received *Skipping Stones*' Nature and Ecology Honor Award.

Nonfiction: Young readers: activity books, animal, arts/crafts, cooking, geography, health, hobbies, how-to, multicultural, music/dance, nature/environment, science, self-help. Does not want to see textbooks, picture books, fiction. "We are looking for books in which learning and doing are inseparable." Recently published *The Kids' Wildlife Book*, by Warner Shedd, illustrated by Loretta Trezzo Bracen (exploring animal worlds through indoor/outdoor experiences); *The Little Hands Art Book*, by Judy Press, illustrated by Loretta Trezzo Bracen (exploring arts/crafts); and *Tales Alive!*, retold by Susan Miloz, illustrated by Michael A. Donuto (multicultural tales with activities).

How to Contact/Writers: Query; submit outline/synopsis and 2 sample chapters. Reports on queries in 3-4 months; mss in 6 months. Publishes book, "depending on graphics, about one year" after acceptance. Will consider simultaneous submissions.

Illustration: Works with 3 illustrators/year. Will review artwork for future assignments. Uses primarily b&w artwork.

Photography: Buys photos from freelancers. Buys stock and assigns work. Contact: Susan Williamson, editorial director.

Terms: Pays authors royalty based on wholesale price. Offers advances. Pays illustrators by the project. Sends galleys to authors. Book catalog available for 8½ × 11 SAE and 4 first-class stamps; ms guidelines available for SASE.

Tips: Interested in "creative, packed-with-interesting information, interactive learning books written for young readers ages 2-6 and 4-10. In nonfiction children's publishing, we are looking for authors with a depth of knowledge shared with children through a warm, embracing style—a respite in a rough world that tells not only how, but affirms that children can."

WILLOWISP PRESS, 801 94th Ave. N., St. Petersburg FL 33702-2426. Division PAGES, Inc. Imprints: Worthington Press, Riverbank Press, Hamburger Press. Book publisher. Writers contact: Acquisitions Editor. Illustrators contact: Art Director. Publishes 15-20 picture books/year; 6-8 young readers/year; 6-8 middle readers/year. 25% of books by first-time authors.

Fiction: Picture books: adventure, animal, contemporary, folktales, history, humor, multicultural, nature/environment, rhymes, concept books for preschool. Young readers: adventure, animal, contemporary, fantasy, folktales, history, humor, multicultural, nature/environment, sports, suspense/mystery. Middle readers: adventure, animal, anthology, contemporary, folktales, history, humor, multicultural, nature/environment, problem novels, romance, sports, suspense/mystery. Young adults: adventure, animal, anthology, contemporary, folktales, history, humor, multicultural, nature/environment, problem novels, romance, sports, suspense/mystery. No religious or violence. Average word length: picture books—350-1,000; beginning chapter books—3,000-4,000; middle readers—14,000-18,000; young adult—20,000-24,000. Recently published *Now That Andi's Gone*, by Karle Dickerson (grades 5 and up, novel); *Jake's Journal*, by Ruth E. Kelley (grades 4-7, novel); *The Little Ant*, by David Novak (grades K-3, picture book).

Nonfiction: Picture books: activity books, animal, biography, geography, history, how-to, multicultural, nature/environment, reference, science. Young readers: activity books, animal, arts/crafts, biography, geography, history, how-to, multicultural, nature/environment, reference, science, sports. Middle readers: activity books, animal, biography, careers, geography, history, hobbies, how-to, multicultural, nature/environment, reference, science, social issues, sports. Young adults: animal, biography, careers, concept, geography, history, hobbies, how-to, multicultural, nature/environment, reference, science, social issues, sports. No religious. Recently published *A Look Around Rain Forests*, by Ed Perez (ages K-3, environment); *10 Women: Political Pioneers*, by Carol Perry (grades 5 and up, biography); *Wonderful Wolves of the Wild*, by Arlene Erlbach (grades 1-3, animal).

How to Contact/Writers: Fiction: Query. Submit outline/synopsis and 2 sample chapters. Nonfiction: Query. Submit outline/synopsis and 1 sample chapter. "Only *one* manuscript at a time! Do *not* send original work when querying." Reports on queries/mss in 6-8 weeks. Publishes a book 6-12 months after acceptance. Will consider simultaneous submissions (if so noted). "SASE a must."

Illustration: Works with 10-12 illustrators/year. Will review ms/illustration packages "though almost all art is assigned independent of manuscript." Will review artwork for future assignments.

How to Contact/Illustrators: Ms/illustration packages: Query; submit ms with dummy. Illustrations only: Query with samples that can be kept on file; provide résumé. Reports in 2-3 months. Samples returned with SASE (and on request). Original artwork not returned at job's completion.

Photography: Purchases photos from freelancers. Contact: Acquisitions Editor. Buys stock and assigns work. Seeking photos related to environment, sports, animals. Photo captions required. Uses color slides. Submit cover letter, résumé, published samples, stock photo list.

Terms: Pays authors royalty or work purchased outright. Offers advance. Pays illustrators by the project. Photographers paid by the project or per photo. "Our terms are highly variable, both in reference to royalties and outright purchase." Book catalog available for 9×12 SAE and 5 first-class stamps. Ms and art guidelines available for SASE.

Tips: "Our books are intended for children to be able to read *themselves*, so please make sure language, length and sentence structure are age-appropriate. And keep the adult voice out!"

■**WINSTON-DEREK PUBLISHERS, INC.**, P.O. Box 90883, Nashville TN 37209. (615)321-0535. Book publisher. Estab. 1972. Editorial contact as follows: picture books: Matalyn Rose Peebles; young reader titles: Maggie Staton; middle reader/young adult titles: George Adderly. Publishes 35-40 picture books/year; 25-30 young readers/year; 10-15 middle readers/year; 10-15 young adults/year. 50% of books by first-time authors; 5% of books from agented authors; 20% of books subsidy published.

Fiction: Picture books: contemporary, folktales, history, religion. Young readers: adventure, folktales, history, religion. Middle readers: adventure, contemporary, folktales, history, religion, suspense/mystery. Young adults: adventure, contemporary, folktales, history, problem novels, religion, suspense/mystery. Average word length: picture book – 600-1200; young reader – 3,000-5,000; middle reader – 2,000; young adult – 10,000-40,000. Published *The Color of My Fur*, by Nanette Brophy; *The Other Little Angel*, by Fred Crump; *Mystery at Loon Lake*, by Michele Biernot.

Nonfiction: Picture books: biography, careers, religion, textbooks. Young readers, middle readers and young adults: biography, careers, history, religion, textbooks/basal readers, African-American biographies. Average word length: picture book – 600-800; young readers – 2,500-4,000; middle reader – 1,000-2,500; young adult – 10,000-30,000.

How to Contact/Writers: Fiction: Query or submit outline/synopsis and sample chapters. Nonfiction: Submit complete ms. Reports on queries in 6 weeks; mss in 8 weeks. Publishes a book 1 year after acceptance. Will consider simultaneous submissions.

Illustration: Will review ms/illustration packages. Contact: J.W. Peebles, editor. Will review work for possible assignments. Uses b&w artwork only.

How to Contact/Illustrators: Ms/illustration packages: Submit 3 chapters of ms with 1 piece of final art. Illustrations only: Submit résumé and tearsheets. Reports in 3 weeks. Original artwork returned at job's completion.

Terms: Pays authors royalties of 10-15% based on wholesale price. Also pays in copies and offers some subsidy arrangements. Separate authors and illustrators: 12½% royalty to writer and 2½% royalty to illustrator. Pays illustrators $30-150 or 2½-8½% royalty. Sends galleys to author; dummies to illustrator. Book catalog for SASE; ms/artist's guidelines free on request.

Tips: In illustration, looks for "action, good work and variety of subjects such as male/female." In mss, looks for "educational, morally sound subjects, multi-ethnic; historical facts."

WOMEN'S PRESS, 233-517 College Street, Toronto, Ontario M6G 4A2 Canada. (416)921-2425. Book publisher. Children's Editor: Martha Ayim. Publishes 1-2 picture books/year; 0-1 middle readers/year; 0-1 young adults/year. 60% of books by first-time authors. "We give preference to authors who are Canadian citizens or those living in Canada."

Fiction: Picture books: contemporary, social issues, health and family problems. Young readers, middle readers and young adults: contemporary, problem novels. Average length: picture books—24 pages; young readers—70-80 pages; middle readers—60-70 pages; young adult/teens—80-150 pages. Published *Asha's Mums*, by Elwin & Paulse (4-8, picture-issue).
Nonfiction: Picture books: contemporary, social issues. Young adults: sex, health.
How to Contact/Writers: Fiction/Nonfiction: Query. Reports on queries in 3 months (minimum); mss in 3-6 months. Publishes a book 1 year after acceptance.
Illustration: Will review ms/illustration packages (Canadian only).
Terms: Pays authors in royalties of 10% minimum based on retail price. Sends galleys to authors; dummies to illustrators. Book catalog and/or ms guidelines free on request.

WOODBINE HOUSE, 5615 Fishers Lane, Rockville MD 20852. (301)468-8800. Book publisher. Editor: Susan Stokes. Production Manager: Robin Dhawan. Publishes 0-2 picture books/year; 0-2 young adult titles/year. 80% of books by first-time authors. "All children's books are for or about children with disabilities."
Fiction: Picture books: special needs (disability-related). "No fiction unless disability-related." Average length: picture books—24 pages. Published *Charlie's Chuckle*, by Clara Berkus (ages 5-11); and *My Brother, Matthew*, by Mary Thompson (ages 5-11).
Nonfiction: All levels: special needs (disabilities). Does not want to see anything other than subjects about disabilities; does not want "books written *primarily* to impart messages about people with disabilities to people without disabilities—e.g., 'Everyone is different and that's OK!' "
How to Contact/Writers: Fiction/nonfiction: Submit complete ms. Reports on queries in 1 month; mss in 2-3 months. Publishes a book 18 months after acceptance. Will consider simultaneous submissions and previously published work.
Illustration: Works with 0-2 illustrators/year. Will review ms/illustration packages. Will review artwork for future assignments. Contact: Robin Dhawan, production manager.
How to Contact/Illustrators: Ms/illustration packages: Submit entire ms with 2-3 pieces of art (color photocopies OK). Illustrations only: Query with samples; provide promo sheet, tearsheets. Reports back only if interested.
Terms: Pays authors royalty of 10-12% based on wholesale price. Pays illustrators by the project. Sends galleys to authors. Book catalog available for 6×9 SAE and 3 first-class stamps. Ms guidelines available for SASE.
Tips: "Unless you have actually lived or worked with a child with a disability, it is unlikely that you will be able to write something that appeals to us."

JANE YOLEN BOOKS See Harcourt Brace & Co.

*ZINO PRESS CHILDREN'S BOOK, Division of Knowledge Unlimited, 2348 Pinehurst Dr., Middleton WI 53562. (608)836-6660. Fax: (608)831-1570. Book publisher. Acquisitions Editor: Dave Schreiner. Publishes 3-4 picture books/year. Publishes rhyming stories and multicultural literature.
Fiction: Picture books, young readers, middle readers: adventure, animal, contemporary, history, multicultural, poetry, special needs. "Text and art that is original and unique and not a retold folktale. Works must reflect a range of lifestyles accurately and without stereotyping, and should express values that lead to tolerance, greater awareness of self and others, kindness and compassion." Does not want to see folktales, books about colors, vegetables, etc. or books without a plot. Average length: picture books—32 pages. Recently published *The Extra Nose*, by Daniel DiPrima, illustrated by Persche; *Slumgullion, the Executive Pig*, by Matt Cibala, illustrated by Tamara Boudreau.

Market conditions are constantly changing! If you're still using this book and it is 1996 or later, buy the newest edition of Children's Writer's & Illustrator's Market *at your favorite bookstore or order directly from Writer's Digest Books.*

Nonfiction: Picture books, young readers: history, multicultural, special needs. For multi-cultural work, author should be of culture written about or author should work with consultant of that culture. Does not want to see biographies of famous people. Average length: picture books — 32-48 pages. Recently published *Be a Friend: The Story of African-American Music in Song, Words and Pictures,* by Leotha Stanley, illustrated by Henry Hawkins.

How to Contact/Writers: Fiction/Nonfiction: Submit complete ms. Reports in 8-10 weeks. Publishes a book 12-16 months after acceptance. Will consider simultaneous submissions.

Illustration: Works with 3-4 illustrators/yearly. Will review ms/illustration packages. Contact: Dave Schreiner, acquisitions editor. Will review artwork for future assignments. Uses color artwork only.

How to Contact/Illustrators: Ms/illustration packages: Submit ms with dummy. Illustrations only: Query with samples. Reports in 1 month. Samples returned with SASE. Some samples filed.

Photography: Buys photos from freelancers. Buys stock images.

Terms: Pays authors royalty based on wholesale price. "We are contemplating using both per project and royalty payments for illustrators depending on artistic input." Sends galleys to authors; dummies to illustrators. Ms guidelines available for SASE.

Tips: "We're looking for both first-time and established writers and illustrators."

Book Publishers/'94-'95 changes

The following markets were included in the 1994 edition of *Children's Writer's & Illustrator's Market* but do not have listings in this edition. The majority did not respond to our request to update their listings. If a reason was given for exclusion, it appears in parentheses after the market's name.

Addison-Wesley Publishing Co.
Appalachian Mountain Club Books
Black Moss Press
Capstone Press Inc. (booked through 1996)
Cloverdale Press (currently not accepting mss)
Council for Indian Education (currently overstocked)
Crown Publishers

Dutton Children's Books
Humanics Limited Press
Jordan Enterprises Publishing Co.
Lothrop, Lee & Shepard Books
March Media, Inc.
Meriwether Publishing Ltd. (changing format)
Merrill Publishing
Quarry Press (per request)
Scholastic Hardcover (no

longer accepting unsolicited mss)
Stone Books
Treasure Chest Publications, Inc. (company being sold)
Trophy Books
Volcano Press (booked for several years)
YMAA Publication Center (no longer publishing children's books)

Magazines

For writers and illustrators who lack previous publication, magazines are an ideal place to break into the business. Collecting bylines and illustration credits is essential in building credibility in the children's field. And, while many magazine editors are partial to working with established writers and illustrators, room still exists for newcomers who have not yet made their marks in the publishing industry.

The good news, in fact, is that the number of juvenile magazines which writers and illustrators may approach is growing. There are now close to 200 kids' magazines found in homes, libraries and classrooms. More than 100 of these magazines—about a dozen of which are new to this edition—are listed in this section.

Among them, you won't find magazines devoted to licensed characters (be it Batman or Barney), or publications that serve as promotions for toys, movies or TV shows (these are primarily produced inhouse). What you will find, however, are diverse magazines aimed at children of all ages and interests.

Increasing variety

Publishers have acknowledged that children—and their interests—are as varied as adults. In this section, for instance, you'll find magazines targeting boys and magazines targeting girls—just as you might find newsstand publications specifically for men or women. Magazines for youngsters affiliated with almost every religious denomination are also listed here. (For more information on the religious market for kids, see Don't Miss Out! Explore the Children's Religious Market beginning on page 22.) You'll also notice specialized magazines devoted to certain sports, such as *Soccer Jr.*; news publications such as *Kids Copy*; and even magazines like *Poem Train* devoted to poetry for and by kids (all three of these magazines, by the way, are new to this edition).

Another plus for the children's magazine industry is that teachers are utilizing fact-based educational publications—such as those teaching history, math or science—as supplements in their classrooms. (For example, see the Insider Report with Al Matano of *Scienceland* on page 206.) As a result, it's not unusual for children to want summer subscriptions, or even their own personal subscriptions, after initially being exposed to the magazines at school.

Above all, children today are more worldly and desire to know what's going on around them. Since magazines have the advantage of timeliness, they can relay information about current events or interests in much less time than books—and at less cost. The average one-year subscription, in fact, is about the same as the cost of one hardcover picture book.

Market concerns

Some of the listings in this section are religious-oriented or special interest publications, others are general interest magazines, and a few are adult magazines with special children's sections. Though the large circulation, ad-driven publications will generally offer a better pay rate than religious or nonprofit magazines, smaller magazines are more open to reviewing the work of newcomers. They also provide an excellent vehicle for you to compile clippings as you work your way toward more lucrative markets.

It's not uncommon, however, for juvenile magazines to purchase all rights to both stories and artwork. Though work for hire is generally frowned upon among freelancers, selling all rights may prove to be advantageous in the end. *Highlights for Children* buys all rights, as do all of the magazines published by the Children's Better Health Institute. Yet these magazines are very reputable, and any clips acquired through them will be valuable. (For more information about the CBHI publications, see the Insider Report with Editor Steve Charles on page 170).

Classic subjects considered by magazines include stories and/or features about the alphabet, outer space, computers and animals (even dinosaurs). As with books, nonfiction features—especially photo features—are popular, and many magazines are devoting more room to such material. Sports stories and articles describing how things work are also marketable. Current needs in the general interest magazine field include environmental issues, historical fiction, retold folktales, mysteries, science fiction and fantasy.

As efforts to supply readers with stories and artwork which include ethnic diversity remain strong, so does the need for multicultural material. You will notice that some publishers have indicated specific needs in their listings. Writers and illustrators should consider creating stories and artwork about groups with only marginal representation in the literature. If you're not a member of the group you are interested in portraying, however, make sure to properly research your subject to insure authenticity. Better yet, pass your work by an expert on the culture before submitting it.

Do your homework

No matter what the trends in the magazine industry, writers and illustrators must know what appeals to today's youth and target their material appropriately. To insure that your work will interest young people—and thus editors—find out what kids are talking about. If in doubt about the relevance of your article or story, read the material to children and see how they respond. By learning what appeals to today's youth, you may find yourself at the beginning of a trend instead of the end.

You must not only know the current interests of children, however, you must also know the topics typically covered by various children's magazines. To help you match your work with the right publications, we include a Subject Index at the back of this book. This index lists both book and magazine publishers by the fiction and nonfiction subjects they are seeking. Use this index in conjunction with the Age-Level Index and you will narrow the list of markets for your work even further.

Targeting the correct age-group with your submission is an important consideration. Few magazines are aimed at children of all ages, so you must be certain your manuscript is written for the audience level of the particular magazine you're submitting to. A report in *Children's Writer* estimates that "more than one-third of all rejection slips are sent because the writer has not targeted a manuscript to the correct age."

To ensure you're targeting the right age level, study both the listings and the actual publications. Each magazine has a different editorial philosophy. Language usage also varies between periodicals, as does the length of feature articles and the use of artwork and photographs. Reading the juvenile magazines you are considering submitting to is the best way to determine if your material is appropriate. As many kids' magazines sell subscriptions via direct mail or schools, you may not be able to find a particular publication at the bookstore or newsstand.

Check your local library, or send for copies of the magazines you're interested in. Most listings in this section have sample copies available and will be glad to send them upon request.

Once you have determined which magazines are potential markets, take another look at their listings to review the preferred method of receiving submissions. Some may wish to see an entire manuscript; others may wish to see a query letter and outline, especially for nonfiction articles (with which accompanying photographs are generally welcome). If you're an artist or photographer, review the listing for the types of samples the art director wants to see.

Finally, be sure to submit your best work. Though the magazine market is a good way for children's writers and illustrators to break in, it is by no means a junkyard for "less-than-your-best" material.

THE ADVOCATE, PKA Publication, 301A Rolling Hills Park, Prattsville NY 12468. (518)299-3103. Articles/Fiction Editor: Remington Wright. Art Director/Photo Editor: CJ Karlie. Bimonthly tabloid. Estab. 1987. Circ. 12,000. "*The Advocate* advocates good writers and quality writings. We publish art, fiction, photos and poetry. *The Advocate's* submitters are talented people of all ages who do not earn their livings as writers. We wish to promote the arts and to give those we publish the opportunity to be published through a for-profit means rather than in a not-for-profit way. We do this by selling advertising and offering reading entertainment."
Fiction: Middle readers and young adults/teens: adventure, animal, contemporary, fantasy, folktales, health, humorous, nature/environment, problem-solving, romance, science fiction, sports, suspense/mystery. Looks for "well written, entertaining work, whether fiction or nonfiction." Buys approximately 42 mss/year. Average word length: 1,500. Byline given. Wants to see more humorous material, nature/environment and romantic comedy.
Nonfiction: Middle readers and young adults/teens: animal, arts/crafts, biography, careers, concept, cooking, fashion, games/puzzles, geography, history, hobbies, how-to, humorous, interview/profile, nature/environment, problem-solving, science, social issues, sports, travel. Buys 10 mss/year. Average word length: 1,500. Byline given.
Poetry: Reviews poetry any length.
How to Contact/Writers: Fiction/nonfiction: send complete ms. Reports on queries in 4-6 weeks/mss in 6-8 weeks. Publishes ms 2-18 months after acceptance.
Illustration: Uses b&w artwork only. Uses cartoons. Reviews ms/illustration packages. Submit a photo print (b&w or color), an excellent copy of work (no larger than 8 × 10) or original. Credit line given.
How to Contact/Illustrators: Ms/illustration packages: Submit complete package with final art. Illustrations only: "Send previous unpublished art with SASE, please." Reports in 2 months. Samples return with SASE; samples not filed. Original work returned upon job's completion. Credit line given.
Photography: Buys photos from freelancers. Model/property releases required. Uses color and b&w prints. Send unsolicited photos by mail with SASE. Reports in 2 months. Wants nature, artistic and humorous photos.
Terms: Pays on publication. Acquires first rights for mss, artwork and photographs. Pays in copies or other premiums. Sample copies for $3. Writer's/illustrator/photo guidelines for SASE.
Tips: "Artists and photographers should keep in mind that we are a b&w paper."

AIM MAGAZINE, America's Intercultural Magazine, P.O. Box 20554, Chicago IL 60620. (312)874-6184. Articles Editor: Ruth Apilado. Fiction Editor: Mark Boone. Photo Editor: Betty Lewis. Quarterly magazine. Circ. 8,000. Readers are high school and college students, teachers, adults interested in helping, through the written word, to create a more equitable world. 15% of material aimed at juvenile audience.
Fiction: Young adults: history, multicultural, "stories with social significance." Wants stories that teach children that people are more alike than they are different. Does not want to see religious fiction. Buys 20 mss/year. Average word length: 1,000-4,000. Byline given.

Nonfiction: Young adults: interview/profile, multicultural, "stuff with social significance." Does not want to see religious nonfiction. Buys 20 mss/year. Average word length: 500-2,000. Byline given.

How to Contact/Writers: Fiction: Send complete ms. Nonfiction: Query with published clips. Reports on queries/mss in 1 month. Will consider simultaneous submissions.

Illustration: Buys 20 illustrations/issue. Preferred theme: Overcoming social injustices through nonviolent means. Reviews ms/illustration packages; reviews artwork for future assignments.

How to Contact/Illustrators: Ms/illustration packages: Query first. Illustrations only: Query with tearsheets. Reports on art samples in 2 months. Original artwork returned at job's completion "if desired." Credit line given.

Photography: Wants "photos of activists who are trying to contribute to social improvement."

Terms: Pays on publication. Buys first North American serial rights. Pays $15-25 for stories/articles. Pays in contributor copies if copies are requested. Pays $5-25 for b&w cover illustration. Photographers paid by the project (range: $10-15). Sample copies for $4.

Tips: "We need material of social significance, stuff that will help promote racial harmony and peace and (illustrate) the stupidity of racism."

AMERICAN GIRL, Pleasant Company, P.O. Box 984, Middleton WI 53562-0984. (608)836-4848. Fiction Editor: Harriet Brown. Editor-in-Chief: Judith Woodburn. Bimonthly magazine. Estab. 1992. Circ. 325,000. "For girls ages 8-12. We run fiction and nonfiction, historical and contemporary."

Fiction: Middle readers: contemporary, historical, multicultural, suspense/mystery, good fiction about anything. No preachy, moralistic tales or stories with animals as protagonists. Only a girl or girls as characters—no boys. Buys approximately 6 mss/year. Average word length: 1,000-2,500. Byline given.

Nonfiction: Any articles aimed at girls ages 8-12. Buys 3-10 mss/year. Average word length: 600. Byline sometimes given.

How to Contact/Writers: Fiction: Send complete ms. Nonfiction: Query with published clips. Reports on queries/mss in 4-6 weeks. Will consider simultaneous submissions.

Illustration: Works on assignment only.

Terms: Pays on acceptance. Buys first North American serial rights. Pays $500 minimum for stories; $300 minimum for articles. Sample copies for $3.95 and SAE with $1.90 in postage (send to Editorial Department Assistant). Writer's guidelines free for SASE.

Tips: "Keep (stories and articles) simple but interesting. Kids are discriminating readers, too. They won't read a boring or pretentious story."

ANIMAL TRAILS, P.O. Box 1264, Huntington WV 25714. Editor: Shannon Bridget Murphy. Quarterly magazine. Estab. 1993. Circ. 500. "A magazine for people of all ages who like to read fiction and true stories about animals, animal issues. Suitable for all ages."

Fiction: All levels: adventure, animal, folktales, history, multicultural, nature/environment, problem-solving, suspense/mystery. "Would like to see more material written by young people and college students." Buys approximately 17-25 mss/year. Average word length: 1,000-7,000. Byline given.

Nonfiction: All levels: animal, biography, games/puzzles, geography, history, how-to, multicultural, nature/environment, problem-solving, science, social issues, travel. Looks for good, well thought out plots with animals as the primary focus of interest; stories that communicate animal/human relationship. Buys 17-25 mss/year. Average word length: 1,000-7,000. Byline given.

Poetry: Reviews poetry. Multiple submissions accepted.

How to Contact/Writers: Reports in 1-2 months. Will consider simultaneous submissions and electronic submissions via disk or modem.

Illustration: Reviews manuscript/illustration package. Reviews artwork for future assignments. Use imagination and be creative." Reviews ms/illustration packages; reviews artwork for future assignments.

How to Contact/Illustrators: Ms/illustration packages: Send complete package with final art, ms with rough sketches. Illustrations only: Submit slides, illustrations. Reports in 1 month. Samples returned with SASE; filed with permission from artist. Credit line given.

Photography: Buys photos from freelancers. Photo captions preferred. Uses color, b&w prints; 35mm, 8 × 10 transparencies. To contact, photographers should send unsolicited photos by mail, provide business card, promotional literature or tearsheets. Reports in 1 month.

Terms: Pays on publication. Buys first rights, one-time rights. Additional payment for ms/illustration packages, when photos accompany articles. Pays photographers by the project, paid per photo. Sample copies for $10. Writer's/illustrator's/photo guidelines for SASE.

APPALACHIAN BRIDE, Teslstar Productions, P.O. Box 1264, Huntington WV 25714. Editor: Shannon Bridget Murphy. Triannual magazine. Estab. 1993. Circ. 500. *"Appalachian Bride* focuses on brides, and traditions in the Appalachian states."

Fiction: All levels: folktales, multicultural. Multicultural needs include: Work must be based on Appalachian family life or traditions. Buys approximately 6-12 mss/year. Average word length: 500-3,000. Byline given.

Nonfiction: All levels: multicultural. Multicultural needs include: work related to Appalachian family life or traditions. Buys 6-12 mss/year. Average word length: 500-3,000. Byline given.

Poetry: Reviews poetry. Multiple submissions welcome.

How to Contact/Writers: Fiction/nonfiction: send complete ms. Reports in 6 weeks. Will consider simultaneous submissions, electronic submissions via disk or modem.

Illustration: "Preferred themes are country and Amish." Reviews ms/illustrations packages; reviews artwork for future assignment.

How to Contact/Illustrators: Ms/illustration packages: Submit complete package with final art, ms with rough sketches. Illustrations only: Submit promo sheet, slides. Reports in 6 weeks. Samples returned with SASE; samples filed with permission of artist. Credit line given.

Photography: Look for interesting photographs that feature Appalachian brides, weddings and family life. Uses color, b&w prints; 35mm, 8 × 10 transparencies. Query with samples; send unsolicited photos by mail; provide business card, promotional literature or tearsheets. Reports in 6 weeks.

Terms: Pays on publication. Buys first rights, one-time rights. Sometimes pays in copies or other premiums. Additional payment for ms/illustration packages, when photos accompany articles. Writer's/illustrator's/photo guidelines for SASE.

ASPCA ANIMAL WATCH, ASPCA, 424 E. 92nd St., New York NY 10128. (212)876-7700, ext. 4441. Art Director: Amber Alliger. Quarterly magazine. Estab. 1951. Circ. 180,000. Focuses on animal issues. 15% of publication aimed at juvenile market.

Illustration: Buys 4 illustrations/issue; 16 illustrations/year. Reviews ms/illustration packages; reviews artwork for future assignments; works on assignment only.

How to Contact/Illustrators: Illustrations only: Send tearsheets, quality photocopies to hold on file. Reports back only if interested. Samples kept on file. Originals returned upon job's completion. Credit line given.

Photography: Looking for animal care, animal abuse, and animal protection. Model/property releases required. Uses 8 × 10, glossy color/b&w prints; 35mm, 2¼ × 2¼ and 4 × 5 transparencies. Photographers should send stock list. Reports in 2 months.

Terms: Buys one-time rights for artwork/photographs. Pays illustrators $100-150 for color cover; $50-100 color inside. Photographers paid per photo (range: $50-100). Sample copies for 9 × 12 SASE. Writer's guidelines not available. Illustrator's/photo guidelines for SASE.

Tips: Trends include "more educational, more interactive" material. Children's section is "Eye on Animals."

ATALANTIK, 7630 Deer Creek Dr., Worthington OH 43085. (614)885-0550. Articles/Fiction Editor: Prabhat K. Dutta. Art Director: Tanushree Bhattacharya. Quarterly magazine. Estab. 1980. Circ. 400. *"Atalantik* is the first Bengali (Indian language) literary magazine published from the USA. It contains poems, essays, short stories, translations, interviews, opinions, sketches, book reviews, cultural information, scientific articles, letters to the editor, serialized novels and a children's section. The special slant may be India and/or education." 10% of material aimed at juvenile audience.

Fiction: Young reader: animal. Middle readers: history, humorous, problem-solving, math puzzles, travel. Young adults: history, humorous, problem-solving, romance, science fiction, sports, spy/mystery/adventure, math puzzles, travel. Does not want to see: "religious, political, controversial or material without any educational value." Sees too many animal and fantasy stories. Buys 20-40 mss/year. Average word length: 300-1,000. Byline given, "sometimes."

Nonfiction: Middle readers: history, how-to, humorous, problem solving, travel. Young adults: history, how-to, humorous, interview/profile, problem-solving, travel, puzzles. Does not want to see: "religious, political, controversial or material without any educational value." Wants to see more educational, math puzzles, word puzzles. Buys 20-40 mss/year. Average word length: 300-1,000. Byline given, "sometimes."

Poetry: Reviews 20-line humorous poems that rhyme; maximum of 5 submissions.

How to Contact/Writers: Fiction/nonfiction: Send complete ms. Reports on queries in 2 weeks; mss in 2-4 months. Will consider simultaneous submissions.

Illustration: Buys 4-20 illustrations/year. Prefers to review juvenile education, activities, sports, culture and recreation. Will review ms/illustration packages, including artwork for future assignments.

How to Contact/Illustrators: Ms/illustration packages: Send "complete manuscript with final art." Illustrations only: Query; send résumé, promo sheet, client list. Reports in 1 month only if interested. Credit line given.

Photography: Purchases photos with accompanying ms only.

Terms: Buys all rights. Usually pays in copies for all circumstances. Sample copy $6. Writer's/illustrator's guidelines free with SASE.

Tips: Writers: "Let subjects be nature, human beings—not abstract ideas. Be imaginative, thorough, flexible and educational. Most importantly, be a child."

BOYS' LIFE, Boy Scouts of America, Box 152079, 1325 W. Walnut Hill Lane, Irving TX 75015-2079. (214)580-2000. Editor: Scott Stuckey. Articles Editor: Doug Daniel. Fiction Editor: Kathleen DaGroomes. Director of Design: Joseph P. Connolly. Art Director: Elizabeth Hardaway Morgan. Monthly magazine. Estab. 1911. Circ. 1,300,000. *Boys' Life* is "a general interest magazine for boys 8 to 18 who are members of the Cub Scouts, Boy Scouts or Explorers. A general interest magazine for all boys."

Fiction: Middle readers: adventure, animal, contemporary, fantasy, history, humor, problem-solving, science fiction, sports, spy/mystery. Does not want to see "talking animals and adult reminiscence." Buys 12 mss/year. Average word length: 1,000-1,500. Byline given.

Nonfiction: "Subject matter is broad. We cover everything from professional sports to American history to how to pack a canoe. A look at a current list of the BSA's more than 100 merit badge pamphlets gives an idea of the wide range of subjects possible. Even better, look at a year's worth of recent issues. Column headings are science, nature, earth, health, sports, space and aviation, cars, computers, entertainment, pets, history, music and others." Average word length: 500-1,500. Columns 300-750 words. Byline given.

How to Contact/Writers: Fiction: Send complete ms. Nonfiction: Query. Reports on queries/mss in 6-8 weeks.

Illustration: Buys 5-7 illustrations/issue; 23-50 illustrations/year. Reviews ms/illustration packages; reviews artwork for possible future assignments; works on assignment only.

How to Contact/Illustrators: Ms/illustration packages: "Query first." Illustrations only: Send tearsheets. Reports on art samples only if interested. Original artwork returned at job's completion.

Terms: Buys first rights. Pays $750 and up for fiction; $400-1,500 for major articles; $150-400 for columns; $250-300 for how-to features.

Tips: "I strongly urge you to study at least a year's issues to better understand type of material published. Articles for *Boys' Life* must interest and entertain boys ages 8 to 18.

Refer to the Business of Children's Writing & Illustrating for up-to-date marketing, tax and legal information.

Write for a boy you know who is 12. Our readers demand crisp, punchy writing in relatively short, straightforward sentences. The editors demand well-reported articles that demonstrate high standards of journalism. We follow *The New York Times* manual of style and usage. All submissions must be accompanied by SASE with adequate postage."

BREAD FOR GOD'S CHILDREN, Bread Ministries, Inc., P.O. Box 1017, Arcadia FL 33821. (813)494-6214. Editor: Judith M. Gibbs. Monthly magazine. Estab. 1972. Circ. 10,000 (US and Canada). "*Bread* is designed as a teaching tool for Christian families." 85% of publication aimed at juvenile market.

Fiction: Young readers, middle readers, young adults/teens: adventure, animal (no speaking animals), contemporary, history, nature/environment, problem-solving, religious, sports, suspense/mystery. Looks for "teaching stories that portray Christian lifestyles without preaching." Buys approximately 20 mss/year. Average word length: 900-1,500 (for teens); 600-900 (for young children). Byline given.

Nonfiction: Preschool-8 years and young readers: arts/crafts, hobbies, how-to, problem-solving, religion. "We do not want anything detrimental of solid family values." Buys 3-4 mss/year. Average word length: 500-800. Byline given.

How to Contact/Writers: Fiction/nonfiction: Send complete ms. Reports on mss in 2 weeks-6 months "if considered for use." Will consider simultaneous submissions and previously published work.

Terms: Pays on publication. Pays $30-40 for stories; $10-20 for articles. Sample copies free for 9 × 12 SAE and 5 first-class stamps (for 3 copies).

Tips: "Know the readership . . . know the publisher's guidelines. Edit carefully for content and grammar."

CALLIOPE, World History for Young People, Cobblestone Publishing, Inc., 7 School St., Peterborough NH 03458. (603)924-7209. Editor-in-Chief: Carolyn P. Yoder. Art Director: Ellen Klempner-Beguin. Picture Editor: Francelle Carapetyan. Magazine published 5 times/year. "*Calliope* covers world history (East/West) and lively, original approaches to the subject are the primary concerns of the editors in choosing material."

Fiction: Middle readers and young adults: adventure, folktales, history, biographical fiction. Material must relate to forthcoming themes. Word length: up to 800.

Nonfiction: Middle readers and young adults: arts/crafts, biography, cooking, games/puzzles, history. Material must relate to forthcoming themes. Word length: 300-800.

Poetry: Maximum line length: 100. Wants "clear, objective imagery. Serious and light verse considered."

How to Contact/Writers: "A query must consist of the following to be considered (please use nonerasable paper): a brief cover letter stating subject and word length of the proposed article; a detailed one-page outline explaining the information to be presented in the article; an extensive bibliography of materials the author intends to use in preparing the article; a self-addressed stamped envelope. Writers new to *Calliope* should send a writing sample with query. If you would like to know if your query has been received, please also include a stamped postcard that requests acknowledgment of receipt. In all correspondence, please include your complete address as well as a telephone number where you can be reached. A writer may send as many queries for one issue as he or she wishes, but each query must have a separate cover letter, outline, bibliography and SASE. Telephone queries are not accepted. Handwritten queries will not be considered. Queries may be submitted at any time, but queries sent well in advance of deadline *may not be answered for several months*. Go-aheads requesting material proposed in queries are usually sent five months prior to publication date. Unused queries will be returned approximately three to four months prior to publication date."

Illustration: Reviews artwork for future assignments.

How to Contact/Illustrators: Illustrations only: Send tearsheets, photocopies. Original work returned upon job's completion (upon written request).

Photography: Buys photos from freelancers. Wants photos pertaining to any forthcoming themes. Uses b&w/color prints, 35 mm transparencies. Send unsolicited photos by mail (on speculation).

Terms: Buys all rights for mss and artwork. Pays 20-25¢/word for stories/articles. Pays on an individual basis for poetry, activities, games/puzzles. "Covers are assigned and paid on an individual basis." Pays photographers per photo ($15-100 for b&w; $25-100 for color). Sample copy for $3.95 and SAE with $1.05 postage. Writer's/illustrator's/photo guidelines for SASE. (See listings for *Cobblestone, The History Magazine for Young People; Faces, The Magazine About People*; and *Odyssey, Science That's Out of This World*).

CAREER WORLD, Curriculum Innovations Group, 60 Revere Dr., Northbrook IL 60062. (708)205-3000. Fax: (708)564-8197. Articles Editor: Carole Rubenstein. Art Director: Kristi Simkins. Monthly (school year) magazine. Estab. 1972. A guide to careers, for students grades 7-12.
Nonfiction: Young adults: education, how-to, interview/profile, career information. Byline given.
How to Contact/Writers: "We do not want any unsolicited manuscripts." Nonfiction: Query with published clips and résumé. Reports on queries in 2 weeks.
Illustration: Buys 5-10 illustrations/year. Reviews ms/illustration packages; reviews artwork for future assignments; works on assignment only.
How to Contact/Illustrators: Query; send promo sheet and tearsheets. Credit line given.
Photography: Purchases photos from freelancers.
Terms: Pays on publication. Buys all rights. Pays $75-250 for articles. Pays illustrators $100-250 for color cover; $25-35 for b&w inside; $50-75 for color inside. Writer's guidelines free, but only on assignment.

CAREERS AND COLLEGES, E.M. Guild, 989 Avenue of the Americas, New York NY 10018. (212)563-4688. Editor-in-Chief: June Rogoznica. Senior Editor: Don Rauf. Art Director: Michael Hofmann. Magazine published 4 times during school year (September, November, January, March). Circ. 500,000. This is a magazine for high school juniors and seniors, designed to prepare students for their futures.
Nonfiction: Young adults: careers, college, health, how-to, humorous, interview/profile, personal development, problem-solving, social issues, travel. Wants more celebrity profiles. Buys 30-40 mss/year. Average word length: 1,000-1,250. Byline given.
How to Contact/Writers: Nonfiction: Query. Reports on queries in 3 weeks. Will consider electronic submissions via disk or modem.
Illustration: Buys 10 illustrations/issue; buys 40 illustrations/year. Will review ms/illustration packages. Works on assignment "mostly."
How to Contact/Illustrators: Ms/illustration packages: Query first. Illustrations only: Send tearsheets, cards. Reports on art samples in 3 weeks if interested. Credit line given. Original artwork returned at job's completion.
Terms: Pays on acceptance. Buys first North American serial rights. Pays $250-300 for assigned/unsolicited articles. Additional payment for ms/illustration packages "must be negotiated." Pays $500-1,000 for color illustration; $300-700 for b&w/color inside illustration. Sample copy $2.50 with SAE and $1.25 postage; writer's guidelines free with SASE.
Tips: Make sure queries address the guidelines. Wants articles that are fresh on the subject of careers and colleges and life after high school.

CEMETERY PLOT, Tellstar Productions, P.O. Box 1264, Huntington WV 25714. Editor: Shannon Bridget Murphy. Quarterly magazine. Estab. 1993. Circ. 500. *Cemetery Plot* is devoted to horror, suspense, mystery and the supernatural. The material is suitable for all ages. 50% of publication aimed at juvenile market.
Fiction: Picture-oriented material: fantasy, multicultural, problem-solving, suspense/mystery. Young readers, middle readers: adventure, fantasy, folktales, multicultural, problem-solving, suspense/mystery, horror. Young adults: adventure, fantasy, folktales, multicultural, problem-solving, suspense/mystery, horror. "Please do not send 'blood and guts' stories." Average word length: 1,000-3,500. Byline given.
Nonfiction: All levels: games/puzzles, history, multicultural, problem-solving. Buys 6-12 mss/year. Average word length: 500-3,500 words. Byline given.
Poetry: Reviews poetry. Multiple submissions welcome. Publishes an annual chapbook of poetry.

How to Contact/Writers: Fiction/nonfiction: Send complete ms. Reports in 1-2 months. Will consider simultaneous submissions, electronic submissions via disk or modem.

Illustration: Reviews ms/illustration packages; reviews artwork for future assignments.

How to Contact/Illustrators: Illustrations only: Query; send promo sheet, slides. Reports in 2-4 weeks. Samples returned with SASE, filed (with permission from artist.) Credit line given.

Photography: Buys photos from freelancers. Looks for "imaginative photos which would be of interest to *Cemetery Plot*." Uses color, b&w prints; 35mm, 8 × 10 transparencies. To contact, query with samples; send unsolicited photos by mail; provide business card, promotional literature or tearsheets.

Terms: Pays on publication. Buys first rights, one-time rights. "Payment depends upon budget. One contributor's copy is provided." Pays photographers per photo. Sample copies for $10. Writer's/illustrator's/photo guidelines for SASE.

Tips: "Wants illustrations with themes of houses, castles, etc; illustrations of children, especially in sets; illustrations that demonstrate the relationship between children and nature or animals with supernatural or mysterious element. The work of young writers and college students welcome."

CHALLENGE, Brotherhood Commission, SBC, 1548 Poplar Ave., Memphis TN 38104. (901)272-2461. Articles Editor: Jeno C. Smith. Art Director: Roy White. Monthly magazine. Circ. 30,000. Magazine contains boy interests, sports, crafts, sports personalities, religious.

Nonfiction: Young adults: arts/crafts, games/puzzles, geography, health, hobbies, how-to, humorous, nature/environment, social issues, sports, youth issues. Looking for stories on sports heroes with Christian testimony. Buys 15 mss/year. Average word length: 700-900. Byline given.

How to Contact/Writers: Nonfiction: Send complete ms. Reports on queries/mss in 1 month. Will consider simultaneous submissions.

Illustration: Buys 1-2 illustrations/issue; 12 illustrations/year. Reviews ms/illustration packages; reviews artwork for future assignments.

How to Contact/Illustrators: Ms/illustration packages: Send complete ms with final art. Illustrations only: Provide promo sheet to be kept on file. Reports back only if interested. Credit line given.

Photography: Purchases photography from freelancers. Wants b&w photos with youth appeal.

Terms: Pays on acceptance. Buys one-time and reprint rights. Pays $25-50 for articles. Pays illustrators $50-100 for color cover; $5-20 for b&w, $10-35 for color inside. Photographers paid per photo (range: $5-100). Sample copies free for #10 SAE and 3 first-class stamps. Writer's/illustrator's guidelines for SAE and 1 first-class stamp.

Tips: Wants to see "teenagers in sports, nature, health, hobbies—no preachy articles."

CHICKADEE, for Young Children from OWL, Young Naturalist Foundation, Suite 306, 56 The Esplanade, Toronto, Ontario M5E 1A7 Canada. (416)868-6001. Editor: Lizann Flatt. Art Director: Tim Davin. Magazine published 10 times/year. Estab. 1979. Circ. 150,000. *Chickadee* is a "hands-on" publication designed to interest 3-9 year olds in science, nature and the world around them.

Fiction: Young readers: adventure, animal, fantasy, folktales, humorous, nature/environment, science fiction, sports. Does not want to see religious, anthropomorphic animal, romance material, material that talks down to kids. Buys 8 mss/year. Average word length: 300-800. Byline given.

Market conditions are constantly changing! If you're still using this book and it is 1996 or later, buy the newest edition of Children's Writer's & Illustrator's Market *at your favorite bookstore or order directly from* Writer's Digest Books.

Nonfiction: Young readers: animal (facts/characteristics), arts/crafts, cooking, games/puzzles, interview/profile, travel. Does not want to see religious material. Buys 2-5 mss/year. Average word length: 20-200. Byline given.

Poetry: Limit submissions to 5 poems.

How to Contact/Writers: Fiction/nonfiction: Send complete ms. SAE and $1 money order for answer and return of ms. Reports on mss in 2 months. Will consider simultaneous submissions.

Illustration: Buys 3-5 illustrations/issue; 40 illustrations/year. Preferred theme or style: realism/humor (but not cartoons). Reviews artwork for future assignments; works on assignment only.

How to Contact/Illustrators: Provide promo sheet or tearsheets to be kept on file. Reports on art samples only if interested. Credit line given.

Photography: Looking for animal (mammal, insect, reptile, fish, etc.) photos. Uses 35mm and 2¼ × 2¼ transparencies. Write to request photo package for $1 money order, attention Robin Wilner, photo researcher.

Terms: Pays on acceptance. Buys all rights for mss. Buys one-time rights for photos. Pays $25-210 for stories. Pays illustrators $100-650 for color inside. Photographers paid per photo (range: $100-350). Sample copies for $4.50. Writer's guidelines free.

Tips: "Study the magazine carefully before submitting material. Fiction most open to freelancers. Kids should be main characters and should be treated with respect."

CHILD LIFE, Children's Better Health Institute, P.O. Box 567, Indianapolis IN 46206. (317)636-8881. Editor: Lise Hoffman. Art Director: Janet Moir. Magazine published 8 times/year. Estab. 1922. Circ. 80,000. "Targeted toward kids ages 9-11, we are the nation's oldest, continuously published children's magazine." Focuses on health, sports, fitness, nutrition, safety, and general interests.

Fiction: Middle readers: adventure, animal, contemporary, health, humorous, multicultural, nature/environment, problem-solving, sports, suspense/mystery. "Health and fitness is an ongoing need." Buys 30-35 mss/year. Maximum word length: 800. Byline given.

Nonfiction: Middle readers: animal, arts/crafts, biography, careers, cooking, games/puzzles, geography, health, history, hobbies, how-to, humorous, interview/profile, multicultural, nature/environment, problem solving, science, social issues, sports, travel. Maximum word length: 800. Byline given.

Poetry: Reviews poetry.

How to Contact/Writers: Fiction/nonfiction: Send complete ms. No queries please. Reports on mss in 8-10 weeks. Will not consider previously published material.

Illustration: Buys 8-10 illustrations/issue. Preferred theme: "Need realistic styles especially." Works on assignment only.

How to Contact/Illustrators: Illustrations only: Send query, résumé and portfolio. Samples must be accompanied by SASE for response and/or return. Credit line given.

Photography: Purchases professional quality photos with accompanying ms only.

Terms: Pays on publication. Writers paid 10-15¢/word for stories/articles. Buys all rights. Pays illustrators $275/cover; $35-90 b&w inside; $70-155 color inside. For artwork, buys all rights. Pays photographers per photo (range: $25-30). Buys one-time rights for photographs. Guidelines available for SASE.

Tips: "We need profiles of young athletes, aged 9-11, and their sports (825 words maximum) and short pieces on outdoor games/exercise (200 words maximum). Examples: planned features on young circus performers, sailors in the Bahamas, jump rope games, and Herqr, an old Scandinavian relay game. We have used adult profiles occasionally. Already covered golf, baseball, basketball, track and hockey. We also need lowfat recipes for mini-meals and healthful snacks for monthly feature. Avoid sugar, whole eggs (egg whites acceptable), red meat, and shortening (when possible). Test recipes before sending them! We do use dessert recipes, but not cakes, cookies, pies, etc., unless they meet above criteria." (See listings for *Children's Digest, Children's Playmate, Humpty Dumpty's Magazine, Jack and Jill, Turtle Magazine* and *U.S. Kids*.)

CHILDREN'S DIGEST, Children's Better Health Institute, Box 567, Indianapolis IN 46206. (317)636-8881. Articles/Fiction Editor: Sandra J. Grieshop. Art Director: Janet K. Moir.

Make Kids Your Specialty

"Writing for kids is a specialty, not simply a place to start your career," says Steve Charles. "You need to use all the skills of good writing you've learned and craft them for younger readers."

As one of five editors at the Children's Better Health Institute (CBHI) in Indianapolis, Indiana, Charles sees many manuscripts in which writers display "subtle condescending attitudes." Other common mistakes include "reworking the same old plot themes over and over; stale, stereotyped characters; and stories written by people who haven't been around kids for a while — revealed through stilted dialogue, unrealistic plot twists, or kids who 'speak' the moral of the story."

Steve Charles

To avoid these problems, Charles suggests spending time with kids to help recall your childhood. "It's not so much a matter of remembering incidents as it is remembering how it felt to be a child," he says. "Remember what it was like to use all of your senses and include those details as you approach your subject [in nonfiction] or add detail to your fiction."

If you're a fiction writer, read the works of the better current writers of children's fiction and pay particular attention to how kids treat each other, Charles adds. "Also pay attention to social issues that concern kids and incorporate them into your work. Examples are AIDS, stay-at-home fathers and homelessness. We often introduce our readers to these subjects through fiction."

Whether you're writing fiction or nonfiction, it's important to know the publisher's philosophy. "The goal of the Children's Better Health Institute is to provide kids with good reading that entertains and encourages a healthful lifestyle," Charles says. And any health-related topic is welcome.

Of special interest are articles concerning sports and fitness. "We run stories about young athletes in traditional sports and also try to introduce readers to new or unusual sports they might enjoy. For example, we've run stories on kids who do spelunking, surf, and drive dog sleds," he says. "Because of our small staff, we depend on freelancers to keep us informed about many of these kids and their pursuits."

In all, CBHI publishes seven magazines, each aimed at a different age-group. Charles is editor of both *Turtle*, a magazine designed to be read to those ages 2-5, and *U.S. Kids*, for readers ages 5-10.

Writers who read CBHI's guidelines will learn that the editors try to present health material in a positive manner, "incorporating humor and a light approach wherever possible without minimizing the seriousness of what we are saying." Those who read sample issues will also discover the magazines have certain personalities, departments and regular features. Each includes a number of age-appropriate activities, such as hidden pictures, dot-to-dots, mazes, acrostics, word searches and games.

While the emphasis on "fitness and fun" continues to distinguish CBHI's publications from most other children's magazines, Charles believes magazines for children are more specialized than five or ten years ago—and much more graphically appealing. "The word-to-picture ratio has continued to move in favor of the picture and more attention is being paid to making the two work together."

When Charles says "picture," he's no longer just referring to illustrations. "We are using more photos in all of our magazines," he says. "Photos are the most effective way to illustrate many of the health- and fitness-related stories we run, and we almost always use photos to accompany profiles on children or new sports. In *U.S. Kids*, we use photos for all but a few departments and the fiction piece. The other six magazines are much more illustration-based. Yet even the magazines for our youngest readers often contain at least one photo feature. That didn't happen very often five years ago."

Though CBHI is open to submissions of short photo features or photos that accompany manuscripts, artwork and drawings are usually assigned. Interested illustrators may send samples for review.

As for writers, Charles is particularly interested in receiving queries for nonfiction articles for *U.S. Kids*. "Because of the amount of information available to writers these days through cable news and computer online services, I've been encouraging people to write me with their nonfiction ideas—*after* they've looked at our magazines," he says. "This leads to more interaction between writers and editors and should give readers a better story, editors less rewriting, and authors more satisfaction."

—*Christine Martin*

BB Sams created this friendly green frog with bulging yellow eyes for "Jump Rabbit," a short feature in Turtle Magazine by Verla Kay. The frog encourages a little bunny who's afraid she's too small to hop, but—after toppling a lily pad—concludes she's really too big.

Magazine published 8 times/year. Estab. 1950. Circ. 125,000. For preteens; approximately 33% of content is health-related.

Fiction: Middle readers: adventure, animal, contemporary, fantasy, folktales, health, history, humorous, nature/environment, problem-solving, science fiction, sports, suspense/mystery. Buys 25 mss/year. Average word length: 500-1,500. Byline given.

Nonfiction: Middle readers: animal, arts/crafts, biography, cooking, education, games/puzzles, geography, health, history, hobbies, how-to, humorous, interview/profile, nature/environment, science, sports, travel. Buys 16-20 mss/year. Average word length: 500-1,200. Byline given.

Poetry: Maximum length: 20-25 lines.

How to Contact/Writers: Fiction/nonfiction: Send complete ms. Reports on mss in 10 weeks.

Illustration: Reviews ms/illustration packages; reviews an illustrator's work for possible future assignments; works on assignment only.

How to Contact/Illustrators: Ms/illustration packages: Query first. Illustrations only: Send résumé and/or slides or tearsheets to illustrate work; query with samples. Reports on art samples in 8-10 weeks. Credit line given.

Photography: Purchases photos with accompanying ms only. Model/property releases required; captions required. Uses 35mm transparencies.

Terms: Pays on acceptance for illustrators, publication for writers. Buys all rights for mss and artwork; one-time rights for photos. Pays 12¢/word for accepted articles. Pays $275 for color cover illustration; $35-90 for b&w, $70-155 for color inside. Photographers paid per photo (range: $10-50). Sample copies for $1.25. Writer's/illustrator's guidelines for SAE and 1 first-class stamp. (See listings for *Child Life, Children's Playmate, Humpty Dumpty's Magazine, Jack and Jill, Turtle Magazine* and *U.S. Kids*.)

CHILDREN'S PLAYMATE, Children's Better Health Institute, Box 567, Indianapolis IN 46206. (317)636-8881. Articles/Fiction Editor: Lise Hoffman. Art Director: Marty Jones. Magazine published 8 times/year. Estab. 1929. Circ. 135,000. For children between 6 and 8 years; approximately 33% of content is health-related.

Fiction: Young readers: animal, contemporary, fantasy, folktales, history, humorous, science fiction, sports, suspense/mystery/adventure. Buys 25 mss/year. Average word length: 200-700. Byline given.

Nonfiction: Young readers: animal, arts/crafts, biography, cooking, games/puzzles, health, history, how-to, humorous, sports, travel. Buys 16-20 mss/year. Average word length: 200-700. Byline given.

Poetry: Maximum length: 20-25 lines.

How to Contact/Writers: Fiction/nonfiction: Send complete ms. Reports on mss in 8-10 weeks.

Illustration: Reviews artwork for possible future assignments; works on assignment only.

How to Contact/Illustrators: Ms/illustration packages: Query first. Illustrations only: Query with samples. Reports on art samples in 8-10 weeks.

Photography: Buys photos with accompanying ms only. Model/property releases required; captions required. Uses 35mm transparencies. Send completed ms with transparencies.

Terms: Pays on acceptance for illustrators, publication for writers. Buys all rights for mss and artwork; one-time rights for photos. Pays 15¢/word for assigned articles. Pays $225 for color cover illustration; $25-100 for b&w inside; $60-125 for color inside. Pays photographers per photo (range: $10-75). Sample copy $1.25. Writer's/illustrator's guidelines for SASE. (See listings for *Child Life, Children's Digest, Humpty Dumpty's Magazine, Jack and Jill, Turtle Magazine* and *U.S. Kids*.)

CHOICES, The Magazine for Personal Development and Practical Living Skills, Scholastic, Inc. 555 Broadway, New York NY 10012. (212)343-6100. Editor: Lauren Tarshis. Art Director: Joan Michaels. Monthly magazine. Estab. 1986 as *Choices* (formerly called *Coed*). "We go to teenagers in home economics and health classes. All our material has curriculum ties: Personal Development, Family Life, Careers, Food & Nutrition, Consumer Power, Child Development, Communications, Health."

Nonfiction: Buys 30 mss/year. Word length varies. Byline given (except for short items).
How to Contact/Writers: Nonfiction: Query with published clips "We don't want unsolicited manuscripts." Reports on queries in 2 weeks.
Illustration: Works on assignment only. "All art is *assigned* to go with specific articles." Pays on acceptance. Sample copy for 9 × 12 SAE and 2 first-class stamps.
Tips: "*Read* the specific magazines. We receive unsolicited manuscripts and queries that do not in any way address the needs of our magazine. For example, we don't publish poetry, but we get unsolicited poetry in the mail."

CLUBHOUSE, Your Story Hour, P.O. Box 15, Berrien Springs MI 49103. (616)471-3701. Articles/Fiction Editor, Art Director: Krista Phillips. Bimonthly magazine. Estab. 1949. Circ. 6,000.
Fiction: Middle readers, young adults: animal, contemporary, health, history, humorous, problem-solving, religious, sports. Does not want to see science fiction/fantasy/Halloween or Santa-oriented fiction. Buys 30 mss/year. Average word length: 800-1,300. Byline given.
Nonfiction: Middle readers, young adults: how-to. "We do not use articles except 200-500 word items about good health: anti—drug, tobacco, alcohol; pro—nutrition." Buys 6 mss/year. Average word length: 200-400. Byline given.
How to Contact/Writers: Fiction/nonfiction: Send complete ms. Reports on queries/mss in 6 weeks. Will consider simultaneous submissions.
Illustration: Buys 20-25 illustrations/issue; more than 120 illustrations/year. Uses b&w artwork only. Reviews artwork for future assignments; works on assignment only.
How to Contact/Illustrators: Illustrations only: Send photocopies, tearsheets or prints of work to be kept on file. Reports on art samples in 6 weeks. Originals usually not returned at job's completion, but they can be returned if desired.
Terms: Pays "about 6 months" after acceptance for authors, within 2 months for artwork. Buys first and one-time rights for mss and artwork. Pays $25-35 for articles. "Writers and artists receive 2 copies free in addition to payment." Pays $30 for b&w cover illustration; $7.50-25 for b&w inside. Sample copies for business SAE and 3 first-class stamps; writer's/illustrator's guidelines free for business SAE and 1 first-class stamp.
Tips: Writers: "Take children seriously—they're smarter than you think! Respect their sense of dignity, don't talk down to them and don't write stories about 'bad kids.' Illustrators: "Keep it clean, vigorous, fresh—whatever your style. Send samples we can keep on file. Black and white line art is best."

COBBLESTONE, The History Magazine for Young People, Cobblestone Publishing, Inc., 7 School St., Peterborough NH 03458. (603)924-7209. Fax: (603)924-7380. Editor: Meg Chorlian. Picture Editor: Francelle Carapetyan. Magazine published 10 times/year. Circ. 38,000. "*Cobblestone* is theme-related. Writers should request editorial guidelines which explain procedure and list upcoming themes. Queries must relate to an upcoming theme. Fiction is not used often, although a good fiction piece offers welcome diversity. It is recommended that writers become familiar with the magazine (sample copies available)."
Fiction: Middle readers, young adults: history. "Authentic historical and biographical fiction, adventure, retold legends, etc., relating to the theme." Buys 6-10 mss/year. Average word length: 800. Byline given.
Nonfiction: Middle readers, young adults: activities, biography, games/puzzles (no word finds), history, interview/profile, travel. All articles must relate to the issue's theme. Buys 120 mss/year. Average word length: 800. Byline given.
Poetry: Up to 100 lines. "Clear, objective imagery. Serious and light verse considered." Pays on an individual basis. Must relate to theme.
How to Contact/Writers: Fiction/nonfiction: Query. "A query must consist of all of the following to be considered (please use nonerasable paper): a brief cover letter stating the subject and word length of the proposed article; a detailed one-page outline explaining the information to be presented in the article; an extensive bibliography of materials the author intends to use in preparing the article; a self-addressed stamped envelope. Writers new to *Cobblestone* should send a writing sample with query. If you would like to know if your query has been received, please also include a stamped postcard that requests acknowledgment of receipt. In all correspondence, please include your complete address

as well as a telephone number where you can be reached. A writer may send as many queries for one issue as he or she wishes, but each query must have a separate cover letter, outline, bibliography and SASE. Telephone queries are not accepted. Handwritten queries will not be considered. Queries may be submitted at any time, but queries sent well in advance of deadline *may not be answered for several months*. Go-aheads requesting material proposed in queries are usually sent five months prior to publication date. Unused queries will be returned approximately three to four months prior to publication date."

Illustration: Buys 3 illustrations/issue; buys 36 illustrations/year. Preferred theme or style: Material that is simple, clear and accurate but not too juvenile. Sophisticated sources are a must. Reviews ms/illustration packages; reviews artwork for future assignments; works on assignment only.

How to Contact/Illustrators: Illustrations only: Send photocopies, tearsheets, or other nonreturnable samples. "Illustrators should consult issues of *Cobblestone* to familiarize themselves with our needs." Reports on art samples in 1-2 months. Original artwork returned at job's completion (upon written request).

Photography: Contact: Francelle Carapetyan, picture editor. Photos must relate to upcoming themes. Send transparencies and/or color/b&w prints. Submit on speculation.

Terms: Pays on publication. Buys all rights to articles and artwork. Pays 20-25¢/word for articles/stories. Pays on an individual basis for poetry, activities, games/puzzles. Pays photographers per photo ($15-100 for b&w; $25-100 for color). Sample copy $3.95 with 7½ × 10½ SAE and 5 first-class stamps; writer's/illustrator's/photographer's guidelines free with SAE and 1 first-class stamp.

Tips: Writers: "Submit detailed queries which show attention to historical accuracy and which offer interesting and entertaining information. Be true to your own style. Study past issues to know what we look for. All feature articles, recipes, activities, fiction and supplemental nonfiction are freelance contributions." Illustrators: "Submit b&w samples, not too juvenile. Study past issues to know what we look for. The illustration we use is generally for stories, recipes and activities." (See listings for *Calliope, The World History Magazine for Young People*; *Faces, The Magazine About People*; and *Odyssey, Science That's Out of This World.*)

COCHRAN'S CORNER, Cochran's Publishing Co., Box 2036, Waldorf MD 20604. (301)843-0485. Articles Editor: Ada Cochran. Fiction Editor/Art Director: Jeanie Saunders. Quarterly magazine. Estab. 1986. Circ. 1,000. "Our magazine is open to most kinds of writing that is wholesome and suitable for young children to read. It is 52 pages, 8½ × 11, devoted to short stories, articles and poems. Our children's corner is reserved for children up to the age of 14. *Right now we are forced to limit our acceptance to subscribers only*." 30% of material aimed at juvenile audience.

Fiction: Picture-oriented material: religious. Young readers: animal, fantasy, humorous, problem solving, religious. Middle readers: religious. Young adults: contemporary, history, religious, romance, science fiction. Does not want to see "anything that contains bad language or violence." Buys 150 mss/year. Maximum word length: 1,000.

Nonfiction: Picture-oriented material: religious, travel. Young readers: animal, how-to, problem solving, religious, travel. Middle readers: religious, travel. Young adults: history, humorous, interview/profile, religious, travel. Does not want to see "editorials or politics." Buys 100 mss/year. Average word length: 150. Byline given.

Poetry: Reviews 20-line poetry on any subject.

How to Contact/Writers: Fiction/nonfiction: Send complete ms. Reports on queries/mss in 3 months. Will consider simultaneous submissions.

Illustration: Reviews ms/illustration packages; reviews work for future assignments.

How to Contact/Illustrators: Reports only if interested. Credit line given.

Terms: "Payment is two contributor's copies for now, but we hope as we grow to begin paying." Sample copy $5 with 9 × 11 SASE. Writer's guidelines free for SASE.

Tips: Must subscribe to be published in this market ($20/1 year; $30/2 years).

COUNSELOR, Scripture Press Pub., Inc., Box 632, Glen Ellyn IL 60138. (708)668-6000. Articles/Fiction Editor: Janice K. Burton. Art Director: Blake Ebel. Newspaper distributed weekly; published quarterly. Estab. 1940. "Audience: children 8-12 years. Papers designed to present everyday living stories showing the difference Christ can make in a child's life. Correlated with Scripture Press Sunday School curriculum."

Fiction: Middle readers: adventure, history, multicultural, nature/environment, problem-solving, sports (all with Christian context). "Actually, true stories preferred by far. I appreciate well-written fiction that shows knowledge of our product. I suggest people write for samples." Buys approximately 12 mss/year. Average word length: 900-1,000. Byline given.

Nonfiction: Middle readers: arts/crafts, biography, games/puzzles, history, interview/profile, nature/environment, problem-solving, religion, science, social issues, sports. Buys approximately 12 mss/year. Average word length: 900-1,000. Byline given.

How to Contact/Writers: Fiction/nonfiction: Send complete ms. Reports on mss in 8-10 weeks. Publishes ms 1-2 years after acceptance (we work a year in advance). Will consider previously published work. Reports on mss in 8-10 weeks.

Illustration: Buys 24-30 illustrations/year. Reviews ms/illustration packages, but not often; reviews artwork for future assignments. Contact: Blake Ebel for details. Credit line sometimes given.

Photography: Purchases photos from freelancers.

Terms: Pays on acceptance. Buys first rights, one-time rights, or all rights for mss. Pays 5-10¢/word for stories or articles, depending on amount of editing required. Sample copies for #10 SAE and 1 first-class stamp. Writers/photo guidelines for SASE.

Tips: "Send copy that is as polished as possible. Indicate if story is true. Indicate rights offered. Stick to required word lengths. Write for our tips for writers, sample copies and theme lists."

CRICKET MAGAZINE, Carus Corporation, P.O. Box 300, Peru IL 61354. (815)224-6656. Articles/Fiction Editor-in-Chief: Marianne Carus. Editor: Deborah Vetter. Art Director: Ron McCutchan. Monthly magazine. Estab. 1973. Circ. 100,000. Children's literary magazine for ages 9-14.

• In addition to *Cricket*, the Carus Corporation publishes *Ladybug* and *Spider* (see listings in this section). The editors have also launched a new publication, *Babybug*, a board book magazine for children under two years old, first appearing in November 1994. Artwork is needed for the magazine ("good multicultural babies"). Contact the above address for submission information.

Fiction: Middle readers, young adults: adventure, animal, contemporary, fantasy, folk and fairy tales, history, humorous, multicultural, nature/environment, science fiction, sports, suspense/mystery. Buys 180 mss/year. Maximum word length: 1,500. Byline given.

Nonfiction: Middle readers, young adults: animal, arts/crafts, biography, environment, experiments, games/puzzles, history, how-to, interview/profile, natural science, problem-solving, science and technology, space, sports, travel. Multicultural needs include articles on customs and cultures. Requests bibliography with submissions. Buys 180 mss/year. Average word length: 1,000. Byline given.

Poetry: Reviews poems, 1-page maximum length. Limit submissions to 5 poems or less.

How to Contact/Writers: Send complete ms. Do not query first. Reports on mss in 2-3 months. Does not like but will consider simultaneous submissions. SASE required for response.

Illustration: Buys 35 illustrations (14 separate commissions)/issue; 425 illustrations/year. Uses b&w and full-color work. Preferred theme or style: "strong realism; strong people, especially kids; good action illustration; no cartoons. All media, but prefer other than pencil." Will review ms/illustration packages "but reserves option to re-illustrate."

How to Contact/Illustrators: Ms/illustration packages: Send complete ms with sample and query. Illustrations only: Provide tearsheets or good quality photocopies to be kept on file. SASE required for response/return of samples. Reports on art samples in 2 months. Original artwork returned at job's completion.

A bullet has been placed within some listings to introduce special comments by the editors of Children's Writer's & Illustrator's Market.

Photography: Purchases photos with accompanying ms only. Model/property releases required. Uses color transparencies, b&w glossy prints.

Terms: Pays on publication. Buys first publication rights in the English language. Buys first publication rights plus promotional rights for artwork. Pays up to 25¢/word for unsolicited articles; up to $3/line for poetry. Pays $750 for color cover; $75-150 for b&w, $150-250 for color inside. Pays $750 for color cover; $75-150 for b&w, $150-250 for color inside. Writer's/ illustrator's guidelines for SASE.

Tips: Writers: "Read copies of back issues and current issues. Adhere to specified word limits. *Please* do not query." Illustrators: "Edit your samples. Send only your best work and be able to reproduce that quality in assignments. Put name and address on *all* samples. Know a publication before you submit — is your style appropriate?"

CRUSADER, Calvinist Cadet Corps, P.O. Box 7259, Grand Rapids MI 49510. (616)241-5616. Editor: G. Richard Broene. Art Director: Robert DeJonge. Magazine published 7 times/year. Circ. 13,000. "Our magazine is for members of the Calvinist Cadet Corps — boys aged 9-14. Our purpose is to show how God is at work in their lives and in the world around them."

Fiction: Middle readers, young adults: Considers all categories but science fiction and romance. Wants to see more adventure, nature and sports. Buys 12 mss/year. Average word length: 800-1,500.

Nonfiction: Middle readers, young adults: considers all categories but fashion. Buys 6 mss/year. Average word length: 400-900.

How to Contact/Writers: Fiction/nonfiction: Send complete ms. Reports on queries/mss in 3-5 weeks. Will consider simultaneous submissions.

Illustration: Buys 1 illustration/issue; buys 6 illustrations/year. Reviews ms/illustration packages; reviews artwork for future assignments; works on assignment only. Credit line given.

How to Contact/Illustrators: Reports in 3-5 weeks.

Photography: Buys photos from freelancers. Wants nature photos and photos of boys.

Terms: Pays on acceptance. Buys first North American serial rights; reprint rights. Pays $10-100 for stories/articles. Pays illustrators $50-200 for b&w cover or inside. Sample copy free with 9×12 SAE and 3 first-class stamps.

Tips: Publication is most open to fiction: write for a list of themes (available yearly in January). See trends in children's magazines in "hard line, real world, to the point and action" material.

CURRENT HEALTH I, The Beginning Guide to Health Education, 60 Revere Dr., Northbrook IL 60062-1563. (708)205-3000. Monthly (during school year September-May) magazine. "For classroom use by students, this magazine is curriculum-specific and requires experienced educators who can write clearly and well at fifth grade reading level."

Nonfiction: Middle readers: health, health-related drugs, behavior, environment, problem-solving. Buys 60-70 mss/year. Average word length: 1,000. "Credit given in staff box."

How to Contact/Writers: Nonfiction: Query with published clips and résumé. Publishes ms 6-7 months after acceptance.

Terms: Pays on publication. Buys all rights. Pays $100-150, "more for longer features." Writer's guidelines available only if writer is given an assignment.

Tips: Needs material about drug education, nutrition, fitness and exercise.

CURRENT HEALTH II, The Continuing Guide to Health Education, 60 Revere Dr., Northbrook IL 60062-1563. (708)205-3000. Monthly (during school year September-May). "For classroom use by students, this magazine is curriculum specific and requires experienced educators who can write clearly and well at a ninth grade reading level."

Nonfiction: Young adults/teens: health, health-related drugs, behavior, environment, problem-solving, sports. Buys 70-90 mss/year. Average word length: 1,000-2,500. Byline given.

How to Contact/Writers: Nonfiction: Query with published clips and résumé. Reports on queries in 2 months. Publishes ms 6-7 months after acceptance.

Terms: Pays on publication. Buys all rights. Pays $100-150 for assigned article, "more for longer features." Writer's guidelines available only if writers are given an assignment.
Tips: Needs articles on drug education, nutrition, fitness and exercise.

DISCOVERIES, Children's Ministries, 6401 The Paseo, Kansas City MO 64131. (816)333-7000. Editor: Rebecca Raleigh. Executive Editor: Mark York. Weekly tabloid. *Discoveries* is a leisure reading piece for third and fourth graders. It is published weekly by WordAction Publishing. "The major purposes of *Discoveries* are to provide a leisure reading piece which will build Christian behavior and values and to provide reinforcement for Biblical concepts taught in the Sunday School curriculum. The focus of the reinforcement will be life-related, with some historical appreciation. *Discoveries'* target audience is children ages 8-10 in grades three and four. The readability goal is third to fourth grade."
Fiction: Young readers, middle readers: adventure, contemporary, problem-solving, religious. "Fiction — stories should vividly portray definite Christian emphasis or character-building values, without being preachy. The setting, plot and action should be realistic." Average word length: 500-700. Byline given.
How to Contact/Writers: Fiction: Send complete ms. Reports on mss in 6-8 weeks.
Illustration: "*Discoveries* publishes a wide variety of artistic styles, i.e., cartoon, realistic, montage, etc., but whatever the style, artwork must appeal to 8-10 year old children. It should not simply be child-related from an adult viewpoint. All artwork for *Discoveries* is assigned on a work for hire basis. Samples of art may be sent for review.
How to Contact/Illustrators: Illustrations only: send résumé, portfolio, client list, tearsheets. Reports back only if interested. Credit line given.
Terms: Pays "approximately one year before the date of issue." Buys multi-use rights. Pays 5¢/word. Pays illustrators $75 for color cover. Contributor receives 4 complimentary copies of publication. Writer's/artist's guidelines free with #10 SAE.
Tips: "*Discoveries* is committed to reinforcement of the Biblical concepts taught in the Sunday School curriculum. Because of this, the themes needed are mainly as follows: faith in God, obedience to God, putting God first, choosing to please God, accepting Jesus as Savior, finding God's will, choosing to do right, trusting God in hard times, prayer, trusting God to answer, Importance of Bible memorization, appreciation of Bible as God's Word to man, Christians working together, showing kindness to others, witnessing." (See listing for *Power and Light*.)

DISNEY ADVENTURES, The Walt Disney Company, 114 Fifth Ave., New York NY 10011-9060. Fiction Editor: Suzanne Harper. Monthly Magazine. Estab. 1990. Circ. 1 million.
  • To learn more about working with *Disney Adventures*, read the interview with Editor Suzanne Harper in the 1994 edition of *Children's Writer's & Illustrator's Market*. (Note: The magazine is now located in New York.)
Fiction: Middle readers: adventure, contemporary, fantasy, humorous, science fiction, sports, suspense/mystery. Buys approximately 6-10 mss/year. Averge word length: 1,500-2,000. Byline given.
Nonfiction: Middle readers: animal, biography, games/puzzles, interview/profile, nature/environment and sports. Buys 100-150 mss/year. Average word length: 250-750. Byline given.
How to Contact/Writers: Fiction: Send complete ms. Nonfiction: Query with published clips. Reports in 1 month. Publishes ms 6-12 months after acceptance. Will consider simultaneous submissions and electronic submissions via disk or modem.
Illustration: Buys approximately 20 illustrations/issue; 250 illustrations/year. Reviews ms/illustration packages; reviews artwork for future assignments; works on assignment only.
How to Contact/Illustrators: Illustrations only: Provide résumé, business card, promotional literature or tearsheets to be kept on file. Reports only if interested. Does not return original artwork.
Photography: Purchases photos separately. Model/property releases required; captions required. Send "anything but originals — everything sent is kept on file." Photographers should provide résumé, business card, promotional literature or tearsheets to be kept on file. Reports only if interested.

Terms: Pays on acceptance. Buys all rights. Purchases all rights for artwork, various rights for photographs. Pays $250-750 for assigned articles. Pays illustrators $50 and up. Photographers paid $100 minimum per project, or $25 minimum per photo. Sample copies: "Buy on newsstand or order copies by calling 1-800-435-0715." Writer's guidelines for SASE.

DOLPHIN LOG, The Cousteau Society, Suite 402, 870 Greenbrier Circle, Chesapeake VA 23320-2641. Editor: Elizabeth Foley. Bimonthly magazine for children ages 7-13. Circ. 80,000. Entirely nonfiction subject matter encompasses all areas of science, natural history, marine biology, ecology and the environment as they relate to our global water system. The philosophy of the magazine is to delight, instruct and instill an environmental ethic and understanding of the interconnectedness of living organisms, including people. Of special interest are articles on ocean- or water-related themes which develop reading and comprehension skills.
Nonfiction: Middle readers, young adult: animal, games/puzzles, geography, interview/profile, nature/environment, science, ocean. Multicultural needs include indigenous peoples, lifestyles of ancient people, etc. Does not want to see talking animals. No dark or religious themes. Buys 10 mss/year. Average word length: 500-700. Byline given.
How to Contact/Writers: Nonfiction: Query first. Reports on queries in 1 month; mss in 2 months.
Illustration: Buys 1 illustration/issue; buys 6 illustrations/year. Preferred theme: Biological illustration. Will review ms/illustration packages; will review artwork for future assignments.
How to Contact/Illustrators: Illustrations only: Query; send résumé, promo sheet, slides. Reports on art samples in 8 weeks only if interested. Credit line given to illustrators.
Photography: Wants "sharp, colorful pictures of sea creatures. The more unusual the creature, the better."
Terms: Pays on publication. Buys first North American serial rights; reprint rights. Pays $25-150 for articles. Pays $25-200/color photos. Sample copy $2 with 9×12 SAE and 3 first-class stamps. Writer's/illustrator's guidelines free with #10 SASE.
Tips: Writers: "Write simply and clearly and don't anthropomorphize." Illustrators: "Be scientifically accurate and don't anthropomorphize. Some background in biology is helpful, as our needs range from simple line drawings to scientific illustrations which must be researched for biological and technical accuracy."

DYNAMATH, Scholastic Inc., 555 Broadway, New York NY 10012-3999. (212)343-6432. Editor: Joe D'Agnese. Art Director: Pam Mitchell. Monthly magazine. Estab. 1981. Circ. 300,000. Purpose is "to make learning math fun, challenging and uncomplicated for young minds in a very complex world."
Nonfiction: All levels: animal, arts/crafts, cooking, fashion, games/puzzles, health, history, hobbies, how-to, humorous, math, multicultural, nature/environment, problem-solving, science, social issues, sports—all must relate to math and science topics.
How to Contact/Writers: Nonfiction: Query with published clips, send ms. Reports on queries in 1 month; mss in 6 weeks. Publishes ms 4 months after acceptance. Will consider simultaneous submissions.
Illustration: Buys 4 illustrations/issue.
How to Contact/Illustrators: Query first; send résumé and tearsheets. Reports back on submissions only if interested. Originals returned to artist at job's completion. Credit line given.
Terms: Pays on acceptance. Buys all rights for mss, artwork, photographs. Pays $50-300 for stories. Pays artists $800-1,000 for color cover illustration; $100-800 for color inside illustration. Pays photographers $300-1,000 per project.

EXPLORING, Boy Scouts of America, 1325 W. Walnut Hill Lane, P.O. Box 152079, Irving TX 75015-2079. (214)580-2365. Executive Editor: Scott Daniels. Art Director: Joe Connally. Photo Editor: Brian Payne. Magazine published "4 times a year—not quarterly." *Exploring* is a 12-page, 4-color magazine published for members of the Boy Scouts of America's Exploring program. These members are young men and women between the ages of 14-21. Interests include careers, computers, life skills (money management, parent/peer relationships, study habits), college, camping, hiking, canoeing.

Nonfiction: Young adults: interview/profile, problem-solving, travel. Buys 12 mss/year. Average word length: 600-1,200. Byline given.

How to Contact/Writers: Nonfiction: Query with published clips. Reports on queries/mss in 1 week.

Illustration: Buys 3 illustrations/issue; buys 12 illustrations/year. Will review artwork for future assignments. Works on assignment only.

How to Contact/Illustrators: Reports on art samples in 2 weeks. Original artwork returned at job's completion.

Terms: Pays on acceptance. Buys first North American serial rights. Pays $300-500 for assigned/unsolicited articles. Pays $1,000 for color cover; $250-500 for b&w inside; $500-800 for color inside. Sample copy with 8½ × 11 SAE and 5 first-class stamps. Free writer's/illustrator's guidelines.

Tips: Looks for "short, crisp career profiles of 1,000 words with plenty of information to break out into graphics."

FACES, The Magazine About People, Cobblestone Publishing, Inc., 7 School St., Peterborough NH 03458. (603)924-7209. Fax: (603)924-7380. Editor-in-Chief: Carolyn P. Yoder. Art Director: Ellen Klempner-Beguin. Picture Editor: Francelle Carapetyan. Magazine published 9 times/year (September-May). Circ. 15,000. "Although *Faces* operates on a by-assignment basis, we welcome ideas/suggestions in outline form. All manuscripts are reviewed by the American Museum of Natural History in New York before being accepted. *Faces* is a theme-related magazine; writers should send for theme list before submitting ideas/queries."

Fiction: Middle readers: anthropology; young adults: contemporary, folktales, history, multicultural, religious. Does not want to see material that does not relate to a specific upcoming theme. Buys 9 mss/year. Maximum word length: 800. Byline given.

Nonfiction: Middle readers and young adults: anthropology, arts/crafts, games/puzzles, history, interview/profile, religious, travel. Does not want to see material not related to a specific upcoming theme. Buys 63 mss/year. Average word length: 300-800. Byline given.

How to Contact/Writers: Fiction/nonfiction: Query with published clips and 2-3 line biographical sketch. "Ideas should be submitted six to nine months prior to the publication date. Responses to ideas are usually sent approximately four months before the publication date."

Illustration: Buys 3 illustrations/issue; buys 27 illustrations/year. Preferred theme or style: Material that is meticulously researched (most articles are written by professional anthropologists); simple, direct style preferred, but not too juvenile. Reviews ms/illustration packages; reviews artwork for future assignments; works on assignment only.

How to Contact/Illustrators: Ms/illustration packages: Illustration is done by assignment. Roughs required. Illustrations only: Send samples of b&w work. "Illustrators should consult issues of *Faces* to familiarize themselves with our needs." Reports on art samples in 1-2 months. Original artwork returned at job's completion (upon written request).

Photography: Wants photos relating to forthcoming themes.

Terms: Pays on publication. Buys all rights for mss and artwork. Pays 20-25¢/word for articles/stories. Covers are assigned and paid on an individual basis. Pays photographers per photo ($15-100 for b&w; $25-100 for color). Sample copy $3.95 with 7½ × 10½ SAE and 5 first-class stamps. Writer's/illustrator's/photo guidelines free with SAE and 1 first-class stamp.

Tips: "Writers are encouraged to study past issues of the magazine to become familiar with our style and content. Writers with anthropological and/or travel experience are particularly encouraged; *Faces* is about world cultures. All feature articles, recipes and activities are freelance contributions." Illustrators: "Submit b&w samples, not too juvenile.

The Subject Index, located before the General Index, lists book and magazine publishers by their fiction and nonfiction needs.

Study past issues to know what we look for. The illustration we use is generally for retold legends, recipes and activities." (See listing for *Calliope, The World History Magazine for Young People*; *Cobblestone, The History Magazine for Young People*; and *Odyssey, Science That's Out of This World*.)

FALCON MAGAZINE, Falcon Press, 48 Last Chance Gulch, P.O. Box 1718, Helena MT 59624. (406)442-6597. Executive Editor: Kay Morton Ellerhoff. Associate Editor: Carolyn Zieg Cunningham. Design Editor: Bryan Knaff. Bimonthly magazine. Estab. 1993. Circ. 55,000. "A magazine for young conservationists."
Nonfiction: Middle readers: animal, arts/crafts (nature-oriented), cooking (outdoor), nature/environment. Average word length: 800 maximum. Byline given.
How to Contact/Writers: Fiction/nonfiction: Query. Reports in 2 months.
Illustration: Buys 6 illustrations/issue; 75 illustrations/year. Reviews ms/illustration packages; reviews artwork for future assignments. Prefers work on assignment.
How to Contact/Illustrators: Illustrations only: Query; send slides, tearsheets. Reports in 2 months. Samples returned with SASE; samples sometimes filed. Original work returned upon job's completion. Credit line given.
Photography: *Must* be submitted in 20-slide sheets and individual protectors, such as KYMAL. Looks for "children outdoors—camping, fishing, doing 'nature' projects." Model/property releases required. Photo captions required. Uses 35mm transparencies. To contact photographers should query with samples. Reports in 2 months.
Terms: Pays on publication. Buys one-time rights for mss. Purchases one-time rights for photographs. Pays $200 minimum for articles. Additional payment for ms/illustration packages ($200). Pays illustrators $40 b&w inside; $250 color cover; $50-100 color inside. Photographers paid by the project ($50 minimum); per photo (range: $50-100). Sample copies for 8½ × 11 SAE. Writer's/illustrator's/photo guidelines for SASE.

FFA NEW HORIZONS, The Official Magazine of the National FFA Organization, 5632 Mt. Vernon Memorial Hwy., Alexandria VA 22309. (703)360-3600. Fax: (703)360-5524. Managing Editor: Lawinna McGary. Bimonthly magazine. Estab. 1952. Circ. 425,000. "*FFA New Horizons* strives to strengthen the aims and purposes of FFA by bringing to our readers living examples of how these are being fulfilled daily by individual FFA members."
Nonfiction: Young adults: animal, biography, careers, education, health, hobbies, how-to, humorous, interview/profile, nature/environment, problem-solving, sports. "All stories must be directed toward teens and have an FFA connection." Does not want to see stories that have no FFA connection at all. Average word length: 600-1,000.
How to Contact/Writers: Nonfiction: Query with published clips. Send complete ms. Reports on queries/mss in 1 month. Publishes ms 2-4 months after acceptance. Will consider simultaneous submissions and electronic submissions via disk or modem.
Illustration: Buys 6 illustrations/year. Reviews ms/illustration packages; reviews artwork for future assignments; works on assignment only.
How to Contact/Illustrators: Ms/illustration packages: Query. Illustrations only: Query with samples. Reports in 1 month. Original work not returned.
Photography: Looking for "photos that show the FFA member and illustrate the story." Uses 5 × 7 color and b&w prints; 35mm transparencies. Reports in 1 month.
Terms: Pays on acceptance. Buys all rights for mss, artwork and photographs. Pay varies. Photographers paid per photo. Sample copies for 9 × 12 SAE and 5 first-class stamps. Writer's/illustrator's/photo guidelines for SASE.

*FIELD & STREAM, Times Mirror Magazines, 2 Park Ave., New York NY 10016. (212)779-5000. Articles Editor: Duncan Barnes. Art Director: Daniel J. McClain. Bimonthly magazine. Estab. 1989. Circ. 2 million. "Field & Stream Jr.," a special 3- to 4-page section of *Field & Stream*, is designed to teach young sportsmen about hunting, fishing and related topics. "We publish straightforward how-to pieces, crafts and projects, puzzles, adventure stories, and fillers about hunting and fishing."
Nonfiction: Middle readers: animal, games/puzzles, how-to, interview/profile, nature/environment, hunting/fishing. "We are looking for articles that are related to hunting and/or fishing. We see too many articles not connected to these topics, and too many 'my first

fishing trip' type stories." Buys 25 mss/year. Average word length: 25 to 600 (25 for fillers). Byline given.

How to Contact/Writers: Nonfiction: Query with published clips. Reports on queries/ mss in 1 month. Publishes ms 3-12 months after acceptance. Will consider electronic submissions via disk or modem.

Illustration: Buys 5 illustrations/issue; 30 illustrations/year. Reviews ms/illustration packages; reviews artwork for future assignments; works on assignment only.

How to Contact/Illustrators: Ms/illustration packages: Query. Illustrations only: Send résumé, promo sheet and portfolio. Samples returned with SASE; samples filed. Original work returned at job's completion. Credit line given.

Photography: Buys photos from freelancers. Uses 35mm transparencies. Query with samples. Reports in 1 month.

Terms: Pays on acceptance. Buys first North American serial rights for mss, artwork and photographs. Pays $75-650 for articles. Additional payment for ms/illustration packages and for photos accompanying articles. Pays illustrators $300-800 for color inside. Pays photographers per photo ($450). Sample copies for $4. Writer's/photo guidelines for SASE.

Tips: "Study back issues of magazines to see what kinds of articles they use and what topics they cover. For 'Field & Stream Jr.,' we are looking for manuscripts that cover hunting and fishing and related topics, such as conservation, natural history and sporting ethics. Most photos or illustrations are requested by the editors in order to complement and illustrate stories. We also include writing by children."

FOCUS ON THE FAMILY CLUBHOUSE; FOCUS ON THE FAMILY CLUBHOUSE JR., Focus on the Family, 8605 Explorer Dr., Colorado Springs CO 80920. (719)531-3400. Editors: Lisa Brock and Marianne Hering. Art Director: Timothy Jones. Monthly magazine. Estab. 1987. Combined circulation is 250,000. "*Focus on the Family Clubhouse* is a 16-page Christian magazine, published monthly, for children ages 8-12. Similarly, *Focus on the Family Clubhouse Jr.* is published for children ages 4-8. We want fresh, exciting literature that promotes biblical thinking, values and behavior in every area of life."

Fiction: Picture-oriented material and young readers: adventure, animal, contemporary, humorous, multicultural, religious. Middle readers: adventure, contemporary, humorous, multicultural, nature/environment, religious, suspense/mystery. Buys approximately 6-10 mss/year. Average word length: *Clubhouse*, 500-1,400; *Clubhouse Jr.*, 250-1,100. Byline given on all fiction; not on puzzles.

Nonfiction: Picture-oriented material, young readers and middle readers: animal, arts/ crafts, biography, cooking, games/puzzles, hobbies, how-to, humorous, interview/profile, nature/environment, religion. Buys 3-5 mss/year. Average word length: 200-1,000. Byline given.

Poetry: Wants to see "humorous or biblical" poetry. Maximum length: 25 lines.

How to Contact/Writers: Fiction/nonfiction: send complete ms. Reports on queries/mss in 4-6 weeks. Publishes ms 4-6 months after acceptance.

Illustration: "Most illustrations are done on assignment." Reviews ms/illustration packages; reviews artwork for future assignments; works on assignment mostly.

How to Contact/Illustrators: Ms/illustration packages: submit ms with rough sketches. Illustrations only: send résumé, promo sheet, portfolio, slides and tearsheets. Reports in 1 month. Samples returned with SASE; samples kept on file. Original work returned at job's completion. Credit line given.

Photography: Buys photos from freelancers. Uses 35mm transparencies. Photographers should query with samples; provide résumé and promotional literature or tearsheets. Reports in 2 months.

Terms: Pays on acceptance. Buys first North American serial rights and reprint rights (occasionally) for mss. Buys first rights or reprint rights for artwork and photographs. Additional payment for ms/illustration packages. Only interested in agented material. Pays photographers by the project or per photo. Sample copies for 9 × 12 SAE and 3 first-class stamps. Writers'/illustrator/photo guidelines for SASE.

Tips: "The best stories avoid moralizing or preachiness, and are not written *down* to children. They are the products of writers who share in the adventure with their readers, exploring the characters they have created without knowing for certain where the story will lead. And they are not always explicitly Christian, but are built upon a Christian foundation (and, at the very least, do not contradict biblical views or values)."

© 1994 F. Joseph VanSeveren.

Joe VanSeveren's pleasingly quirky gouache and airbrush illustration (one of two) accompanied "An Awesome Deal," by Katherine G. Bond in the August 1994 issue of Focus on the Family Clubhouse. VanSeveren captured the caring spirit in Bond's story about a young boy and his sick, aged friend. Art Director Tim Jones says he has gotten good reactions from readers about the artist's bright, fun style.

FOR SENIORS ONLY, Campus Communications, Inc., 339 N. Main St., New City NY 10956. (914)638-0333. Articles/Fiction Editor: Judi Oliff. Art Director: Randi Wendelkin. Semiannual magazine. Estab. 1971. Circ. 350,000. Publishes career-oriented articles for high school students, college-related articles, and feature articles on travel, etc.

Fiction: Young adults: health, humorous, sports, travel. Byline given.

Nonfiction: Young adults: careers, games/puzzles, health, how-to, humorous, interview/profile, social issues, sports, travel. Buys 4-6 mss/year. Average word length: 1,000-2,500. Byline given.

How to Contact/Writers: Fiction/nonfiction: Query; query with published clips; send complete ms. Publishes ms 2-4 months after acceptance. Will consider simultaneous submissions, electronic submissions via disk or modem and previously published work.

Illustration: Reviews ms/illustration packages; reviews artwork for future assignments.

How to Contact/Illustrators: Ms/illustration packages: Query; submit complete package with final art; submit ms with rough sketches. Illustrations only: Query; send slides. Reports back only if interested. Samples not returned; samples kept on file. Original work returned upon job's completion. Credit line given.

Photography: Model/property release required. Uses 5½ × 8½ and 4⅞ × 7⅜ color prints; 35mm and 8 × 10 transparencies. Photographers should query with samples; send unsolicited photos by mail. Reports back only if interested.

Terms: Pays on publication. Buys exclusive magazine rights. Payment is byline credit. Writer's/illustrator's/photo guidelines for SASE.

FREEWAY, Scripture Press Publications, Inc., Box 632, Glen Ellyn IL 60138. (708)688-6000. Articles/Fiction Editor: Amy J. Cox. Art Director: Blake Ebel. Photo Editor: Joe DeLeon. Quarterly in weekly issues. Estab. 1973. *"FreeWay* is a Sunday School take-home paper aimed at high school and college age Christian youth. It's primary objective is to show how biblical principles for Christian living can be applied to everyday life."

Fiction: Young adults/teens: contemporary, humorous, multicultural, nature/environment, problem-solving, religious, sports. "All material must have a clear, spiritual 'take-away' value based on a biblical principle. Stories should be specifically Christian, not just moral." Buys approximately 45 mss/year. Average word length: 400-1,200. Byline given.

Nonfiction: Young adults/teens: careers, games/puzzles, humorous, interview/profile, multicultural (missionaries, personal experience, teens in other cultures), nature/environment, problem-solving, religion, social issues, sports. "We're looking for true stories—personal experience, profiles, and 'as told to.' We also buy articles on teen issues: dating, peer pressure, family relationships, social issues, daily Bible study and prayer, etc. All must have clear, biblical basis." Buys approximately 75 mss/year. Average word length: 400-1,200. Byline given.

Poetry: Maximum length: 25 lines. Limit submissions to 5 poems.

How to Contact/Writers: Fiction/nonfiction: Send complete ms. Reports on mss in 3-4 months. Publishes ms at least one year after acceptance. Will consider simultaneous submissions and previously published work.

Illustration: Buys 15 illustrations/year. Uses b&w artwork only. Reviews artwork for future assignments; works on assignment only.

How to Contact/Illustrators: Illustrations only: Send résumé, promo sheet and tear-sheets. Reports only if interested. Original work returned at job's completion. Credit line given.

Photography: Looks for "action shots, minorities, mood shots, relationship shots, sports, school, teen hangouts, etc. Modest clothing, jewelry, etc." Model/property releases required. Uses b&w 8 × 10 or 5 × 7 prints. Photographers should query with samples. Reports only if interested.

Terms: Pays on acceptance. Buys one-time rights for mss. Purchases one-time rights for artwork and photographs. Pays $25-120 for stories; $25-120 for articles. Payment for illustrations negotiated with designer. Sample copies for #10 SAE and 1 first-class stamp. Writer's/photo guidelines for SASE.

Tips: *"FreeWay* is a great break-in point. We rely heavily upon freelancers. Each weekly issue contains at least 2 freelance-written features plus at least 2 photographs or illustrations. However, we have a narrow audience. We want stories and articles which will help our readers grow in the Christian faith—without being unrealistic or preachy."

THE FRIEND MAGAZINE, The Church of Jesus Christ of Latter-day Saints, 50 E. North Temple, Salt Lake City UT 84150. (801)240-2210. Managing Editor: Vivian Paulsen. Art Director: Richard Brown. Monthly magazine. Estab. 1971. Circ. 350,000. Magazine for 3-11 year olds.

Fiction: Picture material, young readers, middle readers: adventure, animal, contemporary, folktales, history, humorous, problem-solving, religious, ethnic, sports, suspense/mystery. Does not want to see controversial issues, political, horror, fantasy. Average word length: 400-1,000. Byline given.

Nonfiction: Picture material, young readers, middle readers: animal, arts/crafts, biography, cooking, games/puzzles, history, how-to, humorous, problem-solving, religious, sports. Does not want to see controversial issues, political, horror, fantasy. Average word length: 400-1,000. Byline given.

Poetry: Reviews poetry. Maximum length: 20 lines.

How to Contact/Writers: Fiction/nonfiction: Send complete ms. Reports on mss in 2 months.

How to Contact/Illustrators: Illustrators only: Query with samples; arrange personal interview to show portfolio; provide résumé and tearsheets for files.

Terms: Pays on acceptance. Buys all rights for mss. Pays 9-11¢/word for unsolicited articles. Contributors are encouraged to send for free sample copy with 9 × 11 envelope and $1 postage. Free writer's guidelines.

Tips: "*The Friend* is published by The Church of Jesus Christ of Latter-day Saints for boys and girls up to twelve years of age. All submissions are carefully read by the *Friend* staff, and those not accepted are returned within two months when a self-addressed, stamped envelope is enclosed. Submit seasonal material at least eight months in advance. Query letters and simultaneous submissions are not encouraged. Authors may request rights to have their work reprinted after their manuscript is published."

THE GOLDFINCH, Iowa History for Young People, State Historical Society of Iowa, 402 Iowa Ave., Iowa City IA 52240. (319)335-3916. Fax: (319)335-3924. Editor: Amy Ruth. Quarterly magazine. Estab. 1975. Circ. 2,500. "The award-winning *Goldfinch* consists of 10-12 nonfiction articles, short fiction, poetry and activities per issue. Each magazine focuses on an aspect or theme of history that occurred in or affected Iowa."
Fiction: Middle readers: historical fiction only. "Study past issues for structure and content. Most manuscripts written inhouse." Average word length: 500-1,500. Byline given.
Nonfiction: Middle readers: arts/crafts, biography, games/puzzles, Iowa history, how-to, interview/profile, travel. Uses 20-30 mss/year. Average word length: 500-800. Byline given.
Poetry: Reviews poetry. No minimum or maximum word length; no maximum number of submissions. "All poetry must reflect an Iowa theme."
How to Contact/Writers: Fiction/nonfiction: Query with published clips. Reports on queries/mss in 2-4 weeks. Publishes ms 1 month-1 year after acceptance. Will consider electronic submissions via disk or modem.
Illustration: Buys 4 illustrations/issue; 20 illustrations/year. Uses b&w artwork only. Prefers cartoon, line drawing. Reviews ms/illustration packages; reviews artwork for future assignments; works on assignment only.
How to Contact/Illustrators: Ms/illustration packages: Query. Illustrations only: Query with samples. Reports in 2-4 weeks. Original work returned upon job's completion.
Photography: Types of photos used vary with subject. Model/property releases required with submissions. Uses b&w prints; 35mm transparencies. Query with samples. Reports in 2-4 weeks.
Terms: Pays on acceptance (artwork only). Buys all rights. Payment for mss is in copies at this time. Pays illustrators $10-150. Photographers paid per photo (range: $10-100). Sample copies for $4. Writer's/illustrator's/photo guidelines free for SASE.
Tips: "The editor researches the topics and determines the articles. Writers, most of whom live in Iowa, work from primary and secondary research materials to write pieces. The presentation is aimed at children 8-14 and the writing of E.B. White is a model for the prose. All submissions must relate to an upcoming theme. Please send for our writer's guidelines and theme lists before submitting manuscripts."

GUIDE MAGAZINE, Review and Herald Publishing Association, 55 W. Oak Ridge Dr., Hagerstown MD 21740. (301)791-7000. Articles Editor: Jeannette Johnson. Art Director: Bill Kirstein. Weekly magazine. Estab. 1953. Circ. 40,000. "Ours is a weekly Christian journal written for middle readers and young adults, presenting true stories relevant to the needs of today's young person, emphasizing positive aspects of Christian living."
Nonfiction: Middle readers, young adults: adventure, animal, biography, character-building, contemporary, games/puzzles, humorous, nature/environment, problem-solving, religious, social issues, sports, suspense/mystery. "We need true, or based on true, happenings, not merely true-to-life. Our stories and puzzles must have a spiritual emphasis." No violence. No articles. "We always need humorous adventure stories." Buys 300 mss/year. Average word length: 500-600 minimum, 1,000-1,200 maximum. Byline given.
How to Contact/Writers: Nonfiction: Send complete ms. Reports in 1-2 weeks. Will consider simultaneous submissions. "We can only pay half of the regular amount for simultaneous submissions." Reports on queries/mss in 1 week. Credit line given.
Terms: Pays on acceptance. Buys first North American serial rights; first rights; one-time rights; second serial (reprint rights); simultaneous rights. Pays 3-5¢/word for stories and articles. "Writer receives several complimentary copies of issue in which work appears." Sample copy free with 5 × 9 SAE and 2 first-class stamps. Writer's guidelines for SASE.
Tips: Children's magazines "want mystery, action, discovery, suspense and humor—no matter what the topic."

GUIDEPOSTS FOR KIDS, (formerly *Faith 'n Stuff*), Guideposts Associates, Inc., 16 E. 34th St., New York NY 10016. Editor: Mary Lou Carney. Articles Editor: Sailor Metts. Fiction Editor: Lurlene McDaniel. Art Director: Mike Lyons. Photo Editor: Mary Ann Tanner. Bimonthly magazine. Estab. 1990. Circ. 160,000. *"Guideposts for Kids* is published bi-monthly by Guideposts Associates, Inc. for kids 7-12 years old (emphasis on upper end of that age bracket). It is a Bible-based, direct mail magazine that is *fun* to read. It is *not* a Sunday school take-home paper or a miniature *Guideposts*."

Fiction: Middle readers: adventure, animal, contemporary, folktales, historical, humorous, multicultural, nature/environment, problem-solving, religious, sports, suspense/mystery. Multicultural needs include: Kids in other cultures—school, sports, families. Does not want to see preachy fiction. "We want real stories about real kids doing real things—conflicts our readers will respect; resolutions our readers will accept. Problematic. Tight. Filled with realistic dialogue and sharp imagery. No stories about 'good' children always making the right decision. If present at all, adults are minor characters and *do not* solve kids' problems for them." Buys approximately 10 mss/year. Average word length: 500-1,500. Byline given.

Nonfiction: Middle readers: animal, games/puzzles, history, hobbies, how-to, humorous, interview/profile, math, multicultural, nature/environment, problem-solving, religious, science, social issues, sports, travel. "Make nonfiction issue-oriented, controversial, thought-provoking. Something kids not only *need* to know, but *want* to know as well." Buys 10 mss/year. Average word length: 200-1,300. Byline usually given.

How to Contact/Writers: Fiction: Send complete ms. Nonfiction: Query. Reports on queries in 6 weeks; on mss in 2 months.

Illustration: Reviews ms/illustration packages; reviews artwork for future assignments.

How to Contact/Illustrators: Query; send résumé, promo sheet, tearsheets. Reports back only if interested. Credit line given.

Photography: Looks for "spontaneous, *real* kids in action shots."

Terms: Pays on acceptance. Buys all rights for mss. Buys first rights for artwork. "Features range in payment from $200-350; fiction from $200-300. We pay higher rates for stories exceptionally well-written or well-researched. Regular contributors get bigger bucks, too." Additional payment for ms/illustration packages "but we prefer to acquire our own illustrations." Sample copies for $3.25. Writer's guidelines free for SASE.

Tips: "Make your manuscript good, relevant and playful. No preachy stories about Bible-toting children. *Guideposts for Kids* is not a beginner's market. Study our magazine. (Sure, you've heard that before—but it's *necessary!*) Neatness *does* count. So do creativity and professionalism. SASE essential."

HIGH ADVENTURE, Assemblies of God, 1445 Boonville Ave., Springfield MO 65802. (417)862-2781, Ext. 4181. Fax: (417)862-0416. Editor: Marshall Bruner. Quarterly magazine. Circ. 86,000. Estab. 1971. Magazine is designed to provide boys with worthwhile, enjoyable, leisure reading; to challenge them in narrative form to higher ideals and greater spiritual dedication; and to perpetuate the spirit of Royal Rangers through stories, ideas and illustrations. 75% of material aimed at juvenile audience.

Fiction: Buys 100 mss/year. Average word length: 1,000. Byline given.

Nonfiction: Articles: Christian living, devotional, Holy Spirit, salvation, self-help; biography; missionary stories; news items; testimonies, inspirational stories based on true-life experiences.

How to Contact/Writers: Fiction/nonfiction: Send complete ms. Reports on queries in 6-8 weeks. Will consider simultaneous submissions. Will review ms/illustration packages.

How to Contact/Illustrators: Ms/illustration packages: Send complete ms with final art. Illustrations only: "Most of our artwork is done in-house."

Always include a self-addressed, stamped envelope (SASE) with submissions within your own country. When sending material to other countries, include a self-addressed envelope (SAE) and International Reply Coupons (IRCs).

Terms: Pays on acceptance. Buys first and second rights. Pays 2-3¢/word for articles. Sample copy free with 9×12 SASE. Free writer's/illustrator's guidelines for SASE.

HIGHLIGHTS FOR CHILDREN, 803 Church St., Honesdale PA 18431. (717)253-1080. Manuscript Coordinator: Beth Troop. Art Director: Charlie Cary. Monthly magazine. Estab. 1946. Circ. 2.8 million. "Our motto is 'Fun With a Purpose.' We are looking for quality fiction and nonfiction that appeals to children, encourages them to read, and reinforces positive values. All art is done on assignment."
Fiction: Picture-oriented material: animal, contemporary, fantasy, folktales, history, humorous, sports. Young readers, middle readers: adventure, animal, contemporary, fantasy, folktales, history, humorous, problem-solving, science fiction, sports, suspense/mystery. Does not want to see war, crime, violence. "We see too many stories with overt morals." Would like to see more suspense/stories/articles with world culture settings, sports pieces, action/adventure. Buys 150 mss/year. Average word length: 400-800. Byline given.
Nonfiction: Picture-oriented material: animal, arts/crafts, biography, health, history, how-to, humorous, nature/environment, problem-solving, science. Young readers, middle readers: animal, arts/crafts, biography, careers, foreign, health, history, how-to, humorous, interview/profile, nature/environment, problem-solving, science, sports. Does not want to see trendy topics, fads, personalities who would not be good role models for children, guns, war, crime, violence. "We'd like to see more nonfiction for younger readers—maximum of 600 words. We still need older-reader material, too—600-900 words." Buys 75 mss/year. Maximum word length: 900. Byline given.
How to Contact/Writers: Send complete ms. Reports on queries/mss in 4-6 weeks.
Illustration: Preferred theme or style: Realistic, some stylization, cartoon style acceptable. Reviews artwork for future assignments; works on assignment only.
How to Contact/Illustrators: Ms/illustration packages: Art is done on assignment only. Illustrations only: Photocopies, promo sheet, tearsheets, or slides. Résumé optional. Portfolio only if requested. Reports on art samples in 4-6 weeks. Credit line given.
Terms: Pays on acceptance. Buys all rights for mss. Pays 14¢/word and up for unsolicited articles. Pays illustrators $1,025 for color cover; $25-200 for b&w, $25-600 for color inside. Writer's/illustrator's guidelines free on request.
Tips: "Know the magazine's style before submitting. Send for guidelines and sample issue if necessary." Writers: "At *Highlights* we're paying closer attention to acquiring more nonfiction for young readers than we have in the past." Illustrators: "Fresh, imaginative work encouraged. Flexibility in working relationships a plus. Illustrators presenting their work need not confine themselves to just children's illustrations as long as work can translate to our needs. We also use animal illustrations, real and imaginary. We need party plans, crafts and puzzles—any activity that will stimulate children mentally and creatively. We are always looking for imaginative cover subjects."

HOB-NOB, 994 Nissley Rd., Lancaster PA 17601. (717)898-7807. Articles/Fiction/Poetry Editor, Art Director: M. K. Henderson. Quarterly magazine. Circ. 350. *Hob-Nob* began as a "family" publication and prefers to avoid any material that could or should not be read by younger readers. There is now a separate "Family Section" in the magazine, approximately 20 pages of material for young children to teens. 30% of prose in current issue aimed at juvenile audience.
Fiction: Picture-oriented material (preschool-8 years): animal, fantasy, humorous, multicultural. Young readers: adventure, animal, folktales, humorous, nature/environment. Middle readers: adventure, animal, contemporary, fantasy, folktales, history, humorous, nature/environment, problem-solving, science fiction, sports, suspense/mystery. Young adults: adventure, contemporary, fantasy, history, humorous, nature/environment, problem-solving, religious, romance, science fiction, sports, spy/mystery/adventure, suspense/mystery. Does not want to see religious proselytizing material geared to specific denominations or categories of denominations (i.e., "fundamentalist"); "clean" only, no bathroom language. Buys 100 mss/year (all age levels; juvenile—18 in current issue). Maximum word length: 1,500. Byline given.
Nonfiction: Picture-oriented material: arts/crafts, games/puzzles, hobbies, how-to, humorous. Young readers: animal, art/crafts, biography, games/puzzles, humorous, hobbies, how-

Illustrator Gary Undercuffler's fresh watercolor style was perfect for depicting this realistic, urban scene featuring friends frolicking in the froth of a fire hydrant for Highlights for Children. *The magazine's art director sought work conveying "fun and lightheartedness, even in the oppressive city heat," to accompany a poem entitled "August," by Myra Cohn Livingston in (of course) the magazine's August 1994 issue.*

to, nature/environment. Middle readers: animal, arts/crafts, biography, careers, hobbies, humorous, interview/profile, nature/environment, problem-solving, science, sports. Young adults: animal, arts/crafts, biography, careers, hobbies, humorous, interview/profile, nature/environment, problem-solving, science, sports. Buys 15-20 mss/year, (all ages; juvenile—4 in current issue). Maximum word length: 750. Byline given.

How to Contact/Writers: Fiction/nonfiction: Send complete ms. SASE (IRC) for answer to query/return of ms. Reports on queries/mss in 2 months or less. Will consider photocopied and computer printout submissions.

Illustration: "I don't have space for large illustrations so I use cuts, suitable drawings from miscellaneous small ones sent by certain readers." Uses b&w artwork only, no intermediate values. Will review ms/illustration packages. Will review small picture(s) appropriate to a submitted ms.

How to Contact/Illustrators: Ms/illustration packages: Send complete ms and final b&w drawing, small size (or I'll reduce it). Reports on art samples in 2 months or less. Original artwork returned at job's completion if requested and SASE supplied.

Terms: Acquires first or one-time rights. Pays in contributor copies. Sample copy for $2.50. Writer's guidelines free or sent with sample if requested. $5 paid for illustrations used to illustrate stories (serendipitously found!); $10 prize per issue for best children's story (or poem) as selected by readers.

Tips: Will consider short poetry (up to 16 lines) by and for juveniles. "Write what children will enjoy—test out on your own children if possible." Looks for: "shorter fiction, especially humor or whimsy. First time contributors may submit only in January and February; established contributors may submit September through February only." Publication most open to cartoons. Current minimum of two years before new contributors' work can appear.

HOBSON'S CHOICE, P.O. Box 98, Ripley OH 45167. (513)392-4549. Editor: Susannah C. West. Bimonthly magazine. Estab. 1974. Circ. 2,000. "*Hobson's Choice* is a science fiction magazine which also publishes science and technology-related nonfiction along with stories. Although the magazine is not specifically aimed at children, we do number teenagers among our readers. Such readers are the type who might enjoy reading science fiction (both young adult and adult), attending science fiction conventions, using computers, and be interested in such things as astronomy, the space program, etc."

Fiction: Young adults: fantasy, science fiction. "I'm really not interested in seeing fiction other than science fiction and fantasy. Nor am I interested in horror and cyberpunk, although these can be considered subgenres of fantasy and science fiction. I also see too much hackneyed science fiction and fantasy." Buys 12-15 mss/year. Average word length 2,000-10,000.

Nonfiction: Young adults: how-to (science), interview/profile, science. Does not want to see crafts. Buys 8-10 mss/year. Average word length: 1,500-5,000. Byline given.

How to Contact/Writers: Fiction: Send complete ms. Nonfiction: Query first. Reports on queries/mss in 4 months maximum. ("After 4 months, author should feel free to withdraw ms from consideration.") Will consider submissions via disk (Macintosh MacWrite, WriteNow, IBM PC or compatible on 3½ disks).

Illustration: Buys 2-5 illustrations/issue; 20-30 illustrations/year. Uses b&w artwork only. Prefers to review "science fiction, fantasy or technical illustration." Reviews ms/illustration packages; reviews artwork for future assignments.

How to Contact/Illustrators: Ms/illustration packages: "Would like to see clips to keep on file (b&w only, preferably photocopies)." Illustrations only: Query with tearsheets to be kept on file. "If we have an assignment for an artist, we will contact him/her with the ms we want illustrated. We like to see roughs before giving the go-ahead for final artwork." Reports in 4 months "if requested and if request accompanied by SASE." Original artwork returned at job's completion, "sometimes, if requested. We prefer to retain originals, but a high-quality PMT or Velox is fine if artist wants to keep artwork." Credit line given.

Photography: Purchases photos with accompanying ms only. Uses b&w prints. Wants photos for nonfiction.

Terms: Pays 25% on acceptance, 75% on publication. Buys first North American serial rights for mss, artwork and photographs. Pays $20-100 for stories/articles. Pay illustrators $25-50 for b&w cover; $5-25 for b&w inside. Pays photographers per photo (range: $5-25).

Sample copies for $2.75. Writer's/illustrator's guidelines free with business-size SAE and 1 first-class stamp. "Specify fiction or nonfiction guidelines, or both." Tip sheet package for $1.25 and business-size envelope with 1 first-class stamp (includes all guidelines and tips on writing science fiction and nonfiction).

Tips: Writers: "Read lots of children's writing in general, especially specific genre if you're writing a genre story (science fiction, romance, mystery, etc.). We list upcoming needs in our guidelines; writers can study these to get an idea of what we're looking for. We're always looking for nonfiction." Illustrators: "Study illustrations in back issues of magazines you're interested in illustrating for, and be able to work in a genre style if that's the type of magazine you want to publish your work. Everything is open to freelancers, as almost all our artwork is done out-of-house. (We occasionally use public domain illustrations, copyright-free illustrations and photographs.)"

*HODGEPODGE, Thimblesqueak Press, Suite 217, 301 Thelma Dr., Casper WY 82609. (307)265-8041. Fiction Editors: Misty Geer, D. Lees. Bimonthly magazine. Estab. 1994. "Our main goal is to get kids reading! That's why our magazine is just what the title implies: it's a mish-mash. A collection of this and that. With hopefully, a little something for everyone. If we can get our audience (aged 4-8) reading, and loving it, they'll continue."

Fiction: Young readers: adventure, animal, contemporary, fantasy, folktales, health, history, humorous, multicultural, nature/environment, problem-solving, religious, science fiction, sports, suspense/mystery. "We want to make kids aware of and curious about other cultures. We do not want heavy moralizing, cliché or overdone 'lessons.' If you can tell a fun story and get a point across discreetly, fantastic! Otherwise, just have fun." Buys 55 mss/year. Average word length: 3,000. Byline given.

Poetry: Reviews poetry. Anything fun, interesting, enjoyable to read. Maximum length: 24 lines. Limit submissions to 10 poems.

How to Contact/Writers: Fiction: Send complete ms. Reports on queries in 2 weeks; 2-4 weeks on mss. Publishes ms 3 months after acceptance. Will consider simultaneous submissions, electronic submissions and previously published work.

Illustration: Buys 15 illustrations/issue; 90 illustrations/year. Uses b&w artwork only. "Pen and ink are best for us. 8½ × 11 or smaller. Any style or theme." Reviews ms/illustration packages; reviews artwork for future assignments.

How to Contact/Illustrators: Ms/illustration packages: Submit complete package with final art. Submit ms with rough sketches. Illustrations only: Send résumé, promo sheet, portfolio and tearsheets. Reports only if interested. Samples kept on file. Credit line given.

Terms: Pays on publication. Acquires one-time rights. "We are a new publication with a very limited budget. We'll pay in copies, until we get established." Sample copies for 6 × 9 SAE and 2 first-class stamps. Writer's guidelines free for SASE.

Tips: "Children are smart. Don't talk down to them. Half of the reason so few children love to read, is that there is so little out there that talks to them, not at them. Think like a child. Dig out your coloring books and crayons. Sit on the floor and color. Get into the swing of things. Then write a story you'd love to read. If it doesn't sound right to you, it won't sound right to a child! Illustrators: Again, think like a child. Remember their perspective is different from ours. Get down on your knees for a while and view the world from their level. Draw from what you see there. *Hodgepodge* welcomes freelance work in all areas. In fact almost 90% of our magazine comes from freelancers. Our favorite stories by far are the ones that made us laugh out loud as we read them; the ones that stick with us for days afterwards. Write freely, submit professionally. We use illustrations from freelancers heavily throughout the magazine. Some of the portfolios have contained pieces that were accepted immediately, because they fit perfectly in a poem or story we were working on! In others we find the style of the the author and illustrator blend perfectly. Every author has the illustrator who will complement him perfectly. Just let your style be your own, and a mate will be found for you."

 The asterisk before a listing indicates the listing is new in this edition.

THE HOME ALTAR, Meditations for Families with Children, Augsburg Fortress, 426 S. Fifth St., Box 1209, Minneapolis MN 55440. Articles/Fiction Editor: Carol A. Burk. Quarterly magazine. Circ. approximately 70,000. This is a booklet of daily devotions, used primarily by Lutheran families. Each day's reading focuses on a specific Bible passage. 98% of material aimed at juvenile audience.

Fiction: Young readers, middle readers: contemporary, folktales, problem-solving, religious. Buys 365 mss/year. Average word length: 125-170. Byline given.

Nonfiction: Young readers, middle readers: interview/profile, problem-solving, religious. Average word length: 125-170. Byline given.

How to Contact/Writers: Fiction/nonfiction: Query with published clips.

Illustration: Buys 100 illustrations/year. Works on assignment only.

How to Contact/Illustrators: Reports on art samples only if interested.

Terms: Pays on acceptance. Buys all rights. Pays $10 for assigned articles. Free writer's guidelines for 6×9 SAE and 98¢ postage.

HOPSCOTCH, The Magazine for Girls, The Bluffton News Publishing and Printing Company, 103 N. Main St., Bluffton OH 45817. (419)358-4610. Editor: Marilyn Edwards. Bimonthly magazine. Estab. 1989. Circ. 9,000. For girls from 6 to 12 years, featuring traditional subjects—pets, games, hobbies, nature, science, sports, etc.—with an emphasis on articles that show girls actively involved in unusual and/or worthwhile activities."

- In June 1995, Bluffton will begin publishing *Boys' Quest*, a magazine of "hands-on adventure for boys of elementary school age." The editors encourage unsolicited article, artwork and photo submissions. Send SASE to the above address for guidelines.

Fiction: Young readers and middle readers: adventure, animal, contemporary, fantasy, folktales, health, history, humorous, multicultural, nature/environment, problem-solving, sports, suspense/mystery. Does not want to see stories dealing with dating, sex, fashion, hard rock music. Buys 24 mss/year. Average word length: 300-700. Byline given.

Nonfiction: Young readers and middle readers: animal, arts/crafts, biography, careers, cooking, games/puzzles, health, history, hobbies, how-to, humorous, interview/profile, math, multicultural, nature/environment, problem-solving, science. Does not want to see pieces dealing with dating, sex, fashion, hard rock music. "Need more nonfiction with quality photos about a Hopscotch-age girl involved in a worthwhile activity." Buys 46 mss/year. Average word length: 400-700. Byline given.

Poetry: Reviews traditional, wholesome, humorous poems. Maximum word length: 400; maximum line length: 40. Will accept 6 submissions/author.

How to Contact/Writers: Fiction: Send complete ms. Nonfiction: Query, send complete ms. Reports on queries in 3 weeks; on mss in 2 months. Publishes ms 1-2 years after acceptance. Will consider simultaneous submissions.

Illustration: Buys 8-12 illustrations/issue; buys 50-60 illustrations/year. "Generally, the illustrations are assigned after we have purchased a piece (usually fiction). Occasionally, we will use a painting—in any given medium—for the cover, and these are usually seasonal." Uses b&w artwork only for inside; color for cover. Will review ms/illustration packages. Will review artwork for future assignments.

How to Contact/Illustrators: Query first or send complete ms with final art. Illustrations only: Send résumé, portfolio, client list and tearsheets. Reports on art samples with SASE in 2 weeks. Original artwork returned at job's completion. Credit line given.

Photography: Purchases photos separately (cover only) and with accompanying ms only. Looking for photos to accompany article. Model/property releases required. Uses 5×7, b&w prints; 35mm transparencies. Black and white photos should go with ms. Should have girl or girls ages 6-12.

Terms: For manuscripts, pays a few months ahead of publication. For mss, artwork and photos, buys first North American serial rights; second serial (reprint rights). Pays $30-100 for stories/articles. "We always send a copy of the issue to the writer or illustrator." Text and art are treated separately. Pays $100-150 for color cover; $5-15 for b&w inside. Photographers paid per photo (range: $5-15; $150 for color cover photo). Sample copy for $3. Writer's/illustrator's guidelines free for #10 SASE.

Tips: "Please look at our guidelines and our magazine . . . and remember, we use far more nonfiction than fiction. If decent photos accompany the piece, it stands an even better chance of being accepted. We believe it is the responsibility of the contributor to come up with photos. Please remember, our readers are 6-12 years—most are 7-10—and your text should reflect that. Many magazines try to entertain first and educate second. We try to do the reverse of that. Our magazine is more simplistic like a book, to be read from cover to cover."

HUMPTY DUMPTY'S MAGAZINE, Children's Better Health Institute, 1100 Waterway Blvd., P.O. Box 567, Indianapolis IN 46206. (317)636-8881. Editor: Janet Flynn Hoover. Art Director: Lawrence Simmons. Magazine published 8 times/year—Jan/Feb; Mar; April/May; June; July/Aug; Sept; Oct/Nov; Dec. *HDM* is edited for children approximately ages 4-6. It includes fiction (easy-to-reads; read alouds; rhyming stories; rebus stories), nonfiction articles (some with photo illustrations), poems, crafts, recipes and puzzles. Much of the content encourages development of better health habits. "We especially need material promoting fitness."
Fiction: Picture-oriented material: animal, contemporary, fantasy, humorous, sports, health-related. Young readers: adventure, animal, contemporary, fantasy, humorous, science fiction, sports, suspense/mystery, health-related. Does not want to see "bunny-rabbits-with-carrot-pies stories! Also, talking inanimate objects are very difficult to do well. Beginners (and maybe everyone) should avoid these." Buys 35-50 mss/year. Maximum word length: 500. Byline given.
Nonfiction: Picture-oriented material, young readers: animal, how-to, humorous, interview/profile, health-related. Does not want to see long, boring, encyclopedia rehashes. "We're open to almost any subject (although most of our nonfiction has a health angle), but it must be presented creatively. Don't just string together some facts." Looks for a fresh approach. Buys 6-10 mss/year. Prefers very short nonfiction pieces—350 words maximum. Byline given.
How to Contact/Writers: Send complete ms. Nonfiction: Send complete ms with bibliography if applicable. "No queries, please!" Reports on mss in 8-10 weeks.
Illustration: Buys 13-16 illustrations/issue; 90-120 illustrations/year. Preferred theme or style: Realistic or cartoon. Reviews ms/illustration packages; reviews artwork for future assignments; works on assignment only.
How to Contact/Illustrators: Fiction: Ms/illustration packages: Send slides, printed pieces or photocopies. Illustrations only: Send slides, printed pieces or photocopies. Reports on art samples only if interested.
Terms: Writers: Pays on publication. Artists: Pays within 1-2 months. Buys all rights. "One-time book rights may be returned if author can provide name of interested book publisher and tentative date of publication." Pays up to 22¢/word for stories/articles; payment varies for poems and activities. 10 complimentary issues are provided to author with check. Pays $250 for color cover illustration; $35-90 per page b&w inside; $60-120 for 2-color inside; $70-155 for color inside. Sample copies for $1.25. Writer's/illustrator's guidelines free with SASE.
Tips: Writers: "Study current issues and guidelines. Observe, especially, word lengths and adhere to requirements. It's sometimes easier to break in with recipe or craft ideas, but submit what you do best. Don't send your first, second, or even third drafts. Polish your piece until it's as perfect as you can make it." Illustrators: "Please study the magazine before contacting us. Your art must have appeal to three- to seven-year-olds." (See listings for *Child Life, Children's Digest, Children's Playmate, Jack and Jill, Turtle Magazine* and *U.S. Kids.*)

INTERNATIONAL GYMNAST, Paul Zierst and Associates, 225 Brooks, Box 2450, Oceanside CA 92054. (619)722-0030. Editor: Dwight Normile. Published 10 times/year. "We are a magazine about gymnasts for ages 9 and up."
Fiction: Young adults: problem-solving and sports stories for gymnasts.
Nonfiction: Young adults: biography, health, interview/profile, sports. Gymnastics material only.

How to Contact/Writers: Query with published clips. Will consider simultaneous submissions (please advise).

Illustration: Will review ms/illustration packages. Uses b&w artwork only, but "very rarely." Usually prefers cartoons — 8½ × 11 camera ready.

How to Contact/Illustrators: Ms/illustration packages: Query. Illustrations only: Send slides or prints.

Photography: Looking for clear action/personality photos. Photo captions required. Uses 5 × 7 or 8 × 10, b&w, glossy prints; 35mm transparencies. To contact, send unsolicited photos by mail.

Terms: Pays on publication by arrangement. Buys one-time rights for mss, artwork and photos. Pays $15-25 for articles. Pays illustrators per b&w inside illustration (range: $10-15). Photographers paid per photo (range: $5-50).

Tips: "For us, gymnastics knowledge is necessary. Standard kidstuff with tenuous gym orientation doesn't cut it."

JACK AND JILL, Children's Better Health Institute, 1100 Waterway Blvd., Indianapolis IN 46206. (317)636-8881. Articles, Fiction Editor: Danny Lee. Art Director: Karen Neligh. Magazine published 8 times/year. Estab. 1938. Circ. 360,000. "Write entertaining and imaginative stories *for* kids, not just *about* them. Writers should understand what is funny to kids, what's important to them, what excites them. Don't write from an adult 'kids are so cute' perspective. We're also looking for health and healthy lifestyle stories and articles, but don't be preachy."

Fiction: Young readers: animal, contemporary, fantasy, history, humorous, problem-solving. Middle readers: contemporary, humorous. Buys 30-35 mss/year. Average word length: 900. Byline given.

Nonfiction: Young readers: animal, history, how-to, humorous, interview/profile, problem-solving, travel. Buys 8-10 mss/year. Average word length: 1,000. Byline given.

Poetry: Reviews poetry.

How to Contact/Writers: Fiction/nonfiction: Send complete ms. Reports on queries in 2 weeks; mss in 8-10 weeks. Will consider simultaneous submissions.

Terms: Pays on publication; minimum 10¢/word. Buys all rights.

Tips: See listings for *Child Life, Children's Digest, Children's Playmate, Humpty Dumpty's Magazine, Turtle Magazine* and *U.S. Kids.*

*JUNIOR SCHOLASTIC, Scholastic Inc., 555 Broadway, New York NY 10012. (212)343-6295. Articles Editor: Lee Baier. Art Director: Glenn Davis. Photo Editor: Deborah Thompson. Magazine published biweekly during school year. Estab. 1937. Circ. 585,000. Social studies and current events classroom magazine for students in grades 6-8.

Nonfiction: Middle readers, young adults: geography, history, interview/profile, multicultural, nature/environment, social issues, foreign countries. "We mainly buy stories on countries in the news, that include interviews and profiles of kids 11-14." Buys 20 mss/year. Average word length: 500-1,000. Byline given.

How to Contact/Writers: Nonfiction: Query with published clips. Reports on queries in 2 months; mss in 6 months. Publishes ms 2 months after acceptance.

Illustration: Buys 1 illustration/issue; 20 illustrations/year. Reviews ms/illustration packages; reviews artwork for future assignments; works on assignment only.

How to Contact/Illustrators: Illustrations only: send portfolio. Reports back only if interested. Samples returned with SASE; samples filed. Credit line given.

Photography: Buys photos from freelancers. Wants "photos of young teens in foreign countries; teens relating to national issues." Uses b&w/color prints and 35mm transparencies. Query with samples. Reports back only if interested.

Terms: Pays on publication. Buys all rights. Pays $300-600 for articles. Additional payment for photos accompanying articles. Pays illustrators $800 for color cover; $1,000 for color inside. Sample copies for 9 × 11 SAE. Writers/photo guidelines for SASE.

JUNIOR TRAILS, Gospel Publishing House, 1445 Boonville Ave., Springfield MO 65802. (417)862-2781. Articles/Fiction Editor: Sinda S. Zinn. Art Director: Leonard Bailey. Quarterly magazine. Circ. 70,000. *Junior Trails* is an 8-page take-home paper for fifth and sixth graders. "Its articles consist of fiction stories of a contemporary or historical nature. The stories have a moral slant to show how modern-day people can work out problems in acceptable ways, or give examples in history from which we can learn."

Fiction: Middle readers: adventure, animal, contemporary, history, humorous, multicultural, nature/environment, problem-solving, religious, suspense/mystery. Does not want to see science fiction, mythology, ghosts and witchcraft. Wants to see more stories about "kids struggling with a problem in Christian living and solving it through biblical principles." Also looking for stories of ethnic background. Buys 100 mss/year. Average word length: 800-1,500. Byline given.

Nonfiction: Middle readers: animal, history, humorous, nature/environment, problem-solving, religious. Buys 30 mss/year. Average word length: 300-800. Byline given.

Poetry: Wants to see poetry with a religious emphasis.

How to Contact/Writers: Fiction/nonfiction: Send complete ms. Reports on mss in 2-4 weeks. Will consider simultaneous submissions.

Illustration: Uses color artwork only. Reviews artwork for future assignments.

How to Contact/Illustrators: Illustrations only: provide résumé, promo sheet or tearsheets to be kept on file; or arrange personal interview to show portfolio. Reports only if interested. Credit line sometimes given.

Photography: Uses 2¼ × 2¼ transparencies. To contact, photographers should query with samples; provide résumé, promo sheet or tearsheets to be kept on file. Wants photos of "children involved with activity or with other people."

Terms: Pays on acceptance. For mss, buys one-time rights. Buys all rights to artwork; one-time rights to photographs. Pays 2-3¢/word for articles/stories. Pays illustrators $150-200/ for color cover. Photographers paid per photo (range: $30-100). Sample copy free with 9 × 12 SASE.

Tips: "Make the characters and situations real. The story should unfold through their interaction and dialogue, not narration. Don't fill up space with unnecessary details. We are always in need of good fiction stories." Looks for: "fiction that presents believable characters working out their problems according to Bible principles. Present Christianity in action without being preachy; articles with reader appeal, emphasizing some phase of Christian living, presented in a down-to-earth manner; biography or missionary material using fiction technique; historical, scientific or nature material with a spiritual lesson; fillers that are brief, purposeful, usually containing an anecdote, and always with a strong evangelical emphasis."

KEYNOTER, Key Club International, 3636 Woodview Trace, Indianapolis IN 46268. (317)875-8755. Articles Editor: Julie A. Carson. Art Director: James Patterson. Monthly magazine. Estab. 1915. Circ. 133,000. "As the official magazine of the world's largest high school service organization, we publish nonfiction articles that interest teenagers and will help our readers become better students, better citizens, better leaders."

Nonfiction: Young adults: how-to, humorous, problem-solving. Does not want to see first-person accounts; short stories. Buys 15 mss/year. Average word length: 1,500-1,800. Byline given.

How to Contact/Writers: Nonfiction: Query. Reports on queries/mss in 1 month. Will consider simultaneous submissions.

Illustration: Buys 2-3 illustrations/issue; 15 illustrations/year. Reviews ms/illustration packages; works on assignment only.

How to Contact/Illustrators: Ms/illustration packages: "Because of our publishing schedule, we prefer to work with illustrators/photographers within Indianapolis market." Reports on art samples only if interested. Original artwork returned at job's completion if requested.

Terms: Pays on acceptance. Buys first North American serial rights. Pays $150-350 for assigned/unsolicited articles. Sample copy free with 8½ × 11 SAE and 65¢ postage. Writer's guidelines free with SAE and 1 first-class stamp.

Refer to the Business of Children's Writing & Illustrating for up-to-date marketing, tax and legal information.

Tips: "We are looking for light or humorous nonfiction, self-help articles." Also looking for articles about education reform, national concerns and trends, teen trends in music, fashion, clothes, ideologies, etc.

*KID CITY, Children's Television Workshop, 1 Lincoln Plaza, New York NY 10023. (212)595-3456. Articles Editor: Maureen Hunter-Bone. Fiction Editor: Lisa Rao. Art Director: Michele Weisman. Photo Editor: Jacqui Wong. Monthly magazine. Estab. 1971. Circ. 330,000.
Fiction: Young readers, middle readers: adventure, animal, contemporary, fantasy, folktales, history, humorous, multicultural, nature/environment, science fiction, sports. Does not want to see "cutesie, overly moralistic, preachy material." Buys 3-4 mss/year. Average word length: 200-500. Byline given.
Nonfiction: Young readers, middle readers: animal, careers, geography, history, how-to, humorous, interview/profile, multicultural, nature/environment, problem-solving, science, social issues, sports, travel. Does not want to see puzzle and game submissions. Buys 12 mss/year. Average word length: 200-500. Byline given.
How to Contact/Writers: Fiction: Send complete ms. Nonfiction: Query or send complete ms. Reports on queries/mss in 1 month. Will consider simultaneous submissions (if notified).
Illustration: Buys more than 5 illustrations/issue; 50-60 illustrations/year. Reviews ms/ illustration packages; reviews artwork for future assignments; works on assignment only.
How to Contact/Illustrators: Artists send samples (promo sheet, tearsheets). Reports back only if interested. Originals returned to artist at job's completion. Credit line given.
Terms: Pays on publication. Buys one-time rights for mss, artwork, photographs. Pays $250-400 for stories, $250-350 for assigned/unsolicited articles. Pays $300-400 per page for inside color illustrations. Sample copy with 8 × 11 SASE and $1.50. Writer's guidelines free with SASE.
Tips: Writers: "Use concrete, colorful, direct language. We use short-short stories – 2 pages, 100 lines at 45 characters per line. Don't talk down to children. Be funny. Be brief." Illustrators: "Avoid the cute. Use hot colors. Don't make kids you illustrate look like kewpie dolls. Don't be afraid of detail. Use a sense of humor. Send lots of sample cards to art directors. Write or call to bring in portfolios." (See listing for *3-2-1 Contact.*)

*KIDS COPY, The monthly newspaper, Kids Copy Inc., P.O. Box 42, Wyncote PA 19095. (800)352-5444. Editor: Kim Landry. Monthly (September-June) tabloid newspaper. Estab. 1992. Circ. 200,000. Includes the types of news and features found in any newspaper, written by professional journalists for kids 8-13.
Nonfiction: Young readers, middle readers: nature/environment, science, social issues, sports. "We want timely articles tied to current events." Buys 100 mss/year. Average word length: 300-500. Byline given.
How to Contact/Writers: Nonfiction: Query. Reports in 3 weeks. Publishes ms 2 months after acceptance. Will consider electronic submissions via disk or modem.
Terms: Pays on publication. "We buy the copyright and the rights to syndicate the article to the full extent that *Kids Copy* itself is syndicated." Pays $100 for articles. Additional payment $15/photo used. Sample copies free for 9 × 12 SAE and 52¢ postage. Writers guidelines for 9 × 12 SAE and 52¢ stamp.
Tips: "I want *Kids Copy* to be fun, fresh, topical and targeted to the age group 8-13. I want each issue to contain a balance of brain candy and intellectual nutrition. Getting kids to like the brain candy is no challenge. The challenge is to make the nutrition appealing. Without being preachy, *Kids Copy* reflects some values, among them: appreciation of cultural diversity, respect for self and others, the benefits of a healthy lifestyle, the importance of an educated and informed citizenry, concern for the environment and global awareness. We believe the media can play an important part in empowering kids to exercise their rights and accept their responsibilities."

LADYBUG, THE MAGAZINE FOR YOUNG CHILDREN, Carus Corporation, P.O. Box 300, Peru IL 61354. (815)224-6643. Editor-in-Chief: Marianne Carus. Editor: Paula Morrow. Art Director: Ron McCutchan. Associate Art Director: Suzanne Beck. Monthly magazine.

Estab. 1990. Circ. 130,000. Literary magazine for children 2-6, with stories, poems, activities, songs and picture stories.

• In addition to *Ladybug*, the Carus Corporation publishes *Cricket* and *Spider* (see listings in this section). The editors have also launched a new publication, *Babybug*, a board book magazine for children under two years old, first appearing in November 1994. Artwork is needed for the magazine ("good multicultural babies"). Contact the above address for submission information.

Fiction: Picture-oriented material: adventure, animal, fantasy, folktales, humorous, multicultural, nature/environment, problem-solving, science fiction, sports, suspense/mystery. "Open to any easy fiction stories." Buys 50 mss/year. Average word length 300-750 words. Byline given.

Nonfiction: Picture-oriented material: activities, animal, arts/crafts, concept, cooking, humorous, math, nature/environment, problem-solving, science. Buys 35 mss/year.

Poetry: Reviews poems, 20-line maximum length; limit submissions to 5 poems. Uses lyrical, humorous, simple language.

How to Contact/Writers: Fiction/nonfiction: Send complete ms. Queries not accepted. Reports on mss in 2 months. Publishes ms up to 2 years after acceptance. Does not like, but will consider simultaneous submissions.

Illustration: Buys 12 illustrations/issue; 145 illustrations/year. Original artwork returned at job's completion. Prefers "bright colors; all media, but use watercolor and acrylics most often; same size as magazine is preferred but not required."

How to Contact/Illustrators: To be considered for future assignments: Submit promo sheet, slides, tearsheets, color and b&w photocopies. Reports on art samples in 2 months.

Terms: Pays on publication for mss; after delivery of completed assignment for illustrators. For mss, buys first publication rights; second serial (reprint rights). Buys first publication rights plus promotional rights for artwork. Pays up to 25¢/word for prose; $3/line for poetry; $25 minimum for articles. Pays $750 for color (cover) illustration, $50-100 for b&w (inside) illustration, $250/page for color (inside). Sample copy for $4. Writer's/illustrator's guidelines free for SASE.

Tips: Writers: "Get to know several young children on an individual basis. Respect your audience. Wants "less cute, condescending or 'preach-teachy' material. Less gratuitous anthropomorphism. More rich, evocative language, sense of joy or wonders." Set your manuscript aside for at least a month, then reread critically." Illustrators: "Include examples, where possible, of children, animals, and — most important — action and narrative (i.e., several scenes from a story, showing continuity and an ability to maintain interest)." Keep in mind that "people come in all colors, sizes, physical conditions. Be inclusive in creating characters."

*LIGHTHOUSE, Lighthouse Publications, Box 1377, Auburn WA 98071-1377. Editor/Publisher: Tim Clinton. Quarterly magazine. Estab. 1986. Circ. 300. Magazine contains timeless stories and poetry for family reading. 25% of material aimed at juvenile audience.

Fiction: Young readers, middle readers, young adults: adventure, history, humorous, nature/environment, problem-solving, sports, suspense/mystery. Young adults: romance. Does not want to see anything not "G-rated," any story with a message that is not subtly handled or stories without plots. Buys 36 mss/year. Average word length: 2,000. Byline given.

Poetry: Reviews poetry. Maximum line length: 50. Limit submissions to 5 poems.

How to Contact/Writers: Fiction: Send complete ms and SASE with sufficient postage for return of ms. Reports on mss in 3 months.

Terms: Pays on publication. Buys first North American serial rights; first rights. Pays $5-50. Sample copy for $3 (includes guidelines). Writer's guidelines free with regular SAE and 1 first-class stamp.

Tips: "All sections are open to freelance writers — just follow the guidelines and stay in the categories listed above. Try to think of a *new* plot (see so many stories on bullies, storms and haunted houses)."

LISTEN, Celebrating Positive Choices, 55 West Oak Ridge Dr., Hagerstown MD 21740. (301)791-7000, ext. 2535. Monthly magazine. Circ. 50,000. *Listen* offers positive alternatives to drug use for its teenage readers.

Fiction: Young adults: contemporary, health, humorous, nature/environment, problem solving activities, sports. Buys 12 mss/year. Average word length: 1,200-1,500. Byline given.

Nonfiction: Young adults: arts/crafts, hobbies, health, nature/environment, problem solving activities, sports. Wants to see more factual articles on drug abuse. Buys 50 mss/year. Average word length: 1,200-1,500. Byline given.

How to Contact/Writers: Fiction/nonfiction: Send complete ms. Reports on queries/mss in 2 months.

Illustration: Reviews ms/illustration packages; reviews work for future assignments.

How to Contact/Illustrators: Query, send promo sheet and slides. Reports in 1 month. Credit line given.

Photography: Purchases photos from freelancers. Looks for "youth oriented – action (sports, outdoors), personality photos."

Terms: Pays on acceptance. Buys exclusive magazine rights for ms. Buys one-time rights for artwork and photographs. Pays $50-250 for stories/articles. Pays illustrators $150-300 for b&w cover; $250-600 for color cover; $75-150 for b&w inside; $100-300 for color inside. Pays photographers by the project (range: $200-500) or per photo (range: $50-500). Sample copy for $1 and SASE. Writer's guidelines free with SASE.

Tips: "*Listen* is a magazine for teenagers. It encourages development of good habits and high ideals of physical, social and mental health. It bases its editorial philosophy of primary drug prevention on total abstinence from alcohol and other drugs. Because it is used extensively in public high school classes, it does not accept articles and stories with overt religious emphasis. Four specific purposes guide the editors in selecting materials for *Listen*: (1) To portray a positive lifestyle and to foster skills and values that will help teenagers deal with contemporary problems, including smoking, drinking and using drugs. This is *Listen*'s primary purpose. (2) To offer positive alternatives to a lifestyle of drug use of any kind. (3) To present scientifically accurate information about the nature and effects of tobacco, alcohol and other drugs. (4) To report medical research, community programs and educational efforts which are solving problems connected with smoking, alcohol and other drugs. Articles should offer their readers activities that increase one's sense of self-worth through achievement and/or involvement in helping others. They are often categorized by three kinds of focus: (1) Hobbies. (2) Recreation. (3) Community Service.

THE MAGAZINE FOR CHRISTIAN YOUTH!, United Methodist Publishing House, Box 801, 201 Eighth Ave. S., Nashville TN 37202. (615)749-6319. Articles Editor: Tony Peterson. Art Procurement Director: David Dawson. Art Director/Photo Editor: Phillip Francis. Monthly magazine. Estab. 1985. Circ. 35,000. "*Youth!* is a leisure reading magazine whose purpose is to help teenagers develop Christian identity and live the Christian faith in their contemporary culture."

• *Christian Youth!* only solicits fiction material from teens.

Fiction: Young adults: adventure, animal, contemporary, fantasy, folktales, health, humorous, multicultural, nature/environment, problem-solving, religious, science fiction, sports, suspense/mystery. "We appreciate fiction that allows non-white teens to be main characters. We do not want occultic fiction. We appreciate realistic fiction that also takes Christian faith seriously." Buys 5-10 mss/year. Average word length: 500-2,000. Byline given.

Nonfiction: Young adults: animal, arts/crafts, biography, careers, concept, health, history, hobbies, how-to, humorous, interview/profile, multicultural, nature/environment, problem-solving, religion, science, social issues, sports, travel. Does not want to see "heavily moralistic" nonfiction. Buys 10-30 mss/year. Average word length: 500-2,000. Byline given.

How to Contact/Writers: Fiction/nonfiction: Query; send complete ms. Reports on queries in 2 months; mss in 4 months. Will consider simultaneous and electronic submissions via disk or modem and previously published work.

Illustration: Reviews ms/illustration packages; reviews artwork for future assignments.

How to Contact/Illustrators: Ms/illustration packages: Query; submit ms with rough sketches. Illustrations only: Query; send promo sheet, portfolio, slides and tearsheets. Contact: David Dawson. Reports in 2 months. Samples returned with SASE. Samples filed. Original work returned upon job's completion. Credit line given.

Photography: Purchases photography from freelancers. Wants "color transparencies of youth with good ethnic mix and range of ages. Photos used for mood." Model/property release required and must be submitted with images. Uses b&w glossy prints; 35mm, 2¼ × 2¼ transparencies. Query with samples; send unsolicited photos by mail; submit portfolio for review; provide business card, promotional literature and tearsheets. Contact: David Dawson. Reports in 2 months.

Terms: Pays on acceptance. Buys first North American serial rights, first rights, one-time rights, reprint rights or all rights for mss. Buys all rights for artwork; user rights or all rights for photographs. Pays 5¢/word (maximum $150) for stories/articles. Additional payment for ms/illustation packages. Pays illustrators $50-150/b&w cover; $25-50 b&w inside; $150-300/color cover; $25-150 color inside. Photographers paid per photo (range: $25-300). Writer's/illustrator's/photo guidelines for SASE. Wants "color transparencies of youth with good ethnic mix and range of ages. Photos used for mood."

Tips: "Refrain from talking down to teens, use 'your' instead of 'they' language." Aspiring illustrators/photographers: "Make the work as racially inclusive as possible, but avoid stereotyping situations. Transparencies are more versatile than photos."

MAGIC REALISM, Pyx Press, P.O. Box 620, Orem UT 84059-0620. Editor: C. Darren Butler. Managing Editor: Julie Thomas. Associate Editor: Patricia Hatch. Associate Editor: Lisa S. Laurencot. Magazine published 3 times/year. Estab. 1990. Circ. 1,000. "We publish magic, realism, exaggerated realism, literary fantasy; glib fantasy of the sort found in folktales, fables, myth." 10-20% of publication aimed at juvenile market.

Fiction: Middle readers and young adults: fantasy, folktales. Sees too much of wizards, witches, card readings, sword-and-sorcery, silly or precious tales of any sort, sleight-of-hand magicians. Especially needs short-shorts. Buys approximately 40 mss/year. Byline given.

Poetry: Reviews poetry. Length: prefers 3-30 lines. Limit submissions to 3-8 poems.

How to Contact/Writers: Fiction: send complete ms. Reports on queries in 1 month; mss in 3-6 months. Publishes ms 4 months-2 years after acceptance. "Simultaneous and previously published submissions are welcome if clearly labeled as such."

Illustration: Uses b&w artwork only. Reviews ms/illustration packages; reviews work for future assignments.

How to Contact/Illustrators: Ms/illustration packages: Query; submit complete package with final art or submit ms with rough sketches. Illustrations only: Query or send résumé and portfolio. Reports in 3 months. Samples returned with SASE. Original work returned at job's completion. Credit line given.

Photography: "We consider photos, but have received very few submissions." Model/property releases preferred. Photographers should query with samples and résumé of credits; submit portfolio for review.

Terms: Pays on publication. Buys first North American serial rights or one-time rights and reprint rights for ms, artwork and photographs; also buys worldwide Spanish language rights for Spanish edition published 1-2 years after English edition. Pays $2-30 for stories; $3/magazine page and 1 copy for poetry. Pays illustrators $10 for b&w cover; $1-3 for b&w inside. Photographers paid per photo (range: $1-10). Sample copies for $4.95 (back issue); $5.95 (current issue). Writer's guidelines for SASE.

Tips: "Only a fraction of the material we publish is for children. We rarely use anthropomorphic tales. Most material for children is related to folklore. Pyx Press will be relocating in 1995 or 1996; watch for a change of address. Significant changes in editorial policy are planned for 1995; new guidelines will be available by June '95."

MY FRIEND, A Magazine for Children, Daughters of St. Paul/St. Paul Books and Media, 50 St. Paul's Ave., Jamaica Plain, Boston MA 02130. (617)522-8911. Articles/Fiction Editor: Sister Anne Joan, fsp. Art Director: Sister M. Joseph, fsp. Magazine published 10 times/year. Estab. 1979. Circ. 12,000. *"My Friend* is a magazine of inspiration and entertainment for a predominantly Catholic readership. We reach ages 6-12."

Fiction: Young readers and middle readers: adventure, Christmas, contemporary, history, humorous, religious, suspense/mystery. Does not want to see poetry, animals as main characters in religious story, stories whose basic thrust would be incompatible with Catholic values. Buys 50 mss/year. Average word length: 450-750. Byline given.

Nonfiction: Young readers: arts/crafts, games/puzzles, health, history, hobbies, humorous, problem-solving, religious. Middle readers: arts/crafts, games/puzzles, health, history, hobbies, how-to, humorous, interview/profile, media literacy, nature/environment, problem-solving, religion, science, sports. Does not want to see material that is not compatible with Catholic values; no "New Age" material. Buys 10 mss/year. Average word length: 450-750. Byline given.

How to Contact/Writers: Fiction/nonfiction: Send complete ms. Reports on queries in 1 month; mss in 1-2 months.

Illustration: Buys 8 illustrations/issue; buys 60-80 illustrations/year. Preferred theme or style: Realistic depictions of children, but open to variety! "We'd just like to hear from more illustrators who can do *humans*! (We see enough of funny cats, mice, etc.)" Looking for a "Bible stories" artist, too. Reviews artwork for future assignments.

How to Contact/Illustrators: Ms/illustration packages: Send complete ms with copy of final art. Illustrations only: Send résumé, promo sheet and tearsheets. Reports only if interested. Original artwork returned at job's completion. Credit line given.

Photography: Wants photos of "children at play or alone; school scenes."

Terms: Pays on acceptance for mss. Buys first rights for mss; variable for artwork. Pays $20-150 for stories/articles. Pays illustrators $50-100/b&w (inside); $50-175/color (inside). Sample copy $1 with 9×12 SAE and 4 first-class stamps. Writer's/illustrator's guidelines free with SAE and 1 first-class stamp.

Tips: Writers: "Right now, we're especially looking for articles and activities on media literacy and items that would appeal to boys. We are not interested in poetry unless it is humorous. Fiction needs are *amply* provided for already." Illustrators: "Please contact us! For the most part, we need illustrations for fiction stories." In the future, sees children's magazines "getting more savvy, less sappy. Suspect that electronic media styles will penetrate a greater number of magazines for kids and adults alike; literary or intellectual publications would be less affected."

NATIONAL GEOGRAPHIC WORLD, National Geographic Society, 1145 17th St. NW, Washington DC 20036-4688. (202)857-7000. Editor: Susan M. Tejada. Illustrations Director: Chuck Herron. Art Director: Ursula Vosseler. Monthly magazine. Circ. 1.2 million. "*National Geographic World* features factual stories on outdoor adventure, natural history, sports, science and history for children ages 8 and older. Full-color photographs are used to attract young readers and the text easily guides them through the story." Does not publish fiction.

• "*World* does not accept unsolicited manuscripts."

Nonfiction: Picture material: animal, history, how-to, travel. Middle readers, young adults: animal, history, humorous, multicultural, nature/environment, sports. Story ideas that lend themselves to photo stories will be considered. Average word length: 90-600.

How to Contact/Writers: Nonfiction: Query only—no mss please. Reports on queries in 4 months.

Illustration: Works on assignment only. Reviews artwork for future assignments. Illustrations only: Query; send client list and tearsheets.

How to Contact/Illustrators: Illustrations only: Query with samples; arrange personal interview to show portfolio. Reports in 4 months. Credit line given.

Photography: Buys photos separately. Looking for "imaginative, eye-catching action transparencies." Model/property releases and photo captions required. Uses 35mm transparencies. To contact, photographers should query with proposal and outline of photo possibilities.

Market conditions are constantly changing! If you're still using this book and it is 1996 or later, buy the newest edition of Children's Writer's & Illustrator's Market *at your favorite bookstore or order directly from Writer's Digest Books.*

Terms: Pays on publication. Buys all rights for mss and artwork. Buys one-time rights for photos. Pays 80¢/word for stories/articles. Pays $600 for color cover, $100-300 for color inside photos. Photographers are paid per published page. Free sample copy; contributor's guidelines available free.

Tips: "All *World* stories are written by staff. For *World*, the story proposal is the way to break in. Think through the focus of the story and outline what action photos are available. Keep in mind that *World* is a visual magazine. A story will work best if it has a very tight focus and if the photos show children interacting with their surroundings as well as with each other."

NATURE FRIEND MAGAZINE, Pilgrim Publishers, 22777 State Road 119, Goshen IN 46526. (219)534-2245. Articles Editor: Stanley Brubaker. Monthly magazine. Estab. 1983. Circ. 9,000. Monthly magazine.

Nonfiction: Picture-oriented material, young readers, middle readers, young adults: animal, nature. Does not want to see evolutionary material. Buys 50-80 mss/year. Average word length: 350-1,500. Byline given.

How to Contact/Writers: Nonfiction: Send complete ms. Reports on mss in 1-4 months. Will consider simultaneous submissions.

Illustration: Works on assignment only.

Terms: Pays on publication. Buys one-time rights. Pays $15-75. Payment for illustrations: $15-80/b&w inside. Two sample copies for $4 with 7×10 SAE and 85¢ postage. Writer's/illustrator's guidelines for $1.

Tips: Looks for "main articles, puzzles and simple nature and science projects. Please examine samples and writer's guide before submitting."

NEW ERA MAGAZINE, Official Publication for Youth of the Church of Jesus Christ of Latter-Day Saints, 50 E. North Temple St., Salt Lake City UT 84150. (801)240-2951. Articles/Fiction Editor: Richard M. Romney. Art Director: B. Lee Shaw. Monthly magazine. Estab. 1971. Circ. 200,000. General interest religious publication for youth ages 12-18 who are members of The Church of Jesus Christ of Latter-Day Saints (Mormons).

Fiction: Young adults: adventure, contemporary, fantasy, humorous, problem-solving, religious, romance, science fiction, sports. "All material must relate to Mormon point of view." Does not want to see "formula pieces, stories not sensitive to an LDS audience." Buys 20 mss/year. Average word length: 250-2,500. Byline given.

Nonfiction: Young adults: biography, careers, education, fashion, games/puzzles, humorous, interview/profile, problem-solving, religion, travel, sports; "general interest articles by, about and for young Mormons. Would like more about Mormon youth worldwide." Does not want to see "formula pieces, articles not adapted to our specific voice and our audience." Buys 150-200 mss/year. Average word length: 250-2,000. Byline given.

Poetry: Reviews poems, 30-line maximum. Limit submissions to 10 poems.

How to Contact/Writers: Fiction/nonfiction: Query. Reports on queries/mss in 2 months. Publishes ms 1 year or more after acceptance. Will consider electronic submissions via disk.

Illustration: Buys 5 illustrations/issue; 50-60 illustrations/year. "We buy only from our pool of illustrators. We use all styles and mediums." Works on assignment only.

How to Contact/Illustrators: Illustrations only: Submit portfolio for review; provide résumé, business card, promotional literature and tearsheets to be kept on file. Reports on art samples in 2 months. Original artwork returned at job's completion. Credit line given.

Terms: Pays on acceptance. For mss, buys first rights; right to publish again in other church usage (rights reassigned on written request). Buys all or one-time rights for artwork and photos. Pays $25-375 for stories; $25-350 for articles. Pays illustrators and photographers "by specific arrangements." Sample copies for $1. Writer's guidelines free for #10 SASE.

Tips: Open to "first-person and true-life experiences. Tell what happened in a conversational style. Teen magazines are becoming more brash and sassy. We shy away from the outlandish and trendy, but still need a contemporary look."

ODYSSEY, Science That's Out of This World, Cobblestone Publishing, Inc., 7 School S/ Peterborough NH 03458. (603)924-7209. Editor: Elizabeth E. Lindstrom. Editor-in-Cℎ

Carolyn P. Yoder. Art Director: Ellen Klempner-Beguin. Picture Editor: Francelle Cara-petyan. Magazine published 10 times/year. Estab. 1979. Circ. 35,000. Magazine covers astronomy and space exploration for children ages 8-14. All material must relate to the theme of a specific upcoming issue in order to be considered.

Fiction: Middle readers and young adults: adventure, folktales, history, biographical fiction. Does not want to see anything not theme-related. Average word length: 750 maximum.

Nonfiction: Middle readers and young adults: arts/crafts, biography, cooking, games/puzzles (no word finds), science. Don't send anything not theme-related. Average word length: 200-750, depending on section article is used in.

How to Contact/Writers: "A query must consist of all of the following to be considered (please use nonerasable paper): a brief cover letter stating the subject and word length of the proposed article; a detailed one-page outline explaining the information to be presented in the article; an extensive bibliography of materials the author intends to use in preparing the article; a SASE. Writers new to *Odyssey* should send a writing sample with query. If you would like to know if your query has been received, please also include a stamped postcard that requests acknowledgment of receipt. In all correspondence, please include your complete address as well as a telephone number where you can be reached. A writer may send as many queries for one issue as he or she wishes, but each query must have a separate cover letter, outline, bibliography, and SASE. Telephone queries are not accepted. Handwritten queries will not be considered. Queries may be submitted at any time, but queries sent well in advance of deadline *may not be answered for several months*. Go-aheads requesting material proposed in queries are usually sent five months prior to publication date. Unused queries will be returned approximately three to four months prior to publication date."

Illustration: Reviews artwork for future assignments.

How to Contact/Illustrators: Illustrations only: Send tearsheets, photocopies. Original artwork returned upon job's completion (upon written request).

Photography: Wants photos pertaining to any of our forthcoming themes. Uses b&w and color prints; 35mm transparencies. Photographers should send unsolicited photos by mail on speculation).

Terms: Buys all right for mss and artwork. Pays 20-25¢/word for stories/articles. Covers are assigned and paid on an individual basis. Pays photographers per photo ($15-100 for b&w; $25-100 for color). Sample copy for $3.95 and SASE with $1.05 postage. Writer's/illustrator's/photo guidelines for SASE. (See listings for *Calliope, The World History Magazine for Young People*; *Cobblestone, The History Magazine for Young People*; and *Faces, The Magazine About People*.)

*ON COURSE, A Magazine for Teens, General Council of the Assemblies of God, 1445 Boonville Ave., Springfield MO 65802. (417)862-2781. Editor: Melinda Booze. Assistant Editor: Valorie Hurd. Art Director: Richard Harman. Quarterly magazine. Estab. 1991. Circ. 162,000. *On Course* is a religious quarterly for teens "to encourage Christian, biblical discipleship; to promote denominational post-secondary schools; to nurture loyalty to the denomination."

Fiction: Young adults: humorous, religious, Christian discipleship. Average word length: 1,000. Byline given.

Nonfiction: Young adults: careers, humorous, interview/profile, religion, social issues, college life, Christian discipleship.

How to Contact/Writers: Fiction/nonfiction: Send complete ms. Reports on mss in 3 months. Publishes ms 6-24 months after acceptance. Will consider simultaneous submissions, electronic submissions via disk or modem and previously published work.

Photography: Buys photos from freelancers. "Teen life, church life, college life; unposed; often used for illustrative purposes." Model/property releases required. Uses color glossy prints and 35mm or 2¼ × 2¼ transparencies. Query with samples; send business card, promotional literature, tearsheets or catalog. Reports only if interested.

Terms: Pays on acceptance. Buys first or reprint rights for mss. Buys one-time rights for photographs. Pays 6¢/word for stories/articles. Pays photographers "as negotiated." Sample copies free. Writer's guidelines for SASE.

Tips: Also publishes writing by teens.

ON THE LINE, Mennonite Publishing House, 616 Walnut Ave., Scottdale PA 15683. (412)887-8500. Editor: Mary Clemens Meyer. Magazine published "monthly in weekly parts." Estab. 1970. Circ. 10,000.

Fiction: Young adults: contemporary, history, humorous, problem-solving, religious, sports and suspense/mystery. "No fantasy or fiction with animal characters." Buys 60 mss/year. Average word length: 900-1,200. Byline given.

Nonfiction: Middle readers, young adults: animal, arts/crafts, biography, cooking, games/ puzzles, health, history, hobbies, how-to, humorous, nature/environment, problem-solving. Does not want to see articles written from an adult perspective. Average word length: 200-600. Byline given.

Poetry: Wants to see light verse, humorous poetry. Maximum length: 24 lines.

How to Contact/Writers: Fiction/nonfiction: Send complete ms. Reports on queries/mss in 1 month. Will consider simultaneous submissions.

Illustration: Buys 1-2 illustrations/issue; buys 52 illustrations/year. "Illustrations are done on assignment only, to accompany our stories and articles—our need for new artists is very limited."

How to Contact/Illustrators: Illustrations only: "Prefer samples they do not want returned; these stay in our files." Reports on art samples only if interested. Original art work returned at job's completion.

Photography: Looking for photography showing ages 12-14, both sexes, good mix of races, wholesome fun. Uses 8×10 glossy b&w prints. Photographers should send unsolicited photos by mail.

Terms: Pays on acceptance. For mss buys one-time rights; second serial (reprint rights). Buys one-time rights for artwork and photos. Pays 2-5¢/word for assigned/unsolicited articles. Pays $25-50 for color inside illustration. Photographers are paid per photo, $15-50 (cover). Sample copy free with 7×10 SAE. Free writer's guidelines.

Tips: "We will be focusing on the age 12-13 group of our age 0-14 audience. (Focus was somewhat younger before.)"

OWL MAGAZINE, The Discovery Magazine for Children, Young Naturalist Foundation, Suite 306, 56 The Esplanade, Toronto, Ontario M5E 1A7 Canada. (416)868-6001. Editor: Nyla Ahmad. Art Director: Tim Davin. Magazine published 10 times/year. Circ. 160,000. "*OWL* helps children over eight discover and enjoy the world of science and nature. We look for articles that are fun to read, that inform from a child's perspective, and that motivate hands-on interaction. *OWL* explores the reader's many interests in the natural world in a scientific, but always entertaining, way."

Nonfiction: Middle readers, young adults: animal, biology, games/puzzles, high-tech, humor, interview/profile, travel. Especially interested in puzzles and game ideas: logic, math, visual puzzles. Does not want to see religious topics, anthropomorphizing. Buys 20 mss/ year. Average word length: 1,500. Byline given.

How to Contact/Writers: Nonfiction: Query with published clips. Reports on queries in 4-6 weeks; mss in 6-8 weeks.

Illustration: Buys 3-5 illustrations/issue; 40-50 illustrations/year. Uses color artwork only. Preferred theme or style: lively, involving, fun, with emotional impact and appeal. "We use a range of styles." Works on assignment only.

How to Contact/Illustrators: Illustrations only: Send tearsheets and slides. Reports on art samples only if interested. Original artwork returned at job's completion.

Photography: Looking for shots of animals and nature. "Label the photos." Uses $2\frac{1}{4} \times 2\frac{1}{4}$ and 35mm transparencies. Photographers should query with samples.

Terms: Pays on acceptance. Buys first North American and world rights for mss, artwork and photos. Pays $200-500 (Canadian) for assigned/unsolicited articles. Pays up to $650 (Canadian) for illustrations. Photographers are paid per photo. Sample copies for $4.28. Free writer's guidelines.

Tips: Writers: "Talk to kids and find out what they're interested in; make sure your research is thorough and find good consultants who are doing up-to-the-minute research. Be sure to read the magazine carefully to become familiar with *OWL*'s style." (See listing for *Chickadee*.)

POCKETS, Devotional Magazine for Children, The Upper Room, 1908 Grand, P.O. Box 189, Nashville TN 37202. (615)340-7333. Articles/Fiction Editor: Janet R. Knight. Art Director: Chris Schechner, Suite 207, 3100 Carlisle Plaza, Dallas TX 75204. Magazine published 11 times/year. Estab. 1981. Circ. 96,000. "Stories should help children 6 to 12 experience a Christian lifestyle that is not always a neatly wrapped moral package but is open to the continuing revelation of God's will."

Fiction: Young readers, middle readers: contemporary, fantasy, history, religious, "retold Bible stories." Does not want to see violence or talking animal stories. Buys 26-30 mss/year. Average word length: 800-2,000. Byline given.

Nonfiction: Young readers, middle readers: history, interview/profile, religious, "communication activities." Does not want to see how-to articles. "Our nonfiction reads like a story." History is in form of role-model stories, as is profile. Buys 10 mss/year. Average word length: 800-2,000. Byline given.

How to Contact/Writers: Fiction/nonfiction: Send complete ms. "Prefer not to deal with queries." Reports on mss in 2-4 weeks. Will consider simultaneous submissions.

Illustration: Buys 30 illustrations/issue. Preferred theme or style: varied; both 4-color and 2-color. Reviews artwork for future assignments; works on assignment only.

How to Contact/Illustrators: Illustrations only: Send promo sheet, tearsheets and slides to Chris Schechner, Suite 207, 3100 Carlisle Plaza, Dallas TX 75204. "Include samples of both 2-color and 4-color, if you have them." Reports on art samples in 3 months. Original artwork returned at job's completion. Credit line given.

Photography: Purchases photography from freelancers. Buys photos with accompanying ms only.

Terms: Pays on acceptance. Buys first North American serial rights for mss; one-time rights for artwork and photos. Pays 12-15¢/word for stories/articles. Pays $500-600 for color cover illustration; $50-400 for color inside; $50-250 (2-color). Pays $25 for color transparencies accompanying articles; $500 for cover photos. Sample copy free with 8 × 10 SAE and 4 first-class stamps. Writer's/illustrator's guidelines free with SASE.

Tips: "Ask for our themes first. They are set yearly in the fall. Also, we are looking for articles about real children involved in environment, peace or similar activities."

*POEM TRAIN, Rock Ridge Publishing, P.O. Box 203, Jarrettsville MD 21084. Editor: Lisa Ancarrow. Quarterly magazine. Estab. 1993. Circ. 100. Literary magazine of poetry for children. Publishes poetry written by adults for children, as well as "The Caboose" section of poetry written by children.

Poetry: Reviews poetry. Wants "light, funny, touching poetry. No taboo subjects." Maximum length: 25 lines or less. Limit submissions to 6 poems.

How to Contact/Writers: Fiction: Send complete ms. Reports on mss in 2 months. Publishes ms 6-12 months after acceptance. Will consider simultaneous submissions ("just let us know") and/or previously published work ("if rights are cleared").

Illustration: Uses b&w artwork only. Reviews ms/illustration packages.

How to Contact/Illustrators: Ms/illustration packages: Submit complete package with final art. Illustrations only: Send poetry with artwork (illustrations accompany each poem in issue). Reports in 6 weeks. Samples returned with SASE; some samples filed. Original work not returned at job's completion. Credit line given.

Terms: Pays in copies. Acquires one-time rights for mss/artwork. Sample copies for $3.75 postpaid. Writer's guidelines for SASE.

Tips: "Request guidelines, or better yet, a sample copy. For poetry, avoid clichéd subjects, try to look at everyday things through the fresh eyes of a child. Also, avoid overused rhyme schemes!"

POWER AND LIGHT, Children's Ministries, 6401 The Paseo, Kansas City MO 64131. (816)333-7000. Editor: Beula Postlewait. Executive Editor: Mark York. Weekly story paper. "*Power and Light* is a leisure reading piece for fifth and sixth graders. It is published weekly by the Department of Children's Ministries of the Church of the Nazarene. The major purposes of *Power and Light* are to provide a leisure reading piece which will build Christian behavior and values; provide reinforcement for Biblical concepts taught in the Sunday School curriculum. The focus of the reinforcement will be life-related, with some historical appreciation. *Power and Light*'s target audience is children ages 11-12 in grades five and six."

Fiction: Middle readers: adventure, contemporary, multicultural, nature/environment, problem-solving, religious. "Avoid fantasy, science fiction, abnormally mature or precocious children, personification of animals. Also avoid extensive cultural or holiday references, especially those with a distinctly American frame of reference. Our paper has an international audience. We need stories involving multicultural preteens in realistic settings dealing with realistic problems with God's help." Average word length: 500-700. Byline given.

How to Contact/Writers: Send complete ms. Reports on queries in 1 month; mss in 2 months. Publishes ms 2 years after acceptance.

Illustration: *Power and Light* publishes a wide variety of artistic styles, i.e., cartoon, realistic, montage, etc., but whatever the style, artwork must appeal to 11-12 year old children. Reviews artwork for future assignments.

How to Contact/Illustrators: Illustrations only: Query; send résumé, promo sheet and portfolio. Reports back only if interested. Credit line given.

Photography: Buys "b&w archaeological/Biblical for inside use and color preteen/contemporary/action for cover use."

Terms: Pays on publication. "Payment is made approximately one year before the date of issue." Buys one-time rights, all rights and multiple use rights for mss. Purchases all rights and first/one-time rights for artwork and photographs. Pays 3.5-5¢/word for stories/articles. Pays illustrators $40 for b&w, $75 for color cover; $40 for b&w, $50-75 for color inside. Photographers paid per photo (range: $35-45; $200 maximum for cover color photo). Writer's/illustrator's guidelines for SASE.

Tips: "Themes and outcomes should conform to the theology and practices of the Church of the Nazarene, Evangelical Friends, Free Methodist, Wesleyan and other Bible-believing Evangelical churches." Looks for "bright, colorful illustrations; concise, short articles and stories." (See listing for *Discoveries*.)

PRIMARY DAYS, Scripture Press Pub., Inc., Box 632, Glen Ellyn IL 60138. (708)668-6000. Articles/Fiction Editor: Janice K. Burton. Art Director: Blake Ebel. Distributed weekly; published quarterly. Estab. 1935. "Our audience is children 6-8 years old."

Fiction: Young readers: adventure, multicultural, nature/environment, problem-solving, religious, sports (Christian concepts only). Average word length: 600-700.

Nonfiction: Young readers: arts/crafts, biography, games/puzzles, history, interview/profile, multicultural, hobbies, how-to, nature/environment, problem-solving, religion, sports (all need Christian slant). Multicultural needs include: Stories that have their settings in other countries and deal with ethnic family situations. Average word length: 400.

How to Contact/Writers: Fiction/nonfiction: Send complete ms. Reports on mss in 8-10 weeks. Publishes ms 1-2 years after acceptance. (We work 1 year ahead.) Will consider previously published work.

Illustration: Buys 24-30 illustrations/year.

How to Contact/Illustrators: Credit line sometimes given. Contact: Blake Ebel, art director, for submission information.

Photography: Buys photos from freelancers.

Terms: Pays on acceptance. Buys all rights, first rights or one-time rights for mss. Pays 5-10¢/word for stories/articles depending on amount of editing required. Sample copies for #10 SASE. Writer's/photo guidelines for SASE.

Tips: "I'm not interested in material that lacks any spiritual element. Stories/articles must be appropriate for a Sunday School take-home paper. Write for Tips to Writers, sample copies, theme lists."

RACING FOR KIDS, Griggs Publishing Company Inc., P.O. Box 500, Concord NC 28026. (704)786-7132. Editor: Gary McCredie. Monthly magazine. Estab. 1990. Circ. 10,000. Publication caters to kids interested in racing.

Nonfiction: Young readers: auto racing, health, nature/environment, multicultural, science, sports. Middle readers and young adults: animal, arts/crafts, cooking, fashion, health, history, hobbies, interviews/profile, math, multicultural, nature/environment, science, sports—all as they relate to auto racing. Multicultural needs include: sensitivity to minorities in racing—women and African-Americans; with foreign drivers, tell a little about their home country. Buys 12-20 mss/year. Average word length: 400-1,200. Byline given.

How to Contact/Writers: Nonfiction: Query. Reports on queries in 2 months only if interested. Publishes ms 6-12 months after acceptance.

Terms: Pays on publication. Buys exclusive magazine rights for mss. Pays $50-150 for stories, $50-150 for articles. Additional payment for photos that accompany article.

Tips: "Know the subject matter, study publication. All stories are racing-related. We like stories about NASCAR, NHRA and Monster Truck drivers. No fiction please."

R-A-D-A-R, Standard Publishing, 8121 Hamilton Ave., Cincinnati OH 45231. (513)931-4050. Editor: Elaina Meyers. Weekly magazine. Circ. 120,000. *R-A-D-A-R* is a weekly take-home paper for boys and girls who are in grades 3-6. "Our goal is to reach these children with the truth of God's Word, and to help them make it the guide of their lives. Many of our features, including our stories, now correlate with the Sunday school lesson themes. Send for a quarterly theme list and sample copies of *R-A-D-A-R*. Keep in mind that others will be submitting stories for the same themes—this is not an assignment."

Fiction: Middle readers: adventure, animal, contemporary, history, humorous, problem-solving, religious, sports, suspense/mystery. Does not want to see fantasy or science fiction. Buys 150 mss/year. Average word length: 400-1,000. Byline given.

Nonfiction: Middle readers: animal, history, how-to, humorous, interview/profile, problem-solving, religious, travel. Buys 50 mss/year. Average word length: 400-1,000. Byline given.

Poetry: Reviews poetry. Maximum length: 16 lines.

How to Contact/Writers: Fiction/nonfiction: Send complete ms. Reports on queries/mss in 6-8 weeks. Will consider simultaneous submissions (but prefers not to). Reprint submissions must be retyped.

Illustration: Reviews all illustration packages. "Works on assignment only; there have been a few exceptions to this."

How to Contact/Illustrators: Illustrations only: Send résumé, tearsheets or promo sheets; samples of art can be photocopied. Reports on art samples only if interested.

Photography: Purchases photos from freelancers. Model/property releases required. Send résumé, business card, promotional literature or tearsheets to be kept on file.

Terms: Pays on acceptance. Buys first rights, one-time rights, second serial, first North American rights for mss. Purchases all rights for artwork. Pays 3-7¢/word for unsolicited articles (few are assigned). Contributor copies given "not as payment, but all contributors receive copies of their art/articles." Pays $70-125 for color illustrations; $125-150 for color cover; $40-60 for line art only. Photographers paid $125 maximum per photo. Sample copy and writer's guidelines free with 9⅜ × 4¼ SASE.

Tips: "Write about current topics, issues that elementary-age children are dealing with. Keep illustrations/photos current." (See listing for *Straight*.)

RANGER RICK, National Wildlife Federation, 8925 Leesburg Pike, Vienna VA 22184. (703)790-4000. Editor: Gerald Bishop. Design Director: Donna Miller. Monthly magazine. Circ. 850,000. "Our audience ranges from ages six to twelve, though we aim the reading level of most material at nine-year-olds or fourth graders."

• To learn more about working with *Ranger Rick*, read the interview with Editor Gerald Bishop in the 1994 edition of *Children's Writer's & Illustrator's Market*.

Fiction: Middle readers: animal (wildlife), fantasy, humorous, science fiction. Buys 4-6 mss/year. Average word length: 900. Byline given.

Nonfiction: Middle readers: animal (wildlife), conservation, outdoor adventure, humorous. Buys 20-30 mss/year. Average word length: 900. Byline given.

A bullet has been placed within some listings to introduce special comments by the editors of Children's Writer's & Illustrator's Market.

How to Contact/Writers: Fiction: Query with published clips; send complete ms. Nonfiction: Query with published clips. Reports on queries/mss in 6 weeks.
Illustration: Buys 6-8 illustrations/issue; 75-100 illustrations/year. Preferred theme: nature, wildlife. Reviews artwork for future assignments; works on assignment only.
How to Contact/Illustrators: Illustrations only: Send résumé, tearsheets. Reports on art samples in 6 weeks. Original artwork returned at job's completion.
Terms: Pays on acceptance. Buys all rights (first North American serial rights negotiable). Pays up to $575 for full-length of best quality. For illustrations, buys one-time rights. Pays $250-1,000 for color (inside, per page) illustration. Sample copies for $2. Writer's guidelines free with SASE.
Tips: "Fiction and nonfiction articles may be written on any aspect of wildlife, nature, outdoor adventure and discovery, domestic animals with a 'wild' connection (such as domestic pigs and wild boars), science, conservation or related subjects. To find out what subjects have been covered recently, consult our annual indexes and the *Children's Magazine Guide*. These are available in many libraries. The National Wildlife Federation (NWF) discourages the keeping of wildlife as pets, so the keeping of such pets should not be featured in your copy. Avoid stereotyping of any group. For instance, girls can enjoy nature and the outdoors as much as boys can, and mothers can be just as knowledgeable as fathers. The only way you can write successfully for *Ranger Rick* is to know the kinds of subjects and approaches we like. And the only way you can do that is to read the magazine. Recent issues can be found in most libraries or are available from our office for $2 a copy."

SCHOLASTIC MATH MAGAZINE, Scholastic, Inc., 555 Broadway, New York NY 10012-3999. (212)343-6100. Editor: Tracey Randinelli. Senior Designer: Leah Bossio. Art Director: Joan Michael. Magazine published 14 times/year, September-May. Estab. 1980. Circ. 265,000. "We are a math magazine for seventh, eighth and ninth classrooms. We present math in current, relevant, high-interest topics. Math skills we focus on include whole number, fraction and decimal computation, percentages, ratios, proportions, geometry."
Nonfiction: Young adults: animal, arts/crafts, careers, cooking, fashion, games/puzzles, geography, health, history, hobbies, how-to, humorous, interview/profile, math, multicultural, nature/environment, problem solving, science, social issues, sports, travel. No fiction. Does not want to see "anything dealing with *very* controversial issues—e.g., teenage pregnancy, etc." Buys 20 mss/year. Byline given.
How to Contact/Writers: Query. Reports on queries in 2 months. Will consider simultaneous submissions.
Illustration: Buys 4 illustrations/issue; 56 illustrations/year. Prefers to review "humorous, young adult sophistication" types of art. Will review ms/illustration packages. Works on assignment only.
How to Contact/Illustrators: Ms/illustration packages: Query first. × Illustrations only: Query with samples; submit portfolio for review. Reports back only if interested. Original artwork returned at job's completion.
Terms: Pays on publication. Buys all rights for mss. Pays $25 for puzzles and riddles; maximum of $350 for stories/articles. Photographers are paid by the project.
Tips: "For our magazine, stories dealing with math concepts and applications in the real world are sought."

SCHOOL MATES, USCF's Magazine for Beginning Chess Players, United States Chess Federation, 186 Rt. 9W, New Windsor NY 12553. (914)562-8350. Fax: (914)561-CHES. Articles Editor: Brian Bugbee. Fiction Editor: Cheryl Lemire. Art Director: Jami Anson. Bimonthly magazine. Estab. 1987. Circ. 23,000. Magazine for beginning chess players. Offers instructional articles, features on famous players, scholastic chess coverage, games, puzzles, occasional fiction, listing of chess tournaments.
Fiction: Young readers, middle readers, young adults: chess. Middle readers: humorous (chess-related). Average word length: 1,000-5,000 words.
Nonfiction: Young readers, middle readers, young adults: games/puzzles, chess. Middle readers, young adults: interview/profile (chess-related). "No *Mad Magazine* type humor. No sex, no drugs, no alcohol, no tobacco. No stereotypes. We want to see chess presented as a wholesome, non-nerdy activity that's fun for all. Good sportsmanship, fair play, and

Teaching Science and Reading Through Pictures

Did you know there are four different kinds of zebras and you can tell them apart by their stripes? Or that there's a tiny insect called the spittelbug that blows frothy bubbles in which to lay its eggs? Do you know what happens to an aluminum can when it's recycled?

Al Matano

Kids who read *Scienceland: To Nurture Scientific Thinking* get a wealth of these kinds of facts in every issue. The picture-oriented magazine was started 18 years ago by Al Matano, who serves as publisher, editor and art director. *Scienceland* is aimed at preschool and primary-grade children, including those who are read to, those just learning to read, and those who read independently. The magazine, which is published eight times a year, relies on large, colorful photos and illustrations to teach science and nature *and* reading skills.

Like any picture-oriented publication, *Scienceland* depends on photographers and illustrators, not writers, to supply story ideas. "We're looking for very high quality work that has continuity and is captioned as much as possible," says Matano. In almost all cases, staff members of *Scienceland* do thorough research to check the factual accuracy of the captioned material they receive.

Scienceland's artwork is purchased directly from photographers and illustrators, as well as from photo agencies. Matano also frequently discovers illustrations that might interest his young readers in other publications. What he needs most are series of photographs or illustrations depicting subjects in natural or physical science. For example, he's used four photos documenting the metamorphosis of a developing dragonfly and several photos of animals that hatch from eggs, including a frog, a minnow, a mantis, a lizard, a turtle and a crayfish.

Most issues of *Scienceland* have a theme such as "The Long-Necked Giraffe," "How Some Insects are Born" or "Giant Earthmoving Vehicles." Themes are usually initiated by the visuals the staff receives or finds. Information is not presented in article form, but rather in simple captions and descriptions that accompany bright, bold pictures. A young reader will find difficult words spelled phonetically and defined for them throughout each 26-page issue. Most issues also feature a maze or puzzle (done by freelance illustrators) that relates to the theme. For example, a maze featuring true-and-false questions about recycling (whose answers point readers in different directions) is included in the "Can Recycling" issue.

"The editorial approach to *Scienceland* is to interest children in what educators refer to as 'content reading,' " explains Matano. "We use graphics to introduce very simple science to trigger their curiosity, to stimulate children to think as they read, rather than being concerned with rote reading."

As you may have guessed, *Scienceland* is almost exclusively used in classrooms, and offers teachers' editions of each issue. However, individual subscriptions are also available and Matano says teachers often request them for friends and relatives. If you'd like to check out a few issues of the magazine, it can also be found in libraries.

"*Scienceland* is structured to overcome passive reading and dislike of reading," says Matano, "to draw the child into the subject through high-quality visuals, large print, short sentences, notes in smaller print, and occasional questions strategically placed to stimulate response. It integrates the benefits offered by a picture book, a reading book and a workbook."

In reviewing submissions, Matano says, "It's much faster for us to view a series of photos with captions describing the action, whether it's natural or physical science, or a series of illustrations that are connected and tell a story. When I say story," he stresses, "I'm referring to captions or detailed descriptions." In *Scienceland*, a picture is worth a thousand words.

—Alice P. Buening

To Nurture Scientific Thinking

Scienceland

Vol. 17 No. 133   Giant Earthmoving Vehicles

133

Scienceland *Editor/Art Director Al Matano chose this fun photo by Sekai Bunka for the cover of their issue on "Giant Earthmoving Vehicles." The interior photos, also by Bunka, feature the same children wielding tiny shovels amid a monstrous mound of dirt and learning about colossal bulldozers, dumptrucks and power shovels. Matano likes to use photos featuring children in* **Scienceland** *whenever possible.*

'thinking ahead' in chess as in life are extremely desirable in articles. Also, celebrities who play chess."

Poetry: Infrequently published. Must be chess related.

How to Contact/Writers: Send complete ms. Reports on queries/mss in 5 weeks.

Illustration: Buys 2-3 illustrations/year. Prefers b&w and ink; cartoons OK.

How to Contact/Illustrators: Query first. Reports back only if interested. Credit line sometimes given. "Typically, a cover is credited while an illustration inside gets only the artist's signature in the work itself."

Photography: Purchases photos from freelancers. Wants "action shots of chess games (at tournament competitions), well-done portraits of popular chess players."

Terms: Pays on publication. Buys one-time rights for mss, artwork and photos. For stories/ articles, pays $40/1,000 words. Pays illustrators $50-75 for b&w cover; $25-45 for b&w inside. Pays photographers per photo (range: $25-75). Sample copies free for 9 × 12 SAE and 2 first-class stamps. Writer's guidelines free on request.

Tips: Writers: "Lively prose that grabs and sustains kids' attention is desirable. Don't talk down to kids or over their heads. Don't be overly 'cute.' " Illustration/photography: "Whimsical shots are often desirable."

SCIENCE WEEKLY, Science Weekly Inc., P.O. Box 70638, Chevy Chase MD 20813. (301)680-8804. Fax: (301)680-9240. Editor: Deborah Lazar. Magazine published 16 times/ year. Estab. 1984. Circ. 250,000.

Nonfiction: Young readers, middle readers, (K-8th grade): science/math education, education, problem-solving. "Author must be within the greater DC, Virginia, Maryland area."

Terms: Pays on publication. Prefers people with education, science and children's writing background. *Send résumé.*

SCIENCELAND, To Nurture Scientific Thinking, Scienceland Inc., #2108, 501 Fifth Ave., New York NY 10017-6165. (212)490-2180. Fax: (212)490-2187. Editor/Art Director: Al Matano. Magazine published 8 times/year. Estab. 1977. Circ. 16,000. This is "a content reading picture-book for the preschool youngster being read to, the first-grader learning to read and for the second and third grader beginning to read independently."

Nonfiction: Picture-oriented material, young readers: animal, art/crafts, biography, careers, cooking, education, games/puzzles, health, history, how-to, nature/environment, problem-solving. Does not want to see unillustrated material; All material must be illustrated in full color.

Poetry: Reviews poetry. Maximum length: 12 lines.

How to Contact/Writers: *Must* be picture or full-color illustrated stories.

Illustration: Prefers to review "detailed, realistic, full color art. No abstracts or fantasy." Uses color artwork only. Will review captioned/illustration packages; reviews artwork for future assignments.

How to Contact/Illustrators: Captioned/illustration packages: "Query first." Illustrations only: Send unsolicited art by mail; provide résumé, promotional literature or tearsheets to be kept on file. Reports back in 3-4 weeks. "Exclusively contracted original artwork retained at our option for exhibits, etc. Others returned at job's completion."

Photography: Wants to see "physical and natural science photos with children in scenes whenever possible." Model/property release and photo captions required where applicable. Uses 35mm transparencies. Photographer should submit portfolio for review; provide résumé, promotional literature or tearsheets to be kept on file.

Terms: Pays on publication. Buys nonexclusive rights to artwork and photos. Payment for captioned/illustration packages: $50-500 and up. Payment for illustrations: $25-300 and up for color cover; $25-300 and up for color inside. Photographers paid by the project. Sample copy free with 9 × 12 SASE.

Tips: "Must be top notch illustrator or photographer. No amateurs."

SEVENTEEN MAGAZINE, K-III Magazines, 850 Third Ave., New York NY 10022. (212)407-9700. Executive Editor: Shelley Youngblut. Fiction Editor: Joe Bargmann. Senior Editor: Eileen Livers. Art Director: Daniel Pfeffer. Monthly magazine. Estab. 1944. Circ. 1,750,000. "General interest magazine for teenage girls."

Fiction: Young adults: adult, contemporary, fantasy, humorous, religious, romance, science fiction, sports, spy/mystery/adventure. "We consider all good literary short fiction." Buys 12-20 mss/year. Average word length: 1,000-4,000. Byline given.
Nonfiction: Young adults: how-to, humorous, interview/profile, problem-solving, reporting, social issues. Buys 150 mss/year. Word length: Varies from 800-1,000 words for short features and monthly columns to 800-2,500 words for major articles. Byline given.
Poetry: Reviews poetry "only by writers younger than 21 for 'Voice.' "
How to Contact/Writers: Fiction: Send complete ms. Nonfiction: Query with published clips or send complete ms. Reports on queries/mss in 3 weeks. Will consider simultaneous submissions.
Illustration: Uses 1 illustration per short story. Will review ms/illustration packages. Pays illustrators by the project. Writer's guidelines for business-size SASE.

SHARING THE VICTORY, Fellowship of Christian Athletes, 8701 Leeds, Kansas City MO 64129. (816)921-0909. Fax: (816)921-8755. Articles/Photo Editor: John Dodderidge. Art Director: Frank Grey. Monthly magazine. Estab. 1982. Circ. 55,000. "Purpose is to present to coaches and athletes, and all whom they influence, the challenge and adventure of receiving Jesus Christ as Savior and Lord."
Nonfiction: Young adults: interview/profile, sports. Buys 20-25 mss/year. Average word length: 400-900. Byline given.
Poetry: Reviews poetry. Maximum length: 50-75 words.
How to Contact/Writers: Nonfiction: Query with published clips. Reports in 3 weeks. Publishes ms 3 months after acceptance. Will consider simultaneous submissions, electronic submissions via disk or modem and previously published work.
Photography: Purchases photos separately. Looking for photos of sports action. Uses color, b&w prints and 35mm transparencies.
Terms: Pays on publication. Buys first rights and second serial (reprint) rights. Pays $50-250 for assigned and unsolicited articles. Photographers paid per photo (range: $50-300). Sample copies for 9×12 SASE and $1. Writer's/photo guidelines for SASE.
Tips: "Be specific—write short. Take quality photos that are useable." Wants interviews and features. Interested in colorful sports photos.

SHOFAR, 43 Northcote Dr., Melville NY 11747. (516)643-4598. Managing Editor: Gerald H. Grayson. Magazine published monthly October through May—double issues December/January and April/May. Circ. 17,000. For Jewish children ages 8-13.
Fiction: Middle readers: cartoons, contemporary, humorous, poetry, religious, sports. All material must be on a Jewish theme. Buys 10-20 mss/year. Average word length: 500-700. Byline given.
Nonfiction: Middle readers: history, humorous, interview/profile, puzzles, religious. Buys 10-20 mss/year. Average word length: 500-1,000. Byline given.
How to Contact/Writers: Fiction/nonfiction: Send complete ms (preferred) with SASE. Queries welcome. Publishes special holiday issues. Submit holiday theme pieces at least 4 months in advance. Reports on queries/mss in 1 month. Will consider simultaneous submissions.
Illustration: Buys 3-4 illustrations/issue; buys 15-20 illustrations/year. Works on assignment only.
How to Contact/Illustrators: Ms/illustration packages: Query first. Illustrations only: Send tearsheets. Works on assignment only. Reports on art samples only if interested. Original artwork returned at job's completion.
Terms: Buys first North American serial rights or first serial rights for mss and artwork. Pays on publication. Pays 10¢/word plus 5 contributor's copies. Photos purchased with mss at additional fees. Pays $25-100/b&w cover illustration; $50-150/color (cover). Sample copy free with 9×12 SAE and 98¢ postage. Free writer's/illustrator's guidelines.

THE SINGLE PARENT, Journal of Parents Without Partners, Inc., 401 N. Michigan Ave., Chicago IL 60611. (312)644-6610, ext. 3226. Fax: (312)245-1082. Articles/Fiction Editor/Art Director: Mercedes Vance. Quarterly magazine. Estab. 1957. Circ. 90,000. Members of PWP are single parents who are divorced, widowed or never married. "*The Single*

Parent looks at the positive side of the single parent's situation and is interested in all aspects of parenting, and the particular situation of single parenting." 10% of material aimed at juvenile audience.

Fiction: Young readers, middle readers, young adults: contemporary, humorous, problem-solving, suspense/mystery/adventure (only stories with single parent angle). No sad stories or sports, romance, or religious material. Buys commissioned and noncommissioned mss. Average word length: 800-1,500. Accompanying photos/graphics strongly encouraged. Byline given.

Nonfiction: Primarily for adult readers: careers, cooking, education, health, history, humorous, interview/profile, problem-solving. Does *not* want to see material unrelated to single-parent children and families. Average word length: 800-1,500. Buys commissioned and noncommissioned mss. Byline given.

How to Contact/Writers: Fiction/nonfiction: Send complete ms with accompanying photos/graphics and author photo and bio. Mss must be submitted in WordPerfect/ASCII format on 3½" disk with hardcopy. Mss nonreturnable. Editor contacts *only* those authors whose mss will be published. *TSP* reserves copyright for all published articles.

SKIPPING STONES, A Multicultural Children's Quarterly, P.O. Box 3939, Eugene OR 97403. (503)342-4956. Articles/Photo Editor: Arun N. Toké. Fiction Editor: Amy Brandt. Quarterly magazine. Estab. 1988. Circ. 3,000. "*Skipping Stones* is a multicultural nonprofit children's magazine designed to encourage cooperation, creativity and celebration of cultural and environmental richness. We encourage submissions by minorities and under-represented populations."

Fiction: Middle readers, young adult/teens: animal, contemporary, humorous. All levels: folktales, multicultural, nature/environment. Multicultural needs include: bilingual or multilingual pieces; use of words from other languages; settings in other cultures or multiethnic communities.

Nonfiction: Middle readers, young adult/teens: cooking. All levels: animal, biography, cooking, games/puzzles, history, humorous, interview/profile, nature/environment, problem-solving, religion and cultural celebrations, sports, travel, multicultural and environmental awareness. Does not want to see preaching or abusive language; no poems by authors over 18 years old; no suspense or romance stories for the sake of the same. Average word length: 500. Byline given.

How to Contact/Writers: Fiction: Query. Nonfiction: Send complete ms. Reports on queries in 2 months; mss in 4 months. Will consider simultaneous submissions. Please include your name on each page.

Illustration: Prefers b&w drawings especially by young adults. Will consider all illustration packages. Reviews artwork for future assignments.

How to Contact/Illustrators: Ms/illustration packages: Query; submit complete ms with final art; submit tearsheets. Reports back in 4 months (only if interested). Original artwork returned at job's completion. Credit line given.

Photography: Black & white photos preferred, but color photos will be considered. Children 7-15, international, nature, celebration.

Terms: Pays on publication. Buys first or reprint rights for mss and artwork; reprint rights for photographs. Pays in copies for authors, photographers and illustrators; $50-75 for b&w cover. Sample copies for $4 with SAE and 4 first-class stamps. Writer's/illustrator's guidelines for 4×9 SASE.

Tips: Wants material "meant for children" with multicultural or environmental awareness theme. "Think, live and write as if you were a child. Let the 'inner child' within you speak out—naturally, uninhibited." Wants "material that gives insight on cultural celebrations, lifestyle, custom and tradition, glimpse of daily life in other countries and cultures. Photos, songs, artwork are most welcome if they illustrate/highlight the points. Translations are welcome if your submission is in a language other than English. In 1995, our themes will include homeless and street children, world religions and cultures, African-American experiences, bilingual issue, indigenous architecture, songs from various cultures, world in 2025 A.D., Native American culture, nutrition and foods from around the world, hospitality, death and loss."

SLEUTH, Tellstar Productions, P.O. Box 1264, Huntington WV 25714. Articles Editor: Shannon Bridget Murphy. Semiannual magazine. Estab. 1993. Circ. 500. "Mystery magazine for children/young adult readers."

Fiction: All levels: adventure, multicultural, problem-solving, suspense/mystery. Middle readers, young adults: history. "Please do not send stories too complex for children or young readers. I would like to see children's stories that feature children." Average word length: 500-2,000.

Nonfiction: All levels: games/puzzles, how-to, multicultural, mystery, problem-solving, science. "I would like to see practical problem-solving nonfiction articles." Average word length: 500-2,000. Byline given.

Poetry: Reviews poetry. Multiple poetry submissions welcome.

How to Contact/Writers: Fiction/nonfiction: Send complete ms. Reports in 1-2 months. Will consider simultaneous submissions, electronic submissions via disk or modem.

Illustration: Looks for illustrations that feature children; illustrations of children in sets. Reviews ms/illustration packages; reviews artwork for future assignments. .

How to Contact/Illustrators: Illustration only: Query; send portfolio, slides. Reports in 2-4 weeks. Samples returned with SASE, filed with permission of artist. Original work returned upon job's completion. Credit line given.

Photography: Uses color, b&w prints; 35mm, 8×10 transparencies. Query with samples; send unsolicited photos by mail; provide business card, promotional literature or tearsheets. Wants photographs that instruct and entertain children and young people.

Terms: Pays on publication. Buys first rights, one-time rights for mss. Additional payment for ms/illustration packages; when photos accompany articles. Sample copies for $10. Writer's/illustrator's/photo guidelines for SASE.

Tips: "Work of young writers and college students welcome."

*SOCCER JR., The Soccer Magazine for Kids, Triplepoint Inc., 27 Unquowa Rd., Fairfield CT 06430. (203)259-5766. Articles/Fiction Editor: Priscilla Williams. Bimonthly magazine. Estab. 1992. Circ. 100,000. *Soccer Jr.* is for soccer players 8 to 16 years old. It offers "instruction, inspiration and fun."

Fiction: Middle readers, young adults: sports (soccer). Does not want to see "cute," preachy or "moralizing" stories. Buys 3-4 mss/year. Average word length: 1,000-2,000. Byline given.

Nonfiction: Young readers, middle readers, young adults: games/puzzles—soccer-themed. Buys 10-12 mss/year.

How to Contact/Writers: Fiction/nonfiction: Send complete ms. Reports on mss in 2-3 months. Publishes ms 3-12 months after acceptance. Will consider simultaneous submissions.

Illustration: Uses color artwork only. Reviews artwork for future assignments; works on assignment only.

How to Contact/Illustrators: Illustrations only: Send samples to be filed. Samples not returned. "We have a small pool of artists we work from, but look for new freelancers occasionally, and accept samples for consideration."

Terms: Pays on acceptance. Buys first rights for mss. Sample copies for 9×12 SAE and 5 first-class stamps.

Tips: "Read *Soccer Jr.*. An astonishing number of manuscripts are submitted either by people who've never seen the publication or who send non-soccer-related material." The magazine also accepts stories written by children.

*SPIDER, The Magazine for Children, Carus Corporation, P.O. Box 300, Peru IL 61354. Editor-in-Chief: Marianne Carus. Associate Editor: Christine Walske. Art Director: Ron McCutchan. Monthly magazine. Estab. 1994. Circ. 73,400. *Spider* publishes high-quality literature for beginning readers, primarily ages 6-9.

● In addition to *Spider*, the Carus Corporation publishes *Cricket* and *Ladybug* (see listings in this section). The editors have also launched a new publication, *Babybug*, a board book magazine for children under two years old, first appearing in November 1994. Artwork is needed for the magazine ("good multicultural babies"). Contact the above address for submission information.

This bold, comic-book-style illustration by Redondo appeared in the September/October 1994 issue of Soccer Jr. It accompanied "The Wilshire Wildcats," a short story by Connie Levesque told from the point of view of Martha, a heavyset fullback whose coach puts her in the game as a forward. Soccer Jr. Editor Priscilla Williams thought Redondo portrayed the main character as "brave and stolid, even though outmatched. He has a realistic and compassionate style, with a slightly romanticized edge."

Fiction: Young readers: adventure, animal, contemporary, fantasy, folktales, history, humorous, multicultural, nature/environment, problem-solving, science fiction, sports, suspense/mystery. "Authentic, well-researched stories from all cultures are welcome. We would like to see more multicultural material. No didactic, religious, or violent stories, or anything that talks down to children." Average word length: 300-1,000. Byline given.

Nonfiction: Young readers: animal, arts/crafts, cooking, games/puzzles, geography, history, math, multicultural, nature/environment, problem-solving, science. "Well-researched articles on all cultures are welcome. Would like to see more games, puzzles and activities, especially ones adaptable to *Spider*'s takeout pages. No encyclopedic or overtly educational articles." Average word length: 300-800. Byline given.

Poetry: Serious, humorous, nonsense rhymes. Maximum length: 20 lines.

How to Contact/Writers: Fiction/nonfiction: Send complete ms. Reports on mss in 4 months. Publishes ms 1-2 years after acceptance. Will consider simultaneous submissions and previously published work.

Illustration: Buys 20 illustrations/issue; 240 illustrations/year. Uses color artwork only. "Any medium—preferably one that can wrap on a laser scanner—no larger than 20 × 24. We use more realism than cartoon-style art." Reviews ms/illustration packages; reviews artwork for future assignments; works on assignment only.

How to Contact/Illustrators: Ms/illustration packages: Submit ms with rough sketches. Illustrations only: Send promo sheet and tearsheets. Reports in 6 weeks. Samples returned with SASE; samples filed. Original work returned at job's completion. Credit line given.

Photography: Buys photos from freelancers. Buys photos with accompanying ms only. Model/property releases required; captions required. Uses 35mm or 2¼ × 2¼ transparencies. Send unsolicited photos by mail; provide résumé and tearsheets. Reports in 6 weeks.

Terms: Pays on publication for text; within 45 days from acceptance for art. Buys first, one-time or reprint rights for mss. Buys first and promotional rights for artwork; one-time rights for photographs. Pays 25¢/word for stories/articles. Authors also receive 2 complimentary copies of the issue in which work appears. Additional payment for ms/illustration packages and for photos accompanying articles. Pays illustrators $750 for color cover; $200-300 for color inside. Pays photographers per photo (range: $25-75). Sample copies for $4. Writer's/illustrator's guidelines for SASE.

Tips: "Writers: Read back issues before submitting."

STORY FRIENDS, Mennonite Publishing House, 616 Walnut Ave., Scottdale PA 15683. (412)887-5181. Fax: (412)887-3111. Editor: Marjorie Waybill. Art Director: Jim Butti. Magazine published monthly in weekly issues. Estab. 1905. Circ. 9,000. Story paper that reinforces Christian values for children ages 4-9.

Fiction: Young readers: contemporary, humorous, problem-solving, religious, relationships. Buys 45 mss/year. Average word length: 300-800. Byline given.

Nonfiction: Picture-oriented and young readers: interview/profile, nature/environment. Buys 10 mss/year. Average word length: 300-800. Byline given.

Poetry: "I like variety—some long story poems and some four-lines."

How to Contact/Writers: Fiction/nonfiction: Send complete ms. Reports on mss in 2-3 weeks. Will consider simultaneous submissions.

Illustration: Reviews artwork for future assignments; works on assignment only.

How to Contact/Illustrators: Send tearsheets with SASE. Reports in 2 months. Credit line given.

Photography: Buys photos from freelancers. Wants photos of children ages 4-8.

Terms: Pays on acceptance. Buys one-time rights or reprint rights for mss and artwork. Pays 3-5¢/word for stories and articles. Pays $50 for color cover; $25 for b&w inside. Writer's guidelines free with SAE and 2 first-class stamps.

STRAIGHT, Standard Publishing, 8121 Hamilton Ave., Cincinnati OH 45231. (513)931-4050. Articles/Fiction Editor: Carla J. Crane. Magazine published quarterly in weekly parts. Circ. 40,000. *Straight* is a magazine designed for today's Christian teenagers.

Fiction: Young adults: humorous, problem solving, religious, sports. Does not want to see science fiction, fantasy, historical. Buys 100-115 mss/year. Average word length: 1,100-1,500. Byline given.

Nonfiction: Young adults: humorous, interview/profile, problem-solving, religion. Does not want to see devotionals. Buys 24-30 mss/year. Average word length: 500-1,000. Byline given.

Poetry: Reviews poetry from teenagers only.

How to Contact/Writers: Fiction/nonfiction: Query or send complete ms. Reports on queries in 1-2 weeks; mss in 1-2 months. Will consider simultaneous submissions.

Illustration: Buys 40-45 illustrations/year. Uses color artwork only. Preferred theme or style: Realistic, cartoon (full-color only). Reviews artwork for future assignments. Works on assignment only.

How to Contact/Illustrators: Ms/illustration packages: Query first. Illustrations only: Submit promo sheets or tearsheets. Reports back only if interested. Credit line given.

Photography: Buys photos from freelancers. Looking for photos of contemporary, modestly-dressed teenagers. Model/property release required. Uses 5×7 or 8×10 b&w prints and 35mm transparencies. Photographer should send unsolicited photos by mail.

Terms: Pays on acceptance. Buys first rights and second serial (reprint rights) for mss. Buys full rights for artwork; one-time rights for photos. Pays 3-7¢ per word for stories/articles. Pays illustrators $150-300/color inside. Pays photographers per photo (range: $75-125). Sample copy free with business SASE. Writer's/illustrator's guidelines free with business SASE.

Tips: "The main characters should be contemporary teens who cope with modern-day problems using Christian principles. Stories should be uplifting, positive and character-building, but not preachy. Conflicts must be resolved realistically, with thought-provoking and honest endings. Accepted length is 1,100 to 1,500 words. Nonfiction is accepted. We use devotional pieces, articles on current issues from a Christian point of view and humor. Nonfiction pieces should concern topics of interest to teens, including school, family life, recreation, friends, part-time jobs, dating and music." (See listing for *R-A-D-A-R*.)

The Subject Index, located before the General Index, lists book and magazine publishers by their fiction and nonfiction needs.

STUDENT LEADERSHIP JOURNAL, InterVarsity Christian Fellowship, P.O. Box 7895, Madison WI 53707. (608)274-9001, ext. 425. Editor: Jeff Yourison. Quarterly magazine. Estab. 1988. Circ. 11,000.
Fiction: Young adults: multicultural, religious. Multicultural themes include: Forming campus fellowships that reflect the ethnic makeup of the campus and demonstrating *reconciliation* beyond celebrating difference. "I see too much aimed at young teens. Our age group is 18-30 years old." Buys 4 mss/year. Average word length: 300-1,800. Byline given.
Nonfiction: Young adults/teens: history, interview/profile, multicultural, nature/environment, religion, social issue. Multicultural themes include: Affirming the need for ethnic validation and reconciliation. "We don't affirm all lifestyles—therefore we are promoting multi-ethnicity but not full-orbed multiculturalism. We prefer articles on issues, leadership, spiritual growth, sexual healing, dysfunctionality, etc." Buys 6-8 mss/year. Average word length: 1,100-2,200. Byline given.
Poetry: Wants to see free verse; lots of good imagery. Maximum length: 18 lines. Limit submissions to 5 poems.
How to Contact/Writers: Fiction/nonfiction: Send complete ms. Reports on queries/mss in 6 months. Publishes ms 1-2 years after acceptance. Accepts IBM-compatible word processing files on diskettes.
Illustration: Buys 5 illustrations/issue; 20 illustrations/year. Uses b&w line art only. Prefers cartoon pen & ink 5×7 or 8×10 stand alone campus/religious humor. Reviews artwork for future assignments.
How to Contact/Illustrators: Illustrations only: Send promo sheet, portfolio and tearsheets. Reports only if interested. Samples not returned; samples kept on file. Original work returned at job's completion. Credit line given.
Photography: Looks for campus shots—all types: single faces, studying, thinking, "mood"—pairs and groups: praying, studying, talking, playing. 18-22 year old subjects or professor-types. Model/property release preferred. Uses color and b&w 5×7 glossy prints; 2¼×2¼, 4×5 or 35mm transparencies. Photographers should query with samples; send unsolicited photos by mail; provide business card, promotional literature or tearsheets. "Send photocopies I can keep. I'll call for the print." Reports only if interested.
Terms: Pays on acceptance for ms; on publication for photos and cartoons. Buys first North American serial rights, first rights and reprint rights for ms. Purchases first rights for artwork; one-time rights for photographs. Pays $50-75 for stories; $50-125 for articles; and contributor's copies. Pays illustrators $50-100 for b&w cover; $25-75 for b&w inside. Photographers paid per photo (range: $25-50). Sample copies for $3. Writer's/illustrator/ photo guidelines for SASE.
Tips: "Please write and photograph according to the audience. Research the age group and the subculture. Older teens are really sensitive to tokenism and condescension toward their generation. They want to be treated as sophisticated even though they are frequently uninformed and hurting. To reach this audience requires credibility, vulnerability, transparency and confidence!"

SUPERSCIENCE BLUE, Scholastic, Inc., 555 Broadway, New York NY 10012-3099. (212)343-6100. Editor: Kathy Burkett. Art Director: Susan Kass. Monthly (during school year) magazine. Estab. 1989. Circ. 375,000. "News and hands-on science for children in grades 4-6. Designed for use in a class setting; distributed by teacher. Articles make science fun and interesting for a broad audience of children. Issues are theme-based."
Nonfiction: Middle readers: animal, how-to (science experiments), nature/environment, problem-solving, science topics. Does not want to see "general nature stories. Our focus is science with a *news* or *hands-on* slant. To date we have never purchased an unsolicited manuscript. Instead, we assign articles based on clips—and sometimes queries." Write for editorial calendar. Average word length: 250-800. Byline sometimes given.
How to Contact/Writers: Nonfiction: Query with published clips. (Most freelance articles are assigned.) Reports on queries in 4-6 weeks. Publishes ms 4 months after acceptance.
Illustration: Buys 2-3 illustrations/issue; 10-12 illustrations/year. Works on assignment only.
How to Contact/Illustrators: Illustrations only: Send résumé and tearsheets. Reports on art samples only if interested. Original artwork returned at job's completion.

Terms: Pays on acceptance. Buys all rights. Pays $100-600. Illustrations only: $75 minimum for b&w inside; $150-1,200 for color inside (complicated spreads only). Writer's guidelines free on request.

Tips: Looks for "news articles and photo essays. Good journalism means always going to *primary* sources—interview scientists in the field, for example, and *quote* them for a more lively article."

TEEN LIFE, (formerly *Hicall*), Gospel Publishing House, 1445 Boonville Ave., Springfield MO 65802-1894. (417)862-2781, ext. 4359. Articles/Fiction Editor: Tammy Bicket. Art Director: Richard Harman. Photo Editor: Carol Arnold. Quarterly newspaper (Sunday school take-home paper). Estab. 1920. Circ. 80,000. "Slant articles toward the 15- to 19-year-old teen. We are a Christian publication, so all articles should focus on the Christian's responses to life. Fiction should be realistic, not syrupy nor too graphic. Fiction should have a Christian slant also."

Fiction: Young adults: adventure, contemporary, humorous, multicultural, problem-solving, religious, sports (all with Christian slant). Also wants fiction based on true stories. Buys 50 mss/year. Average word length 700-1,500. Byline given.

Nonfiction: Young adults: "thoughtful treatment of contemporary issues (i.e., racism, preparing for the future); interviews with famous Christians who have noteworthy stories to tell. Buys 50 mss/year. "Looking for more articles and fewer stories." Average word length: 1,000. Byline given.

How to Contact/Writers: Fiction/nonfiction: Send complete ms. Do *not* send query letters. Reports on mss in 2-3 months. Will consider simultaneous submissions.

Illustration: Buys 10-30 illustrations/year. Uses color artwork only. Reviews mss/illustration packages; reviews artwork for future assignments; works on assignment only. "Freelance art used only when in-house art department has a work overload." Prefers to review "realistic, cartoon, youth-oriented styles. Any art sent will be referred to the art department. Art department will assign freelance art."

How to Contact/Illustrators: Illustrations only: Query with samples; send résumé, portfolio and client list. Reports only if interested. Credit line sometimes given.

Photography: Buys photos from freelancers. Wants "teen photos that look spontaneous. Ethnic and urban photos urgently needed." Uses color prints, 35mm, 2¼ × 2¼, 4 × 5 transparencies. Send unsolicited photos by mail.

Terms: Pays on acceptance. For mss, buys first North American serial rights, first rights, one-time rights, second serial (reprint rights), simultaneous rights. For artwork, buys one-time rights for cartoons, all rights for assigned illustrations; one-time rights for photos. Pays $25 minimum for stories; $25-75 for articles. Pays $75-100/color cover photo; $35-45/ b&w inside photo; $50-60/color inside photo. Sample copy free with 6 × 9 SASE. Writer's guidelines free with SASE.

Tips: "We want contemporary, real life articles, or fiction that has the same feel. We work on specific themes for each quarter, so interested writers should request current writers guidelines and topic list."

*'TEEN MAGAZINE, Petersen Publishing Co., 6420 Wilshire Blvd., Los Angeles CA 90048. (310)854-2950. Editor: Roxanne Camron. Managing/Fiction Editor: Karle Dickerson. Art Director: Laurel Finnerty. Monthly magazine. Estab. 1957. Circ. 1,100,000. "We are a pure junior high and senior high female audience. 'TEEN teens are upbeat and want to be informed."

Fiction: Young adults: contemporary, humorous, problem-solving, romance, suspense/ mystery. Does not want to see "that which does not apply to our market—i.e., science fiction, history, religious, adult-oriented." Buys 12 mss/year. Length for fiction: 10-15 pages typewritten, double-spaced.

Nonfiction: Young adults: careers, cooking, health, multicultural, problem-solving, social issues, travel. Does not want to see adult-oriented, adult point of view." Buys 25 mss/year. Length for articles: 10-20 pages typewritten, double-spaced. Byline given.

How to Contact/Writers: Fiction/nonfiction: Query. Reports on queries in 3 weeks; mss in 3-4 weeks. Prefer submissions hard copy and disk.

Illustration: Buys 0-4 illustrations/issue. Reviews mss/illustrations packages; reviews artwork for future assignments. Uses various styles for variation. Use a lot of b&w illustration. Light, upbeat." Will review ms/illustration packages; artwork for future assignments.

How to Contact/Illustrators: Ms/illustration packages: "Query first." Illustrations only: "Want to see samples whether it be tearsheets, slides, finished pieces showing the style." Reports back only if interested. Credit line given.

Terms: Pays on acceptance. Buys all rights. Pays $100-400 for stories; $50-400 for articles. Pays $25-250/b&w inside; $100-400/color inside. Writer's/illustrator's guidelines free with SASE.

Tips: Illustrators: "Present professional finished work. Get familiar with magazine and send samples that would be compatible with the style of publication." There is a need for artwork with "fiction/specialty articles. Send samples or promotional materials on a regular basis."

TEEN POWER, Scripture Press Publications, Inc., P.O. Box 632, Glen Ellyn IL 60138. (708)668-6000. Editor: Amy J. Cox. Quarterly magazine. Estab. 1965. "*Teen Power* is an eight-page Sunday School take-home paper aimed at 11-16 year olds in a conservative Christian audience. Its primary objective is to help readers see how principles for Christian living can be applied to everyday life."

Fiction: Young adults: adventure, contemporary, humorous, multicultural, problem-solving, religious, sports. Does not want to see "unrealistic stories with tacked-on morals. Fiction should be true-to-life and have a clear, spiritual take-away value." Buys 50 mss/year. Average word length: 400-1,200. Byline given.

Nonfiction: Young adults: biography, games/puzzles, how-to, humorous, interview/profile, multicultural, problem-solving, religion, social issues, sports. Multicultural themes include: Christian teens in foreign countries, missions, missionary kids, ethnic Christian teens in US and Canada. Does not want to see "articles with no connection to Christian principles." Buys 30 mss/year. Average word length: 250-700. Byline given.

How To Contact/Writers: Fiction/nonfiction: Send complete ms. Reports on mss in 3-4 months. Publishes ms "at least one year" after acceptance. Will consider simultaneous submissions.

Illustration: Reviews artwork for future assignments.

How to Contact/Illustrators: Send résumé, promo sheet, tearsheets. Reports back only if interested. Credit line given.

Photography: Buys photos from freelancers. Looks for mood shots: teen fads and hang outs; sport and school activities shots.

Terms: Pays on acceptance. Buys one-time rights. Pays $25-120 for stories/articles. Negotiates illustrators' fees. Photographers paid per photo. Sample copies and writer's guidelines for #10 SAE and 1 first-class stamp.

Tips: "Take-home papers are a great "break-in" point. Each weekly issue contains at least 2 freelance-written features. However, we are very specific about the type of material we are looking for. We want stories and articles to reinforce our Sunday School lessons and help our readers apply what they learned in Sunday School throughout the week. All submissions must have a spiritual emphasis—not merely a moral lesson."

TEENAGE CHRISTIAN MAGAZINE, Christian Publishing Inc., P.O. Box 549, Murray KY 42071. Articles/Fiction Editor: Marty Dodson, P.O. Box 11276, Nashville TN 37222-1276. Bimonthly magazine. Circ. 13,000. "We publish articles that challenge Christian teenagers to grow in their Christian faith."

Fiction: Young adults/teens: adventure, contemporary, humorous, problem-solving, religious, sports, suspense/mystery. "We get too many articles about perfect people where everything works out in the end. We like to see real-life stories." Buys 15-20 mss/year. Average word length: 1,000-1,750. Byline sometimes given.

Nonfiction: Young adults/teens: animal, arts/crafts, biography, careers, games/puzzles, health, history, hobbies, how-to, humorous, interview/profile, problem-solving, religion, social issues, sports, travel. Work needs to be in touch with Christian teen perspective." Buys 20 mss/year. Average word length: 500-1,500. Byline given.

Poetry: Reviews religious teen-oriented poetry. Maximum length: 20-25 lines. Limit submissions to 3 poems.

How to Contact/Writers: Fiction: Query. Nonfiction: Send complete ms. Reports on queries in 1 month/mss in 2 months. Publishes ms 4-6 months after acceptance. Will consider simultaneous and previously published submissions.

Terms: Pays on publication. Buys one-time rights for ms. Pays $15-25 (occasionally more) for stories/articles. Sample copies for 9 × 12 SAE and 98¢ postage.

Tips: "We look at anything that would help our audience. It is obvious when writers have read the magazine and when they have not. We use freelance writers almost exclusively for fiction. We use well-written pieces on nonfiction topics such as dating, alcohol, finding jobs, etc."

3-2-1 CONTACT, Children's Television Workshop, One Lincoln Plaza, New York NY 10023. (212)595-3456. Articles Editor: Curtis Slepian. Art Director: Gretchen Grace. Magazine published 10 times/year. Estab. 1979. Circ. 440,000. This is a science and technology magazine for 8- to 14-year-olds. Features all areas of science and nature.

Fiction: "Our fiction piece is an on-going series called 'The Time Team.' It is written in-house."

Nonfiction: Middle readers, young adults: animal, health, how-to, interview/profile, multicultural, nature/environment, science. Multicultural needs include: how kids live in other countries (with a science hook; profiles of minority scientists). Does not want to see religion, travel or history. "We see too many research reports on the life of a toad. We'd like to see more articles about scientists doing exciting work (in the field) with lots of quotes." Buys 20 mss/year. Average word length: 750-1,000. Byline given.

How to Contact/Writers: Nonfiction: Query with published clips. Reports on queries in 3 weeks.

Illustration: Buys 15 illustrations/issue; buys 150 illustrations/year. Works on assignment only.

How to Contact/Illustrators: Illustrations only: Send tearsheets, portfolio. Reports on art samples only if interested. Original artwork returned at job's completion. Credit line given.

Photography: Buys photos from freelancers.

Terms: Pays on acceptance. Buys all rights for mss (negotiable). Buys one-time rights for photos unless on assignment. Pays $100-600 for assigned/unsolicited articles. Pays $500-1,000 for color cover illustration; $150-300 for b&w inside; $175-500 for color inside. Pays photographers per photo (range: $150-750). Sample copy for $1.75 and 8 × 14 SASE; writer's/illustrator's guidelines free with 8½ × 11 SASE.

Tips: Looks for "features. We do not want articles based on library research. We want on-the-spot interviews about what's happening in science now."

*TOGETHER TIME, WordAction Publishing Co., 2923 Troost Ave., Kansas City MO 64131. (816)931-1900. Contact: Lynda T. Boardman. Weekly magazine. Estab. 1981. Circ. 27,000. *"Together Time* is a story paper that correlates with the Sunday School Curriculum for three- and four-year-olds. Each paper contains a story, a poem, an activity, and an article directed to the parents."

Fiction: "We would like to see more realistic stories. We don't like them to seem staged. We also do not purchase stories that give life and feeling to inanimate objects." Buys 50 mss/year. Average word length: 100-150. Byline given.

Poetry: Reviews poetry. Maximum length: 8 lines. Limit submissions to 10 poems.

How to Contact/Writers: Fiction: Send complete ms. Reports on queries in 1 month; mss in 3 months. Publishes ms one year after acceptance.

Illustration: Buys 2 illustrations/issue from freelancers. "We do assignment only and like both realistic and cartoon. Must be age-appropriate." Reviews ms/illustration packages; reviews artwork for future assignments; works on assignment.

How to Contact/Illustrators: Ms/illustration packages: Submit ms with rough sketches. Send résumé and portfolio. Reports in 1 month. Sample returned with SASE. Credit line given.

Photography: Buys photos from freelancers. Looks for outdoor or indoor pictures of 3- and 4-year-old children. Uses color and b&w prints; 35mm transparencies. Query with samples. Reports in 1 month.

Terms: Pays on publication. Buys all rights for mss. Buys all rights for artwork; multiuse rights for photographs. Pays $25 maximum for stories. "Writers receive payment and contributor copies." Pays illustrators $40 for b&w, $75 for color cover; $40 for b&w, $75 for color inside. Pays photographers per photo (range: $30-75). Sample copies for #10 SASE. Writer's/illustrator's/photo guidelines for SASE.

Tips: "Make sure that the material you submit is geared to three- and four-year-old children. Request a theme list with the guidelines and try to submit things that apply."

*TOTALLY KIDS MAGAZINE, Peter Green Design/Fox Kids Network, 4219 W. Burbank Blvd., Burbank CA 91505. (818)953-2210. E-mail: bananadog@aol.com. Articles Editor: Scott Russell. Art Director: Debra Hintz. Quarterly magazine. Estab. 1990. Circ. 4 million. Features "fun and hip articles, games and activities for Fox Kids Club members ages 6-13, with special section for kids 2-6, promoting Fox Kids shows."

Fiction: "We use very little fiction. Occasional comic strips or short stories for young kids." Buys 4 mss/year. Average word length: 200-500. Byline sometimes given.

Nonfiction: Picture-oriented material, young readers, middle readers: Any material tied in to a Fox Kids Network show or "one of our other features (no religious material)." Buys 30 mss/year. Average word length: 200-500.

How to Contact/Writers: Fiction/nonfiction: Query with published clips. Reports on queries/mss in 1 month. Publishes mss 2-6 months after acceptance. Will consider simultaneous submissions and electronic submissions via disk or modem.

Illustration: Buys 5 illustrations/issue. Uses color artwork only. Prefers "cartoon character work, must be *on model*." Reviews ms/illustration packages; reviews artwork for future assignments; works on assignment only.

How to Contact/Illustrators: Ms/illustration packages: Query. Illustrations only: Send résumé, promo sheet, tearsheets. Reports only if interested. Samples returned with SASE; samples filed. Original work returned at job's completion. Credit line given.

Photography: Buys photos from freelancers. Uses a variety of subjects, depending on articles. Model/property release required. Uses color prints and 4×5 or 35mm transparencies. Query with résumé, business card, tearsheets. Reports only if interested.

Terms: Pays 30 days from acceptance. Buys all rights. Pays $100-400 for stories/articles. Additional payment for ms/illustration packages and for photos accompanying articles. Sample copy $1. Writer's guidelines for SASE.

Tips: "Practice. Write well. Read. Come up with some good ideas. We try to give kids cutting edge information. Licensing is the key to everything today, marketing-wise. Almost all of our articles are tied into Fox Kids shows."

TOUCH, Calvinettes, Box 7259, Grand Rapids MI 49510. (616)241-5616. Managing Editor: Carol Smith. Art Director: Chris Cook. Monthly (with combined issues May/June, July/August) magazine. Circ. 16,000. "*Touch* is designed to help girls ages 9-14 see how God is at work in their lives and in the world around them."

Fiction: Middle readers, young adults: animal, contemporary, history, humorous, problem-solving, religious, romance. Does not want to see unrealistic stories and those with trite, easy endings. Buys 40 mss/year. Average word length: 400-1,000. Byline given.

Nonfiction: Middle readers, young adults: how-to, humorous, interview/profile, problem-solving, religious. Buys 5 mss/year. Average word length: 200-800. Byline given.

How to Contact/Writers: Send for biannual update for publication themes. Fiction/nonfiction: Send complete ms. Reports on mss in 2 months. Will consider simultaneous submissions.

 The asterisk before a listing indicates the listing is new in this edition.

Illustration: Buys 1-2 illustrations/issue; buys 10-15 illustrations/year. Prefers illustrations to go with stories. Works on assignment only.

How to Contact/Illustrators: Ms/illustration packages: "We would prefer to consider finished art with a ms."

Terms: Pays on publication. Buys first North American serial rights, first rights, second serial (reprint rights) or simultaneous rights. Pays $20-50 for assigned articles; $5-30 for unsolicited articles. "We send complimentary copies in addition to pay." Pays $25-50 for b&w cover illustration; $15-25 for b&w inside illustration. Writer's guidelines free with SASE.

Tips: Writers: "The stories should be current, deal with adolescent problems and joys, and help girls see God at work in their lives through humor as well as problem-solving."

TURTLE MAGAZINE, For Preschool Kids, Children's Better Health Institute, P.O. Box 567, Indianapolis IN 46206. (317)636-8881. Editor: Steve Charles. Art Director: Bart Rivers. Monthly/bimonthly magazine published January/February, March, April/May, June, July/August, September, October/November, December. Circ. 550,000. *Turtle* uses read-aloud stories, especially suitable for bedtime or naptime reading. Also used are poems, simple science experiments, and health-related articles. All but 2 pages aimed at juvenile audience.

Fiction: Picture-oriented material: adventure, animal, contemporary, fantasy, folktales, health-related, history, holiday themes, humorous, nature/environment, problem-solving, sports, suspense/mystery. "Need very simple experiments illustrating basic science concepts. Also needs action rhymes to foster creative movement." Does not want to see stories about monsters or scary things. Avoid stories in which the characters indulge in unhealthy activities like eating junk food. Buys 50 mss/year. Average word length: 150-600. Byline given.

Nonfiction: Picture-oriented material: animal, arts/crafts, games/puzzles, health, multicultural, nature/environment, science, sports. Buys 20 mss/year. Average word length: 150-600. Byline given.

How to Contact/Writers: Fiction/nonfiction: "Prefer complete ms to queries." Reports on mss in 8-10 weeks.

Illustration: Buys 20-25 illustrations/issue; 160-200 illustrations/year. Prefers "realistic and humorous illustration." Reviews artwork for future assignments.

How to Contact/Illustrators: Illustrations only: Send résumé, promo sheet, slides, tearsheets. Reports back only if interested. Credit line given.

Photography: Buys photos from freelancers with accompanying ms only.

Terms: Pays "a few weeks prior to publication." Buys all rights for mss/artwork; one-time rights for photographs. Pays up to 22¢/word for articles (depending upon length and quality) and 10 complimentary copies. Pays $250 for color cover illustration, $30-70 for b&w inside; $65-140 for color inside; $20 for color slide inside. Sample copy $1.25. Writer's/illustrator's guidelines free with SASE.

Tips: "We're beginning to edit *Turtle* more for the very young preschooler, so we're looking for stories and articles that are written more simply than those we've used in the past. Our need for health-related material, especially features that encourage fitness, is ongoing. Health subjects must be age-appropriate. When writing about them, think creatively and lighten up! Fight the tendency to become boringly pedantic. Nobody—not even young kids—likes being lectured. Always keep in mind that in order for a story or article to educate preschoolers, it first must be truly entertaining—warm and engaging, exciting, or genuinely funny. Understand that writing for *Turtle* is a difficult challenge. Study the magazine to see if your manuscript is right for *Turtle*—magazines have distinct personalities that can't be understood by reading market listings alone. There is a trend toward leaner, lighter writing. There will be a growing need for interactive activities. Writers might want to consider developing an activity to accompany their very concise manuscripts." (See listings for *Child Life*, *Children's Digest*, *Children's Playmate*, *Humpty Dumpty's Magazine*, *Jack and Jill* and *U.S. Kids*.)

2 HYPE/HYPE HAIR, Word Up Publication, Suite 401, 210 Route 4 E., Paramus NY 07652. (201)843-4004. Art Director: Stuart Koban. Bimonthly magazine. Estab. 1990. Publishes articles about music (rap and R&B) — fashion, hair trends, health, grooming, games, contests — all dealing with music.

Nonfiction: Young adults: careers, fashion, games/puzzles, health, hobbies, how-to, interview/profile, problem-solving. Byline given.

How to Contact/Writers: Nonfiction: Query with published clips. Publishes ms 5 months after acceptance. Will consider electronic submissions via disk or modem.

Illustration: Buys 10 illustrations/issue. Illustrations should be done on 8½ × 11 paper. Reviews ms/illustration packages; reviews artwork for future assignments; works on assignment only.

How to Contact/Illustrators: Ms/illustration packages: Submit complete package with final art. Illustrations only: Send promo sheet, portfolio, tearsheets. Reports back only if interested. Samples not filed. Original work returned upon job's completion. Credit line given.

Photography: Model/property releases and photo captions required. Uses b&w and color prints. Photographers should send unsolicited photos by mail. Reports back only if interested.

Terms: Pays on publication. Buys one-time rights to mss. Pays $75-100 for articles. Additional payment for ms/illustration packages. Pays illustrators $50-75. Photographers paid per photo (range $35-150). Writer's/illustrator's/photo guidelines free for SASE.

Tips: "Send fun ideas for people with short attention spans."

U.S. KIDS, P.O. Box 567, Indianapolis IN 46202. (317)636-8881. Editor: Steve Charles. Art Editor: Mary Pesce. Magazine published 8 times a year. Estab. 1987. Circ. 250,000.

Fiction: Young readers and middle readers: adventure, animal, contemporary, health, history, humorous, multicultural, nature/environment, problem-solving, sports, suspense/mystery. "I see too many stories with no real story line. I'd like to see more mysteries and contemporary humor stories." Buys approximately 8-16 mss/year. Average word length: 500-800. Byline given.

Nonfiction: Young readers and middle readers: animal, arts/crafts, cooking, games/puzzles, health, history, hobbies, how-to, humorous, interview/profile, multicultural, nature/environment, science, social issues, sports, travel. Wants to see interviews with kids ages 5-11, who have done something unusual or different. Buys 30-40 mss/year. Average word length: 500-600. Byline given.

Poetry: Maximum length: 32 lines.

How to Contact/Writers: Fiction: Send complete ms. Nonfiction: Query. Reports on queries and mss in 1 month. Publishes ms 6 months after acceptance. Will consider simultaneous submissions, electronic submissions via disk or modem and previously published work.

Illustration: Buys 8 illustrations/issue; 70 illustrations/year. Color artwork only. Reviews ms/illustration packages; reviews artwork for future assignments; works on assignment only.

How to Contact/Illustrators: Ms/illustration packages: Query. Illustrations only: Send résumé and tearsheets. Reports back only if interested. Samples returned with SASE; samples kept on file. Does not return originals. Credit line given.

Photography: Purchases photography from freelancers. Looking for photos that pertain to children ages 5-11. Model/property release required. Uses color and b&w prints; 35mm, 2¼ × 2¼, 4 × 5 and 8 × 10 transparencies. Photographers should provide résumé, business card, promotional literature or tearsheets to be kept on file. Reports back only if interested.

Terms: Pays on publication. Buys all rights for mss. Purchases all rights for artwork. Purchases one-time rights for photographs. Pays 10¢/word minimum. Additional payment for ms/illustration packages. Pays illustrators $140/page for color inside. Photographers paid by the project or per photo (negotiable). Sample copies for $2.50. Writer's/illustrator/photo guidelines for SASE.

Tips: "Write clearly and concisely without preaching or being obvious." (See listings for *Child Life, Children's Digest, Children's Playmate, Humpty Dumpty's Magazine, Jack and Jill* and *Turtle Magazine*.)

VENTURE, Christian Service Brigade, P.O. Box 150, Wheaton IL 60189. (708)665-0630. Articles/Fiction Editor: Deborah Christensen. Art Director: Robert Fine. Bimonthly magazine. Estab. 1937. Circ. 19,000. The magazine is designed "to speak to the concerns of boys from a biblical perspective. To provide wholesome, entertaining reading for boys."

Fiction: Middle readers: adventure, animal, humorous, nature/environment, problem-solving, religious, sports, suspense/mystery. Does not want to see fantasy, romance, science fiction or anything without Christian emphasis. "We see too much 'new kid in town' stories. We'd like to see more humor." Buys 12 mss/year. Average word length: 500-1,000. Byline given.

Nonfiction: Middle readers: animal, arts/crafts, interview/profile, nature/environment, religion, science. Buys 6 mss/year. Average word length: 500-1,000. Byline given.

How to Contact/Writers: Fiction/nonfiction: Send complete ms. Reports on queries/mss in 1-2 weeks. Will consider simultaneous submissions.

Illustration: Buys 3 illustrations/issue; 18 illustrations/year. Reviews ms/illustration packages; reviews artwork for future assignments.

How to Contact/Illustrators: Ms/illustration packages: Send complete ms. Illustrations only: Send résumé, promo sheets, portfolio or tearsheets. Reports on art samples only if interested. Original artwork returned at job's completion. Credit line given.

Photography: Buys photos from freelancers. Wants photos of boys 8-11 years old.

Terms: Pays on publication for mss, artwork and photos. Buys first North American serial rights; first rights; second serial (reprint rights). Pays 5-10¢/word for stories/articles. Pays $75-125 for color cover illustration—usually photos only; $35-250 for color inside illustration (includes photos). "We're still figuring out payment because we've just started color with September/October 1994 issue." Sample copy $1.85 with 9 × 12 SAE and 98¢ postage. Writer's/illustrator's guidelines free with SASE.

Tips: "Know kids and their language. Too many writers use the vernacular of their childhood instead of contemporary language. I've seen illustrations and stories become more wild and exciting. Kids like movement."

WITH, The Magazine for Radical Christian Youth, Faith & Life Press, 722 Main, P.O. Box 347, Newton KS 67114. (316)283-5100. Editors: Eddy Hall, Carol Duerksen. Published 8 times a year. Circ. 6,100. Magazine published for teenagers, ages 15-18, in Mennonite, Brethren and Mennonite Brethren congregations. "We deal with issues affecting teens and try to help them make choices reflecting an Anabaptist-Mennonite faith."

Fiction: Young adults: adventure, contemporary, fantasy, folktales, health, humorous, multicultural, nature/environment, problem-solving, religious, science fiction, sports. Multicultural needs include: race relations, first-person stories featuring teens of ethnic minorities. "Would like to see more humor and parables/allegories." Buys 15 mss/year. Average word length: 1,000-2,000. Byline given.

Nonfiction: Young adults: first-person teen personal experience (as-told-to), humorous, multicultural, nature/environment, problem-solving, religion. Buys 15-20 mss/year. Average word length: 500-1,500. Byline given.

Poetry: Wants to see religious, humorous, nature. "We're cutting back on poetry." Maximum length: 50 lines.

How to Contact/Writers: Send complete ms. Query on first-person teen personal experience stories and how-to articles. (Detailed guidelines for first-person stories and how-tos available for SASE.) Reports on queries in 1 month; mss in 6 weeks. Will consider simultaneous submissions.

Illustration: Buys 6-8 illustrations/issue; buys 50-60 illustrations/year. Uses b&w and 2-color artwork only. Preferred theme or style: candids/interracial. Reviews ms/illustration packages; reviews artwork for future assignments.

How to Contact/Illustrators: Ms/illustration packages: Query first. Illustrations only: Query with portfolio (photocopies only) or tearsheets. Reports only if interested. Original artwork returned at job's completion upon request. Credit line given.

Photography: Buys photos from freelancers. Looking for candid photos of teens (ages 15-18), especially ethnic minorities. Uses 8 × 10 b&w glossy prints. Photographers should send unsolicited photos by mail.

Terms: Pays on acceptance. For mss buys first rights, one-time rights; second serial (reprint rights). Buys one-time rights for artwork and photos. Pays 5¢/word for unpublished manuscripts; 3¢/word for reprints. Will pay more for assigned as-told-to stories. Pays $35-50 for b&w cover illustration; $25-40 for b&w inside illustration. Pays photographers per photo (range: $35-50, cover only). Sample copy for 9×12 SAE and $1.21 postage. Writer's/illustrator's guidelines free with SASE.

Tips: "We're hungry for stuff that makes teens laugh—fiction, nonfiction and cartoons. It doesn't have to be religious, but must be wholesome."

WONDER TIME, Beacon Hill Press, 6401 The Paseo, Kansas City MO 64131. (816)333-7000. Editor: Lois Perrigo. Weekly magazine. Circ. 45,000. "*Wonder Time* is a full-color story paper for first and second graders. It is designed to connect Sunday School learning with the daily living experiences and growth of the primary child. Since *Wonder Time*'s target audience is children ages six to eight, the readability goal is to encourage beginning readers to read for themselves. The major purposes of *Wonder Time* are to: Provide a life-related paper which will build Christian values and encourage ethical behavior and provide reinforcement for the biblical concepts taught in the Word Action Sunday School curriculum."

● *Wonder Time* has purchased all the stories, poems and activities needed for its present two-year cycle. They will welcome submissions again in 1996.

Fiction: Young readers: contemporary, problem-solving, religious. Buys 52 mss/year. Average word length: 300-400. Byline given.

Nonfiction: Young readers: religious.

Poetry: Reviews religious poetry of 4-8 lines.

How to Contact/Writers: Fiction/nonfiction: Send complete ms. Reports on queries/mss in 1 month. Will consider simultaneous submissions.

Illustration: Buys 100 illustrations/year. Reviews illustration packages. Works on assignment only.

How to Contact/Illustrators: Ms/illustration packages: Ms with sketch. Illustrations only: Samples of work. Reports on art samples only if interested. Credit line given.

Terms: Pays on publication. Pays $25 per story for rights which allow the publisher to print the story multiple times in the same publication without repayment. Pays illustrators $40 for b&w cover or inside; $75 for color cover or inside. Photographers paid per photo (range: $25-75). Sends complimentary contributor's copies of publication. Sample copy and writer's guidelines with 9½×12 SAE and 2 first-class stamps.

Tips: "Basic themes reappear regularly. Please write for a theme list."

YOUNG CHRISTIAN, Tellstar Productions, P.O. Box 1264, Huntington WV 25714. Articles Editor: Shannon Bridget Murphy. Semiannual magazine. Estab. 1993. Circ. 500. "We publish Christian based stories aimed at a young audience."

Fiction: All levels: history, multicultural, problem-solving, religious, romance, suspense/mystery. "I would like to see more material with holiday themes." Average word length: 500-1,500. Byline given.

Nonfiction: All levels: biography, games/puzzles, history, how-to, multicultural, problem-solving, religion, social issues. Average word length: 500-1,500. Byline given.

Poetry: Reviews poetry. Multiple poetry submissions welcome.

How to Contact/Writers: Fiction/nonfiction: Send complete ms. Reports in 1-2 months. Will consider simultaneous submissions; electronic submissions via disk or modem.

Illustration: Reviews ms/illustration packages; reviews artwork for future assignments.

How to Contact/Illustrators: Ms/illustration packages: Submit complete package with final art; submit ms with rough sketches. Illustrations only: Send promo sheet, portfolio, slides. Reports in 1 month. Samples returned with SASE, filed with permission of artist. Original work returned upon job's completion. Credit line given.

Photography: Buys photos from freelancers. Looks for photographs that feature children in religious or nature-oriented settings. Uses color, b&w prints; 35mm, 8×10 transparencies. To contact, photographers should query with samples; send unsolicited photos by mail; provide business card, promotional literature or tearsheets. Reports in 1 month.

Terms: Pays on publication. Buys first rights, one-time rights. Additional payment for ms/illustration packages, when photos accompany articles. Sample copy for $10. Writer's/illustrator's/photo guidelines for SASE.

Tips: "Work of young writers and college students welcome."

YOUNG NATURALIST FOUNDATION See listings for *Chickadee* and *Owl*.

YOUNG SALVATIONIST, The Salvation Army, 615 Slaters Lane, P.O. Box 269, Alexandria VA 22313. (703)684-5500. Monthly magazine. Estab. 1984. Circ. 50,000. "We accept material with clear Christian content written for high school age teenagers. *Young Salvationist* is published for teenage members of The Salvation Army, a fundamental, activist denomination of the Christian Church."

Fiction: Young adults: multicultural, religious, sports (with Christian perspective). Buys 12-20 mss/year. Average word length: 750-1,200. Byline given.

Nonfiction: Young adults: religious — hobbies, how-to, interview/profile, multicultural, nature/environment, problem-solving, social issues. Buys 40-50 mss/year. Average word length: 750-1,200. Byline given.

Poetry: Reviews 16-20 line poetry dealing with a Christian theme. Send no more than 6 submissions.

How to Contact/Writers: Fiction/nonfiction: Query with published clips or send complete ms. Reports on queries in 2-3 weeks; mss in 1 month. Will consider simultaneous submissions.

Illustrations: Buys 2-3 illustrations/issue; 20-30 illustrations/year. Reviews ms/illustration packages; reviews artwork for future assignments.

How to Contact/Illustrators: Ms/illustration packages: Query or send ms with art." Illustrations only: Query; send résumé, promo sheet, portfolio, tearsheets. Reports on artwork in 2-3 weeks (with SASE). Original artwork returned at job's completion "if requested." Credit line given.

Photography: Purchases photography from freelancers. Looking for teens in action.

Terms: Pays on acceptance. Buys first North American serial rights, first rights, one-time rights or second serial (reprint) rights for mss. Purchases one-time rights for artwork and photographs. For mss, pays 10¢/word. Pays $100-150 color (cover) illustration; $50-100 b&w (inside) illustration; $100-150 color (inside) illustration. Sample copy for 9×12 SAE and 3 first-class stamps. Writer's/illustrator's guidelines free for #10 SASE.

Tips: "Ask for theme list/sample copy! Write 'up,' not down to teens. Aim at young *adults*, not children." Wants "less fiction, more 'journalistic' nonfiction."

YOUTH UPDATE, St. Anthony Messenger Press, 1615 Republic St., Cincinnati OH 45210. (513)241-5615. Articles Editor: Carol Ann Morrow. Art Director: June Pfaff. Monthly newsletter. Estab. 1982. Circ. 30,000. "Each issue focuses on one topic only. *Youth Update* addresses the faith and Christian life questions of young people and is designed to attract, instruct, guide and challenge its audience by applying the gospel to modern problems and situations. The students who read *Youth Update* vary in their religious education and reading ability. Write for average high school students. These students are 15-year-olds with a C+ average. Assume that they have paid attention to religious instruction and remember a little of what 'sister' said. Aim more toward 'table talk' than 'teacher talk.' "

Nonfiction: Young adults/teens: religion. Buys 12 mss/year. Average word length: 2,300-2,400. Byline given.

How to Contact/Writers: Nonfiction: Query. Reports on queries/mss in 6 weeks. Will consider computer printout and electronic submissions via disk.

Photography: Buys photos from freelancers. Uses photos of teens (high-school age) with attention to racial diversity and with emotion.

Terms: Pays on acceptance. Buys first North American serial rights for mss. Buys one-time rights for photographs. Pays $325-400 for articles. Pays photographers per photo ($40 minimum). Sample copy free with #10 SASE. Writer's guidelines free on request.

Always include a self-addressed, stamped envelope (SASE) with submissions within your own country. When sending material to other countries, include a self-addressed envelope (SAE) and International Reply Coupons (IRCs).

Tips: "Read the newsletter yourself—3 issues at least. In the past, our publication has dealt with a variety of topics including: dating, Lent, teenage pregnancy, baptism, loneliness, rock and roll, confirmation and the Bible. When writing, use the *New American Bible* as translation. More interested in church-related topics. It seems that religious magazines have become more doctrinal or exclusive to their denominations."

Magazines/'94-'95 changes

The following markets were included in the 1994 edition of *Children's Writer's & Illustrator's Market* but do not have listings in this edition. The majority did not respond to our request to update their listings. If a reason was given for exclusion, it appears in parentheses after the market's name.

BK News
Brilliant Star
Cat Fancy
Day Care and Early Education
Insights

The Kiln
The Mythic Circle
Noah's Ark (ceased publication)
Otterwise (ceased publication)

Sassy
Street Times
Writer's Open Forum

Audiovisual & Audiotape

The business of kids' music and video is not just a sideline anymore. Kids' media is growing, changing, and getting a lot of attention. And as the industry matures, the different segments of children's media are beginning to blend. Children's record companies are producing work in videotape format. Production houses and book publishers alike are releasing story books in audio and video versions. Stores stock material for kids on both CD and CD-ROM.

After a 1991 surge in major record companies signing children's acts, many big labels realized that the market for kids' music was too unlike the one for adults, and they just weren't equipped to promote their children's acts. The labels proceeded to drop all but a few artists in favor of TV and product tie-ins with a built-in fan base. Although there may not be a great demand for performers as of late, there is still a need for good, original songs for children's acts. And while video still dominates the children's market, children's audio—both music and story tapes—still enjoys steady sales.

Licensing rules

Just as in the children's book industry, however, the use of licensed characters in both audio and video is booming. The top titles of the past year have been dominated by Disney movie characters, Barney the dinosaur, and the Mighty Morphin Power Rangers.

And though the market is flooded with these character-driven products, this may help, not hinder, the sales of other audio and video titles. According to Joseph Porrello, senior vice president of Product Development for Peter Pan Industries, "When you have over 300 items featuring the Power Rangers available, . . . that brings people into the stores who will ultimately buy other [audio and video] products." (For more on Porello's view on the industry, see the Insider Report on page 244.)

Organizing children's media

In March 1994, the Children's Entertainment Association (CEA), with a mission "to raise awareness of children's entertainment within the industry and among the general public," was founded by children's entertainment attorney Howard Leib, organizer of the Kids' Music Seminar, which will hold its third annual meeting in 1995. Leib is forming regional chapters of CEA around the country with membership including children's artists and writers, record-label and video executives, independent producers and managers. (The Children's Entertainment Association can be contacted through Leib at 75 Rockefeller Plaza, Suite 327, New York NY 10019. Fax: (212)275-3835. E-mail: askcea@aol.com.)

In an effort to promote work not tied to the tube, the Coalition for Quality Children's Video has waged a campaign to increase awareness of titles driven neither by film nor TV. This nonprofit organization, based in Santa Fe, New Mexico, publishes Kids First!, a list of endorsed children's videos, and they're kicking off a program to have a Kids First! section in participating retail stores (Kids First! stickers are attached to endorsed products).

Expanding industry

The children's sections of video stores have been well-stocked with titles in recent years, but record stores are just beginning to devote more space to kids' music. The first children's-only record store, Tunesville, has been operating in Williamsville, New York for close to two years, with "okay, but not great" sales, according to a report in *Billboard*.

Children's music has also been getting more radio airtime. This year, the children's Media Network will nationally launch KidStar, a network of stations programming exclusively children's music and shows. KidStar will add AM stations to its roster in Boston, Chicago, Dallas, Houston, Los Angeles, New York, Philadelphia, San Francisco and Washington DC. It joins The Children's Satellite Network out of Minneapolis (which has 19 affiliates), as the only two just-kids radio networks in the country.

And while the number of children's-only radio stations continues to grow, a Los Angeles-based television production company, R.C. Entertainment, has an "MTV" for the very young in the works. Kids Music Network is scheduled to start up sometime this year and feature video clips of kids' acts, as well as other youth-oriented features, with separate programming to appeal to several different age-groups between 2 and 12.

With so much happening in the world of children's entertainment, there are growing opportunities for a great many talents. In the Audiovisual Markets and Audiotape Markets sections that follow, you'll find record companies, book publishers, museums, video production houses and more. Many of the companies listed work with a variety of projects and may need anything from songs and short stories to illustration and clay animation.

To keep up on the dynamic world of children's entertainment, read "Child's Play," Moira McCormick's *Billboard* magazine column, as well as *Publishers Weekly*, which often covers audio and video in its children's section. Industry publications such as *Variety* and *Hollywood Reporter* may also offer useful information on kids' video.

Audiovisual Markets

The production houses listed here don't produce just video cassettes. Many also create filmstrips, slide sets, multimedia productions — even television shows. These studios and production houses are in need of illustration, video graphics, special effects, and a variety of animation techniques, including stop motion, cell, clay and computer animation. They also need the work of writers for everything from animation scripts to educational filmstrips, but be aware that audiovisual media rely more on the "visual" to tell the story.

A number of listings create highly specialized material. Sea Studios, for example, produces only natural history videos, while Films for Christ (new to this edition) focuses on Christian titles. (For more on the religious market for children, see Don't Miss Out! Explore the Children's Religious Market on page 22.) Also note that technology in the world of video production is advancing. Companies such as Porter Versfelt & Associates are already producing CD-ROM and interactive titles for kids, and producers like Jeffrey Aikman of JEF Films believe that computer imaging is becoming the norm in kids' video, so it's important that illustrators stay up-to-date on these emerging techniques. (For more on Aikman's views of the market, see the Insider Report on page 232.)

AERIAL IMAGE VIDEO SERVICES, 137 W. 19th St., New York NY 10011. (212)229-1930. Fax: (212)229-1929. President: John Stapsy. Estab. 1979. Type of company: Video production and post production, and audio production, post production, and computer-based program production. Uses videotapes and audio. (For list of recent productions consult the Random House catalog of children's videos.)

Children's Writing: Does not accept unsolicited material. Submissions returned with proper SASE. Reports in "days."

Illustration/Animation: Does not accept unsolicited material. Hires illustrators for computer and hand animation, storyboarding, live action and comprehensives. Types of animation produced: cel animation, clay animation, stop motion, special effects, 3-D, computer animation, video graphics, motion control and live action. To submit, send cover letter, résumé and demo tape. Art samples returned with proper SASE. Reports in "weeks." Pays "per project."

Tips: When reviewing a portfolio/samples, looks for "application to a project, general talent and interests based on examples."

*AIMS MEDIA, 9710 DeSoto Ave., Chatsworth CA 91311. (818)773-4300. Fax: (818)341-6700. Vice President Production: Michael Wright. Estab. 1956. Producer/Distributor. Audience: ages 6-adult. Produces multimedia productions, films and videotapes. Uses 5 freelance writers/year; buys 15 writing projects per year; uses 1 freelance artist/year.

Children's Writing: Needs: Grade school picture books K-3 level. Query. Submissions are returned with proper SASE. Reports in 2 weeks. Guidelines/catalog free on request. Pays royalty or buys material outright.

Illustration/Animation: Hires for background plates. Types of animation produced: cel animation, clay animation, stop motion, computer animation and video graphics. Submit cover letter, résumé and demo tape (VHS or ¾"). Art samples returned with proper SASE; art samples not filed. Reports in 2 weeks.

ARTICHOKE PRODUCTIONS, 4114 Linden St., Oakland CA 94608. (510)655-1283. Producer/Director: Paul Kalbach. Estab. 1981. Production House (live action and computer graphics/animation). Audience: General. Produces films, videotapes.

Children's Writing: To submit, query with synopsis. Submissions returned with proper SASE. Reports back only if interested. Pay depends on project.

Illustration/Animation: Hires illustrators for character development. Types of animation produced: cel animation, stop motion, special effects, computer animation, video graphics, live action. Art samples returned with proper SASE. Reports back only if interested.

BENNU PRODUCTIONS INC., 626 McLean Ave., Yonkers NY 10705. (914)964-1828. Fax: (914)964-2914. Producer: Wayne J. Keeley. Contact: JoAnne Birkman. Estab. 1985. Film and video production house. Audience: General public, businesses, schools, etc. Uses multimedia productions, films and videotapes. Recent children's productions: "Street Signs," written by Wayne J. Keeley (elementary reading video); and "Don Quixote: An Intro," written by Sergio McLean (literature video for ages 7-12). 25% of writing is by freelancers; 25% of illustrating/animating is by freelancers. Uses 50 freelance writers/year. Uses 10 freelance artists/year.

Children's Writing: Needs: Educational material on all relevant topics for all age levels. Subjects include: substance abuse, environment, history, health, science, art, etc. To submit, query. Submissions returned with proper SASE. Reports back only if interested. Work purchased outright.

Illustration/Animation: Hires illustrators for animation (computer and graphic), storyboarding, character development, live action, comprehensives, pencil testing. Types of animation produced: special effects, computer animation, video graphics, live action. To submit, send cover letter, résumé, demo tape (VHS) and business card. Art samples returned with proper SASE. Reports back only if interested. Pay varies.

Tips: "Educationally stimulating material should be submitted." Looks for "creativity, innovation, flexibility."

*BRIDGESTONE MULTIMEDIA GROUP, 1979 Palomar Oaks Way, Carlsbad CA 92009. (619)431-9888. Fax: (619)431-0489. Estab. 1986. Video management and distribution, soft-

ware publisher. Audience: Family, children. Produces multimedia productions. Recent children's productions: "Everyone Is Special," written by Tony Salerno (self-esteem video for ages 3-10); "Christmas Past," written by various (comedy clips video for family).
Illustration/Animation: Submit demo tape (VHS). Guidelines/catalog free on request.

BROADCAST QUALITY, INC., #316, 5701 Sunset Dr., South Miami FL 33143. (305)665-5416. President: Diana Udel. Estab. 1978. Video production and post production house. Produces videotapes. Children's productions: "It's Ours to Save — Biscayne National Park," written by Jack Moss, produced by Diana Udel/BQI, Betacam SP/1″ Master, (Environmental awareness for grades 4-7); "The Wildlife Show at Parrot Jungle," written by Amy Smith, produced by BQI, Betacam SP/1″ Master, (Hands on to Florida's Wildlife for K-8th grade). Uses 2-5 freelance writers/year; purchases various projects/year.
Tips: "Send a résumé and demo reel. Seeks variety, knowledge of subject and audience."

CENTRE COMMUNICATIONS, Suite #207, 1800 30th St., Boulder CO 80301. (303)444-1166. Contact: Deborah Bodin. Estab. 1975. Production and distribution company. Audience: schools, libraries and television. Produces films and videotapes. Recent children's productions: "Legend of the Spirit Dog," (drama, environmental feature film for ages 5-12); and "Pepper and All the Legs," written by Dick Gackenbach (children's story video for ages 4-8). Uses 2-3 freelance writers/year; purchases 5-6 writing projects/year.
Children's Writing: Needs: educational material, documentaries and live action. "We only commission work or distribute finished products." Reports back only if interested. Buys material outright.
Illustration/Animation: "We're considering using illustrations for CD-ROMs." Send cover letter, résumé, demo tape and b&w print samples.

CLEARVUE/eav, 6465 N. Avondale, Chicago IL 60631. (312)775-9433. Editor/Producer: Mary Watanabe. Estab. 1969. Type of company: production and distribution house. Audience: educational pre-school through high school. Uses filmstrips, slide sets, CD-ROM, videodiscs, videotapes. 70% of illustrating/animating is by freelancers.
Children's Writing: "At this time we are only accepting for review *finished* video projects that we will consider for distribution." Query with résumé. Reports back only if interested. Pays 5-10% royalty.
Illustration/Animation: Hires illustrators for computer animation of company-owned filmstrips. Send cover letter, résumé, demo tape (VHS). Reports in 2 weeks only if interested. Video samples returned. Guidelines/catalog free. Pay: "open."
Tips: "Programs must be designed for educational market — not home or retail. We are looking for good animators with equipment to scan in our filmstrips and animate the characters and action according to prepared directions that allow for artistic variations."

*COUNTDOWN PRODUCTIONS, INC., P.O. Box 190537, Dallas TX 75219. Phone/fax: (214)321-3233. President: Thomas C. Crocker. Estab. 1986. Video Production. Audience: Children. Produces videotapes. Recent children's productions: "Mr. Donut and the Donut Factory," (Christian/morality video for ages 3-12); and "I've Got a Dream — Chuck E. Cheese," (love between siblings video for ages 4-12). Uses 5-6 freelance writers/year; buys 2 writing projects/year. Uses 5-6 artists/year; buys 10-12 art projects/year.
Children's Writing: Query with synopsis, résumé. Submissions cannot be returned; submissions filed. Reports only if interested. Buys material outright.
Illustration/Animation: Hires illustrators for computer/video, animation, storyboarding, live action. Types of animation produced: cel animation, clay animation, stop motion, computer animation, video graphics, live action. Submit cover letter, demo tape (VHS). Art samples not returned; art samples filed. Reports only if interested. Pays $45-85/hour for storyboarding/comp work; $50-100/hour for animation work.
Tips: "Have a ready-for-TV concept, developed characters and story line. Sequels or 13 weeks of material assist in the sale process."

DIMENSION FILMS, 15007 Gault St., Van Nuys CA 91405. (818)997-8065. President: Gary Goldsmith. Estab. 1962. Production house. Audience: schools and libraries. Uses film strips, films, videotapes. 10% of writing is by freelancers; 100% of illustrating/animating is by freelancers.

Children's Writing: Needs: educational material and documentaries for kindergarten-12th-grade audience. To submit, query. Submissions filed. Reports "in a matter of weeks. Call for guidelines." Pays in accordance with Writer's Guild standards.

Illustration/Animation: Hires illustrators for storyboarding, comprehensives. Types of animation produced: cel animation, video graphics, live action. To submit, send cover letter and résumé. Reports "in a matter of weeks. Call for guidelines." Pays $30-60/frame.

Tips: Illustrators/animators: looking for "imagination, clarity and purpose." Portfolio should show "strong composition; action in stillness."

EDUCATIONAL VIDEO NETWORK, 1401 19th St., Huntsville TX 77340. (409)295-5767. Executive Editor: Gary Edmondson. Estab. 1954. Production house. Audience: educational (school). Uses videotapes. 20% of writing by freelancers; 20% of illustrating/animating is by freelancers. Recent children's productions: "Gods and Heroes of Greece and Rome," written by Mary Lee Nolan (mythology/literature video for junior high-college); and "Cut the Fat from Your Diet," written and illustrated by Christina Vuckovic (nutrition video for junior high-college). Uses 1-2 freelance artists/year; buys 2-3 art projects/year.

Children's Writing: Needs: "Curriculum-oriented educational material" for junior high through college audiences. Query. Submissions returned with proper SASE. Reports in 1 month. Guidelines/catalog free. Pays writers royalties of 6-10% or buys material outright.

Illustration/Animation: Hires illustrators for acetate cels, animation. Types of animation produced: cel animation stills, video graphics, limited computer animation. To submit, send cover letter and VHS demo tape. Art samples returned with proper SASE. Reports in 1 month. Guidelines/catalog free. Pays $10-30/cel for animation work.

Tips: "Materials should fill a curriculum need for junior high to college. We seldom assign projects to freelancers. We want to be approached by people who know a particular subject and who have a plan for getting that information across to students. Programs should feature professional production techniques and involve the viewers in the message."

FILM CLASSIC EXCHANGE, 143 Hickory Hill Circle, Osterville MA 02655. (508)428-7198. President: J.H. Aikman. Estab. 1916. Distribution/production house. Audience: Pre-school through college. Produces films, videotapes. Recent children's productions: "The Good Deed," written by William P. Pounder, illustrated by Karen Losaq (film on family values aimed at preschool); "Willie McDuff's Big Day," written and illustrated by Joe Fleming (anti-drug film aimed at ages 12 and up). Uses 6 freelance writers and artists/year. Purchases 6 writing and 6 art projects/year.

Children's Writing: Needs: Preschool. Subjects include: Anti-drug. Query with synopsis or submit completed script. Submissions are returned with proper SASE. Reports back only if interested. Buys material outright.

Illustration/Animation: Hires illustrators for cel/video animation, storyboarding, character development, live action, comprehensives, pencil testing. Types of animation produced: cel animation, clay animation, stop motion, special effects, computer animation, video graphics, motion control, live action. To submit, send cover letter, résumé, demo tape (VHS), color print samples. Art samples returned with proper SASE. Reports back only if interested.

Tips: "Keep sending updated résumés/samples of work."

*FILMS FOR CHRIST, INC., (aka, "Eden Productions"), 2628 W. Birchwood Circle, Mesa AZ 85202. (602)894-1300. Fax: (602)894-8406. Production Director: Paul S. Taylor. Estab. 1961. Producer/distributor of films, videos and books. Audience: Christian families and church audiences. Produces multimedia productions, films, videotapes, books. Recent children's productions: "The Great Dinosaur Mystery," written by Paul S. Taylor, illustrated by Charles Zilch, Gary Webb, Paul S. Taylor (documentary on creation vs. evolution, 7-adult); and "The Great Dinosaur Mystery and the Bible," written by Paul S. Taylor, illustrated by C. Zilch, G. Webb, T. Tennant, J. Chong, P.S. Taylor (creation vs. evolution book, 7-adult). Uses 0-1 freelancer/year. Uses 1-2 artists/year; buys 3-8 art projects/year.

Children's Writing: Needs: documentaries (ages 5-8, 9-12, adult). Subjects include: creation vs. evolution. Query with synopsis; submit résumé. Submissions cannot be returned; submissions filed. Reports only if interested. Catalog free on request. Pays royalty or buys material outright.

Illustration/Animation: Hires illustrators for animation, live action, detailed renderings. Types of animation produced: cel animation, special effects, computer animation, video graphics. Submit cover letter, résumé, demo tape if available (VHS), color print samples. Art samples are filed if interested. Reports only if interested. Catalog is free on request. Rates negotiable, based on anticipated marketability of each project.

Tips: "As a nonprofit, evangelical ministry, we are most interested in developing working relationships with artists and illustrators who are anxious to use their gifts and talents to help propagate the life-changing truths of the Bible."

FINE ART PRODUCTIONS, 67 Maple St., Newburgh NY 12550. (914)561-5866. Director: Richie Suraci. Estab. 1989. "We cover every aspect of the film, video, publishing and entertainment industry." Audience: All viewers. Uses filmstrips, films, slide sets, videotapes, multimedia productions, any format needed. Children's productions: "1991 Great Hudson River Revival," illustrated by various artists (35mm film and print on environment, clearwater sailing ship); and "Wheel and Rock to Woodstock Bike Tour," written and illustrated by various artists (film, print, video on exercise, health, music and volunteerism). Percent of freelance illustrators/animators used varies.

Children's Writing: To submit, query with synopsis, or submit synopsis/outline, completed script, résumé. Submissions are filed, or returned with proper SASE. Reports in 1 month if interested. Pay is negotiated.

Illustration/Animation: Hires illustrators for animation, storyboarding, character development, live action, comprehensives, pencil testing. Types of animation produced: cel animation, clay animation, stop motion, special effects, computer animation, video graphics, motion control, live action. To submit, send cover letter, résumé, demo tape (VHS or ¾"), b&w print samples, color print samples, tearsheets, business card. Art samples are filed, or returned with proper SASE. Reports in 1 month if interested. Guidelines/catalog for SAE. Pay is negotiated.

HOME, INC., 731 Harrison Ave., Boston MA 02118. (617)266-1386. Director: Alan Michel. Estab. 1974. Nonprofit video production and postproduction facility which produces some teen television programming for the local Boston market. Audience: teenagers, teachers, instructors, education administrators, parents, social workers and court intervention professionals. Uses videotapes. Children's productions: "Going to Court," written by Ken Cheeseman, graphics by Alan Michel (¾" videotape puppet drama explaining the court for ages 3 through teens); "Stand Back from Crack," written by Young Nation, graphics by Alan Michel (¾" videotape, anti-drug public service video for teen and pre-teen). 90% of writing is by freelancers; 15% of illustrating/animating is by freelancers.

Children's Writing: Needs: scripts, curriculum, educational support material for videos, proposal writing for elementary through high school. Subjects include social or cultural content/sometimes career or health care oriented. To submit, send synopsis/outline and résumé. Submissions are filed and cannot be returned. Reports back only if interested. Payment negotiated/commissioned.

Illustration/Animation: Hires illustrators for storyboarding and graphics. Types of animation produced: special effects, computer animation and video graphics. To submit send cover letter, résumé, VHS demo tape, b&w and color print samples. Samples are filed and not returned. Reports back only if interested. Payment negotiated. Pays $250-4,000/project for specialized animation.

 The asterisk before a listing indicates the listing is new in this edition.

Tips: "We look for cooperative associates who have a commitment to quality and to their profession. This includes their presentation and follow-through in their dealings with us prior to project engagement."

I.N.I. ENTERTAINMENT GROUP, INC., Suite 700, 11150 Olympic Blvd., Los Angeles CA 90064. (310)479-6755. Fax: (310)479-3475. Chairman of the Board/CEO: Irv Holender. President: Michael Ricci. Estab. 1985. Producer/International Distributor. Audience: children of all ages. Uses films. Children's productions: "The Adventures of Oliver Twist," screenplay written by Fernando Ruiz (updated version of the Dickens tale for ages 4-12); "Alice Through the Looking Glass," screenplay written by James Brewer (updated and upbeat version of Carroll's book for ages 4-12). 100% of writing is by freelancers; 100% of illustrating/animating is by freelancers.

Children's Writing: Needs: animation scripts. "Anything from fantasy to fable." To submit, query with synopsis. Submit synopsis/outline, completed script, résumé. Submissions returned with proper SASE. Reports back only if interested. Pay varies.

Illustration/Animation: Type of animation produced: computer animation. To submit, send cover letter, résumé, demo tape (VHS), color print samples, business card. Art samples are filed, returned with proper SASE or not returned. Reports back only if interested.

Tips: "We are gearing to work with fairytales or classic stories. We look for concise retelling of older narratives with slight modifications in the storyline, while at the same time introducing children to stories that they would not necessarily be familiar with. We are currently in production doing 'International Family Classics, Part II.' We don't hire illustrators for animation. We hire the studio. The illustrators that we hire are used to create the advertising art."

JEF FILMS, 143 Hickory Hill Circle, Osterville MA 02655. (508)428-7198. President: Jeffrey H. Aikman. Estab. 1973. Production house. Audience: schools/libraries/video retailers. Produces slide sets, multimedia productions, films, videotapes. Children's productions: "The Reward," written and illustrated by Dennis Chatfield (film on animation aimed at pre-school); "Kiddy Kartoon Korner," written by Carolyn Elckoff, illustrated by Bill Wicksdorf (35mm film on animation aimed at ages 5-8.) Uses 20-24 freelance writers/year; purchases 20-24 writing projects/year. Uses 20-24 freelance artists/year; purchases 20-24 art projects/year.

Children's Writing: Needs: animation scripts for ages 5-8. Subjects include: tales with messages. To submit, send synopsis/outline. Submissions returned with proper SASE. Reports in 2 months. Buys outright.

Illustration/Animation: Hires illustrators for cel/video/clay animation, storyboarding, character development, live action, comprehensives, pencil testing. Types of animation produced: cel animation, clay animation, stop motion, special effects, video graphics, motion control, live action. To submit, send cover letter, résumé, demo tape (VHS), b&w print samples, color print samples, tearsheets, slides, promo sheet. Samples returned with proper SASE; samples filed. Reports in 2 months.

Tips: "Be persistent. We receive a great number of inquiries and can not always use everyone who submits work. Keep us updated on all new projects. Everything sent to us is kept on file. We look for unique styles unlike other works on market."

KENSINGTON FALLS ANIMATION, Suite 200, 2921 Duss Ave., Ambridge PA 15003. (412)266-0329. Fax: (412)266-4016. Producer: Michael Schwab. Estab. 1979. Animation studio. Audience: entertainment, educational. Uses films, videotapes. 100% of writing is by freelancers; 50% of illustrating/animating is by freelancers. Uses 1-5 freelance writers/year; purchases 1-3 writing projects/year. Uses 1-10 freelance artists/year.

Children's Writing: Needs: animation scripts, educational material. To submit, query with résumé. Submissions are filed. Reports back only if interested. Writers paid in accordance with Writer's Guild standards.

Illustration/Animation: Hires illustrators for character animation, storyboarding, character development, pencil testing, background illustration, ink and paint production. Types of animation produced: cel animation, computer animation, video graphics. To submit, send cover letter, résumé, demo tape (VHS or ¾"). Art samples returned with proper

Illustrators May Find Outlet in Children's Video

Motion pictures have dominated Jeffrey Aikman's life since he was 13 years old. It was at that tender age, that he started his own film company.

After receiving a Super 8 video projector as a Christmas gift from his father, a frustrated Aikman realized few 8mm films were available to show on it. So he headed straight to the doors of major Hollywood film studios and asked to buy rights to 8mm motion pictures. Many of the studios said yes to young Jeff, and he began to amass his private collection.

Twenty-two years later, JEF Films is booming. Aikman has an archive of about 35,000 motion pictures (the world's largest). He's a collector, film historian and film producer. And included in his company's offerings are children's productions,

Jeffrey Aikman

among them videotapes, slide sets, multimedia productions and television shows.

Aikman recognizes the trend in using licensed characters (like Mickey Mouse and Barney) in children's titles. "Unfortunately, the industry is going more and more that route," he says. "Consumers will mostly be going for recognized characters, and I don't think other shows are going to do as well in the future." Despite this forecast, Aikman perseveres in producing films for kids and has several projects on the horizon.

Recently, JEF Films has been experimenting with CD-ROMs. Aikman hopes to have his first consumer-oriented CD-ROM title out sometime this year. "I see more and more computer images, tons of stuff being done on desktop, instead of artists picking up a pen or pencil," he says. "I think that's going to be more and more the norm in kids' video."

With a fulltime staff of just four, JEF Films uses a lot of freelancers. "When we get going on a production, the number can change from four to about forty," Aikman says. Like many production companies, a portion of JEF Films' children's projects are produced for limited use in classrooms and libraries, and some are produced for mass consumption. Among their yearly offerings are two or three full-length features for kids, as well as 10 to 15 short subject films, half of which are animated and half live action.

Freelancers wishing to work for JEF Films or similar production houses should be persistent. "I get in so much stuff, and would assume that other companies in the industry do as well," says Aikman. "The people I'm hiring are constantly sending me updates to their portfolios or résumés—if they've done something, they'll write me a little note, and I think that helps a lot."

Aikman advises artists to show all the styles they're capable of when submitting to a production company. He may use artists for anything from clay animation to storyboards, pulling from the "tons" of submissions he receives through the mail. "I keep everything on file, give people a phone call, and try them out as I need them." He looks for creativity and something "a little bit out of the norm" in both artwork and scriptwriting. Although Aikman's company is a film producer, he rarely receives submissions in videotape form, and actually prefers reviewing printed pieces or work on disk.

Aikman's most recent children's project is a 65-episode, syndicated, half-hour television series for the six-and-under age-group. It's called *Brook Corner*. "Of the animated stuff we've done, a lot has been just limited animation, but this series has full animation, Disney-style," he says.

Brook Corner is set in England and all of the characters are animals. "It's set in the territory where Sherlock Holmes was, in London and the British countryside," Aikman explains. "The main character runs a detective agency. In each episode, the characters are going to be solving some kind of mystery." Viewers will be given clues in order to solve the puzzle along with the animal detectives.

"It's going to be very educational for children," says Aikman, "but it won't be educational to the point of being preachy or shoving it down kids' throats, and hopefully, kids will be able to pick up on it."

Contingent on the success of *Brook Corner*, Aikman would like to start two or three series of the same genre every year. Interested illustrators should spend less time in the libraries and bookstores and keep a watchful eye on their television sets.

—*Alice P. Buening*

© JEF Films.

Burrows (a mole), Squiggly (a weasel) and Harry Hedgehog are three English "gentlemen" detectives in *JEF Films'* Brook Corner, a syndicated, half-hour cartoon series for ages six and under. The animated trio gathers clues for each episode's mystery—which viewers try to solve along with them—as they attempt to outwit arch enemies Willie Whippet, Chutney Joe Ferret, Coy Lou and Crafty Sam.

SASE. Guidelines/catalog free on request. Pays: $10-50/hour for storyboarding/comp work; $20-50/hour for animation work.
Tips: "We offer apprenticeships."

KIDVIDZ: Special Interest Video for Children, 618 Centre St., Newton MA 02158. (617)965-3345. Partner: Jane Murphy. Estab. 1987. Home video publisher. Audience: preschool and primary-age children, 2-12 years. Produces videotapes. Children's productions: "Paws, Claws, Feathers and Fins: A Kids Video Guide to Pets," "Piggy Banks to Money Markets: A Kids Video Guide to Dollars and Sense," "Hey, What About Me: A Kids Video Guide for Brothers and Sisters of New Babies," "Kids Get Cooking: The Egg." Uses 2 freelance writers/year. Uses 3 freelance artists/year. Submissions filed.

KJD TELEPRODUCTIONS, 30 Whyte Dr., Voorhees NJ 08043. (609)751-3500. Fax: (609)751-7729. President: Larry Scott. Creative Director: Kim Davis. Estab. 1989. Location production services (Betacam SP) plus interformat edit and computer animation. Audience: industrial and broadcast. Uses slide sets, multimedia productions, videotapes. Children's productions: "Kidstuff," written by Barbara Daye, illustrated by Larry Scott (educational vignettes for ages 6-16). 10% of writing is by freelancers; 25% of animating/illustrating by freelancers.
Children's Writing: Needs: animation. To submit, query. Submissions are filed. Reports in 2 weeks. Pays royalty or buys material outright.
Illustration/Animation: Hires illustrators for animation. Types of animation produced: computer animation. To submit, send cover letter, résumé, demo tape (VHS or ¾"), b&w print samples, tearsheets, business card. Art samples are filed. Reports in 2 weeks. Pay varies.

MARSHMEDIA, P.O. Box 8082, Shawnee Mission KS 66208. (816)523-1059. Fax: (816)333-7421. Production Director: Joan K. Marsh. Estab. 1969. Production and marketing house. Audience: grades K-12. 100% of writing is by freelancers; 100% of illustrating/animating is by freelancers.
Children's Writing: Needs: educational materials, self-esteem stories for K-3: animal protagonist, significant geographical setting, strong non-sexist self-esteem message, 1,500 words. To submit, query with synopsis and submit completed scripts, résumé. Submissions returned with proper SASE. Buys material outright.
Illustration/Animation: To submit, send résumé and VHS demo tape. Art samples returned with proper SASE. Reports in 1 month.

NATIONAL GALLERY OF ART, Education Dept., Washington DC 20565. (202)737-4215. Fax: (202)789-2681. Head, Dept. of Teacher and School Programs: Kathy Walsh-Piper. Estab. 1941. Museum. Audience: teachers and students. Uses film strips, slide sets, videotapes, reproductions. Children's productions: "The Magic Picture Frame," written by Maura Clarkin (reproductions of paintings for NGA Museum Guide for ages 7-10). 50% of writing is by freelancers.
Children's Writing: Needs: educational material for all levels. Subjects include knowledge of art-making and art history. To submit, send résumé. Submissions are filed. Reports back only if interested. Guidelines/catalog not available. Buys material outright.

NEW & UNIQUE VIDEOS, 2336 Sumac Dr., San Diego CA 92105. (619)282-6126. Fax: (619)283-8264. Acquisitions Managers: Candy Love, Mark Schulze. Estab. 1985. Video production and distribution services. "Audience varies with each title." Uses films and videotapes. Children's productions: "Battle at Durango: The First-Ever World Mountain Bike Championships," written by Patricia Mooney, produced by Mark Schulze (VHS video mountain bike race documentary for 12 and over); "John Howard's Lessons in Cycling," written by John Howard, direction and camera by Mark Schulze (VHS video on cycling for 12 and over). 50% of writing is by freelancers; 85% of illustrating/animating is by freelancers.
Children's Writing: Needs: Completed videotape productions whose intended audiences may range from 1 and older. "Any subject matter focusing on a special interest that can

be considered 'new and unique.' " To submit, query. Submissions are returned with proper SASE. Reports in 2-3 weeks. Payment negotiable.

Illustration/Animation: Hires illustrators for film or video animation. Types of animation produced: computer animation and video graphics. To submit, send cover letter. Art samples returned with proper SASE. Reports back in 2-3 weeks. Payment negotiable.

Tips: "As more and more video players appear in homes across the world, and as the interest in special interest videos climbs, the demand for more original productions is rising meteorically."

TOM NICHOLSON ASSOC., INC., Eighth Floor, 295 Lafayette St., New York NY 10012. (212)274-0470. Estab. 1987. Interactive multimedia developer. Audience: children ages 6-13. Produces multimedia. Recently produced a worldwide series of multi-discipline educational titles (CD-ROM and floppy disk for ages 6-13). Uses 6-10 freelance writers/year. Uses 6-10 freelance artists/year.

Children's Writing: Needs: documentary film, animation scripts, educational/entertainment. Subjects include: science, humanities, nature, etc. To submit, query. Reports back only if interested. Pay is negotiable.

Illustration/Animation: Hires illustrators for animation, storyboarding, character development, live action, comprehensives. Types of animation produced: cel animation, computer animation. To submit, send VHS demo tape, tearsheets, promo sheets. Art samples not returned; samples filed. Reports back only if interested.

Tips: "Samples of past projects are essential and are the basis for all hiring decisions." Looks for "ability to present educational information in a clear, yet highly engaging, manner."

*NORTHWEST IMAGING & FX, #100, 2339 Columbia St., Vancouver, British Columbia V5Y-3Y3 Canada. (604)873-9330. Fax: (604)873-9339. General Manager: Alex Tkach. Estab. 1956. Animation studio and production facility. Audience: Children 2-15. Produces videotapes.

Children's Writing: Query with synopsis. Submissions filed. Reports in 1 month. Pays in accordance with Writer's Guild standards.

Illustration/Animation: Hires illustrators for cel by cel animation. Types of animation produced: cel animation, special effects, computer animation, motion control. Art samples not returned; art samples filed. Reports only if interested. Pay based on experience.

NTC PUBLISHING GROUP, 4255 W. Touhy Ave., Lincolnwood IL 60646. (708)679-5500. Fax: (708)679-2494. Art Director: Karen Christoffersen. Estab. 1960. Type of company: publisher. Audience: all ages. Uses film strips, multimedia productions, videotapes, books and audiocassettes. Children's production: "Let's Learn English Picture Dictionary," illustrations by Marlene Goodman (versions in Spanish, French, German and Italian for ages 7-11). 40% of writing is by freelancers; 50% of illustrating/animating is by freelancers.

Children's Writing: Needs: educational material for ages 5-14. Subjects include: "mostly foreign language, travel and English." To submit, include synopsis/outline, completed script, résumé and samples. Submission returned with proper SASE only. Reports in 2 months. Guidelines/catalog free. Pays writers in royalties or buys material outright—"depends on project."

Illustration/Animation: Hires illustrators for character development, comprehensives, pencil testing. Types of animation produced: stop motion, video graphics. To submit, send cover letter, résumé, color print samples, tearsheets, business card. Art samples returned with proper SASE. Reports in 2 months. Guidelines/catalog free.

Tips: Looking for "experienced professionals only with proven track record in the *educational* field."

OLIVE JAR ANIMATION, 35 Soldiers Field Place, Boston MA 02135. (617)783-9500. Fax: (617)783-9544. Executive Producer: Matthew Charde. Estab. 1984. Animation studio. Audience: all ages. Uses films, videotapes. 75% of writing is by freelancers; 75% of illustrating/animating is by freelancers.

Illustration/Animation: Hires illustrators for animation (all types), storyboarding, pencil testing, design, ink paint, sculpture, illustration. Types of animation produced: cel and clay animation, stop motion, special effects. To submit, send cover letter, résumé, demo tape, b&w print samples, color print samples, tearsheets, business card. Art samples are filed. Reports back only if interested. Pays flat rate according to job.

Tips: Looks for "someone who is really good at a particular style or direction as well as people who work in a variety of mediums. Attitude is as important as talent. The ability to work with others is very important."

MICHAEL SAND INC., 157 Aspinwall Ave., Brookline MA 02146. (617)566-5599. Fax: (617)566-3966. President: Michael Sand. Estab. 1964. Museum planning consultants. Audience: museum visitors. Produces multimedia productions, films, videotapes and interactive video disks. Children's productions: "The Big Dig," written by Doug Smith, illustrated by Robert Barner (hands-on highway planning for upper elementary-adult); and "Whale Discover Center," written by Richard Ellis, illustrated by Tom Vann-Bishop (computer games on marine ecology for lower elementary-adult). Uses 4 freelance writers/year; buys 12 writing projects/year. Uses 8 freelance artists/year; buys 30 art projects/year.

Children's Writing: Needs: animation scripts, educational material, documentaries (ages 5-8, 9-11, 12 and older). Subjects include: history, science, art. To submit, query with synopsis, completed script, résumé, samples. Submissions are returned with proper SASE; submissions sometimes filed. Reports in 1 month. Guidelines/catalog not available. Buys material outright (pay varies).

Illustration/Animation: Hires illustrators for computer-based animation, storyboarding, character development, comprehensives, pencil testing, exhibit renderings, models, 3-D illustration. Type of animation produced: cel animation, stop motion, special effects, computer animation, video graphics, motion control, live action. Submit cover letter, résumé, demo tape (VHS), b&w print samples, color print samples, tearsheets, slides, promo sheet. Samples somtetimes filed. Reports in 1 month if interested. Guidelines/catalog not available. Pays minimum $25/hour.

SEA STUDIOS, INC., 810 Cannery Row, Monterey CA 93940. (408)649-5152. Fax: (408)649-1380. Office Manager: Melissa Lewington. Estab. 1985. Natural history video production company. Audience: general. Uses multimedia productions, videotapes. 50% of writing is by freelancers; 50% of illustrating/animating is by freelancers.

Children's Writing: Needs: educational material—target age dependent on project. To submit, send résumé (no phone calls please). Submissions returned with proper SASE. Reports back only if interested. Pay negotiable.

Illustration/Animation: To submit, send cover letter, résumé (no phone calls please). Art samples returned with proper SASE. Reports back only if interested.

SHADOW PLAY RECORDS & VIDEO, P.O. Box 180476, Austin TX 78718. (512)345-4664. Fax: (512)345-9734. President: Peter J. Markham. Estab. 1984. Children's music publisher. Audience: families with children ages 3-10. Uses videotapes. Children's productions: "Joe's First Video," written by Joe Scruggs, illustrated by various artists (VHS children's music videos for preschool-10 years). 5% of writing is by freelancers; 100% of illustrating/animating by freelancers.

Children's Writing: Needs: poems or lyrics for children's songs. To submit, send query. "No unsolicited submissions accepted!" Submissions returned with proper SASE. Reports in 6 weeks. Pays royalty or buys material outright.

Illustration/Animation: Hires illustrators for animation, storyboarding, live action, pencil testing. Types of animation produced: cel animation, clay animation, stop motion, special

---

Always include a self-addressed, stamped envelope (SASE) with submissions within your own country. When sending material to other countries, include a self-addressed envelope (SAE) and International Reply Coupons (IRCs).

effects, computer animation, video graphics, live action. To submit, send cover letter, résumé, demo tape (VHS), color print samples, business card. Art samples returned with proper SASE. Reports in 6 weeks. Pay varies by project and ability of artist.

SISU HOME ENTERTAINMENT, 10th Floor, 18 W. 27th St., New York NY 10001. (212)779-1559. Fax: (212)779-7118. President: Haim Scheinger. Estab. 1988. Video and audio manufacturers (production, distribution). Audience: Children (educational videos and entertainment videos). Uses videotapes and audio. Children's productions: "Lovely Butterfly—Chanuka," written by IETV (Israel Educational TV), illustrated by IETV (Jewish holiday-program for ages 2-5). 25% of writing is by freelancers.
Children's Writing: Needs: publicity writing—all ages. To submit, arrange interview.
Illustration/Animation: Types of animation produced: clay animation, video graphics illustrations for video box covers. To submit, send résumé. Art samples filed. Reports back only if interested.

TREEHAUS COMMUNICATIONS, INC., 906 W. Loveland Ave., P.O. Box 249, Loveland OH 45140. (513)683-5716. President: Gerard A. Pottebaum. Estab. 1968. Production house. Audience: preschool through adults. Produces film strips, multimedia productions, videotapes. Children's production: "Seeds of Self-Esteem" series, written by Dr. Robert Brooks, Jane Ward and Gerard A. Pottebaum, includes two books for teachers, four in-service teacher training videos and 27 posters for children from primary grades through junior high school, distributed by American Guidance Service, Inc. 30% of writing is by freelancers; 30% of illustrating/animating is by freelancers.
Children's Writing: Needs: educational material/documentaries, for all ages. Subjects include: "social studies, religious education, documentaries on all subjects, but primarily about people who live ordinary lives in extraordinary ways." To submit, query with synopsis. Submissions returned with proper SASE. Reports in 1 month. Guidelines/catalog for SAE. Pays writers in accordance with Writer's Guild standards.
Tips: Illustrators/animators: "Be informed about movements and needs in education, multi-cultural sensitivity." Looks for "social values, originality, competency in subject, global awareness."

*PORTER VERSFELT & ASSOCIATES TELEVISION PRODUCTIONS, P.O. Box 5262, Atlanta GA 30307. (800)946-4646. PIN # 2487647. Executive Producer/President: Porter Versfelt III. Estab. 1984. Video, television and interactive multimedia production company. Audience: all ages (depends upon the project). Produces multimedia productions, films and videotapes. Recent children's productions: "Admissions Decisions: Should Immigrants Be Restricted?", written by Jane Stuart (educational, national public policy documentary video for ages 15 and above); "Behind Closed Doors" (public service announcement/anti-drug abuse message video aimed at ages 10-25). Uses 5 freelance writers/year; buys 5 writing projects/year. Uses 5 freelance artists/year; buys 5 art projects/year.
Children's Writing: Needs: Educational material, documentaries, television series. All ages. Query with synopsis; submit synopsis/outline, résumé and video demo reel of past work on VHS. Submissions returned with proper SASE; submissions filed. Reports in 1 month. Guidelines/catalog free on request. Buys material outright; pays $500 (negotiable).
Illustration/Animation: Hires illustrators for computer-generated animation, storyboarding, character development and live action. Types of animation produced: computer animation and video graphics. Submit cover letter, résumé, demo tape (VHS), color print samples and promo sheet. Art samples returned with proper SASE; art samples filed. Reports in 1 month. Guidelines/catalog free on request. Pays $25/hour for storyboarding/comp work; $100/frame for storyboarding/comp work; $500/project for storyboarding/comp work; $25/hour for animation work; $100/cel for animation work; $500/project for animation work; $50/hour for specialized animation work; $150/frame or cel for specialized animation; $1,000/project for specialized animation. (All figures negotiable.)
Tips: "I am only interested in freelance artists. I hire on a per project basis so I am interested in seeing what talent is out there wherever you are. I am also looking for solid creative concepts for TV series, feature motion pictures and educational videos and documentaries, so I am receptive to concept submissions. I am interested in all subjects, styles

and capabilities. Interactive multi-media and interactive television is the real growth industry for the foreseeable future. I am very interested in concepts and capabilities in this area, including computer programming. I want to publish children's books (both educational and edutainment) on CD-ROM and other interactive technologies. Abilities in this area are especially valuable to me."

Audiotape Markets

In these listings, ten of which are new to this edition, you'll find companies with a range of offerings. Several listings, such as Barron's Educational Series and Dutton's Children's Books, publish exclusively story tapes. More often, however, the companies listed publish and produce music as well as stories. In either case, these companies provide opportunities for songwriters and writers to showcase their work on tape or compact disk.

Among the record companies listed you'll find both large producers and distributors, like Music for Little People and Peter Pan Industries (see Insider Report on page 244), as well as smaller independent studios such as Teeter Tot Records (new to this edition). Included, too, are a few kids' radio stations looking for stories, plays and tunes to fill their airwaves. For more information about the children's entertainment industry, see the Audiovisual & Audiotape introduction on page 225.

ALISO CREEK PRODUCTIONS, INC., P.O. Box 8174, Van Nuys CA 91409. (818)787-3203. President: William Williams. Record company, book publisher. Estab. 1987.
Music: Releases 2 LPs-cassettes; 2 CDs/year. Records 20 children's songs/year. Works with composers, lyricists, team collaborators. For songs recorded pays musicians/artists on record contract and songwriters on royalty contract. Write first and obtain permission to submit material. Submit 3-5 songs with lyric sheets on demo cassette. SASE/IRC for return of submission. Reports in 3 weeks. Recorded songs: "Brontosaurus Stomp," by Bob Menn and William Williams, recorded on Aliso Creek Records label (dixieland music for ages 3-8); "What Make a Car Go, Dad?," by Bob Menn and William Williams, recorded on Aliso Creek Records label (Gilbert & Sullivan-type music for ages 3-8).
Music Tips: "We're looking for music in a variety of styles that doesn't talk down to children or isn't preachy, but does convey positive values or educate."
Stories: Publishes 2 book/cassette packages/year; 2 cassettes/CDs/year. 100% of stories are fiction. Will consider all types of fiction, but story and songs must be related. "We publish musical plays on cassette aimed at ages 3-8." Will consider all types of nonfiction aimed at ages 3-8. Authors are paid negotiable royalty based on retail price; work purchased outright. Submit both cassette tape and ms. Reports on queries in 3 weeks. Catalog is free for #10 SASE. Published: *Take a Trip with Me*, by Bob Menn and William Williams, narrated by Kevin Birkbeck and Katy Morkri (ages 3-8); *Move!*, by Bob Men and William Williams, narrated by Katy Morkri (ages 3-8, a family adjusts to moving to a different city).
Story Tips: "We publish song and story cassettes with an illustrated lyric book so we need writers and illustrators to create a unified product."

AMERICAN MELODY, P.O. Box 270, Guilford CT 06437. (203)457-0881. President: Phil Rosenthal. Music publisher, record company (American Melody), recording studio, book publisher. Estab. 1985.
Music: Releases 4 LPs/year. Member of BMI. Publishes 20 children's songs/year; records 30 children's songs/year. Works with composers, lyricists, team collaborators. For music published pays standard royalty of 50%; for songs recorded pays musicians/artists on record contract, musicians on salary for inhouse studio work, and songwriters on royalty contract. Call first and obtain permission to submit material. Submit demo cassette with lyric sheet. SASE/IRC for return of submission. Reports in 1 month. Recorded songs: "The Bremen Town Song," by Max Showalter and Peter Walker, recorded by Max Showalter on American Melody label (folk music for ages 2-10); "My Little Dog and Me," by Phil Rosenthal, recorded by Phil Rosenthal on American Melody label (bluegrass music for ages 1-8); and

"I Can't Wait for Spring," by Sarah Pirtle, recorded by Linda Schrade and Dave Kiphuth on American Melody label (folk for ages 3-10).
Music Tips: "Submit as nice a demo as possible, with understandable lyrics."

ART AUDIO PUBLISHING COMPANY/TIGHT HI-FI SOUL MUSIC, Dept. CWIM, 9706 Cameron Ave., Detroit MI 48211. (313)893-3406. President: Albert M. Leigh. Music publisher. Estab. 1962.
Music: Works with composers and lyricists. For music published pays standard royalty of 50%. Submit demo tape by mail; unsolicited submissions OK. Submit demo cassette with 1-3 songs, lyric and/or lead sheet. SASE/IRC for return of submission. Reports in 2 weeks.
Music Tips: "We are looking for songs with a strong hook, strong words. We are looking for hits, such as "Little Teddy Bear," "Duckey Lucky" or "Chicken Little." Can be songs or musical stories for movie soundtracks. Videocassette top sales and rentals and also for major record companies, uptempo dance. All lyrics are up-front: words are clearly understandable."

***AUDIO-FORUM,** 96 Broad St., Guilford CT 06437. (203)453-9794. Fax: (203)453-9774. Publicity & Reviews: Nancy Grant. Estab. 1972.
Stories: "We publish for children foreign language educational materials on audio/video cassettes. Also children's level educational cassettes about music." Recently published story tapes: *Phrase-a-Day English for Hispanic Children*, by Judith White, narrated by Judith White and Susan Gomez-Ibanez (ages 4-8, language teaching program); *French Songs for Beginners*, by Charlotte Crosnier, narrated by Charlotte Crosnier and French children (ages 8-15, foreign language learning aid).

***BARRON'S EDUCATIONAL SERIES,** 250 Wireless Blvd., Haupauge NY 11788. (516)434-3311. Fax: (516)434-3723. Managing Editor/Director of Acquisitions: Grace Freedson. Book publisher. Estab. 1940.
Stories: Publishes 3 book/cassette packages/year. For fiction, will consider foreign language. Pays authors royalty. Query. Catalog free for SAE. Ms guidelines free for SASE. Recently recorded story tapes: *Bon Jour Mes Amis*, by Irene Bowers (ages 3-5, foreign language).

BRENTWOOD MUSIC, INC., 316 Southgate Court, Brentwood TN 37027. (615)373-3950. Fax: (615)373-8612. Creative Director: Dale Mathews. Music publisher, book publisher, record company, children's video. Estab. 1980.
Music: Releases 40 cassettes/year; 24-30 CDs/year. Member of ASCAP, BMI and SESAC. Publishes 60-120 children's songs/year. Works with composers. Pays standard royalty of 50% of net receipts for music published. Submit demo cassette tape by mail; unsolicited submissions OK; 2 songs and lyric sheet or lead sheet. "No music can be returned unless you include a self-addressed, stamped envelope. Do not send stamps or postage only. If you want it back, send an *envelope* big enough to hold all material with the *proper* postage affixed. No exceptions." Reports in 3-6 months. Recently recorded songs: "Once Upon an Orchestra," by Don and Lorie Marsh on Designer Music label (orchestral story—like "Peter & The Wolf," ages 3-7); "It's A Cockadoodle Day," by Janet McMahan-Wilson, Tom McBryde, Mary Jordan on Brentwood Kids Co. label (sing along for ages 2-7).
Stories: Will consider fictional animal, fantasy or adventure aimed at preschool through 3rd or 4th grades. Author's pay is negotiable, depending on project. Query. Reports in 3 months. Recently recorded story tapes: *The Leap Year Frog*, by Freddy Richardson, narrated by Mother Goose (ages 2-6, birthday); *How the Donkey Got His Tail*, by Freddy Richardson, narrated by Mother Goose (ages 2-6, birthday).
Tips: "Songs and stories with a Christian or Bible theme fill more of our product development needs than other topics or themes."

BRIDGER PRODUCTIONS, INC., P.O. Box 8131, 4150 Gloryview, Jackson WY 83001. (307)733-7871. Contact: Mike Emmer. Music publisher, film and video production corporation. Estab. 1990.

Music: Releases 2 singles/year. Publishes 1 children's song/year. Hires staff writers for children's music. Works with composers and lyricists, team collaborators. Pays contracted price. Submit demo tape by mail; unsolicited submissions OK. Submit demo cassette, VHS or ¾" SP videocassette if available with 3 songs. Include lyric sheet, lead sheet. Cannot return material. Reports in 3 weeks. We've recorded mostly adults music lately but we are interested in contracting artists to record in our studios—we pay a one time (buyout) fee."
Music Tips: "Songs must be in conjunction with a film/video project for us to be interested."
Stories: Publishes 1 book/cassette package/year. 100% of stories are nonfiction. Will consider all genres of nonfiction. Pays contracted price. Reports on queries/ms in 3 weeks.
Story Tips: "Stories must be in conjunction with a film/video paying project."

BROADCAST PRODUCTION GROUP, 1901 S. Bascom Ave., Campbell CA 95008. (408)559-6300. Fax: (408)559-6382. Creative Director: Dan Korb. Video and film production group. Estab. 1986.
Music: Hires staff writers for children's music. Works with composers and/or lyricists, team collaborators. "Our projects are on a single-purchase basis." Pays per project for songs recorded. Submit demo tape by mail; unsolicited submissions okay. Submit demo cassette, résumé and videocassette if available. Not necessary to include lyric or lead sheets. Reports in 3 weeks.

CENTER FOR THE QUEEN OF PEACE, Suite 412, 3350 Highway 6, Houston TX 77478. Music publisher, book/video publisher and record company. Record labels include Cosmotone Records, Cosmotone Music. Estab. 1984.
Music: Releases 1 single, 1 12-inch single and 1 LP/year. Member of ASCAP. Works with team collaborators. Pays negotiable royalty for music published; for songs recorded pays musicians on salary for inhouse studio work, songwriters on royalty contract. Write for permission to submit material. "Will respond only if interested."

CHILDREN'S MEDIA PRODUCTIONS, P.O. Box 40400, Pasadena CA 91114. (818)797-5462. Fax: (818)797-7524. President: C. Ray Carlson. Video publisher. Estab. 1983.
Music: Works with composers and/or lyricists. For songs recorded pays musicians/artists on record contract. Write for permission to submit material.
Tips: "We use only original music and songs for videos.We serve markets worldwide and must often record songs in foreign languages. So avoid anything provincially *American*. Parents choose videos that will '*teach* for a lifetime' (our motto) rather than entertain for a few hours. State concisely what the 'message' is in your concept and why you think parents will be interested in it. How will it satisfy new FCC regulations concerning 'educational content?' We like ethnic and/or multi-racial stories and illustrations."

THE CHRISTIAN SCIENCE PUBLISHING SOCIETY, One Norway Street, Boston MA 02115. (617)450-2033. Fax: (617)450-2017. General Publications Product Manager: Rhoda M. Ford. Book publisher, "but we do issue some recordings." Estab. 1898.
Music: Works with team collaborators on audiocassettes. Submit query letter with proposal, references, résumé. Does not return unsolicited submissions unless requested. Reports in 3-4 months.
Stories: 100% of stories are nonfiction. Will consider nonfiction for beginning readers, juveniles, teens based on the Bible (King James Version). Authors are paid royalty or work purchased outright, "negotiated with contract." Submit query letter with proposal, references and résumé. Include Social Security number. Reports on queries in 3-4 months. Trade Kit available.
Tips: "Since we are part of The First Church of Christ, Scientist, all our publications are in harmony with the teachings of Christian Science."

CREDENCE CASSETTES, 115 E. Armour Blvd., Kansas City MO 64111. (816)531-0538. Fax: (816)531-7466. Director: Clarence Thomson. Religious/spoken word recording company. Estab. 1973.

Stories: Publishes 20 book/cassette packages/year. 10% of stories are fiction; 90% nonfiction. Will consider religious Kindergarten-adult. Authors are paid 10% royalty based on retail price. Submit cassette tape or story. Reports on queries in 3 weeks. Catalog free on request. Ms guidelines not available. Recorded story tapes: *The Friendship Song*, by Karen Blomgren/C. Thomson, narrated by Karen Blomgren (ages 6-12, story of bird who couldn't sing); *The Pine Tree's Christmas Dream*, by C. Thomson, narrated by Karen Blomgren (ages 4-10, a pine tree becomes Christmas tree).

Tips: Looks for "religious, but symbolic—not fundamentalist, 15-20 minutes long. We're just starting into children's fiction (we've done adult Christian material for 20 years.)"

DERCUM AUDIO, P.O. Box 1425, West Chester PA 19380. (610)889-2410. Fax: (610)889-2412. Contact: Amy Lewis. Audio book producer. Estab. 1985.

Stories: For fiction, will consider fantasy, spy, mystery, etc. Recently produced story tapes: *Culpepper Adventure Series* (6 books), by Gary Paulsen, narrated by Bill Fantini (ages 8-14, mystery/adventure). Pays authors 10% maximum royalties based on wholesale price. Offers $500 average advance. Query. Submit outline/synopsis and sample chapters. Reports on queries/mss in 2-3 months.

DOVE AUDIO, Suite 203, N. Cañon Dr., Beverly Hills CA 90210. (310)273-7722. Fax: (310)273-0365. Customer Service Supervisor: Maryann Camarillo. Audio book publisher. Estab. 1985.

Stories: Publishes approximately 100/year (audio tapes only). 50% of stories are fiction; 50% nonfiction. Submit through agent only. Reports in 2 weeks. Catalog is free on request. Recorded story tapes include *Enchanted Tales*, narrated by Audrey Hepburn (ages 5 and up); *Rap, Rap, Rapunzel*, narrated by Patti Austin (ages 3 and up).

DUTTON CHILDREN'S BOOKS, 375 Hudson St., New York NY 10014. (212)366-2600. Fax: (212)366-2011. President and Publisher: Christopher Franceschelli. Book publisher.

Stories: Publishes 3 book/cassette packages/year. 100% of stories are fiction. Will consider animal and fantasy. Story tapes aimed at ages 2-10. Authors are paid 5-12% royalties based on retail price; outright purchase of $2,000-20,000; royalty inclusive. Average advance $3,000. Submit outline/synopsis and sample chapters through agent. Reports on queries in 3 weeks; on mss in 6 months. Catalog is available for 8×11 SAE and 8 first-class stamps. Ms guidelines available for #10 SASE. Children's story tapes include *Noah's Ark*, narrated by James Earl Jones.

Tips: "Do not call publisher. Get agent. Celebrity readers sell."

ROY EATON MUSIC INC., 595 Main St., Roosevelt Island NY 10044. (212)980-9046. Fax: (212)980-9068. President: Roy Eaton. Music publisher, TV and radio music production company. Estab. 1982.

Music: Member of BMI. Hires staff writers for children's TV commercial music only. Works with composers, lyricists, team collaborators. For music published pays standard royalty of 50%. Write or call for permission to submit material. Submit demo cassette with lyric sheet.

Tips: "Primarily interested in commericals for children."

FINE ART PRODUCTIONS, 67 Maple St., Newburgh NY 12550. (914)561-5866. Contact: Richie Suraci. Music publisher, record company, book publisher. Estab. 1989.

Music: Member of ASCAP and BMI. Publishes and records 1-2 children's songs/year. Hires staff writers for children's music. Works with composers, lyricists, team collaborators. For music published pays standard royalty of 50% or other amount; for songs recorded pays musicians/artists on record contract, musicians on salary for inhouse studio work, songwriters on varying royalty contract. Submit ½" demo tape by mail; unsolicited submis-

---

Refer to the Business of Children's Writing & Illustrating for up-to-date marketing, tax and legal information.

sions OK. Submit demo cassette. Not neccessary to include lyric or lead sheets. SASE/IRC for return of submission. Reports in 3-4 months.
Stories: Publishes 1 book/cassette package and 1 audio tape/year. 50% of stories are fiction; 50% nonfiction. Will consider all genres for all age groups. Authors are paid varying royalty on wholesale or retail price. Submit both cassette tape and ms. Reports in 3-4 months. Catalog is not available. Ms guidelines free with SASE.

GORDON MUSIC CO. INC./PARIS RECORDS, P.O. Box 2250, Canoga Park CA 91306. (818)883-8224. Owner: Jeff Gordon. Music publisher, record company. Estab. 1950.
Music: Releases 3-4 CDs/year. Member of ASCAP and BMI. Publishes 6-8 children's songs/year; records 10-15 children's songs/year. Works with composers, lyricists, team collaborators. For music published pays standard royalty of 50%; for songs recorded, arrangement made between artist and company. Call first and obtain permission to submit. Submit 3-4 videocassette tapes, lyric and lead sheets. Does not return unsolicited submissions. Recorded song: "Izzy, the Pest of the West," recorded by Champ on Paris label.

HIGH WINDY AUDIO, 260 Lambeth Walk, Fairview NC 28730. (704)628-1728. Fax: (704)628-4435. Owner: Virginia Callaway. Record company.
Music: Releases 2 LPs-cassettes/year; 2 CDs/year. Member of BMI, AFTRA. Records 12 children's songs/year. Works with storytellers, musicians. Pays musicians/artists on record contract plus one time studio work.
Stories: Publishes 2 CDs/year. 100% of stories are fiction. Will consider animal, fantasy, history, scary, sports, spy/mystery/adventure. Authors are paid royalty based on retail price. Query. Reports on queries in 3 weeks. Catalog free on request. Submission guidelines not available. Recently recorded story tapes: *Hairyman*, narrated by David Holt (ages 4-adult, folktale); *The Boy Who Loved Frogs*, narrated by Jaay O'Callahan (ages 4-adult, animal story).
Tips: "Call first."

*HIGH-TOP PRODUCTIONS, #925, 6290 Sunset Blvd., Hollywood CA 90028. (213)957-5600. Fax: (213)957-3153. Publisher: Donald Allen. Audio book publisher. Estab. 1990.
Stories: Publishes 35 book/cassette packages/year. 25% of stories are fiction; 75% nonfiction. For fiction/nonfiction, will consider sports aimed at ages 5-14. Pays authors 10% royalty. Offers $300 average advance. Submit complete ms, both cassette tape and ms. Reports on queries/mss in 6 weeks. Catalog free on request. Ms guidelines free for SASE. Recently recorded story tapes: *Willies Last at Bat*, by Sussian Koulor and narrated by Sussian Koulor (ages 8-14, sports).
Tips: "We like sports themes for our children's stories. The book should have a specific moral with a very good story base."

*HOME, INC., 731 Harrison Ave., Boston MA 02118. (617)266-1386. Director: Alan Michel. Nonprofit video production company. Estab. 1973.
Music: Paymaster through to AFTRA/SAG. Works with composers, lyricists, team collaborators. For music published pay negotiated on a project-to-project basis. Submit demo tape by mail; unsolicited submissions OK. Submit demo cassette with 3-6 songs. "I am usually looking for versatility and range in demos submitted." Cannot return material. Reports back only if interested in the work. Recorded songs: "Going to Court," music only by Don Dinicola, recorded by Don Dinicola used on video tape as sound track (country for preschool-preteen); "Stand Back From Crack," by Young Nation, recorded by Frank King, used on video tape (rap for teen).
Music Tips: "We are not a publisher or record company. We work with independent publishers who are attempting to meet some social need through communications. We specialize in developing teen- and preteen-related programming."
Stories: Publishes 5 videos/year. 100% of stories are fiction. Will consider drama, music videos, public service announcements, training for preteens and teens. For nonfiction, considers animal, education and others as may be needed. Payment negotiated. Submit outline/synopsis and sample chapters with résumé. If interested, reports in 2-3 weeks (if solicited only).

KKDS-AM 1060–THE IMAGINATION STATION, P.O. Box 57760, Salt Lake City UT 84157. (801)262-5624. Fax: (801)266-1510. Program Director: Steve Carlson. Radio station. Estab. 1967.
Music: Member of ASCAP, BMI, SESAC. Write for permission to submit material. Submit demo cassette. Send finished cassette to station.
Tips: "We play children's stories on storytime each day. Play music that fits the station. Call first."

LISTENING LIBRARY, INC., One Park Ave., Old Greenwich CT 06870. (203)637-3616. Fax: (203)698-1998. Contact: Editorial Review Committee. Spoken word recording company.
Stories: Buys material outright. Submit completed script. SASE/IRC for return of submission. Reports in 2 months. Recorded books: *A Wrinkle in Time*, by Madeleine L'Engle (ages 9-12); and *Superfudge*, by Judy Blume (ages 5-12).
Tips: "We primarily produce works that are already published. However, we occasionally find that an audio project will arise out of original material submitted to us."

*MAMA-T ARTISTS/THE FOLKTELLERS, P.O. Box 2898, Asheville NC 28802. (704)258-1113. Contact: Rose Smith. Inhouse publisher of storytelling tapes. Estab. 1981.
Stories: Publishes audio tapes and video. 70% of stories are fiction; 30% nonfiction. Will consider all genres for varying age groups. Authors are paid 2-8% royalties based on retail price; or work purchased outright. Negotiable. Average advance $100. Submit demo or mss—"we perform the stories ourselves." Reports on queries/mss in 2-3 months. Catalog free on request. Recorded story audiotapes: *Stories for the Road*, narrated by The Folktellers (traditional and contemporary stories for children of all ages); *Christmas at the Homeplace* (family concert of funny and heartwarming Appalachian stories and Christmas carols). Recently recorded videotapes: *Pennies Pets & Peanut Butter* (30 minute concert of funfilled stories for children ages 4-11; performed live with PBS audience of students grades 2-5).

MEDICINE SHOW MUSIC, INC., 19 Beech Court, Fishkill NY 12524. Phone/fax: (914)896-9359. President: Karan Bunin. Estab. 1991.
Music: Member of BMI. Publishes and records 12 children's songs/year. Hires staff writers for children's music. Works with composers and/or lyricists, team collaborators. Pay varies with projects. Submit demo tape by mail; unsolicited submissions OK. Submit demo cassette (videocassette if available), press kits. Include lyric sheet. Cannot return material. Recently recorded songs: "Skating on the Moon," by Karan Bunin and Jeff Waxman, recorded by Karan & The Musical Medicine Show on 200M Express/BMG Kidz (children's music for ages preschool-adult); "Coming to Your Town," by Karan Bunin, recorded by Karan & The Musical Medicine Show on 200M Express/BMG Kidz (Children's music for ages preschool-adults).
Tips: Send tapes with information about project and intentions (goals). Follow up with phone call 2 weeks after sending.

MELODY HOUSE, INC., 819 NW 92nd St., Oklahoma City OK 73114. (405)840-3383. Fax: (405)840-3384. President: Stephen Fite. Record company. Estab. 1972.
Music: Releases 6 LPs/year. Records 72 children's songs/year. Works with composers, lyricists, team collaborators. For songs recorded pays musicians on salary for inhouse studio work or standard mechanical royalty per song; pay songwriters on royalty contract (10%). Submit demo tape by mail; unsolicited submissions OK. Submit demo cassette (5 songs or more) with lyric and lead sheets. SASE/IRC for return of submission. Reports in 2 months. Recently recorded songs: "Bop 'Til You Drop," written and recorded by Mr. Al on Melody House label (technopop for ages 3-9); "Sleighbells Jingling," written and recorded by Fred Koch on Melody House label (children's folk for ages 3-8).
Tips: "The music and the lyrics should reach out and grab the child's attention. Children are much more sophisticated in their listening than their parents were at the same age. Children's music is definitely taking on the characteristics of the pop market with the sounds and even the hype in some cases. Even some of the messages are now touching on

Music Market Open Despite Return of Licensing

As the oldest independent record company in the United States, Peter Pan Industries has entertained children for more than 50 years, selling more than 100 million records and tapes. With such a long history in the industry, the company has seen trends come and go, and knows what it takes to keep kids entertained.

Joseph Porrello, senior vice president of product development at Peter Pan, sees the children's music industry growing by leaps and bounds. "Today's children's music market is huge, it's phenomenally growing," he says. "On the video side alone, it dominates a large percentage of every video sold. Forty percent of the people who walk into Kmart and buy a video, buy a children's video."

Joseph Porrello

One of the biggest trends in the children's market recently is the return of licensed characters. "Licensed product is coming back to the forefront again," Porrello says. "When I first started here in 1980, I produced audio products with the Flintstones, Jetsons and Scooby Doo. Soon that faded out with the emergence of artists like Raffi; Sharon, Lois and Bram; and other performers. And now interest in that is down, and licensed products such as the Power Rangers and Barney are coming back."

With all the emphasis on licensed characters, it may seem like original performers and songwriters are being pushed aside. But Porrello sees it differently. "I think it's definitely helping the industry," he says of licensed product, "because with the licensed characters, merchandising programs are in effect. When you have over 300 items featuring the Power Rangers available, from lunchboxes to bed sheets, that brings people into the stores who will ultimately buy other products." Those other products are most likely audio and video by children's artists and songwriters.

When looking for artists for the Peter Pan label, Porrello has definite ideas about what works in today's market. "We look for what I call the Bruce Springsteens or Billy Joels for kids," he says. "More than someone sitting on a stool playing guitar—someone who has charisma. Songs have to be very hooky and very sing-along." And to compete with the likes of Raffi or Barney, songs have to work on the toughest critics—kids. "If there were three or four writers or artists we were interested in, and I had to make the decision to sign one, I'd do a focus study," he says. "I would go into daycare centers, run a cassette by a few hundred kids over a month's period and get their reactions." If it's a big hit with them, Peter Pan's interested.

For a children's performer or writer just starting out in the business, Porrello sees the odds of breaking into the children's market as better than the rock or pop markets. "I think it's easier," he says. "Odds are five thousand to one that a band could become another Guns 'N' Roses. To become another children's artist like Raffi, I'd say it's one thousand to one."

Connections within the industry are vital to the aspiring children's artist, and the only way to achieve them is through finding an audience and attracting the attention of those working in the industry. Porrello says about 90 percent of new children's acts are signed through word-of-mouth within companies. "Perhaps Raffi would say, 'I just heard this new children's performer, she opened up for me at the Hollywood Bowl, she's wonderful,' " he says. "And the label would listen to Raffi and sign that performer. Most signings take place like that or through a big-time management company that has affiliations with record companies. Cold turkey, just sending out tapes, it's unbelievably hard."

But it's hardly impossible. Porrello advises beginning performers and songwriters to test their work wherever they can and attempt to build an audience. "In any market, you must have perseverance," he says. "You have to learn to accept the word 'no.' If you're really going to go after it, you have to keep driving and driving; sooner or later you'll break through. Go to the elementary schools as a children's performer. Offer a free concert for the second grade and see what kind of reaction you get. If you see the kids' faces light up, and the teachers want you back, then you know you've got something."

— Cindy Laufenberg

Rock-n-Troll, donning mirrored shades and roller skates, appears with his friends on the cover of this songbook which accompanies the Trollies Radio Show Sing-A-Long *cassette. The Trollies is the supergroup of singing Trolls created by Peter Pan Industries. Their sing-a-long cassette features covers of such timeless tunes as "Kokomo" by the Beach Trolls and "Old Time Rock 'N' Troll," as well as Trollies originals, interspersed with witty radio repartee from WTROLL deejays.*

© 1992 Peter Pan Industries.

issues such as divorce/separation, the environment and social consciousness, both in the U.S. and the world."

MUSIC FOR LITTLE PEOPLE, P.O. Box 1460, Redway CA 95560. (707)923-3991. Fax: (707)923-3241. Contact: Barbara Ellis. Record company.
Music: Releases 6-12 cassettes/year; 6-12 CDs/year. Records 40 children's songs/year. Works with composers and/or lyricists, team collaborators. Pays musicians/artists on record contract. Write for permission to submit material. Cannot return material. Reports in 2-6 months. Recently recorded songs: "Water from Another Time," by John McCutcheon, recorded by Scott Petito (folk for ages 3-8); "Three Little Birds," by Bob Marley, recorded at Banquet Studios—Santa Rosa on Music for Little People (reggae, ages 3-8).
Stories: Publishes 2-6 book/cassette packages/year. 100% nonfiction. For nonfiction, considers cultural and musical history; biography (ages 3-8). Work purchased outright, $500 minimum. Query. Reports on queries in 2-6 months. Catalog is free on request. Submission guidelines not available.

NATIVE AMERICAN PUBLIC BROADCASTING CONSORTIUM, INC., P.O. Box 83111, Lincoln NE 68501. (402)472-3522. Fax: (402)472-8675. Public television and radio production and distribution. Estab. 1977.
Music: Call first and obtain permission to submit material. Submit demo cassette, VHS videocassette if available. Reports in 3 months.
Stories: Will consider anything about Native Americans for all audiences. Catalog free on request. Submission guidelines not available.
Story Tips: "We are looking for programs that can be aired on public radio and on the American Indian Radio On Satellite Network (AIROS) and by or about Native Americans. There is a growing demand for good multicultural programs as well as quality children's multicultural programs. With more and more states passing legislation that mandates multicultural programs be incorporated into the school curriculums, the demand has become tremendous."

OAK STREET MUSIC, 1067 Sherwin Rd., Winnipeg, Manitoba R3H 0T8 Canada. (204)957-0085. Contact: Lynn Burshtien. Record company. Estab. 1987.
Music: Releases 8 LPs-cassettes/year; 3 CDs/year. Member of SOCAN and PROCAN. Publishes and records 10 children's songs/year. Works with team collaborators. Pays standard royalty of 50% for music published; for songs recorded pays musicians/artists on record contract; songwriters on royalty contract. Submit demo tape by mail; unsolicited submissions OK. Include demo cassette (VHS videocassette if available); 3-5 songs, lead sheets. SASE/IRC for return of submission. Recently recorded songs: "What a Day," by F. Penner and D. Donahue, recorded by Fred Penner on Oak Street Music label (children's music for ages 3-7); and "Company Coming," by F. Penner, recorded by Fred Penner on Oak Street Music label (children's music for ages 3-7).
Stories: Publishes 2 book/cassette packages/year. 50% of stories are fiction; 50% nonfiction. Interested in all types of fiction for children ages 5-8. Interested in all types of nonfiction. Submit both cassette tape and ms.
Tips: "Listen to our products for an idea of what we need or choose a specific artist like Fred Penner to write for."

PETER PAN INDUSTRIES, 88 St. Francis St., Newark NJ 07105. (201)344-4214. Fax: (201)344-0465. Vice President of Sales: Shelly Rudin. Music publisher, record company. Record labels include Parade Music, Compose Music, Peter Pan. Estab. 1927.
Music: Releases 20 singles/year; 45 CDs/year. Member of ASCAP and BMI. Publishes 50 children's songs/year; records 80-90 songs/year. Works with composers, lyricists, team collaborators. For music published pays standard royalty of 50%; for songs recorded pays musicians/artists on record contract, songwriters on royalty contract. Submit a 15 IPS reel-to-reel demo tape or VHS videocassette by mail—unsolicited submissions OK. SASE (or SAE and IRCs) for return of submissions. Reports in 4-6 weeks.
Stories: Publishes 12 book/cassette packages/year. 90% of stories are fiction; 10% nonfiction. Will consider all genres of fiction and nonfiction aimed at 6-month to 9-year-olds.

Authors are paid in royalties based on wholesale price. Query. Reports on queries in 4-6 weeks. Book catalog, ms guidelines free on request.
Tips: "Tough business but rewarding. Lullabies are very popular."

PRAKKEN PUBLICATIONS, INC., Suite 1, 275 Metty Dr., P.O. Box 8623, Ann Arbor MI 48103. (313)769-1211. Fax: (313)769-8383. Publisher: George Kennedy. Magazine publisher. Estab. 1934.
Stories: Publishes 4 book/cassette packages/year. 100% of stories nonfiction. Will consider any genre of nonfiction (ages 3-8). Authors are paid 10% royalty based on net sales. Other payment negotiable. Advance not standard practice but possibly negotiable. Submit outline/synopsis and sample chapters. Reports on queries in 2 weeks; on mss in 6 weeks if return requested and SASE enclosed. Catalog free on request. Submission free with SASE.
Tips: "We are presently a publisher of magazines and books for educators. We now seriously seek to expand into such areas as children's books and other than print media."

PRODUCTIONS DIADEM INC., C.P. 11 Rouen St., Québec J8T 1G9 Canada. (819)561-4114. President: Denyse Marleau. Record company. Record label Jouvence. Estab. 1982.
Music: Releases 1-2 LPs/year; 1-2 CDs/year. Member of CAPAC. Records 16-20 songs/year. Works with composers, lyricists. For songs recorded pays musicians/artists on record contract, musicians on salary for inhouse studio work, songwriters on 10% royalty contract. Making contact: Write first and obtain permission to submit a cassette tape with 3 songs and a lyric sheet. SASE (or SAE and IRCs). Reports in 1 month. Recorded songs: "Vive l'hiver," by Marie Marleau, (children's contemporary music); "Chers grands-parents," by Denyse Marleau, (children's contemporary music); "Mon ami l'ordinateur," (children's popular music), all recorded by DIADEM on the Jouvence label.

RHYTHMS PRODUCTIONS/TOM THUMB MUSIC, P.O. Box 34485, Los Angeles CA 90034. President: R.S. White. Record company, cassette and book packagers. Record label, Tom Thumb – Rhythms Productions. Estab. 1955.
Music: Member of ASCAP. Works with composers and lyricists. For songs recorded pays musicians/artists on record contract, songwriters on royalty contract. Submit a cassette demo tape or VHS videotape by mail – unsolicited submissions OK. Requirements: "We accept musical stories. Must be produced in demo form, and must have educational content or be educationally oriented." Reports in 2 months. Recorded songs: *Adventures of Professor Whatzit & Carmine Cat,* by Dan Brown and Bruce Crook (6 book and cassette packages); and *First Reader's Kit* (multimedia learning program); all on Tom Thumb label.

*SATURN, A Division of Rock Dog Records, P.O. Box 3687, Hollywood CA 90028. (213)661-0259. Vice President, A&R: Gerry North. Record company. Estab. 1987.
Music: Releases 3-4 cassettes/year; 3-4 CDs/year. Member of BMI. Records 5 children's songs/year. Hires staff writers for children's music. Works with composers, lyricists and team collaborators. Pay open to negotiation. Write for permission to submit material. Submit demo cassette with lyric sheet (3-5 songs) and SASE. "No phone calls; send letter of query first. When a submission is made, please include a SASE for a reply." SASE for return of submissions. Reports in 1 month. Recently recorded songs: "Endless Youth," recorded by Pat Connolly (folk/acoustic); and "The Never Ending Recess," recorded by Gerald Cannizzaro (novelty/humor).
Tips: "Submit the best material you have – only the best."
Stories: Publishes 3 cassettes/CDs/year. 99% of stories are fiction; 1% nonfiction. For fiction, will consider fantasy, adventure, mystery, animal (ages 3-5). Payment negotiable. Query. "No phone calls please." Reports on queries in 1 month.

 The asterisk before a listing indicates the listing is new in this edition.

CHARLES SEGAL MUSIC, 16 Grace Rd., Newton MA 02159. (617)969-6196. Fax: (617)969-6114. Contact: Charles Segal. Music publisher and record company. Record labels include Spin Record. Estab. 1980.
Music: Publishes 24 children's songs/year. Works with composers and/or lyricists, team collaborators. For music published pays standard royalty of 50%; for songs recorded pays musicians/artists on record contract. Submit demo tape by mail; unsolicited submissions OK. Submit demo cassette if available with 1-3 songs and lyric or lead sheets. Reports in 6-7 weeks. Recorded songs: "Animal Concert," by Colleen Hay, recorded by Concert Kids on CBS label (sing along for ages 4-13); "Everyday Things," recorded by Charles Segal on MFP label (kids pop music for ages 6-15).
Music Tips: "Must be of educational value, entertaining easy listening. The lyrics should not be focused on sex, killing, etc.
Stories: Publishes 6 book/cassette packages/year. 50% of stories are fiction; 50% nonfiction. Will consider all genres aimed at ages 6-15. For nonfiction, considers all aimed at ages 6-15. Authors are paid royalty. Submit complete ms or submit both cassette tape and ms. Reports on queries in 6 weeks; mss in 2 months.
Story Tips: "I always look for the experienced writer who knows where he's going and not beating around the bush; in other words, has a definite message – a simple, good storyline."

SMARTY PANTS AUDIO/VIDEO, Suite #2, 15104 Detroit, Lakewood OH 44107. (216)221-5300. Fax: (216)221-5348. President: S. Tirk. Music publisher, book publisher, record company. Record labels include Smarty Pants, Smarty Time, High Note, S.P.I. Estab. 1988.
Music: Releases 25 LPs/year; 25 CDs/year. Member of BMI. Publishes 5-10 songs/year; records 10-20 songs and stories/year. Hires staff writers for children's music. Works with composers, lyricists, team collaborators. Buys all rights to material. Call first and obtain permission to submit material. Submit demo cassette and videocassette if available; 3 or 4 songs and lyric sheet. Material must be copyrighted. SASE/IRC for return of submission. Reports in 2 weeks. Recently recorded songs: "Beatrix Potter," by S. Tirk/Kathy Garver, recorded by Kathy Garver on the Smarty Pants label (children's music for ages 3-8); "Flopsy Bunnies," by S. Tirk/Kathy Garver, recorded by Kathy Garver on the Smarty Pants label (children's music for ages 3-8).
Music Tips: "Keep it upbeat, topical and clear." Sees big name artists trying to crack children's market.
Stories: Publishes 8 book/cassette packages/year; 2 cassettes/CDs/year. 100% of stories are fiction. Considers animal, fantasy aimed at ages 3-8. Work purchased outright. Submit both cassette tape and manuscript. Reports on queries/mss in 2 weeks. Catalog free on request. Call for guidelines. Recently published and recorded story tapes: *The Tale of Squirrel Nutkin*, by Beatrix Potter, narrated by Kathy Garver (ages 3-8); *The Tale of Benjamin Bunny*, by Blanche Fisher Wright, narrated by Kathy Garver (ages 3-8).

SOUND PUBLICATIONS, INC., Suite 108, 10 E. 22nd St., Lombard IL 60148. (708)916-7071. President: Cheryl Basilico. Music publisher, record company. Record labels include Sound Publications. Estab. 1991.
Music: Releases 10 LPs/year. Publishes and records 50 children's songs/year. For music published pays standard royalty of 50%; songs recorded on joint venture. Call or write for permission to submit material. Submit demo cassette with 3-5 songs, lyric sheet. "Music is to be educational." SASE/IRC for return of submission. Reports in 3 months.

SOUNDPRINTS, 165 Water St., P.O. Box 679, Norwalk CT 06856. (203)838-6009. Assistant Editor: Dana Meacher. Book publisher. Estab. 1988.
Stories: Publishes 6-7 book/cassette packages/year. Almost 100% of stories are fiction. Will consider realistic animal stories for preschool-3rd grade. Query with SASE. Reports on queries in 2 weeks; mss in 1 month. Catalog free on request. Ms guidelines free with SASE. Published and recorded story tapes: *Jackrabbit and the Prairie Fire*, by Susan Saunders, narrated by Peter Thomas (black-tailed jackrabbit on the Great Plains for preschool-3rd grade); *Seasons of a Red Fox*, by Susan Saunders, narrated by Peter Thomas (the first year in the life of a red fox for preschool-3rd grade).
Tips: "Be realistic. Much of what I get is not worth reading."

*STEMMER HOUSE PUBLISHERS, 2627 Caves Rd., Owings Mills MD 21117. (410)363-3690. Fax: (410)363-8459. President: Barbara Holdridge. Book publisher.
Stories: Catalog is free for 9×12 SAE and 75¢ postage. Ms guidelines free for SASE. Recently recorded story tapes: *The Wily Witch*, by Godfried Bomans, narrated by Tammy Grimes, John Houseman (ages 5-10, fairy tales).

*TEETER-TOT RECORDS, RR 1, Box 1658-1, Couch MO 65690. (815)947-3137. Owners/A&R Directors: Chad and Terri Sigafus. Music publisher, record company. Estab. 1988.
Music: Releases 4 records-cassettes/year. Member of ASCAP. Publishes and records 50 children's songs/year. Works with composers and lyricists. Pays standard royalty of 50% for music published; songwriters on royalty contract. Write for permission to submit material. Submit demo cassette with lyric sheet (4 songs). Reports in 1 month. Recently recorded songs: "The Bravest Little Cowboy," by Chad and Terri Sigafus, recorded by Chad and Terri Sigafus on the Teeter-Tot Records label (children's lullabies); and "Elephants and Kangaroos," by Steve Lundquist, recorded by Steve Lundquist on the Teeter-Tot Records label (children's music for ages 2-5).
Tips: "Quality is a must. Children's music is a growing field with a lot of opportunity."
Stories: Publishes 2 stories set to music/year. 50% of stories are fiction; 50% nonfiction. For fiction, will consider all types (pre-school-10 years). For nonfiction, will consider all types. Submit cassette tape of story. Reports in 1 month. Catalog is free on request. Ms guidelines free with SASE. Recently recorded story tapes: *The Ugly Duckling*, by Hans Christian Andersen, narrated by Terri Sigafus (fairy tale to music—original score, all ages).
Story Tips: "Be patient—submit finished work that is quality! The children's music industry is growing very quickly—so much opportunity."

TVN-THE VIDEO NETWORK, 31 Cutler Dr., Ashland MA 01721. (508)881-1800. Fax: (508)881-1800. Producer: Gregg C. McAllister. Video publisher. Estab. 1986.
Music: Member of ASCAP and BMI. Publishes and records 8 children's songs/year for video and multimedia projects. Hires staff writers for children's music. Pays on a work-for-hire basis. Pays musicians on salary for inhouse studio work. Submit demo cassette, VHS videocassette if available. "Reports on an as needed basis only." Recently recorded "Tugboat" and "My Dad and Me."

*TWIN SISTERS PRODUCTIONS, INC., Suite D, 1340 Home Ave., Akron OH 44310. (216)633-8900. Fax: (216)633-8988. President: Kim Thompson. CEO: Karen Hilderbrand. Music publisher, record company. Estab. 1987.
Music: Releases 6 LPs-cassettes/year. Publishes and records 50 children's songs/year. Works with composers and teams collaborators. Pays musicians on salary for inhouse studio work. Call first and obtain permission to submit material. Submit demo cassette with lyric sheet and VHS videocassette. Not necessary to include lyric or lead sheets. List past history of successes. SASE/IRC for return of submission. Reports in 1 month. Recently recorded songs: "Sammy Sue," by Kim Thompson and Karen Hilderbrand, recorded by Hal Wright on the Twin Sisters Productions label (children's music for ages 2-6); "Name the Animals," by Kim Thompson and Karen Hilderbrand, recorded by Kim Thompson on the Twin Sisters Productions label (children's, language for ages 4-12).
Tips: "Children's music is going to be a niche market business. Disney so heavily dominates the mainstream markets that only niche players will succeed."

UPSTREAM PRODUCTIONS, 35 Page Ave., P.O. Box 8843, Asheville NC 28814. (704)258-9713. Fax: (704)258-9727. Owner: Steven Heller. Music composer and producer and record company. Estab. 1982.
Music: Releases 1-3 LPs and 1-3 CDs/year. Member of ASCAP and BMI. Publishes and records 5-8 children's songs/year. Works with composers and lyricists. For music published pays standard royalty of 50%. "Submit letter first for cassette request. Cassettes should have 1-3 songs." Cassettes not returned.

WATCHESGRO MUSIC PUBLISHING CO., Watch Us Climb, ASCAP. 9208 Spruce Mountain Way, Las Vegas NV 89134-6024. (702)363-8506. President: Eddie Lee Carr. Music publisher, record company. Record labels include Interstate 40 Records, Tracker Records. Estab. 1970.

Music: Releases 10 singles/year; 5 12-inch singles/year; 1 LP/year; 1 CD/year. Member of BMI. Publishes 15 children's songs/year; records 4 children's songs/year. Works with composers, lyricists. For music published pays standard royalty of 50%; for songs recorded pays musicians/artists on record contract, musicians on salary for inhouse studio work. Write or call first and obtain permission to submit a cassette tape. Does not return unsolicited material. Reports in 1 week.

WE LIKE KIDS!, produced by KTOO-FM, 224 Fourth St., Juneau AK 99801. (907)586-1670. Fax: (907)586-3612. Producer: Jeff Brown. Producer of nationwide children's radio show.

Music: Releases 50 programs/year. Member of Children's Music Network; National Storytelling Association. Submit demo tape by mail; unsolicited submissions OK. Submit demo cassette, vinyl, CD.

Music Tips: "The best advice we could give to anyone submitting songs for possible airplay is to make certain that you give your best performance and record it in the best way possible. A mix of well-honed songwriting skills, an awareness of a variety of international musical styles, and the advent of home studios have all added up to a delightful abundance of quality songs and stories for children."

Stories: "Our show is based on themes most of the time. Send us your *recorded* stories. We play an average of one story per show, *all* from pre-recorded cassettes, LPs and CDs. Please do not send us *written* stories. Many storytellers have discovered We Like Kids! as a way of sharing their stories with a nationwide audience.

WORLD LIBRARY PUBLICATIONS, A Division of J.S. Paluch Co., 3815 N. Willow Rd., Schiller Park IL 60176. (708)678-0621. General Editor: Laura Dankler. Music publisher. Estab. 1945.

Music: Publishes 10-12 children's songs/year. Works with composers. For music published pays 10% of sales. Making contact: Submit demo cassette tape and lead sheet by mail; unsolicited submissions OK. "Should be liturgical. We are primarily a Roman Catholic publisher." Reports in 3 months. Published children's songs: "Let the Children Come to Me," written and recorded by James V. Marchionda, on WLP cassette 7845 label (religious/catechetical); "Gather You Children," written by Peter Finn and James Chepponis (religious/catechetical); and "Mass of the Children of God," written by James V. Marchionda OP, on WLP Cassette 7664 label (liturgical).

WUVT-FM; HICKORY DICKORY DOCK SHOW, P.O Box 99, Pilot VA 24138. (703)382-4975. Producer: Linda DeVito. Radio producer of children's show which features music, stories, poems. Estab. 1989.

Music: Submit demo cassette. SASE/IRC for return of submission.

Music Tips: "Write material that the whole family can enjoy. Sing-songy is out. Current topics and acoustic/folk melodies are great!"

Stories: Will consider animal, fantasy, sports, adventure. For nonfiction, considers animal, sports (ages 4-10).

WXPN-FM; KID'S CORNER, 3905 Spruce St., Philadelphia PA 19104. (215)898-6677. Fax: (215)573-2152. Host/Producer: Kathy O'Connell, Robert Drake. Radio program. Estab. 1988.

Market conditions are constantly changing! If you're still using this book and it is 1996 or later, buy the newest edition of Children's Writer's & Illustrator's Market *at your favorite bookstore or order directly from Writer's Digest Books.*

Music: Member of Children's Music Network, National Federation of Community Broadcasters, National Association of Independent Record Distributors. Submit demo tape by mail; unsolicited submissions OK. Submit demo cassette, CD, include lyric sheet. Cannot return material. Recently played songs: "Mine," by Idlet/Grimwood, recorded by Trout Fishing in America on Trout Records (rock/folk/children's, ages 7 and up); "Nobody," by Idlet/Grimwood, recorded by Trout Fishing in America on Trout Records (children's, ages 7 and up).

Tips: "Make it funny! Make it appealing to adults. Better production! Funnier/wittier lyrics!"

Audiovisual & Audiotape changes/'94-'95

The following markets were included in the 1994 edition of *Children's Writer's & Illustrator's Market* but do not have listings in this edition. The majority did not respond to our request to update their listings. If a reason was given for exclusion, it appears in parentheses after the market's name.

BES Creative
Chesire Corp.
Crystal Sound Recording, Inc.
Discovery Music
Martin Ezra & Associates
Paul French & Partners, Inc.

(doesn't need children's material)
KDOC-TV (no longer using freelancers)
Landyvision (no longer producing children's material)

Virtual Mountain, Inc.
Quiet Tymes, Inc.
Song Wizard Records (too many submissions)
Treehouse Radio®

Scriptwriter's Markets

Any play for kids, whether an original script or a classical adaptation, must captivate its audience. One way to enthrall a group of youngsters is to use plenty of rhythm, repetition and effective dramatic action. Also make sure the dialogue is realistic, relate the play directly to the experience of the audience, and include an element of surprise, says an article in *Children's Writer*. And avoid using subplots, which lengthen the play. (Most plays for children average less than an hour.)

"Fourth wall" plays, or plays where actors perform as if they are unaware of the audience, are still the standard in this field. But interactive plays which involve the audience are gaining popularity.

Since many theater groups have limited budgets, scripts containing elaborate staging and costumes might not meet their needs. Touring theaters also want simple sets—ones that can be easily transported. Many touring productions are plays that consist of three to six actors. More characters might exist in your play than available actors, so think about how the roles can be doubled up.

Plays using adult roles *and* plays with children's roles are being solicited by the nearly 50 markets in this section. Note the percentages of how many plays produced are for adult roles, and how many are for children's roles. Above all, become familiar with the types of plays the listed markets are seeking. Most listings mention specific plays recently produced or published. Some markets may also supply additional information and/or catalogs upon request.

Finally, payment for playwrights usually comes in the form of royalties, outright payments or a combination of both. The pay scale isn't going to be quite as high as screenplay rates, but playwrights *do* benefit by getting to see their work performed live.

A.D. PLAYERS, 2710 W. Alabama, Houston TX 77098. (713)526-2721. Literary Manager: Martha Doolittle. Estab. 1967. Produces 4-5 children's plays/year in new Children's Theatre Series; 1-2 musical/year. Produces children's plays for professional productions. 99-100% of plays/musicals written for adult roles; 0-1% for juvenile roles. "Cast must utilize no more than four actors. Need minimal, portable sets for proscenium or arena stage with no fly space and no wing space." Recently produced plays: *The Selfish Giant*, by Dr. Gillette Elugren Jr. (a story of a child's sacrificial love, for ages 5-12); and *The Lion, the Witch and the Wardrobe*, dramatized by le Clanche du Rand, story by C.S. Lewis (Lewis's classic story of love, faith, courage and giving, for ages 5-14). Does not want to see large cast or set requirements or New Age themes. Will consider simultaneous submissions and previously performed work. Submission method: Query with synopsis, character breakdown and set description; no tapes until requested. Reports in 6-12 months. Buys some residual rights. Pay negotiated. Submissions returned with SASE.
   • A.D. Players has received the Dove family approval stamp; an award from the Columbia International Film & Video Festival; and a Silver Angel Award.
Tips: "Children's musicals tend to be large in casting requirements. For those theaters with smaller production capabilities, this can be a liability for a script. Try to keep it small and simple, especially if writing for theaters where adults are performing for children. We are interested in material that reflects family values, emphasizes the importance of responsibility in making choices, encourages faith in God and projects the joy and fun of telling a story."

AMERICAN STAGE, P.O. Box 1560, St. Petersburg FL 33731. (813)823-1600. Artistic Director: Victoria Holloway. Estab. 1977. Produces 3 children's plays/year. Produces children's plays for professional children's theater program, mainstage, school tour, performing arts halls. Limited by budget and performance venue. Subject matter: classics and original work for children (ages K-12) and families. Recently produced plays: *Beauty and the Beast*, by Philip Hall and Lee Ahlin (grades K-6); and *The Jungle Books*, adapted by Victorian Holloway, music by Lee Ahlin (Kipling's classic tale of Mowgli the Mancub, and his life being raised in the jungle, for grades K-6). Does not want to see plays that look down on children. Approach must be that of the child or fictional beings or animals. Will consider simultaneous submissions, electronic submissions via disk or modem and previously performed work. Submissions method: Query with synopsis, character breakdown and set description. Reports in 6 months. Purchases "professional rights." Pays writers in royalties (6-8%); $25-35/performance. SASE for return of submission.
Tips: Sees a move in plays toward basic human values, relationships and multicultural communities.

ART EXTENSIONS THEATER, 11144 Weddington, N. Hollywood CA 91601. (818)760-8675. Fax: (818)508-8613. Artistic Director: Maureen Kennedy Samuels. Estab. 1991. Produces 2 plays/year; 1 musical/year. Small budget. Equity waiver. 90% of plays/musicals written for adult roles; 10% for juvenile roles. Produced plays: *Working Without Annette*, by Debbie Devine (about fear of change). Will consider simultaneous submissions and previously performed work. Submission method: Query with synopsis, character breakdown and set description; submit complete ms and score. Reports in 6 weeks. Pays writers in royalties of 5-10%; pays $10-25/performance. SASE for return of submission.

ARTREACH TOURING THEATRE, 3074 Madison Rd., Cincinnati OH 45209. (513)871-2300. Fax: (513)871-2501. Artistic Director: Kathryn Schultz Miller. Estab. 1976. "ArtReach has cast requirement of 3–2 men and 1 woman. Sets must look big but fit in large van." Professional theater. Produced plays: *Young Cherokee*, by Kathryn Schultz Miller (history and culture of early Cherokee tribe as seen through the eyes of a young brave, for primary students and family audiences); and *The Trail of Tears*, by Kathryn Schultz Miller (a companion play to *Young Cherokee* depicting story of Cherokee removal and unjust destruction of their culture, for intermediate through adult audiences). Does not want to see musicals, holiday plays, TV type scripts (about drugs, child abuse etc.) or fractured fairy tales. Will consider simultaneous submissions and previously performed work. Submission method: Query with synopsis, character breakdown and set description. Reports in 10 days to 6 weeks. Author retains rights. Pays writers in royalties. SASE for return of submission.
Tips: "Type script in professional form found in *Writer's Digest Book of Manuscript Formats*. Do not submit plays that are less than 45 pages long. Look to history, culture or literature as resources."

BAKER'S PLAYS, 100 Chauncy St., Boston MA 02111. (617)482-1280. Fax: (617)482-7613. Associate Editor: Raymond Pape. Estab. 1845. Publishes 5-8 children's plays/year; 2-4 children's musicals/year. 80% of plays/musicals written for adult roles; 20% for juvenile roles. Subject matter: "touring shows for 5- to 8-year-olds, full lengths for family audience and full lengths and one act plays for teens." Submission method: Submit complete ms, score and tape of songs. Reports in 3-8 months. Obtains worldwide rights. Pays writers in royalties (amount varies).
Tips: "Know the audience you're writing for before you submit your play anywhere. 90% of the plays we reject are not written for our market."

*BIRMINGHAM CHILDREN'S THEATRE, P.O. Box 1362, Birmingham AL 35201. (205)324-0470. Artistic Director: James W. Rye, Jr.. Estab. 1947. Produces 9 children's plays/year; 1 children's musical/year. "BCT is an adult professional theater performing for youth and family audiences September-May." 99% of plays/musicals written for adult roles; 1% for juvenile roles. "Our 'Wee Folks' Series is limited to four cast members and should be written with preschool-grade 2 in mind. We prefer interactive plays for this age group. We commission plays for our 'Wee Folks' Series (preschool-grade 2), our Children's Series

(K-6) and our Young Adult (6-12)." Recently produced plays: *Mother Goose*, by Jack Cannon (adults revisit Mother Goose Land and relearn rhymes and fun of their youth, for preschool-grade 2); *Young King Arthur*, by Michael Price Nelson (Young Arthur finds out what it's like to grow up and he learns of his birthright—the kingship, for K-6). Does not want plays which have references to witches, spells, incantations, evil magic or devils. No adult language. Will consider musicals, interactive theater for preschool through grade 2 and plays for 4-7 cast members. Submission method: Query first, query with final draft of script. Reports in 4 months. Buys negotiable rights. Buys material outright for $500-4,000. Submissions returned with SASE.

Tips: "We would like our commissioned scripts to teach as well as entertain. Keep in mind the age groups that our audience is composed of. Make sure that your material is interesting and entertaining to adults as well. Send submissions to the attention of Jack Cannon or Joe Zellner."

BOARSHEAD: MICHIGAN PUBLIC THEATER, 425 S. Grand Ave., Lansing MI 48933. (517)484-7800. Artistic Director: John Peakes. Estab. 1966. Produces 4 children's plays/year. Produces children's plays for professional production. Majority of plays written for adult roles. Produced plays: *1,000 Cranes*, by Amy Schultz (story of radiation death years after Hiroshima, for ages 6-15); *Charlotte's Web*, by E.B. White (pigs 'n stuff, for ages 6-12). Does not want to see musicals. Will consider previously performed work. Submission method: Query with synopsis, character breakdown and set description. Send "Attention: Educational Director." Include 10 pages of representative dialogue. Reports in 2 weeks on queries; 4 months on submissions. Pays writers $15-25/performance. Submissions returned with SASE. If no SASE, send self-addressed stamped post card for reply.

CHILDREN'S STORY SCRIPTS, Baymax Productions, Suite 130, 2219 W. Olive Ave., Burbank CA 91506. (818)563-6105. Fax: (818)563-2968. Editor: Deedra Bebout. Estab. 1990. Produces 3-10 children's scripts/year. "Except for small movements and occasionally standing up, children remain seated in Readers Theatre fashion." Publishes scripts sold to schools, camps, churches, scouts, hotels, cruise lines, etc.; wherever there's a program to teach or entertain children. "All roles read by children except K-2 scripts, where kids have easy lines, leader helps read the narration." Subject matter: Scripts on all subjects. Targeted age range—K-8th grade, 5-13 years old. Recently published plays: *Mother Mouse Saves Ten*, by Ruth Kelley (chain-reaction story which highlights counting, for grades K-2); *The Story of Io*, by Deanna Peters (Greek myth, for grades 5-8). No stories that preach a point, stories about catastrophic disease or other terribly heavy topics, theatrical scripts with no narrative prose to move the story along, or stories that have only one speaking character. Will consider simultaneous submissions and previously performed work (if rights are available). Submission method: Submit complete ms. Reports in 2 weeks. Purchases all rights; authors retain copyrights. "We add support material and copyright the whole package." Pays writers in royalties (10-15% on sliding scale, based on number of copies sold). SASE for reply and return of submission.

Tips: "We're only looking for stories related to classroom studies—educational topics with a freshness to them." Writer's guidelines packet available for business-sized SASE with 2 first-class stamps. Guidelines explain what Children's Story Scripts are, give 4-page examples from 2 different scripts, give list of suggested topics for scripts.

THE CHILDREN'S THEATRE COMPANY, 2400 Third Ave. S., Minneapolis MN 55404. (612)874-0500. Artistic Director: Jon Cranney. Estab. 1965. Produces 9 children's plays/year; 1-3 children's musicals/year. Produces children's plays for professional, not-for-profit productions. 60% of plays/musicals written for adult roles; 40% for juvenile roles in all productions. Produced plays: *Ramona Quimby*, by Len Jenkin (family life of the Quimbys, for all ages); *On the Wings of the Hummingbird: Tales of Trinidad*, by Beverly Smith-Dawson (life in Trinidad during carnival, for all ages). Does not want to see plays written for child performers only. Will consider simultaneous submissions and previously performed work. Submission method: Submit complete ms and score (if a musical). Reports in 2-6 months. Rights negotiable. Pays writers in royalties (2%). Submissions returned with SASE.

Tips: "The Children's Theatre Company rarely (if ever) produces unsolicited manuscripts; we continue a long tradition of producing new works commissioned to meet the needs of our audience and catering to the artistic goals of a specific season. Though the odds of us producing submitted plays are very slim, we always enjoy the opportunity to become acquainted with the work of a variety of artists, particularly those who focus on young audiences."

CIRCA '21 DINNER THEATRE, P.O. Box 3784, Rock Island IL 61204-3784. (309)786-2667. Producer: Dennis Hitchcock. Estab. 1977. Produces 2-3 children's plays/year; 3 children's musicals/year. "Prefer a cast no larger than ten." Produces children's plays for professional productions. 95% of plays/musicals written for adult roles; 5% written for juvenile roles. Submission method: Query with synopsis, character breakdown, tape and set description. Reports in 3 months. Payment negotiable.

I.E. CLARK, PUBLISHER, P.O. Box 246, Schulenburg TX 78956. (409)743-3232. Fax: (409)743-4765. Estab. 1956. Publishes 3 children's plays/year; 1 or 2 children's musicals/ year. Medium to large casts preferred. Publishes plays for all ages. Published plays: *Wind of a Thousand Tales*, by John Glore (story about a young girl who doesn't believe in fairy tales, for ages 5-12); *Rock'n'Roll Santa*, by R. Eugene Jackson (Santa's reindeer form a rock band, for ages 4-16). Does not want to see plays that have not been produced. Will consider simultaneous submissions and previously performed work. Submission method: Submit complete ms and audio or video tape. Reports in 4-8 months. Pays writers in negotiable royalties. SASE for return of submission.
Tips: "We publish only high quality literary works."

COMMUNITY CHILDREN'S THEATRE OF KANSAS CITY INC., 8021 E. 129th Terrace, Grandview MO 64030. (816)761-5775. Contact: Blanche Sellens. Estab. 1951. Produces 5 children's plays/year. Prefer casts of between 6-8. Produces children's plays for amateur productions for ages K-6. Produced play: *Red Versus the Wolf*, by Judy Wolferman (musical, for K-6 audience). Submission method: Query first then submit complete ms. Reports in a matter of months. "Winning script is performed by one of the units for two years."
Tips: "Write for guidelines and details for The Margaret Bartle Annual Playrwriting Award."

CONTEMPORARY DRAMA SERVICE, Division of Meriwether Publishing Ltd., 885 Elkton Dr., Colorado Springs CO 80907. (719)594-4422. Fax: (719)594-9916. Editor: Arthur Zapel. Estab. 1979. Publishes 45 children's plays/year; 6-8 children's musicals/year. 15% of plays/ musicals written for adult roles; 85% for juvenile roles. Recently published plays: *And Then There Was One*, by Michael Druce (a whodunit mystery comedy, for ages teen-adult); and *The Fables by Thurber*, by James Thurber (Reader's Theatre dramatizations, for ages teen-adult). "We do not publish plays for elementary level except for church plays for Christmas and Easter. All of our secular plays are for teens or college level." Does not want to see "full-length, 3-act plays (unless they have production history) or plays with dirty language." Will consider simultaneous submissions or previously performed work. Submission method: Query with synopsis, character breakdown and set description; "query first if a musical." Reports in 1 month. Purchases first rights. Pays writers royalty (10%) or buys material outright for $100-1,000. SASE for return of submission.

THE COTERIE, 2450 Grand, Kansas City MO 64108. (816)474-6785. Fax: (816)474-6785. Artistic Director: Jeff Church. Estab. 1979. Produces 7 children's plays/year; 1 children's musical/year. "Prefer casts of between five-seven, no larger than 15." Produces children's plays for professional productions. 80% of plays/musicals written for adult roles; 20% for juvenile roles. "We produce original plays, musicals and literary adaptations for ages five through adult." Produced plays: *Amelia Lives*, by Laura Annawyn Shamas (one-woman show on Amelia Earhart, for 6th grade through adult); *Dinosaurus*, by Ed Mast and Lenore Bensinger (Mobil Oil workers discover cavern of dinosaurs, for ages 5 through adult). "We do *not* want to see 'camp' adaptations of fairytales." Submission method: Query with synopsis, sample scene, character breakdown and set description. Reports in 8-10 months. Rights purchased "negotiable." Pays writers in royalties per play of approximately $500-1,500. SASE for return of submission.

Tips: "We're interested in adaptations of classic literature with small casts, simple staging requirements; also multicultural topics and biography plays of Latin and African-American figures. There is a need for non-condescending material for younger age groups (5-8) and for middle school (ages 9-13)."

CREEDE REPERTORY THEATRE, P.O. Box 269, Creede CO 81130. (719)658-2541. Fax: (719)658-2343. Artistic Director: Richard Baxter. Estab. 1966. Produces 1 children's play/year; 1 musical/year. Limited to 4-6 cast members and must be able to tour. Produces children's plays for summer theater, school or professional productions. 100% of plays/musicals written for adult roles. Publishes plays for ages K-12. Recently produced plays: *Coyote Tails*, by Daniel Kramer and Company (Native American Coyote legend, for grades K-6); and *The Two of Us*, by Michael Frayn (contemporary relationship story, for ages 12-adult). Does not want to see historical plays. Will consider simultaneous submissions and previously performed work. Submission method: Query first, submit complete ms and score, or query with synopsis, character breakdown and set description. Reports in 1 year. Pays writers in royalties (5%); pays $25-30 per performance.
Tips: Sees trends in "non-sexist, non-traditional casting and Native American/Hispanic American interest. No fairy tales unless non-traditional."

DRAMATIC PUBLISHING, INC., 311 Washington St., Woodstock IL 60098. (815)338-7170. Fax: (815)338-8981. Estab. 1885. Publishes 5-8 children's plays/year; 4-6 children's musicals. Recently published: *Song for the Navigator*, by Michael Cowell (integrating cultural heritage with "modern" life, for ages 8-14); and *A Woman Called Truth*, by Sandra Fenichel Asher (life and times of Sojourner Truth, includes some period music, for ages 11-18). Submission method: Submit complete ms/score and cassette/video tape (if a musical); include SASE if materials are to be returned. Reports in 4-6 months. Pays writers in royalties.
  • Dramatic Publishing's plays have won several awards recently. Both *A Women Called Truth* and *Song for the Navigator* won A.A.T.E. Distinguished Play Award for 1994. *A Play About the Mothers of Plaza de Mayo*, by Alisa Palmer, won the Canadian Children's Award for Best New Play.
Tips: "Scripts should be from ½ to 1½ hours long, and not didactic or condescending. Original plays dealing with hopes, joys and fears of today's children are preferred to adaptations of old classics."

ELDRIDGE PUBLISHING CO. INC., P.O. Box 1595, Venice FL 34284. (813)496-4679. Fax: (813)496-9680. Editor: Nancy Vorhis. Estab. 1906. Publishes approximately 30 children's plays/year (5 for elementary; 20 for junior and senior high); 2-3 high school musicals/year. Prefers simple staging; flexible cast size. "We publish for middle, junior and high school, all genres." Recently published plays: *Hollywood Hillbillies*, by Tim Kelly (comedy about country folks who strike it rich, for high school community theater audiences); and *Theatre for a Small Planet*, by Jules Tasca (3 plays for children from different countries, for elementary and up). Does not want to see adult material with strong language or sexual context. Will consider simultaneous submissions ("please let us know, however") and previously performed work. Submission method: Submit complete ms, score and tape of songs (if a musical). Reports in 2 months. Purchases all dramatic rights. Pays writers royalties of 50%; 10% copy sales; buys material outright for $200-500.
Tips: "We're always on the lookout for large-cast comedies which provide a lot of fun for our customers. But other more serious topics which concern teens, as well as intriguing mysteries, and children's theater programs are of interest to us as well. We know there are many new talented playwrights out there and we look forward to reading their fresh scripts."

A bullet has been placed within some listings to introduce special comments by the editors of Children's Writer's & Illustrator's Market.

ENCORE PERFORMANCE PUBLISHING, P.O. Box 692, Orem UT 84059. (801)225-0605. Estab. 1978. Publishes 10-20 children's plays/year; 8-15 children's musicals/year. Prefers equal male/female ratio if possible. Adaptations for K-12 and older. 60% of plays written for adult roles; 40% for juvenile roles. Recently published plays: *Nine Candles for David*, by Barbara Schaap (Hanukkah musical, a treatment of the history behind Hanukkah, for ages 8-14 and families); and *Tales From the Enchanted City*, by L. Don Swartz (modern setting of Brothers Grimm fairy tales, for ages 6-16 and families). Will only consider previously performed work. Looking for issue plays and unusual fairy tale adaptations. Submission method: Query first with synopsis, character breakdown, set description and production history. Reports in 2-4 weeks. Purchases all publication and production rights. Author retains copyright. Pays writers in royalties (50%). SASE for return of submission.
Tips: "Give us issue and substance, be controversial without offence. Use a laser printer! Don't send old manuscript. Make yours look the most professional."

FLORIDA STUDIO THEATRE, 1241 N. Palm Ave., Sarasota FL 34236. (813)366-9017. Artistic Director: Richard Hopkins. Estab. 1980. Produces 3 children's plays/year; 1-3 children's musicals/year. Produces children's plays for professional productions. 50% of plays/musicals written for adult roles; 50% for juvenile roles. "Prefer small cast plays that use imagination more than heavy scenery." Will consider simultaneous submissions and previously performed work. Submission method: Query with synopsis, character breakdown and set description. Reports in 3 months. Rights negotiable. Pay negotiable. Submissions returned with SASE.
Tips: "Children are a tremendously sophisticated audience. The material should respect this."

*THE FOOTHILL THEATRE COMPANY, P.O. Box 1812, Nevada City CA 95959. (916)265-9320. Artistic Director: Philip Charles Sneed. Estab. 1977. Produces 0-2 children's plays/year; 0-2 children's musicals/year. Professional nonprofit theater. 95% of plays/musicals written for adult roles; 5% for juvenile roles. "Small is better, but will consider anything." Recently produced *The Golden Grotto*, by Cleve Haubold/James Alfred Hitt (fantasy about a frog prince, comedy for all ages); *The Best Christmas Pageant Ever*, by Barbara Robinson (family Christmas comedy, for all ages). Does not want to see traditional fairy tales. Will consider simultaneous submissions and previously performed work. Submission method: Query with synopsis, character breakdown and set description. Reports in 6 months. Buys negotiable rights. Payment method varies. Submissions returned with SASE.
Tips: "Trends in children's theater include cultural diversity, real life issues (drug use, AIDS, etc.), mythological themes with contemporary resonance. Don't talk down to or underestimate children."

THE FREELANCE PRESS, P.O. Box 548, Dover MA 02030. (508)785-1260. Managing Editor: Narcissa Campion. Estab. 1979. Produces 3 musicals and/or plays/year. Casts are comprised of young people, ages 8-15, and number 25-30. "We publish original musicals on contemporary topics for children and adaptations of children's classics (e.g., Rip Van Winkle)." Published plays: *Velveteen Rabbit* (based on story of same name, for ages 8-11); *Monopoly*, (young people walk through board game, for ages 11-15). No plays for adult performers. Will consider simultaneous submissions and previously performed work. Submission method: Submit complete ms and score with SASE. Reports in 3 months. Pays writers 10% royalties. SASE for return of submission.

SAMUEL FRENCH, INC., 45 W. 25th St., New York NY 10010. (212)206-8990. Fax: (212)206-1429. Editor: Lawrence Harbison. Estab. 1830. Publishes 2 or 3 children's plays/year; "variable number of musicals." Subject matter: "all genres, all ages. No puppet plays. No adaptations of any of those old 'fairy tales.' No 'Once upon a time, long ago and far away.' No kings, princesses, fairies, trolls, etc." Submission method: Submit complete ms and demo tape (if a musical). Reports in 2-8 months. Purchases "publication rights, amateur and professional production rights, option to publish next 3 plays." Pays writers "book royalty of 10%; professional production royalty of 90%; amateur production royalty of 80%." SASE for return of submissions.

Tips: "Children's theater is a very tiny market, as most groups perform plays they have created themselves or have commissioned."

EMMY GIFFORD CHILDREN'S THEATER, 3504 Center St., Omaha NE 68105. (402)345-4852. Artistic Director: James Larson. Estab. 1949. Produces 9 children's plays/year; 1 children's musical/year. Produces children's plays for professional productions. 100% of plays/musicals written for adult roles. Need plays with small casts, no fly space necessary. Produced plays: *Pippi Longstocking*; *Bye Bye Birdie*. Does not want to see adult plays. Will consider simultaneous submissions, electronic submissions via disk or modem, or previously performed work. Submission method: Query first. Reports in 6 months. Pays writers in royalties (6%). Submissions returned with SASE.

THE GREAT AMERICAN CHILDREN'S THEATRE COMPANY, P.O. Box 92123, Milwaukee WI 53202. (414)276-4230. Fax: (414)276-2214. Artistic Director: Teri Solomon Mitze. Estab. 1975. Produces 2 children's plays/year. Produces children's plays for professional productions; 100% written for adult roles. Produced plays: *The Secret Garden*, by Brett Reynolds (children's classic, for grades K-8); *Charlie & the Chocolate Factory*, by Richard R. George (children's classic, for grades K-8). Will consider previously performed work. Submission method: Query with synopsis, character breakdown and set description. Reports in weeks. Rights and payment negotiable.

*THE GROWING STAGE THEATRE, P.O. Box 132, Chester NJ 07930. (908)879-4946. Artistic Director: Stephen L. Fredericks. Estab. 1982. Produces 8 children's plays/year; 3 children's musicals/year. "We have a 5-person professional company that works with our community performers." 60% of plays/musicals written for adult roles; 40% for juvenile roles. Recently produced plays: *Aladdin*, by Perry Arthur Kroeger, (adaptation from classic tale, for K-8th grade); and *Where Do You Get Your Ideas?* by Sandy Fenichel Asher (storyteller poet and playwright share their perspective in writing, grades 3-6). Plays for adult audiences only. Will consider previously performed work. Submission method: Query with synopsis, character breakdown and set description. Reports in 2 months. "Contracts are developed individually." Pays $25-75/performance. Submissions returned with SASE.
Tips: "There's an overabundance on issue-oriented plays. Creativity, quality, the standards we place on theater aimed at adults should not be reduced in preparing a script for young people. We, together, are forming the audience of tomorrow. Don't turn them off by making the theater another resource for the infomercial—nurture, challenge and inspire them."

HAYES SCHOOL PUBLISHING CO. INC., 321 Pennwood Ave., Wilkinsburg PA 15221. (412)371-2373. Fax: (412)371-6408. Estab. 1940. Produces plays. Wants to see supplementary teaching aids for grades K-12. Interested in all subject areas. Will consider simultaneous and electronic submissions or previously performed work. Submission method: Query first with synopsis, character breakdown and set description, or with complete ms and score. Reports in 3-4 weeks. Purchases all rights. Work purchased outright. SASE for return of submissions.

HONOLULU THEATRE FOR YOUTH, 2846 Ualena St., Honolulu HI 96819. (808)839-9885. Fax: (808)839-7018. Artistic Director: Pamela Sterling. Estab. 1955. "Cast size should be limited to ten; six is ideal." Produces 7 children's plays/year; 1 children's musical. Produces children's plays for professional productions. Subject matter: Looks for plays "celebrating cultures of the Pacific Rim, especially. Also, plays that deal with issues of concern to today's young audiences (varying in age from 6-18)." Produced plays: *The Council*, by William S. Yellow Robe, Jr. (a man's relationship with the environment, for age 10 through adult); *The Giant's Baby*, by Allan Ahlberg (a "modern" fairytale, for ages 5 years through adult). Does not want to see "campy, technical extravanganzas." Will consider simultaneous submissions and previously performed work. Submission method: Query first with cast requirements and synopsis. Reports in 6 months. SASE required for each script requested. Pays writers in royalties (4%) and by commission fee ($2,000-5,000). Rights negotiable.
Tips: "Obviously, I look for smaller casts, less technical machinery, more imaginative use of resources. I have to balance a season with some 'title' recognition, i.e. adaptations of

well-known books or fairy-tales, but I am more interested in good, *original* theatrical literature for young audiences."

INDIANA REPERTORY THEATRE, 140 W. Washington, Indianapolis IN 46204. (317)635-5277. Artistic Director: Libby Appel. Estab. 1971. Produces 3 children's plays/year. Produces children's plays for professional productions. 100% of plays written for adult roles. Limit 8 in cast, 75 minutes running time. Recently produced plays: *Tales from the Arabian Nights*, by Michael Dixon; *Red Badge of Courage*, adaptation by Thomas Olson. Does not want to see preschool and K-4 material. Will consider previously performed work. Submission method: Query with synopsis, character breakdown and set description to Janet Allen, Associate Artistic Director. Reports in 6 months. Pays writers negotiable royalty (6%) or commission fee. Submissions returned with SASE.

*JEWISH ENSEMBLE THEATRE, 16600 W. Maple Rd., West Bloomfield MI 48322. (810)788-2700. Artistic Director: Evelyn Orbach. Estab. 1989. "We are considering children's plays for the first time." Produces children's plays for professional productions. Prefers small casts.

THE MUNY STUDENT THEATRE, 634 N. Grand, St. Louis MO 63103. (314)652-5213. Artistic Director: Christopher Limber. Estab. 1979. Produces 5 children's plays/year; 1 or 2 children's musicals/year. "We produce a touring and mainstage season September-May and offer extensive theater classes throughout the entire year." 100% of plays/musicals written for adult roles; 40% for juvenile roles. Prefers cast of 4 or 5 equity actors, children's parts unlimited. "Tour sets are limited in size." Produced plays: *Flat Stanley*, by Jeff Brown/adapted by Larry Pressgrove (based on children's book, for ages K-3); *BOCON!*, written by Lisa Loomer (a young boy's travels from El Salvador to Los Angeles, for ages 4-6). Will consider simultaneous submissions and previously performed work. Submission method: Query with synopsis, character breakdown and set description. Rights negotiable.
Tips: "We emphasize diverse ethnic and cultural backgrounds. Tour shows should fit into the school curriculum. The Muny Student Theatre's mission is to introduce theater to young people, to encourage creative learning and to develop future theater audiences. The company is now one of the most comprehensive theater education programs in Missouri. Each year the company reaches more than 100,000 students through its resident touring company, professional storytellers, mainstage productions and theater classes."

THE NEW CONSERVATORY THEATRE CENTER, 25 Van Ness Ave., San Francisco CA 94102. (415)861-4914. Fax: (415)861-6988. Executive Director: Ed Decker. Estab. 1981. Produces 6-10 children's plays/year; 1-2 children's musicals/year. Limited budget. Produces children's plays as part of "a professional theater arts training program for youths ages 4-19 during the school year and two summer sessions. The New Conservatory also produces educational plays for its touring company." 100% written for juvenile roles. "We do not want to see any preachy or didactic material." Submission method: Query with synopsis, character breakdown and set description, or submit complete ms and score. Reports in 3 months. Rights purchased negotiable. Pays writers in royalties. SASE for return of submission.
Tips: Sees trend in: "addressing socially relevant issues for young people and their families."

NEW PLAYS INCORPORATED, P.O. Box 5074, Charlottesville VA 22905. (804)979-2777. Artistic Director: Patricia Whitton. Estab. 1964. Publishes 4 plays/year; 1 or 2 children's musicals/year. Publishes "generally material for kindergarten through junior high." Recently published musicals: *Tales from the Rebbe's Table*, by Flora Atkin (Jewish folklore, for grades K-6); and *Rockway Cafe*, by Max Bush (rock star fantasy, for preteens and teens). Does not want to see "adaptations of titles I already have. No unproduced plays; no junior high improvisations." Will consider simultaneous submissions and previously performed work. Submissions method: Submit complete ms and score. Reports in 2 months. Purchases exclusive rights to sell acting scripts. Pays writers in royalties (50% of production royalties; 10% of script sales). SASE for return of submission.

NEW YORK STATE THEATRE INSTITUTE, 155 River St., Troy NY 12180. (518)274-3200. Fax: (518)274-3815. Producing Director: Patricia B. Snyder. Estab. 1976. Produces 1-2 children's plays/year; 1-2 children's musicals/year. Produces family plays for professional theater. 90% of plays/musicals are written for adult roles; 10% for juvenile roles. Does not want to see plays for children only. Produced plays: *The Secret Garden*, adapted by Thomas W. Olson (for all ages); *To Kill a Mockingbird*, adapted by Christopher Sergel (for grade 8 and up). Will consider simultaneous submissions and previously performed work. Submission method: Query with synopsis, character breakdown and set description; submit complete ms and tape of songs (if a musical). Reports in 2-3 months on submissions; 1 month for queries. SASE for return of submission.
Tips: Writers should be mindful of "audience *sophistication*. We do not wish to see material that is childish. Writers should submit work that is respectful of young people's intelligence and perception—work that is appropriate for families, but that is also challenging and provocative."

THE OPEN EYE: NEW STAGINGS, 270 W. 89th St., New York NY 10024. (212)769-4143. Fax: (212)595-0336. Artistic Director: Amie Brockway. Estab. 1972 (theater). Produces plays for a family audience. Most productions are with music, but are not musicals. "Casts are usually limited to six performers because of economic reasons. Technical requirements are kept to a minimum for touring purposes." Produces professional productions using members of Actor's Equity Association. Most plays/musicals written for adult roles. Produced plays: *The Wise Men of Chelm*, by Sandra Fenichel Asher (weaving of several Jewish folk tales, for ages 8 through adult); *Freedom is My Middle Name*, by Lee Hunkins (unsung African-American heroes, for ages 8 through adult). "No videos or cassettes. Letter of inquiry only." Will consider previously performed work. Rights agreement negotiated with author. Pays writers one time fee or royalty negotiated with publisher. SASE for return of submission.
Tips: "We are seeing a trend toward plays that are appropriate for a family audience and that address today's multicultural concerns."

PIONEER DRAMA SERVICE, P.O. Box 4267, Englewood CO 80155. (303)779-4035. Fax: (303)779-4315. Producer: Steven Fendrich. Artistic Director: Elizabeth Berry. Estab. 1960. Publishes 7 children's plays/year; 7 children's musicals/year. Subject matter: Publishes plays for ages 9-high school. Recently published plays/musicals: *Characters*, by Nikki Leigh Mondschein (insightful character study by young playwright, for junior high school-adult audiences); and *Gone with the Breeze*, by Tim Kelley and Bill Francoeur (musical farce on the movie industry, for ages 8-adult). Wants to see "script, scores, tapes, pics and reviews." Will consider simultaneous submissions, CAD electronic submissions via disk or modem, previously performed work. Submission method: Query with synopsis, character breakdown and set description. Submit complete ms and score (if a musical). Reports in 2 months. Purchases all rights. Pays writers in royalties (10% on sales, 50% royalties on productions); or buys material outright for $200-1,000.

PLAYERS PRESS, INC., P.O. Box 1132, Studio City CA 91614-0132. (818)789-4980. Vice President: R. W. Gordon. Estab. 1965. Publishes 5-50 children's plays/year; varying children's musicals/year. Subject matter: "We publish for all age groups." Recently published plays: *Tall Betsy and the Cracker Barrel Tales*, by Jacque Wheeler (children's musical based on folktales, for grades 3-7); and *Try a Little Shakespeare* (Shakespearean play modernized, for grades 4-7). Considers previously performed work only. Submission method: Query with synopsis, character breakdown and set description; include #10 SASE with query. Reports on query in 2-4 weeks; submissions in 3-12 months. Purchases stage, screen, TV rights. Payment varies; work purchased possibly outright upon written request. Submissions returned with SASE.
Tips: "Entertainment quality is on the upswing and needs to be directed at the world, no longer just the U.S. Please submit with two #10 SASEs plus ms-size SASE. Please do not call."

THE PLAYHOUSE JR., 222 Craft Ave., Pittsburgh PA 15213. (412)621-4445. Fax: (412)687-3606. Director: Wayne Brinda. Estab. 1949. Produces 5 children's plays/year; 1 children's

musical/year. Produces children's plays for semi-professional production with a college theater department. 100% of plays/musicals written for adult roles. Produced plays: *The Three Musketeers*, by Bruce Hurlbut (adaptation of Dumas's classic, for age 3-middle school); *Jack and the Beantree*, by Paul Laurakas (musical, Appalachian adaptation of the fairytale, for grades K-4). Does not want to see "strong social problem plays." Will consider simultaneous submissions or previously produced work. Submission method: Query with synopsis, character breakdown and set description (first drafts); submit complete ms and score (if a musical). Reports in 6 weeks. Purchases performance rights; negotiable. Pays writers commission/royalty. SASE for return of submission.
Tips: Looks for "clearly developed plot lines, imaginative use of the space, rather than realistic interiors. Plays should stimulate the imaginations of the director/producer, casts, designers and, ultimately, the audiences."

PLAYS FOR YOUNG AUDIENCES, P.O. Box 4267, Englewood CO 80155. (303)779-4035. Fax: (303)779-4315. Producer: Steven Fendrich. Artistic Director: Elizabeth Berry. Estab. 1989. Publishes 7 children's plays/year; 7 children's musicals/year. Subject matter: Publishes plays for preschool-12th grade audience. Recently produced musicals: *The Enchantment of Beauty and the Beast*, by Vera Morris and Bill Francoeur (new musical adaptation, for ages pre-school-12); *The Beautiful Princess Sasha*, by Jules Tasca (stylized parable on the danger of beauty, for ages 12-adult). Wants to see "script, score, tape, pictures and reviews." Will consider simultaneous submissions, electronic submissions via disk or modem, previously performed work. Submission method: Query with synopsis, character breakdown and set description; submit complete ms and score (if a musical). Reports in 2 months. Purchases all rights. Pays writers in royalties (10% in sales, 50% on productions).

PLAYS, THE DRAMA MAGAZINE FOR YOUNG PEOPLE, 120 Boylston St., Boston MA 02116-4615. (617)423-3157. Managing Editor: Elizabeth Preston. Estab. 1941. Publishes 70-75 children's plays/year. "Props and staging should not be overly elaborate or costly. Our plays are performed by children in school." 100% of plays written for juvenile roles. Subject matter: Audience is lower grades through junior/senior high. Published plays: *Moonlight Is When*, by Kay Arthur (a shy young researcher finds romance in an unexpected place — the Museum of Natural History); *Express to Valley Forge*, by Earl J. Dias, (a courageous patriot saves the day for George Washington's army); and *Kidnapped*, (a dramatization of the Herman Melville classic, adapted by Adele Thane). Send nothing downbeat — no plays about drugs, sex or other 'heavy' topics." Submission methods: Query first on adaptations of folk tales and classics; otherwise submit complete ms. Reports in 2-3 weeks. Purchases all rights. Pay rates vary. Guidelines available; send SASE. Sample copy $3.50.
Tips: "Above all, plays must be entertaining for young people with plenty of action and a satisfying conclusion."

ST. LOUIS BLACK REPERTORY COMPANY, Suite 10 F, 634 N. Grand Blvd., St. Louis MO 63103. (314)534-3807. Artistic Director: Ron Himes. Estab. 1976. Produces 6 children's plays; 2-3 children's musicals/year. Produces children's plays for professional productions. "The St. Louis Black Rep is a professional production company which includes a mainstage and touring component. The touring component produces 3-4 plays per year for young audiences." Produces "African and African-American stories for preschoolers-adults." 100% of plays/musicals written for adult roles. "The touring shows are designed to be flexible and totally self-contained." Produced/published *The Eighth Voyage of Sinbad*, by Patton Hasegawa (story of Sinbad's greatest and most dangerous journey, for grades K-6); *A Long Hard Journey*, by Patricia McKissack, adapted by Eric Wilson (a fascinating train ride brings to life the story of the men who brought the system to its knees by yelling "No more!", for grade 6-adult). Will consider previously performed work. Submission method: Submit complete ms; query with synopsis, character breakdown and set description; submit complete ms and score (if musical). Rights are mutually agreed upon via contract. Pays writers per performance ($20-35). Submissions returned with SASE.
Tips: "Our touring company consists of four-five actors, therefore we need plays written for at least four or a maximum of five characters. If a play calls for more than five roles, the actors must be able to double and interchange them."

*SANTA MONICA GROUP THEATRE, 1211 4th St., Santa Monica CA 90401. (310)394-9779. Artistic Directors: Evelyn Rudie and Chris DeCarlo. Estab. 1962. Produces 11-12 children's plays/year; 10 children's musicals/year. Produces professional and student workshop productions. 30% of plays/musicals written for adult roles; 70% for juvenile roles. Cast size limited to 30 because of size of the stage. Recently produced *Cap'n Jack and the Beanstalk*, by Evelyn Rudie and Chris DeCarlo, (a merry musical romp to a magical kingdom in the clouds, ages 2-92); and *Dear Gabby: The Confesssions of an Over-achiever*, by Evelyn Rudie and Chris DeCarlo (pain and passion of growing up, for teens and their families). Does not want to see clichéd material, material that talks down to young people. Will consider simultaneous submissions and previously performed work. Submission method: Query with synopsis, character breakdown and set description. Reports in 6 months. Pays writers in royalties (4%). Submissions returned with SASE.
Tips: "As an intimate, 99-seat theater—with a stage of 22 feet wide × 18 feet deep, we are limited in what we can use—material should be appropriate for the space available."

*SEATTLE CHILDREN'S THEATRE, P.O. Box 9640, Seattle WA 98109. Literary Manager and Dramaturg: Deborah Frockt. Estab. 1975. Produces 6-8 children's plays/year; 1 children's musical/year. Produces children's plays for professional productions (September-June). 95% of plays/musicals written for adult roles; 5% for juvenile roles. "We generally use adult actors even for juvenile roles." Prefers no turntable, no traps. Recently produced *The Rememberer*, adapted by Steven Dietz (Native American girl struggles to maintain her cultural legacy when she is forced to attend boarding school in 1912, for ages 8 and up); *Afternoon of the Elves*, adapted by Y. York, book by Janet Taylor Lisle (friendship, imagination getting to know those you think are different, for 8 and up). Does not want to see anything that condescends to young people—anything overly broad in style. Will consider simultaneous submissions and previously performed work. Submission method: Query, with synopsis, maximum 10 sample pages of dialogue, résumé or bio. Include SASE. Reports in 3-6 months on synopsis; 6-12 months on mss. Rights vary. Payment method varies. Submissions returned with SASE.
Tips: "Please *do not* send unsolicited manuscripts. We welcome queries by all populations and encourage queries by women and minorities. We prefer sophisticated material (our weekend performances have an audience that is half adults). All shows SCT produces are multiracially cast."

STAGE ONE: THE LOUISVILLE CHILDREN'S THEATRE, 425 W. Market, Louisville KY 40202. (502)589-5946. Fax: (502)589-5779. Producing Director: Moses Goldberg. Estab. 1946. Produces 8-10 children's plays/year; 1-4 children's musicals/year. Stage One is an Equity company producing children's plays for professional productions. 100% of plays/musicals written for adult roles. "Sometimes we do use students in selected productions." Recently produced plays: *Diary of Anne Frank*, by Goodrich and Hackett (teenager grows up in hiding from the Holocaust, for ages 10-up); and *Cinderella*, by Moses Goldberg (story of family dysfunction, abused children, faith and love, for ages 6-12). Does not want to see "camp or condescension." Will consider simultaneous submissions, electronic submissions via disk or modem and previously performed work. Submission method: Submit complete ms, score and tape of songs (if a musical); include the author's résumé if desired. Reports in 3-4 months. Pays writers in royalties (5-6%) or $25-75/performance.
Tips: Looking for "stageworthy and respectful dramatizations of the classic tales of childhood, both ancient and modern; plays relevant to the lives of young people and their families; and plays directly related to the school curriculum."

TADA!, 120 W. 28th St., New York NY 10001. (212)627-1732. Artistic Director: Janine Nina Trevens. Estab. 1984. Produces 3-4 staged readings of children's plays and musicals/year; 2-3 children's musicals/year. "All actors are children, ages 6-17." Produces children's

 The asterisk before a listing indicates the listing is new in this edition.

plays for professional, year-round theater. 100% of plays/musicals written for juvenile roles. Recently produced musicals: *Everything About Camp (Almost)*, scenes by Michael Slade, music and lyrics by many writers including Eric Rockwell, Robby Merkin, David Lawrence and Jamie Bernstein (musical revue about summer camp, ages 3-adult); and *Sleepover*, book by Philip Freedman, music and lyrics by James Beloff (story of girls' sleep-over party crashed by boys, ages 3-adult). Does not want to see fairy tales or material that talks down to children. Submission method: Query with synopsis, character breakdown and set description; submit complete ms, score and tape of songs (if a musical). Reports in 6 months "or in February following the January deadline for our playwriting competition." Rights purchased "depend on the piece." Pays writers in royalties of 1-6% or pays commissioning fee. SASE for return of submissions.

Tips: "Too many authors are writing productions, not plays. Our company is multi-racial and city-oriented. We are not interested in fairy tales. We like to produce material that kids relate to and that touches their lives today."

*TAKE ONE RADIO THEATRE, 11519 Inglewood Court, Riverside CA 92503. (909)359-5475. Artistic Director: William Shockley. Estab. 1993. Produces 50-100 children's plays/year. Produces "very short" professional radio plays. 100% of plays written for adult roles. As a small a cast as possible; as few and as simple sound effects as possible. Recently produced *The Fable of the Wombat & the Tasmanian Devil*, by W.M. Shockley (animal extinction for ages 6-adult). Does not want to see cutesy material; things which write down to audience; no religious. Will consider simultaneous submissions, electronic submissions via disk or modem and previously performed work. Submission method: Submit complete ms. Reports in 2-3 weeks. Acquires the right to produce and distribute the play only; all other rights remain with author. Pays writers in royalties (10%). Submissions returned with SASE.

Tips: "We're looking for short 3-10 page scripts in the proper format (we sell a booklet 'The Radio Play & How to Write It' for $6 which describes our preferred format). Stories should be for children but with adult overtones."

THEATRE FOR YOUNG AMERICA, 4881 Johnson Dr., Mission KS 66205. (913)831-2131. Artistic Director: Gene Mackey. Estab. 1974. Produces 7 children's plays/year; 3-5 children's musicals/year. "We use a small cast (4-7), open thrust stage." Theatre for Young America is a professional equity company. 90% of plays/musicals written for adult roles; 10% for juvenile roles. Produced plays: *The Wizard of Oz*, by Jim Eiler and Jeanne Bargy (for ages 6 and up); *A Partridge in a Pear Tree*, by Lowell Swortzell (deals with the 12 days of Christmas, for ages 6 and up); *Three Billy Goats Gruff*, by Gene Mackey and Molly Jessup (Norwegian folk tales, for ages 6 and up). Submission method: Query with synopsis, character breakdown and set description. Will consider simultaneous submissions and previously performed work. Reports in 2 months. Purchases production rights, tour rights in local area. Pays writers in royalties or $10-50/performance.

Tips: Looking for "cross-cultural material that respects the intelligence, sensitivity and taste of the child audience."

THEATREWORKS/USA, 890 Broadway, New York NY 10003. (212)677-5959. Artistic Director: Jay Harnick. Estab. 1960. Produces 2 children's plays/year; 8 children's musicals/year. Cast of 5 or 6 actors. Play should be 1 hour long, tourable. Professional children's theatre comprised of adult equity actors. 100% of musicals are written for adult roles. Produced plays: *Curious George*, book and lyrics by Thomas Toce, music by Tim Brown (adaptation, for grades K-3); *Little Women*, by Allan Knee, incidental music by Kim Olen and Alison Hubbard (adaptation, for grades 4-8). No fractured, typical "kiddy theater" fairy tales or shows written strictly to teach or illustrate. Will consider previously performed work. Submission method: Query first with synopsis, character breakdown and set description. Reports in 6 months. Pays writers royalties of 6%. SASE for return of submission.

Tips: "Plays should be not only entertaining, but 'about something.' They should touch the heart and the mind. They should not condescend to children."

WEST COAST ENSEMBLE, 6240 Hollywood Blvd., Hollywood CA 90028. (213)871-8673. Artistic Director: Les Hanson. Estab. 1982. Produces 1 children's play/year or 1 children's musical/year. "We operate under an Equity Theatre for Young Audiences contract or under the Los Angeles 99-seat Theatre Plan." 90% of plays/musicals written for adult roles; 10% for juvenile roles. Prefers simple sets; casts of no more than 8. There are no limits on style or subject matter. Will consider simultaneous submissions (no more than 2) and previously performed work. Submission method: Submit complete ms and score (if a musical). Purchases exclusive rights to perform play/musical in Southern California. Pays writers $25-50 per performance. Submissions returned with SASE.

THE YOUNG COMPANY, P.O. Box 225, Milford NH 03055. (603)673-4005. Producing Director: Jerry Smith-Niles. Estab. 1984. Produces 4-6 children's plays/year; 1-2 children's musicals/year. "Scripts should not be longer than an hour, small cast preferred; very small production budgets, so use imagination." The Young Company is a professional training program associated with American Stage Festival, a professional theater. Produced plays/musicals: *Dancing on the Ceiling*, by Austin Tichenor (adaptation of Kafka's *Metamorphosis*, for ages 7 and up); *High Pressure Zone*, music by Andrew Howard, book and lyrics by Austin Tichenor (musical about addictive behavior, for middle school and older audience); *The First Olympics*, by Eve Muson and Austin Tichenor (deals with mythology/Olympic origins, for 6 year old through adult audience). Prefers adaptations with name recognition to young audiences. Does not want to see condescending material. Submission method: Query with synopsis, character breakdown and sample score. Purchases first production credit rights on all future materials. Pays small fee and housing for rehearsals.
Tips: Looks for "concise and legible presentation, songs that further dramatic action. Develop material with strong marketing possibilities. See your work in front of an audience and be prepared to change it if your audience doesn't 'get it.' Don't condescend to your audience. Tell them a *story*."

Special Markets

Walk into any children's-only bookstore—or even the children's department of any book superstore—and you'll find a variety of ancillary products. In fact, posters, coloring books, activity books, stickers, greeting cards, giftwrap, puzzles and games may all have spaces on bookstore shelves, in addition to their usual places in department stores, card shops and toy stores. The reason is simple: Booksellers have discovered such sidelines are valuable.

First, these products act as bait to lure customers who might not visit the bookstore if it only carried books. Prominently displayed sidelines increase the visual attractiveness and enhance the image of a bookstore. As a result, the more inviting atmosphere is more likely to draw customers. Second, booksellers like selling sidelines because they offer a higher margin of profit than books, therefore making them a good source of supplemental revenue. Bookstore owners are especially interested in products which are book-related or education-oriented.

What follows are 57 special markets that produce, among other items, greeting cards, comic books, games and puzzles for children and are interested in using the services of freelancers. As these markets create a potpourri of products, their needs vary greatly. Carefully read through the listings (17 of which are new to this edition) to determine desired subjects and methods of submission. If more specific guidelines are available from companies, write to request them. As in other areas of the children's market, remember the materials created must not only appeal to children but also to the adults who will purchase them.

ALEF JUDAICA, 8440 Warner Dr., Culver City CA 90232. (310)202-0024. Owner: Guy Orner. Greeting card and paper products company. Publishes Judaica card line, gift wrap and party goods. Publishes greeting cards (Hanukkah card line), books and novelties (Hanukkah party goods).
Writing: Needs freelance writing for children's greeting cards and books. Makes 50 writing assignments/year. To contact, send cover letter and writing samples. Reports only if interested. For greeting cards, pays flat fee of $100-200. For other writing, pays by the project (range: $1,000-5,000). Pays on publication. Purchases all rights and exclusive product rights. Credit line given.
Illustration: Needs freelance illustration for children's greeting cards and party goods. Makes about 50 illustration assignments/year. To contact, send published samples, photocopies and portfolio. Reports only if interested. Keeps materials on file. For children's greeting cards, pays flat fee of $100-200. For other artwork, payment "depends on how complicated the project is." Pays on publication. Buys all rights, exclusive product rights. Credit line sometimes given.
Tips: 25% of products are made for kids or have kids' themes. Seasonal material should be submitted 1 year in advance.

AMERICAN ARTS & GRAPHICS, INC., 10915 47th Ave. W., Mukilteo WA 98275. (206)353-8200. Licensing Director: Tina Gilles. Estab. 1948. Paper products company. Publishes and distributes posters "for many large retail chains, specialty stores, bookstores and independent accounts."
Writing: Needs posters. Makes 1-3 writing assignments/month; 12-20/year. To contact, send cover letter, pieces suited for children's posters. Reports in "weeks." Pays $250-1,000 advance against 10% royalties. Pays on acceptance. Purchases exclusive product rights. Credit line given.

Illustration: Needs freelance illustration for children's posters. Makes 1-3 illustration assignments/month; 12-20/year. "Prefers airbrush (bright colors), to fit a 22×34 format—fantasy, cute or funny animals, other popular children and teen subjects." Uses color artwork only. To contact, send cover letter, color photocopies, portfolio, promo pieces, slides. Reports in "weeks." Returns material with SASE; materials sometimes filed. Pay is negotiable—usually $500-1,000 against 10% royalty for 2-3 years. Pays on acceptance. Buys exclusive product rights. Credit line given. Artist's guidelines available for SASE.

Photography: Purchases photography from freelancers. Buys stock and assigns work. Buys 30 stock images/year; makes 12 assignments/year. Wants "exotic sports cars, cute and/or funny animals, wildlife (especially tigers, panthers), sports." Uses 2¼×2¼ and 4×5 transparencies. To contact, send cover letter, slides and portfolio. Reports in "weeks;" materials returned with SASE; materials sometimes filed. Pays $500-1,000 advance against 10% royalties. Pays on acceptance. Buys exclusive product rights. Credit line given. Photographer's guidelines available for SASE.

ARISTOPLAY, LTD., P.O. Box 7529, Ann Arbor MI 48107. (313)995-4353. Fax: (313)995-4611. Product Development Director: Lorraine Hopping Egan. Estab. 1979. Produces educational board games and card decks, activity kits—all educational subjects.

Illustration: Needs freelance illustration and graphic designers (including art directors) for games and card decks. Makes 2-6 illustration assignments/year. To contact, send cover letter, résumé, published samples or color photocopies. Reports back only if interested. For artwork, pays by the project, $500-5,000. Pays on acceptance (½-sketch, ½-final). Buys all rights. Credit line given.

Tips: "Creating board games requires a lot of back and forth in terms of design, illustration, editorial and child testing; the more flexible you are, the better. Also, factual accuracy is important." Target age group 4-14. "We are an educational game company. Writers and illustrators working for us must be willing to research the subject and period of focus."

A/V CONCEPTS CORP., 30 Montauk Blvd., Oakdale NY 11769. (516)567-7227. Fax: (516)567-8745. Editor: Laura Solimene. President: Philip Solimene. Estab. 1969. "We are an educational publisher. We publish books for the K-12 market—primarily language arts and math and reading."

Writing: Needs freelance writing for classic workbooks only: adaptations from fine literature. Makes 5-10 assignments/year. To contact, send cover letter and writing samples. Reports in 3 weeks. For writing assignments, pays by the project ($700-1,000). Pays on publication. Buys all rights.

Illustration: Needs freelance illustration for classic literature adaptations, fine art, some cartoons, super heros. Makes 15-20 illustration assignments/year. Needs "super hero-like characters in four-color and b&w." To contact, send cover letter and photocopies. Reports back in 3 weeks. For artwork, pays by the project (range: $200-1,000). Pays on publication. Buys all rights.

AVANTI PRESS, INC., 2500 Penobscot Bldg., Detroit MI 48226. (313)961-0022. Submit images to this address: Avanti, Suite 602, 84 Wooster, New York NY 10012. (212)941-9000. Art Researcher: Sylvia Bors. Estab. 1979. Greeting card company. Publishes photographic greeting cards—nonseasonal and seasonal.

Photography: Purchases photography from freelancers. Buys stock and assigns work. Buys approximately 50-75 stock images/year. Makes approximately 20-30 assignments/year. Wants "narrative, storytelling images, graphically strong and colorful!" Uses b&w/color prints; 35mm, 2¼×2¼ and 4×5 transparencies. To contact, "Call for submission guidelines—no originals!!" Reports in 2 weeks. Returns materials with SASE. "We pay either a flat fee or a royalty which is discussed at time of purchase." Pays on acceptance. Buys exclusive product rights (world-wide card rights). Credit line given. Photographer's guidelines for SASE.

Tips: At least 50% of products have kids' themes. Submit seasonal material 9 months-1 year in advance. "All images submitted should express some kind of sentiment which either fits an occasion or can be versed and sent to the recipient to convey some feeling."

*THE BEISTLE COMPANY, P.O. Box 10, Shippensburg PA 17257. (717)532-2131. Product Manager: C. Michelle Luhrs-Wiest. Art Director: Brad Clever. Estab. 1900. Paper products company. Produces decorations and party goods, bulletin board aides, posters—baby, baptism, birthday, holidays, educational.

Illustration: Needs freelance illustration for decorations, party goods, educational aides. Makes 20 illustration assignments/year. Prefers fanciful style, cute 4- to 5-color illustration in gouache. To contact, send cover letter, résumé, client list, promo piece. To query with specific ideas, phone or write. Reports only if interested. Materials returned with SASE; materials filed. Pays by the project (range: $325-400 or by contractual agreement; price varies according to type of project). Pays on acceptance. Buys all rights. Artist's guidelines available for SASE.

Photography: Buys photography from freelancers. Buys stock and assigns work. Buys 10-15 stock images/year. Makes 30-50 assignments/year. Uses 35mm, 2¼ × 2¼, 4 × 5 transparencies. To contact, send cover letter, résumé, slides, client list, promo piece. Reports only if interested. Materials returned if accompanied with SASE; materials filed. Pays on acceptance. Buys first rights. Credit line sometimes given—depends on project. Guidelines available for SASE.

Tips: 50% of products are made for kids or have kids' themes. Submit seasonal material 6-8 months in advance.

BEPUZZLED/LOMBARD MARKETING, INC., 22 E. Newberry Rd., Bloomfield CT 06002. (203)769-5723. Fax: (203)769-5799. Creative Services Manager: Judith Dorry. Estab. 1987. Publishes mystery jigsaw puzzles, mystery dinner games.

Writing: Needs freelance writing for short mystery stories. Makes 10-15 writing assignments/year. To contact, send cover letter and writing samples. Reports back only if interested. Pays by the project ($1,800). Pays on publication. Buys all rights. No credit line given.

Illustration: Needs freelance illustration for mystery jigsaw puzzles. Makes 25-30 illustration assignments/year. Preferences announced when needed. To contact, send cover letter, résumé, client list and color promo pieces. Reports back only if interested. Pays by the project ($1,500-3,000). Pays on publication. Buys all rights.

Tips: "Send SASE for guidelines. Submissions should be short and include idea of writing style, and an outline of ideas for visual and literal clues (six each, some with red herrings)."

RUSS BERRIE & COMPANY, INC., 111 Bauer Dr., Oakland NJ 07436. (201)337-9000. Director, Greeting Cards: Angelica Urra. Estab. 1963. Greeting card and paper products company. Manufactures "all kinds of paper products and impulse gifts—photo frames, mugs, buttons, baby gift products, cards, plaques, plush, ceramics, toys, bibs, booties, etc."

Writing: Needs freelance writing for children's books, booklets, greeting cards and other children's products (T-shirts, buttons, bookmarks, stickers, diaries, address books, plaques, perpetual (undated) calendars). "We seek material for children's books with strong story lines and characters that can effectively stand alone as plush, dolls, toys, ceramics, etc. We also seek short, short stories or character sketches revolving around a character (plush or toy) that you have developed. The short, short story would then be used on a two- to four-page small hang tag for the item itself, rather than as a separate book. Educatational or environmental themes are welcome, but please, no preaching . . . an engaging story is most important." Makes 10-50 writing assignments/month. Tired of children's greeting card writing which talks down to kids. To contact, send writing samples. Reports in 2-3 months. Materials returned with SASE; files materials "if we think there may be interest later." For greeting cards, pays flat fee of $50-100 per piece of copy. For books, plaques and other writing, pays more, depending on the project. Pays on acceptance. Buys all rights or exclusive product rights. Writer's guidelines for SASE.

Illustration: Needs freelance illustration for children's greeting cards and other children's products. Makes 10-50 illustration assignments/month. Artwork should be "contemporary, eye catching, colorful—professional. Because we also do products for parents and parents-to-be, we seek both juvenile *and* adult looks in products about children." To contact, send client list, published samples, photocopies, slides and/or promo piece. To query with specific ideas, send tight roughs. Reports in 2 months. Returns material with SASE; files material "if future interest is anticipated." For greeting cards, pays flat fee of $250-500. Pays on acceptance. Buys all rights or exclusive product rights. Credit line sometimes given. Artist's guidelines for SASE.

Photography: Buys photography from freelancers. Buys stock and assigns work. Buys 100 stock images/year. Makes 100 assignments/year. Photos should be "humorous with animals or children; unusual, eye catching, interesting, contemporary—not too arty." Uses b&w prints; 35mm, 2¼ × 2¼, 4 × 5 and 8 × 10 transparencies. To contact, send slides, client list, published samples, promo piece, portfolio, prints. Reports in 2 months. Materials returned with SASE; files photos "if there will be future interest." Pays per photo or by the project. Pays on acceptance. Buys all rights or exclusive product rights. Credit line sometimes given. Photographer's guidelines for SASE.

Tips: "One third of our products are made for kids or have kids' themes. Seasonal material should be submitted 18 months in advance. We're using more freelance illustrators and freelance writers who can submit a concept rather than single piece of writing. We are upbeat, with a large, diverse baby/children's line. Send all material to greeting card director—if it is for another product it will be passed along to the appropriate department."

BRILLIANT ENTERPRISES, 117 W. Valerio St., Santa Barbara CA 93101. Art Director: Ashleigh Brilliant. Estab. 1967. Publishers greeting cards—a wide range of humorous concepts; unrhymed.
Writing/Illustration: Reports in 3 weeks. Pays for greeting cards $40 minimum. Pays on acceptance. Buys all rights. Writer's/illustrator's guideline sheet for $2 and SAE.

BURGOYNE INC., 2030 E. Byberry Rd., Philadelphia PA 19116. (215)677-8000. Art Studio Manager: Mary Beth Burgoyne. Creative Director: Jeanna Lane. Estab. 1907. Greeting card company. Publisher of Christmas and everyday cards.
Illustration: Interested in illustrations for children's greeting cards. To contact, send cover letter. To query with specific ideas, send slides, published samples or original art. Reports in 2 months. Materials filed. Pays on acceptance. Buys greeting card US and worldwide rights. Credit line sometimes given. Artist's guidelines for SASE.
Tips: "We are looking for new traditional Christmas artwork with a detailed children's book look. We are also looking for juvenile birthday and all-occasion artwork year round."

CONTEMPORARY DESIGNS, 213 Main St., Gilbert IA 50105. (515)232-5188. Fax: (515)232-3380. Editor and Art Director: Sallie Abelson. Estab. 1977. Publishes greeting cards, coloring books and puzzles and games. "Greeting cards should be funny—for children who go to camp."
Writing/Illustration: 25% of material is written by freelancers; 20% illustrated by freelancers. Buys 50 freelance projects/year; receives 150 submissions/year. Materials returned with SASE. Reports in 1 month. Pays $40 for greeting cards. Pays on acceptance. Buys all rights on accepted material; negotiable amount for coloring books and puzzles. Writer's/illustrator's guidelines for SASE.
Tips: Submit seasonal material 1 year in advance. "Wants greeting cards for campers and Jewish markets only. Puzzles, games and coloring books should be Judaic."

CREATE-A-CRAFT, P.O. Box 330008, Fort Worth TX 76163-0008. Contact: Editor. Estab. 1967. Produces greeting cards, giftwrap, games, calendars, posters, stationery and paper tableware products for all ages.
Illustration: Works with 3 freelance artists/year. Buys 3-5 designs/illustrations/year. Prefers artists with experience in cartooning. Works on assignment only. Buys freelance designs/illustrations mainly for greetings cards and T-shirts. Also uses freelance artists for calligraphy, P-O-P displays, paste-up and mechanicals. Considers pen & ink, watercolor, acrylics and colored pencil. Prefers humorous and "cartoons that will appeal to families. Must be cute, appealing, etc. No religious, sexual implications or off-beat humor." Produces material for all holidays and seasons. Contact only through artist's agent. Some samples are filed; samples not filed are not returned. Reports only if interested. Write for appointment to show portfolio of original/final art, final reproduction/product, slides, tearsheets, color and b&w. Original artwork is not returned. "Payment depends upon the

assignment, amount of work involved, production costs, etc. involved in the project." Buys all rights. For guidelines and sample cards, send $2.50 and #10 SASE.

Tips: Submit 6 months in advance. "Demonstrate an ability to follow directions exactly. Too many submit artwork that has no relationship to what we produce. No phone calls accepted."

DESIGN DESIGN INC., P.O. Box 2266, Grand Rapids MI 49501. (616)774-2448. President: Don Kallil. Creative Director: Tom Vituj. Estab. 1986. Greeting card company.

Writing: Needs freelance writing for children's greeting cards. For greeting cards, prefers both rhymed and unrhymed verse ideas. To contact, send cover letter and writing samples. Reports in 3 weeks. Materials returned with SASE; materials not filed. For greeting cards, pays flat fee of $50 maximum. Buys all rights or exclusive product rights; negotiable. No credit line given. Writer's guidelines for SASE.

Illustration: Needs freelance illustration for children's greeting cards, notecards, wrapping paper. Makes 30 illustration assignments/month. Uses color artwork only. To contact, send cover letter, published samples, color or b&w photocopies color or b&w promo pieces or portfolio. Reports in 3 weeks. Returns materials with SASE. Pays by the project or royalty. Buys all rights or exclusive product rights; negotiable. Artist's guidelines available for SASE.

Photography: Purchases photography from freelancers. Buys stock and assigns work. Uses 4×5 transparencies or high quality 35mm slides. To contact, send cover letter with slides, stock photo list, published samples and promo piece. Reports in 3 weeks. Materials returned with SASE; materials not filed. Pays per photo or royalties. Pays on usage. Buys all rights or exclusive product rights; negotiable. Photographer's guidelines for SASE.

ECLIPSE COMICS, P.O. Box 1099, Forestville CA 95436. (707)887-1521. Fax: (707)887-7128. Editor-in-Chief: Catherine Yronwode. "Publishes comic books, graphic albums, trading cards, books and posters for young adult and adult market. Most are fictional, but we also have factual, educational lines." Estab. 1978.

• Eclipse is no longer accepting submissions.

Writing: Payment varies—"impossible to answer as books, comic books, trading cards all have different rates. We always pay an advance and royalty." Pays on acceptance. Rights negotiable. Credit line given.

Illustration: "Pay varies by project—all jobs pay an advance plus royalty." Pays on acceptance. Rights negotiable. Credit line given.

Tips: "Send #10 SASE for writers'/artists' guidelines. Painters interested in remaining on file for trading cards, send slides, promo pieces—color only."

*ENGLISH CARDS, LTD., 40 Cutter Mill Rd., Great Neck NY 11021. (516)775-8100. Contact: Douglas Evans. Estab. 1965. Greeting card company. "Greeting cards—birthday, get well, anniversary, friendship, thank you notes, invitations, announcements, boxed stationery. Full line of Christmas cards. All cards are sold in a box to retail outlets."

Illustration: Needs freelance illustration for children's, baby boomers' and senior citizens' greeting cards. Wants juvenile; bright colors (watercolor)—purple, pink vivid colors. Teddys, balloon designs. Also humorous and comic cards with funny verses to match the illustrations for baby boomers." Uses color artwork only. To contact, send cover letter and published samples. To query with specific ideas, send pencil sketches with color written out. Reports in 2-4 weeks. Materials filed. For greeting cards, pays flat fee of $150. For other artwork, pays by the project. Pays on acceptance. Buys all rights.

Photography: Buys photography from freelancers. Buys stock. Wants "clean, vivid, emotional, happy scenes of family, friends, *warmth*!" Uses prints and 4×5 transparencies. Also interested in retro, duo-tone and color-tinted photography. To contact, send stock photo list. Reports in 2-4 weeks. Keeps materials on file. Pays on acceptance. Buys all rights.

Tips: "Call for further information."

EPHEMERA BUTTONS, P.O. Box 490, Phoenix OR 97535. President: Ed Polish. Estab. 1980. Novelty pin back buttons and magnets with slogans and art (for children and adults).

Writing/Illustration: 95% of material written and 5% illustrated by freelancers. Buys over 200 freelance projects/year; receives over 2,000 submissions/year. Needs simple and bold line art that would work on a button. SASE for return of submission. Reports in 6 weeks. Material copyrighted. Pays on publication. Pays $25 per slogan or design. Guideline sheets for #10 SAE and 1 first-class stamp.

Tips: Looks for "very silly and outrageously funny slogans. We also are looking for provocative, irreverent and outrageously funny *adult* humor, and politically correct/incorrect slogans."

*EUROPEAN TOY COLLECTION, 6643 Melton Rd., Portage IN 46368. (219)763-3234. Fax: (219)762-1740. Children's Book Development Director: Beth Mullaney. New Artist Director: Kristin Scott. Estab. 1985. Children's toy, gift and publishing company. "We started our company about ten years ago with the intention of bringing high quality, well-designed products to the marketplace. To reach our goals we hope to find dedicated, talented artists with whom we can work . . . . artists with vision and imagination . . . . both artists who have established reputations as well as new, undiscovered artists." Manufactures novelties, coloring books, puzzles, games, children's picture books, novelty books, activity books, wooden toys, textile toys, etc.

Writing: "We are *opening up a new division* which will be publishing children's books—primarily for ages 2-6—usually, but not always, with product tie-ins."

Illustration: Need freelance illustrations for a wide range of children's products. "We plan on making 2-3 assignments/month; 24-36/year. Subject matter, themes and styles will vary according to project. We use a wide variety of themes and styles." To contact, send résumé, photocopies of artwork that can be kept on file. Submit idea in either detailed sketches and samples or in rough prototype. Reports back only if interested. Materials not returned; materials filed. "Payment for artwork will be competitive. We believe in having a fair, honest relationship with artists so they are fairly compensated for their efforts according to their talents, experience, name recognition, etc. For most unknown artists, payment will usually be by flat fees." Pays on acceptance. "We prefer to purchase all rights." Credit line sometimes given. 98% of products are made for kids or have kids' themes.

Tips: "We are looking for talented artists who care about children, about other people, about the world in which we live . . . artists who have special artistic gifts which they can share. We ask you to be special . . . to 'Wow Us' to 'Astonish Us' with your boldness or your understatement, with your simplicity or your complexity . . . with your imagination or insight or playfulness or poetry of soul or sense of humor. We are looking forward to hearing from you."

*FANTAGRAPHICS BOOKS, INC., 7563 Lake City Way NE, Seattle WA 98115. (206)524-1967. Fax: (206)524-2104. Contact: Submissions Editor. Art Director: Dale Yarger. Estab. 1975.

Writing/Illustration: 100% of material written and illustrated by freelancers. Buys 10-15 freelance projects/year; receives 300 submissions/year. Comic books: "We print comics of quality mostly aimed at adults, but a few for younger readers. We like projects that come wholly from the creator (writer and artist); any subject or style is fine. The only thing an illustrator should be aware of is that we rarely print comics in color; we prefer b&w art. All submissions must be accompanied with a SASE." Reports in 6 weeks. Purchases one-time rights. Pays on publication. Pays 4% minimum for comic books. Guideline sheets for #10 SASE.

Tips: Submit seasonal comic books 9 months in advance.

FAX-PAX USA, INC., 37 Jerome Ave., Bloomfield CT 06002. (203)242-3333. Fax: (203)242-7102. Editor: Stacey L. Savin. Estab. 1990. Buys 1 freelance project/year. Publishes educational picture cards. Needs include US history, natural history.

Writing/Illustration: Buys all rights. Pays on publication. Cannot return material.
Tips: "Well-written, interesting U.S. history sells best."

*FIRST IDEAS, INC., 338 Meadowbook Dr., Huntington Valley PA 19006. President: Craig Richardson. Estab. 1992. Greeting card, novelty items company. Publishes greeting cards (Kabloons), comic books and puzzles.
Writing: Needs freelance writing for children's greeting cards, other children's products. Other needs for freelance writing include television shows and comics. To contact, send cover letter, résumé, client list. To query with specific ideas, send with release. Reports in 2 weeks. Materials returned with SASE; materials filed. Pays on acceptance. Rights negotiable. Credit line sometimes given.
Illustration: Needs freelance illustration for children's greeting cards, TV shows and comic books.

FOTOFOLIO/ARTPOST, 536 Broadway, New York NY 10012. (212)226-0923. Editorial Director: Ron Schick. Estab. 1976. Greeting card company. Also publishes fine art and photographic postcards, notecards, posters, calendars. New children's line.
Illustration: Needs freelance illustration for children's greeting cards, calendars and coloring books. To contact, send cover letter, published samples, photocopies, slides, promo piece. Reports back only if interested. Returns materials with SASE; materials not filed. Rights negotiable. Credit line given. Artist's guidelines not available.
Photography: Buys photography from freelancers. Buys stock. To contact, send cover letter, slides, stock photo list, published samples and promo piece. Reports back only if interested. Returns material with SASE. Pays on usage. Rights negotiable. Credit line given. Photographer's guidelines not available.

*FROM MY HEART, 812 Oriole Lane, Chaska MN 55318. (612)448-6108 or (800)526-5863. Owner: Colleen DeBower. Estab. 1984. Greeting card company. Publishes greeting cards, including children's paper products, invitations, etc.
Writing: Needs freelance writing for children's greeting cards. For greeting cards, prefers both rhymed and unrhymed verse ideas. Looks for humorous greeting card writing. To contact, send cover letter, résumé, client list, writing samples. Reports in 3 weeks. Materials returned; materials filed. Pays flat fee (negotiable). Pays on publication. Buys all rights. Credit line sometimes given.
Illustration: Needs freelance illustration for children's greeting cards and stationery. "Just starting to look for illustrators."

GALISON BOOKS, Suite 910, 36 W. 44th St., New York NY 10036. (212)354-8840. Estab. 1978. Paper products company. Publishes museum-quality gift products, including notecards, journals, address books and jigsaw puzzles. Publishes children's greeting cards and puzzles.
Illustration: Needs freelance illustration for adults and children's greeting cards, jigsaw puzzles. Makes 30 illustration assignments/year. Uses color artwork only. To contact, send cover letter, published samples and color promo piece. To query with specific ideas, write for disclosure form first. Reports back only if interested. Returns materials with SASE; materials filed. For greeting cards, pays flat fee (range: $250-1,000). Pays on publication. Buys one-time rights; negotiable. Credit line given. Artist's guidelines not available.
Photography: Buys photography from freelancers. Buys stock. Buys 40 stock images/year. Uses 35mm, 2¼ × 2¼ and 4 × 5 transparencies. To contact, send cover letter, stock photo list, published samples and color promo piece. Reports back only if interested. Returns materials with SASE; materials filed. Pays $250/photo. Pays on publication. Buys one-time rights; negotiable. Credit line given. Photographer's guidelines available for SASE.
Tips: 10% of products are made for kids or have kids' themes. Seasonal material should be submitted 1 year in advance.

Refer to the Business of Children's Writing & Illustrating for up-to-date marketing, tax and legal information.

THE GIFT WRAP COMPANY, 28 Spring Ave., Revers MA 02151. (503)689-3900. Product Development and Marketing Coordinator: Betsey Cavallo. Estab. 1904. Paper products company. "We manufacture gift wrap and ribbons. Also sell greeting cards (Christmas only)/gift bags."
Illustration: Needs freelance illustration for gift wrap and gift bag designs. Number of illustration assignments "depends on our needs"—20 maximum/year. Looking for baby prints, juvenile birthday, wedding and shower. Uses color artwork only. To contact, send cover letter, résumé, color photocopies and non-returnable art. Reports back only if interested. Returns materials with SASE; materials filed. Pays by the project (range: $150-300). Pays on acceptance. Buys all rights. No credit line given.
Tips: 20-30% of products are made for kids or have kids' themes. Seasonal material should be submitted 4 months in advance. "We look for general designs that will fill our mass market and upscale lines."

GIRLS' LIFE MAGAZINE/THE AVALON HILL GAME CO., 4517 Harford Rd., Baltimore MD 21214. (410)254-9200. Fax: (410)254-0991. President: Jack Dott. Editor: A. Eric Dott. Art Director: Chris Kim. Estab. 1958. Produces comic books (*Tales from the Floating Vagabond*), magazine for girls ages 7-14 and an extensive line of games. 50% of material written and illustrated by freelancers. Buys 50 freelance projects/year; receives 500 submissions annually.
Writing: Makes 6 writing assignments/month; 36/year. To contact send cover letter, résumé, client list, writing samples. Reports back only if interested. Pays on publication. Buys all rights. Credit line sometimes given.
Illustration: Makes 2-3 illustration assignments/month; 30/year. Prefers styles pertaining to general interest topics for girls. To contact send cover letter, résumé, published samples, portfolio. Reports in 1 month. Pays on acceptance. Buys all rights. Credit line sometimes given.

GREAT AMERICAN PUZZLE FACTORY, INC., 16 S. Main St., S. Norwalk CT 06854. (203)838-4240. Fax: (203)838-2065. Art Director: Pat Duncan. Estab. 1976. Produces puzzles.
Illustration: Needs freelance illustration for puzzles. Makes 50 freelance assignments/year. Not interested in seasonal. To contact, send cover letter, color photocopies and color promo pieces with SASE. Reports in 2 months. Rights purchased vary. Buys all rights to puzzles. Pays on publication. Pay varies.
Tips: Wants "whimsical, fantasy" material. Targets ages 4-12 and adult.

GREAT SEVEN, INC., Unit 503, 3870 Del Amo Blvd., Torrance CA 90503. (310)371-4555. Vice President: Ronald Chen. Estab. 1984. Paper products company. Publishes educational and fun stickers for children and teenager markets.
Illustration: Needs freelance illustration for children's fun stickers. Makes 120 illustration assignments/year. Wants "kid themes." To contact, send published samples and b&w photocopies. To query with specific ideas, write to request disclosure form first. Reports back only if interested. Returns material with SASE; materials filed. Pays on acceptance. Buys all rights. No credit line given. Artist's guidelines not available.
Tips: 100% of products are made for kids or have kids' themes. Seasonal material should be submitted 10 months in advance.

HANDPRINT SIGNATURE, INC., P.O. Box 22682, Portland OR 97269. (503)295-1925. Fax: (503)295-3673. President: Paula Carlson. Greeting card company. "Manufacturer of greeting cards especially designed for kids to send. Each card to be 'signed' with a child's handprint or footprint."
   • For more information about Handprint Signature's illustration needs, see the interview with Paula Carlson in the 1994 edition of *Children's Writer's & Illustrator's Market*.
Illustration: Needs freelance illustration for children's greeting cards. "All art must tie in with general theme of Handprint Signature—cards for kids to send. Pure colors." To contact, send cover letter, résumé, published samples and acknowledgement that he/she

has seen and understands Handprint Signature card line (sample packet is available). Reports in 1 month. Returns materials with SASE; materials not filed. For greeting cards, pays advance and 4% royalty for national/life of card. Pays on publication. Credit line given. Artist's guidelines available.

Tips: 100% of products are made for kids or have kids' themes. "Even though an artist's work must tie in with other artists already published, the design and presentation must stand out as his or her own unique interpretation. The card design and the text should be harmonious and always conscious that even though the parent (adult) is buying the card, the card is from a child."

INTERCONTINENTAL GREETINGS LTD., 176 Madison Ave., New York NY 10016. (212)683-5830. Contact: Robin Lipner. Estab. 1964. 100% of material freelance written and illustrated. Produces greeting cards, scholastic products (notebooks, pencil cases), novelties (gift bags, mugs), tin gift boxes, shower and bedding curtains.

Writing: "Greeting card (style) artwork in series of three or more. We use very little writing except for humor." Makes 4 writing assignments/year. To contact, send cover letter, résumé, client list and writing samples with SASE. Reports in 4-6 weeks. Pays advance of $20-100 and royalty of 20% for life. Pays on publication. Purchases exclusive product rights. Credit line sometimes given.

Illustration: Needs children's greeting cards, notebook cover, photo albums, gift products. Makes 15 illustration assignments/month. Prefers primarily greeting card subjects, suitable for gift industry. To contact, send cover letter, résumé, client list, published samples, photocopies, slides and promo piece with SASE. Reports in 4-6 weeks. For greeting cards pays advance of $75 against 20% royalty for life. For other artwork pays 20% royalty for life. Pays on publication. Buys exclusive product rights. Credit line sometimes given.

Tips: Target group for juvenile cards: ages 1-10. Illustrators: "Use clean colors, not muddy or dark."

JILLSON & ROBERTS GIFTWRAP, INC., 5 Watson Ave., Irvine CA 92718. (714)859-8781. Art Director: Josh Neufeld. Estab. 1973. Paper products company. Makes giftwrap/gift-bags.

Illustration: Needs freelance illustration for children's giftwrap. Makes 6-12 illustration assignments/year. Wants children/baby/juvenile themes. To contact, send cover letter. Reports in 1 month. Returns material with SASE; materials filed. For wrap and bag designs, pays flat fee of $250. Pays on publication. Rights negotiable. No credit line given. Artist's guidelines for SASE.

Tips: 20% of products are made for kids or have kids' themes. Seasonal material should be submitted up to 1 month in advance. "We produce two lines of giftwrap per year: one everyday line and one Christmas line. The closing date for everyday is June 30th and Christmas is September 15th."

KINGDOM PUZZLES, 7231 Vanalden Ave., Reseda CA 91335-2580. (818)705-4572. Fax: (818)705-2480. Owner: M. Oldenkamp. Estab. 1987. Produces puzzles.

Making Contact & Terms: Include SASE with submission. Reports in 2 months. Pay varies.

Tips: Submit seasonal puzzles 1 year in advance. Wants "wildlife, nature" material for children and adults.

*THE LANG COMPANIES, 514 Wells St., Delafield WI 53018. (414)646-5555. Art Director: Andrew Lang. Estab. 1982. Greeting card and paper product company. Publishes greeting cards (Lang Graphics, Main Street Press, R.A. Lang Card Company), rubber stamps, calendars, stickers.

Writing: Needs freelance writing for children's greeting cards, story books. For greeting cards, prefers both rhymed and unrhymed verse ideas. Other needs for freelance writing include books. To contact, send cover letter, résumé, client list, writing samples. To query with specific ideas write to request disclosure form first. Reports back in 1 month. Materials returned; materials filed. Pays on publication. Rights negotiable. Credit line sometimes given.

Illustration: Needs freelance illustration for children's greeting cards. To contact, send cover letter, résumé, client list, published samples, color photocopies. To query with specific ideas write to request disclosure form first. Reports back in 1 month. Materials returned; materials filed. Pays on publication. Rights negotiable. Credit line sometimes given.
Photography: Buys photography from freelancers. Buys stock and assigns work. Uses 4×5 transparencies. To contact, send cover letter, résumé, client list, published samples. Reports back in 1 month. Materials returned; materials filed. Pays on usage. Rights negotiable. Credit line sometimes given.

*LOVE GREETING CARD CO. INC., 1717 Opa-Locka Blvd., Opa-Locka FL 33054. (305)685-5683. Editor: Norman Drittel. Estab. 1980. Greeting card, paper products and children's book company. Publishes greeting cards (Muffy 'N' Pebbles), posters, small books.
Writing: Needs freelance writing for children's greeting cards. Makes 2 writing assignments/month; 12/year. Prefers rhymed verse ideas. To contact, send writing samples. To query with specific ideas, contact Norman Drittel. Reports in 2 months. Materials returned with SASE; materials filed. For greeting cards, pays flat fee of $50-100. Pays on acceptance. Buys one-time rights, reprint rights; negotiable. Credit line given. Writer's guidelines available for SASE.
Illustration: Needs freelance illustration for children's greeting cards, book material. Makes 2 illustration assignments/month; 12/year. Prefers 8-10 page books. Uses color artwork only. To contact, send published samples, portfolio. Reports in 2 months. Materials returned with SASE; materials filed. For greeting cards, pays flat fee of $100-250. For other artwork, pays by the project (range: $500-2,500). Pays on acceptance. Rights negotiable. Credit line given. Artist's guidelines available for SASE.
Photography: Buys photography from freelancers. Buys stock and assigns work. Buys 20 stock images/year. Makes 5 assignments/year. Wants children, any subject. Uses color prints; 8×10 transparencies. To contact, send slides, portfolio. Reports in 2 months. Materials returned with SASE; materials filed. Pays per photo (range: $100-150) for b&w/color. Pays on acceptance. Rights negotiable. Credit line given. Guidelines available for SASE.
Tips: 20% of produces are made for kids or have kids' themes. Submit seasonal material 6 months in advance.

MAGIC MOMENTS GREETING CARDS, 10 Connor Lane, Deer Park NY 11729. (516)595-2300, ext. 1206. Art Director: A. Braunstein. Estab. 1938. Greeting card company. Publishes greeting cards.
Illustration: Needs freelance illustration for children's greeting cards. Uses color artwork only. To contact, send color photocopies and slides. Reports in 1 week. Returns materials with SASE; materials not filed. For greeting cards, pays flat fee of $75-135. Pays on acceptance. Buys exclusive product rights. No credit line given. Artist's guidelines not available.

MAYFAIR GAMES, 5641 Howard St., Niles IL 60714. (708)647-9650. Fax: (708)647-0939. Editorial Director: Doug Tabb. Art Director: Christine Vande Vort. Estab. 1981. Produces role playing, board, card and strategy games for teens and adults. 100% of material is written and illustrated by freelancers.
Writing: Buys 25 freelance projects/year; receives 100 submissions/year. SASE. Reports in 2 months. Pays on acceptance and publication. Writer's guideline sheet for SASE.
Tips: Target age group: 14- to 40-years-old.

*FRANCES MEYER, INC., 104 Coleman Blvd., Savannah GA 31408. (912)748-5252. Stationery Brand Manager: Katherine Trosdal. Estab. 1979. Manufacturer of stationery, gift wrap, notes, birth announcements and party supplies.
Illustration: Needs freelance illustration. Makes 10-20 illustration assignments/year. To contact, send portfolio or photocopies, slides, color promo piece. Reports in 2-3 weeks. Materials returned upon request with SASE.

NATIONAL POLY CONSUMER PRODUCTS, P.O. Box 4309, Mankato MN 56002-4309. (507)386-4420. Manager of Sales and Marketing: Germaine Nowacki. Estab. 1960. Plastic products manufacturer. Prints plastic table covers, table skirting, aprons, bibs (adult and child), gloves and boots. Manufactures children's bibs (printed with animals).

Illustration: Makes 3-4 illustration assignments/year. Uses b&w artwork only. To contact, send cover letter, photocopies, slides. To query with specific ideas, write to request disclosure from first. Reports in 2 weeks. For artwork, pays by the project (range: $150-2,000). Material not filed. Pays on acceptance. Buys one-time rights. Credit line given.

Tips: About 3% of the products are made for kids or have kids' themes. Seasonal material should be submitted 6 months in advance.

P.S. GREETINGS/FANTUS PAPER PRODUCTS, 5060 N. Kimberly Ave., Chicago IL 60630. (312)384-0909. Art Director: Bill Barnes. Greeting card company. Publishes boxed and individual counter cards. Publishes greeting cards (Kards for Kids — counter; Kids Kards — boxed; Christmas).

Writing: Needs freelance writing for children's greeting cards. Makes 1-10 writing assignments/year. Looks for writing which is "appropriate for kids to give to relatives." To contact, send writing samples. Reports in 6 months. Material returned only if accompanied with SASE; materials filed. For greeting cards, pays flat fee. Pays on acceptance. Buys all rights. Credit line sometimes given. Writer's guidelines for SASE.

Illustration: Needs freelance illustration for children's greeting cards. Makes 50-100 illustration assignments/year. "Open to all mediums, all themes — use your creativity!" To contact, send published samples (up to 20 samples of any nature) and photocopies. Reports in 6 months. Returns materials with SASE; materials filed. For greeting cards, pays flat fee. Pays on acceptance. Buys all rights. Credit line sometimes given. Artist's guidelines for SASE.

Photography: Buys photography from freelancers. Buys stock. Buys 10-20 stock images/year. Wants florals, animals, seasonal (Christmas, Easter, valentines, etc.). Uses transparencies (any size). To contact, send slides. Reports in 6 months. Materials returned with SASE; materials filed. Pays on acceptance. Buys all rights. Credit line sometimes given. Photographer's guidelines for SASE.

Tips: "Only 7% of products are made for kids or have kids' themes, so it needs to be great stuff!" Seasonal material should be submitted 6 months in advance. "We are open to all creative ideas — generally not fads, however. All mediums are considered equally. We have a great need for 'cute' Christmas subjects."

PAINTED HEARTS & FRIENDS, 1222 N. Fair Oaks Ave., Los Angeles CA 91103. (818)798-3633. Fax: (818)793-7385. Chairman of the Board: David Mekelburg. Co-owner: Susan Kinney. Estab. 1988. Material produced includes greeting cards.

Illustration: Buys 5 freelance projects/year. Material returned with SASE. Reports in 1 week. Pays on publication.

Tips: Submit seasonal material 1 year in advance.

PALM PRESS, INC., 1442A Walnut St., Berkeley CA 94709. (510)486-0502. Assistant Photo Editor: Theresa McCormick. Estab. 1980. Greeting card company. Publishes high quality greeting cards from photos.

Photography: Buys photography from freelancers. Buys stock. Wants unusual images for birthday cards, new baby, friendship, get well, Valentines, Mother's Day, Christmas. Uses 35mm, 2¼×2¼ and 4×5 transparencies. Reports in 1 month. Materials returned with SASE. Pays per photo (range: $150-1,000) or royalties of 6½%. Pays on usage. Buys exclusive product rights. Credit line given. Photographer's guidelines for SASE.

Tips: 15% of products are made for kids or have kids' themes. Seasonal material should be submitted 1½ years in advance.

PEACEABLE KINGDOM PRESS, 1051 Folger Ave., Berkeley CA 94710. (510)644-9801. Fax: (510)644-9805. Art Director: Olivia Hurd. Estab. 1983. Produces posters and greeting cards. Uses images from classic children's books.

Illustration: Needs freelance illustration for children's greeting cards and posters. Makes 5 illustration assignments/month; 60/year. To contact, send cover letter and color photocop-

ies. Reports in 3 weeks. Pays on publication with advance. Pays 5-10% of wholesale for greeting cards. Buys rights to distribution worldwide.
Tips: "We only choose from illustrations that are from published children's book illustrators, or commissioned art by established children's book illustrators. Submit seasonal posters and greeting cards 6 months in advance."

PEACOCK PAPERS, INC., 273 Summer St., Boston MA 02210. New Product Manager: Mia Miranda. Estab. 1982. Manufactures children's and infants' T-shirts and sweatshirts.
Writing: Needs freelance writing for apparel (Ts and sweats). Makes 5 writing assignments/year. To contact, send letter and SASE. To query with specific ideas, submit on 8½×11 paper, double spaced. Reports in 3 weeks. Materials returned with SASE; materials filed. Pays $50 for first use. Pays on acceptance. Buys exclusive product rights. Writer's guidelines for SASE.
Tips: "Send only *original*, humorous one-liners (quick reads) that relate to *all* children and infants."

*PLUM GRAPHICS, P.O. Box 136, Prime St. Station, New York NY 10012. (212)966-2573. Owner: Yvette Cohen. Estab. 1983. Greeting card company. Produces die-cut greeting cards for ages 5-105. Publishes greeting cards (paper zoo line) and message boards.
Writing: Needs freelance writing for children's greeting cards. Makes 4 writing assignments/year. Looks for greeting card writing which is fun. Tired of writing which is boring. To contact, send SASE for guidelines. Reports in 2 months. Materials returned with SASE; materials filed. For greeting cards, pays flat fee of $40. Pays on publication. Buys all rights.
Illustration: Needs freelance illustration for children's greeting cards. Makes 3 illustration assignments/year. Prefers very tight artwork, mostly realism. Uses color artwork only. To contact, send b&w photocopies. Reports only if interested. Materials returned with SASE; materials filed. For greeting cards, pays flat fee of $350-450 "plus $50 each time we repeat." Pays on publication. Buys exclusive product rights. Credit line given sometimes—depends on project.
Tips: 40% of products are made for kids or have kids' themes. Submit seasonal material 1 year in advance. "Go to a store and look at our cards and style before submitting work."

*POPSHOTS, 735 Post Rd. E., Westport CT 06880. (203)454-9700. Founder: Paul Zalon. Estab. 1976. Greeting card and paper products company. Publishes greeting cards (Popshots, high end pop-up cards).
Illustration: Needs freelance illustration for children's greeting cards. Makes 4 illustration assignments/month; 60/year.

PORTAL PUBLICATIONS, LTD., 770 Tamalpais Dr., Corte Madera CA 94925. (415)924-5652. Posters/Art Director: Wendy Lagerström. Card/Art Director: Patricia Collette. Estab. 1955. Publisher and distributor of posters, cards, calendars, art prints, gift bags and T-shirts.
Illustration: Needs freelance illustration for children's greeting cards and posters. Makes 200-300 illustration assignments/year. Prefers animals. Uses color artwork only. To contact, send published samples, slides (not originals). Reports in 2-3 months. Returns materials if accompanied with SASE; materials filed. For greeting cards pays flat fee of $200-350, royalty of 5% for 4 years or life of card or advance of $100-200 against 5% royalty for life of card. For other artwork, pays $500-800 flat fee or $400-600 advance against 5% royalty. Pays on publication. Buys first rights. Credit line given. Artist's guidelines available.
Photography: Buys photography from freelancers. Buys stock and assigns work. Buys 150-250 stock images/year. Makes 200-250 assignments/year. Uses transparencies of all sizes. To contact, send slides (not originals), published samples and promo piece. Materials returned with SASE. Pays per photo (range: $150-1,500 flat fee for photo), or royalties of

The asterisk before a listing indicates the listing is new in this edition.

3-5%. Pays on usage. Buys first rights. Credit line given. Photographer's guidelines for SASE.
Tips: 10% of products are made for kids. Seasonal material should be submitted 9 months in advance. "Contemporary decor colors and trends are important to our products—e.g. cows, wolves, pigs, dogs, cats and whales are popular; sunflowers and environmental themes too."

*PRATT & AUSTIN CO., P.O. Box 587, Holyoke MA 01041. (413)532-1491. Product Development: Lorilee Costello. Estab. 1934. Paper products company. Targets women ages 16-60: stationery, tablets, envelopes, calendars, children's craft items. Produces calendars, paper dolls, paper airplanes, mobiles, etc.
Illustration: Needs freelance illustration for paper airplanes, crafts, paper dolls, calendars, storage boxes. Makes 2-4 illustration assignments/month; 30-40/year.

*PUZZLING POSTCARD CO., 21432 Vintage Way, Lake Forest CA 92630. (714)951-3784. President: Tom Judge. Estab. 1991. Greeting card company, puzzle card producer. Produces Puzzling Postcard™, jigsaw puzzle greeting card. Publishes greeting cards, puzzles.
Illustration: Needs freelance illustration for children's greeting cards. Makes 12-24 illustration assignments/year. Uses color artwork only. To contact, send cover letter, client list, published samples, color photocopies. To query with specific ideas, call to discuss. Reports only if interested. Materials returned with SASE; materials filed. For greeting cards, pays flat fee of $100-200, royalty of 3% for 2 years, advance of $50 against negotiable royalty for negotiable period. Pays on publication. Buys negotiable rights.
Photography: Buys photography from freelancers. Buys stock images. To contact, send cover letter, stock photo list, published samples. Reports only if interested. Materials returned with SASE; materials filed. Pays on usage. Buys negotiable rights.

*RECO INTERNATIONAL CORP., 138-150 Haven Ave., Pt. Washington NY 11050. (516)767-2400. President: Heio W. Reich. Estab. 1967. Collector's plate producer.
Illustration: Needs freelance illustration for collector's plates—children's subjects. Makes 60-100 assignments/year. Uses color artwork only. To contact, send portfolio. Submit specific ideas. Reports in 6 weeks. Materials returned with SASE; materials filed. For greeting cards, pays flat fee and royalty. For other artwork, pays royalty and advance. Pays on acceptance. Buys exclusive product rights. Artist's guidelines available for SASE after review of portfolio.
Tips: 60% of products are made for kids or have kids' themes. Submit seasonal material 6-10 months in advance (although rarely uses seasonal work).

*RED FARM STUDIO, 1135 Roosevelt Ave., P.O. Box 347, Pawtucket RI 02862. (401)728-9300. Contact: Production Coordinator. Estab. 1949. Greeting card company. Publishes coloring books and paintables.
Illustration: Needs freelance illustration for children's traditional subject greeting cards, coloring books and paintables. Makes 1 illustration assignment/month; 6-12/year. Prefers "watercolor, realistic styles yet cute." For first contact, request art guidelines with SASE. Reports in 2-4 weeks. Returns materials with SASE. Appropriate materials are kept on file. "We work on assignment using ink line work (coloring books) or pencil renderings (paintables)." For full color painting pays flat fee of $200-275. For b&w artwork, pays flat fee of $150-175 per page for color books and paintables. Pays on acceptance. Buys all rights. No credit line given but artist may sign artwork. Artist's guidelines for SASE.
Tips: 20% of products are made for kids or have kids' themes. Majority of freelance assignments made during January-May/yearly. "Research companies before sending submissions to determine whether your styles are compatible."

RUBBER STAMPEDE, 967 Stanford, Oakland CA 94608. (510)843-8910. Fax: (510)843-5906. Art Director: Rita Wood. Estab. 1978. Produces puzzles, rubber stamps. Themes: nature, Victorian, teddy bears, cute animals, fantasy.
Illustration: Needs freelance illustration for rubber stamps and packaging. Makes 12 illustration assignments/year. Prefers "cute and realistic." To contact, send cover letter, pub-

lished samples, b&w photocopies and promo pieces. Reports only if interested. Buys all rights. Pays by the project. Pays on acceptance.

Tips: Target age is 3 to 103. Submit seasonal special games, puzzles or comic books 4 months in advance. "No beginners, please. We are looking for a high level of technical expertise."

*MARCEL SCHURMAN COMPANY, 2500 N. Watney Way, Fairfield CA 94533. Editor: Meg Schutte. Creative Director: Diane Ruhl. Greeting card company. Publishes greeting cards, gift wrap, stationery, bags.

Writing: Needs freelance writing for children's greeting cards. Makes 2-3 writing assignments/month; 50/year. For greeting cards, prefers unrhymed verse ideas. To query with specific ideas, write to request disclosure form first. Reports in 6 weeks. Materials returned with SASE; sometimes files material. For greeting cards, pays flat fee of $75-125. Pays on acceptance. Credit line sometimes given. Writer's guidelines available for SASE.

Illustration: Needs freelance illustration for children's greeting cards. Makes 60 illustration assignments/month; 800/year. Uses color artwork only. To contact, send color photocopies. To query with specific ideas, send letter with or without samples. Reports in 1 month. Materials returned if accompanied by SASE; materials filed. For greeting cards pays advance of $300 against 5% royalty for 3 years. Pays "when final art is approved." Credit line sometimes given. Artist's guidelines available for SASE.

Photography: Buys photography from freelancers. Buys stock and assigns work. Uses 4×5 transparencies. To contact, send slides. Reports in 1 month. Materials returned; materials filed. Pays advance of $250 and 5% royalties. Pays "when final art is approved." Buys exclusive product rights, worldwide, 3-year period. Credit line sometimes given. Guidelines for SASE.

Tips: 20% of products are made for kids or have kids' themes.

SHULSINGER SALES, INC., 50 Washington St., Brooklyn NY 11201. (718)852-0042. Art Director: Daniel Deutsch. Estab. 1950. Greeting card and paper products company. "We are a Judaica company, distributing products such as greeting cards, books, paperware, puzzles, games, novelty items – all with a Jewish theme." Publishes greeting cards, novelties, coloring books and puzzles.

Writing: Looks for greeting card writing which can be sent by children to adults and sent by adults to children (of all ages). To contact, send cover letter. To query with specific ideas, write to request disclosure form first. Reports in 2 weeks. Materials returned with SASE; materials filed. For greeting cards, pays flat fee (this includes artwork). Pays on acceptance. Buys exclusive product rights.

Illustration: Needs freelance illustration for children's greeting cards, books, novelties, games. Makes 10-20 illustration assignments/year. "The only requirement is a Jewish theme." To contact, send cover letter and photocopies, color if possible. To query with specific ideas, write to request disclosure form first. Reports in 2 weeks. Returns materials with SASE; materials filed. For children's greeting cards, pays flat fee (this includes writing). For other artwork, pays by the project. Pays on acceptance. Buys exclusive product rights. Credit line sometimes given. Artist's guidelines not available.

Tips: 40% of products are made for kids or have kids' themes. Seasonal material should be submitted 6 months in advance.

STANDARD PUBLISHING, 8121 Hamilton Ave., Cincinnati OH 45231. (513)931-4050. Fax: (513)931-0904. Director: Mark Taylor. Children's Editor: Diane Stortz. Estab. 1866. Publishes children's books and teacher helps for the religious market. Publishes board books, easy readers, coloring books, puzzles, games and activity books.

Writing: Needs freelance writing for children's books. Makes 6-12 writing assignments/year. Reports in 2 months. Pays on acceptance. Buys all rights. Credit line given.

Illustration: Needs freelance illustration for puzzle, activity books, teacher helps. Makes 6-10 illustration assignments/year. Freelance artwork needed for activity books, etc. (b&w line art). To contact, send cover letter and photocopies. Reports back only if interested. Pays on acceptance. Buys all rights. Credit line given.

Tips "We look for upbeat manuscripts with a Christian perspective."

THE STRAIGHT EDGE, INC., 296 Court St., Brooklyn NY 11231. (718)643-2794. President: Amy Epstein. Estab. 1983. Manufactures placemats, shower curtains with educational themes for children and adults.

Illustration: Needs freelance illustration for placemats and shower curtains. Makes approximately 6-10 illustration assignments/year. Wants "line art; no rendering; realistic drawings with a sense of humor." Uses color artwork only. To contact, send cover letter and b&w photocopies. Reports back only if interested. Returns materials if requested; otherwise materials are filed. For artwork, pays by the project (range: $400-500 per mechanical per design). Pays on completion of mechanical. Buys exclusive product rights.

SUNRISE PUBLICATIONS, INC., P.O. Box 4699, Bloomington IN 47402. (812)336-9900. Fax: (812)336-8712. Editor: Sheila Gerber. Art Review Coordinator: Mary Henderson McClain. Estab. 1974. Greeting card lines: general greetings, holidays, note cards. Greeting cards: unrhymed verse.

Writing/Illustration: Buys 600 freelance projects/year. Receives 1,000/year. Reports in 10 weeks. Material copyrighted. Pays on acceptance. Pay for greeting cards $40-125 (versing); $350 per design. Guideline sheets for #10 SAE and 1 first-class stamp.

Tips: Looks for "bright, festive, not-too-wordy verse; occasion-specific illustration. Submit seasonal greeting cards 6-8 months in advance."

*TALICOR, INC., 190 Gentry St., Pomona CA 91767. (909)593-5877. President: Lew Herndon. Estab. 1971. Game manufacturer. Publishes games (adult and children's).

Illustration: Needs freelance illustration for games. Makes 14 illustration assignments/ year. To contact, send promo piece. Reports only if interested. Materials returned with SASE; materials filed. For artwork, pays by the hour or by the project or negotiable royalty. Pays on acceptance. Buys negotiable rights.

Photography: Buys photography from freelancers. Buys stock and assigns work. Buys 6 stock images/year. Makes 6 assignments/year. Uses 4×5 transparencies. To contact, send color promo piece. Reports only if interested. Materials returned with SASE; materials filed. Pays per photo, by the hour, by the day or by the project (negotiable rates). Pays on acceptance. Buys negotiable rights.

Tips: 80% of products are made for kids or have kids' themes. Submit seasonal material 6 months in advance.

WARNER PRESS, P.O. Box 2499, Anderson IN 46018. Product Editor: Robin Fogle. Art Department Manager: Roger Hoffman. Photo Editor: Millie Corzine. Estab. 1880. Publishes children's greeting cards, coloring and activity books and posters, all religious-oriented. "Need fun, up-to-date stories for coloring books, with religious emphasis. Also considering activity books for Sunday school classroom use."

Writing: Needs freelance writing for children's greeting cards, coloring and activity books. To contact, request guidelines first. Reports in 4-6 weeks. For greeting cards, pays flat fee (range: $20-30). Pays on acceptance. Buys all rights. Credit line sometimes given.

Illustration: Needs freelance illustration for children's greeting cards, coloring and activity books. Wants religious, cute illustrations. To contact, send published samples, photocopies and promo pieces (all nonreturnable). Reports in 1 month. For greeting cards, pays flat fee (range: $250-350). Pays on acceptance. Buys all rights. Credit line given.

Tips: Write for guidelines before submitting. Looking for "high quality art on flexible material for scanning. Meeting deadlines is important for children's illustrations. We publish simple styles. Material that does not follow guidelines will not be reviewed."

Special Markets/'94-'95 changes

The following markets were in the 1994 edition of *Children's Writer's & Illustrator's Market* but do not have listings in this edition. A few did not update their listings; if a reason was given for exclusion, it is in parentheses after the market's name.

Everything Personalized, Inc.
Lucy & Company

MU Press (doesn't need children's material)

Rivercrest Industries
TLC Greetings (company sold)

Young Writer's & Illustrator's Markets

The 55 listings in this section are special because they seek work from talented youths. Some are magazines exclusively for children. Others are adult magazines that have set aside special sections to feature the work of younger writers and illustrators. And a few, such as Tyketoon Young Author Publishing Company (see the Insider Report on page 292), are book publishers seeking children's stories and artwork.

Just like markets for adults, markets for children expect you to be familiar with their editorial needs *before* submitting. And the best way to discover a publication's needs is to read several issues. You will easily find some magazines, such as *American Girl* and *Stone Soup*, on newsstands or in libraries. However, many juvenile magazines, particularly small and/or literary publications, are primarily distributed through schools, churches or home subscriptions, and may be difficult to locate. If you can't find a copy of publications such as *Ink Blot*, *Poem Train* or *Writes of Passage* (all new to this edition), write to the editors and see if sample copies are available (and at what cost). Most editors will gladly supply sample copies for a nominal fee.

It is also important to send a self-addressed, stamped envelope (SASE)—with proper postage affixed—with each submission. This way, if the market is not interested in your work, it will be sent back to you. If you do not send a SASE with your submission, chances are you will not get your work returned. Make sure to read the Business of Children's Writing & Illustrating at the beginning of this book for more information about proper submission procedures.

If your material is rejected the first time you send it out, rest assured you are not the only one this has happened to. Many of our best known writers and artists were turned down at the beginning of their careers more times than they can count. The key to becoming published lies in persistence as well as talent. Keep sending out stories and artwork as you continue to improve your craft. Someday, an editor may decide your work is just what he or she needs.

To locate competitions open to young writers and illustrators, turn to Contests & Awards. Listings in that section which are designated by a double dagger (‡) are contests open to students (sometimes exclusively). Additional opportunities for writers can also be found in the *Market Guide for Young Writers* by Kathy Henderson (Writer's Digest Books). You might also be interested in reading Jeff Aikman's story (on page 232 in Audiovisual Markets). It's a great example of how a young person can succeed. At the age of 13, Jeff started his own film company which has grown into a business worth millions.

THE ACORN, 1530 Seventh St., Rock Island IL 61201. (309)788-3980. Newsletter. Estab. 1989. Audience consists of "kindergarten-12th grade, teachers and other adult writers." Purpose in publishing works for children: to expose children's manuscripts to others and provide a format for those who might not have one. Children must be K-12 (put grade on manuscripts). Guidelines available for SASE.

Magazines: 100% of magazine written by children. Uses 6 fiction pieces (500 words), 20 pieces of poetry (32 lines). No payment; purchase of a copy isn't necessary to be printed. Sample copy $2. Subscription $10 for 6 issues. Submit mss to Betty Mowery, editor. Send complete ms. Will accept typewritten, legibly handwritten and/or computer printout. SASE. Reports in 1 week.

Artwork/Photography: Publishes artwork by children. Looks for "all types; size 4 × 5. Use black ink in artwork." No payment. Submit artwork either with manuscript or separately to Betty Mowery. SASE. Reports in 1 week.

Tips: "My biggest problem is not having names on the manuscripts. If the manuscript gets separated from the cover letter, there is no way to know whom to respond to."

AMERICAN GIRL, 8400 Fairway Place, Middleton WI 53562. (608)836-4848. Bimonthly magazine. Audience consists of girls ages 7-12 who are joyful about being girls. Young writers must be 7-12 years old. Writer's guidelines available with #10 SASE.

Magazines: 5% of magazine written by young people. "A few pages of each issue are set aside for children and feature articles that answer questions or requests that have appeared in a previous issue of *American Girl*." Pays in copies. Submit to Harriet Brown, editor. Will accept legibly handwritten ms. SASE. Reports in 2 months.

THE APPRENTICE WRITER, % Gary Fincke, Susquehanna University, Selinsgrove PA 17870. (717)372-4164. Magazine. Published annually. "Writing by high school students and for high school students." Purpose in publishing works by young people: to provide quality writing by students which can be read for pleasure and serve as a text for high school classrooms. Work is primarily from eastern and northeastern states, but will consider work from other areas of US. Students must be in grades 9-12. Writer's guidelines available for SASE.

Magazines: Uses 15 short stories (prefers under 5,000 words); 15 nonfiction personal essays (prefers under 5,000 words); 60 poems (no word limit) per issue. Pays in copies to writers and their schools. Submit mss to Gary Fincke, editor. Submit complete ms. Will accept typewritten mss. SASE. Submit ms by March 15. Responds by May of each year.

Artwork/Photography: Publishes artwork and photography by children. Looks for b&w. Pays in copies to artists and their schools. Submit originals or high quality copies. Submit art and photographs to Gary Fincke, editor. SASE. Submit artwork by March 15. Responds by May of each year.

BEYOND WORDS PUBLISHING, INC., 4443 NE Airport Rd., Hillsboro OR 97124. (503)693-8700. Book publisher. Publishes 1-2 books by children per year. Looks for "books that encourage creativity and an appreciation of nature in children." Wants to "encourage children to write, create, dream and believe that it is possible to be published. The books must be unique, be of national interest and the child must be personable and promotable."

Books: Publishes stories and joke books.

BOODLE, P.O. Box 1049, Portland IN 47371. (219)726-8141. Magazine published quarterly. "Each quarterly issue offers children a special invitation to read stories and poems written by others. Children can learn from the ideas in these stories and the techniques of sharing ideas in picures and written form. Audience is ages 6-12. We hope that publishing children's writing will enhance the self-esteem of the authors and motivate other children to try expressing themselves in this form." Submission requirements: "We ask that authors include grade when written, current grade, name of school, and a statement from parent or teacher that the work is original."

Magazines: 100% of magazine written by children. Uses 12 short stories (100-500 words), 1 usually animal nonfiction piece (100-500 words), 30 poems (50-500 words), 2 puzzles and mazes (50-500 words) per issue. Pays 2 copies of issue. Submit mss to Mavis Catalfio, editor. Submit complete ms. Will accept typewritten and legibly handwritten mss. Include SASE.

Artwork/Photography: Wants "mazes, cartoons, drawings of animals or seasons or sports which will likely match a story or poem we publish." Pays 2 copies of issue. "Drawings should be done in black ink or marker." Submit artwork to Mavis Catalfio, editor. Reports in 2 months.

Tips: Submit seasonal materials at least a year in advance. "We love humor and offbeat stories. We seldom publish sad or depressing stories about death or serious illness."

BOYS' LIFE, 1325 W. Walnut Hill Ln., P.O. Box 152079, Irving TX 75015-2079. (214)580-2366. Magazine published monthly. Audience consists of children ages 7-17. *Boys' Life* is published by the Boy Scouts of America to make available to children ages 7-17 the highest caliber of fiction and nonfiction, to stimulate an interest in good reading and to promote the principles of scouting. Must be 18 or under to submit.

Magazines: Small percentage of magazine written by young people. Uses hobby and collecting tips for "Hobby Hows" and "Collecting" columns. Pays $10/tip. Uses jokes for "Think & Grin" column. Pays choice of $2 or copy of *Scout Handbook* or *Scout Fieldbook/* joke accepted. Several times/year uses personal stories (500 words maximum) for "Readers' Page." Pays $25. Submit mss to column. Submit complete ms. Will accept typewritten and legibly handwritten mss.

Tips: For nonfiction mss, query first. All fiction mss should be double-spaced and typed copy, 1,000-1,500 words. Pays $750 and up for accepted stories. Story categories: humor, mystery, science fiction, adventure. Send to Features Editor, Kathleen Da Groomes one copy of story plus cover letter. Study one year's worth of recent magazines before submitting.

CHICKADEE MAGAZINE, Suite 306, 56 The Esplanade, Toronto, Ontario M5E 1A7 Canada. (416)868-6001. Magazine published 10 times/year. "*Chickadee* is for children ages 3-9. Its purpose is to entertain and educate children about science, nature and the world around them. We publish children's drawings to give readers the chance to express themselves. Drawings must relate the topics that are given in the 'Chirp' section of each issue."

Artwork/Photography: Publishes artwork by children. No payment given. Mail submissions with name, age and return address for thank you note. Submit to Mitch Butler, Chirp editor. Reports in 3 months.

*CHILD LIFE, Children's Better Health Institute, P.O. Box 567, Indianapolis IN 46206. (317)636-8881. Editor: Lise Hoffman. Magazine. Published 8 times/year. "Targeted toward kids ages 9-11, we are the nation's oldest continuously published children's magazine." Focuses on health, sports, fitness, nutrition, safety and general interest.

Magazines: "Publishes jokes, riddles, poems and original stories (250 words maximum) by children." Submit complete mss for fiction and nonfiction. Include name, address, phone number (for office use) and school photo. "No mass duplicated, multiple submission."

CHILDREN'S DIGEST, Children's Better Health Institute, P.O. Box 567, Indianapolis IN 46206. (317)636-8881. Magazine. Published 8 times/year. Audience consists of preteens. Purpose in publishing works by children: to encourage children to express themselves through writing. Requires proof of originality before publishing stories. Writer's guidelines available on request.

Magazines: 10% of magazine written by children. Uses 1 fiction story (under 500 words), 6-10 poems, 15-20 jokes/riddles per issue. "There is no payment for manuscripts submitted by readers." Submit mss to *Children's Digest*, Sandra J. Grieshop, editor. Submit complete ms. Will accept typewritten, legibly handwritten and computer printout mss. "We don't respond unless the material will be published. Sorry, no materials can be returned."

CHILDREN'S PLAYMATE, Children's Better Health Institute, P.O. Box 567, Indianapolis IN 46206. (317)636-8881. Editor: Lise Hoffman. Magazine. Estab. 1928. Audience consists of children between 6 and 8 years of age. Emphasizes health, fitness, safety, good nutrition, and *good* humorous fiction for beginning readers. Writer's guidelines available on request with SASE.

Artwork/Photography: Publishes artwork by children. "Prefers black line drawings on white paper. No payment for children's artwork published." No material can be returned.

We've just made getting your words published a little easier

Subscribe to WRITER'S DIGEST now, and get this invaluable guide, *Getting Published: What Every Writer Needs to Know*, FREE with your paid subscription.

INSIDE: How to write irresistible query letters and prepare polished manuscripts. How to give an editor nothing to do—except buy your work. Where to find ideas. And the "test" every editor gives...14 questions you can use to evaluate your freelancing savvy.

Use the card below to start your subscription today!

Subscription Savings Card

☐ Yes! I want professional advice on how to write publishable material and sell it to the best-paying markets. Start my 1-year (12 issues) subscription to WRITER'S DIGEST for just $18.97...a **46% savings off the newsstand price.**

Name _____

Address _____

City _____

State _____Zip _____

☐ Payment enclosed. Send my FREE gift right away!
☐ Bill me, and send my free gift upon payment.
Charge my ☐ Visa ☐ MasterCard

Card # _____Exp. _____

Signature _____

Guarantee: If you aren't completely satisfied with your subscription at any time, simply cancel and receive a full refund on all unmailed issues due you.
Outside the U.S. add $10 (includes GST) and remit in U.S. funds. Newsstand rate $35.40.

T7CW6

No other source offers so much information and instruction...

on writing...

WRITER'S DIGEST is packed with expert advice that can make you a better writer. Whatever your challenge...from generating plot ideas to overcoming writer's block. Whatever your specialty...from writing poetry to children's stories.

and selling what you write!

In every issue you'll learn the secrets of top-dollar freelancers. Like how to slant your writing for multiple sales. Negotiate contracts with editors and publishers. And how to make (and keep) contacts that help your career. Find out which markets are hot for your work right now, how much they're paying, and how to contact the right people.

Subscribe today and save 46% off the newsstand price!

*THE CLAREMONT REVIEW, 4980 Wesley Rd., Victoria, British Columbia V8Y 1Y9 Canada. (604)658-5221. Magazine. Publishes poetry and fiction with literary value by students aged 13-19 anywhere in North America. Purpose in publishing work by young people: to provide a literary venue.

Magazines: Uses 8-10 fiction stories (200-2,500 words), 25-35 poems. Pays in copies. Submit mss to editors. Submit complete ms. Will accept typewritten mss. SASE. Reports in 1 month.

Artwork: Publishes artwork by children. Looks for b&w imaginative art. Pays in copies. Send picture for review. Negative may be requested. Submit art and photographs to editors. SASE. Reports in 1 month.

CLUBHOUSE, P.O. Box 15, Berrien Springs MI 49103. (616)471-9009. Director of Publications: Elaine Trumbo. Magazine. Estab. 1949. Published monthly. Occasionally publishes items by kids. "Audience consists of kids ages 9-14; philosophy is God loves kids, kids are neat people." Purpose in publishing works by young people: to give encouragement and demonstration of talent. Children must be ages 9-14; must include parent's note verifying originality.

Magazines: Uses adventure, historical, everyday life experience (fiction/nonfiction-1,200 words); health-related short articles; poetry (4-24 lines of "mostly mood pieces and humor"). Pays in prizes for children, money for adult authors. Query. Will accept typewritten, legibly handwritten and computer printout mss. "Will not be returned without SASE." Reports in 6 weeks.

Artwork/Photography: Publishes artwork by children. Looks for all types of artwork— white paper, black pen. Pays in prizes for kids. Send b&w art to Elaine Trumbo, editor. "Won't be returned without SASE."

Tips: "All items submitted by kids are held in a file and used when possible. We normally suggest they do not ask for return of the item."

CREATIVE KIDS, P.O. Box 8813, Waco TX 76714. (800)998-2208. Editor: Andrea Harrington. Magazine published 6 times/year. Estab. 1979. "All of our material is by children, for children." Purpose in publishing works by children: "to create a product that provides children with an authentic experience and to offer an opportunity for children to see their work in print." Writers ages 8-14 must have statement by teacher or parent verifying originality. Writer's guidelines available on request with SASE.

Magazines: Uses "about 6" fiction stories (200-750 words); "about 6" nonfiction stories (200-750 words); poetry, plays, ideas to share 200-750 words/issue. Pays in "free magazine." Submit mss to submissions editor. Will accept typewritten mss. SASE. Reports in 1 month.

Artwork/Photography: Publishes artwork by children. Looks for "any kind of drawing, cartoon, or painting." Pays "free magazine." Send original or a photo of the work to submissions editor. No photocopies. SASE. Reports in 1 month.

Tips: "*Creative Kids* is a magazine by kids, for kids. The work represents children's ideas, questions, fears, concerns and pleasures. The material never contains racist, sexist or violent expression. The purpose is to provide children with an authentic experience. A person may submit one piece of work per envelope. Each piece must be labeled with the student's name, birth date, grade, school, home address and school address. Include a photograph, if possible. Recent school pictures are best. Material submitted to *Creative Kids* must not be under consideration by any other publication. Items should be carefully prepared, proofread and double checked. All activities requiring solutions must be accompanied by the correct answers."

CREATIVE WITH WORDS, *We Are Writers, Too!*, Creative with Words Publications, P.O. Box 223226, Carmel CA 93922. Editor: Brigitta Geltrich. Quarterly anthology. Estab. 1975. "We publish the creative writing of children." Audience consists of children, schools, libraries, adults, reading programs. Purpose in publishing works by children: to offer them an opportunity to get started in publishing. "Work must be of quality, original, unedited, and not published before; age must be given (up to 19 years old)." SASE must be enclosed with all correspondence and mss. Writer's guidelines available on request.

Books: Considers all categories except those dealing with death, violence, pornography and overly religious. Uses fairy tales, folklore items (1,000 words) and poetry (not to exceed 20 lines, 46 characters across). Published *Impossible Loves* (children and adults) and *Animals* (children and adults). Pays 20% discount on each copy of publication in which fiction or poetry by children appears. Submit mss to Brigitta Geltrich, editor. Query; teacher or parent must submit; teacher and/or parents must verify originality of writing. Will accept typewritten and/or legibly handwritten mss. SASE. Reports in 2 months after deadline.

Artwork/Photography: Publishes artwork and computer artwork by children (language art work). Pays 20% discount on every copy of publication in which work by children appears. Submit artwork to Brigitta Geltrich, editor.

FREE SPIRIT PUBLISHING INC., Suite 616, 400 First Ave. North, Minneapolis MN 55401. (612)338-2068. "Our first book by a child will be released this year." Published 8-12 books/year since starting in 1983. "We specialize in SELF-HELP FOR KIDS®. Our main interests include the development of self-esteem, self-awareness, creative thinking and problem-solving abilities, assertiveness, and making a difference in the world. Children have a lot to share with each other. They also can reach and teach each other in ways adults cannot. "We accept submissions from young people ages 14 and older. Plese send a letter from a parent/guardian/leader verifying originality." Writer's guidelines available on request (specify student guidelines).

Books: Publishes psychology, self-help, how-to, education. Pays advance and royalties. Submit mss to M.E. Salzmann, editorial assistant. Send query. Will accept typewritten mss. SASE. Reports in 3-4 months.

FUTURIFIC, INC., the Foundation for Optimism, Futurific, T-3, 150 Haven Ave., New York NY 10032. Publisher: B. Szent-Miklosy. (212)297-0502. Magazine published monthly. Audience consists of people interested in an accurate report of what is ahead. "We do not discriminate by age. We look for the visionary in all people. They must write what will be. No advice or 'may-be.' We've had 18 years of accurate forecasting." Sample copy for $5 postage and handling. Writer's guidelines available on request with SASE.

Magazines: Submit mss to B. Szent-Miklosy, publisher. Will accept typewritten, legibly handwritten, computer printout, 5.25 or 3.5 inch WordPerfect diskette mss.

Artwork/Photography: Publishes artwork by children. Looks for "what the future will look like." Pay is negotiable. Send b&w drawings or photos. Submit artwork to B. Szent-Miklosy, publisher.

THE GOLDFINCH, 402 Iowa Ave., Iowa City IA 52240. (319)335-3916. Magazine published quarterly. Audience is fifth and sixth graders. "Magazine supports creative work by children: research, art, writing." Submitted work must go with the historical theme of each issue.

Magazines: 10-20% written by children. Uses at least 1 nonfiction essay, poem, story/issue (500 words). Pays complimentary copies. Submit mss to Amy Ruth, editor. Submit complete ms. Will accept typewritten, legibly handwritten, computer disk (Apple) mss. Reports in 1 month.

Artwork/Photography: Publishes artwork/photographs by children. Art and photos must be b&w. Pays complimentary copies. Query first to Amy Ruth.

HIGH SCHOOL WRITER, P.O. Box 718, Grand Rapids MN 55744. (218)326-8025. Magazine published monthly during the school year. "The *High School Writer* is a magazine written *by* students *for* students. All submissions must exceed contemporary standards of decency." Purpose in publishing works by young people: "To provide a real audience for student writers—and text for study." Submissions by junior high and middle school students accepted for our junior edition. Senior high students' works are accepted for our senior high edition. Students attending schools that subscribe to our publication are eligible to submit their work." Writer's guidelines available on request.

Magazines: Uses fiction, nonfiction (2,000 words maximum) and poetry. Submit mss to Roxanne Kain, editor. Submit complete ms (teacher must submit). Will accept typewritten, computer-generated (good quality) mss.

Tips: "Submissions should not be sent without first obtaining a copy of our guidelines. Also, submissions will not be considered unless student's school subscribes."

HIGHLIGHTS FOR CHILDREN, 803 Church St., Honesdale PA 18431. (717)253-1080. Magazine published monthly. "We strive to provide wholesome, stimulating, entertaining material that will encourage children to read. Our audience is children ages 2-12." Purpose in publishing works by young people: to encourage children's creative expression. Age limit to submit is 15.

Magazines: 15-20% of magazine written by children. Uses 4-6 fiction stories (50-150 words), 15-20 poems (4-12 lines)/year. Also uses jokes, riddles, tongue twisters. Features which occur occasionally: "What Are Your Favorite Books?" (8-10/year), Recipes (8-10/year), "Science Letters" (15-20/year). Special features which invite children's submissions on a specific topic: "Tell the Story" (15-20/year), "You're the Reporter" (8-10/year), "Your Ideas, Please" (8-10/year), "Endings to Unfinished Stories" (8-10/year). Pays in copies. Submit complete mss to the editor. Will accept typewritten, legibly handwritten and computer printout mss. Reports in 3-6 weeks.

Artwork/Photography: Publishes artwork by children. No payment given. No cartoon or comic book characters. No commercial products. Submit b&w or color artwork for "Our Own Pages." Features include "Creatures Nobody Has Ever Seen" (5-8/year) and "Illustration Job" (18-20/year). Reports in 3-6 weeks.

HOW ON EARTH!, Youth supporting compassionate, ecologically sound living, P.O. Box 3347, West Chester PA 19381. (717)529-8638. Newsletter. Published quarterly. Youth audience. "Through providing a voice for youth, *How on Earth!* honors youth visions and expressions in creating and exploring options for compassionate, ecologically-sound living. *HOE!* acknowledges the interconnectedness of animal, environmental, human rights, peace and other social change issues and explores these relationships through the thoughts and feelings of youth." Must be ages 13-24 and work must be original. Articles well-referenced. "Please send SAE with 1 first-class stamp for submission guidelines."

Magazines: 95% of magazine written by youth. Uses 1-2 creative writing stories, 2-5 research or informative articles, 4-5 poems per issue. Submit mss to: Sally Clinton, coordinator. Query for articles. Will accept typewritten and legibly handwritten mss or 3.5" disk (Macintosh). SASE "only if they want it returned." Reports in 2 months.

Artwork: Publishes artwork and photographs taken by youth. "We accept material depicting nature, animals, ecology, social justice, activism, vegetarian food and anything concerning issues related to these topics. Full color art or photos accepted for cover. Cartoons welcome as well. Pen & ink or dark pencil only." No pay: "All volunteer at this point." Submit artwork and photos to: Sally Clinton, coordinator. SASE "only if they want it returned." Reports in 2 months.

*INK BLOT, 519 S. Pin High Court, Pueblo West CO 81007. (719)547-9744. Newsletter. Published monthly (or as material is received to complete an issue). "I want young writers to do their best work, learn proper form and have their work shared with others. We put our newsletter in libraries, hospitals, waiting rooms and copies to contributors." Purpose in publishing works by young people: To give children an outlet for publishing their talents. To have them write using their imagination and creativity and to share it with others. Accepts manuscripts from all ages. If student, please include age, grade and school name. Only prints original works from contributors. Material is accepted from across the United States and Canada. Typewritten preferred—handwritten *neatly* OK.

Artwork: Publishes artwork by children. Wants small 1½ × 3 b&w ink drawings only; especially drawings that accompany poetry and short stories. No derogatory or obscene pictures accepted. Pays in copies. Submit art to Margaret Larkin, editor, or Vicki Larkin, assistant editor. SASE. Reports in 3 months.

Tips: Sample copy and guidelines available for $1 (check made out to M. Larkin, editor) and SASE. Maximum length 500 words (stories).

*INTERRACE/BIRACIAL CHILD, P.O. Box 12048, Atlanta GA 30355. Editor: Candy Mills. Magazine.

Magazines: 5% of magazine written by young people. Uses fiction (750-1,500 words), nonfiction (600-1,500 words), poetry (25+ lines). Pays $25-75 for articles. Submit mss to Candy Mills, editor. Submit complete mss for fiction and nonfiction. Will accept typewritten, legibly handwritten, Mac disk mss. SASE. Reports in 1-6 months.
Artwork/Photography: Publishes artwork (high quality) and photography by and of children. Pays $10-25. Submit art and photographs to Candy Mills, editor. SASE. Reports in 1-6 months.

IOWA WOMAN, P.O. Box 680, Iowa City IA 52244. (319)987-2879. Published quarterly. "We publish quality fiction, essays, interviews, poetry, book reviews and feature articles for women everywhere. We welcome submissions by girls and young women to encourage them to communicate and share their creative work. If work is by children, we prefer it not be rewritten by an adult. We welcome drawings and visual art, too. Guidelines available for SASE.
Magazines: Less than 1% of magazine written by young people (we hardly ever get submissions). Last year, used 1 nonfiction personal essay about relationship with mother (1,200 words); 2 poetry departments (varying word lengths). Pays $5/published page and 2 copies of issue. Submit complete ms. Mss must be typewritten (diskette if accepted). SASE. Reports in 6 weeks-3 months.
Artwork/Photography: Publishes artwork and photography by children. Looks for "specific illustrations for fiction and essays we've accepted; illustration by child for her own written work." Pays $15 for illustration per story, any genre (b&w only). No payment for photos accompanying a ms. "Ask to be on artist list or send photocopy samples." SASE. Submit art and photographs to Marianne Abel, editor. SASE. Reports in 3 weeks.
Additional Comments: "We welcome submissions for 'Under 21' a column/department open to any genre of work by younger writers."

KIDSART, P.O. Box 274, Mt. Shasta CA 96067. (916)926-5076. Newsletter published quarterly. Publishes "hands-on art projects, open-ended art lessons, art history, lots of child-made art to illustrate." Purpose in publishing works by children: "to provide achievable models for kids—give young artists a forum for their work. We always phone before publishing works to be sure it's OK with their folks, name is spelled correctly, etc."
Artwork/Photography: Publishes artwork/photographs by children. Any submissions by children welcomed. Pays free copies of published work. Submit artwork/photos to Kim Solga, editor. "Your originals will be returned to you in 4-6 weeks." SASE desired, but not required. Free catalog available describing *KidsArt* newsletter. Sample copy $3.

KOPPER BEAR PRESS, P.O. Box 19454, Boulder CO 80308-2454. (303)786-9808. Publishes as material is available. "We believe that young people have important things to say—to everyone!" Purpose in publishing works by young people: To give young people another outlet for their feelings/ideas. Must be 13-21 years old. Must be able to prove work is original. Guidelines available on request.
Books: Publishes stories, essays, novels, novellas and collections. Will review any length. Pay depends on work. For poems, short stories, would like copyright outright. For longer works, advance and royalty. Submit mss to Howard Bashinski. Submit complete ms. Will accept typewritten and legibly handwritten mss. "No electronic submissions." SASE. Reports in 3-6 months.

THE LOUISVILLE REVIEW—CHILDREN'S CORNER, Dept. of English, University of Louisville, 315 Bingham Humanities, Louisville KY 40292. (502)852-6801. Semiannual magazine. "We are a contemporary literary journal." Purpose in publishing works by young people:

Always include a self-addressed, stamped envelope (SASE) with submissions within your own country. When sending material to other countries, include a self-addressed envelope (SAE) and International Reply Coupons (IRCs).

to encourage children to write with fresh images and striking metaphors. Not interested in the "cute" moral lesson on highly rhymed and metered verse. Must supply SASE and permission slip from parent stating that work is original and giving permission to publish if accepted. Only accepts typewritten mss.

Magazines: 10-20% of magazine written by children. Uses 10-25 pages of fiction, essays and poetry, any length. Pays in copies. Submit mss to Children's Corner. Submit complete ms. Will accept typewritten mss. SASE. Reports in 3 months.

*THE MCGUFFEY WRITER, 5128 Westgate Dr., Oxford OH 45056. (513)523-7742. Magazine published 3 times per year. "We publish poems and stories by children that compel the editors to read them to the end because of extraordinary originality of content or facility with language given the age of the child author." Purpose in publishing works by children: to reward by recognition those who strive to create in words and/or drawings and to motivate other children to try to meet a standard set in a sense by their peers. Requirements: be in grades K-12, no geographic restriction, originality must be attested to by adult parent or teacher. Writer's guidelines available on request.

Magazines: 100% of magazine written by young people. Uses 3-5 fiction short stories (500 or fewer words), 0-3 nonfiction stories (500 or fewer words), 5-10 poems (30 lines or less). "We do not publish trite, violent, teen 'romance' or gloom and doom selections. We look for fresh, original writing on topics students know well." Pays 2 copies. Submit mss to Submissions Editor. Submit complete ms. "Send copy—we do not return submissions." Will accept typewritten form and legible handwriting. Responds in 3 months to those who are published.

Artwork/Photography: Publishes black & white illustrations to fit 7½×8 page—any theme. Pays 2 contributor copies. Submit art and photographs to Linda Sheppard, art editor. Responds in 3 months.

*THE MAGAZINE FOR CHRISTIAN YOUTH!, 201 Eighth Ave. S, Box 801, Nashville TN 37202. (615)749-6319. Magazine. Published monthly. Audience consists of youth, ages 11-18. "The purpose of *Youth!* is to help teenagers develop Christian identity and live the Christian faith in their contemporary culture." Purpose in publishing works by young people: To give youth an outlet for creativity, encourage others to submit poetry and serve our readers and the church. "We accept fiction only from teens (ages 11-18). Fiction/poetry must be original. There is a yearly writing contest. Winners are published and paid freelance rates. The contest is announced in our February '94 issue."

Magazines: "Our all-teen issue in November tries for all copy written by teens." Some work by teens appear in other issues as well (30%). Uses 1-3 fiction short stories (60-1,500 words), 1-3 nonfiction articles (60-1,500 words) and 5-8 other features (50-100 words). Pays 5¢/word ($150 maximum). Submit mss to Tony Peterson, editor. Queries preferred, but will accept mss. Will accept typewritten, legibly handwritten, on disk mss. SASE. Reports in 4-6 weeks.

Artwork/Photography: "All-teen issue in November has art and photos by teens. Also, teens illustrate our monthly poetry pages." Submit art and photographs to Tony Peterson, editor. SASE. Reports in 4-6 weeks.

MERLYN'S PEN: The National Magazine of Student Writing, P.O. Box 1058, East Greenwich RI 02818. (800)247-2027. Magazine. Published every 2 months during the school year, September-May. "We publish a Senior Edition (grades 9-12) and an Intermediate Edition (grades 6-9) including 150 manuscripts annually by students in grades 6-12. The entire magazine is dedicated to young adults' writing. Our audience is classrooms, libraries and students from grades 6-12." Writers must be in grades 6-12 and must follow submission guidelines for preparing their mss. When a student is accepted, he/she, a parent and a teacher must sign a statement of originality.

Magazines: Uses 25 short stories (less than 4,000 words), plays; 8 nonfiction essays (less than 3,000 words); 10 pieces of poetry; letters to the editor; editorials; reviews of previously published works; and reviews of books, music, movies per issue. Pays for ms in 3 contributor's copies. Also, a discount is offered for additional copies of the issue. Submit complete ms. Will only accept typewritten mss. "All rejected manuscripts receive an editor's constructive critical comment in the margin." Reports in 10 weeks.

Artwork/Photography: Publishes artwork and photography by young adults, grades 6-12. Looks for b&w line drawings, cartoons, color art for cover. Pays in 3 contributor's copies and a discount is offered for additional copies. Send unmatted original artwork. SASE. Reports in 10 weeks.

Tips: "All manuscripts and artwork must be submitted with a cover sheet listing: name, age and grade, home address, home phone number, school name, school phone number, school address, teacher's name and principal's name. SASE must be large enough and carry enough postage for return."

NATIONAL GEOGRAPHIC WORLD, 17th and M St. NW, Washington DC 20036-4688. (202)857-7000. Magazine published monthly. Picture magazine for ages 8 and older. Writer's guidelines available on request.

Artwork/Photography: Publishes art, letters, poems, games, riddles, jokes and craft ideas by children in mailbag section only. No payment given. Send by mail to: Mailbag. "Sorry, but *World* cannot acknowledge or return your contributions."

THE PIKESTAFF FORUM, P.O. Box 127, Normal IL 61761. (309)452-4831. Magazine published annually; "We hope to eventually get out two issues per year. The basic audience of *The Pikestaff Forum* is adult; in each issue we have a Young Writers feature publishing writing and artwork by young people aged 7-17. Our purpose in publishing works by young people is twofold: (1) to put excellent writing by young people before the general public, and (2) to encourage young people in developing their self-confidence and powers of literary expression. Work must be by young people aged 7-17; it must be original, previously unpublished, and submitted by the authors themselves (we do *not* wish parents or teachers to submit the work); the person's age at the time the piece was written must be stated and SASE must be included." Writer's guidelines available on request.

Magazines: 10% of magazine written by children. Uses 1-3 fiction stories, 7-10 poems per issue. Poetry always welcome. Author or artist receives 3 free copies of the issue in which the work appears, and has the option of purchasing additional copies at a 50% discount. Submit mss to Robert D. Sutherland, editor/publisher. Submit complete ms. Will accept typewritten, legibly handwritten, computer printout mss. SASE. Reports in 3 months.

Artwork/Photography: Publishes artwork by children. No restrictions on subject matter; "should be free-standing and interesting (thought-provoking). *Black & white only* (dark image); we cannot handle color work with our format." Artist receives three free copies of the issue in which the work appears, and has the option of purchasing additional copies at a 50% discount off cover price. In b&w, clearly mark with artist's name, address and age at the time the work was created. Submit artwork to Robert D. Sutherland, editor/publisher. Reports in 3 months. "We do not wish teachers to submit for their students, and we do not wish to see batches of works which are simply the product of school assignments."

*POEM TRAIN, P.O. Box 203, Jarettsville MD 21084. Magazine. Published quarterly. Literary magazine of poetry for children. "We publish poetry written by adults, as well as 'The Caboose' section of poetry written by children."

●*Poem Train* reviews poems of 25 lines or less. See their listing in the magazine section for more information on submissions.

*THE RED ALDER TRUNK, The Magazine of Young Writers, P.O. Box 48652 Bentall Centre, Vancouver, British Columbia V7X 1A3 Canada. (604)435-9871. Magazine. Published 3 times a year. "The goal of *The Red Alder Trunk* is to encourage the love of writing; to move ideas from the inside, out! Our audience is all ages, including children, à la Lewis Carroll." Purpose in publishing works by young people: To provide exposure for writers who are beginning in their careers.

Magazines: 75% of magazine written by young people. Uses 4 fiction stories (400-3,000 words, must be suitable for a younger audience) and 8 poems (50+ words) per issue. Published mss are not paid for. Submit mss to Liane Chapman, editor. Submit complete mss for fiction and poetry. Will accept typewritten or legibly written mss. Reports in 1 month.

Artwork/Photography: Publishes artwork by children. Looks for freehand illustrations, any size. Published artwork is not paid for. Wants black ink or pencil on white background. Submit art to Liane Chapman, editor. SASE. Reports in 1 month.
Tips: *"The Red Alder Trunk* is carried in several Canadian libraries and bookstores."

SHOFAR MAGAZINE, 43 Northcote Dr., Melville NY 11747. (516)643-4598. Magazine published 6 times/school year. Audience consists of American Jewish children age 9-13.
Magazines: 10-20% of magazine written by young people. Uses fiction/nonfiction (500-750 words), Kids Page items (50-150 words). Submit mss to Gerald Grayson, managing editor. Submit complete ms. Will accept typewritten, legibly handwritten mss and computer disk (Mac only). SASE. Reports in 1-2 months.
Artwork/Photography: Publishes artwork and photography by children. Pays "by the piece, depending on size and quantity." Submit original with SASE. Reports in 1-2 months.

SKIPPING STONES, Multicultural Children's Quarterly, P.O. Box 3939, Eugene OR 97403. (503)342-4956. Articles/Fiction Editor: Arun N. Toké. Quarterly magazine. Estab. 1988. Circulation 3,000. *"Skipping Stones* is a multicultural, nonprofit, children's magazine to encourage cooperation, creativity and celebration of cultural and environmental richness. It offers itself as a creative forum for communication among children from different lands and backgrounds. We prefer work by children up to 17-18 year olds. International, minorities and underrepresented populations receive priority, multilingual submissions encouraged."
- *Skipping Stones* received a 1993 EdPress Honor Award for distinguished Achievement in Educational Journalism. For more information about *Skipping Stones,* read the interview with Editor Arun N. Toké in the 1994 edition of *Children's Writer's & Illustrator's Market.*

Magazines: 50% written by children. Uses 10 fiction short stories, plays (500-750 words); 10 nonfiction articles, interviews, letters, history, descriptions of celebrations (500-750 words); 15-20 poems, jokes, riddles, proverbs (250 words or less) per issue. Pays in contributor's copies. Submit mss to Arun Toké, editor. Query for nonfiction; submit complete ms for fiction or other work; teacher may submit; parents can also submit their contributions. Submissions should include "cover letter with name, age, address, school, cultural background, inspiration for piece, dreams for future . . . " Will accept typewritten, legibly handwritten and computer/word processor mss. SASE. Responds in 3 months. Accepts simultaneous submissions.
Artwork/Photography: Publishes artwork and photography for children. Will review all varieties of ms/illustration packages. Wants comics, cartoons, b&w photos, paintings, drawings (preferably, ink & pen or pencil), 8 × 10, color photos OK. Subjects include children, people, celebrations, nature, ecology, multicultural. Pays in contributor's copies.
Terms: *"Skipping Stones* is a labor of love. No cash payment. You'll receive 1-4 copies (depending on the length of your contribution and illustrations." Reports back to artists in 3 months. Sample copy for $4 and 8½ × 11 SAE with 4 first-class stamps.
Tips: "Let the 'inner child' within you speak out — naturally, uninhibited." Wants "material that gives insight on cultural celebrations, lifestyle, custom and tradition, glimpse of daily life in other countries and cultures. Photos, songs, artwork are most welcome if they illustrate/highlight the points. Upcoming features: African-American experience, drugs and substance abuse, religions and cultures from around the world, death and loss, Spanish-English bilingual issue, Native American cultures, street children, the world in 2025AD, songs and foods from around the world, resource conservation and sustainable lifestyles, indigenous architecture, family, women and young girls in various cultures, games children play, etc."

SKYLARK, 2200 169th St., Hammond IN 46323. (219)989-2262. Editor: Pamela Hunter. Young Writer's Editor: Kathy Natiello. Annual magazine. Circ. 650-1,000. 15% of material written by juvenile authors. Presently accepting material *by* children. *"Skylark* wishes to provide a vehicle for creative writing of all kinds, but only by writers ages five through eighteen, especially in the Illinois/Indiana area who have not ordinarily been provided such an outlet. Children need a place to have their work published alongside that of adults."

Proof of originality is required from parents or teachers for all authors. Writer's guidelines available upon request.

Magazines: 15% of magazine written by young people. Uses 2 mystery, fantasy, humor, good narrative fiction stories (800-1,000 words), 2 personal essays, brief character sketch nonfiction stories (400-650 words), 30 poems (no more than 16 lines). Does not want to see material that is obviously religious or sexual. Pays in contributor's copies. Submit ms to young writers' editor. Submit complete ms. Prefers typewritten ms. Must include SASE for return of material. Reports in 4 months. Byline given.

Artwork/Photography: Publishes artwork and photographs by children. Looks for "photos of animals, landscapes and sports, and artwork to go along with text." Pay in contributor's copies. All artwork and photos must be b&w, 8½×11, unlined paper. Do not use pencil and no copyrighted characters. Markers are advised for best reproduction. Include name and address on the back of each piece. Package properly to avoid damage. Submit artwork/photos to Pamela Hunter, editor. SASE. Reports in 6 months.

SNAKE RIVER REFLECTIONS, 1863 Bitterroot Dr., Twin Falls ID 83301. (208)734-0746. Newsletter. Publishes 10 times/year (not published in October or December). Proof of originality required with submissions. Guidelines available on request.

Magazines: 5% of magazine's poems written by children. Uses poetry (30 lines maximum). Pays in copies only. Submit mss to William White, editor. Submit complete ms. Will accept typewritten and legibly handwritten mss. #10 SASE. Reports in 1 month.

THE SOW'S EAR POETRY REVIEW, 19535 Pleasant View Dr., Abingdon VA 24211-6827. (703)628-2651. Magazine published quarterly. "Our editorial philosophy is to serve contemporary literature by publishing the best poetry we can find. Our audience includes serious poets throughout the US. We publish school-aged poets in most issues to encourage young writers and to show our older audience that able young poets are writing. We request young poets to furnish age, grade, school and list of any previous publication." Writer's guidelines available on request.

Magazines: 3% of magazine written by children. Uses 2-3 poems (1 page) per issue. Pays 1 copy. Submit complete ms. Will accept typewritten, legibly handwritten mss. SASE. Reports in 3 months.

Artwork/Photography: Publishes artwork and photographs by children. "Prefer b&w line drawings or photographs. Any subject or size that may be easily reduced or enlarged." Pays 1 copy. Submit artwork to Mary Calhoun, graphics editor. SASE. Reports in 4 months.

SPRING TIDES, 824 Stillwood Dr., Savannah GA 31419. (912)925-8800. Annual magazine. Audience consists of children 5-12 years old. Purpose in publishing works by young people: To encourage writing. Requirements to be met before work is published: must be 5-12 years old. Writers guidelines available on request.

Magazines: 100% of magazine written by young people. Uses 5-6 fiction stories (1,200 words maximum), autobiographical experiences (1,200 words maximum), 15-20 poems (20 lines maximum) per issue. Writers are not paid. Submit complete ms or teacher may submit. Will accept typewritten mss. SASE.

Artwork/Photography: Publishes artwork by children. "We have so far used only local children's artwork because of the complications of keeping and returning pieces."

STONE SOUP, The Magazine by Children, Children's Art Foundation, P.O. Box 83, Santa Cruz CA 95063. (408)426-5557. Articles/Fiction Editor, Art Director: Ms. Gerry Mandel. Magazine published 5 times/year. Circ. 20,000. "We publish fiction, poetry and artwork by children through age 13. Our preference is for work based on personal experiences and close observation of the world." Purpose in publishing works by young people: To encourage children to read and to express themselves through writing and art. Writer's guidelines available upon request.

Magazines: Uses animal, contemporary, fantasy, history, problem-solving, science fiction, sports, spy/mystery/adventure fiction stories. Uses 5-10 fiction stories (100-2,500 words), 5-10 nonfiction stories (100-2,500 words), 2-4 poems per issue. Does not want to see classroom assignments and formula writing. Buys 65 mss/year. Byline given. Pays on acceptance.

Buys all rights. Pays $10 each for stories and poems, $15 for book reviews. Contributors also receive 2 copies. Sample copy $2. Free writer's guidelines. "We don't publish straight nonfiction, but we do publish stories based on real events and experiences." Send complete ms. Will accept typewritten and legibly handwritten mss. SASE. Reports in 1 month.
Artwork/Photography: Publishes any type, size or color artwork/photos by children. Pays $8 for b&w illustrations. Contributors receive 2 copies. Sample copy $2. Free illustrator's guidelines. Send originals if possible. SASE. Reports in 1 month. Original artwork returned at job's completion. All artwork must be by children through age 13.

STRAIGHT MAGAZINE, Standard Publishing, 8121 Hamilton Ave., Cincinnati OH 45231. (513)931-4050. Magazine published weekly. Estab. 1951. Magazine includes fiction pieces and articles for Christian teens 13-19 years old to inform, encourage and uplift them. Purpose in publishing works by young people: to provide them with an opportunity to express themselves. Children must submit their birth dates and Social Security numbers (if they have one). Writer's guidelines available on request, "included in regular guidelines."
Magazines: 15% of magazine written by children. Uses fiction (500-1,000 words), personal experience pieces (500-700 words), poetry (approximately 1 poem per issue). Pays flat fee for poetry; 5¢/word for stories/articles. Submit mss to Carla J. Crane, editor. Submit complete ms. Will accept typewritten and computer printout mss. Reports in 1-2 months.

TEXAS HISTORIAN, Texas State Historical Association, 2/306 Sid Richardson Hall, University Station, Austin TX 78731. (512)471-1525. Articles Editor: David De Boe. Magazine published 4 times a year in February, May, September and November. "The *Texas Historian* is the official publication of the Junior Historians of Texas. Articles accepted for publication must be written by members of the Junior Historians of Texas."
Magazines: Uses history articles aimed at young adults (about 2,500 words). Does not accept unsolicited mss.

THUMBPRINTS, 928 Gibbs St., Caro MI 48723. (517)673-6653. Newsletter published monthly. "Our newsletter is designed to be of interest to writers and allow writers a place to obtain a byline." Purpose in publishing works by children: to encourage them to seek publication. Statement of originality required. Writer's guidelines available on request, "same guidelines as for adults."
Newsletters: Percentage of newsletter written by children "varies from month to month." Pays in copies. Submit ms to Janet Ihle, editor. Submit complete ms or have teacher submit. Will accept typewritten and computer printout mss. Reports in 6-8 weeks.
Artwork/Photography: Publishes artwork by children. Looks for art that expresses our monthly theme. Pays in copies. Send pencil or ink line drawings no larger than 3 × 4. Submit artwork to Janet Ihle, editor. SASE. Reports in 3 months.
Tips: "We look forward to well written articles and poems by children. It's encouraging to all writers when children write and are published."

TURTLE, Children's Better Health Institute, 1100 Waterway Blvd., P.O. Box 567, Indianapolis IN 46206. (317)636-8881. Editor: Steve Charles. Magazine. "*Turtle* is a health-related magazine geared toward children from ages 2-5." Purpose in publishing works by young people: "We enjoy giving children the opportunity to exercise their creativity." Publishes artwork or pictures that children ages 2-5 have drawn or colored all by themselves. Writer's guidelines available on request.
Artwork/Photography: Publishes artwork by children. There is no payment for children's artwork. All artwork must have the child's name, age and complete address on it. "No artwork can be returned."

TYKETOON YOUNG AUTHOR PUBLISHING COMPANY, 7417 Douglas Lane, Fort Worth TX 76180. (817)581-2876. Picture books. Publishes 8 books/year by children only. "We only want picture books written and illustrated by elementary and middle school students (6-14 year-olds). Our audience should be the same age readers as the author and above." Purpose in publishing works by young people: "1) Provide incentives to write; 2) Publish books that are models of good writing and illustrating; 3) Publish teaching tools and guides,

Revision: Frosting the Cake

"Kids see revision as being as exciting as getting the chicken pox!" says Marty Kusmierski. "I wish kids could see revision with this analogy: Writing the story is like baking a cake. It's good, but it's so much better when it's frosted."

That's just one piece of advice Kusmierski offers to young writers and to parents and teachers promoting the writing process. As an elementary school teacher, she encouraged kids to write stories, illustrate their work, and publish their creations. But she couldn't find a book publisher liberal enough to accept her students' work in the formats they could financially support, such as on regular paper instead of bond, or handwritten instead of typed. So she decided to start her own company, and two years later the Tyketoon Young Author Publishing Company was born.

Marty Kusmierski

Tyketoon publishes books written and illustrated by youngsters in first through eighth grade and aims to publish the best story submitted in each grade level. Text can be fiction, nonfiction or poetry and illustrations can be created in any medium. "Not every kid is an outstanding artist," Kusmierski says, "but every kid needs to have some outstanding artwork with the manuscript and especially on the cover, so we encourage all sorts of collaborations and creations, including noncopyrighted photography and collage."

The first year Tyketoon was open to submissions, Kusmierski received more than 5,000 manuscripts—and read them all, looking for stories with colorful illustrations that everyone would want to read. When it came to making final selections, she read the stories to kids and asked which they'd buy with their own money and why. "It was a difficult job getting down to only eight books," she says. "In fact, it was impossible, so we published our top nine."

In all, ten children became winners as one book was a collaboration. Yet Kusmierski says it isn't just the "winners" who benefit. "Writing for publication pushes the creative-process envelope in most kids. All the children who write have a chance to experience writing *success*, many for the first time."

Submissions to Tyketoon were originally limited to students in Texas, but Kusmierski recently opened her doors to students everywhere. Her ultimate goal is to encourage kids to love writing and to write well. In addition to publishing books by children, she also publishes classroom materials to be used with the books, including step-by-step lesson plans that provide teachers "with everything they need to direct and support the writing experience." Kusmierski also visits schools to give student writing presentations and teacher workshops on "how to get kids to write knock-your-socks-off stories."

When students say they don't know where to begin, she suggests they start by keeping writers' notebooks. "A writer's notebook is a place to jot down experiences and observations that might spark a new story or help elaborate another story idea," Kusmierski explains.

Not only can students create stories based upon things that have happened to them, but they can also create stories based upon things that have happened in the world. "We received a wonderful book about a fish who explored the Midwest when he was washed over the banks during the great flood. Fictionalizing real stories can be a good source of plots," she says.

When reading students' manuscripts, Kusmierski, like most publishers, looks for originality. Stories entitled "Best Friends" which are about girls meeting guys at the mall are not very original, she says. Sometimes such stories are also just lists of events. "Teachers shouldn't accept stories that don't have problems in them. Change must occur for the main character. Characters should be in situations they must get out of, have needs they are trying to meet, goals to reach, wants to satisfy, etc. Students who can identify problems in stories they read understand how to put problems in their own stories."

Overall, she says, "We receive many stories that have not been read or tested before being submitted. We wish authors would read their work to five or ten people, ask for comments and *revise* their work. Many books we receive are 'first-draft' quality. I wish every book I read was one I wanted to publish."

If parents and teachers encourage students to revise their work, "to frost their cakes," so to speak, then perhaps Kusmierski's wish would come true and every child could publish his or her creation.

— *Christine Martin*

Nothing Much Happened at School Today!

written & illustrated by
Danny Gordon

One of the first books Tyketoon published, Nothing Much Happened at School Today!, written and illustrated by third-grader Danny Gordon of Arlington, Texas, is about what happens when Mr. Tickie, the zoo keeper, brings animals to visit the school and Leroy lets them loose. Danny got the idea from his mom, who always asks him what happened in school. Publisher Marty Kusmierski says she knew the book was publishable the first time she read it. "It had almost everything — good beginning, middle with exciting events, good ending, humor, art and characters."

making teaching picture book writing easy." Must be ages 6-14. Writer's/illustrator's guidelines available for SASE. Publishes all types of fiction and nonfiction. Publishes poetry in book format with illustrations—one author's collection of poetry or a collaboration from two or more authors (same age level). Word length: under 5,000. Pays scholarship check. Submit mss to Ms. Marty Kusmierski, publisher. Submit complete ms with SASE to receive a personal critique of the work. Will accept typewritten and legibly handwritten mss or any readable format. Reports in 3 months.

VIRGINIA WRITING, Longwood College, 201 High St., Farmville VA 23909. (804)395-2160. Magazine published twice yearly. "*Virginia Writing* publishes prose, poetry, fiction, nonfiction, art, photography, music and drama from Virginia high school students and teachers. The purpose of the journal is to publish 'promise.' The children must be attending a Virginia high school, preferably in no less than 9th grade (though some work has been accepted from 8th graders). Originality is strongly encouraged. The guidelines are also in the front of our magazine." No profanity or racism accepted.

Magazines: 85% of magazine written by children. Uses approximately 5 fiction and nonfiction short stories, 56 poems and prose pieces per issue. Submit mss to Billy C. Clark, founder and editor. Submit complete ms. Will accept typewritten mss. Reports as soon as possible.

Artwork/Photography: Publishes artwork by children. Considers all types of artwork, including that done on computer. Color slides of artwork are acceptable. All original work is returned upon publication in a non-bendable, well protected package. Submit artwork to Billy C. Clark. Reports as soon as possible.

Tips: "All works should be submitted with a cover letter describing student's age, grade and high school currently attending."

VOICES OF YOUTH, Voices of Youth, Inc., P.O. Box 1869, Sonoma CA 95476. (707)938-8314. Publishes 4 magazines/school year of work by high school youths. Purpose in publishing works by young people: to provide a forum for expression and acknowledge ideas and great work of high school students across the country. Our audience is high school students and anyone else interested in what high school students are doing. Must be in grades 9-12 to submit. Writer's guidelines available on request.

Magazines: Uses 40-50 pieces of student writing (length varies) including fiction, nonfiction, poetry and prose per issue. Pays with complimentary copy when article appears. Submit mss to editor. Submit complete ms. Will accept typewritten mss. SASE.

Artwork/Photography: Publishes artwork and photography by children on "any subject of interest to high school students." Prefers b&w. Pays in copies. Send a copy of artwork. Submit art and photos to editor. SASE. Reports in 3-6 weeks.

WHOLE NOTES, P.O. Box 1374, Las Cruces NM 88004. (505)382-7446. Magazine published twice yearly. "We look for original, fresh perceptions in poems that demonstrate skill in using language effectively, with carefully chosen images, clear ideas and fresh perceptions. Our audience (general) loves poetry. We try to recognize excellence in creative writing by children as a way to encourage and promote imaginative thinking." Writer's guidelines available for SASE. Sample issue is $3.

Magazines: Every fourth issue is 100% by children. Writers should be 21 years old or younger. Uses 30 poems/issue (length open). Pays complimentary copy. Submit mss to Nancy Peters Hastings, editor. Submit complete ms. "No multiple submissions, please." Will accept typewritten and legibly handwritten mss. SASE. Reports in 3 weeks.

Artwork/Photography: Publishes artwork and photographs by children. Looks for b&w line drawings which can easily be reproduced; b&w photos. Pays complimentary copy. Send clear photocopies. Submit artwork to Nancy Peters Hastings, editor. SASE. Reports in 3 weeks.

 A bullet has been placed within some listings to introduce special comments by the editors of Children's Writer's & Illustrator's Market.

WOMBAT: A Journal of Young People's Writing and Art, 365 Ashton Dr., Athens GA 30606. (706)549-4875. Published 4 times a year. "Illiteracy in a free society is an unnecessary danger which can and must be remedied. *Wombat,* by being available to young people and their parents and teachers, is one small incentive for young people to put forth the effort to learn to read and write (and draw) better, to communicate better, to comprehend better and—hopefully—consequently, to someday possess greater discernment, judgment and wisdom as a result." Purpose in publishing works by young people: to serve as an incentive, to encourage them to work hard at their reading, writing and—yes—drawing/art skills, to reward their efforts. Writers must be ages 6-16, from any geographic region and include a statement that work is original.

- According to its publisher, "*Wombat* is, unfortunately, on 'hold' probably throughout this entire school year; therefore, we are asking people to query as to when/if we will resume publication, before subscribing or submitting works to *Wombat* right now."

Magazines: 95% of magazine written by children. Have one 2-4 page "Guest Adult Article" in most issues/when available (submitted). Uses poetry; any fiction (3,000 words maximum; shorter preferred) but avoid extreme violence, religion or explicit sex; any nonfiction of interest to 6-16 year olds (3,000-4,000 words); cartoons, puzzles and solutions, jokes, games and solutions. Pays in copies and frameable certificates. Submit mss to Jacquelin Howe, publisher. Submit complete ms. Teacher can submit; parents, librarians, students can submit. Will accept typewritten, legibly handwritten, computer printout mss. Responds in 1-2 weeks with SASE; up to 1 year with seasonal or holiday works (past season or holiday). Written work is not returned. SASE permits *Wombat* to notify sender of receipt of work.

Artwork/Photography: Publishes artwork by children. Looks for works on paper, not canvas. Photocopies OK if clear and/or reworked for clarity and strong line definition by the artist. Pays in copies and frameable certificates. Submit artwork to Jacquelin Howe, publisher. "Artwork, only, will be returned if requested and accompanied by appropriate sized envelope, stamped with sufficient postage."

WORD DANCE, Playful Productions, Inc., 435R Hartford Turnpike, Vernon CT 06066. (203)870-8614. Magazine. Published quarterly. "We're a magazine of creative writing and art that is for *and* by children in kindergarten through grade 8."

Magazines: Uses adventure, fantasy, humorous, etc. (fiction); travel stories, poems and stories based on real life experiences (nonfiction). Publishes 250 total pieces of writing/year; maximum length: 3 pages. Submit mss to Stuart Ungar, articles editor. Sample copy $3. Free writer's guidelines and submissions form. SASE. Reports in 6-8 months.

Artwork: Illustrations accepted from young people in kindergarten through grade 8. Accepts illustrations of specific stories or poems and other general artwork. Must be high contrast. Query. Submit complete package with final art to Melissa Shapiro, art director. SASE. Reports in 6-8 months.

WRITERS' OPEN FORUM, P.O. Box 516, Tracyton WA 98393. Magazine published bimonthly. Purpose in publishing works by young people: to assist young writers by publishing stories and essays which are then critiqued by readers. Our international readership offers a wide scope of opinions and helpful tips. Guidelines available on request; same as for adults, however. Please state age in cover letter.

Magazines: Publishes Special Juniors Edition at least once per year, featuring all stories and essays (50% of the issue) written either *by* children or *for* children. Also prints 1 or 2 stories (25% of issues) in each standard issue written by children. Uses up to 8 fiction short stories, any genre (400-2,000 words); 4 essays (under 1,500 words) per issue. Pays $5 minimum on acceptance. Submit mss to Sandra E. Haven, editorial director. Submit complete ms with cover letter stating author's age. Will accept typewritten mss. SASE. Reports in 2 months.

THE WRITERS' SLATE, (The Writing Conference, Inc.), P.O. Box 664, Ottawa KS 66067. (913)242-0407. Magazine. Publishes 3 issues/year. *The Writers' Slate* accepts original poetry and prose from students enrolled in Kindergarten-12th grade. The audience is students, teachers and librarians. Purpose in publishing works by young people: to give students the opportunity to publish and to give students the opportunity *to read* quality literature written by other students. Writer's guidelines available on request.

Magazines: 90% of magazine written by young people. Uses 10-15 fiction, 1-2 nonfiction, 10-15 other mss per issue. Submit mss to Dr. F. Todd Goodson, editor, Dept. of English, East Carolina University, Greenville NC 27858-4353. Submit complete ms. Will accept typewritten mss. Reports in 1 month.

Artwork/Photography: Publishes artwork by young people. Bold, b&w, student artwork may accompany a piece of writing. Submit to Carlee N. Vieux, editor. Reports in 1 month.

*WRITES OF PASSAGE, P.O. Box 7676, Greenwich CT 06836. (212)674-5706. Journal. Publishes 2 issues/year by children (spring/summer and fall/winter). "Our philosophy: 'It may make your parents cringe, your teacher blush, but your best friend will understand.'" Purpose in publishing works by young people: To give teenagers across the country a chance to express themselves through creative writing. Writers must be 12 to 18 years old, work must be original, short biography should be included.

Magazines: Uses short stories (up to 4 double-spaced pages) and poetry. Pays in two copies. Will accept typewritten and legibly handwritten mss. SASE. Reports in 2 months. Sample copies available for $5. Writer's guidelines for SASE.

Tips: "We began *Writes of Passage* to encourage teenage reading and writing as fun and desirable forms of expression and to establish an open dialogue between teenagers in every state. Our selection process does not censor topics and presents submissions according to the authors' intentions. It gives teens an opportunity to expand on what they have learned in reading and writing classes in school by opening up a world of writing in which they can be free. As a result, submissions often reveal a surprising candidness on the part of the authors, including topics such as love, fear, struggle and death and they expose the diverse backgrounds of contributors."

WRITING, 60 Revere Drive, Northbrook IL 60062. (708)205-3000. Magazine published monthly September-May. Purpose in publishing work by young people: "to teach students to write and write well; grades 7-12. Should indicate age, address, school and teacher with submission. No formal guidelines; but letter is sent if request received."

Magazines: Small percentage of magazine written by children. Uses 1-10 mss/issue. No pay for student writing. Submit mss to Carol Elliot, editor. Submit complete ms; include student's age, address, school and teacher with submission; either child or child's teacher may submit. Prefers typewritten mss. SASE.

YOUNG VOICES MAGAZINE, P.O. Box 2321, Olympia WA 98507. (206)357-4683. Magazine published bimonthly. "*Young Voices* is by elementary and high school students for people interested in their work." Purpose in publishing work by young people: to provide a forum for their creative work. "Home schooled writers *definitely* welcome, too." Writer's guidelines available on request with SASE.

Magazines: Uses 20 fiction stories, 5 reviews, 5 essays and 20 poems per issue (lengths vary). Pays $3-5 on acceptance (more depending on the length and quality of the writing). Submit mss to Steve Charak, publisher, or Char Simons, editor. Query first; submit complete ms. Will accept typewritten and legibly handwritten mss. SASE. Reports in 2 months.

Artwork/Photography: Publishes artwork and photography by children. "Prefer work that will show up in black and white; anything but tanks and horses." Pays $3-5 on acceptance. Submit artwork to Steve Charak or Char Simons. SASE. Reports in 2 months.

Young Writer's & Illustrator's/'94-'95 changes

The following markets were included in the 1994 edition of *Children's Writer's & Illustrator's Market* but do not have listings in this edition for the reasons indicated.

Kid's Today Mini-Magazine (changing format)

Friend (no longer seeks submissions from young writers)

Contests & Awards

Publication is not the only way to get your work recognized. Contests can also be viable vehicles to gain recognition in the industry. Placing in a contest or winning an award validates the time spent writing and illustrating. Even for those who don't place, many competitions offer the chance to obtain valuable feedback from judges and other established writers or artists.

Not all of the contests here are strictly for professionals. Many are designed for "amateurs" who haven't yet been published. And more than 60 of the contests in this section are open to students (some exclusively). Young writers and illustrators will find all contests open to students marked with a double dagger (‡). Contests new to this edition (and there are 20 of them) are preceded by an asterisk (*).

When considering contests, be sure to study guidelines and requirements. Regard entry deadlines as gospel and note whether manuscripts and artwork should be previously published or unpublished. Also, be aware that awards vary. While one contest may award a significant monetary amount, another may award a certificate or medal instead.

Note that some contests require nominations. For published authors and illustrators, competitions provide an excellent way to promote one's work. If your book is eligible for a contest or award, have the appropriate people at your publishing company nominate or enter your work for consideration. Then make sure enough copies of your book are sent to contest judges and others who must see it.

To select potential contests for your work, read through the listings that interest you, then send for more information about the types of written or illustrated material considered and other important details such as who retains the rights to prize-winning material. If you are interested in knowing who has received certain awards in the past, check your local library or bookstores. In fact, many bookstores have special sections for books which are Caldecott and Newbery Award winners.

JANE ADDAMS CHILDREN'S BOOK AWARD, Jane Addams Peace Association, % Judith Volc, 2015 Bluebell, Boulder CO 80302. (303)441-3103. Award Director: Judith Volc. Annual award. Estab. 1953. Purpose of the award: "The Jane Addams Children's Book Award is presented annually for a book that most effectively promotes the cause of peace, social justice, world community, and the equality of the sexes and all races." Previously published submissions only; year previous to year the award is presented. Deadline for entries: April 1. SASE for award rules and entry forms. No entry fee. Awards a certificate to the author and seals for book jackets to the publisher (at cost). A separate award will be given for a picture book. Judging by a committee of children's librarians, teachers and members of WILPF. Works displayed at an award ceremony.

AIM Magazine Short Story Contest, P.O. Box 20554, Chicago IL 60620. (312)874-6184. Contest Directors: Ruth Apilado, Mark Boone. Annual contest. Estab. 1983. Purpose of the contest: "We solicit stories with social significance. Youngsters can be made aware of social problems through the written word and hopefully they will try solving them." Unpublished submissions only. Deadline for entries: August 15. SASE for contest rules and entry forms. SASE for return of work. No entry fee. Awards $100. Judging by editors. Contest open to everyone. Winning entry published in fall issue of *AIM*. Subscription rate $10/year. Single copy $3.50

‡AMERICA & ME ESSAY CONTEST, Farm Bureau Insurance, Box 30400, 7373 W. Saginaw, Lansing MI 48909. (517)323-7000. Contest Coordinator: Lisa Fedewa. Annual contest. Estab. 1968. Purpose of the contest: to give Michigan 8th graders the opportunity to express their thoughts/feelings on America and their roles in America. Unpublished submissions only. Deadline for entries: mid-November. SASE for contest rules and entry forms. "We have a school mailing list. Any school located in Michigan is eligible to participate." Entries not returned. No entry fee. Awards savings bonds and plaques for state top ten ($500-1,000), certificates and plaques for top 3 winners from each school. Judging by home office employee volunteers. Requirements for entrants: "Participants must work through their schools or our agents' sponsoring schools. No individual submissions will be accepted. Top ten essays and excerpts from other essays are published in booklet form following the contest. State capital/schools receive copies."

‡AMHA LITERARY CONTEST, American Morgan Horse Association Youth, P.O. Box 960, Shelburne VT 05482. (802)985-4944. Contest Director: Erica Richard. Annual contest. The contest includes categories for both poetry and essays. The 1994 theme was "Morgan and Youth Show Jitters." Entrants should write to receive the 1995 entry form and theme. Unpublished submissions only. Submissions made by author. Deadline for entries: December 1. SASE for contest rules and entry forms. No entry fee. Awards $50 cash and ribbons to up to 5th place. "Winning entry will be published in *AMHA News and Morgan Sales Network*, a monthly publication."

*‡AMHA MORGAN ART CONTEST, American Morgan Horse Assocociation, Box 960, Shelburne VT 05482. (802)985-4944. Promotional Recognition Coordinator: Susan Bell. Annual contest. The art contest consists of three categories: Morgan art (pencil sketches, oils, water colors, paintbrush), Morgan cartoons, Morgan speciality pieces (sculptures, carvings). Unpublished submissions only. Deadline for entries: December 1. Contest rules and entry forms sent upon request. Entries not returned. Entry fee is $2. Awards $50 first prize in 3 divisions (for adults) and AMHA gift certificates to top 5 places (for children). "All work submitted becomes property of The American Morgan Horse Association. Selected works may be used for promotional purposes by the AMHA." Requirements for entrants: "We consider all work submitted." Works displayed at the annual convention and the AMHA headquarters; published in *AMAHA News* and *The Morgan Horse Magazine*. The contest divisions consist of Junior (to age 17), Senior (18 and over) and Professional (commercial artists). Each art piece must have its own application form and its own entry fee. Matting is optional.

*THE AMY WRITING AWARDS, The Amy Foundation, 3798 Capital City Blvd., Lansing MI 48906. Director: James Russell. Annual award. Estab. 1984. "The purpose is to recognize creative, skillful writing that presents in a sensitive thought-provoking manner the Biblical position on issues affecting the world today." Previously published submissions only; must be published between January 1 and December 31 of calendar year previous to award. Submissions made by the author. Deadline for entries: January 31st of the year following publication. SASE for award rules. "Entry forms not required." No entry fee. Awards $10,000 first prize and $24,000 additional cash awards. Judging by the Amy Awards Committee and a panel of distinguished judges. Right to use for promotion of Amy Writing Awards acquired. "Entry must contain one passage of scripture and be published in a secular nonreligious publication." Works will be published in annual booklet.

‡ARTS RECOGNITION AND TALENT SEARCH (ARTS), National Foundation for Advancement in the Arts, 8000 Bricknell Ave., Miami FL 33131. (305)377-1140. Contact: Sherry Thompson. Open to students/high school seniors or 17 and 18 year-olds. Annual award. Estab. 1981. "Created to bring exceptional young artists to a higher plateau of excellence, Arts Recognition and Talent Search (ARTS) is an innovative national program of the National Foundation for Advancement in the Arts (NFAA). Established in 1981, ARTS touches the lives of gifted young people across the country, providing financial support, scholarships and goal-oriented artistic, educational and career opportunities. Each year, from a pool of 5,000-7,500 applicants, an average of 250 ARTS awardees are chosen for

NFAA support by panels of distinguished artists and educators. Each ARTS applicant, generally a high school senior, 17-18 years of age, has special talent in music, dance, theater, visual arts or creative writing." Submissions made by the student. Deadline for entries: June 1 and October 1 (late). SASE for award rules and entry forms. Entry fee is $25/35 (late) Fee waivers available based on need. Awards $100-3,000 — unrestricted cash grants. Judging by a panel of authors and educators recognized in the field. Rights to submitted/ winning material: NFAA/ARTS retains the right to duplicate work in an anthology or in Foundation literature unless otherwise specified by the artist. Requirements for entrants: Artists must be high school seniors or, if not enrolled in high school, must be 17 or 18 years old. Works will be published in an anthology distributed during ARTS Week, the final adjudication phase which takes place in Miami.

‡BAKER'S PLAYS HIGH SCHOOL PLAYWRITING CONTEST, Baker's Plays, 100 Chauncy St., Boston MA 02111. (617)482-1280. Contest Director: Raymond Pape. Annual contest. Estab. 1990. Purpose of the contest: to acknowledge playwrights at the high school level and to insure the future of American theater. Unpublished submissions only. Deadline for entries: January 31. SASE for contest rules and entry forms. No entry fee. Awards $500 to the first place playwright and Baker's Plays will publish the play. $250 to the second place playwright with an honorable mention; and $100 to the third place playwright with an honorable mention in the series. Judged anonymously. Open to any high school student. Teachers must not submit student's work. The first place playwright will have his/her play published in an acting edition the September following the contest. The work will be described in the Baker's Plays Catalogue, which is distributed to 50,000 prospective producing organizations. Plays must be accompanied by the signature of a sponsoring high school drama or English teacher, and it is recommended that the play receive a production or a public reading prior to the submission. Please include a SASE.

MARGARET BARTLE ANNUAL PLAYWRITING AWARD, Community Children's Theatre of Kansas City, 8021 E. 129th Terrace, Grandview MO 64030. (816)761-5775. Chairperson: Blanche Sellens. Annual contest. Estab. 1947. "Community Children's Theatre of Kansas City, Inc. was organized in 1947 to provide live theater for elementary aged children. We are now recognized as being one of the country's largest organizations providing this type of service." Unpublished submissions only. Deadline for entries: end of January. SASE for award rules and entry forms. SASE for return of entries. No entry fee. Awards $500. Judging by a committee of 5. "CCT reserves the right for one of the units to produce the prize winning play for two years. The plays are performed before students in elementary schools. Although our 5- to 12-year-old audiences are sophisticated, gratuitous violence, mature love stories, or slang are not appropriate — cursing is *not acceptable*. In addition to original ideas, subjects that usually provide good plays are legends, folklore, historical incidents, biographies and adaptations of children's classics."

‡BAY AREA BOOK REVIEWER'S ASSOCIATION (BABRA), %Chandler & Sharp, 11A Commercial Blvd., Novato CA 94949. (415)883-2353. Fax: (415)883-4280. Contact: Jonathan Sharp. Annual award for outstanding book in children's literature, open to Bay Area authors, northern California from Fresno north. Annual award. Estab. 1981. "BABRA presents annual awards to Bay Area (northern California) authors annually in fiction, nonfiction, poetry and children's literature. Purpose is to encourage Bay Area writers and stimulate interest in books and reading." Previously published submissions only. Must be published the calendar year prior to spring awards ceremony. Submissions nominated by publishers; author or agent could also nominate published work. Deadline for entries: December. No entry forms. Send 3 copies of the book to Jonathan Sharp. No entry fee. Awards $100 honorarium and award certificate. Judging by voting members of the Bay Area Book Reviewer's Association. Books that reach the "finals" (usually 3-5 per category)

The double dagger before a listing indicates the contest is open to students.

displayed at annual award ceremonies (spring). Nominated books are displayed and sold at BABRA's annual awards ceremonies, in the spring of each year.

*‡JOHN AND PATRICIA BEATTY AWARD, California Library Association, 717 K. Street Suite 300, Sacramento CA 95814. (916)447-8541. Executive Director: Mary Sue Ferrell. Annual award. Estab. 1987. Purpose of award: "The purpose of the John and Patricia Beatty Award is to encourage the writing of quality children's books highlighting California, its culture, heritage and/or future." Previously published submissions only. Submissions made by the author, author's agent or review copies sent by publisher. The award is given to the author of a children's book published the preceding year. Deadline for entries: Submissions may be made January-December. Contact CLA Executive Director who will liaison with Beatty Award Committee. Awards cash prize of $500 and an engraved plaque. Judging by a 5-member selection committee appointed by the president of the California Library Association. Requirements for entrants: "Any children's or young adult book set in California and published in the U.S. during the calendar year preceding the presentation of the award is eligible for consideration. This includes works of fiction as well as nonfiction for children and young people of all ages. Reprints and compilations are not eligible. The California setting must be depicted authentically and must serve as an integral focus for the book." Winning selection is announced through press release during National Library Week in April. Author is presented with award at annual California Library Association Conference in November.

THE IRMA S. AND JAMES H. BLACK BOOK AWARD, Bank Street College of Education, 610 W. 112th St., New York NY 10025. (212)222-6700. Contact: Linda Greengrass. Annual award. Estab. 1972. Purpose of the award: "The award is given each spring for a book for young children, published in the previous year, for excellence of both text and illustrations." Entries must have been published during the previous calendar year (between January '95 and December '95 for 1995 award). Deadline for entries: January 1. "Publishers submit books to us by sending them here to me at the Bank Street library. Authors may ask their publishers to submit their books. Out of these, three to five books are chosen by a committee of older children and children's literature professionals. These books are then presented to children in selected second, third and fourth grade classes here and at a few other cooperating schools on the East Coast. These children are the final judges who pick the actual award. A scroll (one each for the author and illustrator, if they're different) with the recipient's name and a gold seal designed by Maurice Sendak are awarded in May."

BOOK OF THE YEAR FOR CHILDREN, Canadian Library Association, 200 Elgin St., Suite 206, Ottawa, Ontario K2P 1L5 Canada. (613)232-9625. Contact: Chairperson, Canadian Association of Children's Librarians. Annual award. Estab. 1947. "The main purpose of the award is to encourage writing and publishing in Canada of good books for children up to and including age 14. If, in any year, no book is deemed to be of award calibre, the award shall not be made that year. To merit consideration, the book must have been published in Canada and its author must be a Canadian citizen or a permanent resident of Canada." Previously published submissions only; must be published between January 1 and December 1 of the previous year. Deadline for entries: January 1. SASE for award rules. Entries not returned. No entry fee. Awards a medal. Judging by committee of members of the Canadian Association of Children's Librarians. Requirements for entrants: Contest open only to Canadian authors or residents of Canada. Winning books are on display at CLA headquarters.

BOOK PUBLISHERS OF TEXAS, Children's/Young People's Award, The Texas Institute of Letters, %TCU Press, P.O. Box 30783, Ft. Worth TX 76129. (817)921-7822. Contact: Judy Alter. Send to above address for list of judges to whom entries should be submitted. Annual award. Purpose of the award: "to recognize notable achievement by a Texas writer of books for children or young people or by a writer whose work deals with a Texas subject. The award goes to the author of the winning book, a work published during the calendar year before the award is given. Judges list available each October. Deadline is first postally operative day of January." Previously published submissions only. SASE for award rules and entry forms. No entry fee. Awards $250. Judging by a panel of 3 judges selected by the TIL Council. Requirements for entrants: The writer must have lived in Texas for 2 consecutive years at some time, or the work must have a Texas theme.

THE BOSTON GLOBE-HORN BOOK AWARDS, The Boston Globe & The Horn Book, Inc., The Horn Book, 11 Beacon St., Suite 1000, Boston MA 02108. (617)227-1555. Award Directors: Stephanie Loer and Anita Silvey. Writing Contact: Stephanie Loer, children's book editor for *The Boston Globe*, 298 North St., Medfield MA 02052. Annual award. Estab. 1967. "Awards are for picture books, nonfiction and fiction. Up to two honor books may be chosen for each category." Books must be published between June 1, 1994 and May 30, 1995. Deadline for entries: May 15. "Publishers usually submit books. Award winners receive $500 and silver engraved bowl, honor book winners receive a silver plate." Judging by 3 judges involved in children's book field who are chosen by Anita Silvey, editor-in-chief for The Horn Book, Inc. (*The Horn Book Magazine* and the *Horn Book Guide*) and Stephanie Loer, children's book editor for *The Boston Globe*. "*The Horn Book Magazine* publishes speeches given at awards ceremonies. The book must have been published in the U.S. The awards are given at the fall conference of the New England Library Association."

‡ANN ARLYS BOWLER POETRY CONTEST, *Read* Mgazine, 245 Long Hill Rd., Middletown CT 06457. (203)638-2406. Contest Director: Kate Davis. Annual contest. Estab. 1988. Purpose of the contest: to reward young-adult poets (grades 4-12). Unpublished submissions only. Submissions made by the author or nominated by a person or group of people. Must include signature of teacher, parent or guardian, and student. Deadline for entries: December 23. SASE for contest rules and entry forms. No entry fee. Awards 6 winners $100 each, silver medals, letter of recognition from the U.S. Poet Laureate and publication. Semifinalists receive $50 each. Judging by *Read* editorial staff. "Entrant understands that prize will include publication, but sometimes pieces are published in other issues." Requirements for entrants: the material must be original. Winning entries will be published in the April issue of *Read* (all-student issue).

BUCKEYE CHILDREN'S BOOK AWARD, State Library of Ohio, 65 S. Front St., Columbus OH 43215-4163. (614)644-7061. Nancy Short, Chairperson. Correspondence should be sent to Floyd C. Dickman at the above address. Award every two years. Estab. 1981. Purpose of the award: "The Buckeye Children's Book Award Program was designed to encourage children to read literature critically, to promote teacher and librarian involvement in children's literature programs, and to commend authors of such literature, as well as to promote the use of libraries. Awards are presented in the following three categories: grades K-2, grades 3-5 and grades 6-8." Previously published submissions only. Deadline for entries: February 1. "The nominees are submitted by this date during the even year and the votes are submitted by this date during the odd year. This award is nominated and voted upon by children in Ohio. It is based upon criteria established in our bylaws. The winning authors are awarded a special plaque honoring them at a banquet given by one of the sponsoring organizations. The BCBA Board oversees the tallying of the votes and announces the winners in March of the voting year in a special news release and in a number of national journals. The book must have been written by an author, a citizen of the United States and originally copyrighted in the U.S. within the last three years preceding the nomination year. The award-winning books are displayed in a historical display housed at the Columbus Metropolitan Library in Columbus, Ohio."

*BYLINE MAGAZINE CONTESTS, P.O. Box 130596, Edmond OK 73013. Contest Director: Marcia Preston. Purpose of contest: *ByLines* runs 4 contests a month on many topics. Past topics include first chapter of a novel, genre fiction, children's poem, romantic fiction, personal essay, greeting card verse, valentine or love poem, etc. Send SASE for contest flier with topic list. Unpublished submissions only. Submissions made by the author. "We do not publish the contests' winning entries." SASE for contest rules and entry forms. Entry fee is $3-4. Awards cash prizes for first, second and third place. Amounts vary. Judging by qualified writers or editors. List of winners will appear in magazine.

‡**BYLINE MAGAZINE STUDENT PAGE**, P.O. Box 130596, Edmond OK 73013. (405)348-5591. Contest Director: Marcia Preston, publisher. Estab. 1981. "We offer student writing contests on a monthly basis, September through June, with cash prizes and publication of top entries." Previously unpublished submissions only. "This is not a market for illustration." Deadline for entries varies. "Entry fee usually $1." Awards cash and publication. Judging by qualified editors and writers. "We publish top entries in student contests. Winners' list published in magazine dated 3 months past deadline." Send SASE for details.

CALDECOTT AWARD, Association for Library Service to Children, Division of the American Library Association, 50 E. Huron, Chicago IL 60611. (312)280-2163. Executive Director ALSC: Susan Roman. Annual award. Estab. 1938. Purpose of the award: to honor the artist of the most distinguished picture book for children published in the US (Illustrator must be US citizen or resident.) Must be published year preceding award. Deadline for entries: December. SASE for award rules and entry forms. Entries not returned. No entry fee. "Medal given at ALA Annual Conference during the Newbery/Caldecott Banquet."

‡**CALIFORNIA WRITERS' CONFERENCE AWARDS**, California Writers' Club, 2214 Derby St., Berkeley CA 94705. (510)841-1217. "Ask for award rules before submitting entries." Award offered every 2 years. Next conference, June 23-25, 1995. Purpose of the award: "To encourage writers." Categories: adult short stories, adult novels, adult nonfiction, juvenile fiction or nonfiction, picture books, poetry and scripts. Unpublished submissions only. SASE for award rules and entry forms. SASE for return of entries. Entry fee is $10 for each submission. Awards are $150 first prize; $100, second; $75, third; honorable mention certificates at judges' discretion. Judging by "published writer-members of California Writers' Club. Open to all."

‡**CALIFORNIA YOUNG PLAYWRIGHTS CONTEST**, Playwrights Project, Suite 215, 1450 Frazee Rd., San Diego CA 92108. (619)298-9242. Director: Deborah Salzer. Open to Californians under age 19. Annual contest. Estab. 1985. "Our organization, and the contest, is designed to nurture promising young writers. We hope to develop playwrights and audiences for live theater. We also teach playwriting." Submissions required to be unpublished and not produced professionally. Submissions made by the author. Deadline for entries: usually April 1. "Call for exact date." SASE for contest rules and entry form. No entry fee. Award is professional productions of 3-5 short plays each year, participation of the writers in the entire production process, with a royalty award of $100 per play. Judging by professionals in the theater community, a committee of 5-7; changes somewhat each year. Works performed "in San Diego at the Cassius Carter Centre Stage of the Old Globe Theatre. Writers submitting scripts of 10 or more pages may receive a detailed script evaluation letter if requested."

CANADA COUNCIL GOVERNOR GENERAL'S LITERARY AWARDS, 350 Albert St., P.O. Box 1047, Ottawa, Ontario K1P 5V8 Canada. (613)566-4376. Officer, Writing and Publishing Section: Josiane Polidori. Annual award. Estab. 1937. Purpose of award: to encourage Canadian authors and illustrators of books for young people as well as to recognize the importance of their contribution to literary activity. Award categories include children's text and children's illustration. Must be published between October 1 and September 30 of award year. Eligible books are submitted by publishers (4 copies must be sent to Canada Council). All entries (books or bound galleys) must be received by August 31. (If the submission is in the form of bound galleys, the actual book must be published and received at the Canada Council no later than September 30.) Submission forms available on request. Entries not returned. No entry fee. Awards $10,000 (Canadian). Judging by practicing writers, illustrators or critics. Contest open to Canadian writers and illustrators only.

‡**CHICKADEE COVER CONTEST**, *Chickadee*, Owl Communications, Suite 500, 179 John St., Toronto, Ontario M5T 3G5 Canada. (416)971-5275. Contest Director: Mitch Butler, Chirp Editor. Annual contest. There is a different theme published each year. See 1994 October/November issue for 1995 theme. Unpublished submissions only. Submissions are submitted by readers. Deadline for entries: November. Announcement published each

October issue. No entry fee. Winning drawing published on cover of February issue. Judging by staff of *Chickadee*. Requirements for entrants: Must be 3- to 9-year-old readers.

‡**CHICKADEE'S GARDEN EVENT**, *Chickadee*, Owl Communications, Suite 500, 179 John St., Toronto, Ontario M5T 3G5 Canada. (416)971-5275. Contest Director: Mitch Butler, Chirp Editor. Annual. *Chickadee* readers are asked "to grow a favorite fruit or vegetable (anything as long as you can eat it) and submit a photo or drawing of you and your plant, and tell us why you chose the plant and who helped you to care for it. Include experiences and humorous adventures along the way." Unpublished submissions only. Contest announced in May issue. Deadline for entries: September. Results published in January. Judging by staff of *Chickadee*. Requirements for entrants: Must be 3-9 year-old readers.

‡**CHILDREN'S BOOK AWARD**, Sponsored by Federation of Children's Book Groups. 30 Senneleys Park Rd., Northfield Birmingham B31 1AL England. (021)427-4860. Coordinator: Jenny Blanch. Purpose of the award: "The C.B.A. is an annual prize for the best children's book of the year judged by the children themselves." Categories: (I) picture books, (II) short novels, (III) longer novels. Estab. 1980. Previously unpublished submissions only. Deadline for entries: December 31. SASE for rules and entry forms. Entries not returned. Awards "a magnificent silver and oak trophy worth over $6,000 and a portfolio of children's work." Silver dishes to each category winner. Judging by children. Requirements for entrants: Work must be fiction and published during the current year (poetry is ineligible). Work will be published in current "Pick of the Year" publication.

CHILDREN'S READING ROUND TABLE AWARD, Children's Reading Roundtable of Chicago, 5551 S. University Ave. Unit #1, Chicago IL 60637. (312)523-2959. Annual award. Estab. 1953. "Annual award to individual who has made outstanding contributions to children's books. Individual is nominated by membership, and selected by a committee from the membership, and finalized by a special committee of members, as well as nonmembers of CRRT." Awards a recognition certificate and stipend of $250. Award recipients have been authors, editors, educators and illustrators. "Note that our award recognizes *contributions* to children's literature. This includes people who are neither writers nor illustrators."

‡**CHILDREN'S WRITER WRITING CONTESTS**, 95 Long Ridge Rd., West Redding CT 06896. (203)792-8600. Contest offered every 4 months by *Children's Writer*, the monthly newsletter of writing and publishing trends. Purpose of the contest: To promote higher quality children's literature. "Each contest has its own theme. Our last three were: (1) An adventure story for ages 7-10; 750 words. (2) A self-help or inspirational article for readers 12-14; 1,000 words. (3) A science fiction story for ages 7-10; 750 words. Any original unpublished piece, not accepted by any publisher at the time of submission, is eligible." Submissions made by the author. Deadline for entries: Last Friday in February, June and October. "We charge a $10 entry fee for nonsubscribers only, which is applicable against a subscription to *Children's Writer*." Awards 1st place – $100 or $1,000, a certificate and publication in *Children's Writer*; 2nd place – $50 or $500, and certificate; 3rd-5th places – $25 or $250 and certificates. One or two contests each year with the higher cash prizes also include $100 prizes plus certificates for 6th-12th places. To obtain the rules and theme for the current contest send a SASE to *Children's Writer* at the above address. Put "Contest Request" in the lower left of your envelope. Judging by a panel of 5 selected from the staff of the Institute of Children's Literature. "We acquire First North American Serial Rights (to print the winner in *Children's Writer*), after which all rights revert to author." Open to any writer. Entries are judged on age targeting, originality, quality of writing and, for nonfiction, how well the information is conveyed and accuracy. "Submit clear photocopies only, not originals; submission will *not* be returned. Manuscripts should be typed double-spaced. No pieces containing violence or derogatory, racist or sexist language or situations will be accepted, at the sole discretion of the judges."

THE CHRISTOPHER AWARD, The Christophers, 12 E. 48th St., New York NY 10017. (212)759-4050. Christopher Awards Coordinators: Peggy Flanagan and Virginia Armstrong. Annual award. Estab. 1969 (for young people; books for adults honored since 1949).

"The award is given to works, published in the calendar year for which the award is given, that 'have achieved artistic excellence, affirming the highest values of the human spirit.' They must also enjoy a reasonable degree of popular acceptance." Previously published submissions only; must be published between January 1 and December 31. "Books should be submitted all year. Two copies should be sent to Peggy Flanagan, 12 E. 48th St., New York NY 10017 and two copies to Virginia Armstrong, 22 Forest Ave., Old Tappan NJ 07675." Entries not returned. No entry fee. Awards a bronze medallion. Books are judged by both reading specialists and young people. Requirements for entrants: "only published works are eligible and must be submitted during the calendar year in which they are first published."

CHRISTOPHER COLUMBUS SCREENPLAY DISCOVERY AWARDS, Christopher Columbus Society of the Creative Arts, #600, 433 N. Camden Dr., Beverly Hills CA 90210. (310)288-1988. Award Director: Mr. Carlos Abreu. Annual and monthly awards. Estab. 1990. Purpose of award: To discover new screenplay writers. Unpublished submissions only. Submissions are made by the author or author's agent. Deadline for entries: December 1st and monthly (last day of month). Entry fee is $45. Awards: (1) Feedback — development process with industry experts. (2) Financial rewards — option moneys up to $10 000. (3) Access to key decision makers. Judging by entertainment industry experts, producers and executives.

‡THE COMMONWEALTH CLUB'S BOOK AWARDS CONTEST, The Commonwealth Club of California, 595 Market St., San Francisco CA 94105. (415)597-6700. Executive Director: James D. Rosenthal. Annual contest. Estab. 1932. Purpose of contest: the encouragement and production of literature in California. Juvenile category included. Previously published submission; must be published from January 1 to December 31, previous to contest year. Deadline for entries: January 31. SASE for contest rules and entry forms. No entry fee. Awards gold and silver medals. Judging by the Book Awards Jury. The contest is only open to California writers/illustrators (must have been resident of California when ms was accepted for publication). "The award winners will be honored at the Annual Book Awards Program." Winning entries are displayed at awards program and advertised in newsletter.

‡CRICKET LEAGUE, *Cricket*, 315 Fifth St., Peru IL 61354. (815)224-6643. Address entries to: Cricket League. Monthly. Estab. 1973. "The purpose of Cricket League contests is to encourage creativity and give children an opportunity to express themselves in writing, drawing, painting or photography. There is a contest each month. Possible categories include story, poetry, art or photography. Each contest relates to a *specific theme* described on each *Cricket* issue's Cricket League page. Entries which do not relate to the current month's theme cannot be considered." Unpublished submissions only. Deadline for entries: the 25th of each month. Cricket League rules, contest themes, and submission deadline information can be found in the current issue of *Cricket*. "We prefer that children who enter the contests subscribe to the magazine, or that they read *Cricket* in their school or library." No entry fee. Awards certificate suitable for framing and children's books or art/writing supplies. Judging by *Cricket* editors. Obtains right to print prize-winning entries in magazine. Refer to contest rules in current *Cricket* issue. Winning entries are published on the Cricket League pages in the *Cricket* magazine 3 months subsequent to the issue in which the contest was announced.

MARGUERITE DE ANGELI PRIZE, Bantam Doubleday Dell Books for Young Readers, 1540 Broadway, New York NY 10036. Estab. 1992. Annual award. Purpose of the award: to encourage the writing of fiction for children that examines the diversity of the American experience, either contemporary or historical, in the same spirit as the works of Marguerite de Angeli; to encourage unpublished writers in the field of middle grade fiction. Unpublished submissions only. Submissions made by author or author's agent. Entries should be postmarked between March 31st and June 30th. SASE for award rules. No entry fee. Awards a $1,500 cash prize plus a hardcover and paperback book contract with a $3,500 advance against a royalty to be negotiated. Judging by Bantam Doubleday Dell Books for Young Readers editorial staff. Open to US and Canadian writers who have not previously published a novel for middle-grade readers. Works published in an upcoming Bantam Doubleday Dell Books for Young Readers list.

DELACORTE PRESS PRIZE FOR A FIRST YOUNG ADULT NOVEL, Delacorte Press, Books for Young Readers Department, 1540 Broadway, New York NY 10036. (212)354-6500. Annual award. Estab. 1982. Purpose of award: to encourage the writing of contemporary young adult fiction. Previously unpublished submissions only. Mss sent to Delacorte Press may not be submitted to other publishers while under consideration for the prize. "Entries must be submitted between Labor Day and New Year's Day. The real deadline is a December 31 postmark. Early entries are appreciated." SASE for award rules. No entry fee. Awards a $1,500 cash prize and a $6,000 advance against royalties on a hardcover and paperback book contract. Judged by the editors of the Books for Young Readers Deptartment of Delacorte Press. Rights acquired "only if the entry wins or is awarded an Honorable Mention." Requirements for entrants: The writer must be American or Canadian and must *not* have previously published a young adult novel but may have published anything else.

DREXEL CITATION, Drexel University, College of Information Studies, Philadelphia PA 19104. (215)895-2447. Director: Shelley G. McNamara. Annual award. Purpose of the award: "The Drexel citation is an award that was established in 1963 and has been given at irregular intervals since that time to honor Philadelphia authors, illustrators, publishers or others who have made outstanding contributions to literature for children in Philadelphia. The award is co-sponsored by The Free Library of Philadelphia. The recipient is selected by a committee representing both the College of Information Studies and The Free Library of Philadelphia. There is only one recipient at any given time and that recipient is recognized at an annual conference on children's literature presented each year in the spring on the Drexel campus. The recipient receives an individually designed and hand-lettered citation at a special award luncheon during the conference." Previously published submissions only. Must be published during calendar year. SASE for award rules and entry forms. No entry fee. Judging by Drexel University faculty and Free Library of Philadelphia staff.

‡SHUBERT FENDRICH MEMORIAL PLAYWRIGHTING CONTEST, Pioneer Drama Service, Inc., P.O. Box 4267, Englewood CO 80155-4267. Director: Steven Fendrich. Annual contest. Estab. 1990. Purpose of the contest: "to encourage the development of quality theatrical material for educational and community theater." Previously unpublished submissions only. Deadline for entries: March 1. SASE for contest rules and entry forms. No entry fee. Awards $1,000 royalty advance and publication. Judging by editors. All rights acquired with acceptance of contract for publication. Restrictions for entrants: Any writers currently published by Pioneer Drama Service are not eligible.

CAROLYN W. FIELD AWARD, Pennsylvania Library Association, 1919 N. Front St., Harrisburg PA 17102. (717)233-3113. Executive Director: Margaret S. Bauer, CAE. Annual award. Estab. 1983. Purpose of the award: "to honor outstanding Pennsylvania children's authors/illustrators. Previously published submissions only; must be published January-December of year of award." Deadline for entries: March 1. SASE for contest rules and entry forms. SASE for return of entries. No entry fee. Awards a medal and citation and holds a luncheon honoring award winner. Judging by "children's librarians." Requirements for entrants: "Writer/illustrator must be a Pennsylvania resident." Works displayed at PLA annual conference each fall.

DOROTHY CANFIELD FISHER CHILDREN'S BOOK AWARD, Vermont Department of Libraries, Vermont State PTA and Vermont Congress of Parents and Teachers, % Southwest Regional Library, Pierpoint Ave., Rutland VT 05701. (802)773-5879. Chairman (currently): Judith Hillman. Annual award. Estab. 1957. Purpose of the award: to encourage Vermont children to become enthusiastic and discriminating readers by providing them with books of good quality by living American authors published in the current year. Deadline for entries: "January of the following year." SASE for award rules and entry forms. No entry fee. Awards a scroll presented to the winning author at an award ceremony. Judging is by the children grades 4-8. They vote for their favorite book. Requirements for entrants: "The book must be copyrighted in the current year. It must be written by an American author living in the U.S."

‡FLORIDA STATE WRITING COMPETITION, Florida Freelance Writers Association, Maple Ridge Rd., North Sandwich NH 03259. (603)284-6367. Executive Director: Dana K. Cassell. Annual contest. Estab. 1984. Picture Books/under 6-year-old readers: 400 words maximum. Short Fiction: all age groups judged together/ages 7-10—400-900 words; ages 12 and up—2,000 words maximum. Book Chapter, fiction or nonfiction: ages 7-10—1,000 words maximum; ages 12 and up—3,000 words maximum. Entry fee is $5 (members), $7 (nonmembers). Awards $100 first prize, certificates for second through fifth prizes. Judging by teachers, editors and published authors. Judging criteria: interest and readability within age group, writing style and mechanics, originality, salability. Deadline: March 15. For copy of official entry form, send #10 SASE.

‡4-H ESSAY CONTEST, American Beekeeping Federation, Inc., P.O. Box 1038, Jesup GA 31545. (912)427-8447. Contest Director: Troy H. Fore. Annual contest. Purpose of contest: to award the best original (750-1,000 words) story on honey bees. "The story can be a simplified story about the honey bee family and its life cycle. It can be about beekeepers and what they do. Or it can be a fanciful story which casts bees as characters. Any style is suitable as long as it covers: (1) the roles each of the three castes of bees—queen, drone, worker—play in the honey bee colony; (2) the life cycle of the honey bee colony as a unit; and (3) the ways in which honey bees benefit mankind." Unpublished submissions only. Deadline for entries: before March 1. No entry fee. Awards 1st place: $250; 2nd place: $100; 3rd place: $50. Judging by American Beekeeping Federation's Essay Committee. "All national entries become the property of the American Beekeeping Federation, Inc., and may be published or used as it sees fit. No essay will be returned. Essayists *should not* forward essays directly to the American Beekeeping Federation office. Each state 4-H office is responsible for selecting the state's winner and should set its deadline so state judging can be completed at the state level in time for the winning state essay to be mailed to the ABF office before March 1, 1995. Each state winner receives a book on honey bees, beekeeping or honey. The National Winner will announced by May 1, 1995." Requirements for entrants: Contest is open to active 4-H Club members only.

DON FREEMAN MEMORIAL GRANT-IN-AID, Society of Children's Book Writers and Illustrators, #106, 22736 Vanowen St., West Hills CA 91307. (818)888-8760. Estab. 1974. Purpose of award: to "enable picture book artists to further their understanding, training and work in the picture book genre."Applications and prepared materials will be accepted between January 15 and February 15. Grant awarded and announced on June 15. SASE for award rules and entry forms. SASE for return of entries. No entry fee. Annually awards one grant of $1,000 and one runner-up grant of $500. "The grant-in-aid is available to both full and associate members of the SCBWI who, as artists, seriously intend to make picture books their chief contribution to the field of children's literature."

AMELIA FRANCES HOWARD GIBBON AWARD FOR ILLUSTRATION, Canadian Library Association, Suite 602, 200 Elgin St., Ottawa, Ontario K2P 1L5 Canada. (613)232-9625. Contact: Chairperson, Canadian Association of Children's Librarians. Annual award. Estab. 1971. Purpose of the award: "to honor excellence in the illustration of children's book(s) in Canada. To merit consideration the book must have been published in Canada and its illustrator must be a Canadian citizen or a permanent resident of Canada." Previously published submissions only; must be published between January 1 and December 31 of the previous year. Deadline for entries: February 1. SASE for award rules. Entries not returned. No entry fee. Awards a medal. Judging by selection committee of members of Canadian Association of Children's Librarians. Requirements for entrants: illustrator must be Canadian or Canadian resident. Winning books are on display at CLA Headquarters.

GOLD MEDALLION BOOK AWARDS, Evangelical Christian Publishers Association, Suite 101, 3225 S. Hardy Dr., Tempe AZ 85282. (602)966-3998. Fax: (602)966-1944. Director: Doug Ross. Annual award. Estab. 1978. Categories include Preschool Children's Books, Elementary Children's Books, Youth Books. "All entries must be evangelical in nature and cannot be contrary to ECPA's Statement of Faith (stated in official rules)." Deadlines for entries: December 1. SASE for award rules and entry form. "The work must be submitted by the publisher." Entry fee is $250 for nonmembers. Awards a Gold Medallion plaque.

GOLDEN KITE AWARDS, Society of Children's Book Writers and Illustrators, #106, 22736 Vanowen St., West Hills CA 91307. (818)888-8760. Coordinator: Sue Alexander. Annual award. Estab. 1973. "The works chosen will be those that the judges feel exhibit excellence in writing, and in the case of the picture-illustrated books—in illustration, and genuinely appeal to the interests and concerns of children. For the fiction and nonfiction awards, original works and single-author collections of stories or poems of which at least half are new and never before published in book form are eligible—anthologies and translations are not. For the picture-illustration awards, the art or photographs must be original works (the texts—which may be fiction or nonfiction—may be original, public domain or previously published). Deadline for entries: December 15. SASE for award rules. Self-addressed mailing label for return of entries. No entry fee. Awards statuettes and plaques. The panel of judges will consist of two children's book authors, a children's book artist or photographer (who may or may not be an author), a children's book editor and a librarian." Requirements for entrants: "must be a member of SCBWI." Winning books will be displayed at national conference in August. Books to be entered, as well as further inquiries, should be submitted to: The Society of Children's Book Writers and Illustrators, above address.

‡**HIGHLIGHTS FOR CHILDREN FICTION CONTEST,** 803 Church St., Honesdale PA 18431. (717)253-1080. Mss should be addressed to Fiction Contest. Editor: Kent L. Brown Jr. Annual contest. Estab. 1980. Purpose of the contest: to stimulate interest in writing for children and reward and recognize excellence. Unpublished submissions only. Deadline for entries: February 28; entries accepted after January 1 only. SASE for contest rules. SASE for return of entries. No entry fee. Awards 3 prizes of $1,000 each in cash and a pewter bowl (or, at the winner's election, attendance at the Highlights Foundation Writers Workshop at Chautauqua). Judging by *Highlights'* editors. Winning pieces are purchased for the cash prize of $1,000 and published in *Highlights*; semifinalists go to out-of-house judges (educators, editors, writers, etc.). Requirements for entrants: open to any writer; student writers must be 16 or older. Winners announced in June. "This year's contest is for humorous stories for children. Length up to 900 words. Stories for beginning readers should not exceed 500 words. Stories should be consistent with *Highlights'* editorial requirements. No violence, war, crime or derogatory humor."

‡**HOOT AWARDS, WRITING CONTEST, PHOTO CONTEST, POETRY CONTEST, COVER CONTEST,** *Owl Magazine*, 179 John St., Suite 500, Toronto, Ontario M5T 3G5 Canada. (416)971-5275. Annual. Purpose of awards: "to encourage children to contribute and participate in the magazine. The Hoot Awards recognize excellence in an individual or group effort to help the environment." Unpublished submissions only. Deadlines change yearly. Prizes/awards "change every year. Often we give books as prizes." Winning entries published in the magazine. Judging by art and editorial staff. Entries become the property of Owl Communications. "The contests and awards are open to children up to 14 years of age."

INDIAN PAINTBRUSH BOOK AWARD, Wyoming Library Association, P.O. Box 1387, Cheyenne WY 82003. (307)632-7622. Award Director: Laura Grott. Annual award. Estab. 1986. Purpose of award: to encourage the children of Wyoming to read good books. Previously published submissions only. Deadline for entries: April 1. Books can only be submitted for the nominations list by the children of Wyoming. No entry fee. Awards a watercolor painting. Judging by the children of Wyoming (grades 4-6) voting from a nominations list of 20. Requirements for entrants: only Wyoming children may nominate; books must be published in last 5 years, be fiction, have good reviews; final list chosen by a committee of librarians.

IOWA CHILDREN'S CHOICE AWARD, Iowa Educational Media Association, 1112½ St. SW, Dyersville, IA 52040. (319)875-8888. Chair: Jean Rubner. Annual award. Estab. 1979. Purpose of the award: to encourage children to read more and better books; to provide an avenue for positive dialogue between teacher, parent and children about books and authors; to give recognition to those who write books for children. Books must have been published between 1991 and 1995 for '96-'97 list. "Writers and illustrators *do not 'enter'* their works themselves. A committee of teachers, librarians and students choose the books that are on the list each year. The list is narrowed down to 20-25 books based on set criteria." The award is unique in that it gives children an opportunity to choose the book to receive the award and to suggest books for the yearly reading list. Deadline for entries: February 15. "Students in grades 3-6 throughout Iowa nominate." Awards a brass-plated school bell. Judging by "students in grades 3-6 throughout Iowa."

IOWA TEEN AWARD, Iowa Educational Media Association, 306 E. H Ave., Grundy Center IA 50638. (319)824-6788. Contest Director: Don Osterhaus. Annual award. Estab. 1983. Previously published submissions only. Purpose of award: to allow students to read high quality literature and to have opportunity to select their favorite from this list. Must have been published "in last 3-4 years." Deadline for entries: April 1995 for '96-'97 competition. SASE for award rules/entry forms. No entry fee. "Media specialists, teachers and students nominate possible entries." Awards an inscribed brass apple. Judging by Iowa students in grades 6-9. Requirements: Work must be of recent publication, so copies can be ordered for media center collections. Reviews of submitted books must be available for the nominating committee. Works displayed "at participating classrooms, media centers, public libraries and local bookstores in Iowa."

*‡ISLAND LITERARY AWARDS, Prince Edward Island Council of the Arts, P.O. Box 2234, Charlottetown, Prince Edward C1A 8B9 Canada. Annual award. Estab. 1988. Purpose of awards: to provide Island writers with the opportunity to enter work in one or more of these categories: poetry, short adult fiction, children's literature, feature article and creative writing by Island youth. Unpublished submissions only (except for Feature Article Award). Submissions made by the author. Deadline for entries: February 15. SASE for contest rules and entry forms. Entry fee is $6. Awards range from $100-500 in adult categories; $25-75 for youth contest. Requirements for entrants: "The competitions are open to individuals who have been residents on Prince Edward Island at least six of the last twelve months. Authors of one or more books published within the last five years are not eligible to enter the genre(s) in which they have published."

IUPUI YOUTH THEATRE PLAYWRITING COMPETITION AND SYMPOSIUM, Indiana University-Purdue University at Indianapolis, 525 N. Blackford St., Indianapolis IN 46202. (317)274-2095. Director: Dorothy Webb. Entries should be submitted to W. Mark McCreary, Literary Manager. Contest every two years; next competition will be 1996. Estab. 1983. Purpose of the contest: "to encourage writers to create artistic scripts for young audiences. It provides a forum through which each playwright receives constructive criticism of his/her work and, where selected, writers participate in script development with the help of professional dramaturgs, directors and actors." Unpublished submissions only. Submissions made by author. Deadline for entries: September 1. SASE for contest rules and entry forms. No entry fee. "Awards will be presented to the top ten finalists. Four cash awards of $1,000 each will be received by the top four playwrights whose scripts will be given developmental work culminating in polished readings showcased at the symposium held on the IUPUI campus. This symposium is always held opposite years of the competition. Major publishers of scripts for young audiences, directors, producers, critics and teachers attend this symposium and provide useful reactions to the plays. If a winner is unable to be involved in preparation of the reading and to attend the showcase of his/her work, the prize will not be awarded. Remaining finalists will receive certificates." Judging by professional directors, dramaturgs, publishers, university professors. Write for guidelines and entry form.

*THE EZRA JACK KEATS NEW WRITER AWARD, Ezra Jack Keats Foundation/Administered by the New York Public Library Early Childhood Resource and Information Center, 66 Leroy St., New York NY 10014. (212)929-0815. Program Coordinator: Hannah Nuba. Biennial award. Purpose of the award: "The award will be given to a promising new writer of picture books for children. Selection criteria include books for children (ages nine and under) that reflect the tradition of Ezra Jack Keats. These books portray: the universal qualities of childhood, strong and supportive family and adult relationships, the multicultural nature of our world." Submissions made by the author, by the author's agent or nominated by a person or group of people. Must be published in the 2-year period preceding the award. SASE for contest rules and entry forms. No entry fee. Awards $1,000 coupled with Ezra Jack Keats Silver Medal. Judging by a panel of experts. "The author should have published no more than six books. Entries are judged on the outstanding features of the text, complemented by illustrations. Candidates need not be both author and illustrator. Entries should carry a 1993 or 1994 copyright (for the 1995 award)." Winning book and author to be presented April 13, 1995 at reception at The New York Public Library. Book should be for ages 9 and under.

‡KENTUCKY STATE POETRY SOCIETY ANNUAL CONTEST, Kentucky State Poetry Society, 3289 Hunting Hills Dr., Lexington KY 40515. (606)271-4662. Contest Director: Miriam Woolfolk. Annual contest. Estab. 1966. Unpublished submissions only. Deadline for entries: July 10. SASE for contest rules and entry forms. Categories 2-6 are free, all others $1. $5 for grand prix. Awards certificates of merit and cash prizes from $1 to $100. Sponsors pick judges. "One-time printing rights acquired for publication of first prizes in *Pegasus*, our annual journal." Contest open to all. "No illustrations, please." "First place winners will be published in *Pegasus* and all other winners will be displayed at our annual awards banquet."

KERLAN AWARD, Ezra Jack Keats/Kerlan Collection Memorial Fellowship, 109 Walter Library, 117 Pleasant St. SE, University of Minnesota, Minneapolis MN 55455. (612)624-4576. Curator: Karen Nelson Hoyle. Annual award. Estab. 1975. "Given in recognition of singular attainments in the creation of children's literature and in appreciation for generous donation of unique resources to the Kerlan Collection." Previously published submissions only. Deadline for entries: November 1. Anyone can send nominations for the award, directed to the Kerlan Collection. No materials are submitted other than the person's name. No entry fee. Award is $1,500 to study at Kerlan Collection, University of Minnesota campus, and a laminated plaque. Judging by the Kerlan Award Committee—3 representatives from the University of Minnesota faculty (from the College of Education, the College of Human Ecology and the College of Liberal Arts); one representative from the Kerlan Collection (ex officio); 1 representative from the Kerlan Friends; 1 representative from the Minnesota Library Association. Requirements for entrants: open to all who are nominated. Anyone can submit names. "For serious consideration, entrant must be a published author and/or illustrator of children's books (including young adult fiction) and have donated original materials to the Kerlan Collection."

 The asterisk before a listing indicates the listing is new in this edition.

JANUSZ KORCZAK AWARDS, Joseph H. and Belle R. Braun Center for Holocaust Studies, Anti-Defamation League, 823 United Nations Plaza, New York NY 10017. (212)490-2525. Fax: (212)867-0779. Award Director: Mark Edelman. Award usually offered every 2 years. Estab. 1980. Purpose of award: "The award honors books about children which best exemplify Janusz Korczak's principles of selflessness and human dignity." Previously published submissions only; for 1996, books must have been published in 1994 or 1995. SASE for award rules and entry forms. No entry fee. Awards $1,000 cash and plaque (first prize); plaque (Honorable Mention). Judging by an interdisciplinary committee of leading scholars, editors, literary critics and educators. Requirements for entrants: Books must meet entry requirements and must be published in English. No entries are returned. They become the property of the Braun Center. Press release will announce winners.

LANDERS THEATRE CHILDREN'S PLAYWRITING AWARD, Landers Theatre, 311 E. Walnut, Springfield MO 65806. (417)869-3869. Contact: Mick Denniston. Estab. 1992. Purpose of the award: to produce full-fledged mainstage production of new musicals for young audiences. Unpublished submissions only. Submissions made by the author. Deadline for entries: to be announced. SASE for award rules and entry forms. No entry fee. Awards $5,000 plus full production. Judging by theater artistic staff and panel. Winning play performed in spring of winning season. Call for more information.

‡ELIAS LIEBERMAN STUDENT POETRY AWARD, Poetry Society of America, 15 Gramercy Park, New York NY 10003. (212)254-9628. Award Director: Elise Paschen. Annual award. Purpose of the award: Award is for the best unpublished poem by a high or preparatory school student (grades 9-12) from the US and its territories. Unpublished submissions only. Deadline for entries: December 22. SASE for award rules and entry forms. Entries not returned. Entry fee is $10. "High schools can send an unlimited number of submissions with one entry per individual student. Fee is $1 for individual entries." Award: $100. Judging by a professional poet. Requirements for entrants: Award open to all high school and preparatory students from the US and its territories. School attended, as well as name and address, should be noted. Line limit: none. "The award-winning poem will be included in a sheaf of poems that will be part of the program at the award ceremony and sent to all PSA members."

MAGAZINE MERIT AWARDS, Society of Children's Book Writers and Illustrators, 2510-G Las Posas Rd., Suite 506, Camarillo CA 93010. (805)482-2343. Award Coordinator: Dorothy Leon. Annual award. Estab. 1988. "Purpose of the award: "To recognize outstanding original magazine work for young people published during that year and having been written or illustrated by members of SCBWI." Previously published submissions only. Entries must be submitted between January 31 and December 15 of the year of publication. For brochure (rules) write Award Coordinator. No entry fee. Must be a SCBWI member. Awards plaques and honor certificates for each of the 3 categories (fiction, nonfiction, illustration). Judging by a magazine editor and two "full" SCBWI members. "All magazine work for young people by an SCBWI member—writer, artist or photographer—is eligible during the year of original publication. In the case of co-authored work, both authors must be SCBWI members. Members must submit their own work." Requirements for entrants: 4 copies each of the published work and proof of publication (may be contents page) showing the name of the magazine and the date of issue. The SCBWI is a professional organization of writers and illustrators and others interested in children's literature. Membership is open to the general public at large.

‡MANNINGHAM POETRY TRUST STUDENT CONTESTS, National Federation of State Poetry Societies, Inc., 701 Sanders St., Auburn AL 36830. (205)821-8749. Chair: Margaret Cutchens. Estab. 1980. "Two separate contests are held each year: grades 6-8; grades 9-12. Poems may have been printed and may have won previous awards." Deadline for entries: April 9. Submit 1 poem neatly typed on standard typewriter paper. Submit 1 original and 1 copy. On copy only, type: (1) name (2) complete home mailing address (3) school (4) grade. Awards $50, first place; $30, second place; $20, third place; and 5 honorable mentions of $5 each. Judging by committee of nationally recognized poets appointed by chair. Winners will be announced at the NFSPS convention, and checks will be mailed shortly beforehand. Winners are published in the NFSPS chapbook. Send SASE if you wish to receive a winner's list.

VICKY METCALF BODY OF WORK AWARD, Canadian Authors Association, Suite 500, 275 Slater St., Ottawa, Ontario K1P 5H9 Canada. (613)233-2846. Fax: (613)235-8237. Contact: Awards Chair. Annual award. Estab. 1963. Purpose: to honor a body of work inspirational to Canadian youth. Deadline for entries: December 31. SASE for award rules and entry forms. Entries not returned. No entry fee. Awards $10,000 and certificate. Judging by panel of CAA-appointed judges including past winners. "The prizes are given solely to stimulate writing for children by Canadian writers," said Mrs. Metcalf when she established the award. "We must encourage the writing of material for Canadian children without setting any restricting formulas."

*VICKY METCALF SHORT STORY AWARD, Canadian Authors Association, Suite 500, 275 Slater St., Ottawa, ON K1P 5H9 Canada. (613)233-2846. Fax: (613)235-8237. Contact: Awards Chair. Annual award. Estab. 1979. Purpose: to honor writing by a Canadian inspirational to Canadian youth. Previously published submissions only; must be published between January 1 and December 31. Deadline for entries: December 31. SASE for contest/award rules and entry forms. Entries not returned. No entry fee. Awards $3,000 to Canadian author and $1,000 to editor responsible for publishing winning story if published in a Canadian periodical or anthology. Judging by CAA-selected panel including past winners.

‡MICHIGAN STUDENT FILM & VIDEO FESTIVAL, Detroit Area Film and Television, Harrison High School, 29995 W. 12 Mile Rd., Farmington Hills MI 48334. (810)489-3491. Contest Director: Margaret Culver. Open to students in grades K-12; *entrants must be Michigan residents*. Annual contest. Estab. 1968. Film entries must be 16mm or film that has been transferred to video; categories for video entries are teleplay, commercials, music, documentary, series, artistic, general entertainment, sports, news, editing, unedited, drug awareness (public service announcement), instructional and animation. Submissions may be made by the student or teacher. Deadline for entries is February 20, 1995. Contest rules and entry form available with SASE. Entry fee is $10. Prizes include certificates and medals for all entries; prizes for Best of Show award range from cameras to scholarships. Judging is done by professionals in media, education and production of film and video. The festival reserves the right to use the material for educational or promotional purposes. Work will be shown at the Detroit Film Theater, Detroit Institute of Arts.

‡MILKWEED PRIZE FOR CHILDREN'S LITERATURE, Milkweed Editions, Suite 400, 430 First Ave. N., Minneapolis MN 55401-1473. (612)332-6192. Award Director: Emilie Buchwald, publisher/editor. Annual award. Estab. 1993. Purpose of the award: to encourage writers to turn their attention to readers in the 8-14 age group. Unpublished submissions only "in book form." Submissions made by the author. Deadline for entries is March 15. Must send SASE for award guidelines. No entry fee required. Prizes include publication by Milkweed Editions and a cash advance of $3,000 against royalties. Judging is done by Milkweed Editions. "We acquire all the usual rights as the publisher of the manuscript when we choose a winner." Winners announced in June. Requirements of entrants: writers of English who have previously published a book of fiction or nonfiction for children or adults, or a minimum of 3 short stories or articles in nationally distributed magazines for children or adults. Students are eligible "as long as they fulfill publication rules." Ms should be 110-350 pages in length, typed double-spaced on good quality white paper.

THE MILNER AWARD, Atlanta-Fulton Public Library/Friends of the Atlanta Fulton Public Library, One Margaret Mitchell Square, Atlanta GA 30303. (404)730-1710. Executive Director: Charlene P. Shucker. Annual award. Estab. 1983. Purpose of the award: "The Milner Award is an annual award to a living American author of children's books. Selection is made by the children of Atlanta, voting for their favorite author during Children's Book Week." Previous winners not eligible. "The winning author is awarded a specially commissioned work of the internationally famous glass sculptor, Hans Frabel, and a $1,000 honorarium." Requirements for entrants: "Winner must be an American author, able to appear personally in Atlanta to receive the award at a formal program." *No submission process.*

*MINNESOTA BOOK AWARDS, Minnesota Center for the Book, 226 Metro Square, Seventh & Robert Sts., Saint Paul MN 55101. (612)224-4801. Coordinator: Roger Sween. #400, 550 Cedar St., Saint Paul MN 55101. (612)296-2821. Fax: (612)296-5418. Annual award. Estab. 1988. Purpose of award: "The Minnesota Book Award recognizes, celebrates and promotes the contributions that resident creators of books make to our quality of life and strengthens the linkages among members of the Minnesota community of the book." Previously published submissions only. Any recommendation for nomination welcome with accompanying form and copy of the book. Must be published between January 1 and December 31 of award year. Deadline for entries: December 31. SASE for contest rules and entry forms. No entry fee. Awards provide recognition of nominees and award winners in publicity, exhibits, public ceremonies. Judging by representatives of the book community who select the nominees from all available publications within the year. Teams of 3 judges agree on awards in each category. Requirements for entrants: must reside in Minnesota at time of book publication; show evidence of state taxes or state driver's license. Exhibit of nominated books appears in entry arcade of Minneapolis Public Library and afterward tours to libraries and library conferences in the state. "Our principal efforts hold up outstanding and exemplary books as representative of the wealth and variety of book creators living in our midst."

*‡MARY MOLLOY FELLOWSHIP IN CHILDREN'S WORKING FICTION, The Heekin Group Foundation, P.O. Box 209, Middlebury VT 05753. (802)388-8651. Children's Literature Division Director: Deirdre M. Heekin. Annual award. Estab. 1994. (The Heekin Group Foundation was established in 1992.) "We are awarding our first children's literature fellowship, the Mary Molloy Fellowship in Children's Working Fiction, in July, 1995. We are accepting manuscripts for the middle readers (ages 8-12) category. We have chosen to award this fellowship for this category as we feel it is an area that has not been developed in recent years." Unpublished submissions only. Submissions made by the author. Deadline for entries: December 1. SASE for award rules and entry forms. Entry fee is $20. Awards $4,000. Judging by a children's literature publisher. The competition is open to all beginning career writers who have not yet been published in children's fiction for middle readers (8-12 years old). "For further information regarding our other fiction and nonfiction fellowships, please contact our headquarters: The Heekin Group Foundation, 68860 Goodrich Rd., Sisters OR 97759."

THE NATIONAL CHAPTER OF CANADA IODE, (formerly Violet Downey Book Award), Violet Downey Book Award, Suite 254, 40 Orchard View Blvd., Toronto, Ontario M5R 1B9 Canada. (416)487-4416. Award Director: Marty Dalton. Annual award. Estab. 1985. Purpose of the award: to honor the best children's English language book, by a Canadian, published in Canada for ages 5-13, over 500 words. Fairy tales, anthologies and books adapted from another source are not eligible. Previously published submissions only. Books must have been published between February 1 and January 30. Submissions made by author, author's agent; anyone may submit. Must have been published during previous calendar year. Deadline for entries: January 31. SASE for award rules and entry forms. No entry fee. Awards $3,000. Judging by a panel of 6, 4 IODE members and 2 professionals.

NATIONAL JEWISH BOOK AWARD FOR CHILDREN'S LITERATURE, Jewish Book Council Inc., 15 E. 26th St., New York NY 10010. (212)532-4949. Awards Coordinator: Dr. Marcia W. Posner. Annual award. Estab. 1950. Previously published submissions only; must be published in 1994 for 1995 award. Deadline for entries: January, 1995. SASE for award rules and entry forms. Entries not returned. Entry fee is $75/title; $100 if listed in 2 categories. Awards $750. Judging by 3 authorities in the field. Requirements for entrants: Jewish children's books, published only for ages 8-14. Books will be displayed at the awards ceremony in NYC during Jewish Book Month, November 18–December 18.

NATIONAL JEWISH BOOK AWARD FOR PICTURE BOOKS, (Marcia & Louis Posner Award), Jewish Book Council, 15 E. 26th St., New York NY 10010. (212)532-4949. Awards Coordinator: Dr. Marcia W. Posner. Annual award. Estab. 1980. Previously published submissions only; must be published the year prior to the awards ceremony—1994 and up to March of 1995 for 1995 award. Deadline for entries: January, 1995. SASE for award rules and entry forms. Entries not returned. No entry fee. Awards $750. Judging by 3 authorities in the field. Requirements for entrants: subject must be of Jewish content, but not necessarily religious. Works displayed at the awards ceremony.

‡NATIONAL PEACE ESSAY CONTEST, United States Institute of Peace, Suite 700, 1550 M St. NW, Washington DC 20005-1708. (202)429-3854. Contest Director: Heidi Schaeffer. Annual contest. Estab. 1987. "The contest gives students the opportunity to do valuable research, writing and thinking on a topic of importance to international peace and conflict resolution. Submissions, instead of being published, can be a classroom assignment"; previously published entries must have appeared between September 1 and January 23 previous to the contest deadline. Deadline for entries: January 23, 1995 (postmark deadline). "Interested students, teachers and others may write or call to receive free contest kits. Please do not include SASE." No entry fee. State Level Awards are college scholarships in the following amounts: first place $750; second place $500; third place $250. National winners are selected from among the 1st place state winners. National winners receive scholarships in the following amounts: first place $10,000; second $5,000; third $3,500. Judging is conducted by education professionals from across the country and by the Board of Directors of the United States Institute of Peace. "All submissions become property of the U.S. Institute of Peace to use at its discretion and without royalty or any limitation, any winning essay. Students grades 9-12 in the U.S., its territories and overseas schools may submit essays for review by completing the application process. U.S. citizenship required for students attending overseas schools. Please—no illustrations. National winning essays for each competition will be published by the U.S. Institute of Peace for public consumption."

*‡NATIONAL WRITERS ASSOCIATION ARTICLE/ESSAY CONTEST, 1450 S. Havana, Suite 424, Aurora CO 80012. (303)751-7844. Executive Director: Sandy Whelchel. Annual contest. Estab. 1971. Purpose of contest: "to encourage writers in this creative form and to recognize those who excel in nonfiction writing." Submissions made by author. Deadline for entries: December 31. SASE for contest rules and entry forms. Entry fee is $12. Awards three cash prizes; choice of books; Honorable Mention Certificate. "Two people read each entry; third party picks three top winners from top five." Top 3 winners are published in an anthology published by National Writers Association, if winners agree to this.

*‡NATIONAL WRITERS ASSOCIATION NOVEL WRITING CONTEST, 1450 S. Havana, Suite 424, Aurora CO 80012. (303)751-7844. Executive Director: Sandy Whelchel. Annual contest. Estab. 1971. Purpose of contest: "to encourage writers in this creative form and to recognize those who excel in novel writing." Submissions made by the author. Deadline for entries: April 1. SASE for contest rules and entry forms. Entry fee is $30. Awards top 3, cash prizes; 4 to 10, choice of books; 10 to 20, Honorable Mention Certificates. Judging by "two people read the manuscripts; a third party picks the three top winners from the top 5. We display our members' published books in our offices."

*‡NATIONAL WRITERS ASSOCIATION SHORT STORY CONTEST, 1450 Havana St., Suite 424, Aurora CO 80012. (303)751-7844. Executive Director: Sandy Whelchel. Annual contest. Estab. 1971. Purpose of contest: "To encourage writers in this creative form and to recognize those who excel in fiction writing." Submissions made by the author. Deadline for entries: July 1. SASE for contest rules and entry forms. Entry fee is $12. Awards 3 cash prizes, choice of books and certificates for Honorable Mentions. Judging by "two people read each entry; third person picks top three winners." Top three winners are published in an anthology published by National Writers Association, if winners agree to this.

‡THE NATIONAL WRITTEN & ILLUSTRATED BY . . . AWARDS CONTEST FOR STUDENTS, Landmark Editions, Inc., P.O. Box 4469, Kansas City MO 64127. (816)241-4919. Contest

Director: Teresa Melton. Annual awards contest with 3 published winners. Estab. 1986. Purpose of the contest: to encourage and celebrate the creative efforts of students. There are 3 age categories (ages 6-9, 10-13 and 14-19). Unpublished submissions only. Deadline for entries: May 1. Contest rules available for SAE with 58¢ postage. "Need to send a self-addressed, sufficiently stamped (at least $3 postage), book mailer with book entry for its return. All entries which do not win are mailed back in November or December of each contest year." Entry fee is $1. Awards publication of book. Judging by national panel of educators, editors, illustrators, authors and school librarians. "Each student winner receives a publishing contract allowing Landmark to publish the book. Copyright is in student's name and student receives royalties on sale of book. Books must be in proper contest format and submitted with entry form signed by a teacher or librarian. Students may develop their illustrations in any medium of their choice, as long as the illustrations remain two-dimensional and flat to the surface of the paper." Winners are notified by phone by October 15 of each contest year. By September of the following year, all winners' books are published—after several months of pre-production work on the books by the students and the editorial and artistic staff of Landmark editions. Works are published in Kansas City, Missouri for distribution nationally and internationally.

‡THE NENE AWARD, Hawaii State Library, 478 S. King St., Honolulu HI 96813. (808)586-3510. Award Director: Diane Teramoto. Estab. 1964. "The Nene Award was designed to help the children of Hawaii become acquainted with the best contemporary writers of fiction, become aware of the qualities that make a good book and choose the best rather than the mediocre." Previously published submissions only. Books must have been copyrighted not more than 6 years prior to presentation of award. Work is nominated. Awards Koa plaque. Judging by the children of Hawaii in grades 4-6. Requirements for entrants: books must be fiction, written by a living author, copyrighted not more than 6 years ago and suitable for children in grades 4, 5 and 6. Current and past winners are displayed in all participating school and public libraries.

‡NEW ERA WRITING WRITING, ART, PHOTOGRAPHY & MUSIC CONTEST, The Church of Jesus Christ of Latter-day Saints, 50 E. North Temple, Salt Lake City UT 84150. (801)240-2951. Managing Editor: Richard M. Romney. Annual contest. Estab. 1971. Purpose of the contest: to feature the creative abilities of young Latter-day Saints. Unpublished submissions only. Submissions made by the author. Deadline for entries: January 6. SASE for contest rules and entry forms. No entry fee. Awards partial scholarships to LDS colleges, cash prizes. Judging by *New Era* magazine editorial and design staffs. All rights acquired; reassigned to author upon written request. Requirements for entrants: must be an active member of the LDS Church, ages 12-23. Winning entries published in each August's issue.

NEWBERY MEDAL AWARD, Association for Library Service to Children, Division of the American Library Association, 50 E. Huron, Chicago IL 60611. (312)280-2163. Executive Director, ALSC: Susan Roman. Annual award. Estab. 1922. Purpose of the award: to recognize the most distinguished contribution to American children's literature published in the US. Previously published submissions only; must be published prior to year award is given. Deadline for entries: December. SASE for award rules and entry forms. Entries not returned. No entry fee. Medal awarded at banquet during annual conference. Judging by Newbery Committee.

THE NOMA AWARD FOR PUBLISHING IN AFRICA, Kodansha Ltd., % Hans Zell Associates, P.O. Box 56, 11 Richmond Rd., Oxford OX1 2SJ England. (0865)511428. Fax: (0865)793298 or (0865)311534. Secretary of the Managing Committee: Hans M. Zell. Annual award. Estab. 1979. Purpose of award: to encourage publications of works by African

The double dagger before a listing indicates the contest is open to students.

writers and scholars in Africa, instead of abroad, as is still too often the case at present. Books in the following categories are eligible: scholarly or academic, books for children, literature and creative writing, including fiction, drama and poetry. Previously published submissions only. 1995 award given for book published in 1994. Deadline for entries: end of February 1995. Submissions must be made through publishers. Conditions of entry and submission forms are available from the secretariat. Entries not returned. No entry fee. Awards $5,000. Judging by the Managing Committee (jury): African scholars and book experts and representatives of the international book community. Chairman: Professor Abiola Irele. Requirements for entrants: Author must be African, and book must be published in Africa. "Winning titles are displayed at appropriate international book events."

*‡NORTH AMERICAN INTERNATIONAL AUTO SHOW SHORT STORY & HIGH SCHOOL POSTER CONTEST, Detroit Auto Dealers Association, 1800 W. Big Beaver Rd., Troy MI 48084-3531. (810)643-0250. Public Relations/Writing: Heidi Knickerbocker. Public Relations/Art: Cristy Maines. Annual contest. Submissions made by the author and illustrator. Deadline for entries: October 21. "We are still trying to improve the contest and are still debating the dates every year." SASE for contest rules and entry forms. No entry fee. 5 winners of the short story contest will each receive $500. Entries will be judged by an independent panel comprised of knowledgeable persons engaged in the literary field in some capacity. Entrants must be Michigan residents, including high school students enrolled in grades 9-12. Junior high school students in 9th grade are also eligible. Winners of the High School Poster Contest will receive $1,000, first place; $500, second; $250, third. Entries will be judged by an independent panel of recognized representatives of the art community. Entrants must be Michigan high school students enrolled in grades 9-12. Junior high students in 9th grade are also eligible. Winners will be announced during the North American International Auto Show in January and may be published in the *Auto Show Program* at the sole discretion of the D.A.D.A.

‡OHIOANA BOOK AWARDS, Ohioana Library Association, 65 S. Front St., Suite 1105, Columbus OH 43215. (614)466-3831. Director: Linda R. Hengst. Annual award. "The Ohioana Book Awards are given to books of outstanding literary quality. Up to six are given each year. Awards may be given in the following categories: fiction, nonfiction, children's literature, poetry and books about Ohio or an Ohioan. Books must be received by the Ohioana Library during the calendar year prior to the year the award is given and must have a copyright date within the last two calendar years." Deadline for entries: December 31. SASE for award rules and entry forms. No entry fee. Winners receive citation and glass sculpture. "Any book that has been written or edited by a person born in Ohio or who has lived in Ohio for at least five years" is eligible.

*‡OKLAHOMA BOOK AWARDS, Oklahoma Center for the Book, 200 NE 18th, Oklahoma City OK 73105. (405)521-2502. Award Director: Ann Hamilton. Annual award . Estab. 1989. Purpose of award: "to honor Oklahoma writers and books about our state." Previously published submissions only. Submissions made by the author, author's agent, or entered by a person or group of people, including the publisher. Must be published during the calendar year preceding the award. Deadline for entries: January 10. SASE for award rules and entry forms. No entry fee. Awards a medal—no cash prize. Judging by a panel of 5 people for each category—a librarian, a working writer in the genre, editors, etc. Requirements for entrants: author must be an Oklahoma native, resident, former resident or have written a book with Oklahoma theme. Book will be displayed at Oklahoma Book Award Ceremony and other times.

*ORBIS PICTUS AWARD FOR OUTSTANDING NONFICTION FOR CHILDREN, National Council of Teachers of English, 1111 W. Kenyon Rd., Urbana IL 61801-1096. (217)328-3870, etx. 268. Chair, NCTE Committee on the Orbis Pictus Award for Outstanding Nonfiction for Children: Evelyn Freeman, The Ohio State University at Newark, Newark Ohio. Annual award. Estab. 1989. Purpose of award: to honor outstanding nonfiction works for children. Previously published submissions only. Submissions made by author, author's agent, by a person or group of people. Must be published January 1-December 31 of contest year. Deadline for entries: December 31. Call for award information. No entry fee. Awards a plaque given at the NCTE Elementary Section Luncheon at the NCTE Annual Convention in November. Judging by a committee.

HELEN KEATING OTT AWARD FOR OUTSTANDING CONTRIBUTION TO CHILDREN'S LITERATURE, Church and Synagogue Library Association, P.O. Box 19357, Portland OR 97280. (503)244-6919. Chair of Committee: Lillian Koppin. Annual award. Estab. 1980. "This award is given to a person or organization that has made a significant contribution to promoting high moral and ethical values through children's literature." Deadline for entries: February 1. "Recipient is honored in July during the conference." Awards certificate of recognition and a conference package consisting of registration, meals and housing and a complementary 1 year membership. "A nomination for an award may be made by anyone. It should include the name, address and telephone number of the nominee plus the church or synagogue relationship where appropriate. Nominations of an organization should include the name of a contact person. A detailed description of the reasons for the nomination should be given, accompanied by documentary evidence of accomplishment. The person(s) making the nomination should give his/her name, address and telephone number and a brief explanation of his/her knowledge of the nominee's accomplishments. Elements of creativity and innovation will be given high priority by the judges."

PEN CENTER USA WEST LITERARY AWARD FOR CHILDREN'S LITERATURE, PEN Center USA West, Suite 41, 672 S. Lafayette Park Place, Los Angeles CA 90057. (213)365-8500. Contact: Chair of the Awards Committee. Open to published authors. Annual award. Estab. 1982. Purpose of the award: "to recognize the work of published writers who live west of the Mississippi. The 1995 awards are for books published in 1994." Categories include Children's Literature. Previously published submissions only. Submissions made by the author, author's agent or publishers. Deadline for entries: December 31. SASE for award rules. Cash award, at least $500, and plaque. Judging by awards committee.

PEN/NORMA KLEIN AWARD FOR CHILDREN'S FICTION, PEN American Center, 568 Broadway, New York NY 10012. (212)334-1660. Awarded in odd-numbered years. Estab. 1990. "In memory of the late PEN member and distinguished children's book author Norma Klein, the award honors new authors whose books demonstrate the adventuresome and innovative spirit that characterizes the best children's literature and Norma Klein's own work." Previously published submissions only. "Candidates may not nominate themselves. We welcome all nominations from authors and editors of children's books." Deadline for entries: January 31. Awards $3,000 which will be given in May. Judging by a panel of 3 distinguished children's book authors. Nominations open to authors of books for elementary school to young adult readers. "It is strongly recommended that the nominator describe in some detail the literary character of the candidate's work and how it promises to enrich American literature for children."

PLEASE TOUCH MUSEUM BOOK AWARD, Please Touch Museum, 210 N. 21st St., Philadelphia PA 19103. (215)963-0667. Director of Research and Child Development: Marzy Sykes, Ph.D. Annual award. Estab. 1985. Purpose of the award: "to recognize and encourage the publication of books for young children by first-time American authors that are of the highest quality and will aid them in enjoying the process of learning through books. Awarded to two picture books that are particularly imaginative and effective in exploring a concept or concepts, one for children age three and younger, and one for children ages four-seven." Previously published submissions only. "To be eligible for consideration a book must: (1) Explore and clarify an idea for young children. This could include the concept of numbers, colors, shapes, sizes, senses, feelings, etc. There is no limitation as to format. (2) Be distinguished in both text and illustration. (3) Be published within the last year by an American publisher. (4) Be written by an American author (award for children three and younger); be the first book by an American author and/or illustrator (award for children four-seven)." Deadline for entries: March 15 (submissions may be made throughout the year). SASE for award rules and entry forms. No entry fee. Judging by selected jury of children's literature experts, librarians and early childhood educators. Education store purchases books for selling at Book Award Celebration Day and throughout the year. Receptions and autographing sessions held in bookstores, the main branch of Philadelphia's library and at the museum.

*POCKETS MAGAZINE FICTION CONTEST, The Upper Room, P.O. Box 189, Nashville TN 37202-0189. (615)340-7333. Associate Editor: Lynn Gilliam. Annual contest. Estab. 1990. Purpose of contest: "to discover new freelance writers for our magazine and to encourage freelance writers to become familiar with the needs of our magazine." Unpublished submissions only. Submissions made by the author. Deadline for entries: August 15. SASE for contest rules and entry forms. No entry fee. Awards $1,000 and publication. Judging by *Pockets'* editors and 3 other editors of other Upper Room publications. Winner and runners-up are published in the magazine.

EDGAR ALLAN POE AWARD, Mystery Writers of America, Inc., 6th Floor, 17 E. 47th St., New York NY 10017. (212)888-8171. Executive Director: Priscilla Ridgway. Annual award. Estab. 1945. Purpose of the award: to honor authors of distinguished works in the mystery field. Previously published submissions only. Submissions made by the author, author's agent; "normally by the publisher." Work must be published/produced the year of the contest. Deadline for entries: December 1 "except for works only available in the month of December." SASE for award rules and entry forms. No entry fee. Awards ceramic bust of "Edgar" for winner; scrolls for all nominees. Judging by professional members of Mystery Writers of America (writers). Nominee press release sent after first Wednesday in February. Winner announced at the Edgar Banquet, held in late April.

‡THE PRISM AWARDS, The Kids Netword, 90 Venice Crescent, Thornhill, Ontario L4J 7T1 Canada. (416)889-2957. Award Director: Lucy La Grassa. Annual award. Estab. 1989. Purpose of the award: Children have an opportunity to submit mss for review. Winners are chosen based on originality of ideas and self-expression. Unpublished submissions only. Deadline for entries: January 12, 1995. SASE for award rules and entry forms. Entry fee is $2. Award consists of $500 cash and editorial training and possible publication. Judging by more than 40 independent judges. Requirements for entrants: a Canadian or landed immigrant in Canada, ages 7-14; story must be written solely by the submitter. No less than 4 pages, no more than 16 pages. Copyright to winning ms acquired by The Kids Netword upon winning.

‡PUBLISH-A-BOOK CONTEST, Raintree Steck/Vaughn Publishers. Send written entries to: PAB Contest, P.O. Box 27010, Austin TX 78755. (800)531-5015. Annual contest. Estab. 1987. Purpose of the contest: to stimulate 2nd-6th graders to write outstanding stories for other children. Unpublished submissions only. Word limits: grades 4-6, 700-900 words; grades 2-3, 300-500 words. Deadline for entries: January 31. SASE for contest rules. Stories must be written on a given theme—for 1995 contest: "The Future." "Entries must be sponsored by a teacher or librarian." Entries not returned. No entry fee. Grand prizes: 5 winning entries are professionally illustrated and published in hardcover editions by Raintree. Each winner will receive a $500 advance against an author royalty contract and 10 free copies of the published book. The sponsor named on each of these entries will receive 20 free books from the Raintree catalog. Honorable mentions: each of the 20 honorable mention writers will receive $25. The sponsor named on each of these entries will receive 10 free books from the Raintree Steck-Vaughn catalog. Judging by an editorial team. Contract issued for Grand Prize winners. Payment and royalties paid. Requirements for entrants: Contest is open only to 2nd-6th graders enrolled in a school program in the United States or other countries. Books will be displayed and sold in the United States and foreign markets. Displays at educational association meetings, book fairs. For information contact Elaine Johnston, (512)795-3230, Fax (512)795-3676.

‡QUILL AND SCROLL INTERNATIONAL WRITING/PHOTO CONTEST, *Quill and Scroll,* School of Journalism, University of Iowa, Iowa City IA 52242. (319)335-5795. Contest Director: Richard Johns. Annual contest. Previously published submissions only. Submissions made by the author or school newspaper adviser. Must be published February 6,

1994 to February 4, 1995. Deadline for entries: February 5. SASE for contest rules and entry forms. Entry fee is $2/entry. Awards engraved plaque to junior high level national winners. each sweepstakes winner receives electric typewriter. Judging by various judges. *Quill and Scroll* acquires the right to publish submitted material in the magazine if it is chosen as a winning entry. Requirements for entrants: must be students in grades 6-9.

‡THE AYN RAND INSTITUTE'S ANTHEM ESSAY CONTEST, P.O. Box 6099, Dept. DB, Inglewood CA 90312. (310)306-9232. Fax: (310)306-4925. Contest Director: Dr. Michael S. Berliner. Contest Coordinator: Donna Montrezza. Open to students. Annual. Estab. 1992. Purpose of the contest: "to encourage analytical thinking and writing excellence, and to introduce young people to the philosophic meaning of Ayn Rand's novelette *Anthem*." Deadline: March 30. SASE for contest rules and entry forms. No entry fee. Total prizes: $5,000. One first prize of $1,000; 10 second prizes of $200; 20 third prizes of $100. Judging: All papers are first read by a national testing service; semi-finalist and finalist papers are read by a panel of writers, professors and high school teachers. Rights to submitted or winning entries: Entry becomes property of the Ayn Rand Institute and will not be returned. Open to all ninth and tenth graders in high school. The Institute publishes the winning essay in its fall newsletter.

‡THE AYN RAND INSTITUTE'S FOUNTAINHEAD ESSAY CONTEST, The Ayn Rand Institute, P.O. Box 6004, Dept. DB, Inglewood CA 90312. (310)306-9232. Fax: (310)306-4925. Contest Director: Dr. Michael S. Berliner. Annual contest. Estab. 1986. Purpose of the contest: "to introduce high school juniors and seniors to the fiction and nonfiction writings, as well as the ideas, of Ayn Rand, novelist and philosopher. To encourage well-organized, analytic writing; to place issues important to young people, such as independence and integrity, before them." Unpublished submissions only. Deadline for entries: April 15. Contest rules and entry forms available to high school juniors and seniors for SASE. No entry fee. Awards one first prize $5,000 cash; 5 second prizes $1,000 each; 10 third prizes $500 each. Judging: entries are read by a national testing service; semifinalists and finalists are chosen by a panel of writers, professors and professional people; winner is selected from top entries by a university professor. Submitted or winning entries become property of the Ayn Rand Institute. Entrant must be in last 2 years of secondary school. The Institute publishes the winning essay in its newsletter.

‡READ WRITING & ART AWARDS, *Read* magazine, 245 Long Hill Rd., Middletown CT 06457. (203)638-2406. Contest Director: Kate Davis. Annual award. Estab. 1978. Purpose of the award: to reward excellence in writing and art in the categories of fiction, essay and art. Unpublished submissions only. Submissions made by the author or nominated by a person or group of people . Must include signature of teacher, parent or guardian and student. Deadline for entries: December 16. SASE for contest/award rules and entry forms. No entry fee. Awards first prize ($100), second prize ($75), third prize ($50). Prizes are given in each category, plus publication of first place winners. Judging by *Read* editorial staff. "Entrant understands that prize will include publication, but sometimes pieces are published in other issues. A story may be bought later." Work must be original. Art can be in color or b&w. Published in April issue of *Read* (all-student issue).

‡ANNA DAVIDSON ROSENBERG AWARD FOR POEMS ON THE JEWISH EXPERIENCE, Judah L. Magnes Museum, 2911 Russell St., Berkeley CA 94705. (510)849-2710. Poetry Award Coordinator: P. Friedman. Annual award. Estab. 1986-87. Purpose of the award: to encourage poetry in English on the Jewish experience (writer does not need to be Jewish). Previously unpublished submissions only. Deadline for entries: August 31. SASE for award rules and entry forms by July 31. SASE for list of winners. Awards $100-first prize, $50-second prize, $25-third prize; honorable mention certificates; $25 Youth Commendation (poets under 19, Emerging Poet Award). Judging by committee of 3 well-published poets with editing/teaching experience. There will be a reading of top award winners in December at Magnes Museum. Prospective anthology of winning entries. "We request permission to use in potential anthologies." Write for entry form and guidelines *first*; entries must follow guidelines and be accompanied by entry form. *Please do not phone.*

CARL SANDBURG LITERARY ARTS AWARDS, Friends of the Chicago Public Library, Harold Washington Library Center, 400 S. State St., Chicago IL 60605. (312)747-4907. Annual award. Categories: fiction, nonfiction, poetry, children's literature. Published submissions only; must be published between June 1 and May 31 (the following year). Deadline for entries: August 1. SASE for award rules. Entries not returned. No entry fee. Awards medal and $1,000 prize. Judging by authors, reviewers, book buyers, librarians. Requirements for entrants: native born Chicagoan or presently residing in the 6-county metropolitan area. Two copies must be submitted by August 1. All entries become the property of the Friends.

‡**THE SCHOLASTIC ART AWARDS**, The Aliance for Young Artists & Writers, 555 Broadway, New York NY 10012-3999. (212)343-6493. Director: Susan Ebersole. Annual award. Estab. 1927. Purpose of awards: encouragement and recognition of student achievement in the visual arts. "There are 15 categories: painting, drawing, computer graphics, video, film and animation, 2-D design, 3-D design, mixed media, printmaking, fiber arts and textile design, sculpture, ceramics, jewelry and metalsmithing, photography. Seniors only may submit art and photography portfolios. Awards consist of cash awards, scholarships and prizes. Unpublished submissions only. Some areas have sponsors who conduct a regional preliminary judging and exhibition." SASE for award rules and entry forms. Entry fees and deadlines vary depending on region in which a student lives. Judging by art educators, artists, photographers and art administrators. All publication rights are given to The Alliance (for 2 years). Requirements for entrants: Students must be in grades 7-12. National winners work on exhibition during the summer. Write to above address for more information.

‡**SCHOLASTIC WRITING AWARDS**, The Alliance for Young Artists & Writers, 555 Broadway, New York NY 10012. (212)343-6493. Director: Susan Ebersole. Annual award. Estab. 1923. Purpose of award: encouragement and recognition of young writers. Open to students in grades 7-12. Group I (grades 7, 8, 9). Group II (grades 10,11,12). There are 7 categories: short story, short short story, essay/nonfiction/persuasive writing, dramatic script, poetry, humor and science fiction. Seniors only may submit portfolios representing their best group of writing. Awards consist of cash awards, scholarships and prizes. Selected works will be published in *Scholastic* magazines. Unpublished submissions only. Entires must be postmarked by January except those from central Pennsylvania and Hains County, TX. Deadlines are indicated on entry forms. All publication rights are given to The Alliance for 2 years. Send SASE for guidelines and entry forms.

SCIENCE WRITING AWARD IN PHYSICS AND ASTRONOMY, The American Institute of Physics, 1 Physics Ellipse, College Park MD 20740. (301)209-3090. Contact: Public Information Division. Annual award. Estab. 1987. Purpose of the award: to stimulate and recognize writing that improves children's understanding and appreciation of physics and astronomy. Previously published submissions only; must be published between July 1 and July 31 (the following year). Deadline for entries: July 24. "Entries may be submitted by the publisher as well as the author." Entries not returned. No entry fee. Awards $3,000, certificate and an engraved chair. Judging by a committee of writers and scientists selected by the Governing Board of the AIP. Requirements for entrants: "Entries must be articles or books, written in English or English translations, dealing primarily with physics, astronomy or related subjects directed at children, from preschool ages up to age 15. Entries must have been available to and intended for young people. Your signature on submission will constitute your acceptance of the contest rules. Postmarked no later than July 24."

> *Always include a self-addressed, stamped envelope (SASE) with submissions within your own country. When sending material to other countries, include a self-addressed envelope (SAE) and International Reply Coupons (IRCs).*

‡**SEVENTEEN FICTION CONTEST**, 9th Floor, 850 Third Ave., New York NY 10022. Fiction Editor: Joe Bargmann. Annual contest. Estab. 1945. Unpublished submissions only. Deadline for entries: April 30. SASE for contest rules and entry forms; contest rules also published in November issue of *Seventeen*. Entries not returned. No entry fee. Awards cash prize and possible publication in December's *Seventeen*. Judging by "external readers, in-house panel of editors." If first prize, acquires first North American rights for piece to be published. Requirements for entrants: "Our annual fiction contest is open to anyone between the ages of 13 and 21 on April 30. Submit only original fiction that has never been published in any form other than in school publications. Stories should be between 1,500 and 3,000 words in length (6-12 pages). All manuscripts must be typed double-spaced on a single side of paper. Submit as many original stories as you like, but each story must include your full name, address, birth date and signature in the top right-hand corner of the first page. Your signature on submission will constitute your acceptance of the contest rules."

CHARLIE MAY SIMON BOOK AWARD, Arkansas Elementary School Council, Arkansas Department of Education, Room 302B, #4 Capitol Mall, Little Rock AR 72201. (501)682-4371. Award Director: James A. Hester. Annual contest. Estab. 1970. Purpose of award: to promote reading—to encourage reading of quality literature and book discussion. Previously published submissions only; must be published between January 1 and December 31 of calendar year preceding award; all books must have recommendations from 3 published sources. "Books are selected based on being published in previous calendar year from time of committee work; *Horn Book* is used as selection guide." Students in grades 4-6 vote on their favorite book on a reading list; the book with the most votes receives the Charlie May Simon Medallion and runner-up receives a trophy; reading list prepared by committee of 25 people representing cooperating organizations. No entry fee. Contest open to any book for children in grades 4-6 provided book is printed in year being considered.

*‡**SKIPPING STONES HONOR AWARDS**, *Skipping Stones*, P.O. Box 3939, Eugene OR 97403. (503)342-4956. Annual award. Purpose of contest: "to recognize youth under age 15 for their contributions to multicultural awareness, nature and ecology, social issues, peace and nonviolence." Submissions made by the author. Deadline for entries: June 25, 1995. SASE for contest rules and entry forms. Entry fee is $2. Judging by *Skipping Stones*' staff. "Ten awards are given in three categories: (1) Compositions—(essays, poems, short stories, songs, travelogues, etc.) should be typed (double-spaced) or neatly handwritten. Fiction or nonfiction should be limited to 750 words; poems to 30 lines. Non-English writings are also welcome. (2) Artwork—(drawings, cartoons, paintings or photo essays with captions) should have the artist's name, age and address on the back of each page. Send the originals with SASE. Black & white photos are especially welcome. (3) Youth Organizations—Tell us how your club or group works to: (a) preserve the nature and ecology in your area, (b) enhance the quality of life for low-income, minority or disabled, or (c) improve racial or cultural harmony in your school or community. Use the same format as for compositions."

SMOKEBRUSH ANNUAL FESTIVAL OF NEW PLAYS FOR CHILDREN, Smokebrush Center for Arts & Theater, 235 South Nevada Ave., Colorado Springs CO 80903-1906. (719)444-0884. Fax: (719)444-0566. Artistic Director: Kat Walter. Submit writing entries to Festival Coordinator: Mary Spengler. Annual contest. Estab. 1994. Unpublished, unproduced, full-length plays for children only. Submissions made by the author or the author's agent. Phone for contest rules. Entry fee is $10. Winning playwright receives an expense paid trip to view a professional production of the play. Judging done by a panel of professionals in the children's writing/theater industry.

*KAY SNOW WRITERS' CONTEST**, Williamette Writers, 9045 SW Barbur Blvd. #5A, Portland OR 97219. (503)452-1592. Contest Director: Leona Grieve. Annual contest. Purpose of contest: "to encourage beginning and established writers to continue the craft." Unpublished, original submissions only. Submissions made by the author or author's agent. Deadline for entries: July 30. SASE for contest rules and entry forms. Entry fee is $10, Williamette Writers' members; $15, nonmembers; $5, student writer. Awards cash prize of $200 per category (fiction, nonfiction, juvenile, poetry, script writing). "Judges are anonymous."

SOCIETY OF MIDLAND AUTHORS AWARDS, Society of Midland Authors, % Phyllis Ford-Choyke, 29 E. Division, Chicago IL 60610. (312)337-1482. Annual award. Estab. 1915. Purpose of award: "to stimulate creative literary effort, one of the goals of the Society. There are seven categories, including children's fiction, children's nonfiction, adult fiction and nonfiction, biography, drama and poetry." Previously published submissions only. Submissions made by the author or publisher. Must be published during calendar year previous to deadline. Deadline for entries: January 15. SASE for award rules and entry forms. No entry fee. Awards plaque given at annual dinner, cash (minimum $300). Judging by panel (reviewers, university faculty, writers, librarians) of 3 per category. "Award is for book published in the awards year or play professionally produced in that year for the first time." Author to be currently residing in the Midlands, i.e., Illinois, Indiana, Iowa, Kansas, Michigan, Minnesota, Missouri, Nebraska, North Dakota, South Dakota, Ohio or Wisconsin.

GEORGE G. STONE CENTER FOR CHILDREN'S BOOKS RECOGNITION OF MERIT AWARD, George G. Stone Center for Children's Books, The Claremont Graduate School, 131 E. 10th St., Claremont CA 91711-6188. (714)621-8000, ext. 3670. Award Director: Doty Hale. Annual award. Estab. 1965. Purpose of the award: to recognize an author or illustrator of a children's book or a body of work exhibiting the "power to please and expand the awareness of children and teachers as they have shared the book in their classrooms." Previously published submissions only. SASE for award rules and entry forms. Entries not returned. No entry fee. Awards a scroll. Judging by a committee of teachers, professors of children's literature and librarians. Requirements for entrants: "Nominations are made by students, teachers, professors and librarians. Award made at annual Claremont Reading Conference in spring (March)."

JOAN G. SUGARMAN CHILDREN'S BOOK AWARD, Washington Independent Writers Legal and Educational Fund, Inc., #220, 733 15th St. NW, Washington DC 20005. (202)347-4973. Director: Isolde Chapin. Open to residents of DC, Maryland, Virginia. Award offered every 2 years. Next awards presented in 1996 for publications done in 1994-1995. Estab. 1987. Purpose of award: to recognize excellence in children's literature, ages 1-15. Previously published submissions only. Submissions made by the author or author's agent or by publishers. Must be published in the 2 years preceeding award year. Deadline for entries: January 31. SASE for award rules and entry forms. No entry fee. Awards $500-1,000. Judging by selected experts in children's books. Requirements for entrants: publication of material; residence in DC, Maryland or Virginia. Works displayed at reception for award winners.

SYDNEY TAYLOR BOOK AWARD, Association of Jewish Libraries, %National Foundation of Jewish Culture, 330 Seventh Ave., 21st Floor, New York NY 10001. Chairman: Claudia Z. Fechter. Annual award. Estab. 1973. Purpose of the award: "to recognize books of quality in the field of Judaic books for children in two categories: picture books for young children and older children's books." Previously published submissions only. Submissions made by publisher. Must be published January-December of the year being judged. Deadline for entries: January 31. SASE for award rules and entry forms. No entry fee. Awards plaque and $1,000 total monies in each category. Judging by a committee of 6 librarians. Requirements for entrants: "Subject matter must be of Judaic content."

‡SYDNEY TAYLOR MANUSCRIPT COMPETITION, Association of Jewish Libraries, 15 Goldsmith St., Providence RI 02906. (401)274-1117. Director: Lillian Schwartz. Annual contest. Estab. 1985. Purpose of the contest: "This competition is for unpublished writers of fiction. Material should be for readers ages 8-11, with universal appeal that will serve to deepen the understanding of Judaism for all children, revealing positive aspects of Jewish life." Unpublished submissions only. Deadline for entries: January 15. SASE for contest rules and entry forms. No entry fee. Awards $1,000. Judging by qualified judges from within the Association of Jewish Libraries. Requirements for entrants: must be an unpublished fiction writer. "AJL assumes no responsibility for publication, but hopes this cash incentive will serve to encourage new writers of children's stories with Jewish themes for all children."

‡VEGETARIAN ESSAY CONTEST, The Vegetarian Resource Group, P.O. Box 1463, Baltimore MD 21203. (410)366-VEGE. Address to Vegetarian Essay Contest. Annual contest. Estab. 1985. Unpublished submissions only. Deadline for entries: May 1 of each year. SASE for contest rules and entry forms. No entry fee. Awards $50 savings bond. Judging by awards committee. Acquires right for The Vegetarian Resource Group to reprint essays. Requirements for entrants: age 18 and under. Winning works may be published in *Vegetarian Journal*, instructional materials for students. "Submit 2-3 page essay on any aspect of vegetarianism, which is the abstinence of meat, fish and fowl. Entrants can base paper on interviewing, research or personal opinion. Need not be vegetarian to enter."

‡VERY SPECIAL ARTS YOUNG PLAYWRIGHTS PROGRAM, Very Special Arts Education Office, The John F. Kennedy Center for the Performing Arts, Washington DC 20566. (202)628-2800. National Programs Coordinator: Elena Widder. Annual contest. Estab. 1984. "All scripts must address or incorporate some aspect of disability." Unpublished submissions only. Deadline for entries: April 15. Write to Young Playwrights Coordinator for contest rules and entry forms. No entries returned. No entry fee. Judging by Artists Selection Committee. "Very Special Arts retains the rights for videotaping and broadcasting on television and/or radio." Entrants must be students age 12-18. "Script will be selected for production at The John F. Kennedy Center for the Performing Arts, Washington DC. The winning play is presented each October."

‡VFW VOICE OF DEMOCRACY, Veterans of Foreign Wars of the U.S., 406 W. 34th St., Kansas City MO 64111. (816)968-1117. Annual contest. Estab. 1960. Purpose of contest: to give high school students the opportunity to voice their opinions about their responsibility to our country and to convey those opinions via the broadcast media to all of America. Deadline for entries: November 15. No entry fee. Winners receive awards ranging from $1,000-20,000. Requirements for entrants: "Tenth-twelfth grade students in public, parochial and private schools in the United States and overseas are eligible to compete. Former national and/or first place state winners are not eligible to compete again. Contact your high school counselor or your local VFW Post to enter."

*‡VIDEO VOYAGES CONTEST, Weekly Reader Corporation and Panasonic Company, 245 Long Hill Rd., Middletown CT 06457. (203)638-2442. Contest Director: Lois Lewis. Annual contest. Estab. 1991. Purpose of contest: to reward original videos made by elementary and upper grade students. Unpublished original student videos only. Submissions made by teams or classes of students. Deadline for entry: March. Deadline varies according to announcement date of contest in Weekly Reader publications. Write or call contest director for rules and entry forms. No entry fee. First Prizes: (2) Panasonic camcorder and 4-head VCR and 20-inch color TV. Second Prizes: (2) choice of Panasonic camcorder or 4-head VCR and 27-inch color TV. Third Prizes: (2) Panasonic 20-inch color TV and VCR combination. Honorable Mention Prizes: (4) ten-pack of blank Panasonic VHS cassettes and a video production handbook. "All video equipment prizes are courtesy of Panasonic Company. All prizes are awarded to the winners' schools." Judging by staff members from Weekly Reader Corp. and Panasonic Company. All entries become the property of Weekly Reader Corp. and none will be returned. Requirements for entrants: open to subscribers of *Weekly Reader Edition 5*, *Weekly Reader Senior Edition*, *Read*, *Know Your World Extra*, *Current Events*, *Current Science*, and students in grades 5-12 from nonsubscribing schools. Each entry form must be signed by the supervising teacher(s).

*VIRGINIA LIBRARY ASSOCIATION/JEFFERSON CUP, Virginia Library Association, 669 S. Washington St., Alexandria VA 22314. Award Director changes year to year. Annual award. Estab. 1983. Purpose of award: to honor a distinguished biography, historical fiction, or American history book for young people, thereby promoting reading about America's past, and encouraging writing of U.S. history, biography and historical fiction. Previously published submissions only. Must be published in the year prior to selection. SASE for contest rules and entry forms. Judging by committee. The book must be about U.S. history or an American person, 1492 to present, or fiction that highlights the U.S. past; author must reside in the U.S. The book must be published especially for young people.

‡THE STELLA WADE CHILDREN'S STORY AWARD, *Amelia,* 329 E St., Bakersfield CA 93304. (805)323-4064. Editor: Frederick A. Raborg, Jr. Annual award. Estab. 1988. Purpose of award: "With decrease in the number of religious and secular magazines for young people, the juvenile story and poetry must be preserved and enhanced." Unpublished submissions only. Deadline for entries: August 15. SASE for award rules. Entry fee is $5 per adult entry; there is no fee for entries submitted by young people under the age of 17, but such entry must be signed by parent, guardian or teacher to verify originality. Awards $125 plus publication. Judging by editorial staff. Previous winners include Maxine Kumin and Sharon E. Martin. "We use First North American serial rights only for the winning manuscript." Contest is open to all interested. If illustrator wishes to enter only an illustration without a story, the entry fee remains the same. Illustrations will also be considered for cover publication. Restrictions of mediums for illustrators: Submitted photos should be no smaller than 5 × 7; illustrations (drawn) may be in any medium. "Winning entry will be published in the most appropriate issue of either *Amelia, Cicada* or *SPSM&H* — subject matter would determine such. Submit clean, accurate copy."

WASHINGTON POST/CHILDREN'S BOOK GUILD AWARD FOR NONFICTION, % Patricia Markun, 4405 "W" St. NW, Washington DC 20007. (202)965-0403. Annual contest. Estab. 1977. Purpose of contest: "to encourage nonfiction writing for children of literary quality. Awarded for the body of work of a leading American nonfiction author." No entry fee. Awards $1,000 and an engraved crystal paperweight. Judging by a jury of Children's Book Guild librarians and authors and a *Washington Post* book critic. "One doesn't enter. One is selected."

‡WE ARE WRITERS, TOO!, Creative With Words Publications, P.O. Box 223226, Carmel CA 93922. Contest Director: Brigitta Geltrich. Semiannual contest. Estab. 1975. Unpublished submissions only. Deadline for entries: June 30 and December 31. SASE for contest rules and entry forms. SASE for return of entries "if not winning poem." No entry fee. Awards publication in an anthology. Judging by selected guest editors and educators. June 15 and December 31 contest open to children only (up to and including 19 years old). Writer should request contest rules. SASE with all correspondence. "Age of child must be stated and manuscript must be verified of its authenticity."
  • 1995 is CWW's 20th anniversary. Write for contest rules for special contest with "Dream" theme. There is an entry fee. Deadline is June 30, 1995.

WESTERN HERITAGE AWARDS, National Cowboy Hall of Fame, 1700 NE 63rd St., Oklahoma City OK 73111. (405)478-2250. Director of Public Relations: Dana Sullivant. Annual award. Estab. 1961. Purpose of award: The WHA are presented annually to encourage the accurate and artistic telling of great stories of the West through 15 categories of western literature, television and film, including fiction, nonfiction, children's books and poetry. Previously published submissions only; must be published the calendar year before the awards are presented. Deadline for entries: December 31. SASE for award rules and entry forms. Entries not returned. No entry fee. Awards a Wrangler award. Judging by a panel of judges selected each year with distinction in various fields of western art and heritage. Requirements for entrants: The material must pertain to the development or preservation of the West, either from a historical or contemporary viewpoint. Historical accuracy is vital. Works recognized during special awards ceremonies held annually third weekend in March at the museum. There is an autograph party preceding the awards. Film clips are shown during the awards presentation. Awards ceremonies are broadcast.

LAURA INGALLS WILDER AWARD, Association for Library Service to Children, Division of the American Library Association, 50 E. Huron, Chicago IL 60611. (312)280-2163. Executive Director, ALSC: Susan Roman. Award offered every 3 years. Purpose of the award: to recognize an author or illustrator whose books, published in the US, have over a period of years made a substantial and lasting contribution to children's literature. Awards a medal presented at banquet during annual conference. Judging by Wilder Committee.

‡PAUL A. WITTY OUTSTANDING LITERATURE AWARD, International Reading Association, Special Interest Group, Reading for Gifted and Creative Learning, School of Education, P.O. Box 32925, Fort Worth TX 76129. (817)921-7660. Award Director: Dr. Cathy Collins Block. Annual award. Estab. 1979. Categories of entries: poetry/prose at elementary, junior high and senior high levels. Unpublished submissions only. Deadline for entries: February 1. SASE for award rules and entry forms. SASE for return of entries. No entry fee. Awards $25 and plaque, also certificates of merit. Judging by 2 committees for screening and awarding. Works will be published in Reading Association publications. "The elementary students' entries must be legible and may not exceed 1,000 words. Secondary students' prose entries should be typed and may exceed 1,000 words if necessary. At both elementary and secondary levels, if poetry is entered, a set of five poems must be submitted. All entries and requests for applications must include a self-addressed, stamped envelope."

PAUL A. WITTY SHORT STORY AWARD, International Reading Association, P.O. Box 8139, 800 Barksdale Rd., Newark DE 19714-8139. (302)731-1600. Contact: Mary Cash. Annual award. Estab. 1986. Purpose of award: The entry must be an original short story appearing in a young children's periodical that regularly publishes short stories for children. (These would be periodicals generally aimed at readers to about age 12.) The short story should serve as a reading and literary standard by which readers can measure other writing and should encourage young readers to read by providing them with enjoyable and profitable reading. Deadline for entries: The entry must have been published for the first time in the eligibility year; the short story must be submitted during the calendar year of publication. Anyone wishing to nominate a short story should send it to the designated Paul A. Witty Short Award Subcommittee Chair by November 1. Deadline for completed entries to the subcommittee chair is December 1. Both fiction and nonfiction writing are eligible; each will be rated according to characteristics that are appropriate for the genre. Interested authors should send inquiry to Mary Cash at above address. Award is $1,000 and recognition at the annual IRA Convention.

‡ALICE LOUISE WOOD OHIOANA AWARD FOR CHILDREN'S LITERATURE, Ohioana Library Association, 65 S. Front St., Suite 1105, Columbus OH 43215. (614)466-3831. Director: Linda R. Hengst. Annual award. Estab. 1991. Purpose of award: "to recognize an Ohio author whose body of work has made, and continues to make, a significant contribution to literature for children or young adults." SASE for award rules and entry forms. Gives monetary award (amount may vary). Requirements for entrants: "must have been born in Ohio, or lived in Ohio for a minimum of five years; established a distinguished publishing record of books for children and young people; body of work has made, and continues to make, a significant contribution to the literature for young people; through whose work as a writer, teacher, administrator, or through community service, interest in children's literature has been encouraged and children have become involved with reading."

WORK-IN-PROGRESS GRANTS, Society of Children's Book Writers and Illustrators, #106, 22736 Vanowen St., West Hills CA 91307. (818)347-8188. Annual award. "The SCBWI Work-in-Progress Grants have been established to assist children's book writers in the completion of a specific project." Five categories: (1) General Work-in-Progress Grant. (2) Grant for a Contemporary Novel for Young People. (3) Nonfiction Research Grant. (4) Grant for a work whose author has never had a book published. (5) Grant for a picture book writer. Requests for applications may be made beginning October 1. Completed applications accepted February 1-May 1 of each year. SASE for applications for grants. In any year, an applicant may apply for any of the grants except the one awarded for a work whose author has never had a book published. (The recipient of this grant will be chosen from entries in all categories.) Five grants of $1,000 will be awarded annually. Runner-up grants of $500 (one in each category) will also be awarded. "The grants are available to both full and associate members of the SCBWI. They are not available for projects on which there are already contracts." Previous recipients not eligible to apply.

‡**WRITER'S EXCHANGE POETRY CONTEST**, R.S.V.P. Press, Box 394, Society Hill SC 29593. (803)378-4556. Contest Director: Gene Boone. Quarterly contest. Estab. 1985. Purpose of the contest: to promote friendly competition among poets of all ages and backgrounds, giving these poets a chance to be published and win an award. Submissions are made by the author. Continuous deadline; entries are placed in the contest closest to date received. SASE for contest rules and entry forms. Entry fee is $1 per poem. Awards 50% of contest proceeds, usually $35-100 varying slightly in each quarterly contest due to changes in response. Judging by Gene Boone or a guest judge such as a widely published poet or another small press editor. "From the entries received, we reserve the right to publish the winning poems in an issue of *Writer's Exchange*, a literary newsletter. The contest is open to any poet. Poems on any subject/theme, any style, to 24 lines, may be entered. Poems should be typed, single-spaced, with the poet's name in the upper left corner."

‡**WRITER'S OPEN FORUM CONTESTS**, *Writer's Open Forum*, P.O. Box 516, Tracyton WA 98393. Contest Director: Sandra E. Haven. Estab. 1991. Purpose of contest: to inspire excellence in the traditional short story format. "We like identifiable characters, strong storylines, and crisp, fresh endings. We particularly like helping new writers, writers changing genres and young writers." Unpublished submissions only. Submissions made by the author. Deadline for entries: December 30. SASE for contest rules and entry forms. No entry fee for subscribers; $5 for nonsubscribers. Awards $50, first place; $25, second place; $10, third place. Judging by *Writer's Open Forum* staff. "We reserve the right to publish first, second and third place winners." Please state genre of story and age of intended audience (as "middle reader, ages 9-11") in cover letter. Contest winners announced and first place published in March/April issue. Word count restrictions vary with each contest. Some contests require following a theme or other stipulation. Please request guidelines for contest you want to enter.

‡**WRITING CONFERENCE WRITING CONTESTS**, The Writing Conference, Inc., P.O. Box 664, Ottawa KS 66067. (913)242-0407. Contest Director: John H. Bushman. Annual contest. Estab. 1988. Purpose of contest: to further writing by students with awards for narration, exposition and poetry at the elementary, middle school and high school levels. Unpublished submissions only. Submissions made by the author or teacher. Deadline for entries: January 6. SASE for contest rules and entry form. No entry fee. Awards plaque and publication of winning entry in *The Writer's Slate*, March issue. Judging by a panel of teachers. Requirements for entrants: must be enrolled in school—K-12th grade.

‡**YEARBOOK EXCELLENCE CONTEST**, *Quill and Scroll*, School of Journalism, University of Iowa, Iowa City IA 52242. (319)335-5795. Executive Director: Richard Johns. Annual contest. Estab. 1987. Previously published submissions only. Submissions made by the author or school yearbook adviser. Must be published between November 1, 1994 and November 1, 1995. Deadline for entries: November 1. SASE for contest rules and entry form. Entry fee is $2 per entry. Awards National Gold Key; the high schools and the winning students receive plaque; seniors eligible for scholarships. Judging by various judges. Winning entries may be published in *Quill and Scroll* magazine. Requirements for entrants: must be in a high school that is a charter member of Quill & Scroll.

YOUNG ADULT CANADIAN BOOK AWARD, The Canadian Library Association, 602-200 Elgin St., Ottawa, Ontario K2P 1L5 Canada. (613)232-9625. Fax: (613)563-9895. Contact: Committee Chair. Annual award. Estab. 1981. Purpose of award: "to recognize the author

---

Refer to the Business of Children's Writing & Illustrating for up-to-date marketing, tax and legal information.

of an outstanding English-language Canadian book which appeals to young adults between the ages of 13 and 18 that was published the preceding calendar year. Information is available for anyone requesting. We approach publishers, also send news releases to various journals, i.e. *Quill & Quire*." Entries are not returned. No entry fee. Awards a leather-bound book. Requirement for entrants: must be a work of fiction (novel or short stories), the title must be a Canadian publication in either hardcover or paperback, and the author must be a Canadian citizen or landed immigrant. Award given at the Canadian Library Association Conference.

YOUNG READER'S CHOICE AWARD, Pacific Northwest Library Association, 133 Suzzallo Library, FM-30, University of Washington, Graduate School of Library and Information Science, Seattle WA 98195. (206)543-1897. Secretary: Carol Doll. Award Director: named annually. Annual award for published authors. Estab. 1940. Purpose of award: "to promote reading as an enjoyable activity and to provide children an opportunity to endorse a book they consider an excellent story." Previously published submissions only; must be published 3 years before award year. Deadline for entries: February 1. SASE for award rules and entry forms. No entry fee. Awards a silver medal, struck in Idaho silver. "Children vote for their favorite (books) from a list of titles nominated by librarians, teachers, students and other interested persons."

THE ANNA ZORNIO MEMORIAL CHILDREN'S THEATRE PLAYWRITING AWARD, University of New Hampshire Theatre in Education Program, Department of Theatre and Dance, Paul Creative Arts Center, 30 College Rd., University of New Hampshire, Durham NH 03824. (603)862-2291. Contact: Carol Fisher. Annual award. Estab. 1979. Purpose of the award: "to honor the late Anna Zornio, an alumna of The University of New Hampshire, for dedication to and inspiration of children's theater playwriting." Unpublished submissions only. Submissions made by the author. Deadline for entries: April 30, 1995. SASE for award rules and entry forms. No entry fee. Awards $250 plus guaranteed production. Judging by faculty committee. Acquires rights to campus production. Write for details.

Contests & Awards/'94-'95 changes

The following listings were included in the 1994 edition of *Children's Writer's & Illustrator's Market* but do not have listings in this edition. The majority did not respond to our request to update their listings. If a reason was given for exclusion, it appears in parentheses after the listing's name.

California Books Awards
City of Foster City Writers' Contest
International Reading Assoc. Children's Book Award
Coretta Scott King Award

Mississippi Valley Poetry Contest
The Scott O'Dell Award for Historical Fiction
Ohio Genealogical Society Essay/Art Contest

(ceased)
Time Education Program Student Writing and Art Competition (ceased)

Resources

Clubs & Organizations

Children's writers and illustrators can benefit from contacts made through organizations such as the ones listed in this section. Professional organizations provide writers and artists with numerous educational, business and legal services. Many of these services come in the form of newsletters, workshops or seminars that provide tips about how to be better writers or artists, as well as what types of business records to keep, health and life insurance coverage to carry and/or competitions to consider.

An added benefit to belonging to an organization is the opportunity to network with those who have similar interests, thus creating a support system to help you through tight creative and financial periods. As in any business, knowing the right people can often help your career, and important contacts can be made through your peers. Membership in a writer's or artist's group also shows publishers you're serious about your craft. Of course, this provides no guarantee your work will be published, but it offers an added dimension of credibility and professionalism.

Some of the organizations listed here welcome anyone with an interest, while others are only open to professionals. Still others, such as the Society of Children's Book Writers & Illustrators, have varying levels of membership. SCBWI offers associate membership to those with no publishing credits, while those who have had work for children published receive full membership. Many national organizations such as SCBWI also have regional chapters throughout the country. Feel free to write or call for more information regarding any group that sounds interesting. Be sure to inquire about local chapters, membership qualifications, and services offered.

AMERICAN ALLIANCE FOR THEATRE & EDUCATION, Theatre Department, Arizona State University, Box 873411, Tempe AZ 85287-3411. (602)965-6064. Administrative Director: Katherine Krzys. Purpose of organization: to promote standards of excellence in theater and drama/theater education by providing the artist and educator with a network of resources and support, a base for advocacy, and access to programs and projects that focus on the importance of drama in the human experience. Membership cost: $75 annually for individual in US and Canada, $100 annually for organization, $38 annually for students, $48 annually for retired people; add $20 outside Canada and US. Annual conference held jointly with the Educational Theatre Association in Minneapolis MN, August, 5-8, 1995. Newsletter published quarterly; must be member to subscribe. Contests held for unpublished play reading project and annual awards for best play for K-8 and one for secondary audience. Award plaque and stickers for published playbooks. Published list of unpublished plays deemed worthy of performance in newsletter and press release, and staged readings at conference.

AMERICAN SOCIETY OF JOURNALISTS AND AUTHORS, 1501 Broadway, New York NY 10036. (212)997-0947. Executive Director: Alexandra Cantor. Qualifications for membership: "Need to be a professional nonfiction writer published 8-10 times in general circulation publications." Membership cost: Initiation fee—$100; annual dues—$165. Group sponsors national conferences; monthly workshops in New York City. Workshops/conferences open to nonmembers. Publishes a newsletter for members that provides confidential information for nonfiction writers.

ARIZONA AUTHORS ASSOCIATION, #117, 3509 E. Shea Blvd., Phoenix AZ 85028-3339. (602)942-4240. President: Iva Martin. Purpose of organization: To offer professional, educational and social opportunities to writers and authors. Membership cost: $40/year professional and associate; $50/year affiliate; $25/year student. Different levels of membership include: Professional—published writers; Associate—writers working toward publication; Affiliate—professionals in publishing industry; student—full-time students. Holds monthly educational workshops; contact office for current calendar. Publishes newsletter providing information useful to writers (markets, book reviews, calendar of meetings and events) and news about members. Non-member subscription $25/year. Sponsors Annual Literary Contest. Awards include total of $1,000 in prizes in several categories. Contest open to non-members.

ASSITEJ/USA, % Jolly Sue Baker, 2707 East Union, Seattle WA 98122. Editor, *TYA Today*: Amie Brockway. Purpose of organization: To service theaters focused on productions for young audiences. Also serves as US Center for International Association of Theatre for Children and Young People. Membership cost: $100 for organizations with budgets below $250,000; $200 for organizations with budgets of $250,000-$999,000; $300 for organizatons with budgets over $1 million; $50 annually/individual; $25 students and retirees; $65 for foreign organizations or individuals outside the US; $30 for library rate. Different levels of membership include: organizations, individuals, students, retirees, corresponding, libraries. Sponsors workshops or conferences. Publishes newsletter that focuses on information on field in US and abroad.

THE AUTHORS GUILD, 29th Floor, 330 W. 42nd St., New York NY 10036-6902. (212)563-5904. Executive Director: Robin Davis Miller. Purpose of organization: To offer services and information materials intended to help authors with the business and legal aspects of their work, including contract problems, copyright matters, freedom of expression and taxation. Guild has 6,700 members. Qualifications for membership: Must be book author published by an established American publisher within 7 years or any author who has had three works, fiction or nonfiction, published by a magazine or magazines of general circulation in the last 18 months. Associate membership also available. Annual dues: $90. Different levels of membership include: associate membership with all rights except voting available to an author who has a firm contract offer from an American publisher. "The Guild and Authors League of America conduct several symposia each year at which experts provide information, offer advice, and answer questions on subjects of interest and concern to authors. Typical subjects have been the rights of privacy and publicity, libel, wills and estates, taxation, copyright, editors and editing, the art of interviewing, standards of criticism and book reviewing. Transcripts of these symposia are published and circulated to members." Symposia open to members only. "The *Author's Guild Bulletin*, a quarterly journal, contains articles on matters of interest to writers, reports of Guild activities, contract surveys, advice on problem clauses in contracts, transcripts of Guild and League symposia, and information on a variety of professional topics. Subscription included in the cost of the annual dues."

THE AUTHORS RESOURCE CENTER, 4725 E. Sunrise Dr., #219, Tucson AZ 85718. (602)325-4733. Executive Director: Martha R. Gore. Purpose of organization: To help writers understand the business and professional realities of the publishing world. Also operates literary agency (opened March 1, 1984) that markets members' books to publishers (interested only in authentic multicultural books). Qualifications for membership: serious interest in writing. Membership cost: $60 per year for aspiring and published members. The *Tarc Report* is published bimonthly and includes information about markets, resources, legal matters, writers workshops, reference sources, announcement of members' new books, reviews and other news important to members. Subscription included in membership fee.

CALIFORNIA WRITERS' CLUB, 2214 Derby St., Berkeley CA 94705. (510)841-1217. Secretary: Dorothy V. Benson. Purpose of organization: "We are a nonprofit professional organization open to writers to provide writing and market information and to promote fellowship among writers." Qualifications for membership: "Publication for active members; expected publication in five years for associate members." Membership cost: entry fee $20; annual dues $35. (Entry fee is paid once.) Workshops/conferences: "Biennial summer conference, June 23-25, 1995, at Asilomar, Pacific Grove, CA; other conferences are held by local branches as they see fit." Conferences open to nonmembers. "Newsletter, which goes out to all CWC members and to newspapers and libraries, publishes the monthly meetings upcoming in the eight branches, plus the achievements of members, and market and contest opportunities." Sponsors contests. CWC's "major contest is every two years, and prizes are cash in each of five categories."

CANADIAN AUTHORS ASSOCIATION, #500, 275 Slater St., Ottawa, Ontario K1P 5H9 Canada. (613)233-2846. Fax: (613)235-8237. Contact: National Secretary. Purpose of organization: to help "emerging" writers and provide assistance to professional writers. Membership is divided into two categories for individuals: Member (voting) — Persons engaged in writing in any genre who have produced a sufficient body of work; Associate (nonvoting) — Persons interested in writing who have not yet produced sufficient material to qualify for full membership, or those who, though not writers, have a sincere interest in Canadian literature. Persons interested in learning to write may join the Association for one year. Membership cost: $123.05 includes GST for members, associates and introductory rate. Life membership is $963, which also includes GST. Workshops/conferences: annual conference, June 15-18 in Victoria, British Columbia. "The conference draws writers, editors and publishers together in a congenial atmosphere providing seminars, workshops, panel discussions, readings by award-winning authors, and many social events." Open to nonmembers. Publishes a newsletter for members only. Also publishes a quarterly journal and a bienniel writer's guide available to nonmembers; latest edition 1992. "The Association created a major literary award program in 1975 to honor writing that achieves literary excellence without sacrificing popular appeal. The awards are in four categories — fiction, (for a full-length novel); nonfiction (excluding works of an instructional nature); poetry (for a volume of the works of one poet); and drama (for a single play published or staged). The awards consist of a handsome silver medal and $5,000 in cash; they are funded by Harlequin Enterprises, the Toronto-based international publisher." Contest open to non-members. Also contests for writing by students and for young readers; sponsors Air Canada Awards.

CANADIAN SOCIETY OF CHILDREN'S AUTHORS, ILLUSTRATORS AND PERFORMERS, (CANSCAIP), Suite 103, 542 Mt. Pleasant Rd., Toronto, Ontario M4S 2M7 Canada. (416)322-9666. Secretary: Nancy Prasad. Purpose of organization: Development of Canadian children's culture and support for authors, illustrators and performers working in this field. Qualifications for membership: Members — professionals who have been published (not self-published) or have paid public performances/records/tapes to their credit. Friends — share interest in field of children's culture. Membership cost: $60 (members dues), $25 (friends dues), $30 (institution dues). Sponsors workshops/conferences. Publishes newsletter: includes profiles of members; news round-up of members' activities countrywide; market news; news on awards, grants, etc; columns related to professional concerns.

LEWIS CARROLL SOCIETY OF NORTH AMERICA, 617 Rockford Rd., Silver Spring MD 20902. (301)593-7077. Secretary: M. Schaefer. "We are an organization of Carroll admirers of all ages and interests and a center for Carroll studies." Qualifications for membership: "An interest in Lewis Carroll and a simple love for Alice (or even the Snark)." Membership cost: $20/year. There is also a contributing membership of $50. Publishes a newsletter.

THE CHILDREN'S BOOK COUNCIL, INC., 568 Broadway, New York NY 10012. (212)966-1990. Purpose of organization: "A nonprofit trade association of children's and young adult publishers, CBC promotes the enjoyment of books for children and young adults, and works with national and international organizations to that end. The CBC has sponsored National Children's Book Week since 1945." Qualifications for membership: Trade publishers of children's and young adult books are eligible for membership. Membership cost: "individuals wishing to receive mailings from the CBC (our semi-annual newsletter, *CBC Features*, and our materials brochures) may be placed on our mailing list for a one-time-only fee of $50. Publishers wishing to join should contact the CBC for dues information." Sponsors workshops and seminars. Publishes a newsletter with articles about children's books and publishing, and listings of free or inexpensive materials available from member publishers.

CHILDREN'S READING ROUND TABLE OF CHICAGO, 5551 S. University Ave., Unit #1, Chicago IL 60637. (312)523-2959. Information Chairperson: Marilyn Singer. Purpose of organization: "To support activities which foster and enlarge children's and young adults' interest in reading and to promote good fellowship among persons actively interested in the field of children's books." Qualifications for membership: "Membership is open to anyone interested in children's books. There are no professional qualifications; however, the majority of our members are authors, freelance writers, illustrators, librarians, educators, editors, publishers and booksellers." Membership cost: $15/year (July 1 through June 30), applicable to members within our Chicago meeting area; Associate Membership $10, limited to persons outside the Metropolitan Chicago Area or who are retired. "All members have same privileges, which include attendance at meetings; newsletter, *CRRT Bulletin*; yearbook published biennially; and access to information about CRRT special activities." Workshops/conferences: Children's Reading Round Table Summer Seminar for Writers & Illustrators, given in odd-numbered years. The 2-day seminar, at a Chicago college campus, usually in August, features guest speakers and a variety of profession-level workshops, ms critiquing and portfolio appraisal. Enrollment is open to members and nonmembers; one fee applicable to all. Meals included, housing extra. Also, Children's Reading Round Table Children's Literature Conference, given in even-numbered years. One-day program, at a Chicago college campus, usually in fall. Program includes guest authors and educators, variety of workshops, exhibits, bookstore, lunch. Enrollment open to members and nonmembers; one fee applicable to all. *CRRT Bulletin, Children's Reading Round Table of Chicago* is published seven times a year, in advance of dinner meetings, and contains articles; book reviews; special sections of news about authors and artists, librarians and educators, publishers and booksellers. An Opportunity Column provides information about professional meetings, workshops, conferences, generally in the Midwest area. The *Bulletin* is available to members on payment of dues. Sample copies may be requested. Awards: "We do give an honorary award, the Children's Reading Round Table Annual Award, *not* for a single book or accomplishment but for long-term commitment to children's literature. Award includes check, lifetime membership, plaque. Nominations can be made *only* by CRRT members; nominees are not limited to membership."

CHRISTIAN WRITERS GUILD, 260 Fern Lane, Hume Lake CA 93628. (209)335-2333. Director: Norman B. Rohrer. Purpose of organization: To offer a 48-unit home study, 3-year correspondence course. Qualifications for membership: The ability to think clearly and a commitment to editorial communication. Membership cost: $495 total: $35 down, $15/month. Different levels of membership. Sponsors workshops and conferences. "Conference held at Hume Lake each year for certain in July, then elsewhere as we have invitations." Publishes a small sheet called the "Quill o' the Wisp."

FLORIDA FREELANCE WRITERS ASSOCIATION, Cassell Network of Writers, Maple Ridge Rd., North Sandwich NH 03259. (603)284-6367. Executive Director: Dana K. Cassell. Purpose of organization: To act as a link between Florida writers and buyers of the written word; to help writers run more effective communications businesses. Qualifications for membership: "None—we provide a variety of services and information, some for beginners and some for established pros." Membership cost: $90/year. Publishes a newsletter focusing on market news, business news, how-to tips for the serious writer. Non-member subscription: $39 — does not include Florida section — includes national edition only. Publishes annual *Directory of Florida Markets* and annual *Guide to Florida Writers*. Sponsors contest: annual deadline March 15. Guidelines available fall of year. Categories: juvenile, adult nonfiction, adult fiction, poetry. Awards include cash for top prizes, certificate for others. Contest open to non-members.

GRAPHIC ARTISTS GUILD, 11 W. 20th St., New York NY 10011-3704. (212)463-7730. Fax: (212)463-8779. Executive Director: Paul Basista. Purpose of organization: "To unite within its membership all professionals working in the graphic arts industry; to improve the economic and social conditions of professional artists and designers; to improve industry standards." Qualification for full membership: 51% of income derived from artwork. Associate members include those in allied fields, students and retirees. Initiation fee: $25. Full memberships $110, $150, $195, $245; student membership $55/year. Associate membership $105/year. Publishes *Graphic Artists Guild Handbook, Pricing and Ethical Guidelines.* "The Guild advocates the advancement and protection of artists' rights and interests. It offers professional education geared toward business issues. Other services include legislative advocacy on health and copyright issues, legal and accounting referrals, insurance plans, and artist to artist hotline. The Guild also represents traditionally employed artists and designers for the purpose of collectively bargaining wages, hours and other conditions of work."

THE INTERNATIONAL WOMEN'S WRITING GUILD, P.O. Box 810, Gracie Station, New York NY 10028. (212)737-7536. Executive Director and Founder: Hannelore Hahn. IWWG is "a network for the personal and professional empowerment of women through writing." Qualifications: open to any woman connected to the written word regardless of professional portfolio. Membership cost: $35 annually; $45 annually for foreign members. "IWWG sponsors 13 annual conferences a year in all areas of the US. The major conference is held in August of each year at Skidmore College in Saratoga Springs NY. It is a week-long conference attracting more than 300 women internationally." Also publishes a 28-page magazine, *Network*, 6 times/year; offers health insurance at group rates.

JEWISH PUBLICATION SOCIETY, 1930 Chestnut St., Philadelphia PA 19103-4599. (215)564-5925. Editor-in-Chief: Dr. Ellen Frankel. Children's Editor: Bruce Black. Purpose of organization: "To publish quality Jewish books and to promote Jewish culture and education. We are a non-denominational, nonprofit religious publisher. Our children's list specializes in fiction and nonfiction with substantial Jewish content for pre-school through young adult readers." Qualifications for membership: "One must purchase a membership of at least $25, which entitles the member to purchase a certain unit number of our books. Our membership is nondiscriminatory on the basis of religion, ethnic affiliation, race or any other criteria." Levels of membership include: JPS member, $25; Associate, $50; Friend, $100; Fellow, $125; Senior member, $200; Sustaining member, $500. "*The JPS Bookmark* reports on JPS Publications; activities of members, authors and trustees; JPS projects and goals; JPS history; children's books and activities." All members receive *The Bookmark* with their membership.

LEAGUE OF CANADIAN POETS, 54 Wolseley St., 3rd Floor, Toronto, Ontario M5T 1A5 Canada. (416)504-1657. Fax: (416)947-0201. Executive Director: Edita Petrauskaite. President: John Weier. Inquiries to Administrative Assistant: Sandra Przewiecki. The L.C.P. is a national organization of published Canadian poets. Our constitutional objectives are to advance poetry in Canada and to promote the professional interests of the members. Qualifications for membership: full — publication of at least one book of poetry by a professional publisher; associate membership — an active interest in poetry, demonstrated by several magazine/periodical publication credits. Membership fees: full — $175/year, associate — $60. Holds an Annual General Meeting every spring; some events open to nonmembers. "We also organize reading programs in schools and public venues. We publish a newsletter which includes information on poetry/poetics in Canada and beyond. Also publish the books *Poetry Markets for Canadians*; *Who's Who in the League of Canadian Poets*;

When is a Poem (teaching guide) and its accompanying anthology of Canadian poetry *Vintage*; plus a series of cassettes. We sponsor a National Poetry Contest, open to Canadians living here and abroad." Rules: Unpublished poems of any style/subject, under 75-lines, typed, with name/address on separate sheet. $6 entry fee (includes GST) per poem. $1,000-1st prize, $750-2nd, $500-3rd; plus best 50 published in an anthology. Inquire with SASE. Contest open to Canadian nonmembers. Organizes two annual awards: The Gerald Lampert Memorial Award for the best first book of poetry published in Canada in the preceding year and The Pat Lowther Memorial Award for the best book of poetry by a Canadian woman published in the preceding year. Deadline for both the poetry contest and award is January 31 each year. Send SASE for more details.

*THE NATIONAL LEAGUE OF AMERICAN PEN WOMEN, 1300 17th St. NW, Washington D.C. 20036-1973. (202)785-1997. National President: Dr. Frances "Fran" T. Carter. Purpose of organization: To promote professional work in art, letters and music since 1897. Qualifications for membership: An applicant must show "proof of sale" in each chosen category – art, letters and music. Membership cost: $30 ($5 processing fee and $25 National dues); Annual fees – $25. Different levels of membership include: Active, Associate, International Affiliate, Members-at-Large, Honorary Members (in one or more of the following classifications: Art, Letters, and Music). Holds workshops/conferences. Publishes newsletter. Its focus emphasizes communication concerning Pen Women. Its name is *The Pen Woman*. Non-members do subscribe. $18 per year. Sponsors contests in areas of Art, Letters and Music. Awards made at Biennial Convention. Also, contests in Art, Letters and Music involving Mature Women. Awards include cash prizes – up to $1,000. Contest open to non-members.

NATIONAL WRITERS ASSOCIATION, Suite 424, 1450 S. Havana, Aurora CO 80012. (303)751-7844. Executive Director: Sandy Whelchel. Purpose of organization: Association for freelance writers. Qualifications for membership: associate membership – must be serious about writing; professional membership – must be published and paid writer (cite credentials). Membership cost: $50-associate; $60-professional; Workshops/conferences: TV/Screenwriting Workshops, NWA Annual Conferences, Literary Clearinghouse, Editing and Critiquing Services, Local Chapters. National Writer's School. Open to non-members. Publishes industry news of interest to freelance writers; how-to articles; market information; member news and networking opportunities. Nonmember subscription $18. Sponsors poetry contest; short story, article contest; novel contest. Awards cash for top three winners; books and/or certificates for other winners; honorable mention certificate places 11-20. Contests open to nonmembers.

NATIONAL WRITERS UNION, Suite 203, 873 Broadway, New York NY 10003. (212)254-0279. Office Manager: Anne Mitchell. Purpose of organization: Advocacy for freelance writers. Qualifications for membership: "Membership in the NWU is open to all qualified writers, and no one shall be barred or in any manner prejudiced within the Union on account of race, age, sex, sexual preference, disability, national origin, religion or ideology. You are eligible for membership if you have published a book, a play, three articles, five poems, one short story or an equivalent amount of newsletter, publicity, technical, commercial, government or institutional copy. You are also eligible for membership if you have written an equal amount of unpublished material and you are actively writing and attempting to publish your work." Membership cost: annual writing income under $5,000 – $75/year; annual writing income $5,000-25,000 – $125/year; annual writing income over $25,000 – $170/year. National union newsletter quarterly, issues related to freelance writing and to union organization. Non-member subscription: $15.

 The asterisk before a listing indicates the listing is new in this edition.

THE NEBRASKA WRITERS GUILD, P.O. Box 30341, Lincoln NE 68503-0341. (402)475-1123. President: Linda Dageforde. Purpose of organization: To provide support and information to professional and aspiring writers. "To be an active member, you must meet at least one of these criteria: Have published and placed on sale through regular channels one or more books; have received payment for 5,000 words of prose published in magazines or newspapers of 2,500 circulation or more; have written for television, radio or other media seen or heard by an authenticated audience of 2,500 or more; present evidence of a continuous body of poetry to be judged on the basis of number and quality of publications, regardless of payment or circulation. If you don't qualify as an active member but are interested in the publishing industry, you may join the NWG as an Associate Member." Membership cost: Active and Associate member, $15/year; youth member (has same benefits as Associate member but for people under 18), $7/year. Different levels of membership include: Active member—professional writers; Associate member—aspiring writers, editors, publishers, librarians, etc.; Youth member—18 or younger. Holds two conferences/year—between April and October. Provides market and how-to information and news about the Guild and its members.

PEN AMERICAN CENTER, 568 Broadway, New York NY 10012. (212)334-1660. Fax: (212)334-2181. Purpose of organization: "To foster understanding among men and women of letters in all countries. International PEN is the only worldwide organization of writers and the chief voice of the literary community. Members of PEN work for freedom of expression wherever it has been endangered." Qualifications for membership: "The standard qualification for a writer to join PEN is that he or she must have published, in the United States, two or more books of a literary character, or one book generally acclaimed to be of exceptional distinction. Editors who have demonstrated commitment to excellence in their profession (generally construed as five years' service in book editing), translators who have published at least two book-length literary translations, and playwrights whose works have been professionally produced, are eligible for membership. An application form is available upon request from PEN Headquarters in New York. Candidates for membership should be nominated by two current members of PEN. Inquiries about membership should be directed to the PEN Membership Committee. Friends of PEN is also open to writers who may not yet meet the general PEN membership requirements. PEN sponsors more than fifty public events at PEN Headquarters in New York, and at the branch offices in Boston, Chicago, New Orleans, San Francisco and Portland, Oregon. They include tributes by contemporary writers to classic American writers, dialogues with visiting foreign writers, symposia that bring public attention to problems of censorship and that address current issues of writing in the United States, and readings that introduce beginning writers to the public. PEN's wide variety of literary programming reflects current literary interests and provides informal occasions for writers to meet each other and to welcome those with an interest in literature. Events are all open to the public and are usually free of charge. The Children's Book Authors' Committee sponsors regular public events focusing on the art of writing for children and young adults and on the diversity of literature for juvenile readers. The PEN/Norma Klein Award was established in 1991 to honor an emerging children's book author. National union newsletter covers PEN activities, features interviews with international literary figures, transcripts of PEN literary symposia, reports on issues vital to the literary community. All PEN publications are available by mail order directly from PEN American Center. Individuals must enclose check or money order with their order. Subscription: $8 for 4 issues; sample issue $2. Pamphlets and brochures all free upon request. Sponsors several competitions per year. Monetary awards range from $700-12,750.

THE PLAYWRIGHTS' CENTER, 2301 Franklin Ave. E., Minneapolis MN 55406. (612)332-7481. Outreach Director: Jerald L. Seifert. Purpose of organization: to serve as a service organization for playwrights, offering development, classes, grants. Qualifications for membership: General members pay annual $35 fee; Associate and Core members apply for membership through a peer selection panel. Levels of membership include: General—space in calendar, discounts on classes, automatic notification of fellowships and grant opportunities; Associate—a one-year term with access to developmental lab (and all the above); Core—a 7-year term (see above). Sponsors workshops/conferences. Publishes newsletter: Playwrights' Center activities and programs; members' achievements. Sponsors awards: PlayLabs developmental workshops; McKnight, Jerome fellowships; Jones commissions; McKnight Advancement grants; Many Voices programs, exchanges and other opportunities by application. Awards include developmental services, cash awards. Awards open to non-members. Contact: Lisa Stevens, Public Relations/Membership Director.

PUPPETEERS OF AMERICA, INC., #5 Cricklewood Path, Pasadena CA 91107. (818)797-5748. Membership Officer: Gayle Schluter. Purpose of organization: To promote the art of puppetry. Qualifications for membership: Interest in the art form. Membership cost: single adult, $35; junior member, $20; retiree, $35 ($25 after member for 5 years); group or family, $55; couple, $45. Membership includes a bimonthly newsletter. Sponsors workshops/conferences. Publishes newsletter. *The Puppetry Journal* provides news about puppeteers, puppet theatres, exhibitions, touring companies, technical tips, new products, new books, films, television, and events sponsored by the Chartered Guilds in each of the eight P of A regions. Subscription: $30.

SCIENCE-FICTION AND FANTASY WRITERS OF AMERICA, INC., #1B, 5 Winding Brook Dr., Guilderland NY 12084. (518)869-5361. Executive Secretary: Peter Dennis Pautz. Purpose of organization: To encourage public interest in science fiction literature and provide organization format for writers/editors/artists within the genre. Qualifications for membership: at least one professional sale or other professional involvement within the field. Membership cost: annual active dues—$50; affiliate—$35; one-time installation fee of $10; dues year begins July 1. Different levels of membership include: active—requires three professional short stories or one novel published; affiliate—requires one professional sale or professional involvement. Workshops/conferences: annual awards banquet, usually in April or May. Open to nonmembers. Publishes newsletter. Nonmember subscription: $15 in US. Sponsors SFWA Nebula® Awards for best published science fiction in the categories of novel, novella, novelette and short story. Awards trophy.

SOCIETY OF CHILDREN'S BOOK WRITERS AND ILLUSTRATORS, Suite 106, 22736 Vanowen St., West Hills CA 91307. (818)888-8760. Chairperson, Board of Directors: Sue Alexander. Purpose of organization: To assist writers and illustrators working or interested in the field. Qualifications for membership: An interest in children's literature and illustration. Membership cost: $40/year. Different levels of membership include: full membership—published authors/illustrators; associate membership—unpublished writers/illustrators. Holds 30-40 events (workshops/conferences) around the country each year. Open to nonmembers. Publishes a newsletter focusing on writing and illustrating children's books. Sponsors grants for writers and illustrators who are members.

SOCIETY OF ILLUSTRATORS, 128 E. 63rd St., New York NY 10021. (212)838-2560. Director: Terrence Brown. Purpose of organization: To promote interest in the art of illustration for working professional illustrators and those in associated fields. Membership cost: Initiation fee—$250. Annual dues for Non-Resident members (those living more than 125 air miles from SI's headquarters) are $234. Dues for Resident Artist Members are $396 per year, Resident Associate Members $462. Different levels of membership: *Artist Members* "shall include those who make illustration their profession" and through which they earn at least 60% of their income. *Associate Members* are "those who earn their living in the arts or who have made a substantial contribution to the art of illustration." This includes art directors, art buyers, creative supervisors, instructors, publishers and like categories. "All candidates for membership are admitted by the proposal of one active member and sponsorship of four additional members. The candidate must complete and sign the application form which requires a brief biography, a listing of schools attended, other training and a résumé of his or her professional career." Candidates for *Artist* membership, in addition to the above requirements, must submit examples of their work. Sponsors "The Annual of American Illustration." Awards include gold and silver medals. Open to nonmembers. Deadline: October 1. Sponsors "The Original Art: The Best of Children's Book Illustration." Deadline: mid-July. Call for details.

SOCIETY OF MIDLAND AUTHORS, % Ford-Choyke, 29 E. Division St., Chicago IL 60610. (312)337-1482. President: Phyllis Ford-Choyke. Purpose of organization: Create closer association among writers of the Middle West; stimulate creative literary effort; maintain collection of members works; encourage interest in reading and literature by cooperating with other educational and cultural agencies. Qualifications for membership: To be author or co-author of a book demonstrating literary style and published by a recognized publisher or author of published or professionally produced play and be identified through residence with Illinois, Indiana, Iowa, Kansas, Michigan, Minnesota, Missouri, Nebraska, North Dakota, Ohio, South Dakota or Wisconsin. Membership cost: $25/year dues. Different levels of membership include: regular — published book authors; associate, nonvoting — not published as above but having some connection with literature, such as librarians, teachers, publishers, and editors. Workshops/conferences: program meetings at 410 Club, Chicago, held 5 times a year, featuring authors, publishers, editors or the like individually or on panels. Usually second Tuesday of October, November, February, March and April. Also holds annual awards dinner at 410 Club, Chicago, in May. Publishes a newsletter focusing on news of members and general items of interest to writers. Non-member subscription: $5. Sponsors contests. "Annual awards in 7 categories, given at annual dinner in May. Monetary awards for books published or plays which premiered professionally in previous calendar year. Send SASE to contact person for details." Contest open to non-members. Deadline for contest: January 1.

SOCIETY OF SOUTHWESTERN AUTHORS, P.O. Box 30355, Tucson AZ 85751-0355. President: Robert J. Fitzpatrick. Purpose of organization: To promote fellowship among members of the writing profession, to recognize members' achievements, to stimulate further achievement, and to assist persons seeking to become professional writers. Qualifications for membership: proof of publication of a book, articles, TV screenplay, etc. Membership cost: $40 initiation plus $15/year dues. The Society of Southwestern Authors has annual Writers' Conference, traditionally held the last Saturday of January (write for more information). Publishes a newsletter, *The Write Word*, about members' activities and news of interest to members. Each spring a short story contest is sponsored. Applications are available in September. Send SASE to the P.O. Box, Attn: Contest.

*WESTERN WRITERS OF AMERICA, INC., 1012 Fair St., Franklin TN 37064. (615)791-1444. Secretary/Treasurer: James A. Crutchfield. Membership cost: $60/year. Different levels of membership include: Active and Associate — the two vary upon number of books published. Holds annual convention. Publishes bimonthly newsletter focusing on market trends, book reviews, etc. Non-members may subscribe for $30 ($40 foreign). Sponsors contests. Spur awards given annually for a variety of types of writing. Awards include plaque, certificate, publicity. Contest open to non-members.

THE WRITERS ALLIANCE, 12 Skylark Lane, Stony Brook NY 11790. (516)571-7080. Executive Director: Kiel Stuart. Purpose of organization: "A support/information group for all types of writers." Membership cost: $10/year, payable to Kiel Stuart. A corporate/group membership costs $15. Publishes newsletter for all writers who use (or want to learn about) computers. Non-member subscription $10 — payable to Kiel Stuart.

WRITERS CONNECTION, P.O. Box 24770, San Jose CA 95154-4770. (408)445-3600. Fax: (408)445-3609. Editor: Jan Stiles. Vice President/Program Director: Meera Lester. Purpose of organization: To provide services and resources for writers. Qualifications for membership: Interest in writing or publishing. Membership cost: $45/year. Conferences: Selling to Hollywood and various genre conferences, including writing for children. Publishes a newsletter focusing on writing and publishing (all fields except poetry), how-to, markets, contests, tips, etc., included with membership.

*WRITERS' FEDERATION OF NEW BRUNSWICK, Box 37, Station A, 103 Church St., Fredericton, New Brunswick E3B 4Y2 Canada. (506)459-7228. Project Coordinator: Anna Mae Snider. Purpose of organization: "to promote the work of New Brunswick writers and to help them at all stages of their development." Qualifications for membership: interest in writing. Membership cost: $25, basic annual membership; $15, student/unemployed; $30, institutional membership; $100, sustaining member; $250, patron; and $1,000, lifetime member. Holds workshops/conferences. Publishes a newsletter with articles concerning the craft of writing, member news, contests, markets, workshops and conference listings. Sponsors annual literary competition (for New Brunswick residents). Categories: Fiction — 3 prizes of $400, $100, $30; nonfiction, poetry, children's literature — 3 prizes per category of $200, $100, $30; Alfred Bailey Prize of $400 for poetry ms. Contest open to members only.

*WRITERS GUILD OF ALBERTA, 10523-100 Ave., Edmonton, Alberta T5J 0A8 Canada. (403)426-5892. Executive Director: Mr. Miki Andrejevic. Purpose of organization: to provide meeting ground and collective voice for the writers in Alberta. Membership cost: $55/year; $20 for seniors/students. Holds workshops/conferences. Publishes a newsletter focusing on markets, competitions, contemporary issues related to the literary arts (writing, publishing, censorship, royalties etc.). Nonmembers may subscribe to newsletter. Subscription cost: $55/year. Sponsors annual literary awards program in 7 categories (novel, nonfiction, short fiction, children's literature, poetry, drama, best first book). Awards include $500, leather-bound book, promotion and publicity. Open to nonmembers.

Clubs & Organizations/'94-'95 changes

The following listing was included in the 1994 edition of *Children's Writer's & Illustrator's Market* but does not have a listing in this edition for the reason indicated within parentheses.

National Story League (unable
    to contact)

Conferences & Workshops

Writers and illustrators eager to expand their knowledge of the children's industry should consider attending one of the many conferences and workshops held each year. Whether you're a novice or seasoned professional, conferences and workshops are great places to pick up information on a variety of topics and network with experts in the publishing industry, as well as your peers.

Many conferences and workshops included here focus on juvenile writing or illustrating and related business issues. Others appeal to a broader base of writers or artists, but still provide information that can be utilized in creating material for children. Illustrators may be interested in painting and drawing workshops, for example, while writers can learn about techniques and meet editors and agents at general writing conferences.

Artists can find a detailed directory of annual art workshops offered around the globe in the March issue of *The Artist's Magazine*. Writers should consult the May issue of *Writer's Digest* or *The Guide to Writers Conferences* (ShawGuides) for more general conferences.

Listings in this section provide details about what conference and workshop courses are offered, where and when they are held, and the costs. Some of the national writing and art organizations also offer regional workshops throughout the year. Write or call them for information.

ANTIOCH WRITERS' WORKSHOP, P.O. Box 494, Yellow Springs OH 45387. (513)866-9060. Director: Judy DaPolito. Writers' workshop geared toward all levels. Emphasizes "basic poetry, fiction, nonfiction—with some emphasis on genre and on screenwriting; little on children's, but we have recently included formal workshops with George Ella Lyon." Workshops held last week of July. Cost of workshop: $450; includes tuition. Room and board extra.

ARIZONA CHRISTIAN WRITERS CONFERENCE, P.O. Box 5168, Phoenix AZ 85010. (602)838-4919. Director: Reg Forder. Writer and illustrator workshops geared toward beginner, intermediate and advanced levels. Classes offered include: fiction, nonfiction, poetry, photography, music, etc. Workshops held November 9-11, 1995. Length of each session: 75 minutes. Maximum class size: 30 (approximate). Cost of conference: $99, 1-day session; $169, 2-day session; $229, 3-day session (discount given if paid before October 15).

THE ART & BUSINESS OF HUMOROUS ILLUSTRATION, Cartoon Art Museum, 665 Third St., San Francisco CA 94107. (415)546-3922. Director: Paola Muggia. Writer and illustrator workshops geared toward professional levels. "Class focus is on cartooning, but we do cover some marketing topics about children's books." Workshops held fall and spring. Length of each session: 10 weeks. Registration limited to 30. Cost of workshop: $145; includes art and writing instruction. Write for more information.

*AUSTIN WRITERS' LEAGUE SPRING AND FALL WORKSHOP SERIES, Suite #E-2, 1501 W. Fifth St., Austin TX 78703. (512)499-8914. Executive Director: Angela Smith. Writer and illustrator workshops geared toward all levels. Sessions include writing children's books and marketing children's books. Annual workshop. Workshop held March, April and May; September, October and November. Weekend seminars are held during the summer. Length of each session: 3-6 hours for workshops; 1½-2 days for seminars. Registration limited to 200. Writing/art facilities available: none at workshop location, but "we do have facilities at the Austin Writers' League Resource Center/Library." Cost of workshop: $35-165; includes tuition, continental breakfasts, break refreshments, consultations. Write for more information. The Austin Writers' League has available audiotapes of past workshop programs.

AUTUMN AUTHORS' AFFAIR, 1507 Burnham Ave., Calumet City IL 60409. (708)862-9797. President: Nancy McCann. Writer workshop geared toward beginner, intermediate, advanced levels. Emphasizes writing for children and young adults. Annual workshop. Workshops held generally the fourth weekend in October. Cost of workshop: $75 for 1 day, $120 for weekend. Write for more information.

BE THE WRITER YOU WANT TO BE – MANUSCRIPT CLINIC, Villa 30, 23350 Sereno Court, Cupertino CA 95014. (415)691-0300. Contact: Louise Purwin Zobel. Writer workshops geared toward beginner, intermediate, advanced levels. "Participants may turn in manuscripts at any stage of development to receive help with structure and style, as well as marketing advice. Manuscripts receive some written criticism and an oral critique from the instructor, as well as class discussion." Annual workshop. Usually held in the spring. Length of each session: 1-2 days. Registration limited to 20-25. Cost of workshop: $40-65/day, depending on the campus; includes an extensive handout.

BLUE RIDGE WRITERS CONFERENCE, Roanoke College, 221 College Lane, Salem VA 24153-3794. (703)375-2207. Writer workshops geared toward beginner, intermediate levels. Illustrator workshops geared toward beginner level. Annual workshops held in late September or early October. Length of each session: 1 day. Registration limited to 200. Cost of conference: $50; includes workshops, lunch, reception and keynote address. No requirements prior to registration unless submitting work for critique. Write for more information (include SASE). "We are a small conference dedicated to inspiring writers and assisting publication. Children's literature is *not* covered every year."

THE BROCKPORT WRITERS FORUM SUMMER WORKSHOPS, Lathrop Hall, State University of New York College at Brockport, Brockport NY 14420. (716)395-5713. Director: Dr. Stan Rubin. Writer workshops geared toward intermediate level. Classes offered include Children's Writing and Writing for Young Adults. Next workshop will be in summer of 1995. Length of each session: 6 days. Registration limited to 10-15/genre (60-80 total in all genres offered). Cost of workshop: approximately $400; includes all seminars, readings, guest writers, editors, etc.; access to videotape library; breakfast, some lunches and dinners. Individual conference. Submission of ms in progress or representative finished work required. Write for more information. "Our workshop has run for 12 years drawing participants from New York State and around the U.S. We are a small, pleasant village on the banks of the Erie Canal, 10 miles from Lake Ontario. Our airport is Rochester International." The children's/YA workshop is *not* offered annually. Check with director for schedule.

CAPE WRITING WORKSHOPS, (formerly Cape Literary Workshops), Cape Cod Writers Center, Route 132, West Barnstable MA 02668. (508)775-4811. Executive Director: Marion Vuilleumier. Writer and illustrator workshops geared toward intermediate, advanced levels. Summer workshops offered in children's book writing and children's book illustration. Workshops held second week in August in Barnstable. (Conference held third week in August at Craigville.) Intensive workshops meet Monday-Friday from 9-1. Afternoons and evenings are used to do assignments and enjoy Cape Cod attractions. Class sizes limited. Cost of workshop: $410; includes registration and tuition. Materials, room and board extra. "It is not necessary to have works-in-progress but those who do will find these workshops especially helpful. Participants are encouraged to send current work in advance." Send for brochure for more information on workshops and accommodations.

*CEDAR HILLS CHRISTIAN WRITERS WEEKEND, 34200 Ridge Rd., #110, Willoughby OH 44094. (216)943-3047. Coordinator: Lea Leever Oldham. Writer workshop geared toward beginner, intermediate and advanced levels. Topics include Christian writing for Christian market and moral teaching for mainstream publishers. Annual workshop. Workshop held in June in Painesville OH. Length of each session: weekend. Registration limited to 70. Cost of workshop: to be announced; will include workshops, room and board. Write for more information.

CHILDREN'S LITERATURE CONFERENCE, 110 Hofstra University, U.C.C.E., 205 Davison Hall, Hempstead NY 11550. (516)463-5016. Writers/Illustrators Contact: Lewis Shena, Director, Liberal Arts Studies. Writer and illustrator workshops geared toward all levels. Emphasizes: fiction, nonfiction, poetry, submission procedures, picture books. Workshops held April 22, 1995, 9:30 a.m.-4:30 p.m. Length of each session: 1 hour. Registration limited to 35/class. Cost of workshop: approximately $50; includes 2 workshops, reception, lunch, panel discussion with guest speakers, e.g. "What An Editor Looks For." Write for more information. Co-sponsored by Society of Children's Book Writers & Illustrators.

*CHRISTIAN WRITERS' INSTITUTE ANNUAL WRITERS' CONFERENCE, CWI, 177 E. Crystal Lake Ave., Lake Mary FL 32746. (407)324-5465. Conference Director: Dottie McBroom. Writer and illustrator workshops geared toward all levels. Annual workshop. Workshop held June 1-4 1995. Length of each session: 1 hour. Cost of workshop: $330 (approximately); includes room, food, tuition. Conference held in Wheaton IL.

*CHRISTIAN WRITERS' INSTITUTE FLORIDA CONFERENCE, CWI, 177 E. Crystal Lake Ave., Lake Mary FL 32746. (407)324-5465. Conference Director: Dottie McBroom. Writer and illustrator workshops geared toward all levels. Annual workshop. Workshop held February 23-26, 1995. Length of each session: 1 hour. Cost of workshop: $199 minimum; includes breakfast, tuition, lunch, Saturday banquet. Write for more information. Conference held in Orlando FL.

*CHRISTIAN WRITERS' INSTITUTE TEXAS CONFERENCE, CWI, 177 E. Crystal Lake Ave., Lake Mary FL 32746. (407)324-5465. Conference Director: Dottie McBroom. Writer and illustrator workshops geared toward all levels. Workshop held October 20-23. Length of each session: 1 hour. Cost of workshop: $199; includes tuition, lunch, breakfast, Saturday evening banquet. Write for more information. Conference held in Carrolton TX (North Dallas).

*CRAFT OF WRITING, University of Texas at Dallas, Center for Continuing Education, P.O. Box 830688, CN1.1, Richardson TX 75083-0688. (214)690-2204. Director: Janet Harris. Writer workshops geared toward intermediate. Sessions include "Don't be Shy! How Authors Can Effectively Promote Themselves and Their Books" and "Self-editing and Rewriting." Annual workshop. Workshop held every September. Length of each session: 2 days. Cost of workshop: $195; includes 2 lunches and banquet. Write for more information. "In addition to a manuscript contest, the conference also offers critiquing sessions as well as a chance to meet and mingle with professional writers, agents and editors."

CREATIVE COLLABORATIVE, P.O. Box 2201, La Jolla CA 92038-2201. (619)459-8897. Director: Penny Wilkes. Writer workshops geared toward intermediate, advanced levels. "Writing topics are geared to stimulating the creative spark and following it through to story development. Sharing of ideas and collaborating to enhance everyone's efforts become the keys to this workshop." Workshops held periodically from October-May. Length of each session: half- to full-day sessions. Registration limited to 20 students. Cost of workshop: $75; includes morning creativity session, afternoon writing and reading. Submission of story (1,500 words) or excerpts not to exceed 5 pages required prior to registration. Write for more information.

PETER DAVIDSON'S WRITER'S SEMINAR; HOW TO WRITE A CHILDREN'S PICTURE BOOK SEMINAR, 12 Orchard Lane, Estherville IA 51334. Seminar Presenter: Peter Davidson. *Peter Davidson's Writer's Seminar* emphasizes writing fiction, nonfiction, magazine articles, poetry, scripts, children's work, personal experiences, etc. *How to Write A Children's Picture Book* is for those interested in both writing and illustrating children's material.

Seminars are presented year round at community colleges. In 1995, Peter Davidson will present seminars in Minnesota, Iowa, Illinois, South Dakota, Missouri, Nebraska, Arkansas and Tennessee (write for a schedule). Length of each session: one day, 9 a.m.-4 p.m. Cost of workshop: varies from $42-59, depending on location; includes approximately 35 pages of handouts. Write for more information.

DILLMAN'S CREATIVE WORKSHOPS, 3305 Sand Lake Lodge Lane, Lac du Flambeau WI 54538. (715)588-3143. Coordinators: Amber Weldon or Dennis Robertson. "All levels of art workshops (watercolor, acrylics, pastels and oils) geared to all different levels." 1995 schedule includes a wide variety. Write for tentative 1995 schedule. Workshops held mid-May through mid-October. Length of each session: usually 5 days/6 nights—sometimes weekends. Registration limited to 25/class. Writing and/or art facilities available: 3-4 separate studios—fully equipped. Cost varies from $600-800; includes room, board and tuition. $100-350 tuition only for people staying off-grounds. Write for brochure (include SASE).

DRURY COLLEGE/SCBWI WRITING FOR CHILDREN WORKSHOP, Drury College, Springfield MO 65802. (417)873-7329. Assistant Director, Continuing Education: Lynn Doke. Writer and illustrator workshop geared toward all levels. Emphasizes all aspects of writing for children and teenagers. Classes offered include: "Between Author and Editor: One Editor's View," "Marketing Yourself," "An Editor Works with Illustrators," "No Place for Cowards: Writing Tough Scenes," "Picture Books, or How to Write for Little Bitty Short People," "Digging Up the Bones: Researching the Nonfiction Book," "Children's Interests: What's in It for Me? and Who's in It for You?" and "Skywalking: Poetry that Kids Love." One-day workshop held in October. Length of each session: 1 hour. Ms and portfolio consultations (by appointment only). Registration limited to 25-30/class. $50 registration fee; individual consultations $25. Send SASE for more information.

DUKE UNIVERSITY WRITERS' WORKSHOP, P.O. Box 90703, Durham NC 27708-0703. Director: Marilyn Hartman. "There are various small groups based on level and genre." Writer workshops geared toward all levels. Classes offered include short short fiction, creative nonfiction, poetry, youth and young adult fiction, novel, etc. Annual workshop. Workshops held in June on the Duke campus. Length of each session: 5 days. Registration limited to 10 in each small group. Cost of workshop: $345; includes registration, instruction materials, a few social meals. "Workshop sections are small; participants work a lot. We're low on large-group stuff, high on productivity."

EDUCATION WRITERS ASSOCIATION NATIONAL SEMINAR, 1001 Connecticut Ave. NW, Washington DC 20036. (202)429-9680. Administrative Coordinator: Kristina Blakey. Writer workshops geared toward all levels. Emphasizes topics in education, education writing, investigative reporting in education, narrative writing. Workshop held April, 1995 in Denver CO (annual meeting); regional conferences. Length of each session: 1-4 days. Cost of workshop: $195 for annual meeting; includes some meals. Write for more information.

*FLORIDA CHRISTIAN WRITERS CONFERENCE, 2600 Park Ave., Titusville FL 32780. (407)269-6702, ext. 202. Conference Director: Billie Wilson. Writer and illustrator workshops geared toward all levels. "We offer 48 one-hour workshops and 5 five-hour classes. Many of these are for the children genre: Writing Children's Picture Books, Writing for Teens, Mysteries for Children Curriculum etc. We have 30 publishers and publications represented by editors teaching workshops and reading manuscripts from the conferees. The conference is limited to 200 people. Usually workshops are limited to 25-30. Advanced or professional workshops are by invitation only via submitted application." Cost of workshop: $360; includes food, lodging and tuition. Write for more information.

FLORIDA SUNCOAST WRITERS' CONFERENCE, Department of English, University of South Florida, Tampa FL 33620. (813)974-1711. Director: Ed Hirshberg. Writer workshops geared toward intermediate, advanced, professional levels. Workshops held first weekend in February. Class sizes range from 30-100. Cost of workshop: $95; $75 for students; includes all sessions, receptions, panels. Conference is held on St. Petersburg campus of USF.

*GREAT LAKES WRITER'S WORKSHOP, Alverno College, 3401 S. 39th St., P.O. Box 343922, Milwaukee WI 53234-3922. (414)382-6176. Director: Debra Pass. Writer workshops geared toward beginner and intermediate levels. Annual workshop. Workshop held second full week in July. Length of each session: 2 hours. Cost of workshop: $99 (in 1994); includes entrance into 6 sessions. Write for more information.

GREEN LAKE CHRISTIAN WRITERS CONFERENCE, American Baptist Assembly, Green Lake WI 54941-9300. (800)558-8898. Writer workshops geared toward beginner, intermediate and advanced levels. Emphasizes poetry, nonfiction, writing for children, fiction. Classes/courses offered include: same as above plus 1-session or 2-session presentations on marketing, devotional writing and retelling Bible stories. Workshops held July 8-15, 1995. Length of conference: Saturday dinner through the following Saturday breakfast. Registration limited to 20/class. Writing and/or art facilities available: housing, conference rooms, etc. "No special equipment for writing." Cost of workshop: $80; includes all instruction plus room and meals as selected. Write for more information. "The conference focuses on helping writers to refine their writing skills in a caring atmosphere utilizing competent, caring faculty. This annual conference has been held every year since 1948."

HEART OF AMERICA WRITERS' CONFERENCE, JCCC, 12345 College Blvd., Overland Park KS 66210. (913)469-3838. Director: Judith Choice. Writer workshops geared toward all levels. Annual workshop. Workshops held April 21-22, 1995. Length of each session: 1-3 hrs. Registration limited to 135. Cost of workshop: $90; includes lunch, reception. Write for more information.

*HIGHLAND SUMMER CONFERENCE, Box 7014 Radford University, Radford VA 24142. (703)831-5366. Director: Grace Toney Edwards. Assistant to the Director: Jo Ann Asbury. Writer workshops geared toward beginner, intermediate and advanced levels. Emphasizes Appalachian literature. Annual workshop. Workshop held June 19-30, 1995 (last 2 weeks in June annually). Length of each session: 1-2 hours. Registration limited to 20. Writing facilities available: computer center. Cost of workshop: Regular tuition (housing/meals extra). Must be registered student or special status student. Write for more information. Past visiting authors include: Wilma Dykeman, Sue Ellen Bridgers, George Ella Lyon, Lou Kassem.

HIGHLIGHTS FOUNDATION WRITERS WORKSHOP AT CHAUTAUQUA, Dept. CWL, 814 Court St., Honesdale PA 18431. (717)253-1192. Conference Director: Jan Keen. Writer workshops geared toward beginner, intermediate and advanced levels. Classes offered include: "Children's Interests," "Writing Dialogue," "Beginnings and Endings," "Rights, Contracts, Copyrights," "Science Writing." Workshops held July 15-22, 1995, Chautauqua Institution, Chautauqua, NY. Registration limited to 100/class. Write for more information.

HOFSTRA UNIVERSITY SUMMER WRITERS' CONFERENCE, 110 Hofstra University, UCCE, 205 Davison Hall, Hempstead NY 11550-1090. (516)463-5016. Director of Liberal Arts Studies: Lewis Shena. Writer workshops geared toward all levels. Classes offered include fiction, nonfiction, poetry, children's literature, stage/screenwriting and other genres. Children's writing faculty has included Pam Conrad, Johanna Hurwitz, Tor Seidler and Jane Zalben, with Maurice Sendak once appearing as guest speaker. Annual workshop. Workshops held July 10-21, 1995. Length of each session: Each workshop meets for 2½ hours daily for a total of 25 hours. Students can register for a maximum of 3 workshops, schedule an individual conference with the writer/instructor and submit a short ms. (less than 10 pages) for critique. Enrollees may register as certificate students or credit students. Cost of workshop: certificate students enrollment fee is approximately $600 plus $26 registration fee; 2-credit student enrollment fee is approximately $800 undergraduate and $835 graduate; 4-credit student enrollment fee is approximately $1,500 undergraduate and $1,550 graduate. On-campus accommodations for the sessions are available for approximately $300/person. Certificate students may attend any of the 5 workshops, a private conference and special programs and social events. Credit students may attend only the workshops they have registered for (a maximum of 2 for 2 credits each) and the special programs and social events.

INTERNATIONAL WOMEN'S WRITING GUILD, P.O. Box 810, Gracie Station, New York NY 10028. (212)737-7536. Executive Director: Hannelore Hahn. Writer and illustrator workshops geared toward all levels. Offers 60 different workshops—some are for children's book writers and illustrators. Also sponsors 13 other events throughout the US. Annual workshops. Workshops held in August. Length of each session: 1½ hours; sessions take place for an entire week. Registration limited to 400. Cost of workshop: $300. Write for more information. "This workshop always takes place at Skidmore College in Saratoga Springs NY."

THE IUPUI NATIONAL YOUTH THEATRE PLAYWRITING SYMPOSIUM, 525 N. Blackford St., Indianapolis IN 46202. (317)274-2095. Literary Manager: W. Mark McCreary. "The purpose of the Symposium is to provide a forum in which we can examine and discuss those principles which characterize good dramatic literature for young people and to explore ways to help playwrights and the promotion of quality drama. Publishers, playwrights, directors, producers, librarians and educators join together to examine issues central to playwriting." Holds playwriting competition. Send SASE for guidelines and entry form. Deadline: September 1, 1996.

I'VE ALWAYS WANTED TO WRITE BUT—BEGINNERS' CLASS, Villa 30, 23350 Sereno Ct., Cupertino CA 95014. (415)691-0300. Contact: Louise Purwin Zobel. Writer workshops geared toward beginner, intermediate levels. "This seminar/workshop starts at the beginning, although the intermediate writer will benefit, too. There is discussion of children's magazine and book literature today, how to write it and how to market it. Also, there is discussion of other types of writing and the basics of writing for publication." Annual workshops. "Usually held several times a year; fall, winter and spring." Sessions last 1-2 days. Cost of workshop: $45-65/day, depending on the campus; includes extensive handout. Write for more information.

MAINE WRITERS WORKSHOP, 2 Central St., Rockport ME 04856. (207)236-8581. Assistant to Director: Alix Taylor. Founder and Director: David H. Lyman. "These workshops are for professional writers who have a history of published work. Newspaper writers may wish to develop their craft in writing novels, or to improve their travel writing. Professional travel writers may wish to begin work on their first novel, or need help overcoming a block. Writers without a history of published work are discouraged from attending, but are accepted if samples of their work show talent and dedication. A résumé *must* accompany your application indicating your publishing career." Workshops held in summer and fall. Length of each session: 1 week. Maximum class size: varies. Write for cost information and brochure on workshops and accommodations.

*MANHATTANVILLE WRITERS' WEEK, Manhattanville College, 2900 Purchase St., Purchase NY 10577. (914)694-3425. Dean, Adult and Special Programs: Ruth Dowd. Writer workshops geared toward beginner, intermediate and advanced levels. Offers 5-day workshop in children's literature. Workshop held last week in June. Length of each session: one week. Cost of workshop: $550 (non-credit); includes a full week of workshops, lectures, readings, etc. Workshop may be taken for 2 graduate credits. Write for more information.

Market conditions are constantly changing! If you're still using this book and it is 1996 or later, buy the newest edition of Children's Writer's & Illustrator's Market *at your favorite bookstore or order directly from Writer's Digest Books.*

MAPLE WOODS COMMUNITY COLLEGE WRITERS' CONFERENCE, 2601 NE Barry Rd., Kansas City MO 64156. (816)437-3010. Coordinator, Continuing Education: Jill Weiler. Writer workshops geared toward beginner, intermediate levels. Various writing topics and genres covered. Conference held in fall. Length of each session: 1 hour. Registration limited to 150/class. Cost of workshop: $45; includes lunch.

MARITIME WRITERS' WORKSHOP, Department Extension & Summer School, P.O. Box 4400, University of New Brunswick, Fredericton, New Brunswick E3B 5A3 Canada. (506)453-4646. Week-long workshop geared to all levels and held in July. Length of each session: 3 hours/day. Group workshop plus individual conferences, public readings, etc. Registration limited to 10/class. Cost of workshop: $250 tuition. Meals and accomodations extra. 10-20 ms pages due before conference (deadline announced). Scholarships available.

MIDLAND WRITERS CONFERENCE, Grace A. Dow Memorial Library, 1710 W. St. Andrews, Midland MI 48640. (517)835-7151. Conference Chair: Barbara Brennan. Writer and illustrator workshops geared toward all levels. "We always have one session each on children's, poetry and basics." Classes offered include: how to write poetry, writing for youth, your literary agent/what to expect. Workshops held June 10, 1995. Length of each session: concurrently, 4 1-hour and 2-hour sessions. Maximum class size: 40. "We are a public library." Cost of workshop: $45; $35 seniors and students; includes choice of workshops and the keynote speech given by a prominent author (last year P.J. O'Rourke). Write for more information.

*MIDWEST WRITERS' CONFERENCE, 6000 Frank Ave. NW, Canton OH 44720. (216)499-9600. Coordinator: Debbie Ruhe. Writer workshops geared toward beginner, intermediate and advanced levels. Emphasizes markets, publications and selling your work. Annual workshop. Workshop held early October. Length of each session: 1 hour. Registration limited to 400 total people. Cost of workshop: $65; includes Friday afternoon workshops, keynote address, Saturday workshops, box lunch, up to 2-ms entries in contest. Write for more information.

MISSISSIPPI VALLEY WRITERS CONFERENCE, Augustana College, Rock Island IL 61265. (309)762-8985. Conference Director: David R. Collins. Writer workshops geared toward all levels. Classes offered include Juvenile Writing—1 of 9 workshops offered. Annual workshop. Workshops held June 4-9, 1995; usually it is the second week in June each year. Length of each session: Monday-Friday, 1 hour each day. Registration limited to 20 participants/workshop. Writing facilities available: college library. Cost of workshop: $25 registration; $40 to participate in 1 workshop, $70 in 2, $30 for each additional; $20 to audit a workshop. Write for more information.

MOUNT HERMON CHRISTIAN WRITERS CONFERENCE, Mount Hermon Christian Conference Center, P.O. Box 413, Mount Hermon CA 95041. (408)335-4466. Fax: (408)335-9218. Director of Public Affairs: David R. Talbott. Writer workshops geared toward all levels. Emphasizes religious writing for children via books, articles; Sunday school curriculum; marketing. Classes offered include: "Suitable Style for Children"; "Everything You Need to Know to Write and Market Your Children's Book"; "Take-Home Papers for Children." Workshops held annually over Palm Sunday weekend: April 7-11, 1995. Length of each session: 5-day residential conferences held annually. Registration limited 45/class, but most are 10-15. Conference center with hotel-style accommodations. Cost of workshop: $425-650 variable; includes tuition, resource notebook, refreshment breaks, full room and board for 13 meals and 4 nights. Write for more information.

THE NATIONAL WRITERS ASSOCIATION CONFERENCE, Suite 424, 1450 S. Havana, Aurora CO 80012. (303)751-7844. Executive Director: Sandy Whelchel. Writer workshops geared toward all levels. Classes offered include marketing, agenting, "What's Hot in the Market." Annual workshop. Workshops held in June 1995. Length of each session: 50-minute sessions for 2½ days. "In 1995 the workshop will be held during a 5-day Alaskan cruise through the Inland Passage." Write for more information.

*NEW LETTERS WEEKEND WRITERS CONFERENCE, University of Missouri—Kansas City, 5100 Rockhill Rd., 215 55B, Kansas City MO 64110-2499. (816)235-2736. Continuing Education Manager: Mary Ann McKinley. Writer and illustrator workshops geared toward intermediate, advanced and professional levels. 1994 topic was "Writing for Love, Money and Immortality." Annual workshop. Workshop held in June. Length of each session: approximately 1 hour. Registration limited to 80. Writing facilities available on request. Cost of workshop: $90 non-credit. "Credit fees vary depending on level. Call for credit information. Those *attending for college credit* from UMKC must submit a manuscript." Write for more information.

CHRISTOPHER NEWPORT UNIVERSITY WRITERS' CONFERENCE, 50 Shoe Lane, Newport News VA 23606-2998. (804)594-7158. Coordinator: Terry Cox-Joseph. Director of Continuing Education: Dr. Sue Jones. Writer workshops geared toward beginner, intermediate, professional levels. Emphasizes all genres. Offers 4 awards: poetry, short stories, juvenile fiction, nonfiction. Call for guidelines and to be on mailing list. Workshop held April 1, 1995. Length of each session: 2¼ hours. Registration limited to 35/class. Cost of workshop: $65.

*OKLAHOMA FALL ARTS INSTITUTES, P.O. Box 18154, Oklahoma City OK 73154. (405)842-0890. Director of Programs: Mary Gordon Taft. Writer and illustrator workshops geared toward intermediate, advanced and professional levels. Writing topics include writing for children, poetry, fiction, nonfiction, art of teaching writing; art topics include drawing, painting, illustrating children's books, sculpture, printmaking. Annual workshop. Workshop held each year in October (1995 dates: October 12-15 and October 26-29). Registration is limited to 20 participants per workshop; 5 workshops each weekend. Cost of workshop: $450; includes tuition, double-occupancy room and board. Write for more information. "Catalogues are available. Each workshop is taught by a professional artist of national reputation. Workshops held at Quartz Mountain Lodge a beautiful, secluded location."

101 WAYS TO MARKET YOUR BOOK, P.O. Box 152281, Arlington TX 76015. (817)468-9924. Seminar Director: Mary Bold. Writer workshops geared toward beginner, intermediate levels. Classes offered include heavy emphasis on how books are marketed to the public and how author and publisher can work together in promoting new titles. Annual workshop. Workshops held (usually), spring and fall. Length of each session: half day. No prior requirements. Write for more information. "Many of my seminars (for both writers and publishers) are sponsored by area universities and learning centers, as well as by the National Association of Independent Publishers."

OZARK CREATIVE WRITERS, INC. CONFERENCE, 6817 Gingerbread Lane, Little Rock AR 72204. (501)565-8889. President: Peggy Vining. Writer's workshops geared to all levels. "All forms of the creative process dealing with the literary arts. We have expanded to songwriting." Always the second weekend in October (October 12-14, 1995) at Inn of the Ozarks in Eureka Springs AR (a resort town). Morning sessions are given to main attraction author . . . 6 1-hour satellite speakers during each of the 2 afternoons. Two banquets. "Approximately 125-150 attend the conference yearly . . . many others enter the creative writing competition." Cost of workshop: $25-30. "This does not include meals or lodging. We do block off 50 rooms prior to September 1 for OCW guests." Send #10 SASE for brochure. "Reserve early."

PERSPECTIVES IN CHILDREN'S LITERATURE CONFERENCE, 226 Furcolo Hall, University of Massachusetts, Amherst MA 01003. (413)545-4325 or (413)545-1116. Director of Conference: Masha K. Rudman. Writer and illustrator workshops geared to all levels. Emphasis varies from year to year. Next conference held April 8, 1995. Length of each session: 9 a.m.-4 p.m. (lunch included). Registration limited to 500. Cost of workshop: about $50. Graduate credit available.

*PIMA WRITERS' WORKSHOP, 2202 W. Anklam Rd., Tucson AZ 85709. Workshop Director: Peg Files. Writer workshop geared toward beginner, intermediate and advanced levels.

"The workshop includes sessions on writing children's and juvenile books and opportunities to meet individually with writers and editors." Annual workshop. Workshop held in May. Length of each session: 3 days. Cost of workshop: $65; includes tuition. Write for more information.

PORT TOWNSEND WRITER'S CONFERENCE, Centrum, P.O. Box 1158, Port Townsend WA 98368. (206)385-3102. Director: Carol Jane Bangs. Writer workshops geared toward intermediate, advanced and professional levels. Emphasizes writing for children and young adults. Classes offered include: Jane Yolen master class; intermediate/advanced writing for children. Workshops held mid-July. Length of each session: 10 days. Registration limited to 20/class. Writing facilities available: classrooms. Cost of workshop: $370; includes tuition, room and board extra. Publication list for master class. Write for more information. $100 deposit necessary. Applications accepted after December 1 for following July; workshops fill by February.

ROBERT QUACKENBUSH'S CHILDREN'S BOOK WRITING AND ILLUSTRATING WORK-SHOP, 460 E. 79th St., New York NY 10021. (212)744-3822. Contact: Robert Quackenbush. Writer and illustrator workshops geared toward all levels. Emphasizes picture books from start to finish. Workshops held fall, winter and summer. Courses offered fall and winter include 10 weeks each — ½ hour/week; July workshop is a full five day (9 a.m.-4 p.m) extensive course. Registration limited to 10/class. Writing and/or art facilities available; work on the premises; art supply store nearby. Cost of workshop: $650 for instruction.

READER'S DIGEST WRITER'S WORKSHOP, Northern Arizona University, P.O. Box 5638, Flagstaff AZ 86011-5638. (602)523-3554. Associate to the President: Ray Newton. Writer workshops geared toward all levels. Classes offered include major emphasis on nonfiction magazine articles for major popular publications. Annual workshops in various locations in US. Length of each session: intensive 2-day sessions, each approximately 1 hour. Registration limited to 250. Cost of workshop: $150 registration fee; includes 3 meals. Does not include travel or lodging."Participants will have opportunity for one-on-one sessions with major editors, writers representing national magazines, including the *Reader's Digest*." Write for more information.

SAN DIEGO STATE UNIVERSITY WRITERS' CONFERENCE, The College of Extended Studies, San Diego CA 92182. (619)594-2514. Extension Director: Jan Wahl. Writer workshops geared toward beginner, intermediate and advanced levels. Emphasizes nonfiction, fiction, screenwriting, advanced novel writing. Classes offered include: "Learning to Think Like an Editor"; "Writing for Television and Motion Pictures"; "Writing Children's Non-fiction and Picture Books." Workshops held third weekend in January each year. Length of each session: 50 minutes. Registration limited to 100/class. Cost of workshop: 1994 fees were $195; included Saturday reception, 2 lunches and all sessions. Write for more information.

*SEATTLE PACIFIC CHRISTIAN WRITERS CONFERENCE, Humanities Department, Seattle Pacific University, Seattle WA 98119. (206)281-2109. Director: Linda Wagner. Writer workshops geared toward beginner, intermediate, advanced levels. Emphasizes "excellence in writing for the religious market. Stress on the craft of writing, usually includes some excellent workshops for children's writers." Workshops held fourth week of June. Length of each session: 70 minutes. Maximum class size: "varies — usually not more than 40." Cost of workshop: $200.

*SOCIETY OF CHILDREN'S BOOK WRITERS AND ILLUSTRATORS — ALABAMA/GEORGIA REGION, 1616 Kestwick Dr., Birmingham AL 35226. (205)979-0270. Regional Advisor: Joan Broerman. "The fall conference, 'Writing and Illustrating for Kids,' is always the third Saturday in October in Birmingham, and offers entry level and professional track workshops as well as numerous talks on craft from early picture books through young adult novels." Cost of workshop: $50-60 for SCBWI members; $60-70 for nonmembers. Write for more information (include SASE). "Our spring conference is in different parts of the two-state region. The 1995 spring conference date is March 11, 1995."

*SOCIETY OF CHILDREN'S BOOK WRITERS & ILLUSTRATORS CONFERENCE IN CHILDREN'S LITERATURE, 610 W. 112th St., New York NY 10025. Conference Chairman: Kimberly Colen. Writer and illustrator conference geared toward all levels. Annual conference. Conference held usually the first or second Saturday in November. Length of each session: 1 hour, 15 minutes. Registration limited to 225. Cost of conference: $65, nonmembers; $60, members; includes continental breakfast, lunch and a day of meeting authors, illustrators, publishers, editors and agents. Write for more information.

SOCIETY OF CHILDREN'S BOOK WRITERS & ILLUSTRATORS – FLORIDA REGION, 2158 Portland Ave., Wellington FL 33414. (407)798-4824. Florida Regional Advisor: Barbara Casey. Writer and illustrator workshops geared toward beginner, intermediate, advanced and professional levels. Subjects to be announced. Workshop held in the meeting rooms of the Palm Springs Public Library, 217 Cypress Lane, Palm Springs FL. Registration limited to 100/class. Cost of workshop: $35 for members, $40 for non-members. Write for more information. "We plan to give one conference a year to be held on the second Saturday in September."

SOCIETY OF CHILDREN'S BOOK WRITERS & ILLUSTRATORS – HAWAII, 98-688 Keikialu St., Aiea HI 96701. (808)486-4086. Regional Advisor: Marion Coste. Writer and illustrator conferences geared toward all levels and others interested in promoting children's literature. Write for more information.

SOCIETY OF CHILDREN'S BOOK WRITERS & ILLUSTRATORS – INDIANA RETREAT, 4810 Illinois Rd., Fort Wayne IN 46804. (219)436-2160. Conference Director: Betsy Storey. Writer and illustrator workshops geared toward all levels. Classes offered include "Nuts and Bolts for Beginners," "First Sales," "Professionalism, Writing the Picture Book" and "Nonfiction for Children." All are geared toward children's writers and illustrators. Workshops held annually in June. Length of each session: 45 minutes to 1½ hours. Cost of workshop: approximately $225; includes accommodations, meals and workshops. Write for more information. "Manuscript and portfolio critiques by published writers and illustrators will be offered at additional charge."

SOCIETY OF CHILDREN'S BOOK WRITERS & ILLUSTRATORS – MID-ATLANTIC WRITERS' ANNUAL CONFERENCE, 616 Old Dominion Dr., Yorktown VA 23692. (804)894-4679. Regional Advisor: Linda Wirkner. Writer workshops geared toward all levels. Illustrator workshops geared toward beginner, intermediate levels. Annual workshop. Workshops held in fall of each year. Length of each session: 1 day. Registration limited to 100. Writing and/or art facilities available: writing contest, display of illustrations. Cost of workshop: $60-70; includes breakfast coffee, luncheon, afternoon soft drinks. Write for more information.

SOCIETY OF CHILDREN'S BOOK WRITERS & ILLUSTRATORS – NEW ENGLAND CONFERENCE, RFD #41A Washington St., Boxford MA 01921. (203)721-8444. Regional Advisor: Cathy Duble. Writer/illustrator workshops geared toward all levels. Emphasizes writing and illustrating for the children's market. 1-day workshop held May 20, 1995 at the Mascomomet High School, Topsfield MA. (location varies from year to year) includes keynote speakers and many workshops. Length of each session: 8-5 p.m. Registration limited to 250. "Specific cost yet to be determined; usually includes all-day conference, lunch. Conference is open to both published and unpublished writers and illustrators of children's books (and magazines) and anyone else interested in those aspects of children's books."

*SOCIETY OF CHILDREN'S BOOK WRITERS & ILLUSTRATORS – SAN DIEGO CHAPTER Writing for Children, the Words and the Pictures, 6506 Mt. Ackerman Dr., San Diego CA 92111. (619)569-7617. Conference Chairman: Lynda Pflueger. Writer and illustrator workshops geared toward all levels. Sessions include "Writing and Illustrating Picture Books," "Writing Nonfiction for Children," "Writing for the Young Adult Market" and

CHILDREN'S WRITER

W hether you're writing for yourself or creating a best-seller, CHILDREN'S WRITER covers the spectrum monthly. It gives you up-to-the-minute information you can't beg, borrow or buy anywhere else.

More than that, CHILDREN'S WRITER deals with the current questions and problems you're most likely to encounter—and it covers all the major markets that buy freelance writing.

"CHILDREN'S WRITER is full of information and articles that touch every writer, published or unpublished," says Patricia Clauson, Batavia, NY. "I think of it as a support group. When your newsletter arrives, everything comes to a halt! It's my favorite companion at the lunch table. I really *do* devour it… It's a wonderful newsletter."

"It helped me get an article accepted…."

"CHILDREN'S WRITER is a great source of reference for me and even helped me get an article accepted for publication," reports Karen Muller, E. Northport, NY. *Hob-Nob's* request for nonfiction pieces in the February CHILDREN'S WRITER was a definite break for me. Thanks for helping my dream come true!"

"The articles about squeezing time out for writing and developing skills were most helpful," writes Carolyn Beck, Rialto, CA, "since I am a busy mother of three young children…As someone getting started at the business of writing, *The Marketplace* section cuts through all the overwhelming array of data to sift through to find an editor who will use my work."

FREE Sample Issue

To get your free issue, just complete the reverse side and mail. *There is no obligation!*

The Monthly Newsletter for the **BOOMING CHILDREN'S MARKET!**

"From the Editor's Desk." Annual workshop. Workshop held on the second or third Saturday in March. Length: all day workshop with 6 1-hour sessions. Cost of workshop: $55-75; includes all day workshop and luncheon. Write for more information. "Meeting other writers, networking and marketing information is stressed during workshop."

SOCIETY OF CHILDREN'S BOOK WRITERS & ILLUSTRATORS—TENNESSEE SPRING CONFERENCE, Box 3342, Clarksville TN 37043-3342. (615)358-9849. Regional Advisor: Cheryl Zach. Writer workshop geared toward all levels. Illustrator workshops geared toward beginner, intermediate levels. Emphasizes writing the picture book, writing and selling chapter books and middle grade fiction, young adult fiction, nonfiction, poetry, and magazine stories and articles. Workshop held in the spring. Length of each session: 1 day. Registration limited to 100. Write for more information. "SCBWI-Tennessee's 1995 conference is scheduled for April 29 in Nashville."

SOCIETY OF CHILDREN'S BOOK WRITERS & ILLUSTRATORS—WISCONSIN ANNUAL FALL RETREAT, 26 Lancaster Court, Madison WI 53719-1433. (608)271-0433. Regional Advisor: Sheri Cooper Sinykin. Writer workshops geared toward all levels. Classes offered include: pre-publication secrets; post-publication problems; workshops on craft; author-editor dialogues on the revision process; working relationships; marketing. "The entire retreat is geared *only* to children's book writing." Annual workshop. Retreat held September 29-October 1, 1995. Length of each session: 1-2 hours; retreat lasts from Friday evening to Sunday afternoon. Registration limited to approximately 60. Cost of workshop: usually $160-180 for SCBWI members, higher for nonmembers; includes room, board and program. "We strive to offer an informal weekend with an award-winning children's writer, an agent or illustrator and an editor from a trade house in New York in attendance." There's usually a waiting list by mid-July. Send SASE for flier.

SOUTHERN CALIFORNIA SOCIETY OF CHILDREN'S BOOK WRITERS & ILLUSTRATORS; ILLUSTRATORS DAY, #105, 11943 Montana Ave., Los Angeles CA 90049. (310)820-5601. Regional Advisor: Judith Enderle. Illustrator workshops geared toward all levels. Emphasizes illustration and illustration markets. Conference includes: presentations by art director, children's book editor and panel of artists/author-illustrators. Workshops held annually in the fall. Length of session: full day. Maximum class size: 100. "Editors and art directors will view portfolios. We want to know if each conferee is bringing a portfolio or not." This is a chance for illustrators to meet editors/art directors and each other. Writers Day held in the spring. National conference for authors *and* illustrators held every August."

*SOUTHWEST WRITERS CONFERENCE, Suite B, 1338 Wyoming Blvd. NE, Albuquerque NM 87112. (505)293-0303. Conference Director: JoAnn Hamlin. Writer workshops geared toward all levels. Covers all genres at all levels of writing. Annual workshop. Workshop held August 24-27, 1995 at Hilton Hotel. Length of each session: Friday-Sunday. Cost of workshop: $240 (approximately); includes all workshops and meals. Write for more information.

STATE OF MAINE WRITERS' CONFERENCE, 16 Colby Ave., P.O. Box 146, Ocean Park ME 04063. (207)934-5034 (summer). (413)596-6734 (winter). Chairman: Richard F. Burns. Writers' workshops geared toward beginner, intermediate, advanced levels. Emphasizes poetry, prose, mysteries, editors, publishers, etc. Annual workshop. Workshops held August 22-25 1995. Cost of workshop: $75 (half price for students 21 and under); includes all sessions and banquet, snacks, poetry booklet. Write for more information.

*TRENTON STATE COLLEGE WRITERS' CONFERENCE, English Dept, Trenton State College, Hillwood Lakes CN 4700, Trenton NJ 08650-4700. (609)771-3254. Director: Jean

 The asterisk before a listing indicates the listing is new in this edition.

Hollander. Writer workshops geared toward all levels. Workshops held April 6, 1995. Length of each session: 2 hours. Registration limited to 50. Cost of workshop: $50 (reduced rates for students); includes conference, workshop and ms critique. Write for more information.

MARK TWAIN WRITERS CONFERENCE, 921 Center St., Hannibal MO 63401. (314)221-2462 or (800)747-0738. Director: James C. Hefley. Writers' workshops geared toward beginner, intermediate and advanced levels. Workshops covering poetry, humor, Mark Twain, newspapers, freelancing, writing for children, the autobiography and working with an agent. Workshops held in June. Length of each session: 50-90 minutes. Registration limited to 12-20/class. Writing facilities available: computers. Cost of workshop: $395; includes all program fees, room, meals and group photo. Write for more information.

*VANCOUVER INTERNATIONAL WRITERS FESTIVAL, 1243 Cartwright St., Vancouver, British Columbia V6H 4B7 Canada. (604)681-6330. Producer: Alma Lee. "The mission of the Vancouver International Writers Festival is to encourage an appreciation of literature and to promote literacy by providing a forum where writers and readers can interact. This is accomplished by the production of special events and an annual Festival which feature writers from a variety of countries, including Canada, whose work is compelling and diverse. The Festival attracts over 8,000 people and presents approximately 40 events in four venues during five days on Granville Island, located in the heart of Vancouver, British Columbia." Workshop held third weekend in October (5-day festival). "All writers who participate are invited by the producer. The events are open to anyone who wishes to purchase tickets."

VASSAR INSTITUTE OF PUBLISHING AND WRITING: CHILDREN'S BOOKS IN THE MARKETPLACE, Box 300, Vassar College, Poughkeepsie NY 12601. (914)437-5903. Program Coordinator: Maryann Bruno. Director: Barbara Lucas. Writer and illustrator workshops geared toward all levels. Emphasizes "the editorial, production, marketing and reviewing processes, on writing fiction and nonfiction for all ages, creating the picture book, understanding the markets and selling your work." Classes offered include: "Writing Fiction," "The Editorial Process," "How to Write a Children's Book and Get It Published." Workshop held July 9-14, 1995. Length of each session: 3½-hour morning critique sessions, afternoon and evening lectures. Registration limited to 40/class (with 3 instructors). Cost of workshop: approximately $800, includes room, board and tuition for all critique sessions, lectures and social activities. "Proposals are pre-prepared and discussed at morning critique sessions. Art portfolio review given on pre-prepared works." Write for more information. "This conference gives a comprehensive look at the publishing industry as well as offering critiques of creative writing and portfolio review."

VENTURA/SANTA BARBARA FALL WORKSHOP, 22736 Vanowen, Suite 106, West Hills CA 91307. (818)888-8760. Regional Advisor: Alexis O'Neill. Writer workshops geared toward all levels. "We invite editors, authors and author/illustrators. We have had speakers on the picture book, middle grade, YA, magazine, religious markets and photographer for photo essay books. Both fiction and nonfiction are covered." Workshop held in October; other events to be announced. Length of each session: 9:00 a.m.-4 p.m. on Saturdays. Cost of workshop: $40; includes all sessions and lunch. Write for more information.

WELLS WRITERS' WORKSHOP, 69 Broadway, Concord NH 03301. (603)225-9162. Coordinator: Victor Andre Levine. Writer workshops geared toward beginner, intermediate levels. "Sessions focus on careful plot preparation, as well as on effective writing (characterization, dialogue and exposition), with lots of time for writing." Workshops which meet on Maine seacoast, are offered twice a year. Length of each session: 5 days. Registration limited to 5/class. Writing facilities available: space, electrical outlets, resident MS-DOS computer. Cost of workshop: $750; some scholarship money available. Cost includes tuition, housing and food. Write for more information. "I invite interested writers to call or write. I'd be happy to meet with them if they're reasonably close by. Workshop stresses the importance of getting the structure right when writing stories for children."

WESLEYAN WRITERS CONFERENCE, Wesleyan University, Middletown CT 06459. (203)685-3604. Director: Anne Greene. Writer workshops geared toward all levels. "This conference is useful for writers interested in how to structure a story, poem or nonfiction piece. Although we don't always offer classes in writing for children, the advice about structuring a piece is useful for writers of any sort, no matter who their audience is." Classes in the novel, short story, fiction techniques, poetry, journalism and literary nonfiction. Guest speakers and panels offer discussion of fiction, poetry, reviewing, editing and publishing. Individual ms consultations available. Workshops held annually the last week in June. Length of each session: 6 days. "Usually, there are 100 participants at the Conference." Classrooms, meals, lodging and word processing facilities available on campus. Cost of workshop: tuition — $430, room — $95, meals (required of all participants) — $173. "Anyone may register; people who want financial aid must submit their work and be selected by scholarship judges." Write for more information.

WESTERN RESERVE WRITERS AND FREELANCE CONFERENCE, Lakeland Community College, 7700 Clocktower Dr., Mentor OH 44060. (216)953-7080. Coordinator: Lea Leever Oldham. Writer workshops geared toward all levels. Emphasizes fiction, photography, greeting card writing, science fiction and fantasy writing, poetry. Classes offered include: "Writing for Children in Whole Language & Curriculum." Workshops held in mid-September. Length of each session: 7 hrs. Cost of workshop: $44 plus lunch. Other workshops held in late March or early April. Write for more information to #110, 34200 Ridge Rd., Willoughby OH 44094. (216)943-3047.

***WESTERN RESERVE WRITERS MINI CONFERENCE**, 34200 Ridge Rd. #110, Willoughby OH 44094. (216)943-3047. Coordinator: Lea Leever Oldham. Writer workshops geared toward beginner, intermediate and advanced levels. Topics include writing and selling children's writing. Annual workshop. Workshop held in March or early April at Lakeland Community College, Mentor OH. Length of each session: half day. Cost of workshop: $25. Write for more information.

WILLAMETTE WRITERS ANNUAL WRITERS CONFERENCE, Suite 5A, 9045 SW Barbur Blvd., Portland OR 97219. (503)452-1592. Writer workshops geared toward all levels. Emphasizes all areas of writing. Opportunities to meet one-on-one with leading literary agents and editors. Workshops held in August.

***THE WRITERS' CENTER AT CHAUTAUQUA**, Box 408, Chautauqua NY 14722. (716)357-2445 or (717)872-8337 (September through May). Director: Mary Jean Irion. Writer workshops geared toward beginner and intermediate levels. Emphasizes poetry, fiction, nonfiction, at least 1 week of which is devoted to writing for children; for example, the elements of writing, slanted for children's writers: setting, characters, plot, conflict, etc. Workshop held sometime between June 23-August 31, 1-3 each afternoon Monday-Friday. Length of each session: 2 hours. Registration limited to 25. Cost of workshop: $60. "Often a leader will invite students to submit their work for class discussion or for comments by the leader, but this is never a requirement." Write for more information. September-May, mail should be addressed to 149 Kready Ave., Millersville PA 17551. "A $10 membership in The Writers' Center at Chautauqua includes full information on each season, mailed out in March, with registration blank."

WRITERS CONNECTION CONFERENCES, (formerly Seminars for Writers), P.O. Box 24770, San Jose CA 95154-4770. (408)445-3600. Fax: (408)445-3609. Program Director: Meera Lester. Conferences are scheduled throughout the year and include "Writing for Children," "Literary Agents' Day," "Writing for Interactive Multimedia," "Selling to Hollywood" and other fiction, nonfiction and scriptwriting programs. Bookstore of writing, reference and how-to books. Monthly newsletter with membership only. Write for more information.

***WRITERS' FORUM**, 1570 E. Colorado Blvd., Pasadena CA 91106-2003. (818)585-7608. Coordinator of Forum: Meredith Brucker. Writer workshops geared toward all levels.

"Last year Eve Bunting spoke on 'Writing the Picture Book.' " Workshop held March 11, 1995. Length of session: 1 hour and 15 minutes including Q & A time. Cost of workshop: $90; includes lunch. Write for more information to Community Education, Pasadena City College, 1570 E. Colorado Blvd., Pasadena CA 91106-2003.

*WRITERS IN THE REDWOODS RETREAT, Alliance Redwoods, 6250 Bohemian Hwy., Occidental CA 95465. (707)874-3507. Guest Services Director: Bob Ward. Writer workshops geared toward beginner and intermediate levels. Topics include how freelancers can and do earn a living; how to write book proposals and get contracts; from idea to published novel; tricks of the trade to keep writing during dry spells. Annual workshop. Workshop held November 3-5, 1995. Registration limited to 100. Cost of workshop: $170-240; includes tuition, room and board, handouts, freebies. For information, write to Writers Information Network, P.O. Box 11337, Bainbridge Island WA 98110.

WRITERS STUDIO SPRING WRITERS CONFERENCE, 3403 45th St., Moline IL 61265. (309)762-8985. Coordinator, Pro Tem: David R. Collins. Writer workshops geared toward intermediate level. Emphasizes basic writing and mechanics. Workshops held in March. Length of each session: 3 hours. Workshop is free. Write for more information.

*YACHATS LITERARY FESTIVAL, 124 NE California St., Yachats OR 97498. (503)547-3271. Director: Frena Gray Davidson. Writer workshops geared toward beginner, intermediate and advanced levels. Offers a 5-day "Writing for Children Workshop" (for participants to work on their own projects). Annual workshop. Workshop held "around September." Length of session: 1 full week. Registration is limited (number varies). Writing facilities available: computer room. Cost of workshop: $250 (approximately); includes workshop for whole week, plus evening events. Food and accommodations plan extra. "Yachats is one of the most beautiful places on the Oregon Coast, by the ocean and an ancient forest."

Conferences & Workshops/'94-'95 changes

The following listings were included in the 1994 edition of *Children's Writer's & Illustrator's Market* but do not have listings in this edition. The majority did not respond to our request to update their listings. If a reason was given for exclusion, it appears in parentheses after the listing's name.

Bennington Writing Workshops
Clarion Science Fiction & Fantasy Writing Workshops
Florida State Writers Conference (per request)
SCBWI-Rocky Mountain Chapter Summer Retreat
University of Kentucky Women Writers Conference
Write to Sell Writer's Conference (per request)
Writing Books for Children

Helpful Books & Publications

The editors of *Children's Writer's & Illustrator's Market* suggest the following books and periodicals to keep you informed on writing and illustrating techniques, trends in the field, business issues and additional markets. Most are available in libraries or bookstores or may be ordered directly from their publishers.

Books

THE ART OF WRITING FOR CHILDREN: SKILLS & TECHNIQUES OF THE CRAFT. By Connie C. Epstein. Archon Books, 1991.

THE ARTIST'S FRIENDLY LEGAL GUIDE. By Floyd Conner, Peter Karlen, Jean Perwin and David M. Spatt. North Light Books, 1991.

GETTING STARTED AS A FREELANCE ILLUSTRATOR OR DESIGNER. By Michael Fleishman. North Light Books, 1990.

GUIDE TO WRITING FOR CHILDREN. By Jane Yolen. The Writer, Inc., 1989.

HOW TO SELL YOUR PHOTOGRAPHS & ILLUSTRATIONS. By Elliott & Barbara Gordon. North Light Books, 1990.

HOW TO WRITE A CHILDREN'S BOOK & GET IT PUBLISHED. By Barbara Seuling. Charles Scribner's Sons, 1991.

HOW TO WRITE AND ILLUSTRATE CHILDREN'S BOOKS. Treld Pelkey Bicknell and Felicity Trotman, editors. North Light Books, 1988.

HOW TO WRITE AND SELL CHILDREN'S PICTURE BOOKS. By Jean E. Karl. Writer's Digest Books, 1994.

HOW TO WRITE, ILLUSTRATE, AND DESIGN CHILDREN'S BOOKS. By Frieda Gates. Lloyd-Simone Publishing Company, 1986.

MARKET GUIDE FOR YOUNG WRITERS. By Kathy Henderson. Writer's Digest Books, 1993.

THE WRITER'S ESSENTIAL DESK REFERENCE. Glenda Tennant Neff, editor. Writer's Digest Books, 1991.

A WRITER'S GUIDE TO A CHILDREN'S BOOK CONTRACT. By Mary Flower. Fern Hill Books, 1988.

WRITING BOOKS FOR YOUNG PEOPLE. By James Cross Giblin. The Writer, Inc., 1990.

WRITING FOR CHILDREN & TEENAGERS. By Lee Wyndham and Arnold Madison. Writer's Digest Books, 1985.

WRITING WITH PICTURES: HOW TO WRITE AND ILLUSTRATE CHILDREN'S BOOKS. By Uri Shulevitz. Watson-Guptill Publications, 1985.

Publications

BILLBOARD. Timothy White, editor-in-chief. 1515 Broadway, New York NY 10036. *Weekly music industry trade publication covering children's audio and video in biweekly "Child's Play" column. Subscription: $239/year. Available on newsstands for $4.95/issue.*

BOOK LINKS. Barbara Elleman, editor. American Library Association, 50 E. Huron St., Chicago IL 60611. *Magazine published six times a year (September-July) for the purpose of connecting books, libraries and classrooms. Features articles on specific topics followed by bibliographies recommending books for further information. Subscription: $20/year.*

CHILDREN'S BOOK INSIDER. Laura Backes, editor. P.O. Box 1030, Fairplay CO 80440-1030. E-mail: JB58@aol.com. *Monthly newsletter covering markets, techniques, and trends in children's publishing. Subscription: $34/year.*

CHILDREN'S WRITER. Susan Tierney, editor. The Institute of Children's Literature, 95 Long Ridge Rd., West Redding CT 06896-1124. *Monthly newsletter of writing and publishing trends in the children's field. Subscription: $24/year.*

THE FIVE OWLS. Susan Stan, editor. Hamline University Crossroads Center, MS-C1924, 1536 Hewitt Ave., St. Paul MN 55104. *Bimonthly newsletter for readers personally and professionally involved in children's literature. Subscription: $20/year.*

THE HORN BOOK MAGAZINE. Anita Silvey, editor. The Horn Book, Inc., 11 Beacon St., Suite 1000, Boston MA 02108. *Bimonthly guide to the children's book world including views on the industry and reviews of the latest books. Subscription: $35/year.*

THE LION AND THE UNICORN: A CRITICAL JOURNAL OF CHILDREN'S LITERATURE. Jack Zipes and Louisa Smith, editors. The Johns Hopkins University Press—Journals Publishing Division, 2175 N. Charles St., Baltimore MD 21218-4319. *Biannual publication serving as a forum for discussion of children's literature featuring interviews with authors, editors and experts in the field. Subscription: $19.50/year.*

ONCE UPON A TIME . . . . Audrey Baird, editor. 553 Winston Court, St. Paul MN 55118. *Quarterly magazine for children's writers and illustrators and those interested in children's literature. Subscription: $17.50/year.*

PUBLISHERS WEEKLY. Nora Rawlinson, editor-in-chief. Bowker Magazine Group, Cahners Publishing Co., 249 W. 17th St., New York NY 10011. *Weekly trade publication covering all aspects of the publishing industry; includes coverage of the children's field (books, audio and video) and spring and fall issues devoted solely to children's books. Subscription: $139/year. Available on newsstands for $3/issue. (Special issues are higher in price.)*

SOCIETY OF CHILDREN'S BOOK WRITERS AND ILLUSTRATORS BULLETIN. Stephen Mooser and Lin Oliver, editors. Society of Children's Book Writers and Illustrators, 22736 Vanowen St., Suite 106, West Hills CA 91307. *Bimonthly organizational newsletter of SCBWI covering news of interest to members. Subscription with $40/year membership.*

Glossary

Advance. A sum of money a publisher pays a writer or illustrator prior to the publication of a book. It is usually paid in installments, such as one half on signing the contract; one half on delivery of a complete and satisfactory manuscript. The advance is paid against the royalty money that will be earned by the book.

All rights. The rights contracted to a publisher permitting the use of material anywhere and in any form, including movie and book club sales, without additional payment to the creator.

Anthropomorphization. The act of attributing human form and personality to things not human (such as animals).

ASAP. As soon as possible.

ASCAP. American Society of Composers, Authors and Publishers. A performing rights organization.

B&W. Black & white.

Backlist. A publisher's list of books not published during the current season but still in print.

Biennially. Occurring once every two years.

Bimonthly. Occurring once every two months.

Biweekly. Occurring once every two weeks.

BMI. Broadcast Music, Inc. A performing rights organization.

Book packager. A company which draws all elements of a book together, from the initial concept to writing and marketing strategies, then sells the book package to a book publisher and/or movie producer. Also known as book producer or book developer.

Business-size envelope. Also known as a #10 envelope. The standard size used in sending business correspondence.

Camera-ready. Refers to art that is completely prepared for copy camera platemaking.

Caption. A description of the subject matter of an illustration or photograph; photo captions include persons' names where appropriate. Also called cutline.

CD-ROM. Compact disc read-only memory. Non-erasable electronic medium used for digitalized image and document storage.

Clean-copy. A manuscript free of errors and needing no editing; it is ready for typesetting.

Concept books. Books that deal with issues, problems and concerns facing young people, such as divorce, birth of a sibling, friendship, moving, or the death of a family member.

Contract. A written agreement stating the rights to be purchased by an editor, art director or producer and the amount of payment the writer, illustrator or photographer will receive for that sale.

Contributor's copies. The magazine issues sent to an author, illustrator or photographer in which her work appears.

Copy. The actual written material of a manuscript.

Copyediting. Editing a manuscript for grammar usage, spelling, punctuation and general style.

Copyright. A means to legally protect an author's/illustrator's/photographer's work. This can be shown by writing ©, the creator's name, and year of work's creation.

Cover letter. A brief letter, accompanying a complete manuscript, especially useful if responding to an editor's request for a manuscript. May also accompany a book proposal. (See The Business of Children's Writing & Illustrating.)

Cutline. See caption.

Division. An unincorporated branch of a company.

Dummy. Handmade mock-up of a book.

E-mail. Electronic mail. Messages sent from one computer to another via a modem or computer network.

Final draft. The last version of a polished manuscript ready for submission to an editor.

First North American serial rights. The right to publish material in a periodical before it appears in book form, for the first time, in the United States or Canada.

Flat fee. A one-time payment.

Galleys. The first typeset version of a manuscript that has not yet been divided into pages.

Genre. A formulaic type of fiction, such as horror, mystery, romance, science fiction or western.

Glossy. A photograph with a shiny surface as opposed to one with a non-shiny matte finish.

Gouache. Opaque watercolor with an appreciable film thickness and an actual paint layer.

Halftone. Reproduction of a continuous tone illustration with the image formed by dots produced by a camera lens screen.

Hard copy. The printed copy of a computer's output.

Hi-Lo. High interest, low reading level. Pertains mostly to books for beginning adult readers.

Imprint. Name applied to a publisher's specific line of books.

IRC. International Reply Coupon. Sold at the post office to enclose with text or artwork sent to a foreign buyer to cover his postage cost when replying or returning work.

Keyline. Identification, through signs and symbols, of the positions of illustrations and copy for the printer.

Kill fee. Portion of the agreed-upon price the author or artist receives for a job that was assigned and worked on, but then canceled.

Layout. Arrangement of illustrations, photographs, text and headlines for printed material.

Line drawing. Illustration done with pencil or ink using no wash or other shading.

Mechanicals. Paste-up or preparation of work for printing.

Middle reader. The general classification of books written for readers ages 9-11.

Modem. A small electrical box that plugs into the serial card of a computer, used to transmit data from one computer to another, usually via telephone lines.

Ms (mss). Manuscript(s).

One-time rights. Permission to publish a story in periodical or book form one time only.

Outline. A summary of a book's contents in 5-15 double-spaced pages; often in the form of chapter headings with a descriptive sentence or two under each heading to show the scope of the book.

Package sale. The sale of a manuscript and illustrations/photos as a "package" paid for with one check.

Payment on acceptance. The writer, artist or photographer is paid for her work at the time the editor or art director decides to buy it.

Payment on publication. The writer, artist or photographer is paid for her work when it is published.

Photostat. Black & white copies produced by an inexpensive photographic process using paper negatives; only line values are held with accuracy. Also called stat.

Picture book. A type of book aimed at preschoolers to 8-year-olds that tells a story primarily or entirely with artwork.

PMT. Photomechanical transfer. Photostat produced without a negative, somewhat like the Polaroid process.

Print. An impression pulled from an original plate, stone, block, screen or negative; also a positive made from a photographic negative.

Production house. A film company which creates video material including animation, special effects, graphics, filmstrips, slides, live action and documentaries.

Proofreading. Reading a manuscript to correct typographical errors.

Query. A letter to an editor designed to capture his interest in an article or book you propose to write.

Reading fee. An arbitrary amount of money charged by some agents and publishers to read a submitted manuscript.

Reprint rights. Permission to print an already published work whose first rights have been sold to another magazine or book publisher.

Response time. The average length of time it takes an editor or art director to accept or reject a query or submission and inform the creator of the decision.

Rights. What are offered to an editor or art director in exchange for printing a manuscript, artwork or photographs.

Rough draft. A manuscript which has been written but not checked for errors in grammar, punctuation, spelling or content. It usually needs revision.

Roughs. Preliminary sketches or drawings.

Royalty. An agreed percentage paid by a publisher to a writer, illustrator or photographer for each copy of her work sold.

SASE. Self-addressed, stamped envelope.

SCBWI. Society of Children's Book Writers and Illustrators.

Second serial rights. Permission for the reprinting of a work in another periodical after its first publication in book or magazine form.

Semiannual. Occurring once every six months.

Semimonthly. Occurring twice a month.

Semiweekly. Occurring twice a week.

Serial rights. The rights given by an author to a publisher to print a piece in one or more periodicals.

Simultaneous submissions. Material sent to several publishers at the same time. (Some publishers refuse to consider such submissions. Simultaneous submissions should not be made without stating so in your cover letter.)

Slant. The approach to a story or piece of artwork that will appeal to readers of a particular publication.

Slush pile. Editors' term for their collections of unsolicited manuscripts.

SOCAN. Society of Composers, Authors and Music Publishers of Canada. A performing rights organization.

Software. Programs and related documentation for use with a particular computer system.

Solicited manuscript. Material which an editor has asked for or agreed to consider before being sent by a writer.

Speculation (Spec). Creating a piece with no assurance from the editor or art director that it will be purchased or any reimbursements for material or labor paid.

Stat. See photostat.

Subsidiary rights. All rights other than book publishing rights included in a book contract, such as paperback, book club and movie rights.

Subsidy publisher. A book publisher which charges the author for the cost of typesetting, printing and promoting a book. Also called a vanity publisher.

Synopsis. A brief summary of a story or novel. Usually a page to a page and a half, single-spaced, if part of a book proposal.

Tabloid. Publication printed on an ordinary newspaper page turned sideways and folded in half.

Tearsheet. Page from a magazine or newspaper containing your printed art, story, article, poem or photo.

Thumbnail. A rough layout in miniature.

Transparencies. Positive color slides; not color prints.

Unsolicited manuscript. Material sent without an editor's or art director's knowledge or consent.

Vanity publisher. See subsidy publisher.

Word processor. A computer that produces typewritten copy via automated typing, text-editing, and storage and transmission capabilities.

Young adult. The general classification of books written for readers ages 12-18.

Young reader. The general classification of books written for readers ages 5-8.

For important market listing information and explanations of symbols used throughout Children's Writer's & Illustrator's Market, *see page 39.*

Age-Level Index

This index is designed to help you more quickly locate book and magazine markets geared to the age-group(s) for which you write, illustrate or take photos. Read each listing carefully and follow the publishers' specific information about the type(s) of manuscript(s) each prefers and the style(s) of artwork and photos each wishes to review. Use this index in conjunction with the Subject Index to further hone your list of possible markets.

Book Publishers

Picture books (preschoolers to 8-year-olds). ABC, All Books for Children 43; Advocacy Press 44; Aegina Press/University Editions 44; Africa World Press 45; African American Images 45; Aladdin Paperbacks 45; Alyson Publications, Inc. 45; American Bible Society 49; American Education Publishing 49; Andersen Press Limited 50; Arcade Pubilshing 50; Atheneum Books for Young Readers 51; Augsburg Fortress, Publishers 51; Bantam Doubleday Dell 53; Barrons Educational Series 54; Behrman House Inc. 55; Bess Press 56; Boyds Mills Press 57; Candlewick Press 59; Carolina Wren Press/Lollipop Power Books 59; Carolrhoda Books, Inc. 60; Chariot Books 61; Charlesbridge 61; Children's Book Press 65; Children's Library Press 65; Childrens Press 65; China Books 66; Chronicle Books 67; Clarion Books 68; Cobblehill Books 68; Concordia Publishing House 69; Cool Kids Press 69; Crocodile Books, USA 70; Crocodile Creek Press/European Toy Collection 70; Crossway Books 71; Crown Publishers (Crown Books for Children) 71; CSS Publishing 71; Dawn Publications 73; Dial Books for Young Readers 73; Dimi Press 74; Distinctive Publishing Corp. 76; Dorling Kindersley, Inc. 77; Down East Books 77; Dutton Children's Books 78; Eakin Press 78; Eerdmans Publishing Company, Wm. B. 78; Falcon Press Publishing Co. 79; Farrar, Straus & Giroux 80; Fitzhenry & Whiteside Ltd. 81; Friendship Press, Inc. 83; Geringer Books, Laura 83; Gibbs Smith, Publisher 84; Godine, Publisher, David R. 85; Golden Books 85; Greenwillow Books 86; Grosset & Dunlap, Inc. 86; Harcourt Brace & Co. 87; HarperCollins Children's Books 88; Harvest House Publishers 89; Hendrick-Long Publishing Company 89; Holiday House Inc. 90; Holt & Co., Inc., Henry 91; Homestead Publishing 91; Houghton Mifflin Co. 91; Huntington House Publishers 92; Hyperion Books for Children 93; Hyperion Press Limited 93; Ideals Children's Books 93; Jalmar Press 94; Jewish Lights Publishing 95; Jewish Publication Society 96; Just Us Books, Inc. 97; Kabel Publishers 97; Kar-Ben Copies, Inc. 98; Knopf Books for Young Readers 99; Kruza Kaleidoscopix, Inc. 99; Laredo Publishing Co. Inc. 102; Lee & Low Books, Inc. 102; Little, Brown and Company 104; Lodestar Books 105; Lucas/Evans Books Inc. 106; Lucky Books 107; McElderry Books, Margaret K. 108; Mage Publishers Inc. 109; Magination Press 109; Meadowbrook Press 110; Metamorphous Press 110; Millbrook Press, The 111; Morehouse Publishing Co. 112; Morris Publishing, Joshua 112; Northland Publishing 114; NorthWord Press, Inc. 114; Open Hand Publishing Inc. 115; Orca Book Publishers 118; Orchard Books 119; Our Child Press 119; Owen Publishers, Inc., Richard C. 119; Pacific Press 120; Parenting Press, Inc. 121; Paulist Press 122; Pavilion Books Ltd. 123; Peachtree Publishers, Ltd. 123; Pelican Publishing Co. Inc. 124; Perspectives Press 124; Philomel Books 125; Pippin Press 125; Polychrome Publishing Corporation 127; Preservation Press, The 128; Price Stern Sloan, Inc. 128; Prometheus Books 130; Pumpkin Press Publishing House/A Way to Grow 130; Putnam's Sons, G.P. 130; Questar Publishers, Inc. 131; Random House Books for Young Readers 131; Read'n Run Books 132; Rosebrier Publishing Co. 133; Sadlier, Inc., William H. 134; St. Paul Books and Media 134; Sasquatch Books 135; Scientific American Books for Young Readers 135; Shoestring Press 137; Silver Moon Press 138; Simon & Schuster Books for Young Readers 139; Soundprints 139; Speech Bin, Inc., The 140; Standard Publishing 141; Starburst Publishers 141; Stemmer House Publishers, Inc. 141; The Summit Publishing Group, The 142; Sunbelt Media, Inc./Eakin Press 143; Sundance Publishers & Distributors 143; Tab Books 144; Transworld Publishers Limited 147; Tricycle Press 147; Troll Associates 148; Trophy Books 148; Tyndale House Publishers, Inc. 149; University Classics, Ltd. Publishers 149; University Editions, Inc. 149; Usborne Publishing Ltd. 150; Victor Books 150; Walker And Co. 152; Waterfront Books 153; Whispering Coyote Press, Inc. 154; Whitebird Books 154; Whitman & Company, Albert 154; Willowisp Press 156; Winston-Derek Publishers, Inc. 157; Women's Press 157; Woodbine House 158; Zino Press Children's Book 158

Young readers (5- to 8-year-olds). ABC, All Books for Children 43; Advocacy Press 44; Aegina Press/University Editions 44; Africa World Press 45; African American Images 45; Aladdin Paperbacks 45; Alyson Publications, Inc. 45; American Bible Society 49; American Education Publishing 49; Andersen Press Limited 50; Arcade Pubilshing 50; Atheneum Books for Young Readers 51; Augsburg Fortress, Publishers 51; Bantam Doubleday Dell 53; Barrons Educational Series 54; Behrman House Inc. 55; Bess Press 56; Bethany House Publishers 56; Bethel Publishing 57; Boyds Mills Press 57; Bright Ring Publishing 58; Candlewick Press 59; Carolina Wren Press/Lollipop Power Books 59; Carolrhoda Books, Inc. 60; Chariot Books 61;

Chicago Review Press 64; Childrens Press 65; China Books 66; Chronicle Books 67; Clarion Books 68; Cobblehill Books 68; Concordia Publishing House 69; Cool Kids Press 69; Coteau Books Ltd. 70; Crocodile Creek Press/European Toy Collection 70; Crossway Books 71; Crown Publishers (Crown Books for Children) 71; CSS Publishing 71; Dawn Publications 73; Denison Co. Inc., T.S. 73; Dial Books for Young Readers 73; Dimi Press 74; Discovery Enterprises, Ltd. 74; Distinctive Publishing Corp. 76; Dorling Kindersley, Inc. 77; Down East Books 77; Dutton Children's Books 78; Eakin Press 78; Eerdmans Publishing Company, Wm. B. 78; Enslow Publishers Inc. 79; Falcon Press Publishing Co. 79; Farrar, Straus & Giroux 80; Fitzhenry & Whiteside Ltd. 81; Franklin Watts 81; Free Spirit Publishing 82; Friendship Press, Inc. 83; Geringer Books, Laura 83; Gibbs Smith, Publisher 84; Godine, Publisher, David R. 85; Golden Books 85; Greenwillow Books 86; Grosset & Dunlap, Inc. 86; Harcourt Brace & Co. 87; HarperCollins Children's Books 88; Harvest House Publishers 89; Hendrick-Long Publishing Company 89; Herald Press 89; Holiday House Inc. 90; Holt & Co., Inc., Henry 91; Homestead Publishing 91; Houghton Mifflin Co. 91; Huntington House Publishers 92; Hyperion Books for Children 93; Hyperion Press Limited 93; Ideals Children's Books 93; Incentive Publications, Inc. 94; Jalmar Press 94; Jewish Lights Publishing 95; Jewish Publication Society 96; Jones University Press/Light Line Books, Bob 96; Just Us Books, Inc. 97; Kabel Publishers 97; Kar-Ben Copies, Inc. 98; Knopf Books for Young Readers 99; Kruza Kaleidoscopix, Inc. 99; Laredo Publishing Co. Inc. 102; Little, Brown and Company 104; Lodestar Books 105; Look and See Publications 106; Lucas/Evans Books Inc. 106; Lucky Books 107; McElderry Books, Margaret K. 108; Magination Press 109; Marlor Press, Inc. 109; Meadowbrook Press 110; Metamorphous Press 110; Millbrook Press, The 111; Morehouse Publishing Co. 112; Morris Publishing, Joshua 112; Northland Publishing 114; NorthWord Press, Inc. 114; Open Hand Publishing Inc. 115; Orca Book Publishers 118; Orchard Books 119; Our Child Press 119; Owen Publishers, Inc., Richard C. 119; Pacific Press 120; Parenting Press, Inc. 121; Paulist Press 122; Pavilion Books Ltd. 123; Peachtree Publishers, Ltd. 123; Peartree 123; Pelican Publishing Co. Inc. 124; Perspectives Press 124; Philomel Books 125; Pippin Press 125; Planet Dexter 126; Players Press, Inc. 126; Polychrome Publishing Corporation 127; Preservation Press, The 128; Price Stern Sloan, Inc. 128; Prometheus Books 130; Pumpkin Press Publishing House/A Way to Grow 130; Putnam's Sons, G.P. 130; Questar Publishers, Inc. 131; Random House Books for Young Readers 131; Read'n Run Books 132; Rizzoli Books For Children 133; Rosebrier Publishing Co. 133; Sadlier, Inc., William H. 134; St. Paul Books and Media 134; Sasquatch Books 135; Scientific American Books for Young Readers 135; Seacoast Publications of New England 136; Seedling Publications, Inc. 137; Shoestring Press 137; Silver Moon Press 138; Simon & Schuster Books for Young Readers 139; Speech Bin, Inc., The 140; Standard Publishing 141; Starburst Publishers 141; Stemmer House Publishers, Inc. 141; Summit Publishing Group, The 142; Sunbelt Media, Inc./Eakin Press 143; Sundance Publishers & Distributors 143; Tab Books 144; Transworld Publishers Limited 147; Tricycle Press 147; Troll Associates 148; Trophy Books 148; Tyndale House Publishers, Inc. 149; University Classics, Ltd. Publishers 149; University Editions, Inc. 149; Usborne Publishing Ltd. 150; Victor Books 150; Victory Publishing 151; W.W. Publications 151; Walker And Co. 152; Waterfront Books 153; Weigl Educational Publishers 153; Weiss Associates, Inc., Daniel 154; Whitman & Company, Albert 154; Williamson Publishing Co. 155; Willowisp Press 156; Winston-Derek Publishers, Inc. 157; Women's Press 157; Woodbine House 158; Zino Press Children's Book 158

Middle readers (9- to 11-year-olds). ABC, All Books for Children 43; Advocacy Press 44; Aegina Press/University Editions 44; Africa World Press 45; African American Images 45; Aladdin Paperbacks 45; Alyson Publications, Inc. 45; American Bible Society 49; Andersen Press Limited 50; Arcade Pubilshing 50; Archway/Minstrel Books 50; Atheneum Books for Young Readers 51; Augsburg Fortress, Publishers 51; Avon Books 52; B&B Publishing, Inc. 53; Bantam Doubleday Dell 53; Barrons Educational Series 54; Beautiful American Publishing Company 54; Behrman House Inc. 55; Bess Press 56; Bethany House Publishers 56; Bethel Publishing 57; Blue Heron Publishing, Inc. 57; Boyds Mills Press 57; Bright Ring Publishing 58; Cambridge Educational 59; Candlewick Press 59; Carolrhoda Books, Inc. 60; Chariot Books 61; Chelsea House Publishers 64; Chicago Review Press 64; Childrens Press 65; China Books 66; Chronicle Books 67; Clarion Books 68; Clear Light Publishers 68; Cobblehill Books 68; Concordia Publishing House 69; Cool Kids Press 69; Coteau Books Ltd. 70; Crossway Books 71; Crown Publishers (Crown Books for Children) 71; CSS Publishing 71; Davis Pubilcations, Inc. 72; Dawn Publications 73; Denison Co. Inc., T.S. 73; Dial Books for Young Readers 73; Dimi Press 74; Discovery Enterprises, Ltd. 74; Distinctive Publishing Corp. 76; Down East Books 77; Dutton Children's Books 78; E.M. Press, Inc. 78; Eakin Press 78; Eerdmans Publishing Company, Wm. B. 78; Enslow Publishers Inc. 79; Facts on File 79; Falcon Press Publishing Co. 79; Farrar, Straus & Giroux 80; Fawcett Juniper 80; Fiesta City Publishers 80; Fitzhenry & Whiteside Ltd. 81; Franklin Watts 81; Free Spirit Publishing 82; Friendship Press, Inc. 83; Geringer Books, Laura 83; Gibbs Smith, Publisher 84; Godine, Publisher, David R. 85; Golden Books 85; Greenhaven Press 86; Greenwillow Books 86; Grosset & Dunlap, Inc. 86; Harcourt Brace & Co. 87; HarperCollins Children's Books 88; Harvest House Publishers 89; Hendrick-Long Publishing Company 89; Herald Press 89; Holiday House Inc. 90; Holt & Co., Inc., Henry 91; Homestead Publishing 91; Houghton Mifflin Co. 91; Huntington House Publishers 92; Hyperion Books for Children 93; Incentive Publications, Inc. 94; Jalmar Press 94; Jewish Publication Society 96; Jones University Press/Light Line Books, Bob 96; Just Us Books, Inc. 97; Kabel Publishers 97; Kar-Ben Copies, Inc. 98; Knopf Books for Young Readers 99; Kruza Kaleidoscopix, Inc. 99; Laredo Publishing Co. Inc. 102; Little, Brown and Company 104; Lodestar Books 105; Look and See Publications 106; Lorimer & Co., James 106; Lucas/Evans Books Inc. 106; Lucent Books 107; Lucky Books 107; McElderry Books, Margaret K. 108; Marlor Press, Inc. 109; Meadowbrook Press 110; Metamorphous Press 110; Milkweed Editions 111; Millbrook Press, The 111; Misty Hill Press 112; Morehouse Publishing Co. 112; Morris Publishing, Joshua 112; Muir Publications, Inc, John 113; Open Hand Publishing Inc. 115; Orca Book Publishers 118; Orchard Books 119; Our Child Press 119; Pacific Press 120; Pando Publications 121; Parenting

Press, Inc. 121; Paulist Press 122; Pavilion Books Ltd. 123; Peachtree Publishers, Ltd. 123; Peartree 123; Pelican Publishing Co. Inc. 124; Philomel Books 125; Pippin Press 125; Planet Dexter 126; Players Press, Inc. 126; Pocahontas Press, Inc. 127; Polychrome Publishing Corporation 127; Preservation Press, The 128; Press of Macdonald & Reinecke, The 128; Price Stern Sloan, Inc. 128; Prometheus Books 130; Pumpkin Press Publishing House/A Way to Grow 130; Putnam's Sons, G.P. 130; Questar Publishers, Inc. 131; Random House Books for Young Readers 131; Read'n Run Books 132; Rizzoli Books For Children 133; Rosebrier Publishing Co. 133; Sadlier, Inc., William H. 134; St. Anthony Messenger Press 134; St. Paul Books and Media 134; Scientific American Books for Young Readers 135; Seacoast Publications of New England 136; Seedling Publications, Inc. 137; Shoestring Press 137; Silver Moon Press 138; Simon & Schuster Books for Young Readers 139; Speech Bin, Inc., The 140; Standard Publishing 141; Starburst Publishers 141; Stemmer House Publishers, Inc. 141; Sterling Publishing Co., Inc. 142; Summit Publishing Group, The 142; Sunbelt Media, Inc./Eakin Press 143; Sundance Publishers & Distributors 143; Tab Books 144; Thistledown Press Ltd. 145; Transworld Publishers Limited 147; Tricycle Press 147; Troll Associates 148; Trophy Books 148; Tudor Publishers, Inc. 148; Tyndale House Publishers, Inc. 149; University Classics, Ltd. Publishers 149; University Editions, Inc. 149; Usborne Publishing Ltd. 150; Victor Books 150; Victory Publishing 151; W.W. Publications 151; Walker And Co. 152; Ward Hill Press 152; Waterfront Books 153; Weigl Educational Publishers 153; Weiss Associates, Inc., Daniel 154; Whitman & Company, Albert 154; Wiley & Sons, Inc., John 155; Willowisp Press 156; Winston-Derek Publishers, Inc. 157; Women's Press 157; Woodbine House 158; Zino Press Children's Book 158

Young adults (ages 12 and up). Aegina Press/University Editions 44; Africa World Press 45; African American Images 45; Aladdin Paperbacks 45; Alyson Publications, Inc. 45; American Bible Society 49; Andersen Press Limited 50; Arcade Pubilshing 50; Archway/Minstrel Books 50; Atheneum Books for Young Readers 51; Augsburg Fortress, Publishers 51; Avon Books 52; Bandanna Books 52; B&B Publishing, Inc. 53; Bantam Doubleday Dell 53; Barrons Educational Series 54; Behrman House Inc. 55; Berkley Publishing Group 55; Bess Press 56; Bethany House Publishers 56; Bethel Publishing 57; Blue Heron Publishing, Inc. 57; Boyds Mills Press 57; Cambridge Educational 59; Candlewick Press 59; Chariot Books 61; Chelsea House Publishers 64; Chicago Review Press 64; Childrens Press 65; Clarion Books 68; Clear Light Publishers 68; Cobblehill Books 68; Concordia Publishing House 69; Cool Kids Press 69; Crossway Books 71; CSS Publishing 71; Davenport, Publishers, May 72; Davis Pubilcations, Inc. 72; Dawn Publications 73; Dial Books for Young Readers 73; Dimi Press 74; Discovery Enterprises, Ltd. 74; Distinctive Publishing Corp. 76; Down East Books 77; Dutton Children's Books 78; E.M. Press, Inc. 78; Eakin Press 78; Eerdmans Publishing Company, Wm. B. 78; Enslow Publishers Inc. 79; Facts on File 79; Farrar, Straus & Giroux 80; Fawcett Juniper 80; Fiesta City Publishers 80; Fitzhenry & Whiteside Ltd. 81; Franklin Watts 81; Free Spirit Publishing 82; Friendship Press, Inc. 83; Geringer Books, Laura 83; Globe Fearon Educational Publisher 84; Greenhaven Press 86; Greenwillow Books 86; Grosset & Dunlap, Inc. 86; Harcourt Brace & Co. 87; HarperCollins Children's Books 88; Harvest House Publishers 89; Hendrick-Long Publishing Company 89; Herald Press 89; Hi-Time Publishing Corporation 90; Holiday House Inc. 90; Holt & Co., Inc., Henry 91; Homestead Publishing 91; Houghton Mifflin Co. 91; Hunter House Publishers 92; Huntington House Publishers 92; Hyperion Books for Children 93; Incentive Publications, Inc. 94; Jalmar Press 94; Jewish Publication Society 96; Jones University Press/Light Line Books, Bob 96; Kabel Publishers 97; Knopf Books for Young Readers 99; Lion Books, Publisher 104; Little, Brown and Company 104; Lodestar Books 105; Lorimer & Co., James 106; Lucas/Evans Books Inc. 106; Lucent Books 107; McElderry Books, Margaret K. 108; Metamorphous Press 110; Milkweed Editions 111; Millbrook Press, The 111; Misty Hill Press 112; Morehouse Publishing Co. 112; Naturegraph Publisher, Inc. 114; Open Hand Publishing Inc. 115; Orca Book Publishers 118; Orchard Books 119; Our Child Press 119; Pacific Press 120; Pando Publications 121; Paulist Press 122; Pavilion Books Ltd. 123; Peachtree Publishers, Ltd. 123; Pelican Publishing Co. Inc. 124; Philomel Books 125; Players Press, Inc. 126; Pocahontas Press, Inc. 127; Polychrome Publishing Corporation 127; Preservation Press, The 128; Press of Macdonald & Reinecke, The 128; Price Stern Sloan, Inc. 128; Prometheus Books 130; Pumpkin Press Publishing House/A Way to Grow 130; Putnam's Sons, G.P. 130; Questar Publishers, Inc. 131; Read'n Run Books 132; Rizzoli Books For Children 133; Rosen Publishing Group, The 133; Sadlier, Inc., William H. 134; St. Anthony Messenger Press 134; St. Paul Books and Media 134; Scientific American Books for Young Readers 135; Shaw Publishers, Harold 137; Shoestring Press 137; Silver Moon Press 138; Simon & Schuster Books for Young Readers 139; Speech Bin, Inc., The 140; Standard Publishing 141; Starburst Publishers 141; Summit Publishing Group, The 142; Sunbelt Media, Inc./Eakin Press 143; Sundance Publishers & Distributors 143; Tab Books 144; Texas Christian University Press 144; Thistledown Press Ltd. 145; Titan Books 146; Tricycle Press 147; Troll Associates 148; Trophy Books 148; Tudor Publishers, Inc. 148; University Classics, Ltd. Publishers 149; University Editions, Inc. 149; Usborne Publishing Ltd. 150; W.W. Publications 151; Walker And Co. 152; Ward Hill Press 152; Waterfront Books 153; Weigl Educational Publishers 153; Weiss Associates, Inc., Daniel 154; Wiley & Sons, Inc., John 155; Willowisp Press 156; Winston-Derek Publishers, Inc. 157; Women's Press 157; Woodbine House 158

Magazines

Picture-oriented material (preschoolers to 8-year-olds). Animal Trails 163; Appalachian Bride 164; Bread for God's Children 166; Cemetery Plot 167; Chickadee 168; Cochran's Corner 174; Focus on the Family Clubhouse; Focus on the Family Clubhouse Jr. 181; Friend Magazine, The 183; Highlights for Children 186; Hob-Nob 186; Humpty Dumpty's Magazine 191; Ladybug, the Magazine for Young Children 194; National Geographic World 198; Nature Friend Magazine 199; Science Weekly 208; Scienceland 208; Skipping Stones 210; Sleuth 211; Story Friends 213; Together Time 217; Turtle Magazine 219; Young Christian 222

Young readers (5- to 8-year-olds). Animal Trails 163; Appalachian Bride 164; ASPCA Animal Watch 164; Atalantik 164; Bread for God's Children 166; Cemetery Plot 167; Chickadee 168; Children's Playmate 172; Cochran's Corner 174; Discoveries 177; DynaMath 178; Focus on the Family Clubhouse; Focus on the Family Clubhouse Jr. 181; Friend Magazine, The 183; Highlights for Children 186; Hob-Nob 186; Hodgepodge 189; Home Altar, The 190; Hopscotch 190; Humpty Dumpty's Magazine 191; Jack and Jill 192; Kid City 194; Kids Copy 194; Lighthouse 195; My Friend 197; Nature Friend Magazine 199; Pockets 202; Primary Days 203; Racing for Kids 203; School Mates 205; Science Weekly 208; Scienceland 208; Single Parent, The 209; Skipping Stones 210; Sleuth 211; Soccer Jr. 211; Spider 211; Story Friends 213; Straight 213; U.S. Kids 220; Wonder Time 222; Young Christian 222

Middle readers (9- to 11-year-olds). Advocate, The 162; American Girl 163; Animal Trails 163; Appalachian Bride 164; ASPCA Animal Watch 164; Atalantik 164; Boys' Life 165; Bread for God's Children 166; Calliope 166; Cemetery Plot 167; Child Life 169; Children's Digest 169; Clubhouse 173; Cobblestone 173; Cochran's Corner 174; Counselor 174; Cricket Magazine 175; Crusader 176; Current Health I 176; Discoveries 177; Disney Adventures 177; Dolphin Log 178; DynaMath 178; Faces 179; Falcon Magazine 180; Field & Stream 180; Focus on the Family Clubhouse; Focus on the Family Clubhouse Jr. 181; Friend Magazine, The 183; Goldfinch, The 184; Guide Magazine 184; Guideposts for Kids 185; High Adventure 185; Highlights for Children 186; Hob-Nob 186; Home Altar, The 190; Hopscotch 190; Jack and Jill 192; Junior Scholastic 192; Junior Trails 192; Kid City 194; Kids Copy 194; Lighthouse 195; Magic Realism 197; My Friend 197; National Geographic World 198; Nature Friend Magazine 199; Odyssey 199; On the Line 201; Owl Magazine 201; Pockets 202; Power and Light 202; Racing for Kids 203; R-A-D-A-R 204; Ranger Rick 204; School Mates 205; Science Weekly 208; Shofar 209; Single Parent, The 209; Skipping Stones 210; Sleuth 211; Soccer Jr. 211; Superscience Blue 214; 3-2-1 Contact 217; Touch 218; U.S. Kids 220; Venture 220; Young Christian 222

Young adults (ages 12 and up). Advocate, The 162; Aim Magazine 162; Animal Trails 163; Appalachian Bride 164; Atalantik 164; Bread for God's Children 166; Calliope 166; Career World 167; Careers and Colleges 167; Cemetery Plot 167; Challenge 168; Clubhouse 173; Cobblestone 173; Cochran's Corner 174; Cricket Magazine 175; Crusader 176; Current Health II 176; Dolphin Log 178; DynaMath 178; Exploring 178; Faces 179; FFA New Horizons 180; For Seniors Only 182; FreeWay 183; Guide Magazine 184; High Adventure 185; Hob-Nob 186; Hobson's Choice 188; International Gymnast 191; Junior Scholastic 192; Lighthouse 195; Listen 195; Magic Realism 197; National Geographic World 198; Nature Friend Magazine 199; New Era Magazine 199; Odyssey 199; On Course 200; On The Line 200; Owl Magazine 201; Racing for Kids 203; Scholastic Math Magazine 205; School Mates 205; Science Weekly 208; Seventeen Magazine 208; Sharing the Victory 209; Single Parent, The 209; Skipping Stones 210; Sleuth 211; Soccer Jr. 211; Student Leadership Journal 214; Teen Life 215; 'Teen Magazine 215; Teen Power 216; Teenage Christian Magazine 216; 3-2-1 Contact 217; Touch 218; 2 Hype/Hype Hair 219; With 221; Young Christian 222; Young Salvationist 223; Youth Update 223

Subject Index

Use this index to more quickly locate the book and magazine publishers seeking the fiction and nonfiction subjects you write about, illustrate or photograph. Read each listing carefully and follow the publishers' specific information about the type(s) of manuscript(s) each prefers and the style(s) of artwork and photos each wishes to review. Use this index in conjunction with the Age-Level Index to further hone your list of possible markets.

Book Publishers: Fiction

Adventure. ABC, All Books for Children 43; Aegina Press/University Editions 44; Africa World Press 45; American Education Publishing 49; Andersen Press Limited 50; Archway/Minstrel Books 50; Avon Books 52; Bantam Doubleday Dell 53; Barrons Educational Series 54; Bess Press 56; Bethany House Publishers 56; Bethel Publishing 57; Blue Heron Publishing, Inc. 57; Boyds Mills Press 57; Candlewick Press 59; Children's Library Press 65; Childrens Press 65; Clarion Books 68; Cobblehill Books 68; Cool Kids Press 69; Crocodile Creek Press/European Toy Collection 70; Crossway Books 71; Dawn Publications 73; Dial Books for Young Readers 73; Dimi Press 74; Distinctive Publishing Corp. 76; Dorling Kindersley, Inc. 77; Down East Books 77; Dutton Children's Books 78; E.M. Press, Inc. 78; Farrar, Straus & Giroux 80; Fitzhenry & Whiteside Ltd. 81; Geringer Books, Laura 83; Gibbs Smith, Publisher 84; Godine, Publisher, David R. 85;

Grosset & Dunlap, Inc. 86; HarperCollins Children's Books 88; Houghton Mifflin Co. 91; Hyperion Books for Children 93; Ideals Children's Books 93; Jewish Publication Society 96; Jones University Press/Light Line Books, Bob 96; Just Us Books, Inc. 97; Knopf Books for Young Readers 99; Laredo Publishing Co. Inc. 102; Little, Brown and Company 104; Lodestar Books 105; Lorimer & Co., James 106; Lucky Books 107; McElderry Books, Margaret K. 108; Milkweed Editions 111; Morris Publishing, Joshua 112; Orca Book Publishers 118; Peachtree Publishers, Ltd. 123; Peartree 123; Philomel Books 125; Pippin Press 125; Polychrome Publishing Corporation 127; Pumpkin Press Publishing House/A Way to Grow 130; Putnam's Sons, G.P. 130; Random House Books for Young Readers 131; Rizzoli Books For Children 133; Rosebrier Publishing Co. 133; Sasquatch Books 135; Seacoast Publications of New England 136; Seedling Publications, Inc. 137; Shaw Publishers, Harold 137; Shoestring Press 137; Simon & Schuster Books for Young Readers 139; Standard Publishing 141; Thistledown Press Ltd. 145; Troll Associates 148; Tyndale House Publishers, Inc. 149; University Editions, Inc. 149; Usborne Publishing Ltd. 150; Victor Books 150; Weiss Associates, Inc., Daniel 154; Whispering Coyote Press, Inc. 154; Whitman & Company, Albert 154; Willowisp Press 156; Winston-Derek Publishers, Inc. 157; Zino Press Children's Book 158

Animal. ABC, All Books for Children 43; Advocacy Press 44; Aegina Press/University Editions 44; American Education Publishing 49; Andersen Press Limited 50; Archway/Minstrel Books 50; Atheneum Books for Young Readers 51; Bantam Doubleday Dell 53; Barrons Educational Series 54; Beautiful American Publishing Company 54; Bess Press 56; Bethel Publishing 57; Blue Heron Publishing, Inc. 57; Boyds Mills Press 57; Candlewick Press 59; Children's Library Press 65; Childrens Press 65; China Books 66; Chronicle Books 67; Clarion Books 68; Cobblehill Books 68; Cool Kids Press 69; Crocodile Books, USA 70; Crocodile Creek Press/European Toy Collection 70; Crown Publishers (Crown Books for Children) 71; Dawn Publications 73; Dial Books for Young Readers 73; Distinctive Publishing Corp. 76; Down East Books 77; Dutton Children's Books 78; Farrar, Straus & Giroux 80; Geringer Books, Laura 83; Gibbs Smith, Publisher 84; Godine, Publisher, David R. 85; Grosset & Dunlap, Inc. 86; Harcourt Brace & Co. 87; HarperCollins Children's Books 88; Holiday House Inc. 90; Houghton Mifflin Co. 91; Hyperion Books for Children 93; Ideals Children's Books 93; Jones University Press/Light Line Books, Bob 96; Knopf Books for Young Readers 99; Kruza Kaleidoscopix, Inc. 99; Laredo Publishing Co. Inc. 102; Little, Brown and Company 104; Lodestar Books 105; Lucky Books 107; Milkweed Editions 111; Morehouse Publishing Co. 112; Morris Publishing, Joshua 112; Northland Publishing 114; NorthWord Press, Inc. 114; Orchard Books 119; Pando Publications 121; Paulist Press 122; Peachtree Publishers, Ltd. 123; Peartree 123; Philomel Books 125; Pippin Press 125; Pumpkin Press Publishing House/A Way to Grow 130; Random House Books for Young Readers 131; Read'n Run Books 132; Sasquatch Books 135; Seacoast Publications of New England 136; Seedling Publications, Inc. 137; Simon & Schuster Books for Young Readers 139; Soundprints 139; Speech Bin, Inc., The 140; Standard Publishing 141; Stemmer House Publishers, Inc. 141; Sunbelt Media, Inc./Eakin Press 143; Thistledown Press Ltd. 145; Transworld Publishers Limited 147; Troll Associates 148; University Classics, Ltd. Publishers 149; University Editions, Inc. 149; Usborne Publishing Ltd. 150; Victor Books 150; Walker And Co. 152; Weiss Associates, Inc., Daniel 154; Whispering Coyote Press, Inc. 154; Whitman & Company, Albert 154; Willowisp Press 156; Zino Press Children's Book 158

Anthology. Bess Press 56; Blue Heron Publishing, Inc. 57; Candlewick Press 59; Children's Library Press 65; Crocodile Creek Press/European Toy Collection 70; Dutton Children's Books 78; Farrar, Straus & Giroux 80; Geringer Books, Laura 83; Houghton Mifflin Co. 91; Hyperion Books for Children 93; Orchard Books 119; Paulist Press 122; Pavilion Books Ltd. 123; Read'n Run Books 132; Rizzoli Books For Children 133; Transworld Publishers Limited 147; Troll Associates 148; Weiss Associates, Inc., Daniel 154; Willowisp Press 156

Concept. ABC, All Books for Children 43; Advocacy Press 44; Africa World Press 45; American Education Publishing 49; Barrons Educational Series 54; Bess Press 56; Children's Library Press 65; Childrens Press 65; Crocodile Creek Press/European Toy Collection 70; Dial Books for Young Readers 73; Farrar, Straus & Giroux 80; Grosset & Dunlap, Inc. 86; HarperCollins Children's Books 88; Herald Press 89; Holiday House Inc. 90; Houghton Mifflin Co. 91; Huntington House Publishers 92; Ideals Children's Books 93; Jalmar Press 94; Jewish Lights Publishing 95; Magination Press 109; Morris Publishing, Joshua 112; Pando Publications 121; Paulist Press 122; Peachtree Publishers, Ltd. 123; Pumpkin Press Publishing House/A Way to Grow 130; Putnam's Sons, G.P. 130; Read'n Run Books 132; Seedling Publications, Inc. 137; Tricycle Press 147; University Classics, Ltd. Publishers 149; Victory Publishing 151; Whitman & Company, Albert 154

Contemporary. ABC, All Books for Children 43; Africa World Press 45; American Education Publishing 49; Andersen Press Limited 50; Archway/Minstrel Books 50; Atheneum Books for Young Readers 51; Avon Books 52; Bantam Doubleday Dell 53; Bess Press 56; Blue Heron Publishing, Inc. 57; Boyds Mills Press 57; Candlewick Press 59; Children's Book Press 65; Children's Library Press 65; Childrens Press 65; China Books 66; Clarion Books 68; Cobblehill Books 68; Cool Kids Press 69; Coteau Books Ltd. 70; Crocodile Books, USA 70; Crocodile Creek Press/European Toy Collection 70; Crossway Books 71; Davenport, Publishers, May 72; Dorling Kindersley, Inc. 77; Dutton Children's Books 78; Farrar, Straus & Giroux 80; Fawcett Juniper 80; Fitzhenry & Whiteside Ltd. 81; Free Spirit Publishing 82; Geringer Books, Laura 83; Harcourt Brace & Co. 87; HarperCollins Children's Books 88; Harvest House Publishers 89; Holiday House Inc. 90; Houghton Mifflin Co. 91; Hyperion Books for Children 93; Ideals Children's Books 93; Jewish Publication Society 96; Jones University Press/Light Line Books, Bob 96; Just Us Books, Inc. 97; Knopf Books for Young Readers 99; Laredo Publishing Co. Inc. 102; Little, Brown and Company 104; Lodestar Books 105; Lorimer & Co., James 106; McElderry Books, Margaret K. 108; Mage Publishers Inc. 109; Milkweed Editions 111;

Northland Publishing 114; Orca Book Publishers 118; Orchard Books 119; Owen Publishers, Inc., Richard C. 119; Paulist Press 122; Pavilion Books Ltd. 123; Peartree 123; Polychrome Publishing Corporation 127; Pumpkin Press Publishing House/A Way to Grow 130; Putnam's Sons, G.P. 130; Read'n Run Books 132; Rizzoli Books For Children 133; St. Paul Books and Media 134; Seacoast Publications of New England 136; Seedling Publications, Inc. 137; Simon & Schuster Books for Young Readers 139; Standard Publishing 141; Thistledown Press Ltd. 145; Titan Books 146; Transworld Publishers Limited 147; Troll Associates 148; Tudor Publishers, Inc. 148; Victor Books 150; Weiss Associates, Inc., Daniel 154; Whitman & Company, Albert 154; Willowisp Press 156; Winston-Derek Publishers, Inc. 157; Women's Press 157; Zino Press Children's Book 158

Fantasy. Advocacy Press 44; Aegina Press/University Editions 44; American Education Publishing 49; Andersen Press Limited 50; Archway/Minstrel Books 50; Atheneum Books for Young Readers 51; Bantam Doubleday Dell 53; Candlewick Press 59; Children's Library Press 65; China Books 66; Clarion Books 68; Coteau Books Ltd. 70; Crocodile Creek Press/European Toy Collection 70; Crossway Books 71; Dial Books for Young Readers 73; Distinctive Publishing Corp. 76; Dutton Children's Books 78; Eerdmans Publishing Company, Wm. B. 78; Farrar, Straus & Giroux 80; Fawcett Juniper 80; Geringer Books, Laura 83; Gibbs Smith, Publisher 84; Godine, Publisher, David R. 85; Harcourt Brace & Co. 87; HarperCollins Children's Books 88; Houghton Mifflin Co. 91; Hyperion Books for Children 93; Knopf Books for Young Readers 99; Kruza Kaleidoscopix, Inc. 99; Laredo Publishing Co. Inc. 102; Little, Brown and Company 104; Lucky Books 107; McElderry Books, Margaret K. 108; Milkweed Editions 111; Morehouse Publishing Co. 112; Orchard Books 119; Philomel Books 125; Pippin Press 125; Rosebrier Publishing Co. 133; Seacoast Publications of New England 136; Seedling Publications, Inc. 137; Seedling Publications, Inc. 137; Simon & Schuster Books for Young Readers 139; Speech Bin, Inc., The 140; Titan Books 146; Transworld Publishers Limited 147; University Editions, Inc. 149; Usborne Publishing Ltd. 150; W.W. Publications 151; Walker And Co. 152; Whispering Coyote Press, Inc. 154; Whitman & Company, Albert 154; Willowisp Press 156

Folktales. Africa World Press 45; American Education Publishing 49; Andersen Press Limited 50; Bess Press 56; Boyds Mills Press 57; Candlewick Press 59; Carolrhoda Books, Inc. 60; Children's Library Press 65; Childrens Press 65; China Books 66; Chronicle Books 67; Clarion Books 68; Crocodile Creek Press/European Toy Collection 70; Dawn Publications 73; Dial Books for Young Readers 73; Dorling Kindersley, Inc. 77; Dutton Children's Books 78; Eerdmans Publishing Company, Wm. B. 78; Farrar, Straus & Giroux 80; Fitzhenry & Whiteside Ltd. 81; Geringer Books, Laura 83; Gibbs Smith, Publisher 84; Godine, Publisher, David R. 85; HarperCollins Children's Books 88; Holiday House Inc. 90; Houghton Mifflin Co. 91; Hyperion Books for Children 93; Hyperion Press Limited 93; Ideals Children's Books 93; Jewish Publication Society 96; Kar-Ben Copies, Inc. 98; Knopf Books for Young Readers 99; Laredo Publishing Co. Inc. 102; Little, Brown and Company 104; Lodestar Books 105; McElderry Books, Margaret K. 108; Mage Publishers Inc. 109; Morehouse Publishing Co. 112; Northland Publishing 114; Open Hand Publishing Inc. 115; Orca Book Publishers 118; Owen Publishers, Inc., Richard C. 119; Pando Publications 121; Paulist Press 122; Pavilion Books Ltd. 123; Peachtree Publishers, Ltd. 123; Pelican Publishing Co. Inc. 124; Philomel Books 125; Pippin Press 125; Press of Macdonald & Reinecke, The 128; Pumpkin Press Publishing House/A Way to Grow 130; Putnam's Sons, G.P. 130; Rizzoli Books For Children 133; Sasquatch Books 135; Seacoast Publications of New England 136; Seedling Publications, Inc. 137; Shoestring Press 137; Simon & Schuster Books for Young Readers 139; Stemmer House Publishers, Inc. 141; Thistledown Press Ltd. 145; Transworld Publishers Limited 147; Tricycle Press 147; Troll Associates 148; Tudor Publishers, Inc. 148; Ward Hill Press 152; Weigl Educational Publishers 153; Whispering Coyote Press, Inc. 154; Whitebird Books 154; Whitman & Company, Albert 154; Willowisp Press 156; Winston-Derek Publishers, Inc. 157

Health. China Books 66; Dial Books for Young Readers 73; Farrar, Straus & Giroux 80; Fitzhenry & Whiteside Ltd. 81; Geringer Books, Laura 83; Houghton Mifflin Co. 91; Laredo Publishing Co. Inc. 102; Little, Brown and Company 104; Magination Press 109; Paulist Press 122; Pumpkin Press Publishing House/A Way to Grow 130; Speech Bin, Inc., The 140; Tricycle Press 147; Troll Associates.148; University Classics, Ltd. Publishers 149; Usborne Publishing Ltd. 150; Waterfront Books 153; Whitman & Company, Albert 154; Women's Press 157

Hi-Lo. Bess Press 56; Childrens Press 65; Fitzhenry & Whiteside Ltd. 81; Globe Fearon Educational Publisher 84; Lorimer & Co., James 106; Peartree 123; Pumpkin Press Publishing House/A Way to Grow 130; Read'n Run Books 132; Seedling Publications, Inc. 137; Simon & Schuster Books for Young Readers 139

History. Africa World Press 45; Augsburg Fortress, Publishers 51; Bandanna Books 52; Bess Press 56; Blue Heron Publishing, Inc. 57; Boyds Mills Press 57; Candlewick Press 59; Carolrhoda Books, Inc. 60; Children's Library Press 65; China Books 66; Chronicle Books 67; Clarion Books 68; Coteau Books Ltd. 70; Crocodile Books, USA 70; Crocodile Creek Press/European Toy Collection 70; Crossway Books 71; Crown Publishers (Crown Books for Children) 71; Davenport, Publishers, May 72; Dial Books for Young Readers 73; Dorling Kindersley, Inc. 77; Down East Books 77; Dutton Children's Books 78; Farrar, Straus & Giroux 80; Geringer Books, Laura 83; Gibbs Smith, Publisher 84; Grosset & Dunlap, Inc. 86; Harcourt Brace & Co. 87; HarperCollins Children's Books 88; Hendrick-Long Publishing Company 89; Herald Press 89; Holiday House Inc. 90; Houghton Mifflin Co. 91; Huntington House Publishers 92; Hyperion Books for Children 93; Ideals Children's Books 93; Jewish Publication Society 96; Jones University Press/Light Line Books, Bob 96; Just Us Books, Inc. 97; Kruza Kaleidoscopix, Inc. 99; Little, Brown and Company 104; Lodestar Books 105; McElderry Books, Margaret K. 108; Milkweed Editions 111; Misty Hill Press 112; Northland Publishing 114;

Open Hand Publishing Inc. 115; Orca Book Publishers 118; Orchard Books 119; Pando Publications 121; Paulist Press 122; Peachtree Publishers, Ltd. 123; Pelican Publishing Co. Inc. 124; Philomel Books 125; Pippin Press 125; Polychrome Publishing Corporation 127; Press of Macdonald & Reinecke, The 128; Putnam's Sons, G.P. 130; Random House Books for Young Readers 131; Rizzoli Books For Children 133; Seacoast Publications of New England 136; Stemmer House Publishers, Inc. 141; Sunbelt Media, Inc./Eakin Press 143; Texas Christian University Press 144; Troll Associates 148; University Editions, Inc. 149; Usborne Publishing Ltd. 150; Walker And Co. 152; Whitman & Company, Albert 154; Willowisp Press 156; Winston-Derek Publishers, Inc. 157; Zino Press Children's Book 158

Humor. Aegina Press/University Editions 44; American Education Publishing 49; Andersen Press Limited 50; Archway/Minstrel Books 50; Avon Books 52; Bantam Doubleday Dell 53; Bess Press 56; Boyds Mills Press 57; Children's Book Press 65; Children's Library Press 65; Childrens Press 65; Cool Kids Press 69; Coteau Books Ltd. 70; Crocodile Creek Press/European Toy Collection 70; Crown Publishers (Crown Books for Children) 71; Davenport, Publishers, May 72; Farrar, Straus & Giroux 80; Fitzhenry & Whiteside Ltd. 81; Gibbs Smith, Publisher 84; HarperCollins Children's Books 88; Houghton Mifflin Co. 91; Hyperion Books for Children 93; Little, Brown and Company 104; Lodestar Books 105; Milkweed Editions 111; Owen Publishers, Inc., Richard C. 119; Peachtree Publishers, Ltd. 123; Pippin Press 125; Pumpkin Press Publishing House/A Way to Grow 130; Putnam's Sons, G.P. 130; Simon & Schuster Books for Young Readers 139; Thistledown Press Ltd. 145; Titan Books 146; Transworld Publishers Limited 147; Whispering Coyote Press, Inc. 154; Willowisp Press 156

Multicultural. ABC, All Books for Children 43; Africa World Press 45; African American Images 45; Andersen Press Limited 50; Augsburg Fortress, Publishers 51; Barrons Educational Series 54; Bess Press 56; Boyds Mills Press 57; Carolina Wren Press/Lollipop Power Books 59; Carolrhoda Books, Inc. 60; Charlesbridge 61; Children's Book Press 65; Children's Library Press 65; Childrens Press 65; China Books 66; Chronicle Books 67; Cool Kids Press 69; Distinctive Publishing Corp. 76; Dorling Kindersley, Inc. 77; Dutton Children's Books 78; Farrar, Straus & Giroux 80; Fitzhenry & Whiteside Ltd. 81; Free Spirit Publishing 82; Friendship Press, Inc. 83; Gibbs Smith, Publisher 84; Globe Fearon Educational Publisher 84; HarperCollins Children's Books 88; Houghton Mifflin Co. 91; Hyperion Books for Children 93; Ideals Children's Books 93; Jewish Lights Publishing 95; Just Us Books, Inc. 97; Kar-Ben Copies, Inc. 98; Laredo Publishing Co. Inc. 102; Little, Brown and Company 104; Lodestar Books 105; Lorimer & Co., James 106; McElderry Books, Margaret K. 108; Mage Publishers Inc. 109; Magination Press 109; Milkweed Editions 111; Morehouse Publishing Co. 112; Northland Publishing 114; Open Hand Publishing Inc. 115; Orchard Books 119; Our Child Press 119; Owen Publishers, Inc., Richard C. 119; Paulist Press 122; Peartree 123; Philomel Books 125; Pippin Press 125; Polychrome Publishing Corporation 127; Pumpkin Press Publishing House/A Way to Grow 130; Read'n Run Books 132; Rizzoli Books For Children 133; Sadlier, Inc., William H. 134; Sasquatch Books 135; Seedling Publications, Inc. 137; Simon & Schuster Books for Young Readers 139; Stemmer House Publishers, Inc. 141; Thistledown Press Ltd. 145; Transworld Publishers Limited 147; Tricycle Press 147; Tudor Publishers, Inc. 148; Ward Hill Press 152; Weigl Educational Publishers 153; Whitman & Company, Albert 154; Willowisp Press 156; Zino Press Children's Book 158

Nature/Environment. ABC, All Books for Children 43; Advocacy Press 44; Andersen Press Limited 50; Barrons Educational Series 54; Beautiful American Publishing Company 54; Bess Press 56; Blue Heron Publishing, Inc. 57; Carolrhoda Books, Inc. 60; Children's Library Press 65; China Books 66; Chronicle Books 67; Clarion Books 68; Cool Kids Press 69; Coteau Books Ltd. 70; Crocodile Creek Press/European Toy Collection 70; Crown Publishers (Crown Books for Children) 71; Dawn Publications 73; Dial Books for Young Readers 73; Distinctive Publishing Corp. 76; Dorling Kindersley, Inc. 77; Down East Books 77; Dutton Children's Books 78; Farrar, Straus & Giroux 80; Fitzhenry & Whiteside Ltd. 81; Geringer Books, Laura 83; Gibbs Smith, Publisher 84; Grosset & Dunlap, Inc. 86; HarperCollins Children's Books 88; Houghton Mifflin Co. 91; Ideals Children's Books 93; Knopf Books for Young Readers 99; Laredo Publishing Co. Inc. 102; Little, Brown and Company 104; Lodestar Books 105; Lucky Books 107; Milkweed Editions 111; Morris Publishing, Joshua 112; Northland Publishing 114; NorthWord Press, Inc. 114; Orca Book Publishers 118; Orchard Books 119; Owen Publishers, Inc., Richard C. 119; Pando Publications 121; Paulist Press 122; Peachtree Publishers, Ltd. 123; Peartree 123; Pelican Publishing Co. Inc. 124; Philomel Books 125; Pippin Press 125; Press of Macdonald & Reinecke, The 128; Pumpkin Press Publishing House/A Way to Grow 130; Read'n Run Books 132; Rosebrier Publishing Co. 133; Sasquatch Books 135; Seacoast Publications of New England 136; Seedling Publications, Inc. 137; Soundprints 139; Stemmer House Publishers, Inc. 141; Transworld Publishers Limited 147; Tricycle Press 147; Troll Associates 148; University Classics, Ltd. Publishers 149; University Editions, Inc. 149; Usborne Publishing Ltd. 150; Weigl Educational Publishers 153; Whispering Coyote Press, Inc. 154; Whitman & Company, Albert 154; Willowisp Press 156

Poetry. Aegina Press/University Editions 44; Boyds Mills Press 57; Candlewick Press 59; China Books 66; Chronicle Books 67; Dial Books for Young Readers 73; Dutton Children's Books 78; Geringer Books, Laura 83; HarperCollins Children's Books 88; Hyperion Books for Children 93; Laredo Publishing Co. Inc. 102; Meadowbrook Press 110; Morehouse Publishing Co. 112; Orchard Books 119; Peachtree Publishers, Ltd. 123; Philomel Books 125; Pumpkin Press Publishing House/A Way to Grow 130; Rizzoli Books For Children 133; Seedling Publications, Inc. 137; Simon & Schuster Books for Young Readers 139; Transworld Publishers Limited 147; Troll Associates 148; University Editions, Inc. 149; Usborne Publishing Ltd. 150; Victory Publishing 151; Willowisp Press 156; Zino Press Children's Book 158

Problem Novels. Avon Books 52; Barrons Educational Series 54; Berkley Publishing Group 55; Bess

Press 56; Bethany House Publishers 56; Chronicle Books 67; Cobblehill Books 68; Cool Kids Press 69; Dial Books for Young Readers 73; Eerdmans Publishing Company, Wm. B. 78; Farrar, Straus & Giroux 80; Free Spirit Publishing 82; Geringer Books, Laura 83; Harcourt Brace & Co. 87; HarperCollins Children's Books 88; Harvest House Publishers 89; Herald Press 89; Houghton Mifflin Co. 91; Hyperion Books for Children 93; Jewish Publication Society 96; Jones University Press/Light Line Books, Bob 96; Lorimer & Co., James 106; Magination Press 109; Milkweed Editions 111; Orca Book Publishers 118; Philomel Books 125; Putnam's Sons, G.P. 130; Read'n Run Books 132; Shaw Publishers, Harold 137; Transworld Publishers Limited 147; Troll Associates 148; Tudor Publishers, Inc. 148; University Classics, Ltd. Publishers 149; Weiss Associates, Inc., Daniel 154; Whitman & Company, Albert 154; Willowisp Press 156; Winston-Derek Publishers, Inc. 157; Women's Press 157

Religious. Aegina Press/University Editions 44; Bethel Publishing 57; China Books 66; Concordia Publishing House 69; Crossway Books 71; CSS Publishing 71; Dial Books for Young Readers 73; Distinctive Publishing Corp. 76; Eerdmans Publishing Company, Wm. B. 78; Friendship Press, Inc. 83; Herald Press 89; Huntington House Publishers 92; Jewish Publication Society 96; Kar-Ben Copies, Inc. 98; Morehouse Publishing Co. 112; Morris Publishing, Joshua 112; Pacific Press 120; Paulist Press 122; Pelican Publishing Co. Inc. 124; Questar Publishers, Inc. 131; Read'n Run Books 132; Rosebrier Publishing Co. 133; Sadlier, Inc., William H. 134; St. Paul Books and Media 134; Shaw Publishers, Harold 137; Standard Publishing 141; Tyndale House Publishers, Inc. 149; Victor Books 150; Winston-Derek Publishers, Inc. 157

Romance. Aegina Press/University Editions 44; Archway/Minstrel Books 50; Avon Books 52; Berkley Publishing Group 55; Bethany House Publishers 56; Cool Kids Press 69; Farrar, Straus & Giroux 80; Fawcett Juniper 80; Harcourt Brace & Co. 87; Harvest House Publishers 89; Houghton Mifflin Co. 91; Hyperion Books for Children 93; Jewish Publication Society 96; Transworld Publishers Limited 147; Troll Associates 148; University Editions, Inc. 149; Weiss Associates, Inc., Daniel 154; Willowisp Press 156

Science Fiction. Aegina Press/University Editions 44; Andersen Press Limited 50; Children's Library Press 65; Clarion Books 68; Crossway Books 71; Dial Books for Young Readers 73; Dutton Children's Books 78; Farrar, Straus & Giroux 80; Fawcett Juniper 80; Harcourt Brace & Co. 87; Houghton Mifflin Co. 91; Hyperion Books for Children 93; Knopf Books for Young Readers 99; Little, Brown and Company 104; Lucky Books 107; Milkweed Editions 111; Orchard Books 119; Titan Books 146; Transworld Publishers Limited 147; Troll Associates 148; University Editions, Inc. 149; Usborne Publishing Ltd. 150; Victor Books 150; Walker And Co. 152

Special Needs. Alyson Publications, Inc. 45; Carolrhoda Books, Inc. 60; Free Spirit Publishing 82; Globe Fearon Educational Publisher 84; Houghton Mifflin Co. 91; Kar-Ben Copies, Inc. 98; Magination Press 109; Orca Book Publishers 118; Our Child Press 119; Paulist Press 122; Philomel Books 125; Putnam's Sons, G.P. 130; Read'n Run Books 132; Sasquatch Books 135; Seedling Publications, Inc. 137; Speech Bin, Inc., The 140; University Classics, Ltd. Publishers 149; Waterfront Books 153; Whitman & Company, Albert 154; Woodbine House 158; Zino Press Children's Book 158

Sports. Aegina Press/University Editions 44; Archway/Minstrel Books 50; Avon Books 52; Bantam Doubleday Dell 53; Bess Press 56; Boyds Mills Press 57; Clarion Books 68; Cobblehill Books 68; Cool Kids Press 69; Dial Books for Young Readers 73; Distinctive Publishing Corp. 76; Farrar, Straus & Giroux 80; Fitzhenry & Whiteside Ltd. 81; Geringer Books, Laura 83; Grosset & Dunlap, Inc. 86; Harcourt Brace & Co. 87; HarperCollins Children's Books 88; Holiday House Inc. 90; Houghton Mifflin Co. 91; Hyperion Books for Children 93; Ideals Children's Books 93; Jewish Publication Society 96; Jones University Press/Light Line Books, Bob 96; Just Us Books, Inc. 97; Knopf Books for Young Readers 99; Orchard Books 119; Pumpkin Press Publishing House/A Way to Grow 130; Random House Books for Young Readers 131; Read'n Run Books 132; Seedling Publications, Inc. 137; Standard Publishing 141; Sunbelt Media, Inc./Eakin Press 143; Thistledown Press Ltd. 145; Transworld Publishers Limited 147; Troll Associates 148; Usborne Publishing Ltd. 150; Victor Books 150; Whitman & Company, Albert 154; Willowisp Press 156

Suspense/Mystery. Aegina Press/University Editions 44; Andersen Press Limited 50; Archway/Minstrel Books 50; Avon Books 52; Bantam Doubleday Dell 53; Barrons Educational Series 54; Berkley Publishing Group 55; Bess Press 56; Bethany House Publishers 56; Boyds Mills Press 57; Children's Library Press 65; Cobblehill Books 68; Cool Kids Press 69; Coteau Books Ltd. 70; Crocodile Books, USA 70; Crossway Books 71; Davenport, Publishers, May 72; Dial Books for Young Readers 73; Distinctive Publishing Corp. 76; Dutton Children's Books 78; Farrar, Straus & Giroux 80; Fitzhenry & Whiteside Ltd. 81; Geringer Books, Laura 83; Harcourt Brace & Co. 87; HarperCollins Children's Books 88; Harvest House Publishers 89; Holiday House Inc. 90; Houghton Mifflin Co. 91; Hyperion Books for Children 93; Jewish Publication Society 96; Jones University Press/Light Line Books, Bob 96; Knopf Books for Young Readers 99; Little, Brown and Company 104; Lodestar Books 105; Milkweed Editions 111; Orca Book Publishers 118; Orchard Books 119; Pelican Publishing Co. Inc. 124; Pippin Press 125; Putnam's Sons, G.P. 130; Random House Books for Young Readers 131; Read'n Run Books 132; Simon & Schuster Books for Young Readers 139; Standard Publishing 141; Thistledown Press Ltd. 145; Titan Books 146; Transworld Publishers Limited 147; Troll Associates 148; Tudor Publishers, Inc. 148; Tyndale House Publishers, Inc. 149; University Editions, Inc. 149; Usborne Publishing Ltd. 150; Victor Books 150; Weiss Associates, Inc., Daniel 154; Whitman & Company, Albert 154; Willowisp Press 156; Winston-Derek Publishers, Inc. 157

Book Publishers: Nonfiction

Activity Books. American Bible Society 49; American Education Publishing 49; Bess Press 56; Boyds Mills Press 57; Bright Ring Publishing 58; Cambridge Educational 59; Chicago Review Press 64; China Books 66; Crocodile Creek Press/European Toy Collection 70; Crown Publishers (Crown Books for Children) 71; Davenport, Publishers, May 72; Davis Pubilcations, Inc. 72; Denison Co. Inc., T.S. 73; Dial Books for Young Readers 73; Dorling Kindersley, Inc. 77; Enslow Publishers Inc. 79; Fitzhenry & Whiteside Ltd. 81; Franklin Watts 81; Friendship Press, Inc. 83; Gibbs Smith, Publisher 84; Grosset & Dunlap, Inc. 86; HarperCollins Children's Books 88; Ideals Children's Books 93; Jalmar Press 94; Just Us Books, Inc. 97; Lion Books, Publisher 104; Little, Brown and Company 104; Lodestar Books 105; Look and See Publications 106; Lucky Books 107; Marlor Press, Inc. 109; Meadowbrook Press 110; Millbrook Press, The 111; Morris Publishing, Joshua 112; NorthWord Press, Inc. 114; Pando Publications 121; Paulist Press 122; Preservation Press, The 128; Pumpkin Press Publishing House/A Way to Grow 130; Read'n Run Books 132; Rizzoli Books For Children 133; Sasquatch Books 135; Speech Bin, Inc., The 140; Sterling Publishing Co., Inc. 142; Summit Publishing Group, The 142; Tab Books 144; Tricycle Press 147; Troll Associates 148; Tyndale House Publishers, Inc. 149; University Classics, Ltd. Publishers 149; Usborne Publishing Ltd. 150; Victory Publishing 151; Weigl Educational Publishers 153; Wiley & Sons, Inc., John 155; Williamson Publishing Co. 155; Willowisp Press 156

Animal. Aegina Press/University Editions 44; American Education Publishing 49; Atheneum Books for Young Readers 51; Beautiful American Publishing Company 54; Boyds Mills Press 57; Candlewick Press 59; Carolrhoda Books, Inc. 60; Children's Library Press 65; Childrens Press 65; Chronicle Books 67; Clarion Books 68; Cobblehill Books 68; Crocodile Creek Press/European Toy Collection 70; Crown Publishers (Crown Books for Children) 71; Denison Co. Inc., T.S. 73; Dial Books for Young Readers 73; Distinctive Publishing Corp. 76; Dorling Kindersley, Inc. 77; Down East Books 77; Dutton Children's Books 78; E.M. Press, Inc. 78; Enslow Publishers Inc. 79; Facts on File 79; Falcon Press Publishing Co. 79; Franklin Watts 81; Golden Books 85; Grosset & Dunlap, Inc. 86; Harcourt Brace & Co. 87; HarperCollins Children's Books 88; Huntington House Publishers 92; Ideals Children's Books 93; Jones University Press/Light Line Books, Bob 96; Knopf Books for Young Readers 99; Knopf Books for Young Readers 99; Kruza Kaleidoscopix, Inc. 99; Little, Brown and Company 104; Lodestar Books 105; Lucky Books 107; Millbrook Press, The 111; Morris Publishing, Joshua 112; Muir Publications, Inc, John 113; Naturegraph Publisher, Inc. 114; Northland Publishing 114; NorthWord Press, Inc. 114; Orca Book Publishers 118; Orchard Books 119; Owen Publishers, Inc., Richard C. 119; Pando Publications 121; Paulist Press 122; Peachtree Publishers, Ltd. 123; Pippin Press 125; Pumpkin Press Publishing House/A Way to Grow 130; Random House Books for Young Readers 131; Read'n Run Books 132; Sasquatch Books 135; Seacoast Publications of New England 136; Seedling Publications, Inc. 137; Simon & Schuster Books for Young Readers 139; Stemmer House Publishers, Inc. 141; Sterling Publishing Co., Inc. 142; Sunbelt Media, Inc./Eakin Press 143; Troll Associates 148; Trophy Books 148; University Classics, Ltd. Publishers 149; University Editions, Inc. 149; Usborne Publishing Ltd. 150; Walker And Co. 152; Whitman & Company, Albert 154; Wiley & Sons, Inc., John 155; Williamson Publishing Co. 155; Willowisp Press 156

Arts/Crafts. Boyds Mills Press 57; Bright Ring Publishing 58; Cambridge Educational 59; Chicago Review Press 64; Childrens Press 65; China Books 66; Chronicle Books 67; Crocodile Creek Press/European Toy Collection 70; Davis Pubilcations, Inc. 72; Denison Co. Inc., T.S. 73; Dorling Kindersley, Inc. 77; Franklin Watts 81; Gibbs Smith, Publisher 84; Grosset & Dunlap, Inc. 86; HarperCollins Children's Books 88; Lion Books, Publisher 104; Little, Brown and Company 104; Millbrook Press, The 111; Muir Publications, Inc, John 113; Pando Publications 121; Paulist Press 122; Philomel Books 125; Pippin Press 125; Read'n Run Books 132; Sasquatch Books 135; Simon & Schuster Books for Young Readers 139; Stemmer House Publishers, Inc. 141; Sterling Publishing Co., Inc. 142; Summit Publishing Group, The 142; Tricycle Press 147; University Classics, Ltd. Publishers 149; Usborne Publishing Ltd. 150; Victory Publishing 151; Wiley & Sons, Inc., John 155; Williamson Publishing Co. 155; Willowisp Press 156

Biography. Atheneum Books for Young Readers 51; Bandanna Books 52; B&B Publishing, Inc. 53; Bess Press 56; Boyds Mills Press 57; Candlewick Press 59; Carolrhoda Books, Inc. 60; Chelsea House Publishers 64; Childrens Press 65; China Books 66; Chronicle Books 67; Clarion Books 68; Crown Publishers (Crown Books for Children) 71; Dial Books for Young Readers 73; Dimi Press 74; Discovery Enterprises, Ltd. 74; Distinctive Publishing Corp. 76; Dutton Children's Books 78; Eerdmans Publishing Company, Wm. B. 78; Enslow Publishers Inc. 79; Facts on File 79; Falcon Press Publishing Co. 79; Fitzhenry & Whiteside Ltd. 81; Franklin Watts 81; Gibbs Smith, Publisher 84; Globe Fearon Educational Publisher 84; Greenhaven Press 86; Grosset & Dunlap, Inc. 86; Harcourt Brace & Co. 87; HarperCollins Children's Books 88; Hendrick-Long Publishing Company 89; Holiday House Inc. 90; Homestead Publishing 91; Huntington House Publishers 92; Ideals Children's Books 93; Jewish Publication Society 96; Jones University Press/Light Line Books, Bob 96; Just Us Books, Inc. 97; Knopf Books for Young Readers 99; Kruza Kaleidoscopix, Inc. 99; Lee & Low Books, Inc. 102; Lion Books, Publisher 104; Little, Brown and Company 104; Lodestar Books 105; McElderry Books, Margaret K. 108; Milkweed Editions 111; Millbrook Press, The 111; Morehouse Publishing Co. 112; Muir Publications, Inc, John 113; Pando Publications 121; Paulist Press 122; Peachtree Publishers, Ltd. 123; Pelican Publishing Co. Inc. 124; Philomel Books 125; Pippin Press 125; Pocahontas Press, Inc. 127; Pumpkin Press Publishing House/A Way to Grow 130; Putnam's Sons, G.P. 130; Random House Books for Young Readers 131; Read'n Run Books 132; Rizzoli Books For Children 133; St. Paul Books and Media 134; Scientific American Books for Young Readers 135; Seacoast Publications of New England 136; Seedling Publications,

Inc. 137; Simon & Schuster Books for Young Readers 139; Stemmer House Publishers, Inc. 141; Sundance Publishers & Distributors 143; Texas Christian University Press 144; Titan Books 146; Troll Associates 148; Trophy Books 148; Tudor Publishers, Inc. 148; University Editions, Inc. 149; Victor Books 150; Walker And Co. 152; Ward Hill Press 152; Willowisp Press 156; Winston-Derek Publishers, Inc. 157

Careers. B&B Publishing, Inc. 53; Cambridge Educational 59; Childrens Press 65; Cool Kids Press 69; Crown Publishers (Crown Books for Children) 71; Denison Co. Inc., T.S. 73; Dial Books for Young Readers 73; Distinctive Publishing Corp. 76; Enslow Publishers Inc. 79; Facts on File 79; Fitzhenry & Whiteside Ltd. 81; Globe Fearon Educational Publisher 84; Lodestar Books 105; Millbrook Press, The 111; Owen Publishers, Inc., Richard C. 119; Paulist Press 122; Pocahontas Press, Inc. 127; Read'n Run Books 132; Rosen Publishing Group, The 133; Seedling Publications, Inc. 137; Summit Publishing Group, The 142; Sundance Publishers & Distributors 143; Tricycle Press 147; Troll Associates 148; University Editions, Inc. 149; Weigl Educational Publishers 153; Whitman & Company, Albert 154; Willowisp Press 156; Winston-Derek Publishers, Inc. 157

Concept. ABC, All Books for Children 43; Africa World Press 45; American Education Publishing 49; B&B Publishing, Inc. 53; Barrons Educational Series 54; Bess Press 56; Cambridge Educational 59; Childrens Press 65; Clarion Books 68; Cool Kids Press 69; Crocodile Creek Press/European Toy Collection 70; Grosset & Dunlap, Inc. 86; HarperCollins Children's Books 88; Jalmar Press 94; Just Us Books, Inc. 97; Little, Brown and Company 104; Lodestar Books 105; Magination Press 109; Millbrook Press, The 111; Muir Publications, Inc, John 113; Pando Publications 121; Paulist Press 122; Pumpkin Press Publishing House/A Way to Grow 130; Seedling Publications, Inc. 137; Standard Publishing 141; Tricycle Press 147; University Classics, Ltd. Publishers 149; Victory Publishing 151; Wiley & Sons, Inc., John 155; Willowisp Press 156

Cooking. Bright Ring Publishing 58; Children's Library Press 65; China Books 66; Chronicle Books 67; Crocodile Creek Press/European Toy Collection 70; Fiesta City Publishers 80; Franklin Watts 81; Gibbs Smith, Publisher 84; Little, Brown and Company 104; Pando Publications 121; Paulist Press 122; Pelican Publishing Co. Inc. 124; Rizzoli Books For Children 133; Sasquatch Books 135; Seedling Publications, Inc. 137; Simon & Schuster Books for Young Readers 139; Victory Publishing 151; Williamson Publishing Co. 155

Educational. Atheneum Books for Young Readers 51; Free Spirit Publishing 82; Incentive Publications, Inc. 94; Metamorphous Press 110; Planet Dexter 126; Waterfront Books 153

Geography. B&B Publishing, Inc. 53; Bess Press 56; Boyds Mills Press 57; Cambridge Educational 59; Charlesbridge 61; Chicago Review Press 64; Children's Library Press 65; Childrens Press 65; China Books 66; Chronicle Books 67; Clarion Books 68; Crocodile Creek Press/European Toy Collection 70; Discovery Enterprises, Ltd. 74; Distinctive Publishing Corp. 76; Dorling Kindersley, Inc. 77; Down East Books 77; Facts on File 79; Falcon Press Publishing Co. 79; Fitzhenry & Whiteside Ltd. 81; Franklin Watts 81; Friendship Press, Inc. 83; HarperCollins Children's Books 88; Little, Brown and Company 104; Lodestar Books 105; Millbrook Press, The 111; Pando Publications 121; Pippin Press 125; Pumpkin Press Publishing House/A Way to Grow 130; Sasquatch Books 135; Seacoast Publications of New England 136; Shoestring Press 137; Sterling Publishing Co., Inc. 142; Sundance Publishers & Distributors 143; Tab Books 144; Tricycle Press 147; John Wiley & Sons, Inc. 155; Williamson Publishing Co. 155; Willowisp Press 156

Health. Childrens Press 65; Crocodile Creek Press/European Toy Collection 70; Crown Publishers (Crown Books for Children) 71; Dial Books for Young Readers 73; Enslow Publishers Inc. 79; Facts on File 79; Fitzhenry & Whiteside Ltd. 81; Franklin Watts 81; Free Spirit Publishing 82; Globe Fearon Educational Publisher 84; Hunter House Publishers 92; Lucent Books 107; Magination Press 109; Millbrook Press, The 111; Parenting Press, Inc. 121; Paulist Press 122; Pelican Publishing Co. Inc. 124; Scientific American Books for Young Readers 135; Speech Bin, Inc., The 140; Summit Publishing Group, The 142; Tricycle Press 147; University Classics, Ltd. Publishers 149; Waterfront Books 153; Weigl Educational Publishers 153; Whitman & Company, Albert 154; Wiley & Sons, Inc., John 155; Williamson Publishing Co. 155; Women's Press 157

Hi-Lo. Barrons Educational Series 54; Bess Press 56; Childrens Press 65; Facts on File 79; Fitzhenry & Whiteside Ltd. 81; Globe Fearon Educational Publisher 84; HarperCollins Children's Books 88; Lucky Books 107; Read'n Run Books 132; Read'n Run Books 132; Rosen Publishing Group, The 133; Seedling Publications, Inc. 137; Sterling Publishing Co., Inc. 142

History. Aegina Press/University Editions 44; Africa World Press 45; Atheneum Books for Young Readers 51; B&B Publishing, Inc. 53; Behrman House Inc. 55; Bess Press 56; Blue Heron Publishing, Inc. 57; Boyds Mills Press 57; Cambridge Educational 59; Candlewick Press 59; Carolrhoda Books, Inc. 60; Chelsea House Publishers 64; Children's Library Press 65; Childrens Press 65; China Books 66; Chronicle Books 67; Clarion Books 68; Crocodile Books, USA 70; Crossway Books 71; Crown Publishers (Crown Books for Children) 71; Denison Co. Inc., T.S. 73; Dial Books for Young Readers 73; Discovery Enterprises, Ltd. 74; Distinctive Publishing Corp. 76; Dorling Kindersley, Inc. 77; Dutton Children's Books 78; E.M. Press, Inc. 78; Eerdmans Publishing Company, Wm. B. 78; Enslow Publishers Inc. 79; Falcon Press Publishing Co. 79; Fitzhenry & Whiteside Ltd. 81; Fitzhenry & Whiteside Ltd. 81; Franklin Watts 81; Gibbs Smith, Publisher 84; Globe Fearon Educational Publisher 84; Golden Books 85; Greenhaven Press 86; Grosset & Dunlap, Inc. 86; Harcourt Brace & Co. 87; HarperCollins Children's Books 88; Hendrick-Long Publishing Company 89; Holiday House Inc. 90; Homestead Publishing 91; Huntington House Publishers 92; Ideals Children's Books 93; Jewish Publication Society 96; Jones University Press/Light Line Books, Bob 96; Just Us Books, Inc. 97; Kruza Kaleidoscopix, Inc. 99; Laredo Publishing Co. Inc. 102; Lion Books, Publisher 104; Little, Brown and Company 104; Lodestar Books 105; Look and See Publications 106; Lucent Books 107; McElderry Books,

Margaret K. 108; Millbrook Press, The 111; Misty Hill Press 112; Open Hand Publishing Inc. 115; Orchard Books 119; Pando Publications 121; Paulist Press 122; Peachtree Publishers, Ltd. 123; Pelican Publishing Co. Inc. 124; Philomel Books 125; Pippin Press 125; Pocahontas Press, Inc. 127; Polychrome Publishing Corporation 127; Preservation Press, The 128; Press of Macdonald & Reinecke, The 128; Pumpkin Press Publishing House/A Way to Grow 130; Putnam's Sons, G.P. 130; Random House Books for Young Readers 131; Rizzoli Books For Children 133; Seacoast Publications of New England 136; Shoestring Press 137; Simon & Schuster Books for Young Readers 139; Sunbelt Media, Inc./Eakin Press 143; Texas Christian University Press 144; Troll Associates 148; University Editions, Inc. 149; Usborne Publishing Ltd. 150; Victor Books 150; Walker And Co. 152; Ward Hill Press 152; Weigl Educational Publishers 153; Whitman & Company, Albert 154; Willowisp Press 156; Winston-Derek Publishers, Inc. 157; Zino Press Children's Book 158

Hobbies. American Education Publishing 49; Avon Books 52; Bright Ring Publishing 58; Carolrhoda Books, Inc. 60; Chicago Review Press 64; Children's Library Press 65; Childrens Press 65; China Books 66; Crown Publishers (Crown Books for Children) 71; Enslow Publishers Inc. 79; Fitzhenry & Whiteside Ltd. 81; Free Spirit Publishing 82; Harcourt Brace & Co. 87; HarperCollins Children's Books 88; Ideals Children's Books 93; Lion Books, Publisher 104; Lucky Books 107; Marlor Press, Inc. 109; Millbrook Press, The 111; Muir Publications, Inc, John 113; Pando Publications 121; Planet Dexter 126; Pocahontas Press, Inc. 127; Random House Books for Young Readers 131; Read'n Run Books 132; Seedling Publications, Inc. 137; Sterling Publishing Co., Inc. 142; Summit Publishing Group, The 142; Troll Associates 148; Usborne Publishing Ltd. 150; Walker And Co. 152; Whitman & Company, Albert 154; Wiley & Sons, Inc., John 155; Williamson Publishing Co. 155; Willowisp Press 156

How-to. Barrons Educational Series 54; Cambridge Educational 59; Chicago Review Press 64; Childrens Press 65; Crocodile Creek Press/European Toy Collection 70; Dimi Press 74; E.M. Press, Inc. 78; Gibbs Smith, Publisher 84; Herald Press 89; Jalmar Press 94; Lion Books, Publisher 104; Magination Press 109; Pando Publications 121; Planet Dexter 126; Sasquatch Books 135; Sterling Publishing Co., Inc. 142; Summit Publishing Group, The 142; Titan Books 146; Tricycle Press 147; Usborne Publishing Ltd. 150; Victory Publishing 151; Wiley & Sons, Inc., John 155; Williamson Publishing Co. 155; Willowisp Press 156

Multicultural. Africa World Press 45; African American Images 45; B&B Publishing, Inc. 53; Bess Press 56; Boyds Mills Press 57; Candlewick Press 59; Carolrhoda Books, Inc. 60; Chelsea House Publishers 64; Childrens Press 65; China Books 66; Chronicle Books 67; Clarion Books 68; Clear Light Publishers 68; Crocodile Creek Press/European Toy Collection 70; Davis Pubilcations, Inc. 72; Dawn Publications 73; Denison Co. Inc., T.S. 73; Dutton Children's Books 78; Facts on File 79; Fitzhenry & Whiteside Ltd. 81; Franklin Watts 81; Free Spirit Publishing 82; Globe Fearon Educational Publisher 84; HarperCollins Children's Books 88; Hendrick-Long Publishing Company 89; Hunter House Publishers 92; Ideals Children's Books 93; Just Us Books, Inc. 97; Laredo Publishing Co. Inc. 102; Lee & Low Books, Inc. 102; Lion Books, Publisher 104; Little, Brown and Company 104; Lodestar Books 105; Lucent Books 107; Mage Publishers Inc. 109; Magination Press 109; Millbrook Press, The 111; Muir Publications, Inc, John 113; Naturegraph Publisher, Inc. 114; Northland Publishing 114; Open Hand Publishing Inc. 115; Orchard Books 119; Our Child Press 119; Owen Publishers, Inc., Richard C. 119; Pando Publications 121; Paulist Press 122; Pelican Publishing Co. Inc. 124; Philomel Books 125; Pippin Press 125; Polychrome Publishing Corporation 127; Putnam's Sons, G.P. 130; Read'n Run Books 132; Rizzoli Books For Children 133; Rosen Publishing Group, The 133; Sasquatch Books 135; Seedling Publications, Inc. 137; Simon & Schuster Books for Young Readers 139; Stemmer House Publishers, Inc. 141; Sundance Publishers & Distributors 143; Tab Books 144; Tudor Publishers, Inc. 148; Ward Hill Press 152; Whitman & Company, Albert 154; Williamson Publishing Co. 155; Willowisp Press 156; Winston-Derek Publishers, Inc. 157; Zino Press Children's Book 158

Music/Dance. Avon Books 52; Bright Ring Publishing 58; China Books 66; Crocodile Creek Press/European Toy Collection 70; Crown Publishers (Crown Books for Children) 71; Denison Co. Inc., T.S. 73; Dial Books for Young Readers 73; Fiesta City Publishers 80; Fitzhenry & Whiteside Ltd. 81; Franklin Watts 81; Harcourt Brace & Co. 87; HarperCollins Children's Books 88; Ideals Children's Books 93; Lodestar Books 105; Metamorphous Press 110; Millbrook Press, The 111; Pelican Publishing Co. Inc. 124; Philomel Books 125; Pippin Press 125; Players Press, Inc. 126; Pumpkin Press Publishing House/A Way to Grow 130; Read'n Run Books 132; Sasquatch Books 135; Seedling Publications, Inc. 137; Stemmer House Publishers, Inc. 141; Titan Books 146; Troll Associates 148; Trophy Books 148; Usborne Publishing Ltd. 150; Walker And Co. 152; Whitman & Company, Albert 154; Williamson Publishing Co. 155

Nature/Environment. ABC, All Books for Children 43; Aegina Press/University Editions 44; American Bible Society 49; Archway/Minstrel Books 50; B&B Publishing, Inc. 53; Beautiful American Publishing Company 54; Blue Heron Publishing, Inc. 57; Boyds Mills Press 57; Bright Ring Publishing 58; Cambridge Educational 59; Candlewick Press 59; Carolrhoda Books, Inc. 60; Charlesbridge 61; Children's Library Press 65; Childrens Press 65; China Books 66; Chronicle Books 67; Clarion Books 68; Cobblehill Books 68; Crocodile Books, USA 70; Crocodile Creek Press/European Toy Collection 70; Crown Publishers (Crown Books for Children) 71; Dawn Publications 73; Denison Co. Inc., T.S. 73; Dial Books for Young Readers 73; Dimi Press 74; Dorling Kindersley, Inc. 77; Down East Books 77; Dutton Children's Books 78; Eerdmans Publishing Company, Wm. B. 78; Enslow Publishers Inc. 79; Facts on File 79; Falcon Press Publishing Co. 79; Fitzhenry & Whiteside Ltd. 81; Franklin Watts 81; Free Spirit Publishing 82; Gibbs Smith, Publisher 84; Globe Fearon Educational Publisher 84; Golden Books 85; Greenhaven Press 86; Grosset & Dunlap, Inc. 86; Harcourt Brace & Co. 87; HarperCollins Children's Books 88; Holiday House Inc. 90; Homestead Publishing 91; Ideals Children's Books 93; Jones University Press/Light Line Books, Bob 96; Knopf Books for Young Readers 99;

Sports. Aegina Press/University Editions 44; Archway/Minstrel Books 50; Avon Books 52; Bess Press 56; Cambridge Educational 59; Chelsea House Publishers 64; Childrens Press 65; China Books 66; Cobblehill Books 68; Crown Publishers (Crown Books for Children) 71; Dial Books for Young Readers 73; Dorling Kindersley, Inc. 77; E.M. Press, Inc. 78; Enslow Publishers Inc. 79; Facts on File 79; Fitzhenry & Whiteside Ltd. 81; Franklin Watts 81; Golden Books 85; Grosset & Dunlap, Inc. 86; Harcourt Brace & Co. 87; Harper-Collins Children's Books 88; Holiday House Inc. 90; Ideals Children's Books 93; Jewish Publication Society 96; Knopf Books for Young Readers 99; Kruza Kaleidoscopix, Inc. 99; Lodestar Books 105; Lucent Books 107; Lucky Books 107; Millbrook Press, The 111; Pando Publications 121; Pelican Publishing Co. Inc. 124; Pocahontas Press, Inc. 127; Random House Books for Young Readers 131; Read'n Run Books 132; Seedling Publications, Inc. 137; Standard Publishing 141; Sterling Publishing Co., Inc. 142; Sunbelt Media, Inc./Eakin Press 143; Troll Associates 148; Tudor Publishers, Inc. 148; University Editions, Inc. 149; Usborne Publishing Ltd. 150; Victor Books 150; Walker And Co. 152; Whitman & Company, Albert 154; Willowisp Press 156

Textbooks. Aegina Press/University Editions 44; Bess Press 56; Davis Pubilcations, Inc. 72; Denison Co. Inc., T.S. 73; Globe Fearon Educational Publisher 84; Jalmar Press 94; Paulist Press 122; Pocahontas Press, Inc. 127; Read'n Run Books 132; Sadlier, Inc., William H. 134; Speech Bin, Inc., The 140; Tudor Publishers, Inc. 148; University Classics, Ltd. Publishers 149; Winston-Derek Publishers, Inc. 157

Magazines: Fiction

Adventure. Advocate, The 162; Animal Trails 163; Atalantik 164; Boys' Life 165; Bread for God's Children 166; Calliope 166; Cemetery Plot 167; Chickadee 168; Child Life 169; Children's Digest 169; Children's Playmate 172; Counselor 174; Cricket Magazine 175; Cricket Magazine 175; Crusader 176; Discoveries 177; Disney Adventures 177; Focus on the Family Clubhouse; Focus on the Family Clubhouse Jr. 181; Friend Magazine, The 183; Guideposts for Kids 185; Hob-Nob 186; Hodgepodge 189; Jack and Jill 192; Junior Trails 192; Kid City 194; Ladybug, the Magazine for Young Children 194; Lighthouse 195; Magazine for Christian Youth!, The 196; My Friend 197; New Era Magazine 199; Odyssey 199; Power and Light 202; Primary Days 203; R-A-D-A-R 204; Seventeen Magazine 208; Single Parent, The 209; Sleuth 211; Spider 211; Teen Life 215; Teen Power 216; Teenage Christian Magazine 216; Turtle Magazine 219; U.S. Kids 220; Venture 220; With 221

Animal. Animal Trails 163; Atalantik 164; Boys' Life 165; Bread for God's Children 166; Chickadee 168; Child Life 169; Children's Digest 169; Children's Playmate 172; Clubhouse 173; Cochran's Corner 174; Cricket Magazine 175; Crusader 176; Focus on the Family Clubhouse; Focus on the Family Clubhouse Jr. 181; Friend Magazine, The 183; Guideposts for Kids 185; Highlights for Children 186; Hob-Nob 186; Hodge-podge 189; Humpty Dumpty's Magazine 191; Junior Trails 192; Kid City 194; Ladybug, the Magazine for Young Children 194; Magazine for Christian Youth!, The 196; R-A-D-A-R 204; Ranger Rick 204; Scholastic Math Magazine 205; Skipping Stones 210; Spider 211; Touch 218; Turtle Magazine 219; U.S. Kids 220; Venture 220

Contemporary. Advocate, The 162; American Girl 163; Boys' Life 165; Bread for God's Children 166; Child Life 169; Children's Digest 169; Children's Playmate 172; Clubhouse 173; Cochran's Corner 174; Cricket Magazine 175; Crusader 176; Discoveries 177; Disney Adventures 177; Faces 179; Focus on the Family Clubhouse; Focus on the Family Clubhouse Jr. 181; FreeWay 183; Friend Magazine, The 183; Guideposts for Kids 185; Highlights for Children 186; Hob-Nob 186; Hodgepodge 189; Home Altar, The 190; Hopscotch 190; Humpty Dumpty's Magazine 191; Jack and Jill 192; Junior Trails 192; Kid City 194; Listen 195; Magazine for Christian Youth!, The 196; My Friend 197; New Era Magazine 199; On the Line 201; Pockets 202; Power and Light 202; R-A-D-A-R 204; Seventeen Magazine 208; Shofar 209; Single Parent, The 209; Skipping Stones 210; Spider 211; Story Friends 213; Teen Life 215; 'Teen Magazine 215; Teen Power 216; Teenage Christian Magazine 216; Touch 218; Turtle Magazine 219; U.S. Kids 220; With 221; Wonder Time 222

Fantasy. Advocate, The 162; Boys' Life 165; Cemetery Plot 167; Chickadee 168; Children's Digest 169; Children's Playmate 172; Cochran's Corner 174; Cricket Magazine 175; Crusader 176; Disney Adventures 177; Highlights for Children 186; Hob-Nob 186; Hobson's Choice 188; Hodgepodge 189; Hopscotch 190; Humpty Dumpty's Magazine 191; Jack and Jill 192; Kid City 194; Ladybug, the Magazine for Young Children 194; Magazine for Christian Youth!, The 196; Magic Realism 197; New Era Magazine 199; Pockets 202; Ranger Rick 204; Seventeen Magazine 208; Spider 211; Turtle Magazine 219; With 221

Folktales. Advocate, The 162; Animal Trails 163; Appalachian Bride 164; Calliope 166; Cemetery Plot 167; Chickadee 168; Children's Digest 169; Children's Playmate 172; Cricket Magazine 175; Crusader 176; Faces 179; Focus on the Family Clubhouse; Focus on the Family Clubhouse Jr. 181; Friend Magazine, The 183; Guideposts for Kids 185; Highlights for Children 186; Hob-Nob 186; Hodgepodge 189; Home Altar, The 190; Hopscotch 190; Kid City 194; Ladybug, the Magazine for Young Children 194; Magazine for Christian Youth!, The 196; Magic Realism 197; Odyssey 199; Spider 211; Turtle Magazine 219; With 221

Health. Advocate, The 162; Child Life 169; Children's Digest 169; Clubhouse 173; Crusader 176; For Seniors Only 182; Hodgepodge 189; Hopscotch 190; Humpty Dumpty's Magazine 191; Listen 195; Magazine for Christian Youth!, The 196; Turtle Magazine 219; U.S. Kids 220; With 221

History. Aim Magazine 162; American Girl 163; Animal Trails 163; Atalantik 164; Boys' Life 165; Bread for God's Children 166; Calliope 166; Children's Digest 169; Children's Playmate 172; Clubhouse 173; Cob-blestone 173; Cochran's Corner 174; Counselor 174; Cricket Magazine 175; Crusader 176; Faces 179; Focus on the Family Clubhouse; Focus on the Family Clubhouse Jr. 181; Friend Magazine, The 183; Goldfinch, The 184; Guideposts for Kids 185; Highlights for Children 186; Hob-Nob 186; Hodgepodge 189; Hopscotch 190; Jack and Jill 192; Junior Trails 192; Kid City 194; Lighthouse 195; My Friend 197; Odyssey 199; On the Line 201; Pockets 202; R-A-D-A-R 204; Sleuth 211; Spider 211; Touch 218; Turtle Magazine 219; U.S. Kids 220; Young Christian 222

Humorous. Advocate, The 162; Atalantik 164; Boys' Life 165; Chickadee 168; Child Life 169; Children's Digest 169; Children's Playmate 172; Clubhouse 173; Cochran's Corner 174; Cricket Magazine 175; Crusader 176; Disney Adventures 177; Focus on the Family Clubhouse; Focus on the Family Clubhouse Jr. 181; For Seniors Only 182; FreeWay 183; Friend Magazine, The 183; Guideposts for Kids 185; Highlights for Children 186; Hob-Nob 186; Hodgepodge 189; Hopscotch 190; Humpty Dumpty's Magazine 191; Jack and Jill 192; Junior Trails 192; Kid City 194; Ladybug, the Magazine for Young Children 194; Listen 195; Magazine for Christian Youth!, The 196; My Friend 197; New Era Magazine 199; On Course 200; On the Line 201; R-A-D-A-R 204; Ranger Rick 204; School Mates 205; Seventeen Magazine 208; Shofar 209; Single Parent, The 209; Skipping Stones 210; Spider 211; Story Friends 213; Straight 213; Teen Life 215; 'Teen Magazine 215; Teen Power 216; Teenage Christian Magazine 216; Touch 218; Turtle Magazine 219; U.S. Kids 220; Venture 220; With 221

Multicultural. Aim Magazine 162; American Girl 163; Animal Trails 163; Appalachian Bride 164; Cemetery Plot 167; Child Life 169; Counselor 174; Cricket Magazine 175; Crusader 176; Faces 179; Focus on the Family Clubhouse; Focus on the Family Clubhouse Jr. 181; FreeWay 183; Friend Magazine, The 183; Guideposts for Kids 185; Hob-Nob 186; Hodgepodge 189; Hopscotch 190; Junior Trails 192; Kid City 194; Ladybug, the Magazine for Young Children 194; Magazine for Christian Youth!, The 196; Power and Light 202; Primary Days 203; Skipping Stones 210; Sleuth 211; Spider 211; Student Leadership Journal 214; Teen Power 216; U.S. Kids 220; With 221; Young Christian 222; Young Salvationist 223

Nature/Environment. Advocate, The 162; Animal Trails 163; Bread for God's Children 166; Chickadee 168; Child Life 169; Children's Digest 169; Counselor 174; Cricket Magazine 175; Crusader 176; Focus on the Family Clubhouse; Focus on the Family Clubhouse Jr. 181; FreeWay 183; Guideposts for Kids 185; Hob-Nob 186; Hodgepodge 189; Hopscotch 190; Junior Trails 192; Kid City 194; Ladybug, the Magazine for Young Children 194; Lighthouse 195; Listen 195; Magazine for Christian Youth!, The 196; Power and Light 202; Primary Days 203; Skipping Stones 210; Spider 211; Turtle Magazine 219; U.S. Kids 220; Venture 220; With 221

Problem-Solving. Advocate, The 162; Atalantik 164; Boys' Life 165; Bread for God's Children 166; Cemetery Plot 167; Child Life 169; Children's Digest 169; Clubhouse 173; Cochran's Corner 174; Counselor 174; Crusader 176; Discoveries 177; FreeWay 183; Friend Magazine, The 183; Guideposts for Kids 185; Highlights for Children 186; Hob-Nob 186; Hodgepodge 189; Home Altar, The 190; Hopscotch 190; International Gymnast 191; Jack and Jill 192; Junior Trails 192; Ladybug, the Magazine for Young Children 194; Lighthouse 195; Listen 195; Magazine for Christian Youth!, The 196; New Era Magazine 199; On the Line 201; Power and Light 202; Primary Days 203; R-A-D-A-R 204; Single Parent, The 209; Sleuth 211; Spider 211; Story Friends 213; Straight 213; Teen Life 215; 'Teen Magazine 215; Teen Power 216; Teenage Christian Magazine 216; Touch 218; Turtle Magazine 219; U.S. Kids 220; Venture 220; With 221; Wonder Time 222; Young Christian 222

Religious. Bread for God's Children 166; Clubhouse 173; Cochran's Corner 174; Counselor 174; Crusader 176; Discoveries 177; Faces 179; Focus on the Family Clubhouse; Focus on the Family Clubhouse Jr. 181; FreeWay 183; Friend Magazine, The 183; Guideposts for Kids 185; Hob-Nob 186; Hodgepodge 189; Home Altar, The 190; Junior Trails 192; Magazine for Christian Youth!, The 196; My Friend 197; New Era Magazine 199; On Course 200; On the Line 201; Pockets 202; Power and Light 202; Primary Days 203; R-A-D-A-R 204; Seventeen Magazine 208; Shofar 209; Story Friends 213; Straight 213; Student Leadership Journal 214; Teen Life 215; Teen Power 216; Teenage Christian Magazine 216; Together Time 217; Touch 218; Venture 220; With 221; Wonder Time 222; Young Christian 222; Young Salvationist 223

Romance. Advocate, The 162; Atalantik 164; Cochran's Corner 174; Hob-Nob 186; Lighthouse 195; New Era Magazine 199; Seventeen Magazine 208; 'Teen Magazine 215; Touch 218; Young Christian 222

Sports. Advocate, The 162; Boys' Life 165; Chickadee 168; Children's Digest 169; Children's Playmate 172; Cochran's Corner 174; Disney Adventures 177; Highlights for Children 186; Hob-Nob 186; Hobson's Choice 188; Hodgepodge 189; Humpty Dumpty's Magazine 191; Kid City 194; Ladybug, the Magazine for Young Children 194; Magazine for Christian Youth!, The 196; New Era Magazine 199; Ranger Rick 204; Seventeen Magazine 208; Spider 211; With 221

Suspense/Mystery. Advocate, The 162; American Girl 163; Animal Trails 163; Atalantik 164; Boys' Life 165; Bread for God's Children 166; Cemetery Plot 167; Child Life 169; Children's Digest 169; Children's Playmate 172; Cricket Magazine 175; Crusader 176; Disney Adventures 177; Focus on the Family Clubhouse; Focus on the Family Clubhouse Jr. 181; Friend Magazine, The 183; Guideposts for Kids 185; Highlights for Children 186; Hob-Nob 186; Hodgepodge 189; Hopscotch 190; Humpty Dumpty's Magazine 191; Junior Trails 192; Ladybug, the Magazine for Young Children 194; Lighthouse 195; Magazine for Christian Youth!, The 196; My Friend 197; On the Line 201; R-A-D-A-R 204; Seventeen Magazine 208; Single Parent, The 209; Spider 211; 'Teen Magazine 215; Teenage Christian Magazine 216; Turtle Magazine 219; U.S. Kids 220; Venture 220; Young Christian 222

Magazines: Nonfiction

Animal. Advocate, The 162; Animal Trails 163; ASPCA Animal Watch 164; Boys' Life 165; Chickadee 168; Child Life 169; Children's Digest 169; Children's Playmate 172; Cochran's Corner 174; Cricket Magazine 175; Crusader 176; Disney Adventures 177; Dolphin Log 178; DynaMath 178; Falcon Magazine 180; FFA New Horizons 180; Field & Stream 180; Focus on the Family Clubhouse; Focus on the Family Clubhouse Jr. 181; Friend Magazine, The 183; Guide Magazine 184; Highlights for Children 186; Hob-Nob 186; Hopscotch 190; Humpty Dumpty's Magazine 191; Jack and Jill 192; Junior Trails 192; Kid City 194; Ladybug, the Magazine for Young Children 194; Magazine for Christian Youth!, The 196; National Geographic World 198; Nature Friend Magazine 199; On the Line 201; Owl Magazine 201; Racing for Kids 203; R-A-D-A-R 204; Ranger Rick 204; Scholastic Math Magazine 205; Scienceland 208; Skipping Stones 210; Spider 211; Superscience Blue 214; Teenage Christian Magazine 216; 3-2-1 Contact 217; Turtle Magazine 219; U.S. Kids 220; Venture 220

Arts/Crafts. Advocate, The 162; Bread for God's Children 166; Calliope 166; Challenge 168; Chickadee 168; Child Life 169; Children's Digest 169; Children's Playmate 172; Cricket Magazine 175; Cricket Magazine 175; Crusader 176; DynaMath 178; Faces 179; Falcon Magazine 180; Focus on the Family Clubhouse; Focus on the Family Clubhouse Jr. 181; Friend Magazine, The 183; Goldfinch, The 184; Highlights for Children 186; Hob-Nob 186; Hopscotch 190; Ladybug, the Magazine for Young Children 194; Listen 195; Magazine for Christian Youth!, The 196; My Friend 197; Odyssey 199; On The Line 200; Primary Days 203; Racing for Kids 203; Scholastic Math Magazine 205; Scienceland 208; Spider 211; Teenage Christian Magazine 216; Turtle Magazine 219; U.S. Kids 220; Venture 220

Biography. Advocate, The 162; Animal Trails 163; Calliope 166; Child Life 169; Children's Digest 169; Children's Playmate 172; Cobblestone 173; Counselor 174; Cricket Magazine 175; Crusader 176; Disney Adventures 177; FFA New Horizons 180; Focus on the Family Clubhouse; Focus on the Family Clubhouse Jr. 181; Friend Magazine, The 183; Goldfinch, The 184; Guide Magazine 184; High Adventure 185; Highlights for Children 186; Hob-Nob 186; Hopscotch 190; International Gymnast 191; Magazine for Christian Youth!, The 196; New Era Magazine 199; Odyssey 199; On the Line 201; Primary Days 203; Scienceland 208; Skipping Stones 210; Teen Power 216; Teenage Christian Magazine 216; Young Christian 222

Careers. Advocate, The 162; Career World 167; Careers and Colleges 167; Child Life 169; Crusader 176; FFA New Horizons 180; For Seniors Only 182; FreeWay 183; Highlights for Children 186; Hob-Nob 186; Hopscotch 190; Kid City 194; Magazine for Christian Youth!, The 196; New Era Magazine 199; On Course 200; Scholastic Math Magazine 205; Scienceland 208; Single Parent, The 209; 'Teen Magazine 215; Teenage Christian Magazine 216; 2 Hype/Hype Hair 219

Concept. Advocate, The 162; Crusader 176; Ladybug, the Magazine for Young Children 194; Magazine for Christian Youth!, The 196

Cooking. Advocate, The 162; Calliope 166; Chickadee 168; Child Life 169; Children's Digest 169; Children's Playmate 172; Choices 172; Crusader 176; DynaMath 178; Falcon Magazine 180; Focus on the Family Clubhouse; Focus on the Family Clubhouse Jr. 181; Friend Magazine, The 183; Hopscotch 190; Ladybug, the Magazine for Young Children 194; Magazine for Christian Youth!, The 196; Odyssey 199; On the Line 201; Racing for Kids 203; Single Parent, The 209; Skipping Stones 210; Spider 211; 'Teen Magazine 215; U.S. Kids 220

Fashion. Advocate, The 162; DynaMath 178; New Era Magazine 199; Racing for Kids 203; 2 Hype/Hype Hair 219

Games/Puzzles. Advocate, The 162; Animal Trails 163; Atalantik 164; Calliope 166; Cemetery Plot 167; Challenge 168; Chickadee 168; Child Life 169; Children's Digest 169; Children's Playmate 172; Cobblestone 173; Counselor 174; Cricket Magazine 175; Crusader 176; Disney Adventures 177; Dolphin Log 178; DynaMath 178; Faces 179; Field & Stream 180; Focus on the Family Clubhouse; Focus on the Family Clubhouse Jr. 181; For Seniors Only 182; FreeWay 183; Friend Magazine, The 183; Goldfinch, The 184; Guide Magazine 184; Guideposts for Kids 185; Hob-Nob 186; Hopscotch 190; Magazine for Christian Youth!, The 196; My Friend 197; New Era Magazine 199; Odyssey 199; On the Line 201; Owl Magazine 201; Primary Days 203; Scholastic Math Magazine 205; School Mates 205; Scienceland 208; Shofar 209; Skipping Stones 210; Sleuth 211; Soccer Jr. 211; Spider 211; Teen Power 216; Teenage Christian Magazine 216; Turtle Magazine 219; 2 Hype/Hype Hair 219; U.S. Kids 220; Young Christian 222

Geography. Advocate, The 162; Animal Trails 163; Challenge 168; Child Life 169; Children's Digest 169; Cricket Magazine 175; Crusader 176; Dolphin Log 178; Junior Scholastic 192; Kid City 194; Magazine for Christian Youth!, The 196; Scholastic Math Magazine 205; Spider 211

Health. Boys' Life 165; Careers and Colleges 167; Challenge 168; Child Life 169; Children's Digest 169; Children's Playmate 172; Choices 172; Crusader 176; Current Health I 176; Current Health II 176; DynaMath 178; FFA New Horizons 180; For Seniors Only 182; Highlights for Children 186; Hopscotch 190; Humpty Dumpty's Magazine 191; International Gymnast 191; Listen 195; Magazine for Christian Youth!, The 196; My Friend 197; On the Line 201; Racing for Kids 203; Racing for Kids 203; Scholastic Math Magazine 205; Scienceland 208; Single Parent, The 209; 'Teen Magazine 215; Teenage Christian Magazine 216; 3-2-1 Contact 217; Turtle Magazine 219; 2 Hype/Hype Hair 219; U.S. Kids 220

History. Advocate, The 162; Animal Trails 163; Atalantik 164; Boys' Life 165; Calliope 166; Cemetery

Plot 167; Child Life 169; Children's Digest 169; Children's Playmate 172; Cobblestone 173; Cochran's Corner 174; Counselor 174; Cricket Magazine 175; Crusader 176; DynaMath 178; Faces 179; Focus on the Family Clubhouse; Focus on the Family Clubhouse Jr. 181; Friend Magazine, The 183; Goldfinch, The 184; Guideposts for Kids 185; Highlights for Children 186; Hopscotch 190; Jack and Jill 192; Junior Scholastic 192; Junior Trails 192; Kid City 194; Magazine for Christian Youth!, The 196; My Friend 197; National Geographic World 198; On the Line 201; Pockets 202; Primary Days 203; Racing for Kids 203; R-A-D-A-R 204; Scholastic Math Magazine 205; Scienceland 208; Single Parent, The 209; Skipping Stones 210; Sleuth 211; Spider 211; Student Leadership Journal 214; Teenage Christian Magazine 216; U.S. Kids 220; Young Christian 222

Hobbies. Advocate, The 162; Bread for God's Children 166; Challenge 168; Child Life 169; Children's Digest 169; Counselor 174; Cricket Magazine 175; Crusader 176; DynaMath 178; FFA New Horizons 180; Focus on the Family Clubhouse; Focus on the Family Clubhouse Jr. 181; Guideposts for Kids 185; Hob-Nob 186; Hopscotch 190; Listen 195; Magazine for Christian Youth!, The 196; My Friend 197; On the Line 201; Primary Days 203; Racing for Kids 203; Scholastic Math Magazine 205; Teenage Christian Magazine 216; 2 Hype/Hype Hair 219; U.S. Kids 220; Young Salvationist 223

How-to. Advocate, The 162; Animal Trails 163; Atalantik 164; Bread for God's Children 166; Career World 167; Careers and Colleges 167; Challenge 168; Child Life 169; Children's Digest 169; Children's Playmate 172; Clubhouse 173; Cochran's Corner 174; Cricket Magazine 175; Crusader 176; DynaMath 178; FFA New Horizons 180; Field & Stream 180; Focus on the Family Clubhouse; Focus on the Family Clubhouse Jr. 181; For Seniors Only 182; Friend Magazine, The 183; Goldfinch, The 184; Guideposts for Kids 185; Highlights for Children 186; Hob-Nob 186; Hobson's Choice 188; Hopscotch 190; Humpty Dumpty's Magazine 191; Jack and Jill 192; Keynoter 193; Kid City 194; My Friend 197; National Geographic World 198; On the Line 201; Primary Days 203; R-A-D-A-R 204; Scholastic Math Magazine 205; Scienceland 208; Seventeen Magazine 208; Sleuth 211; Superscience Blue 214; Teen Power 216; Teenage Christian Magazine 216; 3-2-1 Contact 217; Touch 218; 2 Hype/Hype Hair 219; U.S. Kids 220; Young Salvationist 223

Humorous. Advocate, The 162; Atalantik 164; Careers and Colleges 167; Challenge 168; Child Life 169; Children's Digest 169; Children's Playmate 172; Cochran's Corner 174; Cricket Magazine 175; Crusader 176; DynaMath 178; FFA New Horizons 180; Focus on the Family Clubhouse; Focus on the Family Clubhouse Jr. 181; For Seniors Only 182; FreeWay 183; Friend Magazine, The 183; Guide Magazine 184; Guideposts for Kids 185; Highlights for Children 186; Hob-Nob 186; Hopscotch 190; Humpty Dumpty's Magazine 191; Jack and Jill 192; Junior Trails 192; Keynoter 193; Kid City 194; Ladybug, the Magazine for Young Children 194; Magazine for Christian Youth!, The 196; My Friend 197; National Geographic World 198; New Era Magazine 199; On Course 200; On the Line 201; Owl Magazine 201; R-A-D-A-R 204; Ranger Rick 204; Scholastic Math Magazine 205; Seventeen Magazine 208; Shofar 209; Single Parent, The 209; Skipping Stones 210; Straight 213; Teen Power 216; Teenage Christian Magazine 216; Touch 218; U.S. Kids 220; With 221

Interview/Profile. Advocate, The 162; Aim Magazine 162; Atalantik 164; Career World 167; Careers and Colleges 167; Chickadee 168; Child Life 169; Children's Digest 169; Cobblestone 173; Cochran's Corner 174; Counselor 174; Cricket Magazine 175; Crusader 176; Disney Adventures 177; Dolphin Log 178; Exploring 178; Faces 179; FFA New Horizons 180; Field & Stream 180; Focus on the Family Clubhouse; Focus on the Family Clubhouse Jr. 181; For Seniors Only 182; Goldfinch, The 184; Guideposts for Kids 185; Highlights for Children 186; Hob-Nob 186; Hobson's Choice 188; Home Altar, The 190; Hopscotch 190; Humpty Dumpty's Magazine 191; International Gymnast 191; Jack and Jill 192; Junior Scholastic 192; Kid City 194; Magazine for Christian Youth!, The 196; My Friend 197; New Era Magazine 199; On Course 200; Owl Magazine 201; Pockets 202; Primary Days 203; Racing for Kids 203; R-A-D-A-R 204; Scholastic Math Magazine 205; School Mates 205; Seventeen Magazine 208; Sharing the Victory 209; Shofar 209; Single Parent, The 209; Skipping Stones 210; Story Friends 213; Straight 213; Student Leadership Journal 214; Teen Life 215; Teen Power 216; Teenage Christian Magazine 216; 3-2-1 Contact 217; Touch 218; 2 Hype/Hype Hair 219; U.S. Kids 220; Venture 220; Young Salvationist 223

Math. Crusader 176; DynaMath 178; Guideposts for Kids 185; Hopscotch 190; Ladybug, the Magazine for Young Children 194; Magazine for Christian Youth!, The 196; Racing for Kids 203; Scholastic Math Magazine 205; Spider 211

Multicultural. Aim Magazine 162; Animal Trails 163; Appalachian Bride 164; Cemetery Plot 167; Child Life 169; Counselor 174; Cricket Magazine 175; Crusader 176; Dolphin Log 178; DynaMath 178; FreeWay 183; Guideposts for Kids 185; Hopscotch 190; Junior Scholastic 192; Kid City 194; Magazine for Christian Youth!, The 196; National Geographic World 198; Primary Days 203; Racing for Kids 203; Scholastic Math Magazine 205; Skipping Stones 210; Sleuth 211; Spider 211; Student Leadership Journal 214; Teen Life 215; 'Teen Magazine 215; Teen Power 216; 3-2-1 Contact 217; Turtle Magazine 219; U.S. Kids 220; With 221; Young Christian 222; Young Salvationist 223

Nature/Environment. Advocate, The 162; Animal Trails 163; ASPCA Animal Watch 164; Boys' Life 165; Challenge 168; Child Life 169; Children's Digest 169; Counselor 174; Cricket Magazine 175; Crusader 176; Current Health I 176; Current Health II 176; Disney Adventures 177; Dolphin Log 178; DynaMath 178; Falcon Magazine 180; FFA New Horizons 180; Field & Stream 180; Focus on the Family Clubhouse; Focus on the Family Clubhouse Jr. 181; FreeWay 183; Guide Magazine 184; Guideposts for Kids 185; Highlights for Children 186; Hob-Nob 186; Junior Scholastic 192; Junior Trails 192; Kid City 194; Kids Copy 194; Ladybug, the Magazine for Young Children 194; Listen 195; Magazine for Christian Youth!, The 196; My Friend 197; National Geographic World 198; Nature Friend Magazine 199; On the Line 201; Primary Days

203; Racing for Kids 203; Scholastic Math Magazine 205; Scienceland 208; Skipping Stones 210; Spider 211; Story Friends 213; Student Leadership Journal 214; Superscience Blue 214; 3-2-1 Contact 217; Turtle Magazine 219; U.S. Kids 220; Venture 220; With 221; Young Salvationist 223

Problem-Solving. Advocate, The 162; Animal Trails 163; Atalantik 164; Bread for God's Children 166; Careers and Colleges 167; Cemetery Plot 167; Child Life 169; Counselor 174; Crusader 176; Current Health I 176; Current Health II 176; DynaMath 178; Exploring 178; FFA New Horizons 180; FreeWay 183; Friend Magazine, The 183; Guide Magazine 184; Guideposts for Kids 185; Highlights for Children 186; Hob-Nob 186; Home Altar, The 190; Jack and Jill 192; Junior Trails 192; Keynoter 193; Kid City 194; Ladybug, the Magazine for Young Children 194; Listen 195; Magazine for Christian Youth!, The 196; My Friend 197; New Era Magazine 199; On the Line 201; Primary Days 203; R-A-D-A-R 204; Seventeen Magazine 208; Single Parent, The 209; Skipping Stones 210; Sleuth 211; Spider 211; Straight 213; Superscience Blue 214; 'Teen Magazine 215; Teen Power 216; Teenage Christian Magazine 216; Touch 218; 2 Hype/Hype Hair 219; With 221; Young Christian 222; Young Salvationist 223

Religious. Bread for God's Children 166; Cochran's Corner 174; Counselor 174; Crusader 176; Faces 179; Focus on the Family Clubhouse; Focus on the Family Clubhouse Jr. 181; FreeWay 183; Friend Magazine, The 183; Guide Magazine 184; Guideposts for Kids 185; High Adventure 185; Home Altar, The 190; Junior Trails 192; Magazine for Christian Youth!, The 196; My Friend 197; New Era Magazine 199; On Course 200; Pockets 202; Primary Days 203; Shofar 209; Skipping Stones 210; Straight 213; Student Leadership Journal 214; Teen Power 216; Teenage Christian Magazine 216; Touch 218; Venture 220; With 221; Wonder Time 222; Young Christian 222; Young Salvationist 223; Youth Update 223

Science. Advocate, The 162; Animal Trails 163; Boys' Life 165; Child Life 169; Counselor 174; Cricket Magazine 175; Crusader 176; Dolphin Log 178; DynaMath 178; Focus on the Family Clubhouse; Focus on the Family Clubhouse Jr. 181; Guideposts for Kids 185; Highlights for Children 186; Hob-Nob 186; Hobson's Choice 188; Kid City 194; Kids Copy 194; Ladybug, the Magazine for Young Children 194; Magazine for Christian Youth!, The 196; My Friend 197; Odyssey 199; Racing for Kids 203; Scholastic Math Magazine 205; Science Weekly 208; Sleuth 211; Spider 211; Superscience Blue 214; 3-2-1 Contact 217; Turtle Magazine 219; U.S. Kids 220; Venture 220

Social Issues. Advocate, The 162; Animal Trails 163; Careers and Colleges 167; Challenge 168; Child Life 169; Choices 172; Counselor 174; Crusader 176; DynaMath 178; Focus on the Family Clubhouse; Focus on the Family Clubhouse Jr. 181; For Seniors Only 182; FreeWay 183; Guide Magazine 184; Guideposts for Kids 185; Junior Scholastic 192; Kid City 194; Kids Copy 194; Magazine for Christian Youth!, The 196; On Course 200; Scholastic Math Magazine 205; Seventeen Magazine 208; Student Leadership Journal 214; Teen Life 215; 'Teen Magazine 215; Teen Power 216; Teenage Christian Magazine 216; U.S. Kids 220; Young Christian 222; Young Salvationist 223

Sports. Advocate, The 162; Boys' Life 165; Challenge 168; Child Life 169; Children's Digest 169; Children's Playmate 172; Counselor 174; Cricket Magazine 175; Crusader 176; Current Health II 176; Disney Adventures 177; DynaMath 178; FFA New Horizons 180; Field & Stream 180; Focus on the Family Clubhouse; Focus on the Family Clubhouse Jr. 181; For Seniors Only 182; FreeWay 183; Friend Magazine, The 183; Guide Magazine 184; Guideposts for Kids 185; Highlights for Children 186; Hob-Nob 186; International Gymnast 191; Kid City 194; Kids Copy 194; Listen 195; Magazine for Christian Youth!, The 196; My Friend 197; National Geographic World 198; New Era Magazine 199; Primary Days 203; Racing for Kids 203; Scholastic Math Magazine 205; Sharing the Victory 209; Skipping Stones 210; Teen Power 216; Teenage Christian Magazine 216; Turtle Magazine 219; U.S. Kids 220

Travel. Advocate, The 162; Animal Trails 163; Atalantik 164; Careers and Colleges 167; Chickadee 168; Child Life 169; Children's Digest 169; Children's Playmate 172; Cobblestone 173; Cochran's Corner 174; Cricket Magazine 175; Crusader 176; Exploring 178; Faces 179; For Seniors Only 182; Goldfinch, The 184; Guideposts for Kids 185; Jack and Jill 192; Kid City 194; Magazine for Christian Youth!, The 196; National Geographic World 198; Owl Magazine 201; R-A-D-A-R 204; Scholastic Math Magazine 205; Skipping Stones 210; 'Teen Magazine 215; Teenage Christian Magazine 216; U.S. Kids 220; Spider 211; Straight 213; Teen Life 215; Teen Power 216; Teenage Christian Magazine 216; Turtle Magazine 219; U.S. Kids 220; Venture 220; With 221; Young Salvationist 223

General Index